A HISTORY OF YORK MINSTER

A HISTORY OF
YORK MINSTER

Edited by G. E. AYLMER and REGINALD CANT

CLARENDON PRESS · OXFORD · 1977

Oxford University Press, Walton Street, Oxford OX2 6DP

OXFORD LONDON GLASGOW NEW YORK
TORONTO MELBOURNE WELLINGTON CAPE TOWN
IBADAN NAIROBI DAR ES SALAAM LUSAKA ADDIS ABABA
KUALA LUMPUR SINGAPORE JAKARTA HONG KONG TOKYO
DELHI BOMBAY CALCUTTA MADRAS KARACHI

ISBN 0 19 817199 4

Frontispiece: A King of England, probably
representing Edward II, from the border of a
canopy panel in the Heraldic Window, North Aisle,
Nave. See pages 349–50

*Printed in Great Britain by BAS Printers Limited,
Over Wallop, Hampshire*

PREFACE

This book owes its inception to an initiative from the Dean and Chapter of York in 1968. It was clear by that time that much new knowledge of the Minster's history was becoming available: the staff of the York office of the Royal Commission on Historical Monuments (England) were accumulating material for their forthcoming Inventory; historians belonging to the recently established University of York were turning their attention to the subject; and in 1967 an archaeological investigation of the site had begun in conjunction with the urgently required strengthening of the building's foundations. It was felt that a scholarly book would have a wider than purely academic appeal; and there was general agreement that it must treat the Minster not only as an architectural monument but also as a place of worship and a social unit with a continuing history. Furthermore it was particularly appropriate to mark the 1350th anniversary of the founding of the Minster with this publication in 1977.

An editorial committee was constituted, consisting of Professor A. G. Dickens, C.M.G., Director of the Institute of Historical Research, University of London, who acted as Chairman, Professor Francis Wormald, C.B.E., Professor Owen Chadwick, Regius Professor of Modern History, University of Cambridge, Professor G. E. Aylmer, Professor of History, University of York and Canon Reginald Cant, Chancellor of the Minster, who acted as secretary. After the death of Professor Wormald in 1972, Professor Christopher Brooke, then of Westfield College, London, took his place.

A team of authors was enlisted and the editorial committee wish to express their gratitude to these scholars for their willingness to contribute. Among those who have aided them in their task to whom they would wish to place on record their gratitude are the Royal Commission on Historical Monuments (England); the staff of the Minster Library, particularly Mr Bernard Barr; the Minster archivist, Miss Katharine Longley; the late Mrs Norah Gurney, Dr David Smith, the present Director, and the staff, of the

Borthwick Institute, York; and the Oxford University Press itself, without whose support, patience and skill, the book could never have been produced. They also wish to express gratitude for generous financial assistance, which has enabled the Press to keep down the price of the published volume, from the following bodies: The Dean and Chapter of York, the Oliver Sheldon Memorial Trust (York), the Twenty-Seven Foundation and the Yorkshire Philosophical Society.

Since the majority of the contributors have lived and worked in York during the time of its composition, the book itself has been to an unusual degree a corporate enterprise in which the partners have greatly helped one another and so would wish to record their mutual indebtedness. By far the greater share in the detailed editing of the volume has naturally fallen to the two members of the editorial committee resident in York, and it is the united wish of their colleagues that the book should go out under their names. The two resident editors wish to record their appreciation of the help and support they have received from their colleagues on the editorial committee.

Finally, grateful acknowledgement is made to all those who have given permission to use copyright photographs. Every effort has been made to ensure that the following list is complete, but for any inadvertent omissions the editors express their regret.

ACKNOWLEDGEMENTS

Archaeologia (Society of Antiquaries). Plate 3

The Dean and Chapter of Durham. Plates 4 and 5

The Dean and Chapter of York. Plates 1, 2, 6–10, 86, 92–94, 104, 112, 118, 119, 135–137, 161 164–167, 169–178

J. Haselock. Plates 162 and 163

His Grace the Duke of Norfolk. Plate 134

The Northern Echo. Plates 138, 139, 141, 142, 144–147, 149, 151, 152, 154, 156, 158, 159

D. O'Connor. Plates 87, 88, 106, 111, 116, Colour Frontispiece

Phaidon Press Ltd. Plate 155

D. Phillips, Director of Minster Excavations, Plans I and II (adapted by Dr John H. Harvey); III and IV (from drawings by Miss L. Rowbottom)

Royal Commission on Historical Monuments (England). Plates 11–52, 55–78, 89, 91, 95–103, 105, 107–110, 113–115, 117, 120–131, 133, 140, 143, 148, 150, 153, 157, 178(b)

Shepherd Building Group. Plates 179–182

Trinity College, Cambridge. Plate 170

University of York, Centre for Medieval Studies. Plates 90 and 132

D. Whiteley. Plates 53, 54, 83–85, 160, 168, 171, 178(a)

York City Art Gallery. Plates 79–81 and 177

Yorkshire Architectural and York Archaeological Society. Plate 82

CONTENTS

LIST OF ILLUSTRATIONS

ABBREVIATIONS

Manuscript Collections

BIHR	Borthwick Institute of Historical Research, York
BM *and* BL	British Museum (now including the British Library)
Bodl.	Bodleian Library
PRO	Public Record Office
Torre 'Minster'	James Torre, 'Antiquities of York Minster', 1690–1, manuscript in York Minster Library
YCA	York City Archives, in the City Library
YCL	York City Library
YML	York Minster Library

Printed Works

Place of publication London, unless stated otherwise

AASR	*Associated Architectural and Archaeological Societies' Reports and Papers*
AntJ	*Antiquaries Journal* (Society of Antiquaries)
ArchJ	*Archaeological Journal* (Royal Archaeological Institute)
Bede, *HE*	Bede, *Historia Ecclesiastica*, with page ref. from *Bede's Eccles. History of the English People*, ed. B. Colgrave and R. A. B. Mynors (Oxford Medieval Texts; 1969)
Browne, *Fabric Rolls*	J. Browne, *Fabric Rolls and Documents of York Minster* (York, new edn. 1863)
Browne, *History*	J. Browne, *History of the Metropolitan Church of St. Peter, York* (2 vols., York, 1847)
CChR	*Calendar of Charter Rolls* (HMSO)

CClR   *Calendar of Close Rolls* (HMSO)

CPapR   *Calendar of Papal Registers (Letters, Petitions)*

CPatR   *Calendar of Patent Rolls* (HMSO)

CSPDom   *Calendar of State Papers Domestic* (HMSO)

Clay, *Fasti*   C. T. Clay (ed.), *York Minster Fasti, being notes on the Dignitaries, Archdeacons and Prebendaries in the Church of York prior to the year 1307* (YAS Rec. Ser. cxxiii, cxxiv, 1957–8)

DNB   *Dictionary of National Biography*

Dixon and Raine, *Fasti Ebor.*   W. H. Dixon and J. Raine, *Fasti Eboracenses, Lives of the Archbishops of York*, vol. I (York, 1863)

Drake, *Ebor.*   Francis Drake, *Eboracum* (York and London, 1736, unless a later edition is specified)

EHD   *English Historical Documents*

EHR   *English Historical Review*

Fabric Rolls   J. Raine (ed.), *The Fabric Rolls of York Minster* (Surtees Society, vol. xxxv, 1859)

Harrison, *Medieval College*   F. Harrison, *Life in a Medieval College* (1952)

Herring, *Visit.*   *Archbishop Herring's Visitation Returns*, ed. S. L. Ollard and P. C. Walker (YAS Rec. Ser. lxxi, lxxii, lxxv, lxxvii, lxxix, 1928–31)

Hists. York   *Historians of the Church of York and its Archbishops*, ed. J. Raine (Rolls Series, 3 vols., 1879–94)

Hugh, *York*   *Hugh the Chanter, The History of the Church of York, 1066–1127*, ed. and trans. C. Johnson (Nelson's Medieval Texts, 1961)

JBAA   *Journal of the British Archaeological Association*

JEH   *Journal of Ecclesiastical History*

Le Neve, *Fasti*   J. Le Neve, *Fasti Ecclesiae Anglicanae, etc.*, ed. T. D. Hardy (3 vols., Oxford, 1854)

Le Neve—Horn and Smith   J. Le Neve, *Fasti Ecclesiae Anglicanae 1541–1857*, IV York Diocese, compiled by Joyce M. Horn and David M. Smith (1975)

Le Neve—Jones   J. Le Neve, *Fasti Ecclesiae Anglicanae, 1300–1541*, VI Northern Province, compiled by B. Jones (1963)

Monasticon   Sir William Dugdale, *Monasticon Anglicanum*, ed. J. Caley, H. Ellis, and B. Bandinel (1817–30; reprint 1846 unless specified)

Ornsby, *Dioc. Hist.*   G. Ornsby, *Diocesan Histories: York* (n.d. [1882])

PP	*Parliamentary Papers*
VCH	*Victoria History of the Counties of England* (see under name of county)
VCH York	*Victoria History etc., City of York*, ed. P. M. Tillott (1961)
VCH Yorkshire	*Victoria History etc., County of Yorkshire* (4 vols., 1907–25)
Willis, *Survey*	Browne Willis, *Survey of the Cathedrals of York etc.*, vol. i (1727)
Willis, *York Cathedral*	R. Willis, *The Architectural History of York Cathedral* (1848)
YAJ	*Yorkshire Archaeological Journal* (Leeds, 1869/70–; the first ten volumes are entitled *Yorkshire Archaeological and Topographical Journal*)
YAS Rec. Ser.	Yorkshire Archaeological Society, Record Series
YCR	*York Civic Records*, 8 vols., *YAS Rec. Ser.*, 1939–52
Y. Cour.	*York Courant*
Y. Gaz.	*Yorkshire Gazette*
YH	*York Herald*
Y.M. Hist. Tr.	*York Minster Historical Tracts*, ed. A. Hamilton Thompson (1927)
York Statutes	J. Raine (ed.), *The Statutes etc. of the Cathedral Church of York* (2nd edn., Leeds, 1900)
YP	*Yorkshire Post*

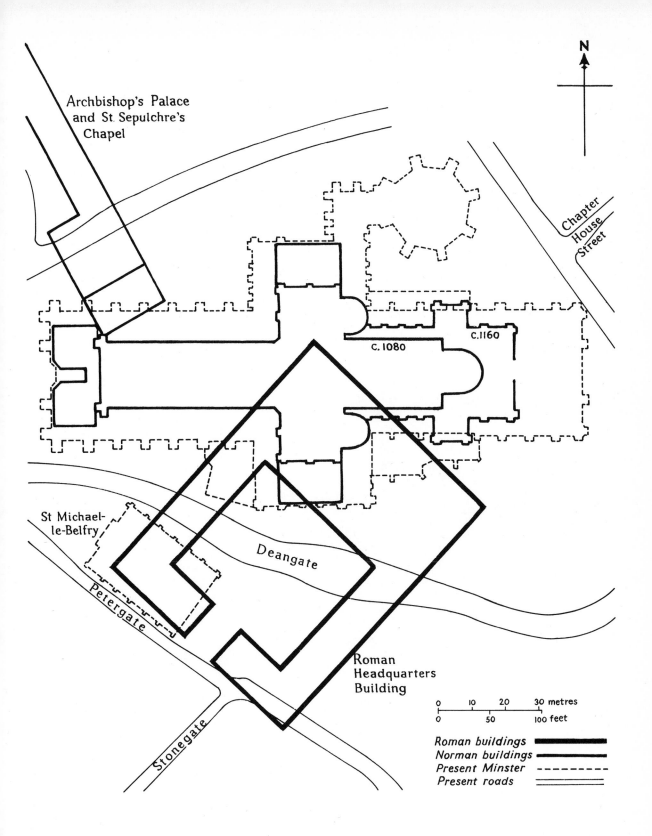

N

Archbishop's Palace
and St. Sepulchre's
Chapel

Chapter
House
Street

c. 1080

c. 1160

St Michael-
le-Belfry

Deangate

Petergate

Roman
Headquarters
Building

Stonegate

0	10	20	30 metres
0		50	100 feet

Roman buildings ▬▬▬▬
Norman buildings ──────
Present Minster ‑ ‑ ‑ ‑ ‑ ‑
Present roads ────────

Plan I The three main periods of building on the site.

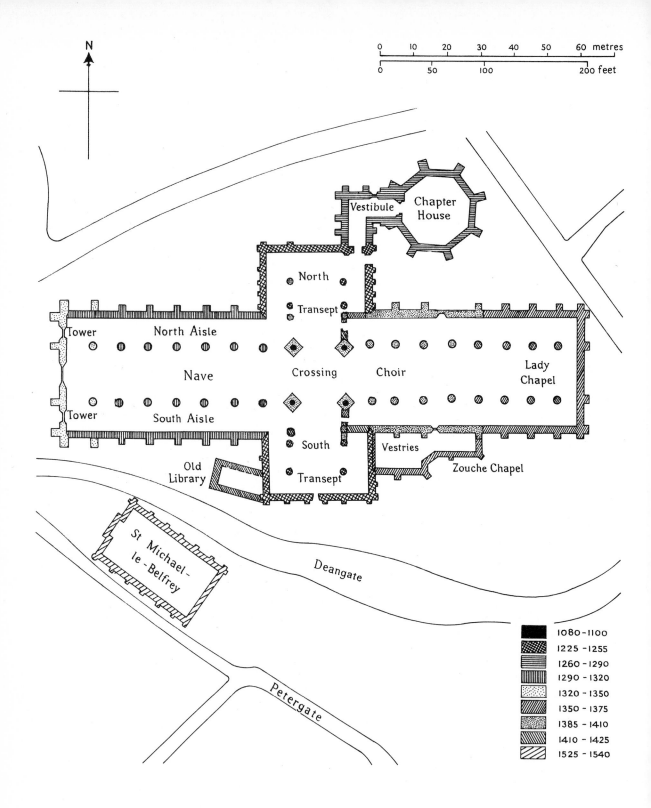

N

	metres
0 10 20 30 40 50 60	metres
0 50 100 200 feet	feet

Chapter House

Vestibule

North Transept

Tower

North Aisle

Nave

Crossing

Choir

Lady Chapel

Tower

South Aisle

South Transept

Old Library

Vestries

Zouche Chapel

St Michael-le-Belfrey

Deangate

Petergate

■	1080–1100
	1225–1255
	1260–1290
	1290–1320
	1320–1350
	1350–1375
	1385–1410
	1410–1425
	1525–1540

Plan II Periods of construction of the present Minster and St. Michael-le-Belfry.

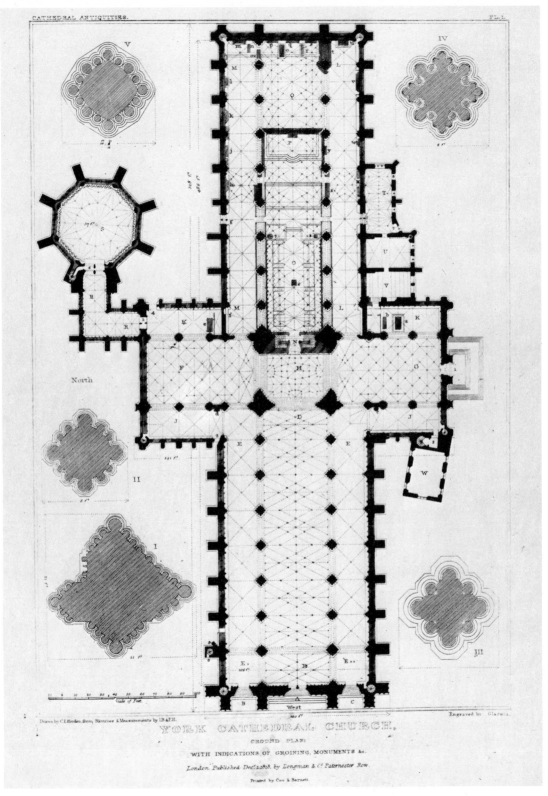

Plan III From John Britton, *The History and Antiquities of the Metropolitical Church of York*, 1819.
A ground plan sufficiently accurate to be used by engineers today.

1 St. Mark from the York Gospels. A genuine relic of the pre-conquest Minster, since this Gospel Book was already in York by about 1020. But it was probably made in Canterbury about 1000. Since the 14th c. it has been used as an oath-book for deans, archdeacons, and canons, and more recently for archbishops. Now Chapter Library, Add. MS. 1, f. 60v.

CHAPTER I

From 627 until the Early Thirteenth Century

Rosalind M. T. Hill and Christopher N. L. Brooke

The Roman legacy[1]

Christianity came to York during the period of the Roman occupation of
Britain, but the exact date of its coming, and the name of the man who
brought it, will probably never be known. Under the Roman Empire the
faith was spread in many ways, by merchants coming from Mediterranean
cities to pick up the British products—slaves, tin, hunting-dogs, and rather
inferior pearls—by slaves (often literate and intelligent men) who came to
Britain in the service of Roman masters, and even, at times, by members of
the army, who contributed some martyrs to Christianity despite the fact that
the military profession was not approved by teachers of the early Church.
York, which from about A.D. 73 onwards was a prosperous and well-
defended settlement, must have attracted its share of all these people. It was
a river-port in a rich hinterland, a *colonia* containing soldiers both active
and retired, and it became, under Septimius Severus, the administrative
capital of Lower Britain. It must also have been an extremely pleasant place
in which to live. Alcuin, who knew and loved it some three and a half
centuries after the end of the Roman occupation, could still describe it as 'a
lofty city with walls and towers', a prosperous port where the Ouse,

[1] For the general history of York and the Minster see *VCH York*, pp. 2–24 (A. G. Dickens and H. G.
Ramm); *The Noble City of York*, ed. A. Stacpoole *et al.* (York, 1972), esp. R. Cant, 'The Minster',
pp. 23–66; H. G. Ramm, 'The growth and development of the city to the Norman Conquest',
pp. 225–54; F. W. Brooks, 'York—1066 to present day', pp. 255–335; *VCH Yorkshire* iii. 375 ff.
(A. Hamilton Thompson). For the history of York before the end of the tenth century see also *An
Inventory of the Historical Monuments in the City of York*, i, *Eburacum: Roman York* (Royal
Commission on Historical Monuments, 1962); A. F. Norman, 'Religion in Roman York' and H. G.
Ramm, 'The End of Roman York' (pp. 143–54, 179–99), in *Soldier and Civilian in Roman Yorkshire*, ed.
R. M. Butler (Leicester, 1971); Rosemary Cramp, *Anglian and Viking York* (Borthwick Papers, no. 33,
York, 1967); J. Lamb, *The Archbishopric of York, the Early Years* (1967); A. L. Binns, *The Viking
Century in East Yorkshire* (East Yorks. Local History Ser. xv, 1963); J. Radley, 'Economic aspects of
Anglo-Danish York', *Medieval Archaeology*, xv (1971), 37–57.

abounding in fish, flowed among the hills and woods through fields covered with flowers.[2]

There may well have been a few Christians in York before the end of the first century A.D. Where they met for worship we do not know. Before the Peace of the Church in A.D. 312 Christians were not subject to continuous, active persecution. Like other minority groups whose ideas were thought to be peculiar they suffered horribly when society needed a scapegoat, and there were martyrs in Britain, although none is actually recorded from York. For long periods, however, the authorities preferred to forget about the Christians so long as they remained unobtrusive and did not openly challenge the cult of the pagan gods or of the emperor's divinity. Christian worship took place all over the empire in private rooms, with a door-keeper to keep watch, or in any out-of-the-way place such as a disused tomb. Some of the rooms seem to have been regular meeting-places, adorned with crypto-Christian symbols such as the *Rotas* word-square or a picture of Bellerophon overcoming the chimera, but it was dangerous to be too openly explicit. To make a public or ostentatious display of Christian belief was to ask for trouble, and although Gildas, writing in the sixth century, speaks of the British Christians after 312 setting to work to 'rebuild the churches which had been levelled to the ground' we have no archaeological evidence to support his statement, and it appears to be inherently improbable.[3]

In 306 Constantine the Great was proclaimed emperor in York; and it is probable that there was then a small Christian congregation among the citizens who acclaimed him. Constantine, in spite of Geoffrey of Monmouth's pleasant tradition that his mother Helena was a British princess and the daughter of Old King Cole himself,[4] had in fact no British blood. His father came from Illyria and his mother from Bithynia, while he himself had been born at Nish and was in Britain, at the time of his imperial acclamation, simply because his father's work had brought the family to that remote province. At the time of his Proclamation as Caesar he was not yet a Christian; it was only five years later that he was to see the vision of the Cross over the Sun which encouraged him to win the Battle of the Milvian Bridge, and to follow it up in 312 with a general edict of toleration for the Christian Church. By the year 314, however, the Christian community in York already had its own bishop. He may or may not have

[2] *Hists. York* i. 349–50.

[3] Gildas, *De excidio*, c. 12. ed. T. Mommsen, *Monumenta Germ. Hist., Auctores antiquissimi*, xiii (1898), 32; for Bellerophon, etc. see J. M. C. Toynbee, 'Pagan motifs and practices in Christian art and Ritual in Roman Britain', in *Christianity in Britain 300–700*, ed. M. W. Barley and R. P. C. Hanson (Leicester, 1968), pp. 177–92.

[4] Geoffrey of Monmouth, *Historia Regum Britanniae*, v. 6, ed. A. Griscom (New York, 1929), p. 338.

been called Eborius—the name is a perfectly possible one, but it is rather suspiciously like the name of the city, Eboracum, from which he came.[5] He attended in 314 the Council of Arles, one of the four pre-Nicene provincial councils of the Church, whose authority was later assumed to be of equal validity with that of the general councils themselves. The existence of this bishop is of considerable importance for the history of the Church in Romano-British York. A bishop was normally the chief priest of a congregation in a city, and his existence usually implied that a Christian community had been in the habit of meeting there for some time. It is most unlikely that the formation of a Christian Church in York, the election of Eborius, and his summons and journey to Arles could all have taken place in the two years which had elapsed since Christianity became an officially respectable religion.

In 359 British bishops again attended a church council, this time at Rimini. We know nothing about them except that they were too poor to pay their own expenses and had to be helped from the public funds, a fact which suggests that Christianity in Britain was not yet attracting the kind of rich and public-spirited convert who could afford to build and endow a large church.[6] Some of the Christian citizens of York seem also to have taken their religion in an equivocal spirit not entirely unknown to their descendants; the burial of a woman, whose grave was found marked by a plaque inscribed with an undoubtedly Christian inscription (*Soror ave, vivas in Deo*), was associated with trinkets and bangles designed to be worn in a very un-Christian heaven.[7]

Theodosius I put an end in 395 to the formal cult of pagan gods throughout the empire, of which York was a small part. How much unofficial worship of the old gods continued is problematical; Gildas describes the country, even in his own time, as being full of idols.[8] Britain in the early fifth century was, however, a Christian province in the formal sense, and the citizens of York must have had at least one church within their walls, although we do not know where it was. There is no evidence to suggest that they tried to convert the Germanic *foederati* who were settled extensively outside the city. The history of north-eastern England in the fifth and sixth centuries is extremely obscure. York itself survived; it retained its Roman name in a somewhat mutilated form, and its fortifications were kept up and even strengthened. Later, and unreliable, traditions incorporated it into the Arthurian legend under the name of Caer

---

[5] Cf. J. C. Mann, 'The Administration of Roman Britain', *Antiquity*, xxxv (1961), 317.

[6] *Councils and Ecclesiastical Documents*, ed. A. W. Haddan and W. Stubbs (Oxford, 1869–73), i. 9–10.

[7] *Inventory of the Historical Monuments in the City of York*, i

[8] Gildas, c. 4, ed. Mommsen, p. 29.

Ebrauc, and Widdrington, writing about 1660, observed sourly that Arthur's habit of holding his Christmas court there was 'the original and spring of all the loose and licentious pranks at York for Christmas',[9] but the stories are clearly quite apocryphal. Bede records the fact that in the eighth century the old Roman title of *municipium* was still remembered and used,[10] but in the year 600 the people of Deira, as the incoming Anglo-Saxons called southern Northumbria, were pagans, except for the small kingdom of Elmet in the south-west. This kept its independence as a British and Christian community until its conquest by Edwin.[11]

Paulinus and the conversion

Gregory the Great's *angeli* were Anglians from Deira, and it was the report of Deiran paganism and that of their king Ælle which moved him to send the first Christian mission to the Anglo-Saxon peoples.[12] The faith was received with tolerance rather than with positive enthusiasm. Ælle's son Edwin is described by Bede as a just and virtuous prince, and both Bede's narrative and the evidence of archaeology suggest that he was an admirer of things Roman, but he accepted Christianity only in middle life and after considerable delay. It was Edwin who caused to be built in York the first church of which we have any record, to serve as a baptistery for himself and his family, and as a base of operations for his bishop Paulinus. Bede tells us that this church was built in a hurry ('citato opere'), that it was made of wood, and that it was small. The fact that he mentions the building, a few years later, of a rectangular stone church designed to enclose the earlier wooden building *in gyro* suggests that it was a round baptistery, perhaps with a narthex for the accommodation of catechumens, a copy in wood of the stone baptisteries such as those at Ravenna, some of which Paulinus had probably seen when he was in Italy. The wooden church must have been ready for Edwin's baptism at Easter of the year 627, and the larger stone church in which it was to be enclosed was begun some time before his death in 632/3. The walls of this church were designed to be higher than those of the wooden structure, and the whole building was clearly meant to be a work worthy of a Romanophil prince who ruled northern England from sea to sea and was accepted as Bretwalda.[13] The pope, following the instructions of Gregory the Great that York was to be the seat of the

[9] T. Widdrington, *Analecta Eboracensia*, ed. C. Caine (1897), p. 31.
[10] Bede, *HE* iii.1, ed. Colgrave and Mynors, pp. 212–13.
[11] Cf. *Historia Brittonum*, ed. T. Mommsen, *Monumenta Germ. Hist., Auctores antiquissimi*, xii. 206–7; trans. in *EHD* i ed. D. Whitelock (1955), p. 237.
[12] Bede, *HE* ii.1, esp. pp. 132–5.
[13] Ibid. ii. 14, pp. 186–7.

northern metropolitan, alternating in seniority with London, sent to Paulinus a pallium in token of his investiture as archbishop, but this did not arrive until after Edwin's death in battle and the flight of his bishop to the south; and Paulinus laid up the pallium in the church of Rochester, where it remained as a venerable relic of no practical significance.[14] The establishment of the archbishopric of York was delayed for another century, but London never became an archbishopric at all. The southern primacy did not move from Canterbury, where it had been firmly established by St. Augustine and his immediate successors. No northern prelate, in residence in his see, ever received the pallium until the time of Ecgbert, to whom it was sent, according to Bede's continuators and to Simeon of Durham, in 735.[15] This slow start, and the vicissitudes suffered by the northern province at the time of the Viking invasions, established the ascendancy of Canterbury to such an extent that even the undoubted dictum of St. Gregory, as reported by Bede, did not suffice to upset it.

The first Minster

Edwin did not live to see his stone church completed. After the year of troubles which followed his death (a year so horrible, according to Bede, that the annalists refused to record it) the building was finished by his successor Oswald, and Edwin's relics were buried in it, in the porticus of St. Gregory.[16] Up to the date of writing (1977) we do not know exactly where this church stood. It was for a long time believed that as at Canterbury, Rochester, and St. Paul's, London, the original church established by the Gregorian mission marked the holy site for its successors, and that therefore Edwin's church must underlie some part of the Minster. The fact that Bede expressly says that Edwin's church was built 'in the city' and therefore somewhere within the circuit of the existing walls, as a proper setting for the king's baptism, strengthened this belief, especially since the Minster occupies a conspicuous site at the top of a slight hill, and lies at the very centre of Roman York. It is possible that as at Winchester the original church may have been orientated in a peculiar way and have lain a little to one side of the later building. It is also possible that the original Romano-British church of York had grown up on a site hallowed by associations with the earliest Christian community, and that this site was not at the official centre of the Roman city. If so, the traditionally holy place may have

[14] Ibid. ii. 20, pp. 204–5.
[15] Bede, *Contin.*, pp. 572–3 (ed. Colgrave and Mynors); *Symeonis Monachi Opera Omnia*, ed. T. Arnold (Rolls Ser., 1882–5), ii. 31; trans. in *EHD* i. 239.
[16] Bede, *HE* ii. 20, pp. 204–5. See also *The Earliest Life of Gregory the Great*, by the Monk of Whitby, ed. B. Colgrave (Lawrence, 1968), pp. 42, 102 ff. The Monk places the whole body at Whitby.

been used as the site of a later church, as happened in the case of San Clemente in Rome. There is, too, the possibility that since Eddi in his *Life of Bishop Wilfrid* mentions no crypt at York in the seventh century although he is careful to describe the 'foundations in the earth' at Hexham and Ripon,[17] Edwin's stone church did not carry deep foundations, and was completely obliterated by later buildings on the site.

In any case, it was clearly not kept in repair during the years of the Celtic Church's ascendancy in Northumbria. St. Aidan, through whose work Christianity was restored in the north after Edwin's death, was a wandering, Celtic bishop whose base of operations, so far as he had one, was in Lindisfarne. We have evidence that he worked in Deira, but no missionary of the Celtic Church was ever likely to set much store by the Roman tradition of basing the Church's administration upon a civic bishopric. Moreover, York at this time was vulnerable to attacks from the formidable combination of Penda of Mercia and the Britons of North Wales; we know that Deira was overrun at least twice and probably three times between the death of Oswald in 641/2 and the Battle of the Winwaed, itself a Yorkshire river, in 654/5. The see of York was restored in 664, probably for St. Wilfrid, but the length of time which he spent over his consecration in Gaul seems to have caused the king to put forward St. Chad in his place. St. Chad was removed for irregular consecration in or soon after 669, but Archbishop Theodore, impressed by the singular holiness of his life, transferred him to Lichfield. St. Wilfred succeeded him at York, although Bede's words suggest that Wilfrid's tenure, among that of his other Northumbrian sees, was intended to be more a matter of temporary administration than of permanent establishment. When he took over York in about 670 he found the structure of Edwin's church to be in a fairly lamentable state, although it had been completed for only about forty years. 'The ridge of the roof owing to its age let the water through, the windows were unglazed and the birds flew in and out, building their nests, while the neglected walls were disgusting to behold, owing to all the filth caused by the rain and the birds.'[18]

Eddi's description sounds accurate rather than rhetorical to anyone who has investigated a neglected English church. Roof-building clearly worried seventh-century English architects. The roof of the 'church of wonderful workmanship' at Lincoln collapsed before many years had passed.[19] Many roofs were thatched. Bede describes the church at Lindisfarne as being covered with a thatch of rushes after the manner of the Irish ('more

[17] Eddi (Eddius Stephanus), *Life of Bishop Wilfrid*, ed. B. Colgrave (Cambridge, 1927), pp. 32–7, 44–7.
[18] Eddi, pp. 34–5.
[19] Bede, *HE* ii. 16, pp. 192–3.

Scottorum'), and he describes a house with a roof of withies and dried grass ('virgis contextum ac foeno tectum') standing somewhere near the site of the Battle of Maserfield in the decade 640–50.[20] His description of thatching with rushes as being an Irish practice suggests that the Anglo-Saxon builders used something else, but we do not learn what it was until St. Wilfrid, faced with the dilapidations at York, 'renewed the ruined roof-ridges, skilfully covering them with pure lead'. Having thus dealt with the problem of the leaky roof, he excluded the birds and the rain by putting glass in the windows (he had, says Eddi, brought with him from Gaul 'masons and artificers of almost every kind').[21] Seventh-century windows, to judge from the example which survives at Jarrow, were exceedingly small, but they would still be wide enough to admit a moderately thin pigeon, as well as the inevitable sparrow and starling. When he had turned out the birds, St. Wilfrid caused the inside of the church to be whitewashed ('secundum prophetam super nivem dealbavit') and he then adorned it with 'various kinds of vessels and furniture'.[22] Descriptions of church architecture given in saints' lives are notably suspect, owing more than a little to reminiscences of Solomon's temple. Nevertheless, by comparing the descriptions given by Eddi of the churches of Ripon and Hexham, finished within ten years of York, with those given by Bede of the churches of Wearmouth and Jarrow, finished a few years later, it is possible to understand something of how Wilfrid's restored church at York would have appeared to the worshipper who entered it. The altar, behind, under, or within which relics were deposited, would have been adorned with hangings of purple and silk, woven in an intricate design. Upon it, raised by a book-rest and set in a jewelled case or binding, would stand the gospel-book, either richly illuminated or written in letters of gold upon parchment stained with the precious purple dye. The walls and probably also the *testudo* (the wooden partition screening the altar, like the Royal Gate in the modern Orthodox church, of which Bede gives evidence at Wearmouth) would be adorned with icons painted upon wooden panels, depicting the types and anti-types of the Old and New Testaments, for example Isaac carrying the wood for Abraham's sacrifice and Christ carrying the cross, or the serpent raised up by Moses in the wilderness and Christ raised up at Calvary.[23] These paintings in churches were of the utmost importance in the evangelization of England. Gregory the Great, who had a curious

---

[20] Ibid. iii. 25, 10, pp. 294–5, 244–5.

[21] Eddi, pp. 30–1.

[22] Ibid. pp. 34–5.

[23] Bede, *Historia abbatum*, ed. C. Plummer (Bede, *Opera Historica*, i, Oxford, 1896), cc. 5–6, pp. 368–70.

intuitive insight into the minds of barbarian converts, had called the painted churches of his own time 'the books of the unlearned',[24] and it is clear that for most of the English no other book was available. As we can see from Bede's *Prose Life of St. Cuthbert*, it was extremely difficult to explain to illiterate Anglian farmers 'how the new worship [was] to be conducted'.[25] Miracles, such as that performed in answer to St. Cuthbert's prayers, helped some of them to learn, but for most of them no saint was made manifest, and they had to depend upon the pictures in the church.

St. Wilfrid held the see of York and of the whole northern Church until 678. There is some suggestion in Bede's narrative that Archbishop Theodore was not happy with an arrangement which made the whole of the Northumbrian lands ecclesiastically dependent upon one man, especially one possessed of a 'countless army of followers arrayed in royal vestments and arms'.[26] In 678, when St. Wilfrid fell out with King Ecgfrith and went into exile, the see of York was given to Bosa, one of St. Hild's pupils, described by Bede as 'a man of singular merit and holiness'.[27] St. Cuthbert came to him at York for consecration to the see of Lindisfarne in 685. Wilfrid returned, with papal support and at least the acquiescence of Theodore, in the following year, but in 691 he quarrelled with King Aldfrith and was again expelled from York, this time permanently. Bosa was restored, and held the see until his death in 705, when he was succeeded by the learned and saintly John of Beverley, patron and friend of Bede and himself a pupil of Theodore of Tarsus and Abbot Hadrian in the famous school at Canterbury. St. John appears in Bede's *Ecclesiastical History* as a vigorous and active bishop, constantly at work, travelling round the diocese to instruct his people and dedicate churches, using the Greek medical knowledge, which he had learned from Theodore, in healing the sick.[28] In 718, when he was already old, he returned to his own monastery of Beverley, which retained his relics and became the centre of his cult. He relinquished his see of York to another Wilfrid, abbot of the monastery of York. This man cannot himself have been young, since he had been a pupil of St. Hild who had died nearly forty years earlier. Alcuin, who must have talked to people who remembered him, described him as a man who commanded honour, reverence, and love, who delighted to enrich and beautify his church, and to decorate the altar and the crosses with

[24] Gregory the Great, *Registrum*, ed. P. Ewald and L. M. Hartmann, *Monumenta Germ. Hist., Epistolae*, i–ii (1887–99), xi. 10, vol. ii, pp. 269–72.
[25] Bede, *Vita S. Cuthberti*, ed. B. Colgrave (Cambridge, 1940), c. iii, pp. 164–5.
[26] Eddi, pp. 48–9.
[27] Bede, *HE* v. 3, pp. 458–61.
[28] Ibid. v. 2–6, pp. 456–69.

gold—'not wishing to hide the treasures, the good bishop displayed them to the glory of God'.[29] He also bestowed gifts on the other churches in York: it was a common custom at the time to establish several churches in the same neighbourhood. It is possible that Wilfrid II was rather less successful than St. John of Beverley as a pastoral bishop. He was still in office when Bede ended the *Ecclesiastical History* in 731, and although Alcuin says that he did not neglect the duties of his see, he may have found it too hard to travel through the difficult countryside. Bede, writing to Wilfrid's successor Ecgbert soon after, says that there were at the time outlying villages 'lying among high mountains or in thick forests' which were infrequently visited by a bishop or even a catechist.[30]

Ecgbert, who held York from 732/4 to 766 and seems to have been the first resident ruler of the see to be recognized as archbishop, was the last prelate of York whom Bede knew personally and the first to exercise a direct influence upon Alcuin. He was a man of great authority, the brother of a reigning king of Northumbria, a friend and perhaps a pupil of Bede, who wrote him a letter full of good advice. Bede urged upon Ecgbert the study of the pastoral epistles of St. Paul and the works of St. Gregory (especially the *Pastoral Care*), and encouraged him to train a household given to serious and godly pursuits 'not like that which is attributed to some bishops' who encourage laughter, jokes, the telling of popular stories, and the attending of parties. Above all, he advised Ecgbert to attend to his pastoral duties and to the teaching and training of his clergy.[31]

His advice was followed. Alcuin, who in his boyhood studied under Ecgbert at York, remembered him as a most distinguished teacher, *egregius doctor*, and as one especially well versed in the study of psalmody. He was famous also for enriching the fabric of his church at York, and Alcuin's statement that he decorated it with gold, silver, jewels, and silken hangings may well be true, although the wording is a little suggestive of a description in common form. Still, Ecgbert was of princely blood, and presumably had gold and jewels to command.[32]

Ecgbert is often regarded as the founder of the famous cathedral school at York, which was in his time known outside England as a centre of learning—St. Boniface, writing to him from Germany in 747, thanks him for a present of books.[33] In reality, the school was already well established

---

[29] *Hists. York* i. 385.

[30] Bede, *Epistola ad Ecgbertum episcopum*, ed. C. Plummer (*Opera Historica*, i), c. 7, p. 410.

[31] Ibid. cc. 3–4, pp. 406–8.

[32] *Hists. York* i. 386.

[33] Boniface, *Epistolae*, ed. M. Tangl, *Briefe des heiligen Bonifatius und Lullus* (Berlin, 1916), no. 75; trans. in *EHD* i. 757–8. Cf. W. Levison, *England and the Continent in the Eighth Century* (Oxford, 1946), pp. 139 ff.

when Ecgbert became bishop. It must go back at least to the time of St. Wilfrid, to whom, as Eddi says, 'men of noble birth gave their sons to be instructed' before 678. Wilfrid was probably influenced more deeply than he cared to admit by the learned tradition already established at Canterbury. St. John of Beverley had a number of young men in his household who had been sent to him to study, and some at least of these were laymen, given at times to racing their horses. John was long remembered at York as a patron and friend of young people, and a miracle recorded at his tomb in the twelfth century shows him restoring to life a boy who had fallen off a roof while watching an Easter play.[34] Bosa and Wilfrid II, both of whom had been trained at Whitby and were described by Bede as 'men of singular merit and holiness', must have passed on the tradition of good learning in which St. Hild had brought them up. Ecgbert appointed as *scholasticus* at York his friend, and ultimately his successor as archbishop, Æthelbert, the man whom Alcuin regarded as his own particular teacher, 'lover of justice, trumpet of law, herald of salvation'.[35] It was this man who gave to Alcuin that love of scholarship which never forsook him, so that at the end of his life he could ask for the epitaph: 'Alcuin was my name, learning I loved.'[36]

Æthelbert drew his scholars to him, says Alcuin, taught them, brought them up, and loved them. The curriculum of his school, based probably on that of Theodore and Hadrian at Canterbury, began with the teaching of the Seven Liberal Arts and progressed to theology, philosophy, some law, and probably also some medicine. There was a splendid library, which Alcuin later celebrated in verse. It contained works in Hebrew, Greek, and Latin, not only the great Christian classics and the works of the western fathers of the Church, of Jerome, Hilary, Augustine, and Gregory, and the works of Bede and Boethius, but also the writings of many classical authors, 'the penetrating Aristotle', Pliny, Cicero, Virgil, and others. Alcuin gives a list of forty-one different authors whose works were represented, and we cannot be sure that this is complete, since it is not easy to preserve bibliographical accuracy when writing in hexameters.[37] It is clear, however, that the schools of York in the second half of the eighth century could have held their own with any centre of learning north of the Alps, and Charlemagne admitted as much when in 782 he invited Alcuin to become master of his own palace school.

During Ecgbert's pontificate, in 741, the Minster church of York was

---

[34] *Hists. York* i. 328–9.
[35] Ibid. i. 390.
[36] Helen Waddell, *Medieval Latin Lyrics* (1929; 4th edn. 1933), pp. 94–5.
[37] *Hists. York* i. 395–6.

burned down. There is no evidence to suggest that this was anything but an accident, and we know from Bede and the *Anonymous Life of St. Cuthbert* that in settlements where most of the buildings were of wood fires were frequent, and often disastrous. Simeon of Durham records another great fire at York in 764, but he does not say that this one destroyed any churches. The fire of 741 seems to have left the old church in ruins, but the people of York were in a position to rebuild it.[38] Alcuin and his fellow student Eanbald, who later succeeded Æthelbert as archbishop, were concerned with the rebuilding in some official capacity. The new church, even allowing for some poetic licence in Alcuin's writings, must have been a work of great splendour. He describes it as lofty, supported by columns, and having round arches and panelled ceilings. It contained thirty altars, and was surrounded by many beautiful *porticus* or side-chapels.[39]

Æthelbert retired from the archbishopric towards the end of his life and was succeeded by Eanbald I (780–96), Eanbald II (796–*c*. 808), and Wulfsige, who probably died some time between 830 and 837. The political situation in Northumbria was disturbed, and in 793, after 'dire portents' in the shape of whirlwinds, lightning, and 'fiery dragons . . . flying in the air' had caused great consternation, the first recorded Viking attacks fell upon the country, destroying the church of Lindisfarne.[40] Alcuin, writing to King Ethelred, warned him that this was a chastisement which the Northumbrians had richly deserved.[41] In another letter, addressed to the clergy of York at the time of the archiepiscopal election of 796, he urges them to avoid the sin of simony, and it is clear that he is afraid of undue influence exercised by rapacious nobles in their struggle to seize the Crown.[42] In the event he seems to have approved of Eanbald II, whom he addresses as his dearest and most faithful son, asking to be remembered in his prayers and advising him to carry St. Gregory's *Pastoral Care* with him wherever he goes. In 801 he sent to Eanbald a hundred pounds of tin for the purpose of roofing the belfry, *domuncula cloccarum*, 'for its own beauty and the reputation of the place', together with four screens of lattice-work, which may have been designed to keep out the birds.[43] Eanbald seems to have been a vigorous archbishop with some interest in learning, for he wrote asking Alcuin questions about the liturgy, and held a synod of the

[38] Simeon of Durham, ed. Arnold, ii. 38, 42; trans. in *EHD* i. 240, 242.
[39] *Hists. York* i. 394.
[40] Anglo-Saxon Chronicle, MS.D, *sub anno* 793, trans. in *EHD* i. 167.
[41] Alcuin, *Epistola* 108, ed. E. Dümmler, *Monumenta Germ. Hist., Epistolae*, iv. 1895; trans. in *EHD* i. 784–5.
[42] *Epistola* 104; *Councils and Ecclesiastical Documents*, ed. Haddan and Stubbs, iii. 500–1.
[43] Alcuin, *Epistola* 226; cf. K. Harrison, 'The Pre-Conquest Churches of York', *YAJ* xl (1959–62), 232–49, *esp.* 237.

Northumbrian Church at an unidentified place called Pincanheale.[44] He was ready to lend books; Alcuin, writing to Charlemagne, mentions his need for books such as he used to have in his own country, which are not obtainable on the other side of the Channel, and asks that they may be brought to him from York by special messengers.[45] Clearly, the intellectual and devotional traditions of York at the end of the eighth century had not yet been seriously disrupted, either by civil wars or the threat of Viking raids.

Of Eanbald II's successors until 900, Wulfsige, Wigmund, and Wulfhere, we know very little. Wulfsige was certainly anxious to preserve the proper tradition of Catholic teaching throughout his province, as may be seen from the letter which the Bishop of Lindisfarne wrote to him in the 830s on the subject of the odd heresies of Nial and Pehtred.[46] Wigmund was a friend of the learned Lupus, abbot of Ferrières, a monastery which was linked with York by the fact that Charlemagne had formerly granted it to Alcuin. As late as 852 this same Lupus wrote to Ealdsige, abbot of York, asking for the loan of some books, the *Quaestiones* on the scriptures of St. Jerome and of Bede, and Quintilian's *Concerning the training of an Orator*.[47] Clearly, despite the increasing attacks of the Vikings, the church of York was still a notable centre of learning in the middle of the ninth century.

The Viking period and the age of St. Oswald
In 855 the Viking army wintered in England for the first time. By 867 the Danes were occupying East Anglia, and in the following year they went north, crossed the Humber, and captured York. The Northumbrians suspended their civil wars for long enough to attack them, and in spite of the death of both their kings the English seem to have negotiated a truce which left them in possession of the city; but in 869 the Danes were in York again. Simeon of Durham, drawing upon earlier northern annals, records the fact that Archbishop Wulfhere, who had received the pallium in 854, was 'reinstated' in 873 and died in 892 in the thirty-ninth year of his episcopate, after which the see was vacant for eight years.[48] Very little of its ancient reputation seems to have survived at York. Asser tells us that King Alfred 'was wont to say' that 'at that time' (the decade after 871) there were

---

[44] *Councils and Ecclesiastical Docs.*, ed. Haddan and Stubbs, iii. 527; Simeon of Durham, ed. Arnold, p. 316.

[45] Alcuin, *Epistola* 121 (p. 177); cf. William of Malmesbury, *Gesta Regum*, ed. W. Stubbs (Rolls Ser., 1887–9), i. 68.

[46] *Councils and Ecclesiastical Docs.*, ed. Haddan and Stubbs, iii. 615–16; *EHD* i. 806–7.

[47] Lupus de Ferrières, *Correspondance*, ii, ed. L. Levillain (Paris, 1935), pp. 78–81; *EHD* i. 808–9.

[48] Simeon of Durham, ed. Arnold, ii. 92; *EHD* i. 251.

'no good scholars in all the kingdom of the West Saxons',[49] and he brought in learned men from abroad and from Western Mercia to fill the gap. Of Northumbria he did not speak at all.

For the first half of the tenth century there is little recorded history of the church of York. The city was occupied in turn by the Danes, the armies of the West Saxon successors of Alfred, and Norse raiders from Ireland. It was not until the reign of Edgar (959–75) that the English were safely in possession of the whole of Northumbria. It does not, however, appear that these years were a time of entire depression, either for the material prosperity of York or for the state of its Christian population. As so often happened the Vikings, who were prepared to trade as well as to ravage, brought a measure of prosperity; the *Anonymous Life of St. Oswald* describes York in about 980 as a densely populated city, full of Danish merchants, even if its buildings were somewhat down-at-heel.[50] Some of the Danes were even showing an interest in Christianity, perhaps as an insurance against risks in the future life, perhaps in order to facilitate relations with the English, and perhaps from genuine conviction. There were archbishops still in York, though they are little more than names to us, and the Minster survived and even remained a centre of Christian worship. As early as 895 a Danish king, Guthfrith, who was converted to Christianity, was buried in it,[51] and in 934 King Athelstan made it a very substantial grant of land.[52] Roger of Wendover, who seems to be using here some earlier source, records that in 946 King Eadred presented it with two large bells.[53]

In 956/8 Oscytel, translated from the see of Dorchester, became archbishop. He was a near relation of the saintly Oda, who since 942 had held the see of Canterbury as a notable reformer, and his undoubtedly Scandinavian name strengthens the probability of the story that Oda's father was a pagan Dane who had come to England in the war-band of Hubba and Ivar the Boneless. Oscytel was a personal friend of St. Dunstan, and therefore almost by definition a reformer, although very little is known of his work. He was succeeded, after the very short pontificate of Edwald,

---

[49] *EHD* i. 266; *Asser's Life of King Alfred*, ed. W. H. Stevenson (Oxford, 1904; rev. edn. 1959), c. 24, p. 21.

[50] *Hists. York* i. 454. On Viking York see refs. above, n. 1.

[51] Æthelweard, *Chronicle*, ed. A. Campbell (Nelson's Medieval Texts, 1962), p. 51.

[52] *Early Yorks. Charters*, i, ed. W. Farrer (Edinburgh, 1914), no. 1, with sceptical comments by W. H. Stevenson; but see *EHD* i. 505–8, where it is defended by Prof. Whitelock; full bibliography in P. H. Sawyer, *Anglo-Saxon Charters* (1968), no. 407.

[53] Roger of Wendover, *Flores Historiarum*, ed. H. O. Coxe (Eng. Hist. Soc., 1841–2), i. 399; *EHD* i. 257.

by his 'near earthly kin'[54] (probably a nephew) St. Oswald, bishop of Worcester. Oswald held the two sees together until his death in 992. This seems to have been a deliberate arrangement, probably made in order to build-up the depleted and exhausted church of York by linking it to one of the richest parts of Western Mercia. Oswald was one of the three outstanding personalities of the tenth-century reformation in England, the others being St. Dunstan and St. Ethelwold. Unfortunately for historians, the man who wrote his biography was a person of flowery style and strongly conventional ideas, and he was also much more interested in Oswald's doings as bishop of Worcester and as abbot of Ramsey than in his activities at York. Desiring above all things to emphasize Oswald's saintliness, he gives us very little of the man's individuality. However, a few facts do emerge. Oswald was distinguished from his youth by a strong desire to learn and to teach, and at the monastery of Fleury, to which he had gone to study the principles of the reformed Benedictine rule, he learned the whole office by heart, 'wishing to teach his own countrymen what he had learned from strangers'.[55] He had a notably beautiful voice and, at least at Ramsey,[56] he established a strong musical tradition. Whenever he came to York, he always went first to his church.[57] In spite of the fact that he suffered painfully from rheumatism[58] he seems to have tried to carry out visitations of his see; it is recorded that he went to Ripon, established monks there in the place of secular clergy, and provided a new shrine for the relics of St. Wilfrid and his companions.[59] The one incident recorded in detail about his life in York is the story of a mouse which died suddenly after eating some of the blessed bread which the archbishop was accustomed to distribute to his guests at the beginning of a feast.[60] It is an odd tale, but it serves at least to illustrate the decorous behaviour which the archbishop expected to prevail at his parties. We may believe that at York, as at Worcester, his death was marked by such public lamentation that 'merchants left their bargaining, and women their distaffs and their weaving'.[61]

The union of two substantial sees in the hands of a single saintly bishop is a puzzle; nor is it made easier by the numerous cases of similar pluralism in

[54] *Hists. York* i. 420.
[55] Ibid. i. 419.
[56] Ibid. i. 417, 464.
[57] Ibid. i. 454; on the *Vita Oswaldi* see Whitelock in *EHD* i. 839 and refs., esp. D. J. V. Fisher, in *Cambridge Historical Jour.* x, iii (1952) 27 ff.
[58] *Hists. York* i. 467.
[59] Ibid. i. 462–3.
[60] Ibid. i. 454–5.
[61] Ibid. i. 472.

the two generations between Oswald's death and the Norman conquest. Some of the bishops were men of exemplary piety, like Oswald's two successors, Ealdwulf, formerly abbot of Peterborough, who held both Oswald's sees from 995 till his death in 1002, and Wulfstan the homilist, translated from London to the double see in 1002.[62] Some of the pluralists seem to have been practising a mere abuse; and this was recognized in the case of one of the later archbishops, Ealdred, who tried to hold Worcester with York at his translation in 1061, but was ousted by the pope from Worcester a year later; it was notorious in the case Ealdred's contemporary at Canterbury, Stigand, who was found to be holding the sees both of Canterbury (1052–70) and of Winchester even after he had complaisantly surrendered the see of East Anglia to his brother.[63] Edward the Confessor was particulary tolerant of bishops who accumulated wealth in unusual ways, and some of the English cathedrals benefited permanently from his tolerance, York included. But in the era of the movement for ecclesiastical reform of which popes like Nicholas II, who drummed Ealdred, were the centre, episcopal pluralism, along with clerical marriage and other ancient customs, were fiercely attacked. Evidently St. Oswald had grounds of a more acceptable character than Ealdred's for combining the sees.

If such pluralism is strange in a saint, even stranger is the contrast between the two cathedrals to which it draws our attention; and this is of particular interest, for it provides us with the first real insight we have into the nature of the Minster's clergy. From the time of St. Oswald until the dissolution of the monasteries Worcester was one of the English cathedrals served by a chapter of monks. Oswald at Worcester and Ethelwold at Winchester were the founders of this practice, often said—with some exaggeration—to be unique to Britain.[64] Under Oswald himself and his immediate successors, and again under the last eminent Old English bishop, Wulfstan II (1062–95), Worcester Cathedral was a notable centre of

---

[62] For what follows see F. Barlow, *The English Church, 1000–1066* (1963); D. Whitelock, 'The Dealings of the Kings of England with Northumbria in the tenth and eleventh centuries' in *The Anglo-Saxons, Studies presented to B. Dickins* (1959), pp. 70 ff; Janet M. Cooper, *The Last Four Anglo-Saxon Archbishops of York* (Borthwick Papers, no. 38, York, 1970). On Ealdwulf see refs. in *Heads of Religious Houses, England and Wales, 940–1216*, ed. D. Knowles, C. N. L. Brooke, and V. C. M. London (Cambridge, 1972), p. 59. On Wulfstan see esp. D. Whitelock, 'Archbishop Wulfstan, homilist and statesman', *Trans. Royal Hist. Soc.*, 4th Ser. xxiv (1942), 25–45; Whitelock, 'Wulfstan at York', in *Franciplegius: Medieval and Linguistic Studies in honor of Francis Peabody Magoun, Jr.*, ed. J. B. Bessinger, Jr., and R. P. Creed (New York, 1965), pp. 214–31; and Whitelock's edn. of *Sermo Lupi ad Anglos* (2nd edn. 1952); trans. in *EHD* i. 854–9; *Homilies*, ed. D. Bethurum (Oxford, 1957).
[63] Barlow, op. cit., pp. 86–90, 76–81.
[64] On their monasticism see D. Knowles, *Monastic Order in England* (Cambridge, 1940; 2nd edn. 1963), Chs. iii–iv; at one time or another a fair number of chapters on the Continent were monastic, and a large number had chapters of canons regular.

monastic observance. York was never monastic, nor were either of the other Minster churches under the archbishops' immediate control—Ripon or Beverley—served by monks in the tenth or any later century; indeed, there were no monastic communities at all in England north of the Trent in the tenth and early eleventh centuries. Northumbria in general, and the vale of York in particular, are full of monastic remains; a few are of the age of St. Wilfrid and Bede; the great majority are monuments to the Norman age; none was late Old English. When Thomas, the first Norman archbishop of York, arrived, he is supposed to have found merely the remnant of a group of secular canons in the Minster—three of a total never more than seven.[65]

Beside this, let us set another contrast. In 1092 the aged Bishop Wulfstan presided over a synod in the crypt of his cathedral which settled many issues, including the status of the parish churches in Worcester itself.[66] It determined that by ancient custom there was only one parish, that of the cathedral, and that the various other ancient churches of the city were subordinate to the cathedral. Such a decision might have been regarded as quite normal by an Italian bishop of the age; it was coming to sound strange to English ears, for the eleventh century saw the proliferation of tiny parishes attached to tiny parish churches in many English towns. By the end of the eleventh century York certainly had eleven, and probably far more; by 1200 it had forty. By then Lincoln, Norwich, and Winchester had even more numerous parish churches, and London almost 100 within the walls.[67]

The reasons most commonly alleged for Oswald's pluralism are the poverty of the see of York and the paganism of its inhabitants. The Viking invasions had made large areas of eastern and northern England pagan at worst, missionary country at best. Oswald and his successors attempted its reconquest from bases in the south and south-west. While they marched out towards York from a base by the Severn, their neighbour the bishop of Dorchester—the vast see which was to be moved to Lincoln after the Norman Conquest—nestled by the Thames.[68] The pagan element among the north-eastern Vikings no doubt made York an insecure base for a bishop in the mid- and late tenth centuries and for a time reduced the temporalities of the see. There has been much argument as to how thickly the Scandinavian invaders settled in the northern Danelaw, in Lincolnshire and Yorkshire. The most striking evidence of the situation at the time of St. Oswald's death

[65] Hugh, *York*, p. 11.

[66] *Cartulary of Worcester Cathedral Priory*, ed. R. R. Darlington (Pipe Roll Soc., 1968), pp. 31–2; cf. C. N. L. Brooke in *Studies in Church History*, vi, ed. G. J. Cuming (Cambridge, 1970), p. 64.

[67] Brooke, *Studies*, pp. 64 ff.; C. N. L. Brooke and G. Keir, *London 800–1216* (1975), Ch. 6.

[68] See Barlow, pp. 163–4, 215–16; D. Whitelock, 'The Conversion of the Eastern Danelaw', in *Saga-Book of the Viking Soc.* xii (1937–45), 159–76.

is provided by the coins struck by the moneyers of York.[69] They show first of all that it was considered a major centre of economic activity; in the mid-eleventh century there were as many moneyers at York as in London itself. By the standards of the day it was a large and prosperous town. A recent analysis of the names of the moneyers on the coins shows a marked preponderance of names of Viking origin. On the coins of the London mint in the reign of Ethelred the Unready (978–1016) all but a handful of the moneyers have Old English names; in Lincoln and the towns of the east Midlands there is a notable Scandinavian element, rising in Chester to a quarter. In York the Scandinavian names amount to 40, swamping the English (13) and Celtic (5). By this date the Vikings had been in York for a century, and some English parents may have been giving their children Norse names. But when all allowances have been made, it is difficult to escape the conclusion of the expert who has analysed this striking evidence, that York was still 'a primarily Norwegian colony', and that 'the integration of the settlers with the native population was far less complete in York than in any other part of England in which the Vikings settled'.[70]

Virtually all the English bishops between the reign of Edgar and the accession of Cnut (959–1016) had been monks before their consecration. From Cnut's time there is an increasing element recruited from the secular clergy, specially from the royal chapel; there is also an increasing element of rich men inclined to add see to see and pile up money and estates. Religious life and pastoral care took two chief forms, as far as we can tell: the monastic communities flourished, as at Worcester, and remained in the eleventh century centres of religious life for the laity as well; elsewhere there was a proliferation of parish churches, reflecting self-help by landowners and merchants, and by parish clergy living close to the people. It is rare for us to have evidence of collaboration between the bishop and the parish priests; the outstanding exception is in the Northumbrian Priests' Laws, which seem to show us the great legislator Archbishop Wulfstan I at work among the rank and file of his clergy in York.[71].

Wulfstan was almost certainly a monk by origin, but he has won renown

---

[69] See the remarkable study by Veronica J. Smart, 'Moneyers of the late Anglo-Saxon coinage, 973–1016' in *Commentationes de nummis saeculorum IX–XI in Suecia repertis*, ii (Stockholm, 1968), pp. 191–276, esp. pp. 227–33 for York. in this period see H. Lindkvist, 'A study on early medieval York', *Anglia*, l (1926), 345–94; J. Radley, 'Economic aspects of Anglo-Danish York', *Medieval Archaeology*, xv (1971), 37–57.

[70] Smart, op. cit., p. 233.

[71] See Whitelock in *EHD* i. 434–9; F. Liebermann, *Gesetze der Angelsachsen* (Halle, 1903–16), i. 380–5; C. N. L. Brooke, in *Studies*, pp. 80–1. Cf. Janet M. Cooper, op. cit., pp. 8–10. Some of the code was drawn from other, earlier codes, adapted to the needs of York. Janet Cooper thinks it was the work of a subordinate, reworked by Wulfstan.

in recent years by the progressive revelation of his work as legislator and pastoral leader; his works consist of eloquent vernacular sermons and legislation both secular and ecclesiastical. 'With great deserts have we merited the miseries which oppress us', he said in his famous Sermon of the Wolf (a play upon his name) to the English—originally a response to the disasters of the end of Ethelred's reign; 'a great breach will require much repair, and a great fire no little water, if the fire is to be quenched at all; and great is the necessity for everyman that he keep henceforward God's laws eagerly and pay God's dues rightly.'[72]

Wulfstan was indeed much interested both in the Church's laws and pastoral care and in its revenues. The first half of the famous cartulary of Worcester Cathedral, Cotton MS. Tiberius A.xiii,[73] was written under Wulfstan's eye, and carefully corrected and annotated by a hand which may well be Wulfstan's own. For another record, also in the British Museum, Harleian MS.55, f.4v, shows us the same hand labelling and correcting a copy of a record of St. Oswald relating to some of the properties of the see of York. It seems clear that Wulfstan's base was at Worcester, and it is probable that we owe the survival of this record to the care of the monks of Worcester for his books. But it also seems clear that he cared for his northern see; and pastorally as well as temporally. *The Law of the Northumbrian Priests* may well be, at least in part, from his hand.[74] It is a puzzling document, but in the main it seems to be a very down-to-earth attempt to deal with the clergy of a teeming city, and we need not doubt that it reflects life in York in Wulfstan's later years. The clergy are gathered into a guild or club which attempts to enforce standards of practice and behaviour by levying fines; they are in many ways very secular—they frequent taverns, are quarrelsome, liable to put 'unsuitable things' in their church, say mass before the church is consecrated, celebrate in wooden chalices, bring weapons into church; they have to be reminded that they can only have one wife (a remarkable concession indeed from a celibate archbishop), that they must 'all love and honour one God . . . and entirely cast out every heathen practice' (*c.* 47). We are shown an active missionary clergy close to their flocks in spirit and manner as well as physically, in the tiny churches in which they are admonished not to celebrate festivals in the wrong order; of the larger presence of the Minster there is no hint.

Wulfstan's work evidently continued; for the Flemish monk Folcard,

---

[72] *EHD* i. 855.

[73] On which see N. R. Ker, 'Hemming's Cartulary', in *Studies in Medieval History presented to F. M. Powicke*, ed. R. W. Hunt, W. A. Pantin, R. W. Southern (Oxford, 1948), pp. 49–75; it was ed. by T. Hearne in 1723. On Harleian 55 see Ker, *Catalogue of Manuscripts containing Anglo-Saxon* (Oxford, 1957) no. 225. See Whitelock, 'Wulfstan at York', esp. p. 216.

[74] See Whitelock in *EHD* i. 434–5.

who wrote the life of St. John of Beverley in the middle of the century, commends Archbishop Ealdred for his synodal reforms.[75] In celebrating the liturgy the holy church of York—cathedral and diocese—had shaken off its ancient rusticity, decent order had been enjoined, and the clergy told to take off their secular garments and put on decent clerical dress. In Folcard's stately phrases one catches the echo of cosmopolitan contempt for semi-educated provincial clergy, but also of the lively worker priests and whisky priests—an interesting combination—suggested by the Northumbrian Priests' Law.

The Norman Conquest

On Christmas Day 1066 Ealdred anointed and crowned William the Conqueror king of the English in Westminster Abbey; and in 1069 he died.[76] The appointment of his successor marked a new departure in the promotion of Norman clergy. Hitherto, William's nominees had either been members of the Norman feudal nobility, like his half-brother, Odo of Bayeux, or Geoffrey de Mowbray of Coutances, or pious reforming monks, like Maurilius of Rouen or Lanfranc, very soon to become archbishop of Canterbury and no doubt already marked out for the office. The English bishops were rarely aristocratic either before or after the Conquest; already in the Confessor's time the majority had come to be recruited from the royal chapel, and although a trickle of monks continued, the majority of William's appointments were of secular clerks who had grown up both in his chapel and household and in the secular cathedrals of Normandy.[77] Many of the bishops of the next generation had held office or a canonry at Bayeux or Rouen; from Bayeux and the Bessin came three of the most remarkable clerical families of the age.[78] First Thomas, treasurer of Bayeux,

---

[75] 'Vita S. Johannis', *Hists. York* i. 241. Cf. Ibid. ii. 342–54, esp. 353–4: a later chronicle, evidently incorporating early material or traditions, which suggests that Ealdred was active in attempting to sustain or revive some kind of communal life in the minsters of his diocese, especially Beverley; and he is said to have built a refectory at York.

[76] See Guy of Amiens, *Carmen de Hastingae Proelio*, ed. C. Morton and H. Muntz (Oxford, 1972), p. lv; Anglo-Saxon Chronicle, MS.D, *sub anno* 1068 for 1069; on Ealdred see Barlow, pp. 86–90. For the effects of the Norman Conquest see esp. J. Le Patourel, 'The Norman Conquest of Yorkshire', *Northern History*, vi (1971), 1–21. On Ealdred's last years and death, *Hists. York* ii. 349–50, cf. 350–4. There is a very interesting reference to the *consuetudo* of the church of York in the time of Edward the Confessor and Archbishop Ealdred in a charter attributed to Henry I (and perhaps genuine): *Hists. York* iii. 34–6.

[77] Barlow, pp. 76 ff; R. and C. Brooke, 'I Vescovi di Inghilterra e Normannia durante il secolo XI: contrasti' in *Miscellanea del Centro di Studi Medioevali*, viii (Milan, forthcoming).

[78] On these families see C. N. L. Brooke, 'Gregorian reform in action: clerical marriage in England, 1050–1200', *Cambridge Hist. Jour.* xii, i (1956), 1–21, esp. 12 ff., repr. *Medieval Church and Society* (1971), pp. 69–99, esp. 86 ff.; also Brooke, 'The Composition of the Chapter of St. Paul's, 1086–1163', *Cambridge Hist. Jour.* x, ii (1951), 111–32, esp. 124.

archbishop of York (1070–1100), whose brother Samson was bishop of Worcester from 1096; and Samson's son, another Thomas, was ultimately to sit on his uncle's throne at York from 1108 to 1114. Next Ranulf Flambard, William II's notorious minister, bishop of Durham (1099–1128), brother and father of other career clerks.[79] Finally Anger or Anskar, Thomas's colleague at Bayeux, who came to London with his wife Popelina and settled in a canonry at St. Paul's; they reared at least two sons, one of whom, Audoen, was successively canon of St. Paul's and bishop of Evreux, the other, Thurstan, canon of St. Paul's and archbishop of York (1114–40).[80] Thurstan began as a favourite clerk of William Rufus, and colleague of Flambard, and ended, in the odour of sanctity, founder of Fountains Abbey and monk of Pontefract. In his own career he reconciled or settled several of the conflicts of the age: a scion of the old abuse (as the age saw it) of clerical marriage and hereditary benefices, a worldly royal clerk, who was yet the friend and patron of monks; and in a world in which Cistercian monks could engage in bitter conflict with Cluniacs, he founded a Cistercian abbey and died clothed in the habit of a Cluniac. He also settled the primacy dispute between Canterbury and York—settled after a fashion, for it has flared up again times out of number since his death; but no archbishop of York has since been compelled to admit the formal superiority of the archbishop of Canterbury.

Thurstan must be one of the heroes of this chapter, for he is the central figure of the one really notable chronicle to come out of York Minster in the Norman period, that of Hugh the Chanter, or Hugh Sottewame, which is mainly a lively and entertaining account of Thurstan's struggles.[81] But Thomas and his family were in their way no less interesting. Samson was evidently a man with a subtle and cunning mind, perhaps the author and chief scribe of the Domesday survey;[82] and Thomas was one of the founders of the type of secular cathedral which was characteristic of medieval England, and, in a modified form, still lives in York Minster.

The foundation of the chapter: dignities and prebends
If we were in a position to ask an instructed clerk of the eleventh or twelfth

---

[79] R. W. Southern, *Medieval Humanism and other studies* (Oxford, 1970), pp. 183–205; Brooke in *Cambridge Hist. Jour.* x, ii (1951), 124, 129 ff corrected by D. E. Greenway, in J. Le Neve, *Fasti Ecclesiae Anglicanae 1066–1300*, i (1968), pp. 97–8.

[80] D. Nicholl, *Thurstan, archbishop of York* (York, 1964); see above, n. 78.

[81] Hugh, *York*; on Hugh, canon and precentor (hence 'Chanter'), see Clay, 'Precentors and chancellors', pp. 116–20; Clay, *Fasti* i. 12, and 51, 53, 84; ii. 41–2, 56, 137–8, 163, for other members of the family Sottewame, esp. Arnulf and Thomas, who were also canons.

[82] As suggested by V. H. Galbraith, 'Notes on the career of Samson bishop of Worcester (1096–1112)', *EHR* lxxxii (1967), 86–101.

centuries what sort of folk peopled cathedrals in his day, he would be able without much difficulty to say 'canons or, in a few places, monks'. But if we asked him what kind of people canons were, we could expect an answer much less clear cut. Traditionally, the word 'canon' was supposed to mean a 'rule', and many canons claimed that they took this name because they lived according to a rule.[83] But notoriously some canons were more regular than others. The distinctions in use in the eleventh century went back to the days of Charlemagne and his successor, Louis the Pious, in the early ninth century. These emperors promulgated edicts and presided over councils which provided, on paper at least, for the reform of the very varied, and often very lax, institutes of their empire, and divided the world into monks and canons in a tolerably clear way. Monks lived according to the Rule of St. Benedict and were in a fair measure separated from the world; canons lived also according to a rule and a number of customary regulations codified, probably by Amalarius of Metz, in the Council of Aachen of 816–17. These regulations were deeply influenced by the Rule of St. Benedict, and, had the canons adhered closely to them, they would have been little different from monks, save that their opportunities to work in the world and serve the communities among which they lived were somewhat greater.

By the twelfth century it was possible for some observers to see two types of canon clearly distinct: canons regular, who lived according to the Rule of St. Augustine and so were frequently known as 'Augustinian', and canons secular, who lived in their own houses and enjoyed separate incomes. Even then there were secular canons who liked to quote the old saying 'canon equals *regula*', and the distinction was nothing like so firm as most modern scholars would have us believe. In the eleventh century it was even less so; for the Rule of St. Augustine, though ancient, and in some of its versions and lineaments possibly even connected with the great bishop of Hippo, was hardly known in England before about 1100; and the way of life of the secular canons, in the form in which it is known to us from the custumals of the twelfth century and later, was hardly recognized as legitimate before about 1090.

The canons of English cathedrals in the two generations before the Conquest, in so far as we have any information about them, all seem to have paid some sort of lip service either to the *Institutio canonicorum* of 816–17,

---

[83] Cf. K. Edwards, *The English Secular Cathedrals in the Middle Ages* (2nd edn., Manchester, 1967), pp. 1 ff. (to which we are much indebted in what follows). See also, on canons regular, J. C. Dickinson, *The Origins of the Austin Canons* . . . (1950); *La Vita Comune del Clero nei secoli xi e xii, Miscellanea del Centro di Studi Medioevali*, iii (Milan, 1962); *Libellus de diversis ordinibus* . . . ed. and trans. G. Constable and B. Smith (Oxford, 1972).

or to a version of the eighth-century Rule of Bishop Chrodegang of Metz, which is sometimes referred to as the expanded Rule of Chrodegang.[84] This bound them to a measure of common life, not only in attending regularly at mass and the round of daily offices in the cathedral, but also eating communal meals in a refectory by day and sleeping together in a dormitory at night. In some, as at St. Paul's, it seems to have been not wholly incompatible with some independent use of money and resources; and at the cathedrals, such as York, where the community was very small, a genuine communal life seems unlikely, and it is quite possible, even probable, that cathedral clerks, like other clergy, lived in the world and married.[85] Folcard's preface, confirmed by later evidence, may indicate that Ealdred embarked on a scheme of reform, but Hugh the Chanter tells us that it was Thomas who in his early years introduced or reintroduced canons living the common life at York; in his later years he converted the chapter to conform with the model to which he had been accustomed in Normandy, a fully secular chapter of canons living in their own houses, enjoying the fruits of separate incomes or 'prebends'.

The history of the secular canons on the Continent has yet to be written, and there is much about it which is totally obscure.[86] But we know that in many parts of northern France (and with local differences, in many other regions too) there had grown up in the preceding centuries a type of cathedral chapter which must have been familiar to many of the Norman invaders. This consisted of a group of between twenty and fifty canons, with individual prebends (literally, a prebend means provisions or provender), who lived in houses in the close, met regularly for mass and offices, and served the cathedral and, traditionally, also the churches of the neighbourhood. They were directed by a group of dignitaries, to whom various special functions were delegated: such as the dean or provost, the head of the chapter under the bishop, the precentor who ruled the choir, the chancellor who ruled the seal and the school, the treasurer who guarded relics, reliquaries and other treasures, and so forth. Such chapters existed, or were in process of formation, in various Norman cathedrals in the second half of the eleventh century, but much more mature examples were to be seen not far off, in Chartres and Paris and elsewhere.

There was little in the custom of such chapters to prevent the secular

---

[84] See D. Whitelock's *R. W. Chambers Memorial Lecture*, 'Some Anglo-Saxon bishops of London' (London, 1975).

[85] See Brooke in *A History of St. Paul's Cathedral*, ed. W. R. Matthews and W. M. Atkins (1957), pp. 11 ff., 361 ff.; cf. A. Morey and C. N. L. Brooke, *Gilbert Foliot and his Letters* (Cambridge, 1965), pp. 188 ff. and refs.; see above, n. 83. For what follows see n. 44 n. 75.

[86] See literature cited above, n. 83.

canons from being absentees, and doubtless already at this date many of them were engaged in various other activities, in the service of dukes and kings and other bishops; perhaps also in trade and commerce—though the great proliferation of petty bureaucracies, and the great growth of schools and universities, still lay well in the future when Thomas was consecrated archbishop in 1070. Already these chapters formed large and diverse groups of men with manifold concerns in the affairs of the world and the Church. Not surprisingly, they were not well regarded by the more ardent reformers of the day. One of the central planks in the platform of the papal reformers was the campaign for celibacy. In cathedral closes, as in parish churches, as far as the evidence allows us to generalize, it was normal in the mid-eleventh century for the clergy to be married. In these circles the programme of the papal reformers spelt social revolution, the downgrading of many ladies of the close from wives to concubines; in the end, their disappearance. From the parishes (in all probability) they never disappeared during the Middle Ages. The reformers saw the secular chapters of canons as haunts of vice; for the canons set what they regarded as a bad example to the clergy at large, and passed on their prebends to their sons or near relations. We have no reason to suppose that they were wrong in this. Celibacy had been enjoined on all clergy in the orders of sub-deacon and above from the fifth century—in many respects the law was even older than that—and canons, whether in orders or not, were included in this ban in various pronouncements of the late eleventh century.

The law of the Church was perfectly clear. Equally so was custom, and custom hallowed these alliances. We have no reason to suppose that Samson's wife and the lady Popelina, mother of Thurstan, were anything but respected and respectable. The reformers were already attacking them, but it was a long time before the law of celibacy deeply affected the life of the close. The best documented cathedral of the late eleventh and early twelfth centuries, in this respect, is that of London; and we know that at least a third of the canons of St. Paul's of that era were married, and a proportion of these passed on their benefices to their sons.[87] The hereditary canons began to disappear in the second quarter of the twelfth century, and were evidently by then regarded by most responsible churchmen as an abuse. But in the eleventh century opinion must have been very divided, and the family-men included both native English and Norman canons. Of York before about 1090 we know little, though doubtless Thomas had some of his Norman associates, and possibly a wife,

---

[87] See D. E. Greenway, in J. Le Neve, *Fasti Ecclesiae Anglicanae, 1066–1300*, i; Brooke in *Cambridge Hist. Jour.*, x, ii (1951), 124 ff.; xii, i (1956), 16 ff.; xii, ii (1956), 187–8.

in his entourage. At the neighbouring cathedral of Durham an elderly, learned, married clerk called Eilaf held the office of treasurer until the Norman Bishop William of Saint-Calais replaced the existing community by monks in 1083; Eilaf and his son lived on for another thirty years as priests of the ancient church of Hexham, until canons regular came to oust him in 1113, sent by Archbishop Thomas II.[88] The younger Eilaf was allowed an honourable pension, but could hardly be expected to welcome this harsh intervention. The next year his small son came to tell him that the archbishop was dead—'True, my son, he is dead who leads an evil life', said he, not believing at first that the boy could know.[89] The son was to grow up to be abbot of the great Cistercian house of Rievaulx, and St. Ailred is a very remarkable link between the world of the hereditary priests and the stern, celibate asceticism of the Order of Cîteaux, which was to be the major spiritual force in Yorkshire in the second quarter of the twelfth century.

It was natural for the papal reformers of the eleventh century, as for the Cistercians in the twelfth, to look askance at secular chapters and secular canons. More positively, the campaign for celibacy was part of a movement to turn all clergy into quasi-monks, to separate them from the entanglements of the world and the flesh, to make communities of canons into quasi-monastic convents. The key moment in the formation of these endeavours was the Council in the Lateran Basilica in Rome in 1059 at which Pope Nicholas II presided over crucial debates and decisions in the formation of the campaign.[90] One such debate was the discussion of the life of canons, the *vita canonica*, which led to a refreshment of the movement and, in the long run, to the discovery, or invention, of the Rule of St. Augustine and the growth of the Augustinian canons. Immediately, it inspired fresh efforts to enforce the *Institutio canonicorum* of 816–17 and to strengthen the institutes which had sprung from it. And one of the most remarkable figures of the council was the eminent theologian and monk Lanfranc of Pavia, by 1059 Lanfranc of Bec, a leading monk in Normandy and already a councillor to Duke William; later to be archbishop of Canterbury (1070–89).

In spite of this council and the movement it fostered, the secular cathedral chapter enjoyed a modest renaissance in the two generations which followed, and this is an ironical aspect of the history of the Church in the wake of the papal reform. In no part of Western Europe did the secular

---

[88] J. Raine, *Priory of Hexham*, i (Surtees Soc., 1864), pp. 1 ff.; F. M. Powicke, in Walter Daniel, *Life of Ailred of Rievaulx* (Nelson's Medieval Texts, 1950), pp. xxxiv f.
[89] Walter Daniel, p. 72.
[90] Dickinson, *Origins of the Austin Canons*, pp. 29 ff.; G. Miccoli, 'Pier Damiani e la vita comune del clero' in *La Vita Comune del Clero* i. 186 ff.

cathedral chapter flourish more than in England and Normandy in the late eleventh century. Norman chapters were re-founded and greatly enlarged and enriched at Bayeux and Coutances, whose bishops were among the Conqueror's leading military advisers and assistants, and represented old corruption in an episcopate well provided with men of more admirable character.[91] In England the situation was complicated by the presence of monastic chapters already at Worcester, Winchester, and Canterbury. These looked strange to Norman eyes, and Lanfranc himself evidently had doubts, or was thought to have doubts, about their suitability. Unlike some of his colleagues, and his more imaginative and sympathetic successor, St. Anselm, he cared little for English traditions and cults. But he rapidly discovered the advantage of a community which was both regular and able to absorb a group of his own Norman monastic colleagues. In later years he gave encouragement to the formation of monastic chapters at Rochester (1080) by his disciple Bishop Gundulf, and to the establishment of the see of Wells in Bath Abbey (1088–90).[92] In the 1080s the bishop of Dorchester–Lincoln seems to have been contemplating a monastic chapter,[93] and such were formed at Durham in 1083 and at Norwich soon after.

What happened elsewhere has never been made entirely clear, although it is well known that secular chapters on the Norman pattern were formed in about 1090 at Salisbury, Lincoln, London, and York. 'When he received the archbishopric', says Hugh the Chanter of Thomas I, 'he found everything deserted and waste; of the seven canons (there had been no more), he found three in the burnt city and ruined church' which he inherited after the rebellion of 1070 and its savage suppression by the Conqueror. 'The rest were dead or driven away by fear and misery. He reroofed and to the best of his ability rebuilt the church to which he restored the canons whom he had found there; he recalled the fugitives to

---

[91] See R. and C. Brooke, op. cit.; D. C. Douglas, 'The Norman Episcopate before the Norman Conquest' in *Cambridge Hist. Jour.* xiii, ii (1957), 101–15; D. R. Bates, 'Biography of Odo bishop of Bayeux, 1049–97' (Univ. of Exeter Ph.D thesis 1970); J. Le Patourel, 'Geoffrey de Montbray, bishop of Coutances, 1049–93', *EHR* lix (1944), 129–61.

[92] R. A. L. Smith 'John of Tours, bishop of Bath, 1088–1122', *Collected Papers* (1947), pp. 74–102; J. Armitage Robinson, *Somerset Hist. Essays* (1921), pp. 54 ff., for the later history of Wells and its relation to Bath.

[93] On Lincoln, see the forthcoming study by P. Kidson; the history of the community at Stow and the scale of Remigius's cathedral at Lincoln suggest that he may have had in mind to form a monastic chapter; it seems clear that the secular chapter was formed only in the last few years of his life, *c.* 1090–1 (see below; Giraldus Cambrensis, *Opera* (Rolls Ser., 1861–91), vii, ed. J. F. Dimock, pp. 18–19; Henry of Huntingdon, *Historia Anglorum*, ed. T. Arnold (Rolls Ser., 1879), pp. 300–3, who claims to have known all Remigius's dignitaries). H. E. Salter in *Cartulary of Eynsham Abbey* (Oxford Hist. Soc., 1907–8), i, pp. x–xii, 32–5, 48–50.

the service of God and the Church and added to their number; he rebuilt the refectory and dormitory. He appointed a provost to preside over the others and to manage their affairs; he gave vills, lands and churches himself and restored those which others had taken away. He bestowed much of his own property on the canons; he assigned wise and diligent men to be archdeacons in the diocese. . . . The canons had long lived in common, but the archbishop, after taking advice, determined to divide some of the lands of St. Peter's which were still waste into separate prebends, to leave room for a growing number of canons, each of whom might be eager to build on and cultivate his own share for his own sake. This was done. Then he appointed a dean, treasurer, and precentor, endowing each of them as befitted the church, himself, and their individual dignities. He had already established a master of the schools. He founded and built the present church'—Hugh was writing in the late 1120s and Thomas's church has long since departed, though substantial remains have in recent years been brought to light and can be inspected in the new undercroft of the Minster—'and adorned and furnished it to the best of his power with clerks, books and ornaments: above all else he desired to have good and reputable clerks'.[94]

Here is the clearest statement for any English chapter of the curious pause which often separates the appointment of the first Norman bishop from the establishment of an openly secular chapter. Yet such a change of mind seems to have been common. In the years between 1089 and 1092 the secular chapter with separate prebends ruled by dean, precentor, treasurer, master of the schools, with archdeacons as dignitaries or at least as canons, makes its début at York, Lincoln, and Salisbury; in every case the bishop was far from being a newcomer. In London the formation of prebends and appointment of dean and archdeacons came about the same time; there and elsewhere the other dignitaries followed later—and in most of the other chapters progress towards the model of Salisbury, Lincoln, and York took at least two generations.[95] At York, as at Lincoln and London, and probably at Salisbury, the division of the diocese into territorial archdeaconries seems to have coincided with the formation of the new chapter.

Of St. Osmund's work at Salisbury we have a contemporary record in the

---

[94] Hugh, *York*, p. 11 (slightly adapted). On Thomas's church see below, Ch. III; and on his work at York, A. Hamilton Thompson in *VCH Yorkshire* iii. 375–82. There is a reference to the use of chrism pennies for his restoration in *Hists. York* iii. 68, in which Thurstan remits the payments, since by his time payment for chrism had come to be regarded as a kind of simony, and was forbidden. The formation of the close is indicated by William II's remarkable writ, *Early Yorks. Charters*, i, ed. W. Farrer (Edinburgh, 1914), no. 127. If space permitted comment could be made on Archbishop Gerard's letter to St. Anselm on the canons and Pope Honorius II's letter about an absentee dean (1125–30), which reveal characteristic problems of such a chapter appearing at an early stage (*Hists. York* iii. 23–6, 47–8).

Institutio, stating the functions and privileges of dignitaries and canons, which is dated 1091, and also in the foundation charter of the same date.[96] At Lincoln, we are told—and other evidence confirms it—that Remigius instituted twenty-one canons 'according to the rite of Rouen Cathedral'.[97] Rouen was thought to have provided the model for the customs and rituals of Salisbury in the time of Osmund, and Salisbury and Osmund the model for the rest of England.[98] So stated, the case is undoubtedly over-simplified, but enshrines a substantial element of truth.

The rites and customs of Rouen had been described in a book written by John of Avranches, archbishop of Rouen from 1067 to 1079.[99] In its original form it contained a remarkable analysis of the possible dignitaries of a cathedral, which in its turn was based on observation among other cathedrals and on a text attributed to St. Isidore. The cathedral which is most likely to have influenced the list of dignitaries, Rouen apart, is Chartres, the most mature among the great chapters of northern France in this age. No doubt too the customs of Bayeux, from which Thomas and many other influential canons of this age sprang, affected its English rivals: in assessing the details we are hampered by the total absence of evidence as to the liturgical practices of Salisbury, or York, or Bayeux, which can with any confidence be traced back to the eleventh century. But it is in any event reasonably clear that the bishops of Salisbury and Lincoln worked out with the archbishop of York, and in some measure with the bishop of London, the new pattern they all established in the years between 1089 and 1092.

[95] See the studies of K. Edwards, D. E. Greenway, and others cited above, nn. 83, 85, 87; the full story is emerging with the publication of the revised Le Neve; see also J. Armitage Robinson, op. cit.; A. Watkin, *Dean Cosyn and Wells Cathedral Miscellanea* (Somerset Record Soc., 1941), pp. xxv f., 87–9 (on Wells); H. Mayr-Harting, *Acta of the Bishops of Chichester, 1091–1207* (Canterbury and York Soc., 1964), pp. 41–8; K. Edwards in *VCH Wilts.* iii. 156 ff. For what follows see A. Morey and C. N. L. Brooke, *Gilbert Foliot and his Letters* (Cambridge, 1965), p. 216 and n.; D. E. Greenway in J. Le Neve, *Fasti . . . 1066–1300*, i, and iii (forthcoming).

[96] W. H. Frere, *Use of Sarum* (Oxford, 1898–1901), i. 257–61; *Register of St. Osmund*, ed. W. H. Rich Jones (Rolls Ser., 1883–4), i. 198–200, 212–15. C. N. L. Brooke has defended the authenticity of these documents in a paper summarized in 'Continental influence on English Cathedral Chapters in the XIth and XIIth centuries', *Résumés des communications* of the 11th International Historical Congress at Stockholm (Stockholm, 1960), pp. 120–1; but see K. Edwards in *VCH Wilts.* iii. 156–8.

[97] Giraldus Cambrensis, *Opera*, vii. 19.

[98] Cf. Brooke, 'Continental influence . . .'; Morey and Brooke, *Gilbert Foliot*, pp. 188 ff.

[99] *De officiis ecclesiasticis*, ed r. Delamare (Paris, 1923), who prints the edition which circulated, but also notes the variant version of which an extract survives in an English twelfth-century MS. in Bodl. 843. It seems that this was more probably the original version; it included a list of orders and dignities which had a literary background (like much in John's work), but it is also reminiscent of the dignitaries of Chartres (cf. E. de Lépinois and L. Merlet, in *Cartulaire de Notre Dame de Chartres* (Paris, 1862–5), esp. ii. 96, cf. i. 127). On John's work and its circulation in England see E. Bishop, 'Holy week rites of Sarum, Hereford and Rouen compared', *Liturgica Historica* (Oxford, 1918), pp. 276–300, esp. 277–8, 299–300.

Thus the formation of the secular chapters belongs precisely to the years when the see of Canterbury was vacant and the provincial chapter of Canterbury, of which the bishop of London is still dean and the bishop of Winchester precentor, was being formed. At first sight it is strange that these men should wait till the end of their days was approaching—all save Maurice of London were elderly, and Thomas and Remigius had both been bishops for twenty years before embarking on such ambitious projects. We may well conclude that it was no chance that it happened in the only period of the late eleventh and early twelfth centuries when Canterbury was not ruled by an eminent monk; to put it another way, when Lanfranc had been removed from the scene, they felt free to found openly secular chapters. Beyond this we cannot go; save only to say that in the grass at Old Sarum, on the hill at Lincoln, and in the undercroft at York, lies the physical evidence of their intentions: the full story of their plans, and changes of mind, will only be known when both the historical and the archaeological evidence have been successfully interpreted.

Temporalities

The temporal wealth of archbishop and chapter in the later Middle Ages was substantial. The landed estates formed a single unit under the archbishop's control and probably remained so down to the eleventh century. William of Malmesbury (*c.* 1125) tells us that Thomas I's successors grumbled that he had impoverished them by being too generous to the chapter;[100] and it seems that a division took place in his time, firstly between his own and the chapter's lands, and secondly between the common fund of the chapter and the individual prebends of the canons. It may well be true that the chapter was relatively well endowed; and it was certainly true in later times that some of the offices and prebends of York were exceptionally rich. No chapter could show inequalities of wealth so great among its canons; and the treasurership and the prebend of Masham, in particular, became famous throughout England and indeed to the gates of Rome and of Avignon, as two of the most desirable plums in Christendom.[101]

[100] William of Malmesbury, *Gesta Pontificum*, ed. N. E. S. A. Hamilton (Rolls Ser., 1870), p. 257. Domesday shows 'the land of St. Peter' comprising about 270 carucates in Yorkshire, mostly in the vale of York and Ryedale (see summary and discussion by A. Hamilton Thompson in *VCH Yorkshire* iii. 11). There have been interesting studies of the holdings of archbishop and chapter in the city, important for study of chapter holdings *c.* 1090, by A. G. Dickens, 'The "shire" and prison of the archbishop in the eleventh century', *YAJ* xxxviii (1952–5), 131–47, and John Harvey, 'Bishophill and the Church of York', *YAJ* xli (1963–6), 377–93.

[101] For all that follows see Clay, *Fasti*, esp. i. 22–30 on the treasurers; ii. 51–5 on the prebend of Masham; see also Clay, 'Treasurers' and next note.

The prebend of Masham was established by Roger de Mowbray in the late twelfth century for his kinsman Roger, son of Sampson d'Aubigny.[102] It is rare for the story of a prebend to be so precisely known, and most prebends were endowed by the action of the archbishop, the generosity of the king, or a substantial gift (as in the case of Masham) from a local baron or landowner of substance. Some were well endowed, no doubt, for favoured clerks and relations; some to provide a tempting bait to bring promising young clergy to York. In many cases deserted or partly deserted lands were assigned to prebends and dignities: sometimes they grew and flourished; sometimes they languished. None was so precarious as the prebend of St. Paul's which fell into the sea—'Consumpta per Mare'—but they were widely scattered from Masham in the north-west, thirty-three miles from York, to the Newbalds and South Cave to the south-east; or Wetwang, Driffield, Langtoft, and Grindale to the east.[103] A nucleus lay among St. Peter's manors close to York (Osbaldwick, Dunnington, Strensall, and Warthill), but the scatter of estates in an area heavily devastated after the Norman Conquest makes it natural that their growth should be very variable, and helps to explain why the distinction between prebends rich and poor became so marked.

A few of these chapter estates lay outside Yorkshire. Of these the most interesting are Axminster in Devon, whose wealthy church had been granted by Edward the Confessor to Ealdred, a favourite clerk of Archbishop Ealdred, in the 1060s, and in which the Minster retained a substantial interest; and Oddington in Gloucestershire, a surviving fragment of Archbishop Ealdred's holdings in that county.[104] He had been a man of great wealth: in addition to his two bishoprics he had a grip on the abbey of Gloucester, and Archbishop Thomas struggled hard to retain Ealdred's Gloucestershire manors in a *cause célèbre* not finally settled until 1157.[105] Some of the archbishop's endowments went much further back: for they had once (in the tenth century) been given the whole of Amounderness—a substantial part of Lancashire—and had received other rich gifts over the centuries from King Edward to the Norman Conquest.[106] Much must have depended on the personal wealth of bishops like Ealdred.

Yet when Thomas arrived in 1070 he entered an impoverished see. The

---

[102] *Charters of the Honour of Mowbray, 1107–91*, ed. D. E. Greenway (1972), nos. 191, 197, 325–6, also pp. xliii, lxvi; Clay, *Fasti* i, nos. 34–7; ii. 52.

[103] See Clay, *Fasti* ii, *passim*, esp. opening map.

[104] Ibid. ii. 35–8, 153–5; *Historia et cartularium mon. S. Petri Gloucestriae*, ed. W. H. Hart (Rolls Ser., 1863–7), ii. 105 ff.

[105] *Hist. et cart. Glouc.* ii. 105 ff. Morey and Brooke, *Gilbert Foliot*, pp. 124 ff.; *Letters and Charters of Gilbert Foliot*, ed. Morey and Brooke (Cambridge, 1967), nos. 128–30.

[106] For Amounderness, above, n. 52; see also the charters in *Early Yorks. Charters*, i, and Clay, *Fasti*.

Conqueror had faced rebellion in the north in 1069 and always feared York and Yorkshire as a centre of Viking sympathizers: he lived under the shadow of the threat of invasion from Denmark or Norway. His answer to his threat was characteristic: a fearful devastation from which the city and the vale took two or three generations to recover fully.[107] The early history of the prebends is not sufficiently clear for us to date their origin with precision. It seems likely that a proportion of both rich and poor prebends goes back to Thomas's time.[108] Early in the twelfth century, in the brief reign of Archbishop Gerard (1100–8), a substantial endowment came from Henry I and Queen Matilda, from which sprang the prebends of Driffield and Laughton; later in his reign Henry added Weighton.[109] The middle and later years of Henry I were to see the rapid spread of the Augustinian canons in the diocese, under his patronage; the later years saw the beginnings of the great Cistercian houses. It looks as if, early in his reign, he considered the Minster an important centre of loyalty and influence. The Norman kings rarely visited York; they greatly relied on the archbishop and the bishop of Durham, and on their chapters, for the peace and prosperity of the north-east.

In the eleventh and twelfth centuries York was somewhat remote from the main centres of political and intellectual activity in the Anglo-Norman world—or so it must have appeared to the Norman career ecclesiastics who filled the see after the Conquest. It was doubtless an important part of Thomas's aim in forming the dignities and prebends to attract men of a calibre to form the nucleus of a flourishing chapter. The evidence is not sufficient to give more than an impressionistic account of the chapter and its members in the twelfth century. But we know enough to see something of the success and failure, of the aims, ambitions, and difficulties of the archbishops and of the leading members of the chapter. The twelfth-century deans included four men who became bishops;[110] but the two at the end of the century—Hubert Walter and Simon of Apulia—were too involved in royal administration to have much time to spare for York. Perhaps the most characteristic figure in the list is Robert de Gant, whose

[107] See esp. T. A. M. Bishop 'The Norman Settlement of Yorkshire', *Studies in Medieval History presented to F. M. Powicke* (Oxford, 1948), pp. 1–12, who points out, however, that the waste lands recorded in 1086 cannot be attributed wholly to the Conqueror's armies.

[108] See Clay, *Fasti* ii, p. v, who gathers evidence which makes it probable that the prebends of Holme, Grindale, Warthill, Givendale, and Sherborne (later three prebends) go back to Thomas's time.

[109] Ibid. and pp. 20, 49, 81; *Early Yorks. Charters*, i. 333 ff. Gerard's pontificate also witnessed the important and interesting list of chapter privileges printed in *Visitations and Memorials of Southwell Minster*, ed. A. F. Leach (Camden Soc., 1891), pp. 190–6.

[110] William of Ste.-Barbe (Durham, 1143–52); Hubert Walter (Salisbury, 1189–93; archbishop of Canterbury, 1193–1205); Henry Marshal (Exeter, 1194–1206); Simon of Apulia (Exeter, 1214–23). See Clay, 'Deans'; Clay, *Fasti*, i. 1–2.

name seems to place him in a well-known baronial family, who was chancellor to King Stephen from 1140–1 until 1154, and who yet managed to be a fairly frequent visitor to York.[111] This combination of service to the chapter and to kings or bishops, or even to the pope, is characteristic of the twelfth century; thereafter the distinction became increasingly clear cut between a small community genuinely resident and a large number of canons and dignitaries living elsewhere, drawing the revenues of their offices in York but rarely sitting in their stalls.

The treasurership attracted such men from an early date. After the promotion of St. William from treasurer to archbishop, it went first to his cousin Hugh du Puiset, nephew of King Stephen and of Henry of Blois, bishop of Winchester, who was more active (so it seems) in his role as archdeacon of Winchester.[112] When the pope consecrated Hugh to the see of Durham in 1153, he gave the treasurership to a favourite clerk of the archbishop of Canterbury, John of Canterbury; and when John—an able and amiable man, and a peacemaker in the troubles between Thomas Becket and Henry II—went on to be bishop of Poitiers (1162) and later archbishop of Lyon (1182), a royal clerk, Ralph de Warneville, succeeded who was also treasurer of Rouen, and seems to have lived in Normandy.[113] He was followed, probably in 1182, by another eminent royal clerk, no less than Geoffrey Plantagenet, the king's illegitimate son, who also seems rarely to have visited York until he became archbishop (1189–1212).[114] Not all the treasurers were absentees—two of those of the early thirteenth century frequently appear as witnesses among their fellow canons; but the treasureship remained a prize, to attract the greatest connoisseur among English pluralists, Bogo de Clare, son of the earl of Gloucester, in 1285; and Bogo's successor was a Colonna.[115]

The chapter and the world: York and Canterbury

The chapter had a life none the less and a feeling of community; and like

---

[111] Clay, 'Deans', pp. 366–70; cf. Clay in *YAJ* xxxvi (1944–7), 281 n. 50. There is little precise evidence of non-residence in this period; cf. the absentee dean of the 1120s (*Hists. York* iii. 47–8) and Thomas Becket, prebendary of Apesthorpe (Clay, *Fasti* ii. 4, cf. p. vii), But it is likely that there was far more than we can have evidence of.

[112] G. V. Scammell, *Hugh du Puiset, bishop of Durham* (Cambridge, 1956), esp. pp. 7–8; Clay, 'Treasurers', pp. 10–11.

[113] *Letters . . . of Gilbert Foliot*, pp. 137–8; Scammell, pp. 12 ff.; Clay, 'Treasurers', pp. 11–24; P. Pouzet, *L'anglais Jean dit Bellesmains . . .* (Lyon, 1927).

[114] On Geoffrey, see below, pp. 37–43; Clay, 'Treasurers', pp. 24–5. The name 'Plantagenet' was applied to Geoffrey's grandfather, Geoffrey of Anjou, by Ralph de Diceto, *Opera Historica*, ed. W. Stubbs, i (Rolls Ser., 1876), p. 291; but otherwise it seems not to have been current till the fifteenth century.

[115] Clay, *Fasti* i. 22–30, esp. pp. 26–8; Clay, 'Treasurers'.

most such amorphous communities it fell prey from time to time to division and faction. The inner story is mostly hidden from us, but the two great *causes célèbres* of the early and mid-twelfth century, Thurstan's fight against the primacy of Canterbury and the case of St. William, illustrate both the cohesion and the faction.

Thurstan was a newcomer when he first visited York as archbishop.[116] The firm determination he was able to sustain from first to last is striking testimony to a solid body of feeling in the chapter itself to help and support him; to inspire him indeed to endless struggles in what has appeared to most modern commentators a dreary suit. It did not so appear to contemporaries, and of this a notable witness is Hugh the Chanter, a writer of great skill and verve and self-confidence, who dedicated almost the whole of his lives of the archbishops to a detailed narrative of Thurstan's struggles.[117]

Thurstan won because, in the end, the pope was bound to recognize that his case had the sounder historical foundation; and it is a notable fact that the York chapter succeeded without forgery—it is the only major religious community in England of whose early muniments we have any substantial remnant, to whom no suspicion of forgery attaches.[118] Essentially, this was because the canons and the archbishop of York fought a short, sharp battle against the primacy of Canterbury, and won, not a total victory, but sufficient to make elaborate invention unnecessary.

The see of Canterbury was older and had been effectively metropolitan much longer than York; and the centres of power and wealth in the kingdom, as well as the centres of monastic observance, made York a northern outpost. Between 900 and 1066 there were no mint-towns north of the Trent save York and Chester, and no monasteries north of the Wash save Burton-on-Trent. When Lanfranc, a man of wide and cosmopolitan outlook and somewhat imperial ambitions, came to Canterbury in the 1070s, it was natural for him both to assume that Britain, like Gaul, had a traditional primacy dispute, and to look to the king as an ally in forming a united English—or rather British—Church, under the primacy of Canterbury. This suited William, who had ambitions, as yet undefined,

[116] See above, n. 78, and esp. D. Nicholl, *Thurstan*.
[117] Hugh, *York*; and above, n. 81. On his reliability see R. W. Southern, *St. Anselm and his biographer* (Cambridge, 1963), pp. 143, 303–9, and below, n. 119.
[118] See Morey and Brooke, *Gilbert Foliot*, ch. viii; Brooke, *Medieval Church and Society* (1971), ch. 5. The statement in the text is bold, and doubt has attached e.g. to Athelstan's grant (but see n. 52); and it may have to be modified when the early professions in York Minster library M2(2)a, fo. 7r–v, have been critically examined. (We owe special thanks to Miss Katharine Longley for help with this reference; study of this and another text of York professions is being undertaken by Mr. A. Makinson and Professor R. Somerville.)

over Wales and Scotland, and a deep suspicion of the folk of Yorkshire. Thus Lanfranc was able to extract from Thomas I profession of obedience, though not without a struggle.[119] Meanwhile Thomas prepared for a counter-attack: he asserted the claims of his province to jurisdiction, not only over the bishopric of Durham, but over Cumbria and Scotland, Lindsey (i.e. most of Lincolnshire) and Worcester; and to round the matter off, for good measure, the diocese of Chester, Coventry, and Lichfield. These disputes raged incessantly in the late eleventh and twelfth centuries, and to set beside Canterbury's notable collection of professions York possesses copies of a few—and perhaps some of them are of doubtful authenticity—from bishops of Scotland and the Isles.[120] But in the end, though Canterbury retained, after a mighty struggle, its lordship over Wales, York lost Scotland and the Isles, and was only compensated with Cumbria, where Henry I and Thurstan set up the new bishopric of Carlisle in 1133, though it was never before 1200 the stable seat of a bishop.[121] Thus York won its measure of independence from Canterbury, and lost its claim to a wider empire.

The kings judged these issues by their political implications; the popes, while never ignoring political expediency, by law and precedent. It is a curious irony that if the archbishops of York had been prepared to submit to Canterbury, they might have had whole-hearted support from the English king and the English Church for their attempts on the Scottish bishops, and might even have won a little more territory in England. They staked much for their own freedom, their own primacy; and one cannot withhold a feeling of admiration and awe for the power of their cause. The canons of York won fervent support even from a newcomer like Thurstan—or, later, from a Canterbury man like Roger of Pont l'Évêque. It is hard for us to recapture the emotions which inspired some of the best minds in Canterbury to cheat and forge,[122] inspired Thurstan and his colleagues at

[119] See *Canterbury Professions*, ed. M. Richter (Canterbury and York Soc., 1973), pp. lvii ff. and no. 34; Dr. Richter's account is mainly based on Lanfranc's own narrative and other Canterbury sources, since for the period down to the election of Thurstan Hugh the Chanter's account is confused and at times 'distorted' (Richter, p. lviii n.). He convincingly argues that Hugh's account of the consecration of St. Anselm is misleading (p. lxix n.). Hugh's credit greatly improves when he becomes an eyewitness and the York case was in the ascendant.

[120] See above, n. 118.

[121] See D. E. Greenway in Le Neve, *Fasti . . . 1066–1300*, ii (1971), p. 19 and refs.; Nicholl, *Thurstan*, pp. 140–50; H. S. Offler, 'A note on the early history of the Priory of Carlisle', *Trans. Cumberland and Westmorland Antiquarian and Archaeol. Soc.*, N.S. lxv (1965), 176–81; J. C. Dickinson, 'Walter the Priest and St. Mary's, Carlisle', *Trans. Cumberland and Westmorland Antiquarian and Archaeol. Soc.*, N.S. lxix (1969), 102–14; M. Brett, *The English Church under Henry I* (Oxford, 1975).

[122] See Southern, *St. Anselm*, pp. 308–9, and 'The Canterbury Forgeries', *EHR* lxxiii (1958), 193–226; cf. above, n. 118.

York to face endless litigation, journeys, possible loss of office, revenue, and career—and all those who are more than names to us were career ecclesiastics by no means indifferent to the world and the flesh. King Henry I shared his father's suspicions of York and the north-east; Thurstan must have seemed at his appointment the very type of the courtier-bishop, and his heroic resistance to archbishop and king an incomprehensible nuisance. In the end he won, and no archbishop of York has made profession of obedience to Canterbury since.

The idea of primacy in the eleventh century, though it took more than one form, essentially involved jurisdiction, and not just an honorific title, set up between the rank and file of the metropolitans and the pope. It could be used, as the archbishop of Lyon sometimes used it, by a close adherent of the papacy set to lord it over the archbishops of Gaul; it could be used, as Lanfranc tried to use it, to establish a local empire in which the primate's authority counted for more than the pope's. In the long run this was the more likely course, and primacy therefore aroused suspicion from the papacy; this, and the very doubtful historical grounds on which the party of Canterbury based its case, secured papal support for Thurstan and the chapter of York. Hugh the Chanter gives a fascinating and probably in the main sound account of the struggles of Thurstan and the canons of York who helped him, culminating in the famous scene in the papal Curia in 1123 when the Canterbury monks produced their privileges 'headed with the names of popes of Rome', but with 'no trace of the style of the Roman chancery. . . .' And when neither seals nor signatures could be found on any of them 'they made up their minds to come back and say that the bulls had either perished or were lost. When they said this, some smiled, others wrinkled their noses, and others laughed aloud; making fun of them and saying that it was a miracle that lead should perish or be lost and parchment survive.'[123] Perhaps Hugh claimed more knowledge of the matter than he really possessed, for although he was right to think the bulls should have been leaden, papyrus not parchment was used in the chancery down to the eleventh century. But he was right that the privileges were mostly forged, and Thurstan deserved his moment of triumph after his long toil.

In his later years Thurstan showed a wide interest in the spiritual welfare of his see, and is especially well known for fostering the new religious orders, Augustinian and Cistercian, and for his share in founding the great abbey of Fountains.[124] He died, much respected, at the Cluniac priory of

[123] Hugh, *York*, pp. 114–15 (slightly adapted).
[124] Nicholl, *Thurstan*, ch. v–vii; on Fountains also D. Bethell, 'The Foundations of Fountains Abbey and the state of St. Mary's York in 1132', *Jour. of Eccles. Hist.* xvii (1966), 11–27; L. G. D. Baker, 'The Foundation of Fountains Abbey', *Northern History*, iv (1969), 29–43.

Pontefract. He had held together in a single grasp the world of Ranulf Flambard and the court of William Rufus, and the new world of St. Bernard and his Yorkshire disciples William, first abbot of Rievaulx, and Henry Murdac, monk of Clairvaux, abbot of Fountains, and ultimately archbishop (1147–53). In the chapter at York, zeal for his great cause and the archbishop's personality seem likewise to have held a peaceful balance. But peace was superficial, and within the chapter, and between the chapter and the new monastic movements, Thurstan's retirement was the signal for fifteen years of strife.

The life and death of William FitzHerbert

The central character in this story was the enigmatic William FitzHerbert, later to enjoy a strange celebrity as St. William of York.[125] William was son of Herbert, chamberlain to Henry I, and came of a family with estates in Yorkshire; his mother was half-sister to King Stephen, and so he must have seemed marked out for promotion in the early years of Stephen's reign, since Stephen's brother Henry of Blois, as bishop of Winchester and papal legate, shared with the king the distribution of patronage, and a rash of nephews and protégés spread over the English Church. The abbot of Fécamp was one of these, and he was marked out for York;[126] but although the chapter argued and the king and legate cajoled for many months, the attempt failed, and the chapter's attention was diverted to a nephew nearer home. We know little of the background to the quarrel which now broke out: the two leading figures in the chapter after the archbishop, Hugh the dean and Hugh the precentor—the Chanter—had recently departed, the dean to become a monk at Fountains, the precentor to another world.[127] The new dean, William of Ste-Barbe, shortly to become bishop of Durham, seems to have tried to be a peacemaker; but he found himself in the midst of a battle of archdeacons. William FitzHerbert himself, treasurer since before 1114 (it seems), was also (as invariably in the twelfth century) archdeacon of the East Riding; his chief opponents were Walter of London, archdeacon of the West Riding, and Osbert of Bayeux, Archbishop Thurstan's nephew, archdeacon of Richmond.[128] In January 1141 a majority in the chapter

---

[125] See D. Knowles, 'The case of St. William of York', rev. edn. in *The Historian and Character and other essays* (Cambridge, 1963), pp. 76–97, with bibliography on pp. 94–6; Clay 'Treasurers', pp. 8–10; life in *Hists. York* ii. 270–91, and in the great window in the north choir transept of the Minster (1422–3).

[126] Knowles, 'The case of St. William', p. 80; cf. *Letters . . . of Gilbert Foliot*, pp. 109–10, 116.

[127] Clay, 'Deans', pp. 363–4; Clay, 'Precentors and Chancellors', pp. 116–20, with notes on the Chanter's family.

[128] Clay, 'Archdeacons', pp. 277–9, 283, 286; Clay, *Fasti* i. 33, 46; Knowles, p. 97; on Osbert see also A. Morey, 'Canonist evidence in the Case of St. William of York', *Cambridge Hist. Jour.* x, iii (1952), 352–3; *Letters . . . of Gilbert Foliot*, pp. 164–5; *Letters of John of Salisbury*, ed. W. J. Millor, H. E. Butler, and C. N. L. Brooke, i (Nelson's Medieval Texts, 1955), pp. 261–2.

elected William the Treasurer as archbishop; but some of the canons, powerfully supported by leaders of the religious orders in the diocese, refused to accept the election, and they carried their protest to the gates of Rome—and also, which was of more consequence, to the gates of Clairvaux, where the prophetic figure of St. Bernard was roused for the destruction of the archbishop-elect.

So great was the dust raised by the controversy that it is difficult to discern the flame within, or to tell what really was the tinder to the conflict. They objected to William's mode of life and to the manner of his election; they treated him (not without justice) as the pawn of royal intervention, an intervention no less obnoxious for the fact that his uncle Henry, papal legate and bishop of Winchester—the whore of Winchester as Bernard politely called him—was evidently playing a more forceful part in the affair than King Stephen. 'O happy Winchester, O second Rome, happy in your choice of so great a name! O city so powerful that you can withstand the authority of your mighty fathers in Curia . . .' wrote Bernard with crushing irony after the long *démarches* of 1141–3 and the archbishop's eventual consecration by his uncle under circumstances of doubtful legality.[129] But his letter was not all irony, for he intended his hearers, pope and cardinals, to shudder and take action. 'Lest such contumacy should become a custom and an example, lest the dignity of Rome should be torn to shreds, lest the authority of Peter succumb to these new and great humiliations, lest religion should grow cold in the diocese of York, yea, lest it be wholly up-rooted and scattered to the winds' Rome must take the hammer and break the idol that the whore of Winchester had set up in Peter's Minster—'May your Holiness grow and flourish'.[130] The pope died, however, and his successor Eugenius III was a disciple of St. Bernard, who knew the fervour and the mettle of the great Yorkshire Cistercians: of Richard of Fountains, devout and normally peaceful, William of Rievaulx, a zealot but in his own way inspired, Henry Murdac, who rather reflected the harsher side of Bernard, Ailred the future abbot of Rievaulx, the most attractive of all the early Cistercians and a man of peace.[131] The idol was removed and Henry Murdac set in his place. Predictably, the king tried to prevent him from taking up office; less predictably perhaps, the people of York showed implacable hostility. After his failure to win papal restoration in 1147–8, William visited

[129] St. Bernard, *Epistola* 235 (in Mabillon's 2nd edn., repr. Migne, *Patrologia Latina*, clxxxii), trans. B. S. James, *Letters of St. Bernard of Clairvaux* (1953), no. 204, pp. 275–6 (slightly adapted, as in Brooke, *Europe in the Central Middle Ages*, 1964, pp. 311–13).

[130] Ibid.; cf. Knowles, 'The case of St. William', pp. 86–7.

[131] See Knowles, 'The case of St. William', also *Monastic Order*, chs. xiii–xiv; Walter Daniel's *Life of Ailred*, ed. and trans. F. M. Powicke; A. Squire, *Aelred of Rievaulx* (1969); Ailred, *Opera Omnia*, ed. A. Hoste and C. H. Talbot (in progress, Turnhout, 1971–   ).

Sicily, whose king was his distant relative, and stayed with the royal chancellor, an old friend from Yorkshire, Robert of Selby.[132] On his return he brought gifts to his uncle at Winchester, which perhaps included Byzantine objects to inspire the famous Byzantinate pages in the Winchester Psalter of this epoch; and it is possible, even likely, that he brought back from the south relics to comfort his own old age, perhaps in the charming box of Sicilian Muslim manufacture which still adorns the Minster at York.[133]

For to York in the end William returned. In 1153 the pope, St. Bernard, and Henry Murdac all died. At Rome an arrangement was made: William was restored to York, another nephew of Stephen and Henry of Blois, Hugh du Puiset, William's successor as treasurer of York, was promoted to the see of Durham, and John of Canterbury became treasurer.[134] St. William's return was a triumphal progress: the famous story of how the bridge at York broke under the throng which gathered to welcome him, and the injured were miraculously restored by his prayers, does not come from a contemporary source; but it seems clearly to represent a consistent tradition at York that William was loved and revered.[135] Even so, it is extremely unlikely that he would have been canonized but for the dramatic conclusion to his earthly story. On his return to England in 1154 he made peace with Fountains, which his supporters had sacked in 1147, and showed every wish to be on good terms with his former enemies. But immediately after celebrating solemn mass in York Minster, he was taken ill, and on 8 June, 1154 he died. Archdeacon Osbert was accused of poisoning him, and although such tales were common and as commonly disbelieved, Osbert failed to clear himself, was unfrocked, and became a minor baron.[136]

From 1154 to 1215: Roger of Pont l'Évêque and Geoffrey Plantagenet
Meanwhile no time was lost in providing William with a successor. With a speed which excited comment at the time—and must certainly rouse our suspicions that the wily archbishop of Canterbury, Theobald, had been engaged in intrigue—the archdeacon of Canterbury, Roger of Pont l'Évêque, was elected archbishop of York.

Roger (1154–81) and his successor Geoffrey Plantagenet (1189–1212),

---

[132] R. H. Pinder-Wilson and C. N. L. Brooke, 'The reliquary of St. Petroc and the Ivories of Norman Sicily', *Archaeologia*, civ (1973), p. 299 and n. 1, for this incident and Robert's name.
[133] Ibid., pp. 285–6, 296, 299; see Pl. 3; on the Winchester Psalter see G. Zarnecki, *Later English Romanesque Sculpture* (1953), p. 30; and, in general, F. Wormald, *The Winchester Psalter* (1973).
[134] See nn. 112, 113.
[135] *Hists. York* ii. 275–6.
[136] Above, n. 128; Knowles, 'The case of St. William of York', pp. 92–4.

Henry II's illegitimate son, each contributed something to the tradition of
the Minster: Roger by inaugurating the first age of sumptuous building
after Thomas I, Geoffrey by persistently quarrelling with the chapter. The
true creators of the Minster and the chapter as it was in 1215 were Thomas I
and Thurstan, heirs of the old style of secular cathedral chapter who yet
had the imagination to make something creative and constructive from it.
Thurstan had tried to patronize both secular and regular clergy in the
spiritual life of the diocese: Ripon, Beverley, Southwell, and the distant
outpost at St. Oswald's Gloucester had been developed along the lines of the
York chapter; Cistercian and Augustinian foundations were aided and
fostered.[137] Compared with the pontificates of the two sons of Bayeux,
Roger's and Geoffrey's seem but an epilogue. Roger was indeed a great
builder, and founder of what became the notable chapel of St. Sepulchre;
and in Geoffrey's time the chapter was more involved in royal and papal
politics than ever before.[138] Each pontificate was in its way a remarkable
episode, if only for the light it sheds on what had already taken place in
York and the vale. But it seems likely that, here as elsewhere, there came to
be a growing divorce between archbishop and chapter, a growing division
between resident and non-resident canons.

If Theobald hoped to see in Roger a subservient colleague, he was
disappointed; and between Roger and Theobald's successor, Thomas
Becket, an implacable feud developed. Roger was seriously suspected of
stirring the murderers of Becket to action, and after the eclipse and
restoration to which Roger had to submit in the early 1170s, the clerks of
Canterbury—led apparently by the eminent humanist John of Salisbury—
accused their one-time colleague of nameless crimes.[139] The truth of all
these accusations is hard to discern. Roger's role in the Becket affair is
unattractive; undoubtedly both he and Becket were urged on to their more
extreme actions by the old rivalry of Canterbury and York, whose share in
the dispute has never been fully unravelled. It is equally clear that the old
archbishop, Theobald, had trusted both of them, and the quality of his
judgement was usually sound; his disciples were men of exceptional parts.
In the diocese of York religion was not cooling off in Roger's time. The rich

---

[137] Nicholl, *Thurstan*, chs. v–vii. St. Oswald's became Augustinian under Archbishop Henry Murdac.
[138] See below; and cf. Alexander III's letter to Roger (1173, *Hists. York* iii. 78). On St. Sepulchre's see
A. Hamilton Thompson, 'The Chapel of St. Mary and the Holy Angels, otherwise known as St.
Sepulchre's Chapel, at York', *YAJ* xxxvi (1944–7), 63–77; Roger's charter of ordinance and
endowment is in *Hists. York* iii. 75–7, dated 1177–81 by Clay, 'Precentors and Chancellors', p. 133.
[139] *Materials for the History of Thomas Becket*, vii, ed. J. C. Robertson and J. B. Sheppard (Rolls Ser.,
1885), no. 777. The attribution to John has been doubted, and the text supposed interpolated, but
the early MSS. leave little doubt that John preserved it among his own letters, as we now have it: see
discussion in *Letters of John of Salisbury*, ii (forthcoming).

2 The Horn of Ulf or Ulphus. An ivory horn, probably from south Italy, early 11th C. It was already in the Minster treasury by *c.* 1400, and tradition asserts that it was a horn of tenure, symbol of a gift of land by the 11th Century thegn Ulf son of Thorald. The silver mounts were added in 1675, when it was restored to the Minster by Henry, Lord Fairfax. It is now in the Undercroft Museum in the Minster.

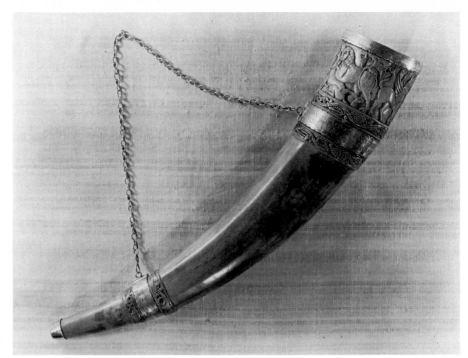

3 Ivory Casket, made by Islamic craftsmen in Sicily or south Italy in the 11–12th C., with incised ornament. These caskets were prized by Christian purchasers all over western Christendom as reliquaries, and one virtually identical in shape is now in the Cathedral Museum at Trento. This casket may have been brought from Sicily by St. William in 1148 (see p. 37; R. H. Pinder-Wilson and C. N. L. Brooke in *Archaeologia*, civ (1973), 261–305, esp. pp. 285–6, 299–300 and pls. lxxix–lxxxi). Preserved in the Minster Treasury and now in the Undercroft Museum.

remnant of his work on the Minster reflects the temporal prosperity that the Church in York enjoyed in the second half of the twelfth century,[140] and the long list of new foundations, Cistercian, Augustinian, and Premonstratensian in particular, reveals an unprecedented flow of recruits and patronage. By the time of Roger's death in 1181 the splendid churches of all the religious houses, and their flocks and fields, must have helped to make Yorkshire a very different heritage from the charred battlefield which Archbishop Thomas I had entered in 1070. Nor need we suppose that Roger played no part in this.

It seems likely that the ferocity of Roger's onslaught on Becket, and his continuing zeal for the rights of his see,[141] reflect a close relationship between Roger and some at least of his chapter; more than personal animosity against a former colleague and rival seems implicit in his dealings with St. Thomas, and there is copious evidence that he became, like Thurstan before him, devoted to the interests of his Church. The mantle of his office weighed on him; to say that he was a worthy successor of Thurstan would be to go beyond the evidence. In his early years he was in a measure ruled by his chapter; in later years we may believe that he ruled them—perhaps not without friction, like his friend Gilbert Foliot of London;[142] but in Roger's case we lack evidence, just as we cannot tell how deep a mark his own appointments made upon the chapter. Whereas the nephews of Gilbert Foliot proliferated in the archdeaconries' and other stalls at Hereford and London, there is no single canon or dignitary of Roger's time who can be proved to be of his family. Very likely this is due to our ignorance; the Norman Jeremiah, archdeacon of Cleveland and probably author of the Lay Folks' Mass Book may well have been a relation as well as a protégé. But it is clear that there was a continuing and important element at York of men already established before his coming. During most of his reign the dean was Robert Butevilain, already archdeacon of York at his arrival, promoted dean in 1157–8. Robert lived until 1186, and after his death continuity came to be symbolized by Hamo, precentor from the early 1170s till the late 1190s, then treasurer (1197–9 to 1217); but of his origin we know nothing. Hamo was evidently a leading figure among the local resident canons; the other treasurers were men of the south, who owed their place to papal or royal patronage, already an important influence in

---

[140] See pp. 28–31.

[141] See esp. *Gesta Henrici secundi . . .* ed. W. Stubbs (Rolls Ser., 1867), i. 104–5, 112–14 (1176); for his part in the events of 1170 see esp. A. Heslin (Mrs. Duggan), 'The Coronation of the Young King in 1170', *Studies in Church History*, ii, ed. G. J. Cuming (1965), pp. 165–78. It is much to be hoped that the materials on Roger prepared by the late Father G. Culkin, now deposited at the Borthwick Institute, will one day form the basis for a full study (now (1977) being undertaken by Dr. M. Lovatt).

[142] Morey and Brooke, *Gilbert Foliot*, pp. 204–11.

the recruitment of the chapter, thought not to the degree it later became. We have met John of Canterbury and Ralph de Warneville; the space between Ralph and Hamo was filled by the 'roaring devil i' the old play', Geoffrey Plantagenet, illegitimate son of Henry II, later himself archbishop.

Geoffrey had the misfortune to earn the dislike of two of the colleagues in his father's Curia to whom we owe much of our knowledge of him, Walter Map the satirist and Roger of Howden the chronicler; more favourable was the view of his biographer, Gerald of Wales.[143] Some recent historians, while marvelling at his exceptional gift for quarrelling with everyone to hand, have reckoned him the one faithful son of Henry II, and have supposed that he may have mellowed in his last years.[144] Of this we cannot be sure, for from 1207 till 1212 he was an exile in Normandy, out of harm's way; but at least it may be said that he seems conscientiously to have objected to his brother King John's high-handed treatment of the Church. For the rest, he arrived in York in 1191, to be enthroned on 1 November, and before two years were out he had quarrelled with the chapter, been reconciled, and quarrelled again. It is hard now to discern precisely what caused the battles, and some episodes in the epic may have been collusive or fictitious. Nor can one avoid the suspicion that some ambitious clerks battened on Geoffrey, knowing full well that patronage slipped rapidly through his fingers. When he came to York he was served by two eminent canonists on the make, Master Simon of Apulia and Master Honorius, author of the *Summa decretalium quaestionum*, one of the most remarkable canon law treatises of its day.[145] In 1193–4 Henry Marshal, dean of York, was promoted to the see of Exeter, and Geoffrey, after an abortive attempt to appoint his own half-brother, Peter, tried to set Simon in his place; but he rapidly transferred his support to the royal nominee, Philip of Poitou. The king was then a prisoner in Germany, and to Germany went Simon, presently to be joined by Hamo the precentor and three archdeacons.

---

[143] Giraldus Cambrensis, *Opera*, iv, ed. J. S. Brewer (Rolls Ser., 1873), 355–431; Walter Map, *De nugis curialium*, v. 6, ed. M. R. James (Oxford, 1914), pp. 238–9, 246 ff.; Howden, *Chronica*, ed. W. Stubbs (Rolls Ser., 1868–71), iii–iv, esp. iv, pp. xxxiv–lxxvii. On Jeremiah see Clay, 'Archdeacons', pp. 412–15.

[144] Stubbs, intro. to Howden, *ut supra*; on Geoffrey and his troubles see Decima L. Douie, *Archbishop Geoffrey Plantagenet and the Chapter of York* (Borthwick Papers, No. 18, York, 1960); Clay, 'Deans', pp. 374 ff.; Clay, 'Treasurers', pp. 24 ff.; Clay, 'Archdeacons', pp. 425–30 and in *Early Yorks. Charters*, iv, pp. xxv–xxvi. For a full study of Geoffrey, including an appraisal of his administration of the diocese, see Marie B. Lovatt, 'The career and administration of Archbishop Geoffrey of York (?1151–1212)' (Univ. of Cambridge Ph.D. thesis 1974–5) (by the author's kindness C. N. L. Brooke has been able to eradicate error from his account with its aid; he regrets it did not come in time to improve his approach to Geoffrey).

[145] For Honorius see preceding note and S. Kuttner and E. Rathbone, 'Anglo-Norman canonists of the twelfth century', *Traditio*, vii (1949–51), 279–358, esp. 296, 304–16.

Richard may have been swayed by the fact that his intolerable half-brother now supported Simon's rival, or he may have accepted the chapter's plea that the deanery was an elective office;[146] from 1194 till 1214 Simon remained dean, then followed Henry Marshal to Exeter, and Hamo ruled in his stead. In 1196 Richard I dropped a penny in the pool; while Geoffrey was absent appealing to the pope he made various appointments, including the presentation of Adam of Thorner—evidently a Yorkshireman—to the archdeaconry of York, in spite of the fact that Geoffrey had already presented his brother Peter, and (for good measure) Peter of Dinan; Richard's nephew Arthur of Brittany urged compromise on the king, and Peter and Adam were permitted to share the profits of the archdeaconry. Adam performed the functions, and when both visited the Minster at the same time, which we may reckon a rare event, they occupied the stall on alternate days.[147]

The archbishop's appetite for disputation was not yet quenched, however, and Adam was not left in peace. Geoffrey's most curious adventure came when he set Master Honorius in the archdeaconry of Richmond in 1198. This vast archdeaconry stretched right across to the Lake District, and its revenues were very substantial. The king wanted it for Roger of St. Edmund; the chapter installed him; and the archbishop quarrelled with Honorius. But Honorius won; he took his suit to Rome, and there the great canonist received the favour of the pope, obtained his suit, and returned to enjoy his triumph from the safe distance of the court of Geoffrey's rival, Hubert Walter, ex-dean of York, now archbishop of Canterbury.[148]

Geoffrey's adventures continued. They provide us with a comic interlude, which yet throws a beam of light into the obscure history of the chapter. The endless disputes cannot have made the Minster an edifying or a comfortable place; they remind us that pope, archbishop, king, and chapter always competed in the later Middle Ages for control of chapter patronage, and that many of the richest stalls were held by absentees. They reflect, almost in caricature, the long disputes common to many chapters over appointments, especially of the dean, and the division of the chapter between resident and absentee. But it is clear that the chapter contained a nucleus of local men who genuinely tried to sustain its services as well as its privileges. In the 1190s these included not only Hamo, evidently a married

---

[146] On this issue see *Hists. York* iii. 92 ff.; Morey and Brooke, *Gilbert Foliot*, pp. 205–6; D. Knowles, *The Episcopal Colleagues of Archbishop Thomas Becket* (Cambridge, 1951), pp. 111–12.

[147] For this, and the later vicissitudes to 1201, when Adam's interest in the archdeaconry finally disappeared, see Clay, 'Archdeacons', pp. 425–7.

[148] See above, n. 144 and refs., and C. R. Cheney, *Hubert Walter* (1967), pp. 164–5.

man or at least a father, reflecting the domesticity of an earlier age; but also Hugh Murdac, nephew of Archbishop Henry Murdac, formerly king's clerk and justice, now an old man in his retirement in the chapter; Adam of Thorner, later to enjoy for a time half the stall of the archdeaconry of York; Reginald Arundel, prebendary of Ulleskelf, and his namesake, presumably a relative, Roger Arundel, son of William Arundel of Foston on the Wolds, a substantial tenant of the Percy see.[149] The list could be extended; the chapter of York, like many, still contained a number of resident canons; and it was more tenacious than most of its liberties and rites. The use of York was one of the few never submerged by the use of Sarum in the late Middle Ages. The Minster today bears eloquent witness that it was a powerful centre of loyalty and devotion in the thirteenth and fourteenth centuries.

At the end of Geoffrey's reign the chapter seems, however, notably unhappy and divided. Beyond this we cannot go; for such general judgements do not do justice to the variety of personality and outlook, of attitude and sentiment, of such diverse groups as made a twelfth-century chapter; nor is the scattered, scanty evidence, like the bridge over the Ouse, strong enough to bear them.

Rosalind Hill and Christopher Brooke are very grateful to the editorial committee, especially to Canon Reginald Cant, Professor G. E. Aylmer, and Professor A. G. Dickens, for their help, advice, and encouragement; to their fellow contributors Dr. Eric Gee and Dr. John H. Harvey, and especially Dr. Barrie Dobson, for copious suggestions and corrections; to Mr. J. G. Beckwith and Professor C. R. Dodwell for assistance with the captions to the plates; for much appreciated help and correction to Miss Katharine Longley and Mr. Bernard Barr of the Minster library, and to the late Mrs. Norah Gurney and to Dr. David Smith, successive directors of the Borthwick Institute; and also to several other friends, in particular to Dr. Marie Lovatt for generously lending her thesis on Archbishop Geoffrey (see p. 144, n. 41).

[149] Clay, 'Treasurers', pp. 28–30; Clay, *Fasti* i, esp. 82–3, 86, 91–2; ii. 20–1, 75, 98, 106–11; Clay, 'Archdeacons', pp. 425–8; Clay in *Early Yorks. Charters*, xi. 197.

CHAPTER II

The Later Middle Ages
1215–1500

Barrie Dobson

Immediately after the singing of vespers on 6 February 1349 a group of supporters of the bishop of Durham entered the Minster to stage a deliberate demonstration against the authority of the metropolitan church of York. Standing under the crucifix at the gates of the choir, they expressed their contempt for the York cathedral clergy by breaking wind, shouting insults, and 'performing other enormities'. This episode, although a comparatively minor and bloodless incident in the long history of jurisdictional contest between the churches of medieval York and Durham, was nevertheless sufficiently disturbing to draw from the then archbishop, William de la Zouche, one of the few recorded general comments on the role of the Minster to survive from the late Middle Ages.

For both the Old and the New Testament teach us that holiness becomes the house of the Lord. As befits a place erected under His authority, His worship there should be performed peacefully and with due reverence. No one should make any noise there and no one should incite or take part in any sort of disturbance. In such a church there should be no contumely at all, no disputes and no public assemblies, far less any profane demonstrations—nothing in fact should happen there to disturb the divine office or offend the eyes of the Divine Majesty.[1]

In placing such emphasis on the importance of tranquillity in his cathedral church, Archbishop Zouche was not only expressing an often unattainable ideal but revealing why it will always be impossible to write the real history of a medieval cathedral. Of all the human qualities, serenity of routine is the one which disarms the historian most completely; and nobody can now hope to re-create in words the continuous rhythms of divine worship in the late medieval Minster. To the canons, vicars choral, and chantry priests who served the church of York between the beginning of the thirteenth and the end of the fifteenth centuries the following

[1] BIHR, Reg. Zouche, fo. 29; *Letters from Northern Registers* (Rolls Ser., 1873), pp. 397–9.

account of their activities would have seemed to stress the least important of their contributions to their own time and posterity. Like all great medieval cathedrals, the metropolitan church of St. Peter at York was an exceptionally complex institution just because it fulfilled so many different purposes. First and most obviously it was the largest and most splendid house of Christian worship in its diocese, a building whose primary *raison d'être* was the *Opus Dei*, the continuous round of communal devotion in the choir and elsewhere. Secondly, it towered above the city of York as a heavenly mansion deliberately designed to 'signify the Holy Catholic Church which is built in Heaven of living stones'. Finally, as a massive business corporation, it served as the most important instrument in the north for diverting economic wealth from local parishes and churches towards a comparatively small group of professional ecclesiastical administrators. Of these three functions the first can only be assessed intermittently and by the uncertain light of chapter ordinances and visitation records, while the second is hidden from us almost completely just because the cathedral clergy took it so absolutely for granted.

By contrast the evidence for both the internal administration of the late medieval Minster and for the careers of the members of the cathedral chapter is almost embarrassingly plentiful. So voluminous indeed are the archives of the dean and chapter for the late medieval period that they have inhibited a long line of York antiquaries and historians from getting to grips with the problems they present. To the pioneering researches of the indefatigable James Torre, Canon James Raine the younger, and Professor A. Hamilton Thompson all students of the medieval cathedral are in permanent debt; but for all three of these gifted, if very different, scholars, interest in the mother church tended to be only an incidental by-product of their wider concern with the general history of the see of York. Only a minute proportion of the muniments of the dean and chapter have yet found their way into print; and for many years to come a definitive history of the cathedral in the later Middle Ages will be an unattainable ideal. The following pages can therefore only provide a very partial and provisional introduction to the administrative practices of one of medieval England's most elaborate institutions. 'Not only in appearance, but constitutionally, a medieval cathedral was a great ship with many decks or departments'.[2] Despite occasional doubts, sometimes expressed by contemporaries themselves, as to whether its voyage was always well directed, the navigation of that enormous ocean liner through the ever-changing currents of the social and religious scene was one of the most remarkable

[2] E. F. Jacob, *The Fifteenth Century* (Oxford, 1961), p. 289.

phenomena of the period between 1215 and 1500. As the present appearance of York Minster itself serves to remind us, at no other period did it call forth such a wealth of religious aspiration and economic enterprise.

Archbishop Walter de Gray and the consolidation of the chapter

The cathedral clergy of medieval York, like their counterparts elsewhere, could only comprehend the history of their church in terms of the archbishops who had presided over the see. Despite the obvious dangers of such an attitude to the past, it would be hard to deny that the accession of Walter de Gray marks the most important turning-point in the story of the medieval Minster. Towards the end of 1215 Pope Innocent III brought a long and unedifying election dispute to a close by telling the representatives of the York chapter at Rome that 'By Saint Peter, virginity is a great virtue; and we will give him to you'.[3] The events of the next forty years were to reveal to the canons of York that chastity was only one of Gray's many qualities. In the first place the crisis of authority which had afflicted the see of York since Archbishop Geoffrey's flight from England in 1207, and in some ways since as long ago as the death of Archbishop Roger in 1181, was at last over. During the previous generation the clerks of the cathedral had suffered severely from the lack of an effective and respected leader. That, at least, was a danger from which the later medieval chapter was to be almost completely spared. Gray's own tenure of the see lasted until his death in May 1255 and was to prove one of the longest in the history of the English Church, unsurpassed at York itself until the pontificate of Archbishop Harcourt in the early nineteenth century. Of the twenty-two vacancies in the see of York between 1215 and 1500, only four (those which followed the deaths of William de Greenfield in 1315, William Melton in 1340, Richard Scrope in 1405, and Henry Bowet in 1423) lasted for more than a few months.[4] In the years immediately after his own translation to the see of York, it was to be Archbishop Gray's role to redefine the position of the archbishop in his diocese and his cathedral. All the evidence we have, and for the first time in the history of York Minster we have a good deal, points to Gray's considerable success in imposing ecclesiastical order on a previously recalcitrant and often turbulent province. Given the size and previous history of his see, it is hard to deny him a place in the front rank of the 'reforming bishops' of thirteenth-

---

[3] *Rogeri de Wendover Flores Historiarum* (Rolls Ser., 1886–9), ii. 153, 160; cf. *Selected Letters of Pope Innocent III concerning England*, ed. C. R. Cheney and W. H. Semple (1953), no. 81; Dixon and Raine, *Fasti Ebor.*, pp. 281–3; A. B. Emden, *A Biographical Register of the University of Oxford to* A.D. *1500* (Oxford, 1957–9), ii. 807–8.
[4] *Hists. York* ii. 403–41; Le Neve–Jones, pp. 3–5.

century England and equally hard not to think it appropriate that his skeleton conveyed 'a sense of quiet dignity and repose' when exposed to modern eyes in May 1968.[5]

Forced upon an unwilling chapter by both king and pope, it was certainly to Gray's advantage in his dealings with his new cathedral and its clergy that he entered York as an ex-chancellor of England, a powerful outsider who had been uninvolved in the local factions and feuds of the previous twenty years. Indeed the history of the church of York between 1215 and 1255 is a testimonial to the reforms that could be made under the aegis of an archbishop with little taste for jurisdictional conflict. Gray's close co-operation with his cathedral chapter was itself dependent upon a broad similarity of attitude to the problems of organizing and administering the Minster. He owed much of his success to his ability to collate to key positions a new group of professional clerical administrators, prepared to dedicate themselves to the burdens of guiding and controlling an increasingly elaborate corporation. Like all developments in the history of a cathedral which depend upon the appearance of new personnel, the change could only be a gradual one. The dean of York during the first four years of Gray's pontificate was that same Hamo who had served the cathedral as its precentor and then its treasurer since the early 1170s.[6] But by the middle of the 1220s, the period at which Archbishop Gray's register begins, it is clear enough that a new generation of canons was in control. Especially conspicuous were the members of Gray's own kindred gradually brought up to York from the south Midlands. The archbishop's own nephews, Henry and Walter de Gray, were both collated to canonries and prebends in the cathedral as well as being succesively rectors of Gargrave in Craven between 1226 and 1271.[7] A third nephew, William de Langton alias de Rotherfield, rose to even higher prominence as a dean of York (c. 1260–79) who would have succeeded his uncle on the archiepiscopal throne at York in 1265 had it not been for papal opposition.[8] As it was, the translation of Walter Giffard, yet another of Archbishop Gray's relatives, to the see of York in the following year ensured the survival of a Gray connection within the cathedral church for many years to come.[9]

[5] M. Gibbs and J. Lang, *Bishops and Reform, 1215–1272* (Oxford, 1934), pp. 18, 52, 159, 176; H. G. Ramm *et al.*, 'The Tombs of Archbishops Walter de Gray (1216–55) and Godfrey de Ludham (1258–65) in York Minster, and their Contents', *Archaeologia*, ciii (1971), 108.

[6] Clay, *Fasti* i. 2–3; 'Treasurers', p. 28; 'Precentors and Chancellors', p. 121; see above, p. 40.

[7] *Reg. Gray*, pp. 7, 15, 68, 191, 195, 261 n.; *CPapR, 1198–1304*, p. 162; Clay, *Fasti* ii. 52–3, 92; *Fasti Parochiales*, iv (YAS Rec. Ser. cxxxiii, 1971), 43.

[8] *Annales Monastici* (Rolls Ser., 1864–9), iv, 161, 184; Clay, *Fasti* i. 7–8.

[9] *Reg. Wickwane*, p. iii; J. L. Grassi, 'Royal Clerks from the Archdiocese of York in the Fourteenth Century', *Northern History*, v (1970), 15–16; see below, p. 80.

In his careful control over the recruitment to the York chapter, Archbishop Gray was of course only exploiting the most powerful instrument in any diocesan's relationship with his cathedral, his right to collate to canonries and prebends. Of even greater importance for the future of the Minster was Gray's determination to involve the residentiary members of the York chapter in the practical business of administering his diocese. On the evidence of the witness lists to the archbishop's charters, many of the York canons were in regular attendance upon him. Master Simon de Evesham, for example, successively prebendary of Weighton, precentor, archdeacon of the East Riding, and archdeacon of Richmond, acted as the archbishop's datary and probably the keeper of his register.[10] Similarly, Master Laurence of Lincoln, prebendary of Wetwang and later archdeacon of York, presided over Gray's ecclesiastical courts as his official before he met a violent death at the hands of a knight in the Minster close.[11] So eager was Gray to use the services of his Minster clergy that in 1227 he took the unusual step of securing from Pope Honorius III permission to keep the four dignitaries of the cathedral in his company despite their statutory commitment to residence at the Minster. Nor is it a coincidence that three of the four dignitaries at that time (Dean Roger de Insula; Precentor Geoffrey of Norwich; and Chancellor Richard of Cornwall) were university graduates.[12] Gray himself, despite an early reputation for inadequate learning, was the first archbishop of York able to receive the benefits of education at the new university of Oxford: between 1215 and the end of the century well over half of the dignitaries and archdeacons of the Minster had followed his example.[13] As the more highly trained and more technically sophisticated canons of the thirteenth century began to replace their predecessors it was natural that the organization of the Minster should be more systematically defined than ever before. Of all the great achievements of Gray's pontificate, perhaps only the rebuilding of the cathedral transepts proved a more enduring legacy to the future than the regulation imposed by himself and his chapter on a previously volatile and often chaotic corporation.

The first important step in this process occurred in 1219–20 when Dean Roger de Insula and a small committee of four York canons were chosen by their colleagues to legislate on residence by members of the chapter. After lengthy discussion with all interested parties and investigation of the practices adopted by other churches, this committee produced—on St.

[10] *Reg. Gray*, pp. xii, 10, 80; Clay, *Fasti* i. 14–15.
[11] *Reg. Gray*, p. 79; Clay, *Fasti* i. 34–5; ii. 85.
[12] *Reg. Gray*, pp. 157–8; Clay, *Fasti* i. 3, 13–14, 18–19; Emden, *Oxford*, i. 490–1.
[13] Dixon and Raine, *Fasti Ebor.*, p. 280; Clay, *Fasti* i. xiii.

Valentine's Day 1222—what now survive as the oldest recorded statutes of the church of York.[14] Brief and inadequate though these early ordinances were, they appear to mark the first serious attempt on the part of the York chapter to impose an intelligible pattern on the administrative confusion caused by the previous century's dramatic and uncontrolled expansion of the cathedral's wealth and personnel. In particular, like secular cathedral chapters everywhere else in England, the chapter of York Minster was forced to come to terms with the potentially alarming problem of completely unregulated non-residence on the part of its own members.[15] Even at this early stage Dean Roger and his colleagues had of course no intention of compelling or even encouraging the great majority of the York canons to live in the cathedral precincts; but it was already imperative to ensure that those who did so should be adequately rewarded and to make explicit the most fundamental of all distinctions within the medieval chapter.

In some ways the *statuta de residentia* of 1222 proved to be more stringent than the realities of later medieval practice would permit. By requiring continuous residence from the four dignitaries or *quatuor personae* of dean, precentor, chancellor, and treasurer, these early statutes were enunciating a principle to be more honoured in the breach than the observance. More important for the future was the rule that all canons who decided to take up residentiary status should spend a minimum of half of the year (later defined as twenty-four weeks) living near the Minster.[16] During that period of ordinary or minor residence the residentiary canon was expected to attend matins, vespers, and the major celebrations of mass unless prevented by illness or the need for periodic bleeding. Even more significantly, York was already one of the five English secular cathedrals in which the intending residentiary had to give evidence of his determination to reside by undergoing a preliminary period of 'greater' residence (twenty-six weeks at York) before he was entitled to receive emoluments from the chapter's common fund. The amount of commons to be received by each residentiary was fixed by the 1222 statutes at the generous rate of 6d. a day, a sum raised to 1s. 0d. on feasts of the nine lessons and 2s. 0d. on double

[14] YML, M1(1)b (Statutes), fos. 9–10; BM, Cotton MS. Vit. A. II, fos. 100–1; *York Statutes*, pp. 14–17. Considerable confusion has been caused in the past by a failure to recognize that those statutes which precede the *statuta de residentia* of 1222 in the numerous manuscript and printed editions of the York cathedral statutes are of a considerably later date. They apparently represent the codification of the *consuetudines, ordinaciones et statuta* of the Minster made as late as 1317: YML, M2(4)g (Misc. Register, 1290–1340), fo. 25.
[15] The closest analogy is provided by the Lincoln *capitula de residentia* of 1236–7: *Statutes of Lincoln Cathedral*, ed. H. Bradshaw and C. Wordsworth (Cambridge, 1892–7), ii. 109, 144–60.
[16] YML, M1(1)b, fo. 8ᵛ; *York Statutes*, p. 11.

feasts. In addition to these daily commons paid for attendance at the canonical hours, residentiaries of York were awarded an equal share of any surplus in the common fund at the end of each half-yearly term. Although, as will be seen, the value of both the daily commons and the half-yearly dividend received by the residentiary canons of York was later to increase in value, Dean Roger de Insula and his fellow canons had taken the all-important step of drawing a clear distinction between canons in and out of residence. In particular, and in response to the claim of Treasurer William de Rotherfield to a double share of the common fund on the grounds that his dignity was comprised of two prebends, the early thirteenth-century chapter accepted the general principle 'that the common fund is not a part of a prebend but is annexed only to residence'.[17]

The steady application of this principle to the operations of the York chapter provides the most important key to the Minster's constitutional and financial arrangements for the rest of the Middle Ages. As early as 1226 Pope Honorius III was well aware that 'very few canons make residence in the church' of York;[18] and ever afterwards the residentiary element within the chapter remained a small and exclusive body. Throughout the following three centuries York Minster was nearly always to be served by fewer residentiary canons than any other cathedral in England.[19] Admittedly, it is only after 1370–1 (the year of the first surviving Minster chamberlain's account roll) that completely comprehensive lists of canons in residence can be properly compiled; and before 1290—the year from which the attendance of canons is recorded in surviving chapter act-books—any estimate of the numbers of residentiary canons is bound to be somewhat hazardous. Nevertheless, enough evidence survives to make it reasonably clear that from the 1220s to the 1290s there were rarely more than eight or nine canons actually living near the Minster at any one time.[20] It was therefore to a comparatively small group of canons, men like John le Romeyn the elder, Geoffrey of Norwich, and Lawrence of Lincoln as well as that triumvirate of future archbishops of the see, Sewall de Boville, Godfrey Ludham, and William Wickwane, that the thirteenth-century York chapter owed its growing sense of continuity and *esprit de corps*. By 1255 these men

[17] YML, M1(1)b, fo. 10; *York Statutes* p. 16.
[18] *CPapR, 1198–1304*, p. 115; *Reg. Gray*, p. 155.
[19] K. Edwards, *The English Secular Cathedrals in the Middle Ages* (2nd. edn., Manchester, 1967), pp. 70–83; 'The Cathedral of Salisbury' (*VCH Wilts*. iii.), pp. 162–81; C. N. L. Brooke, 'The Earliest Times to 1485', *A History of St. Paul's Cathedral*, ed. W. R. Mathews and W. M. Atkins (1957), pp. 39, 53, 89–92.
[20] *Hists. York* iii. 153, 157, 202–3; *Reg. Gray*, pp. 133, 191, 195; *Reg. Giffard*, p. 134; *Memorials of Ripon* (Surtees Soc., 1882–8), i. 271; YML, L 2/1 (Magnum Registrum Album), iv, fos. 4–5; M 2(4)g, fos. 1, 4.

were sufficiently confident of their own position as the real masters of the chapter to call on Pope Alexander IV to censure those of their non-resident colleagues who refused to contribute to the financial burdens of the cathedral.[21]

To an extent perhaps still insufficiently appreciated, the greatest danger facing English secular chapters in the early decades of the thirteenth century had been that the financial claims of absentee canons might divert too large a proportion of the church's wealth away from the cathedral altogether. In their remarkably successful struggle to prevent such a development, the York residentiaries were certainly assisted by the generosity of Archbishop Gray in augmenting their common fund, for example by the church of Hornby in 1221, thus eliminating one possible 'seed of dissension and discord' among themselves.[22] It was equally important to the resident canons that all the York dignities, archdeaconries, and prebends should be put on a sound financial footing in their own right. In 1222 the prebends of the chancellor and archdeacon of Richmond still consisted of a share in the common fund; and it was obviously in the interests of the canons resident in York that such a situation should be succeeded by one in which all the prebends and dignities would be separately endowed and firmly grounded 'in certis possessionibus'.[23] An unascertainable number of money prebends may well have existed at York in the early thirteenth century, but only one of these, the appropriately named Botevant ('lacking profit') survived to the 1290s.[24] The most important developments in the evolution of the thirteenth-century chapter lay not in the foundation of new prebends but in the success of the York canons in persuading successive archbishops to provide existing dignitaries and canons with greater resources. In 1230, for example, Archbishop Gray appropriated the four Yorkshire churches of Mappleton, Wawne, Tunstall, and Withernwick to the archdeaconry of the East Riding, the chancellorship, the succentorship, and the prebend of Holme respectively.[25] More important still was Archbishop Gray's separation of the treasurership from the archdeaconry of the East Riding to which it had previously been annexed: in 1218 he endowed the former with a substantial portion (later to be known as the prebend of Newthorpe) of the

---

[21] YML, L 2/1 (Magnum Registrum Album), iii. fo. 63; *Hists. York* iii. 173.

[22] *Reg. Gray*, pp. 139–40.

[23] YML, M1(1)b, fo. 10; *York Statutes*, p. 17.

[24] Botevant derived its unusual name from a Middle English phrase meaning 'without profit' (Clay, *Fasti* ii. 11). The creation of the prebend of Throckrington in 1224 is best interpreted as an example of the conversion of an existing money prebend into a properly but very poorly endowed one (*CPapR, 1198–1304*, p. 111; *Reg. Gray*, p. 148).

[25] *Reg. Gray*, pp. 22, 52–3; *VCH Yorkshire* iii. 25.

ancient prebend of Sherburn, using the residue to found the new prebends of Wistow and Fenton.[26] Twenty-four years later (in 1242) the prebend of Wilton was created, not to increase the size of the York chapter but to supplement the already wealthy resources of the treasurer, to whose office Wilton was thenceforward to be inseparably annexed.[27]

The comparatively few new prebends founded at York after 1215 were therefore usually an incidental by-product of complicated arrangements made to provide existing benefices in the church with additional financial support. Nor is it difficult to explain why the spate of twelfth-century prebendal creations had now dwindled to a trickle. The multiplication of canonries and prebends in a cathedral church always tended to work to the advantage of the bishop rather than his chapter; but Walter de Gray and his successors must have become rapidly aware that king or pope were more likely than themselves to gain from the provision of an increasingly greater range of ecclesiastical patronage at the Minster. For that reason alone the archbishops were unwilling to apply their own financial resources to the creation of new prebends; and the evidence of the archbishops' registers leaves us in no doubt that it had become increasingly difficult to persuade either religious houses or lay notables in the north to endow prebends in the cathedral. When in the 1290s Archbishop Romeyn embarked upon the only possible alternative, the subdivision of existing prebends, he found his efforts blocked by his own chapter and by Edward I.[28] Towards the end of the century the vested interests involved in the maintenance of the prevailing number of prebends had become too strong for any archbishop to overcome; and with Archbishop Romeyn's creation of the comparatively poor prebend of Bilton in 1294,[29] the total of canonries and prebends in the church of York reached what proved to be its final complement of thirty-six. The evolution of the prebendal system at York had now been completed and was to undergo no major modification until the Reformation.

The cathedral prebends and the rewards of residence
By no means the largest English secular chapter and easily surpassed by those of Lincoln, Wells, and Salisbury (with 58, 55, and 52 canons respectively), the church of York nevertheless presented an exceptionally

---

[26] YML, L2/1 (Magnum Registrum Album), iii. 50–1; *Reg. Gray*, pp. 132–3; *CPapR, 1198–1304*, p. 57; cf. YML, M 2(3)a (Treasurer's Cartulary), fos. 9ᵛ–11.
[27] YML, M1(1)b (Statutes), fo. 47; *Reg. Gray*, p. 198.
[28] *Reg. Romeyn*, ii. 24–5, 27–8 ('Capitulum enim divisioni hujusmodi noluit consentire'); cf. Clay, *Fasti* ii. 48, 53–4.
[29] YML, L 2(2)a (Domesday Book), fo. 121; M 2(2)c, fo. 5; *Reg. Romeyn*, ii. 19–22; Clay, *Fasti* ii. 8.

varied and heterogeneous series of opportunities for the careerist ecclesiastic. Admittedly, two prebends out of the total of thirty-six, those of Bramham and Salton, were appropriated to the two Augustinian priors of Nostell and Hexham respectively. But the assignment of a place in choir and chapter to these two monastic prelates, a practice which can be paralleled at the secular cathedrals of Chichester, Hereford, Salisbury, and Wells, had no major constitutional implications. Although the prior of Hexham held a prebendal house in the cathedral close and both he and the prior of Nostell very occasionally attended chapter meetings, they could inevitably only take an intermittent interest in the affairs of the cathedral church.[30] As we have seen, two other prebends, Newthorpe and Wilton, had been annexed to the dignity of treasurer by Archbishop Gray, an arrangement which caused much contention at the end of the thirteenth century but which was to endure until they both disappeared with the office of treasurer itself at the Reformation.[31] The precentor and the chancellor of the Minster had to wait until 1484 for the existing prebends of Driffield and Laughton to be annexed to their dignities by Archbishop Rotherham;[32] while at no time during the Middle Ages did the dean of York have a prebend attached to his own office. As the possession of a prebend was the essential and necessary qualification for the right to sit in chapter as a canon, the medieval deans, chancellors, and precentors of York would normally expect either to retain the prebend they held at the time of their appointment to their dignities or to secure collation to a vacant prebend as soon as possible thereafter. The curious anomaly whereby the holder of a major dignity in the cathedral choir might yet be without a canonical voice in his cathedral chapter was certainly not unknown at late medieval York; but it was comparatively rare and generally restricted to those dignitaries who had no intention of ever taking up residence at York. Although several of the twenty-four deans of York between 1290 and 1500 had to wait some months or even years to acquire a cathedral prebend, only three (Cardinal Angelicus Grimaud between 1366 and 1380; Cardinal Adam Easton between 1382 and 1385; and the future archbishop of Canterbury, Roger Walden, between 1395 and 1397) never held a prebendal stall in the York chapter-house.[33]

The desirability of providing prebends for the major dignitaries of the cathedral as well as the five archdeacons of the diocese still left the

---

[30] YML, M2(4)g (Misc. Reg., 1290–1340), fos. 25, 27^v–28; cf. *The Priory of Hexham* (Surtees Soc., 1864–5), ii. 152–3.

[31] A. H. Thompson, 'The Treasurership of York and the Prebend of Wilton', printed in *Reg. Greenfield*, i. 299–305; see below, p. 73.

[32] BIHR, Reg. Rotherham, i, fos. 99–100; ii. 99^v; Le Neve–Jones, pp. 45, 65.

[33] Le Neve–Jones, pp. 6–9, and *passim*; Clay, *Fasti* i. 10–12.

archbishop with a most extensive range of patronage at the Minster. What made that patronage so extensive was not only the number of prebends at York but the frequency with which so many of them became vacant. Precisely because they attracted the attentions of papal, royal, and episcopal administrators who trafficked extensively in benefices throughout England, the York prebends tended to change hands at a comparatively rapid rate. By 1325 the cathedral statutes themselves included a clause allowing canons to exchange or resign their prebends after a minimum of three years.[34] Only a minority of canons, a minority which naturally included many of the residentiaries, were ever likely to hold the same prebend for more than a decade; and even the most cursory examination of archiepiscopal registers and the chapter's act-books makes it clear that there can have been few years between the beginning of the fourteenth and the end of the fifteenth centuries when two or three prebends did not become vacant and available for re-collation. In itself the frequency with which the York prebends changed possession only increased the competitive instinct of those clerks who wished to secure one. At various times in the later Middle Ages, and especially in the decades immediately before and after 1300, this competition was so intense that it is often difficult to know who actually held contested prebends at a particular moment of time. The frenetic intensity with which York prebends were pursued was the natural consequence of their financial value. There is no need to labour the point that both the prebends and the dignities of the cathedral of York were primarily assessed in terms of the annual revenue with which they could provide their incumbents. Despite the well-known inadequacies of the assessment for papal taxation made in 1291 and (to a lesser extent) of the *Valor Ecclesiasticus* of 1535, those two national surveys of clerical wealth provide us with our best opportunity to estimate the comparative rewards the York dignities and prebends could bring to their holders.[35]

The most obvious conclusion to emerge from these valuations of York prebends made in 1291 and 1535, whatever their deficiencies as an accurate guide to the real income to be enjoyed by a canon during the later Middle Ages, is the extreme inequality of prebendal wealth. Much more significant however, for such inequalities were a characteristic of prebends

---

[34] *York Statutes*, p. 39.
[35] For the highly artificial and often arbitrary nature of the 1291 *taxacio* see Archbishop Romeyn's own comments two years later (*Reg. Romeyn*, i. 133), and R. Graham, 'The Taxation of Pope Nicholas. IV', *EHR* xxiii (1908), pp. 434–54: the medieval York chapter never produced an alternative valuation of its prebends and relied upon the papal assessment for its own purposes: see YML, M2(2)c, fo. 23.

Table Annual values of York dignities, archdeacons and prebends

	'Taxatio Vetus', 1291[36]			*'Valor Ecclesiasticus', 1535*[37]			
	£	s	d	£	s	d	
Dignitaries							
Dean	373	6	8	307	10	7½	
Precentor	16	13	4	96	4	2	(including prebend of Driffield)
Chancellor	33	6	8	85	6	8	(including prebend of Laughton)
Treasurer	233	6	8	220	—	—	
Subdean	53	6	8	50	14	2	
Succentor	13	6	8	8	—	—	
Archdeacons							
York	68	—	—	90	3	1½	
East Riding	42	6	8	62	14	7	
Cleveland	36	—	—	36	—	10	
Richmond	200	—	—	—	—	—	
Nottingham	17	9	—	61	—	10	
Prebends							
Ampleforth	40	—	—	35	—	—	
Apesthorpe	10	—	—	8	—	—	
Barnby	14	—	—	14	8	4	
Bilton	10	—	—	14	8	9	
Bole	16	—	—	17	17	1	
Botevant	20	—	—	17	17	1	
Bramham	40	—	—	—	—	—	(annexed to priors of Nostell)
Bugthorpe	40	—	—	34	7	1½	
Cave, South	106	13	4	—	—	—	
Driffield	100	—	—	—	—	—	(annexed to precentorship, 1484)
Dunnington	10	—	—	19	10	10	
Fenton	53	6	8	37	15	5	
Fridaythorpe	40	—	—	38	16	0½	
Givendale	12	—	—	10	2	6	
Grindale	10	—	—	9	17	1	

[36] *Taxatio Ecclesiastica . . . Nicholai IV* (Record Commission, 1802), pp. 297–8; cf. *York Statutes*, p. 42.
[37] *Val. Ecc.* v. 1–2, occasionally supplemented by figures in Torre, 'Minster', *passim*.

	£	s	d	£	s	d	
Holme	16	13	4	11	3	9	
Husthwaite	26	13	4	38	17	11	
Knaresborough (with Bichill)	46	13	4	42	18	9	
Langtoft	100	—	—	43	19	7	
Laughton	73	6	8	—	—	—	(annexed to chancellorship, 1484)
Masham[38]	166	13	4	80	—	—	
Newbald, North	53	6	8	40	—	—	
Newbald, South	20	—	—	14	9	7	
Newthorpe	—	—	—	—	—	—	(annexed to treasureship)
Osbaldwick	26	13	4	35	3	4	
Riccall	46	13	4	33	11	8	
Salton	53	6	8	—	—	—	(annexed to priors of Hexham)
Stillington	46	13	4	47	16	$5\frac{1}{2}$	
Strensall	53	6	8	67	7	1	
Thockrington	6	13	4	2	17	1	
Ulleskelf	20	—	—	34	11	8	
Warthill	10	—	—	6	—	—	
Weighton	40	—	—	32	10	5	
Wetwang	120	—	—	80	11	3	
Wilton	33	6	8	—	—	—	(annexed to treasureship)
Wistow	100	—	—	65	16	$0\frac{1}{2}$	

in all English secular cathedrals except Exeter, was the extremely high value of most of the York prebends compared with their counterparts elsewhere. Whereas at Hereford and Lichfield even the richest prebends were rarely assessed for taxation at more than £20 a year, at York in 1291 only ten of the thirty-six prebends were taxed at less than that figure. The cathedral church of York could offer not only Masham, the wealthiest single prebend in England, but also a range of lucrative canonries unsurpassed even by its closest rivals in this field, the cathedrals of Salisbury and Lincoln. Thus the average value of the thirty-six York prebends as assessed in 1291 was as much as £48, approximately £8 higher than the equivalent figure at Lincoln.[39] Prebends like Masham, Wetwang, South Cave,

[38] Masham was valued at £120 a year when held by George Neville in the mid-fifteenth century (*CPapR, 1447–55*, p. 2).

[39] Cf. A. H. Thompson, *The English Clergy and their organization in the later Middle Ages* (Oxford, 1947), p. 102, n.2.

Driffield, Langtoft, and Wistow, together with the even more valuable archdeaconry of Richmond and deanery and treasurership of the cathedral, were among the very richest prizes of the medieval English Church. At one level this exceptional wealth explains why 'canonries at York always led to dispute';[40] at another it demonstrates how large a proportion of the total wealth of the cathedral church could be continuously diverted into the hands of papal and royal candidates who made no direct contribution to the work of the Minster whatsoever.

As an individual clerk's chances of acquiring a prebend always depended on such variable factors as a vacancy in the see, the archbishop's own ability to retain his freedom to collate against external pressures, and the life-expectancy of the previous incumbent, the history of the holders of a particular prebendal stall at York reflects ever-changing patterns. But as a general rule, and as one would expect, the richest prebends tended to be in the possession of non-residents. The golden prebend of Masham itself, for instance, was held not by local York ecclesiastics but by an archbishop's nephew (Walter de Gray), by the most notorious of all English pluralists (Bogo de Clare), and by one of the most outstanding of Edward I's civil servants (John de Drokensford). In the late fifteenth century the fruits of Masham were still being enjoyed *in absentia* by a galaxy of ecclesiastical luminaries best known for their presence at the English court and their subsequent promotion to the episcopal bench.[41] The attachment of such men to the richest York prebends made that chapter the most distinguished in England; but their careers are largely irrelevant to the history of the medieval Minster itself.

Although the York chapter had no alternative but to accept a situation whereby the great majority of its richest benefices formed part of a vast spoils system operating in the interests of papal and governmental officials, it was careful not to abandon its very real control over the integrity of the prebends themselves. At the very least each prebendary was obliged by statute to bequeath a precious cope and a palfrey to the cathedral church, gifts regularly commuted into cash payments from the thirteenth century onwards.[42] The chapter's right to compel non-resident canons to provide financial assistance at times of crisis seems to have been little exercised in practice; but a vacancy in a prebend provided the common fund of the cathedral with substantial if occasional windfalls. In 1294 resident

[40] T. S. R. Boase, *Boniface VIII* (1933), p. 310.
[41] Clay, *Fasti* ii. 52–5; Le Neve–Jones, pp. 66–8.
   Statutes, pp. 2, 39; cf. the *Mortuaria Canonicorum* and *Vacaciones Beneficiorum* sections of the Minster fabric and chamberlains' rolls (YML, E 1 and E 3) respectively for the implementation of this statute.

members of the chapter accordingly agreed that a proper defence of the liberties of their church required the making of 'a book in which should be written down the goods, rights and customs of each prebend one by one'.[43] Extensive although not complete sections of this 'book' still survive and provide a vivid and detailed impression of the financial resources of twenty-one York prebendaries.[44] Although the great majority of the York prebends were based on the revenues of Yorkshire parish churches in which the prebendaries were titular rectors, some were entirely comprised of landed estates: thus the prebendary of Dunnington held eight bovates in demesne and thirty-six in service there together with meadow, woodland, and moor as well as a hall in York. The richer prebendaries possessed one or more manor-houses on their estates and sometimes continued to maintain these as personal residences to the end of the Middle Ages. The detailed administration of his lands and the collection of his rents was delegated by the canon to his own bailiffs: and if he were a perpetual absentee, he would normally farm his entire estate to a local agent. Precisely because they were independently administered, prebendal estates are inadequately documented within the chapter's own archives; but it is clear that the prebendaries' attempts to exact their manorial rights over their tenants aroused much controversy in the fourteenth and fifteenth centuries. At times absentee canons would appeal to the chapter itself to enforce the raising of their rents. Much more common were accusations by the resident members of the chapter that absentee canons had 'wasted' their prebendal estates either by failing to maintain buildings in an adequate state of repair or by selling off the assets, and especially the timber, of the prebend.[45] The canons resident at York might be spared the physical presence of many of their colleagues; but much of their time had to be spent in trying to deal with the problems presented by chronic 'absentee landlordship'.

The complexities of the Minster's financial machinery are such that it will never be possible to provide an absolutely precise assessment of how large a proportion of the revenues of the cathedral church remained at the disposal of the cathedral clergy resident at York. But it seems safe to suggest that at most times in the later Middle Ages between a half and two-thirds of a total cathedral income of well over £2,000 was regularly diverted into the hands of absentee clerks. What remained at York certainly sufficed to place the residentiary dignitaries, archdeacons, and canons among the most

---

[43] *York Statutes*, p. 34.
[44] BM, Cotton MS. Claudius B.III, fos. 166–97; translated as 'Extents of the Prebends of York' in *Miscellanea*, iv. (YAS Rec. Ser. recte xliv, 1937), pp. 1–38: for another, and better, text, see YML, L 2(2)a, fos. 101ᵛ–120ᵛ. A much fuller survey of thirty prebendal estates c. 1500 may be found in M 2(2)c (Repertorium), fos. 43–65ᵛ.

wealthy secular ecclesiastics in England. For those prepared to contemplate long periods of residence at the Minster and able to afford the heavy initial expenses of taking up residence, the rewards seem to have been greater than in any other English secular cathedral. Indeed the variety of methods whereby a residentiary canon could supplement the income he derived from his prebend almost defies analysis. No reader of the great series of late medieval York wills, for example, can fail to be struck by the handsome financial payments made to canons who attended the innumerable funeral services, obits, and anniversaries in the cathedral.[46] Of much greater value was the residentiary's right to share in the profits of the Minster's common fund or *communia*. The practice of reserving a large number of wealthy churches and estates for the common expenses of the chapter was of course as old as the institution of the prebends themselves; and a papal confirmation of capitular possessions in 1194 reveals that by the end of the twelfth century the common fund was already extremely handsomely endowed.[47] Subsequent benefactions greatly enhanced its value and also made possible the creation of a completely separate fabric fund.[48] By the beginning of the fourteenth century the *communia* itself was under the financial management of the Minster's chamberlain, who accounted twice a year and was often a vicar choral of the cathedral. In the 1370s, when his account rolls begin to survive, the chamberlain was in receipt of an income approaching £700 a year, of which approximately two-thirds found its way in payments to the residentiary canons.[49] At the Reformation the York chapter's communal income was assessed at £434 a year, more than the total value of all Lichfield's thirty-two prebends.[50]

As at most other English secular cathedrals, there were three different ways whereby canons in residence at York could receive emoluments from the common fund. In the first place every canon who had passed through

[45] YML, H 2/1 (Chapter Acts, 1400–35), fos. 13ᵛ, 16–18; cf. 'Documents relating to Visitations of the Diocese and Province of York, 1407, 1423' in *Miscellanea*, ii. (Surtees Soc., cxxvii, 1916), p. 240. For the 1445–6 account of the bailiff of the prebendary of Langtoft, a rare survival, see YML, P 1(1)viii.
[46] e.g. *Testamenta Eboracensia* (Surtees Soc., 1836–1902), i. 169, 386; ii. 204, 265; iii. 84, 85, 143; iv. 301; *Hists. York* iii. 300; *CChR, 1226–57*, pp. 270–1.
[47] *The Priory of Hexham* (Surtees Soc., 1864–5), i. 54; Clay, *Fasti* ii. 39 n. 3, 97, 114; *Hists. York* iii. 95–6.
[48] With two earlier exceptions the annual accounts of the *custos fabricae* only begin to survive from 1399: both the income and expenditure of this official (often over £500 per annum in the early fifteenth century) tended to fluctuate considerably (see E 3/1–24, often poorly transcribed in *Fabric Rolls*, pp. 1–94).
[49] YML, E1/1–6. Although no chamberlain's roll survives before 1370, the existence of his office can be traced back to at least the thirteenth century; see e.g. BM, Additional Charter 16,760 for an original acquittance by Geoffrey de Lanum chamberlain in 1307. This *Camerarius Capituli* must of course be sharply distinguished from the chamberlain of the vicars choral (see below, p. 91).
[50] *Val. ecc.* iii. 132; v. 1–2.

the probationary stage of unpaid greater residence was entitled to commons assessed by the number of days in the year on which he was physically present at the main cathedral services. From the late fourteenth century onwards the *communia canonicorum* section of the chamberlains' accounts reveals that commons were normally distributed at the rates of 3s. 0d. on double feasts, 2s. 0d. on feasts of nine lessons, and 1s. 0d. on all other days.[51] As there were nearly fifty designated *festa duplicia* at the late medieval Minster, and almost twice as many feasts of the nine lessons, a canon who resided continuously throughout the year could be assured of an additional income of £26 or £27 from his commons alone. Needless to say, not many canons emulated the example of Canon Nicholas de Ferriby whose faultless record of attendance (fifty-two weeks and one day) in 1400–1 earned him the maximum amount of commons; and most residentiaries were in York for their statutory period of twenty-six weeks and little more.[52] Even these estimates must be treated with some caution in view of the possibility that a canon employed out of York on chapter business might be 'awarded his residence as if he had been personally present'.[53] It is hardly surprising that the great majority of chapter meetings at the late medieval Minster were attended by only a handful of canons.

Much more valuable than his daily commons was the York residentiary's right to an equal share of the surplus of the common fund when this was distributed at Whitsuntide and Martinmas. Here again the evidence of the York chamberlains' accounts, admittedly only available after 1370, fully confirms Dr. Kathleen Edwards's suggestion that 'shares in the division of surplus commons at York were probably exceptionally valuable'.[54] Towards the end of the fourteenth century the chamberlain often had as much as £200 to distribute at the end of each of his half-yearly terms, a sum which declined to approximately £170 a century later. But the exact amount received by each canon naturally depended on the number of his fellows also in residence; thus the eight residentiaries at York in the mid-1370s received portions of less than £40 a year while the three canons

---

[51] YML, E1/1–37; L 2(3)a, fos. 69–70; BIHR, Reg. Rotherham, i. fo. 100; *Fabric Rolls*, p. 123. It remains uncertain at what date these increased rates replaced those originally laid down by the chapter in 1222 (see above, p. 49).

[52] YML E1/1–30. The number of days in which a canon kept his residence throughout the whole year is recorded in all chamberlains' accounts which run from Whitsuntide to Martinmas: the Martinmas–Pentecost rolls only record details of half-yearly residence. For evidence of the gradually increasing number of feasts of the nine lessons and double feasts at the medieval Minster see *Hists. York* iii. 254–65.

[53] *Fabric Rolls*, p. 200. Similar suspicions are raised by the admittedly exceptional and scandalous case of John Barnyngham who kept residence at St. Paul's Cathedral while a residentiary canon of York from 1433 to 1457 (YML, H 2/3, *passim*; *History of St. Paul's*, p. 91).

[54] Edwards, *Secular Cathedrals*, p. 45.

resident at York in 1487–8 obtained well over £100 each from the same source.[55] As is well known, such calculations could easily lead to a vested financial interest in restricting the size of the residentiary body. So too could the third and last of the methods whereby resident canons might exploit the resources of the common fund—the farming of its churches and estates at a fixed rent. By 1291 the complications caused by the ubiquity of this practice induced Dean Henry de Newark and his chapter to produce detailed regulations on the subject. The right of farming estates pertaining to the common fund was not only restricted to the residentiaries in order of seniority but an attempt was made to fix the farms at levels which would enable canons to make a fair but not exorbitant profit.[56] The indirect evidence of the competition among residentiaries to take up farms like those of Copmanthorpe, Bishop Burton, and Weaverthorpe certainly suggests that they could be very profitable indeed.[57]

Perhaps the only certain conclusion to emerge from this necessarily compressed survey of the emoluments at the disposal of the residentiary canons of York is of their quite remarkable value. Only the wealthiest magnates and prelates of northern England can have had a more regular supply of liquid capital at their disposal. As will be seen, this was the wealth which sustained active careers in the service of the chapter and archbishop, endowed chantries, maintained great households, and helped to rebuild the Minster itself. Future research is almost certain to reveal that the residentiaries at York were among the leading money-lenders of the north, the men to whom an impoverished monastery or a financially embarrassed merchant would naturally turn in times of trial.[58] For evidence of their extensive private libraries, magnificent furnishings, and extravagant style of living the historian has to wait until their wills and inventories begin to survive at the end of the fourteenth century; but they must always have impressed their contemporaries, to apply Matthew Paris's comment on John le Romeyn the elder, as clerks 'crammed with rents and treasures'.[59] How large a proportion of that treasure was devoted to the religious and charitable purposes of the cathedral must have depended on the personal interests and aspirations of each residentiary. Committed to an endless round of hospitality and entertainment as well as of administrative

---

[55] YML, E 1/3, 4, 48, 49, 55, 57.

[56] YML, L 2(3)a, fos. 71, 89; *York Statutes*, pp. 27–33; cf. pp. 24–5. For analogies at other secular cathedrals see Edwards, *Secular Cathedrals*, p. 47; *History of St. Paul's*, pp. 60–5.

[57] See e.g. YML, H 2/1, fos. 9, 13[V], 22; M 1(1)b, fos. 29[V], 46[V]; and the *Magne Firme Dominorum Residentium* section of surviving chamberlains' accounts. Cf. BM, Cotton MS. Vit. A II, fo. 115[V].

[58] I. Kershaw, *Bolton Priory, The economy of a northern monastery, 1286–1325* (Oxford, 1973), pp. 139, 177–8, 191–2; *CPatR, 1436–41*, p. 102.

[59] *Matthaei Parisiensis Chronica Majora* (Rolls Ser., 1872–83), v. 534, 544–5.

and judicial business, most of the residentiaries no doubt conceived of their own personal wealth as a reflection of the magnificence of the Minster in whose service they lived and died. The great majority of clerks who took up residence as canons of York certainly remained there forever; and by the end of the Middle Ages the nave and choir of the cathedral were crowded with the long-vanished tombs of successive generations of men whose proudest epitaph was *canonicus residentiarius*.[60] Proudest of all perhaps were those canons who combined residence at York with the possession of one of the four great dignities around which the religious and administrative life of the medieval cathedral was intended to revolve.

The dignitaries of the cathedral

Amidst the extraordinary diversity of constitutional practice at the nine medieval English secular cathedrals, the pride of place given to the four major dignitaries of dean, precentor, chancellor, and treasurer strikes a welcome note of uniformity. At York, as elsewhere, these *quatuor personae* were in theory the rulers of the cathedral, the four corner-stones of the Minster's spiritual as well as material fabric. To Archbishop Thomas of Bayeux the system he applied to the northern metropolitan church in the last decades of the eleventh century must indeed have seemed sensible, logical, and likely to prove effective. To the dean was entrusted the presidency of the chapter as well as general responsibility for the welfare of all the cathedral clergy; the precentor was to supervise the liturgical, and the chancellor the secretarial and educational functions of the cathedral; while the treasurer's duties comprised not only the safe-keeping of the church's plate and relics but also the maintenance of its fabric and furnishings. So essential were these functions to the welfare of the Minster that it is hardly surprising to discover that the earliest recorded statutes of the medieval chapter began with the regulation that all four dignitaries should continue to reside as had been the custom hitherto.[61] In fact, and with much more serious consequences than in the case of the thirty-six York prebends, the pressures to convert these four dignities into incidental rewards for absentee clerks often proved overwhelming. From the middle of the thirteenth century onwards it is difficult to find any occasion on which all of the *quatuor personae* of York were resident near the cathedral at the same time. Indeed the evidence of fourteenth- and fifteenth-century visitation records and chapter ordinances often suggests that the internal organization of the Minster's affairs might have been more efficient and harmonious if the four dignities had never been created: too often the

[60] Drake, *Ebor.*, pp. 500–14, derived from Torre 'Minster' (see p. 134^v for plan of monuments).
[61] YML, M 1(1)b (Statutes), fo. 9^v; *York Statutes*, p. 14.

unexercised authority of an absentee dean, precentor, chancellor, or treasurer positively inhibited the residentiary canons from eradicating obvious abuses.[62] In many ways the constitutional history of the late medieval Minster is a commentary on the difficulties of administering a complex community in the absence of its senior administrators. Nevertheless, the ideal of residentiary dignitaries was never completely discredited; and even in their absence their offices formed the structural basis of the Minster's constitutional and administrative arrangements.

'They say that in the church he is superior to everyone except the archbishop; and in the chapter he is superior to all.'[63] The medieval statutes leave no doubt of the absolute primacy of the dean of York over the rest of his cathedral clergy. When in the cathedral he played the dominant role in all the major ceremonies of the liturgical year, taking the central position in all important processions, reciting the *confiteor* at prime and compline, and celebrating the mass on principal feasts. It was the dean's duty to bless the candles on the day of the Purification, the ashes on Ash Wednesday, and the palms on Palm Sunday: on Maundy Thursday he was expected to wash the feet of the poor.[64] At York as elsewhere the most concrete manifestation of the dean's authority was his right to install a new archbishop on the archiepiscopal throne; and when in the city he also summoned and presided over meetings of the chapter and admitted and invested to all the cathedral prebends and dignities. Above all, the dean was committed to a magnificence of display and largess deliberately designed to emphasize the wealth and prestige of his cathedral. His York residence, the Dean's Place, occupied a conspicuous site to the south-east of the cathedral church; by the fifteenth century the York deanery, fortified in 1302 and extended in 1415, had its own orchard and gateway into Petergate and was capable of providing hospitality on a grand scale.[65] Even more impressive, although very difficult to recapture, must have been the sight of the dean on ceremonial progress through the city and the surrounding area. In 1325 it was decreed that on his visitations of the chapter estates and farms the dean might be accompanied by nineteen horses while the York canon who accompanied him was restricted to five; and on the eve of the Reformation, Dean Brian Higden (1516–39) was still being 'attended to the church on a

---

[62] YML, H 1/2 (Chapter Acts, 1343–70), fo. 6ᵛ; H 1/3 (Chapter Acts, 1352–1426), fo. 51; H 2/1 (Chapter Acts, 1400–35), fo. 20.

[63] *York Statutes*, p. 3.

[64] YML, M 2(2)c (Repertorium), fo. 2; M 1(1)b (Statutes), fos. 5–6; *York Statutes*, pp. 1–4.

[65] For a series of references to the often very elusive history of the medieval deanery see *Early Yorkshire Charters*, ed. W. Farrer (Edinburgh, 1914–16), i. 219–21; *CPatR, 1301–7*, p. 19; *CPatR, 1413–16*, p. 288; *YCR* i. 146; ii. 75; *Testamenta Eboracensia*, iv. 31, 119; *Yorkshire Inquisitions*, iii. (YAS. Rec. Ser. xxxi, 1902), pp. 134–5.

Christmas day by 50 gentlemen before him in tawney coates garded with black velvet and 30 yemen behind him in like coates garded with taffeta'.[66]

Such conspicuous display was inevitably founded on great wealth; and in purely financial terms the deanery of York certainly deserves its reputation as 'the major English benefice below episcopal rank'.[67] With an annual income assessed at over £300 in 1535, the revenues of the dean far surpassed those of his fellow dignitaries and canons. Solidly based on an endowment of over twenty appropriated Yorkshire churches, themselves the basis of the dean's extensive peculiar spiritual jurisdiction, the resources of the deanery provided its holder with the opportunity to accumulate massive reserves of liquid capital. Henry de Newark and William de Hambleton, successively deans of York between 1290 and 1307, lent sums of well over £100 to the monks of Durham and Bolton by a series of complicated and possibly usurious arrangements.[68] Not surprisingly, deans of York were well able to perpetuate their memory by founding chantries and other religious charities. Deans Roger de Insula (d. *c.* 1232), Geoffrey of Norwich (d. 1238), William of Langton (d. 1279), William of Hambleton (d. 1307), the brothers William and Robert Pickering (d. 1312 and 1332), William Felter (d. 1451), and Richard Andrew (d. 1477) were all commemorated by means of perpetual chantries in the Minster itself; and in 1315–18 Dean Robert Pickering founded what was thenceforward one of the city of York's most substantial hospitals, that of St. Mary in Bootham.[69] Wealth on such a scale obviously had a less admirable effect in exciting the acquisitive instincts of senior ecclesiastics in the service of the papacy, the royal government, and the archbishop. To none of the latter could the choice of a dean of York be a matter of indifference; and it followed that succession to this office was characterized by more disputes than any other in the cathedral except the treasurership.

Alone among the dignitaries and prebendaries of the medieval English secular cathedral, the dean was appointed not by the archbishop but as the result of a supposedly 'free' capitular election. After the Fourth Lateran Council of 1215 no archbishop could hope to argue, like Archbishop Geoffrey in 1194, that 'the deanery belonged to his own gift'.[70] But it would

---

[66] *York Statutes*, p. 37; D. M. Palliser, *The Reformation in York, 1534–1553* (Borthwick Papers, no. 40, 1971), p. 2.

[67] R. L. Storey, *Thomas Langley and the Bishopric of Durham, 1406–1437* (1961), p. 9.

[68] *Durham Account Rolls*, ed. J. T. Fowler (Surtees Soc., 1898–1901), ii. 491; Kershaw, *Bolton Priory*, pp. 139, 174–8. For another reference to Dean Hambleton's property transactions see *Feet of Fines, 1300–14* (YAS Rec. Ser. cxxvii, 1965), p. 48.

[69] YML, P2 (St. Peter's School), Box II; *Fabric Rolls*, pp. 277, 283, 285, 287, 288, 290, 294, 301; *Hists. York* iii. 241; *CPatR, 1313–17*, p. 213; *CPatR, 1317–21*, pp. 259–60; *VCH Yorkshire* iii. 345.

[70] *Hists. York* iii. 92–4.

be idle to pretend that the later medieval chapter could ever elect a dean without paying serious consideration to royal and archiepiscopal interests. Nevertheless, much more frequently than in the case of elections to the see itself, there were many decanal elections in which the chapter undoubtedly did find room for complicated manœuvre. The greatest threat to the chapter's own discretion was undoubtedly the possibility of papal provision to the deanery; but against this danger the canons' greatest allies were often the archbishop and the king. Only in the mid-fourteenth century when three successive cardinals, Elias Talleyrand (1342–64), Angelicus Grimaud (1366–80), and Adam Easton (1382–5) were in turn provided to the deanery did capitular election become quite ineffective over a long span of time.[71] The often voluminous but invariably highly formal records of decanal elections at York before and after this period do little to illuminate the intrigues and pressures which usually accompanied these occasions; but they do make it clear that the small group of residentiary canons played a leading role and generally hoped to elect one of their own number as dean.

In the autumn of 1310, for example, William Pickering became dean as the result of an election in which twenty-two canons voted, but only nine were present in the chapter-house; at the election two years later of William's brother, Robert Pickering, only eight of the sixteen canons who participated voted in person.[72] As university graduates in law with a long and varied experience of ecclesiastical and royal administration, the Pickering brothers were in any case two eminently desirable candidates for the York deanery in the eyes of both king and archbishop. But any attempt on the part of the residentiary canons to elect one of themselves as dean in the face of royal or archiepiscopal opposition was almost certainly doomed to failure. The eleven canons who elected their colleague Thomas Sampson to the deanery in November 1342 had their choice rapidly ruled out of court by both Edward III and Pope Clement VI;[73] and in what proved to be the most exciting and contentious decanal election ever held at late medieval York, that of 1452, the residentiary canons were forced to surrender the claims of their own candidate, John Barnyngham, in favour of the king's secretary, Master Richard Andrew.[74] As the Middle Ages drew

---

[71] Le Neve–Jones, pp. 6–7. Cf. BIHR, Reg. Zouche, fos. 16–17; Reg. Thoresby, fo. 64; Reg. A. Neville, i. fo. 12. At Salisbury Cathedral all six deans between 1297 and 1379 were non-resident foreigners (*VCH Wilts.* iii. 170).

[72] *Reg. Greenfield*, i. 44–50, 69–81.

[73] BIHR, Reg. Zouche, fos. 216–17.

[74] See YML, A1(4), and BIHR, RH 74–6, for important collections of original evidence on this disputed election; cf. BIHR, Reg. Kempe, fos. 157–8; *CPapR, 1447–55*, p. 112.

to a close, so too did the York chapter's ability to do more than make a formal election of a dean nominated by the Crown.

For long periods of the later Middle Ages it therefore followed that the material rewards of the York deanery were too great to allow the chapter to elect a candidate on the grounds of his qualifications for the office alone. Of the thirty-four deans between 1215 and 1500 only fifteen or sixteen devoted much personal attention to the responsibilities of their position. Before the early fourteenth century most deans were heavily involved in diocesan administration at York itself and therefore could often play a prominent role in choir and chapter. By contrast, the century between the death of Robert Pickering in 1332 and the election of William Felter in 1436 was characterized by a succession of non-resident deans who held high office in the royal administration and accordingly soon found their way on to the English episcopal bench: of the eight York deans between 1385 and 1436 only John Prophet failed to secure a bishopric. The mid- and late fifteenth century saw a partial revival of the resident dean in the persons of men like William Felter, Richard Andrew, Robert Booth, and William Sheffield, highly experienced and well-connected administrators who nevertheless spent several months of every year in York.[75] In each of these three periods, however, the York chapter had to be able to manage its affairs without a dean *in situ*. Although Archbishop John le Romeyn had once informed Pope Boniface VIII that a vacancy in the York deanery would cause 'burdens and dangers to the church of York by the loss of its prebends, rights and liberties',[76] the canons residentiary found it essential to face these burdens and dangers on their own. The act-books of the late medieval chapter leave no doubt that the routines of the cathedral's administration were little affected by the dean's presence or absence. Almost all of the dean's responsibilities could be delegated to the senior residentiaries; and the dean's own ability to take independent initiatives and to wield authority independent of his chapter was in any case severely limited. As in most other English secular cathedrals, the dean's constitutional position in his chapter was never more than that of a *primus inter pares* and at no time is there evidence of serious jurisdictional conflict between his fellow canons and himself. The Minster clergy certainly continued to cherish the ideal of an active resident dean; but what they apparently valued most was his hospitality, his largess, and his giving of copious alms to the poor and to themselves.[77]

The office of precentor or cantor had been instituted for much more

[75] YML, E1/40–59 (Chamberlains' Accounts, 1463–92); H2/3 (Chapter Acts, 1427–1504), *passim*.
[76] *Reg. Romeyn*, ii. 214–15; cf. *Reg. Greenfield*, i. 42–3.
[77] *York Statutes*, p. 3; Clay, *Fasti* i. 9; cf. Edwards, *Secular Cathedrals*, p. 145.

specific reasons. 'To him pertains the rule of the choir as regards singing and psalmody.'[78] Although the medieval statutes of the cathedral are less than absolutely precise in describing the York precentor's duties, it is clear that he was expected not only to exercise general supervision over the liturgical practices of the choir but also to play a personally prominent role in many of its most important services.[79] His supremacy in the choir is perhaps best symbolized by his prerogative of installing every member of the cathedral clergy from dean to vicar choral. But it was over the admission and training of the choristers of the Minster that the precentor's authority was naturally at its most absolute. By supervising admissions to the cathedral song school, a body over which he exercised complete jurisdictional control, the precentor was in theory able to influence the recruitment of young clerks into the cathedral much more than any of his colleagues. Although York's cathedral song school is much less well documented than its grammar school, it seems clear enough that from the early thirteenth century onwards it enjoyed a continuous if erratic history under the control of a professional choir master, himself appointed by the precentor. A complaint made to Archbishop Thoresby in 1367 by the then precentor, Master Adam of York, that 'various chaplains, holy water carriers and others were maintaining song schools in parish churches, houses and other places in the city of York' makes it incidentally clear that boys trained in the cathedral song school were not all committed to future service in the Minster choir.[80]

Although second in precedence only to the dean, the precentor was far inferior to him in financial terms. Until the wealthy prebend of Driffield was permanently annexed to the dignity by Archbishop Rotherham in 1484, the precentorship was very poorly endowed indeed.[81] Of its thirty-three holders between 1215 and 1500 several were prepared to relinquish it for the chancellorship or even a parochial benefice; and on only one occasion, in 1381, did it attract the attention of an Italian cardinal and become the subject of a papal provision.[82] Such comparative poverty did not, however, preserve the precentorship from the hands of absentee royal clerks. As in the case of the York deanery it is possible to distinguish between the mid-thirteenth and the fifteenth centuries, in which long-serving residentiary precentors were by no means uncommon, and an

[78] *York Statutes*, pp. 5, 14; cf. *Reg. Gray*, p. 52.

[79] BIHR, Reg. Zouche, fo. 221[v]; *York Statutes*, pp. 5–6.

[80] *Early Yorkshire Schools* (YAS Rec. Ser. xxvii, xxxiii, 1899, 1903), i. 22–3; cf. *York Statutes*, pp. 5–6.

[81] BIHR, Reg. Rotherham, i. fos. 99–100; G. Lawton, *Collection Rerum Ecclesiarum de Dioecesi Eboracensi* (1842), pp. 3, 295; *Fasti Parochiales*, iii. (YAS Rec. Ser. cxxix, 1967), 20.

[82] *CPatR, 1381–5*, p. 48; Le Neve–Jones, pp. 10–12.

intervening period when the office was often held for short intervals by prominent administrators and future bishops (Thomas de Cantilupe, Antony Bek, William de la Corner, Thomas de Cobham). Although the precentor's absence from the cathedral, together with his failure to maintain his house within the Minster close, was frequently deplored, it was often unavoidable. It followed that his personal involvement in the round of worship within the cathedral rapidly became less and less essential. As early as the mid-thirteenth century most of the precentor's duties in the choir itself had been delegated to his two deputies, the succentor of the vicars and the *succentor canonicorum*, the latter an office inaugurated during the early years of Archbishop Gray's pontificate.[83] Even a precentor in residence gradually lost his right to precedence in the cathedral to the most senior residentiary canon;[84] and it is hard to resist the conclusion that by the fourteenth century this particular dignity had lost its organic connection with the responsibilities for which it had been originally created.

The right of the chancellor of the Minster to be the third dignitary of the church of York and to 'have priority in all things after the precentor' was firmly based on a judicial decision made in 1191, only a few months after Archbishop Geoffrey had introduced the new title of *cancellarius* to replace that officer's older designation of *magister scholarum*.[85] This change of name, adopted in turn by all secular English cathedrals, was largely a matter of convention; but in most ways the York chancellor's original title provides a more accurate impression of his functions than its successor. The canons and vicars choral of the late medieval Minster never lost sight of the fact that the primary duty of their chancellor was to stimulate and supervise the educational and intellectual life of the cathedral. As late as 1472 his non-residence was singled out for especial criticism because 'he ought to teach (*legere*) and conduct the schools near the church'.[86] Admittedly, the chancellor of the cathedral had important functions in the choir, notably in assigning lessons to the minor clergy; but most of these responsibilities were soon delegated to his deputy, the subchancellor, an officer who had certainly emerged at York by the 1220s.[87] Similarly, the chancellor's statutory obligation to preserve the chapter's seal *ad citationes*

---

[83] *Reg. Gray*, p. 52. The office of *succentor canonicorum* survived throughout the medieval period but it too was increasingly likely to be held by absentee clerks (*CPatR, 1467–77*, p. 268; *Fabric Rolls*, p. 250).

[84] YML, M2(2)c (Repertorium), fo. 15.

[85] YML, L2/1 (Magnum Registrum Album), iii. fos. 94–5; *Hists. York* iii. 90–1; Clay, 'Precentors and chancellors', pp. 135–6; Edwards, *Secular Cathedrals*, p. 179.

[86] *Early Yorkshire Schools*, i. 28; *Fabric Rolls*, p. 250.

[87] *Hists. York* iii. 152; *York Statutes*, p. 7.

seems to have been observed very erratically in practice; and by the late fourteenth and fifteenth centuries the onerous secretarial business of the Minster was entrusted to a long line of specially appointed chapter clerks.[88] Like all dignitaries and residentiary canons of the Minster, the chancellor was also committed to a strenuous variety of administrative work arising from his own estates and churches: this aspect of his position is well illustrated by the fortunate and very rare survival of 'a humble attempt at a letterbook' preserved by William Wickwane as chancellor in the late 1260s.[89] Nevertheless, to his medieval contemporaries as to ourselves, the main interest of the chancellor's office is the extent to which he was able to direct and maintain a tradition of learning at the cathedral.

According to two famous Lateran decrees of 1179 and 1215 metropolitan cathedrals throughout Christendom were required to provide not only a master to teach grammar free of charge to poor scholars and their own clerks but also a theologian to teach the Holy Scriptures 'to priests and others, and especially to those who have a cure of souls'. The extent to which these two decrees were observed in practice remains one of the most mysterious and controversial aspects of the medieval Church.[90] At York, as elsewhere, the provision of elementary educational facilities in grammar is much better documented than that of regular lectures in theology. Although it will never be possible to write a genuine history of the cathedral grammar school in the Middle Ages, there can be no doubt that such an institution did enjoy a continuous existence in the vicinity of the Minster from at least the early twelfth century to the Reformation. Throughout that long period the chancellor's own connection with the Minster's grammar school was no doubt usually remote; but he never lost his right to appoint its master and regularly supported its claims to educational monopoly in the city and surrounding area.[91] Although nothing is known of the internal organization or curriculum of the school, occasional references to successive *magistri scholarum grammaticalium Sancti Petri Eboracensis* provide not only evidence of continuity but also some indication of its development over the

---

[88] The names and activities of the late medieval chapter clerk are fully documented in surviving chapter act-books and chamberlain's rolls (where he is recorded as receiving a pension of 2 marks a year: YML, E1/1–57, *passim*). For the testament of the especially long-serving chapter clerk, Master Thomas Dautre, alias de Alta Ripa, who died in 1437, see *Testamenta Eboracensia*, ii. 59–61; and cf. *ibid*. iv. 84–6.

[89] C. R. Cheney, 'Letters of William Wickwane, Chancellor of York, 1266–68', *EHR* xlvii (1932), 626–42.

[90] J. D. Mansi, *Sacrorum Conciliorum Collectio* (Florence and Venice, 1759–98), xxii, cols. 227–8, 999–1000; and see Edwards, *Secular Cathedrals*, pp. 185–205; N. Orme, *English Schools in the Middle Ages* (1973), pp. 79–86.

[91] YML, H 1/2 (Chapter Acts, 1343–70), fos. 6, 70, 122; *Early Yorkshire Schools*, i. 18–30.

5 The Seal of Dean Robert Pickering of York (1312–33). (Dean and Chapter of Durham Muniments, 1.1 Archid. Dunelm. 5).

4 The Seal of the Chapter of York Minster (late 13th C.): inscribed *'Sigillum Capitolii Sancti Petri Eboracensi Ad Citaciones Tantum'*. (Dean and Chapter of Durham Muniments, 2.2 Archiep. 5).

6 The Chancellor Lecturing to the scholars of the Minster School: from the 'Chancellor's Window' of the south aisle of the nave, *c.* 1330. 'In the 2nd Light sits Chancellor Riplingham . . . reading out of a book in his hand Lectures to his scholars which stand by him' (Torre's description of the Minster in the late 17th C.).

later medieval period. By the fifteenth century the office of grammar schoolmaster, originally assigned to a regent in arts for only three or four years, was usually held for long periods and even for life by a professional and often married *magister*.[92]

The cathedral chancellor's several attempts to suppress York's only other well-established grammar school, that sponsored by the great hospital of St. Leonard's, met with no success; but those attempts make it clear that the Minster school deliberately set out to satisfy the educational needs of the whole city. Although the choristers and junior clergy of the Minster no doubt always attended in considerable numbers, the administration of the cathedral grammar school seems to have become increasingly detached from that of its mother church. So too did its physical location. Before 1289, when the site of the school was transferred to the prebendal house of Dunnington, teaching seems to have taken place within a room in the angle between the Norman nave and the west side of the south transept of the cathedral church itself; and for the rest of the Middle Ages the Minster grammar school, which changed its location on at least one occasion, was apparently situated in or near Petergate.[93] In view of the frequent changes of fortune which seem to have characterized all long-established medieval schools, no general assessment of the value of the educational services provided by the Minster's grammar school can hope to be at all reliable. Nevertheless, it is likely to have been one of the largest and most important schools in the country. In 1369 Richard Beckingham, an advocate of the court of York, bequeathed twopence each to sixty poor and conscientious clerks of the grammar school; and on the eve of the Reformation the monks of St. Mary's Abbey, York, were still accommodating fifty poor scholars of the Minster school in a house called the Conclave or the Clee sited near the gateway of their precinct.[94]

The number of senior clerks who attended the Minster in the hope of receiving more advanced educational instruction in theology must have been considerably fewer. At York, as elsewhere, the ascendancy of Oxford and Cambridge universities from the early thirteenth century onwards reduced the possibility that a secular cathedral might promote a very

[92] *Testamenta Eboracensia*, iii. 143, 198–9; Drake, *Ebor.*, p. 495; *Early Yorkshire Schools*, i. 19–30. From 1380 onwards *magistri scolarium grammaticalium* (not necessarily always those of the cathedral) were occasionally admitted to the franchise of the city of York: *Register of the Freemen of the City of York* (Surtees Soc., 1897–9), i. 77, 98.

[93] *Reg. Romeyn*, i. 381–2; and see below, p. 103. For references to a place called 'Scoles' in the cemetery of St. Michael-le-Belfrey in 1408 and to the meeting of the convocation of York in the 'novis scolis ecclesie Eboracensis' some years later, see A. Raine, *Mediaeval York* (1955), p. 32; and *Records of the Northern Convocation* (Surtees Soc. cxiii, 1907), p. 152.

[94] *Testamenta Eboracensia*, i. 86; *Val. Ecc.* v. 6; Edwards, *Secular Cathedrals*, p. 194.

vigorous centre of higher learning. But sufficient evidence does survive to suggest that the tradition of cathedral lectures in theology was never allowed to languish absolutely. In 1355 a disputation on the Conception of the Virgin was conducted by a Franciscan and a Dominican friar within the chancellor's school at York; and ten years later Bishop Simon Langham encouraged several brethren of St. Leonard's Hospital to attend the local theological school and write down 'what might seem devout and notable'. In the first half of the fourteenth century the fame of the Minster's educational facilities may have spread as far as Exeter where it encouraged a certain John of Cornwall to travel to York 'for the purpose of study'.[95] Much more than its grammar school, the success of the cathedral's lectures in theology seems to have depended on the quality and energy of the successive chancellors of the Minster. In the case of an absentee or senile holder of that office, the chapter might appoint a deputy to deliver the lectures;[96] but the chancellor's statutory duty to lecture in person was certainly never forgotten and often observed. In 1293 Archbishop Romeyn encouraged rectors of churches within his diocese to attend the then chancellor's lectures in theology; and in his will of August 1332 Robert de Ripplingham bequeathed his magisterial chair and desk ('cathedram meam et descum') to his successor as chancellor of the Minster.[97] Appropriately enough, one of the best-preserved medieval representations of a canon or dignitary to survive in the present Minster can still be found in the so-called Chancellor's window of the nave: in the centre panel of the bottom row Ripplingham is depicted in a blue robe as he lectures to his students on the familiar first verse of the Gospel of St. John (Plate 6).[98]

The names of the twenty men who successively held the office of chancellor in the Minster between 1200 and 1500 suggest that the archbishop of York and his cathedral clergy were always at pains to appoint a distinguished scholar to that dignity. The chancellorship, almost alone amongst the York dignities and prebends, was unaffected by papal provision: and it was held continuously by a succession of famous scholars. According to the cathedral statutes 'the chancellor ought to be a master of

[95] A. G. Little, *The Grey Friars in Oxford* (Oxford Historical Soc. xx, 1892), p. 242; Orme, *English Schools in the Middle Ages*, pp. 82–3; *Exeter Freemen, 1266–1967*, ed. M. M. Rowe and A. M. Jackson (Devon and Cornwall Record Soc., Extra Series I, 1973), p. 21.

[96] *Early Yorkshire Schools*, i. 26.

[97] *Hists. York* iii. 220–1; *Early Yorkshire Schools*, i. 17, 24.

[98] Edwards, *Secular Cathedrals*, p. 198; and for the most recent description of the window see P. Gibson, 'The Stained and Painted Glass of York', *The Noble City of York*, ed. A. Stacpoole *et al.* (York, 1972), pp. 98–9. More detailed accounts are provided by Torre, 'Minster', p. 31; G. Benson, *The Ancient Glass Windows in the Minster and Churches of the City of York* (Yorkshire Philosophical Soc., 1915), pp. 42–3.

theology'; and in fact all the chancellors of the Minster between 1290 and 1496 possessed doctorates in theology except for the two canon lawyers, Simon de Beckingham (1350–69) and John Estcourt (1426–7).[99] In the mid-thirteenth century the chancellorship was held by such prominent graduates of Oxford and Paris universities as that *theologus praeelectus*, Master John Blundus, and his immediate successor and future bishop of Winchester, John Gervays of Exeter, 'learned in physical science'.[100] Two centuries later it was a dignity offered to, but characteristically rejected by, one of the most celebrated figures in the Oxford University world, Thomas Gascoigne. After being held by two of the most famous English humanists, Thomas Chaundler and John Gunthorpe, the chancellorship then passed (1498–1528) to William Melton, the tutor of John Fisher at Cambridge and the owner of a library which reveals his dedication to the ideals of Erasmus and early sixteenth-century 'Christian Humanism'.[101] However, only a minority of these learned chancellors resided in York, and one or two (including Chaundler and Gunthorpe) probably never visited the cathedral at all. Nevertheless, the chancellor was perhaps the holder of the only dignity or prebend at the Minster whose appointment was not primarily governed by financial considerations.

In the case of the Minster's fourth major dignity, the exact opposite is true. Partly through a series of historical accidents, partly because of the rapacious acquisitive instincts of early treasurers like the elder John le Romeyn, the treasurership of York was always one of the wealthiest benefices in England.[102] No position in the church of York was more eagerly sought after, and none was a source of greater litigation. During the century which followed the death of Romeyn in 1255, the succession to the treasurership of York continuously provoked legal disputes of almost unfathomable complexity.[103] Singled out for special attention by both papal Curia and English monarch, this was a benefice over which the archbishops of the late thirteenth and early fourteenth centuries could

[99] Clay, *Fasti* i. 17–21; Le Neve–Jones, pp. 9–10.

[100] *Matthaei Parisiensis Chronica Majora* (1872–83), v. 41; Clay, *Fasti* i. 19–20; Emden, *Oxford* i. 206; ii. 757–8.

[101] BIHR, Reg. Neville, i. fos. 4ᵛ–5; YML, H 2/3 (Chapter Acts, 1427–1504), fo. 213; *Testamenta Eboracensia*, v. 258–9; A. B. Emden, *A Biograhical Register of the University of Cambridge to 1500* (Cambridge, 1963), pp. 400–1; cf. J. K. McConica, *English Humanists and Reformation Politics* (Oxford, 1965), p. 91.

[102] For a detailed inventory of the treasurer's property in 1298 see YML, M2(3)d.

[103] See e.g. *CPatR, 1247–58*, pp. 424, 429, 455, 458; *1258–66*, p. 436; *CPapR, 1305–42*, pp. 28, 41, 73; for the particularly acrimonious dispute between Boniface VIII's great-nephew, Francesco Gaetani the younger, and the king's clerk, Walter de Bedewynd, in 1306–7, see *Select Cases before the King's Council, 1243–1482* (Selden Soc. xxxv, 1918), pp. 18–27; cf. Professor Hamilton Thompson's 'The Treasurership of York and the Prebend of Wilton', *Reg. Greenfield*, i. 299–305.

exercise little effective control. Held *in absentia* by royal favourites (John Mansel and Bogo de Clare), by younger sons of prominent English magnates (Amaury de Montfort and Edmund de Mortimer), and by Italian cardinals and relations of the pope (Pietro Colonna and Francesco Gaetani), the treasurership of York was at that time a source of often scandalous controversy.[104] By the fifteenth century, however, most of the treasurers (men like John de Branktre, John Clifford, John Newton, Robert Wolveden, John Barnyngham, John Pakenham, and William Sheffield) did take up residence at the Minster and dispensed lavish hospitality from their house in the cathedral close.[105] At the end of the Middle Ages the archbishops of York had turned the wheel full circle and converted the treasurership into the supreme reward for the heads of their own ecclesiastical administration, and in particular for their vicars-general.[106]

At first sight the presence of the treasurer at York might have seemed all the more welcome to the Minster clergy because of that dignitary's importance to the welfare of the cathedral. As the officer 'who ought to keep the church', the treasurer had in theory a general responsibility not only for the preservation of the church's plate, jewels, and relics but also for the upkeep of the cathedral's fabric and its internal fittings. However, like the three senior dignitaries of the Minster, he delegated most of these duties, in his case to what was in effect a specialized and largely autonomous administrative department. The latter was headed by a subtreasurer, one of the most prominent officials at the Minster and a clerk appointed not by the treasurer but by the dean and chapter.[107] The treasurer's office met the cost of various commodities consumed during the routines of worship at the Minster and also paid for the board and wages of the subtreasurer and his five subordinates. Of these, the two vestry-clerks (*clerici de vestibulo*) had charge of the cathedral's large collection of clerical vestments, themselves washed by a professional launderer.[108] Even more important to the daily conduct of divine worship in the cathedral were the three sacrists. The

[104] *Reg. Wickwane*, pp. 286–7; and cf. Clay, *Fasti* i. 25–30; Le Neve–Jones, pp. 12–13.

[105] It seems probable, although not absolutely certain, that the Treasurer's House or Place occupied the site of the present mansion of that name (which incorporates substantial remains of medieval walling) from the late eleventh century onwards; *Testamenta Eboracensia*, i. 167; iv. 279–89; *YCR* ii. 60; *VCH York*, p. 342; L. P. Wenham, *Gray's Court, York* (York, n.d.), pp. 10–12.

[106] It was no doubt for this reason that very few fifteenth-century treasurers ever left York: of the 14 treasurers between 1360 and 1503, 2 became deans of York, 1 archdeacon of Richmond, and the remainder died in office (Le Neve–Jones, pp. 13–15).

[107] YML, M 1(1)b (Statutes), fos. 7–8, 11ᵛ, 48; *Fabric Rolls*, p. 191; and for other references to the subtreasurer see *Hists. York* iii. 244, 376; *Testamenta Eboracensia*, iii. 91, 117, 178.

[108] YML, H 1/2 (Chapter Acts, 1343–70), fo. 6ᵛ; cf. H 1/3 (Chapter Acts, 1352–1426), fo. 51. Like the sacrists, the vestry clerks received regular courtesy payments from the Minster's common fund (YML, E1/1–57).

recipients of innumerable bequests 'to ryng the belles solemply' at funeral services in the Minster, these sacrists had a chamber of their own and were responsible for the provision of lights in the church, for opening and closing its various doors, and for ordering processions.[109] As the medieval equivalents of the modern cathedral vergers, the three sacrists came under constant criticism at visitations of the Minster for their failure to prevent intolerable noise, to quell unruly groups of boys, and to eject pigeons, dogs, and other animals.[110] The frequency and volume of such complaints points to a central if paradoxical feature of the late medieval Minster's history, the contrast between the great power and wealth of the four dignitaries and their inability to enforce acceptable standards of behaviour on the part of their servants in the church itself. To adapt the words once addressed by Archbishop Wickwane to that most negligent of all York treasurers, Bogo de Clare, the Minster always faced the danger that greed for its milk and wool might lead to the death of the sheep.[111]

The archbishops and the Minster, 1256–1373

Eleven archbishops held the see of York between the death of Walter de Gray in 1255 and that of John Thoresby in 1373. Of their personalities, almost completely concealed from us by the formal phraseology of the voluminous correspondence issued in their names, we can at least know enough to suggest that they were a highly variegated succession of prelates. Thus to Walter Giffard (1266–79), remembered for his stately presence, sociability, and corpulence, there succeeded the austere and intransigent William Wickwane (1279–85), 'esteemed a petty Saint in that age'.[112] Wickwane's own successor, John le Romeyn (1286–96), managed to combine a reputation for exceptional avarice with a magnificence and liberality allegedly unsurpassed by any of his predecessors or successors.[113] From these and similar comments it is comparatively easy to appreciate what qualities the clergy of the diocese and cathedral of York looked for in their leader. As a man he was expected to give evidence of both personal piety and of a commitment to learning; as an archbishop he had to be severe to the transgressor and ruthless to those who defied his authority while remaining hospitable and accessible to the remainder of his flock. Above all

[109] *York Statutes*, pp. 9, 13–14; cf. *Reg. Thomas Langley* (Surtees Soc., 1956–70), i. 159; *Testamenta Eboracensia*, i. 262; iii. 62, 84–5, 234, 281; iv. 52, 303.
[110] YML, H 1/2 (Chapter Acts, 1343–70), fo. 6^v; *Fabric Rolls*, pp. 244, 251, 258, 269.
[111] *Reg. Wickwane*, p. 286.
[112] *Chronicon de Lanercost*, ed. J. Stevenson (Edinburgh, 1839), pp. 71, 103; *Hists. York* ii. 407–8; *Reg. Wickwane*, p. xx.
[113] *Chronicon Henrici Knighton* (Rolls Ser., 1889–95), i. 359; *Hists. York* ii. 409; *Reg. Romeyn*, ii. pp. xxxi–xxxiii.

he had to use his office and the wealth it brought him as a source of munificence and patronage:[114] the fact that he invariably promoted the careers of his own family and servants did his reputation little harm provided that his largess to the churches, and especially the cathedral church, of his diocese never ran completely dry. To this conventional stereotype the characters of all eleven archbishops between 1255 and 1373 could readily be made to conform, but only at the cost of depriving us of a knowledge of the individual strengths and weaknesses which each brought to his conduct of his office. At York, as at most other English cathedral churches, a series of short biographical notices of the holders of the see was compiled at erratic intervals during the course of the later Middle Ages, but these do little to illuminate the exact nature of the archbishops' problems or the way in which they tried to meet them.[115]

Such ignorance must not mislead us into the assumption that these eleven archbishops lacked distinction and force of personality; but it has to be admitted that by comparison with the holders of other English sees those of York failed to earn themselves reputations for either outstanding sanctity or scholarship.[116] Miracles were allegedly performed at the shrine of William Wickwane; but only, one suspects, because that tomb was at Pontigny in Burgundy, the Cistercian abbey already hallowed by its associations with three archbishops of Canterbury, Thomas Becket, Stephen Langton, and St. Edmund Rich. In the sixteenth century Bishop John Bale optimistically included the names of both Wickwane and his predecessor, Sewall de Boville (1256–8), in his catalogue of Britain's famous authors on the strength of works which modern scholarship has hitherto been unable to trace; and how far Archbishop Thoresby (1352–73) had a personal share in the composition of the so-called *Lay-folks' Cathechism* he issued from Cawood Palace in November 1357 for the use of the parish priests of his province remains a highly debatable matter.[117] Neither saints nor creative scholars, the eleven archbishops between Boville and Thoresby all belonged to the ministerial class of professional clerical

[114] For the only detailed study of archiepiscopal patronage at this period see L. H. Butler, 'Archbishop Melton, his Neighbours and his Kinsmen, 1317–40', *Jour. Eccles. Hist.* ii (1951), pp. 54–68.

[115] *Hists. York* ii. 401–45; cf. pp. 446–87 for the even briefer verse tributes to the archbishops preserved in two metrical chronicles of the church of York composed in the late fourteenth and late fifteenth centuries.

[116] M. D. Knowles, *The Medieval Archbishops of York* (Oliver Sheldon Memorial Lecture, York, 1961), pp. 9–11.

[117] J. Bale, *Illustrium Majoris Britanniae Scriptorum Catalogus* (Basle, 1557–9), i. 111–12; ii. 42; *The Lay Folks' Catechism* (Early English Text Soc., Original Series no. 118, 1901), pp. xii–xx, 98; W. A. Pantin, *The English Church in the Fourteenth Century* (Cambridge, 1955), p. 212; Emden, *Oxford* i. 234; iii. 1864, 2228.

administrators who dominated the English episcopal bench throughout the later Middle Ages. Only two, Walter Giffard and William de la Zouche, were members of noble or gentry families; most, and perhaps all, of the others were of comparatively humble origins and seem to have owed their initiation into an administrative career to the patronage of an older churchman or their membership of an existing clerical affinity. In either case the archbishopric of York was reserved for clerks whose skills had been tested in the schools as well as in administrative work. To the generalization that all archbishops had by this time to undergo at least some experience of university education, William Melton (1317–40), a franklin's son from the parish of Welton near Howden, was the only exception.[118] In line with the general trend in the country at large, the educational attainments of the archbishops between 1256 and 1373 reflect a movement away from Paris to Oxford and from the desirability of a doctorate in theology (Boville, Romeyn, Corbridge) to one in canon and civil law.[119]

Nevertheless, and despite several recent attempts to prove otherwise, the episcopal bench of medieval England has always defied precise categorization. Perhaps the only common characteristic of all these eleven archbishops was their readiness to put their considerable administrative experience at the service of their diocese and province. As Professor Hamilton Thompson pointed out fifty years ago, the early volumes of the famous series of York archiepiscopal registers are the best extant memorial to their 'exemplary diligence in diocesan business'.[120] Although these registers do indeed confirm that no archbishop of this period neglected his spiritual responsibilities completely, the amount of time a particular prelate could personally spend within the boundaries of his diocese naturally depended upon the demands made upon his services by the English government. In so far as a meaningful distinction can be made between the various men who held the see, it must certainly be that between those whose administrative careers had always been pursued within the church of York and those who had the wider experience of public life and work at Westminster and in the royal service. During the half-century following the death of Walter Gray the see was ruled by a succession of seven archbishops of whom only one, Walter Giffard, had held high office in the English government. Throughout most of this fifty-year period the interests of the church of York were in the hands of ex-deans of the cathedral (Boville and Ludham), ex-chancellors (Wickwane and Corbridge),

---

[118] BIHR, Reg. Melton, fos. 28, 63; Butler, 'Archbishop Melton', p. 63.
[119] The only archbishop of York before the fifteenth century who is known to have studied at Cambridge University is Walter Giffard (Emden, *Cambridge*, 257).
[120] 'The Medieval Archbishops in their Diocese', *Y. M. Hist. Tr.*, p. 2.

and on one occasion (John le Romeyn) the illegitimate son of an ex-treasurer of the Minster. These archbishops naturally identified themselves almost exclusively with their see: Thomas de Corbridge indeed never left his diocese at all after his enthronement in 1300.[121] With Corbridge's death four years later the surprisingly long succession of York cathedral clergy on the archiepiscopal throne came to an end. Between 1304 and 1373 the see was in the hands of four outstandingly distinguished royal clerks, William de Greenfield, William Melton, William de la Zouche, and John Thoresby, all of whom had served as either the king's chancellor or the keeper of his privy seal. Even in these four cases elevation to the archiepiscopal throne subsequently led to a gradual, if never complete, withdrawal from Crown service to diocesan affairs.

All in all, the cathedral clergy of York could be well satisfied with the choice of their pontiffs between 1256 and 1373. Nor can there be much doubt that until at least the first decade of the fourteenth century the canons in residence at York had often been able to influence that choice. With the exceptions of Walter Giffard and John Thoresby, translated to York from the lesser sees of Bath and Wells and Worcester respectively, all archbishops of this period underwent the process of capitular postulation. Although often subject to later annulment by a pope who wished to exercise his prerogative of provision without rejecting the chapter's candidate, election was still by no means merely formal. In 1255–6 the members of the York chapter secured the pope's consent to their election of their dean, Sewall de Boville, despite royal opposition; and in 1279 and 1285 archbishops Wickwane and Romeyn secured a clear majority of votes at elections conducted in the York chapter-house 'per viam scrutinii'.[122] Even in the fourteenth century the chapter did not always elect 'at the instance of the lord king'; and William de la Zouche became archbishop in 1340 in the teeth of Edward III's preference for William de Kildesby.[123] On the whole, however, archiepiscopal elections at York remained compara-tively free from the disputes and scandals that characterized the succession to so many of the cathedral's dignities and prebends. In so far as the succession of a new archbishop produced complications at all, perhaps the most inconvenient was the delay caused by the elect's journey to the papal Curia to receive the pallium. In his determination to avoid consecration at

---

[121] *Reg. Corbridge*, ii, p. xv.

[122] *CPapR, 1198–1304*, p. 328; Matthew Paris, *Chronica Majora*, v. 516, 522, 570; *Reg. Wickwane*, pp. 304–8; *Reg. Romeyn*, ii, pp. x–xi; *Hists. York* ii. 407–9. At other English cathedrals, too, elections of bishops *de gremio* were at their most frequent in the century after the Fourth Lateran Council of 1215, the only period when the process of free capitular election was given a reasonably fair trial: see e.g. *VCH Wilts*. iii. 166; *History of St. Paul's*, p. 42.

[123] *Hists. York* ii. 415, 417–18; Le Neve–Jones, p. 3.

the hands of the rival primate of Canterbury, every new archbishop not already in episcopal orders between 1256 and 1373 travelled to the Curia, the only exception being Henry de Newark, consecrated at York itself in 1298 by Antony Bek, his flamboyant suffragan bishop of Durham.[124] Partly because it was usually so long delayed, the enthronement of the archbishop on his return to his diocese soon became the occasion for spectacular display and feasting.[125]

'Archbishops who cast themselves humbly before the blessed feet of the Apostles were naturally expected to yield to apostolic demands in the future'.[126] As we have already seen, the cathedral church of York was exceptionally vulnerable to the intrusion of papal provisors into its major dignities, archdeaconries, and prebends. Several recent analyses of the operations of papal provision in thirteenth- and fourteenth-century England have been at pains to defend this so-called system against too sweeping a condemnation; but the registers of the archbishops of York leave no doubt that throughout this period it was always the single most important cause of insecurity and conflict. As elsewhere in England, the invasion of curial officials and especially of cardinals (of whom nine held prebends in the Minster before 1307) was the subject of bitter comment from the reign of Henry III onwards; and only after the outbreak of the Great Schism in 1378 and the second Statute of Provisors twelve years later did the previous spate of alien provisors dwindle to a trickle. Throughout the intervening period successive archbishops fought a series of long and painful battles to prevent the complete erosion of their patronage at the cathedral. Archbishops Boville and Zouche were both excommunicated for their resistance to papal demands; and in a famous letter of 1288 Archbishop Romeyn lamented—somewhat ironically in view of the Italian origins of his own family—the systematic plundering of the church of York for the sake of the 'Romans'.[127] In the following year the pope himself acknowledged that many of the York prebends were held by persons living overseas; and on Romeyn's death in 1296 at least a third of the canons were foreigners.[128] During the subsequent forty years, when the incidence of papal provision at York was at its height, the ratio of aliens to Englishmen in the chapter varied between one to two and one to three.[129] By the end of Archbishop Melton's pontificate the number of papal nominees with

---

[124] *Hists. York* ii. 410.

[125] *Ibid.* 415–16; Dixon and Raine, *Fasti Ebor.*, p. 401. See below, p. 100.

[126] 'The Fourteenth Century', *Y.M. Hist. Tr.*, p. 6.

[127] Matthew Paris, *Chronica Majora*, v. 586, 624, 678–9; *VCH Yorkshire* iii. 39; Dixon and Raine, *Fasti Ebor.*, pp. 342–4; *Reg. Romeyn*, ii. pp. xvii–xviii, 28–9.

[128] *CPapR, 1198–1304*, p. 496; *Reg. Romeyn*, ii. 1–28; *VCH Yorkshire* iii. 378.

[129] *Reg. Corbridge*, ii. 1–32; *Reg. Greenfield*, i, xviii; BIHR, Reg. Melton, fos. 68–122.

expectations of appointments to York canonries and prebends who actually
secured installation had begun to decline and the worst of the invasion was
over. As Archbishop Giffard had pointed out to Cardinal Ottobuono, its
most serious effect was to undermine the archbishop's ability to provide for
his own clerks.[130] On the internal affairs of the chapter the Italians had little
or no direct influence and do not appear even to have voted by proxy at
archiepiscopal or decanal elections.

Aliens were by no means the only beneficiaries of papal provisions; and
as the fourteenth century progressed, these provisions tended to become
one of the more popular methods whereby the English Crown promoted the
careers of its own clerks. Of the thirty-four collations to York prebends
recorded in the register of Archbishop Greenfield (1306–15), only ten were
appointments by the archbishop himself, twelve were papal provisions (of
which five were to Englishmen), and another twelve were nominations by
the royal government.[131] Quite apart from the king's acknowledged right to
present to canonries during vacancies of the see, he was able to place
overwhelming pressure on all archbishops to allocate the lion's share of the
Minster's benefices to his own clerks. By its very nature this pressure has
left only intermittent traces in surviving records; but the great lawsuit for
the treasurership of York between Francesco Gaetani and Walter de
Bedewynd in 1306–7 is only one of many cases to prove that a confrontation
between a papal cardinal and a favourite royal clerk would usually end in
victory for the latter.[132] So valuable were the richest York dignities,
archdeaconries, and prebends that it need occasion us no surprise to
discover that the membership of the medieval chapter reads like a roll-call
of the heads of the English civil service. So much was inevitable and
obvious; but the distinctive feature of the cathedral church of York was, as
Professor Hamilton Thompson first appreciated, that 'it was in no small
degree the training-ground in which servants of the state had their
apprenticeship in official routine'.[133] The existence of a vast but close-knit
affinity of Yorkshire clerks who dominated the English chancery and
wardrobe during the reigns of the three Edwards has now been
demonstrated in considerable detail.[134] Such a remarkable concentration
and continuity of administrative power in the hands of the 'York clerks'

---

[130] *Reg. Giffard*, p. 245.

[131] *Reg. Greenfield*, i, pp. xiv–xv, 289–98; cf. Pantin, *The English Church in the Fourteenth Century*,
p. 60.

[132] A. Deeley, Papal Provision and Royal Rights of Patronage in the early fourteenth century', *EHR* xliii
(1928), p. 151; cf. Clay, *Fasti* i. 29–30.

[133] 'The Medieval Chapter', *Y.M. Hist. Tr.*, p. 13.

[134] J. L. Grassi, 'Royal Clerks from the Archdiocese of York in the Fourteenth Century', *Northern
History*, v (1970), 12–33.

was the consequence of frequent royal visits to the north at this period, of the self-perpetuating nature of medieval clerical dynasties, and above all of the great influence wielded by the central figures of archbishops Giffard (who created the connection), Melton, and Thoresby. Naturally enough many members of this interconnected clan held one or more York prebends during the course of their careers. More important still, very many of them had personal experience of York as young clerks working within the archbishop's own diocesan administration.

The existence of this York affinity makes it more than usually difficult to draw the always shadowy line which separates the active from the non-active members of a medieval chapter. In the years around 1300 residentiary canons were often drawn, like the Pickering brothers, into occasional service on behalf of the king; at the same time several non-residentiaries retained sufficient interest in the affairs of their mother church to find time to attend chapter meetings at the Minster.[135] Nevertheless, and as at all times in the Middle Ages, the small resident nucleus of the chapter consisted of those clerks whose major re-sponsibilities were to the archbishop rather than the king. The number of residentiaries was usually very small. In 1305 John Nassington informed the auditor of the chapter of Beverley that there were then only two York canons in residence; most ordinary chapter meetings at York in the first half of the fourteenth century were attended by only three to five canons; and when the number of residentiaries rose to nine in 1343 there were complaints that the resources of the common fund could not readily support such a number.[136] It is never easy to define what a medieval chapter meant in practice as opposed to constitutional theory; but throughout the late thirteenth and early fourteenth centuries real continuity was main-tained by a handful of archiepiscopal administrators, not only the dignitaries we have already met but men like John de Craucombe (vicar-general at the turn of the century), Richard of Chester (Archbishop Greenfield's chancellor), and Thomas Sampson (official of the archdiocese in the 1330s).[137] Although the archbishops of York had to surrender personal control over the majority of chapter appointments to papal Curia and English government, they had the consolation of knowing that the resident canons at least were their own very carefully selected men.

By a familiar paradox the personal involvement of the residentiary members of the cathedral chapter in the archbishop's service made it easier

[135] YML, M 2(4)g (Misc. Reg., 1290–1340), fos. 1, 4, 11, 25, 26, 27ᵛ; Emden, *Oxford* iii. 1532–4.
[136] YML, M 2(4)g, fos. 12, 26, etc.; *Memorials of Beverley Minster* (Surtees Soc., 1898–1903), i. 62; Harrison, *Medieval College*, pp. 179, 182; Drake, *Ebor.*, App., p. lxxv; *VCH Yorkshire* iii. 378.
[137] Emden, *Oxford* i. 407; iii. 1636; 2165–6.

for them to achieve increasing immunity from his authority in their corporate capacity. It was a situation in which the archbishop had little to gain and much to lose by attempting to define that authority and one in which the constitutional divorce between prelate and chapter accordingly became as complete as their personal relations were cordial. Perhaps the most startling testimony to this divorce is the fact that York seems to have been the only secular cathedral in England to deny its titular head a statutory right to sit in chapter at all: according to statutes codified in the early fourteenth century the dean of York 'in the church is greater than anyone after the archbishop; and in chapter he is greater than all'.[138] By about the same date the archbishops of York seem to have quietly surrendered their rights to participate in the making of cathedral statutes and to exercise detailed supervision over the conduct of life and worship in the Minster. Similarly, the chapter denied to the archbishop any control over decanal elections and tried to ensure that its dean's powers were sufficiently extensive to enable him to personify its increasing independence. By a compromise of 1290 the dean was at last compelled to make an oath of obedience to the archbishop at the time of his confirmation at the hands of the latter; but even this oath, one not sworn by individual canons or by the chapter as a group, was considerably more guarded than that taken by the archbishop himself at the time of his enthronement in the minster.[139] In many ways the archbishop's ability to exercise spiritual jurisdiction was more limited in his cathedral than in any other church of his diocese. Not an absolutely independent 'ecclesiastical republic', the late medieval Minster was nevertheless largely immune from archiepiscopal intervention and interference. The itineraries of the thirteenth- and fourteenth-century archbishops leave no doubt that their visits to their palace north of the cathedral were always occasional. Committed as they were to the pastoral care of an enormous diocese, they perambulated constantly between a dozen or more of their manor-houses; and it was from Bishop Burton, Bishop Wilton, Southwell, Laneham, and Scrooby, and above all from Cawood and Bishopthorpe on the west bank of the Yorkshire Ouse, that the late medieval archbishops ruled their see.[140]

To the general rule that the late medieval archbishops of York were

---

[138] *York Statutes*, p. 3; see above, p. 63.

[139] YML, M 1(1)b (Statutes), fo. 41; A 1(2, 4); *Reg. Greenfield*, i. 50, 81.

[140] See e.g. *Reg. Greenfield*, v. 299–328, the most detailed as well as the latest itinerary in date to be published. For the changing patterns of archiepiscopal residence in the later Middle Ages (a subject still to be investigated in detail), see also H. E. J. Le Patourel and P. Wood, 'Excavation at the Archbishop of York's Manor House at Otley', *YAJ* xlv (1973), pp. 115–41; 'The Medieval Archbishops in their Diocese', *Y.M. Hist. Tr.*, pp. 3–4; *English Episcopal Palaces (Province of York)*, ed. R. S. Rait (1911), pp. 2–8, 32–65.

prepared to tolerate a high degree of autonomy on the part of their cathedral chapter there is, however, one important exception. Throughout the late thirteenth and early fourteenth centuries the debate about the precise constitutional relationship between archbishop and chapter focused on the vexed and often obscure issue of his right to conduct a regular disciplinary visitation of his cathedral church. At a time when the right of bishops to visit their cathedral chapters was being asserted throughout Western Europe, there was never any possibility that the northern province could avoid a constitutional battle on this contentious subject; but what characterized the struggle at York was the chapter's success in ensuring that a defeat on the main issue should be accompanied by restrictions which largely emasculated their visitor's disciplinary powers. As it was, the archbishops of the late thirteenth century were understandably reluctant to open what was bound to be an embarrassing dispute with a formidable adversary. It seems highly likely that even Archbishop Wickwane, whose strenuous attempts to carry out a metropolitan visitation of the church of Durham inaugurated a period of spectacular jurisdictional strife, never carried out a regular visitation of his own cathedral church.[141] It was Wickwane's successor, Archbishop Romeyn, who finally forced the issue of his right to visit the chapter into the open, probably as a by-product of his personal feud with Dean Robert of Scarborough. Only after the latter's compulsory retirement from the scene was an agreement between archbishop and chapter made on 21 November 1290. While accepting the archbishop's right to hold a visitation once every five years, the chapter effectively limited his ability to make much of such occasions: he was to be accompanied by no one but two of the canons themselves and had no right either to put detailed questions in writing or to interrogate individual members of the chapter against their will.[142]

Not surprisingly, few archbishops of the immediately subsequent period seem to have availed themselves of the extremely limited visitatorial rights conceded to them by the compromise of 1290; and it was Archbishop Melton thirty-five years later who finally succeeded in establishing a new and lasting settlement. In the summer of 1328 and under the threat of an appeal to the papacy, the chapter reluctantly conceded that henceforward the archbishop might visit every four years, on which occasions he could not only introduce three or four clerical assessors into the chapter-house but also produce written *corrigenda* on the basis of private examination of

[141] How far Wickwane's two mandates calling for a capitular visitation on 2 January 1280 had real effect remains highly obscure: *Reg. Wickwane*, pp. 2–3, 210; cf. R. Brentano, *York Metropolitan Jurisdiction and Papal Judges Delegate, 1279–96* (Berkeley, 1959), pp. 33–5.

[142] *Reg. Romeyn*, i. 393–5; ii. pp. xviii–xxi; *Hists. York* iii. 216–20; *CPapR, 1198–1304*, p. 517.

individuals.[143] The especially well-recorded visitations of Archbishop Zouche in May 1343 and Archbishop Thoresby in May 1362 show that the chapter was indeed bound by the terms of the 1328 settlement; but any possibility that archiepiscopal visitations might ever have become a genuinely effective means of imposing discipline on the canons was impaired by the comparative infrequency of such events in the later Middle Ages and by the archbishops' inability to enforce corrections upon an unwilling or recalcitrant chapter. When Archbishop Kempe attempted to overcome such recalcitrance in 1428, the chapter prepared a lengthy and largely successful defence of its position.[144] Paradoxically enough, a close reading of the many surviving late medieval visitation *comperta* at York suggests that these occasions were used less to correct the faults of the residentiary canons than to strengthen their own authority over the rest of the cathedral clergy.[145]

Much the greatest memorial to the continuing harmony between the archbishops and their chapters is, however, the support given by the former to the massive enterprise of rebuilding the whole cathedral. It is easy to forget that the clerks of the late medieval Minster worshipped in an atmosphere of almost perpetual building crisis. By the middle of the fourteenth century it is at last possible to gain some impression of the variety of activity within the Minster itself. Not only its fabric, but its internal arrangements and its furnishings and decoration were in a state of continuous flux. As in other major English churches, the general effect of increased liturgical complexity and a rapid multiplication of new altars and chantry foundations had been to convert the Minster into a veritable house of many mansions. The variety of purposes to which St. Peter's Church was applied defies easy analysis. By no means all of these purposes were religious ones; and it often proved impossible to restrict the transaction of secular affairs to the chapter-house or one of the cathedral vestries. Rents were paid inside the Minster, sometimes at the high altar itself; and money, valuables, and documents were deposited in the cathedral for safe keeping by York Jews, by local merchants, and by the royal government.[146]

---

[143] *BIHR*, Reg. Melton, fos. 103–5; printed from Archbishop Kempe's register in *Miscellanea*, ii. (Surtees Soc. cxxvii, 1916), pp. 280–90; cf. YML, M 1 (1)b, fos. 30–5.

[144] YML, M1(1)d; cf. H2/1 (Chapter Acts, 1400–35), fo. 30.

[145] YML, H 1/2 (Chapter Acts, 1343–70), fos. 6^v–7; H 1/3 (Chapter Acts, 1352–1426), fos. 50–1; L2(3)a (Visitation Book), fos. 1–5, and *passim*; cf. BIHR, Reg. Zouche, fo. 217^v. Only a very inadequate impression of the voluminous visitation material among the Minster archives is provided by the selections printed in *Fabric Rolls*, pp. 242–74.

[146] *York Memorandum Book*, iii (Surtees Soc. clxxxvi, 1973), p. 152; R. B. Dobson *The Jews of Medieval York and the Massacre of March 1190* (Borthwick Papers, no. 45, 1974), p. 28; *CPatR, 1258–66*, pp. 344–5; *Testamenta Eboracensia*, ii. 274.

Numerous wooden partitions within the church provided enough seclusion to encourage the use of the Minster for a variety of formal and informal gatherings, including on occasion even meetings of the York city council itself. More regular still were the sessions of the archbishop's consistory and other courts; and of course the Minster was the almost invariable meeting-place of convocations and synods of the northern province.[147] The cathedral church was also often used for the discussion of political affairs by the northern lords at times of national emergency; and in the early 1330s the royal chancery itself met in the chapter-house.[148] At all times the Minster was visited by numerous magnates as well as members of the royal family. Perhaps the most spectacular events ever witnessed at the medieval Minster were the royal weddings celebrated there in 1221, 1251, and 1328. On that last occasion the marriage of Edward III to Philippa of Hainault was attended by virtually every leading member of the English aristocracy.[149]

There are after all worse guides to the success of any cathedral than the number of visitors it attracts. Like modern tourists, the countless hordes of men and women who walked into the late medieval Minster left little trace behind them except handfuls of coins in the collection boxes dispersed throughout the church.[150] Then, as now, perhaps only a minority entered the cathedral in a particularly devout frame of mind; but for those who did so the incentives were of course immeasurably greater than anything in our experience today. To those who visited the Minster on special festivals or contributed to its fabric successive popes and archbishops offered a large variety of indulgences; and it was there too that the inhabitants of York and the surrounding area could hear the preaching of a crusade, listen to prayers for fine weather, or show their enthusiasm for the success of English armies abroad.[151] Visitors from further afield were more likely to be drawn to York by the Minster's rich and variegated collection of relics and, above all, by the growing reputation of its own local saint. Too much has sometimes been made of St. William of York's supposed inferiority to his more famous Yorkshire rivals, saints John of Beverley and Wilfrid of Ripon.

---

[147] E.g. *Reg. Romeyn*, i. 150; *Calendar of Reg. Waldby* (Borthwick Texts and Calendars, ii, 1974), p. 21; BIHR, Reg. Bowet, ii. fo. 10ᵛ; *Reg. W. Booth*, fo. 337; *Reg. Langley*, ii. 41, 99, 142, 160, 182; *Records of Northern Convocation, passim; Handbook of British Chronology*, ed. F. M. Powicke and E. B. Fryde (Royal Historical Soc., 1961), pp. 553–63; *Councils and Synods, 1205–1313*, ed. F. M. Powicke and C. R. Cheney (Oxford, 1964), ii. 1093–6, 1185–6, 1277–84, 1319–48.

[148] *CCIR, 1333–37*, pp. 129, 130, 188.

[149] Matthew Paris, *Chronica Majora*, iii. 67; v. 266–7; *VCH York*, pp. 28, 56.

[150] See the *oblaciones* section of the keeper of the fabric's account rolls (E 3/1–32); cf. *Fabric Rolls*, pp. 30–1.

[151] *CPapR, 1198–1304*, pp. 537, 540; Dixon and Raine, *Fasti Ebor.*, p. 416; *Hists. York* iii. 182; *Letters from Northern Registers*, pp. 93, 101, 402–3.

Against considerable odds the chapter's assiduous campaign to convert one of its obscurer twelfth-century archbishops into the centre of an important cult gradually bore fruit. After St. William's delayed canonization in 1227 and the translation of his remains from the nave to a shrine behind the high altar in 1284, there is evidence that he at last became the subject of intense if energetically promoted local veneration (Plates 7 and 8). In particular the portable shrine of St. William's head, contained within a silver-gilt reliquary studded with jewels, and 'borne with certaine Images brouches beads and bells', became the cathedral's single greatest treasure and attracted more attention as well as more precious gifts than any other.[152] When, on a famous occasion, Margery Kempe was asked to account for her turbulent presence in York she had no hesitation in replying that, 'Syr, I come on pilgrimage to offyr her at Seynt William'.[153] Appropriately enough, a table of St. William's miracles hanging in the Minster vestry still survived as 'the only rags of popery we have left us' until as late as 1736.[154]

Vicars choral and chantry priests

'The story of daily life in the fourteenth-century close is largely the story of the doings of the lesser clergy'.[155] Dr. Kathleen Edwards's generalization can be safely applied to York Minster at all periods of its later medieval history. After 1215 the dignitaries and canons there can never have formed anything but a minute proportion of the total cathedral clergy. Thus of the eighty-two members of that body who appeared in the Minster to commemorate the anniversary of Archbishop Bowet's death in 1424, only seven were canons: but there were then present sixteen 'parsons' or chantry chaplains, thirty-six vicars, six deacons, five thurifers, and seven choristers as well as the two vestry-clerks and three sacrists of the cathedral.[156] The total size of this variegated group of *ministri inferiores* changed remarkably little between the early fourteenth century and the Reformation, and at all times a rigid line of status separated them from the

[152] *CPapR, 1198–1304*, pp. 90–1, 96, 540; *Hists. York* ii. 407–8; iii. 127–30, 133–4, 210–11, 388–9; *Reg. Wickwane*, p. 294; *Testamenta Eboracensia*, ii. 117–18, 233; *YCR* ii. 187. For the deliberate dismantling of this portable shrine, in October 1541, see J. S. Purvis, 'Notes from the Diocesan Registry at York', *YAJ* xxxv (1943), pp. 392–3.
[153] *The Book of Margery Kempe* (Early English Text Soc., o.s. ccxii, 1940), p. 122.
[154] Drake, *Ebor.*, p. 481; cf. BM, Stowe MS. 884, fo. 59. This table is no doubt to be identified with that copied by Roger Dodsworth and printed from Bodl., Dodsworth MS. 125 in *Hists. York* ii. 531–43.
[155] Edwards, *Secular Cathedrals*, p. 251.
[156] *Testamenta Eboracensia*, iii. 85; cf. ibid. iii. 143; iv. 302–3; Harrison, *Medieval College*, p. 169.

7 The translation of St. William's relics to his new shrine behind the High Altar in 1284: a panel from St. William's Window in the north choir aisle, *c.* 1423.

8 The lame and the blind at the shrine of St. William of York: a panel from St. William's Window in the north choir aisle, *c.* 1423.

members of the chapter.[157] The ranks of the lesser clergy, on the other hand, differed from one another in function, age, and experience but not in social origin. The first qualification for the admission of new choristers to the York choir was naturally the possession of a good singing voice; but it was also expected that as they matured they would, 'per processum temporis', become the cathedral's thurifers, deacons, and, eventually, its vicars choral. Worship in the Minster was largely conducted by locally born clerks who devoted the whole of their lives to a career in the cathedral's service.

Little can ever be known of the youngest members of the cathedral clergy. The seven choristers (a number raised to twelve in the fifteenth century thanks to a munificent bequest of £300 by Thomas Dalby, archdeacon of Richmond) received daily commons of a penny each from the common fund and were expected to board together under the supervision of a responsible *custos* or chaplain.[158] The *esprit de corps* of this small group of choir-boys found its most dramatic manifestation in the festivities associated with the election of a boy bishop to commemorate Holy Innocents' Day (28 December). A surviving account of the income and expenses of the York *Episcopus Innocentium* or boy bishop in 1396–7 reveals him collecting substantial sums of money from the residentiary canons and conducting a mock visitatorial progress to places as far away as Bridlington and Fountains as well as presiding over a complicated series of entertainments at intervals between Christmas and Candlemas.[159] Until the early sixteenth century the celebration of this Feast of the Boys was always a regular feature of Minster life at York, where it often caused controversy if not the extreme hostility sometimes encountered in the southern cathedrals.[160] Needless to say such regulated licence at the beginning of the year did not prevent considerable unruliness among the choristers at other times. One of their misdemeanours in 1409 was that of playing football and other games within the close, an offence rather less surprising than that of their successors in 1566 who 'have plaied at the foote ball within the

[157] As their historian pointed out, 'only three vicars-choral of York have ever been made canons of York'—himself and two of his Tudor predecessors (Harrison, *Medieval College*, p. 303). Similar conclusions as to the origins and status of the thirty-two vicars choral at medieval Lichfield emerge from H. Jenkins, 'Lichfield Cathedral in the Fourteenth Century' (unpubl. Univ. of Oxford B.Litt. thesis 1956), i, 101–2.

[158] YML, E 1/1–57 (Chamberlains' Accounts, 1370–1489); M 2(4)g (Misc. Reg., 1290–1340), fo. 25ᵛ; *Early Yorkshire Schools*, i. 21; *Test. Ebor.* i. 262–3; *York Statutes*, pp. 12–13.

[159] 'Two Sermons preached by the Boy Bishop', ed. J. G. Nichols (Camden Society, N.S. xiv, 1875), pp. 31–4; E. K. Chambers, *The Mediaeval Stage* (Oxford, 1903), i. 356–8; ii. 287–9.

[160] YML, L 2(3)a (Visitation Book), fos. 72ᵛ–73; H 2/3 (Chapter Acts, 1427–1504), fos. 187, 190ᵛ, 193ᵛ, 197ᵛ, 228ᵛ; E 3/32 (Fabric Roll, 1498–9); *Fabric Rolls*, pp. 158, 214; Drake, *Ebor.*, p. 481; cf. Edwards, *Secular Cathedrals*, pp. 316–17.

cathedrall churche of Yorke'.[161] More frequent at all times were complaints that the choir-boys had been poorly taught and that they gossiped in the church, the last a charge brought even more frequently against the five thurifers and the six deacons of the cathedral. Thurifers and deacons, who performed their duties under the control of the subchancellor, played so conspicuous a role in Minster services and processions that it was only too easy to notice when they failed to appear in the choir or behaved badly there.[162]

Compared to the sparsity of surviving evidence for the activities of these junior members of the cathedral clergy, that for the body of vicars choral is voluminous and does full and proper justice to their central place in the life and worship of the medieval Minster.[163] As in other English secular cathedrals the office of vicar choral derived from the obligation upon absentee canons to appoint a personal deputy to take their place in the choir. The appearance of numerous cathedral *vicarii* as witnesses to early Yorkshire charters makes it clear that this was already a common practice in the mid-twelfth century; and most, if not all, of the thirty-six York canons must have been regularly presenting their vicars for admission by the chapter long before a statute of 1291 made the maintenance of a vicar in priest's orders (at a standardized cost of forty shillings a year) compulsory on all canons, whether resident or not.[164] Each of the thirty-six vicars choral at York continued to be attached to a particular prebendal stall and might occasionally enjoy some slight personal connection with his master, most notably a somewhat undefined right to hospitality at his table as well as to his choir-habit after his death. But, as the form of the oath sworn on their admission to their stalls makes abundantly clear, the primary loyalties of the vicars choral were due to the chapter on the one hand and to their own corporate body on the other. As early as 1230 the Minster vicars can be found acquiring property and administering chantries and obits as well as using a common seal.[165] It was obviously in the interests of the dean and chapter as well as of would-be benefactors to the cathedral to encourage this development towards fully corporate organization on the part of the

[161] YML, L 2(3)a, fo. 7; *Fabric Rolls*, p. 244; A. Raine, *History of St. Peter's School, York* (1926), p. 83.

[162] YML, H1/2 (Chapter Acts, 1343–70) fo. 6ᵛ; E 1/1–57 (Chamberlains' Accounts, 1370–1489); *Fabric Rolls*, pp. 245, 251; *York Statutes*, p. 7.

[163] For what can only be regarded as a preliminary survey of the vicars' muniments see Harrison, *Medieval College*, to which, however, the same author's earlier and much shorter 'The Bedern College and Chapel', *Proc. of Yorks. Architectural and York Archaeological Soc.* ii (1936), 19–43, is often to be preferred.

[164] YML, L (2)1 (Magnum Registrum Album), iv, fo. 2; *Early Yorkshire Charters*, i. 136, 207, 224; *York Statutes*, p. 27.

[165] YML, M 2 (2)c (Repertorium), fo. 2; *Hists. York* iii. 140–1, 152.

vicars; and in November 1252 Dean Sewall de Boville and his colleagues enacted a series of important statutes whereby an integrated system was imposed on a previously confused situation. Henceforward all vicars choral at York were subjected to detailed regulations which committed them to regular attendance at the daily and nightly hours under penalty of losing their commons if they failed to appear. More important still, the 1252 statutes allowed the vicars to elect one of their own number, alternatively known as their *custos* or as the *succentor vicariorum*, to act as the manager of their internal affairs and as their representative in the world at large. Although the exact legal position of the first succentor, Alan Salvator, and that of his successors remained somewhat controversial until the vicars of St. Peter's Church were formally incorporated as a college by Henry V on 26 May 1421, there is ample evidence that from 1252 onwards the vicars choral were an elaborately organized and largely self-governing body.[166]

It was also in the mid-thirteenth century that the vicars choral were given the opportunity of organizing their common life in an entirely new way. As a result of a bequest by William de Laneham, a canon of York who died in the late 1240s, they secured residential accommodation on a block of property situated little more than 150 yards from the east end of the Minster. The Bedern, to give the common dwelling-place of the vicars the name by which it was universally known after 1275, gradually acquired a chapel (still under construction in 1328–9) and a common dining hall to add to its sets of individual chambers for each vicar choral.[167] Despite the often crowded and sometimes squalid living conditions in the Bedern it was generally successful in its primary purpose of ensuring that the vicars 'shuld be and contynue in the said college att comons, and bed, and not abrode in the cytie'.[168] As time passed the York Bedern, the first such institution to be founded at any English secular cathedral, seems to have become more rather than less comfortable and salubrious. In 1335 it was enlarged by a plot of land at the corner of Aldwark given by the mayor and community of York; and in 1396 a special pedestrian bridge from the solar of the Bedern's gatehouse to that of the gatehouse of the Minster close

[166] *CPatR, 1266–72*, p. 369; *1416–22*, pp. 360–1; *York Statutes*, pp. 17–20; Harrison, *Medieval College*, pp. 27–8, 296–7.

[167] YML L(2)1 (Magnum Registrum Album), iv, fo. 43ᵛ; *Monasticon* vi. 1193, 1475; Harrison, *Medieval College*, pp. 29–42; Harrison, 'The Bedern Chapel, York', *YAJ* xxvii (1923), 197–209; cf. YCA, C 60 (Husgable Accounts, *c.* 1282).

[168] *Yorkshire Chantry Surveys* (Surtees Soc., 1894–5), i. 25. For the congestion caused by piles of wood kept for fuel in the common courtyard of the Bedern see YML, Vicars Choral Cartulary, fo. 135. Since the destruction of the Bedern Chapel in 1961, the most substantial remains of the college to survive are those of its hall (described in *York Civic Trust, Annual Report, 1970–1*, pp. 30–3).

across Goodramgate eliminated the dangers incurred by the vicars walking to and from services in the Minster.[169]

Such attempts to isolate this large and celibate community of vicars from the temptations and distractions of the city around them were bound to be unavailing. Coming as so many of them did from local families, it is hardly surprising that they were sometimes to be seen walking around the streets of York dressed like laymen and with knives and daggers hanging between their legs.[170] The improprieties, the crimes, and above all the adulteries of the vicars choral are the single most astonishing revelation afforded by surviving court records of the fourteenth and fifteenth centuries. Most surprising perhaps are the many vicars who kept their mistresses actually in their rooms within the Bedern, in at least one instance (that of William Benysleve in 1461) so that they could give birth to their children there. Such quasi-domesticity on the part of vicars choral was by no means confined to those of York and probably incurred little social disapproval at the time. Only in the case of exceptionally recalcitrant vicars, like William Easington who in 1417 was faced with six separate charges of fornication as well as an accusation of slander against a fellow vicar, was the chapter at all likely to deprive the offender of his stall.[171] Not surprisingly, it was sometimes almost as difficult to preserve a respectable standard of discipline among the vicars when in the choir itself; serious absenteeism, discordant singing, incessant chattering, and the unauthorized shortening of divine services figure prominently in visitation *comperta* of the fifteenth century. Such evidence is notoriously dangerous to evaluate, and the misbehaviour of the York vicars choral could be easily paralleled elsewhere; but it would be idle to pretend that worship within the late medieval Minster was being conducted by the humble and meek.

The emergence of a large and powerful corporation of vicars choral within the Minster close obviously raised other more general problems. In practice it was the vicars who carried the major responsibility for the detailed administrative as well as religious routines of the cathedral. The many quarrels and disputes between individual inmates of the Bedern did not preclude the growth of a formidable sense of corporate identity on the part of the vicars as a whole. Their common obligation to live together as well as to worship together soon led to a high degree of administrative specialization. The collection of rents from a large and complicated assortment of urban properties became the primary responsibility of the chamberlain, an official who had certainly emerged by 1304. Other vicars

[169] YML, VR8; *1334–8*, p. 163; *1391–6*, p. 712; cf. *VCH Yorkshire* iii. 382–3.
[170] *Fabric Rolls*, pp. 242–3.
[171] J. S. Purvis, *A Mediaeval Act Book* (York, 1943), pp. 14–40.

accounted as the bursars (who distributed commons), repairers, and *brasiatores* in accordance with statutes of ever-increasing complexity produced by the vicars themselves. Above all, the elected warden of the college or *succentor vicariorum* (an office which tended to change hands at irregular but quite frequent intervals) promoted the cohesion of the vicars in his capacity as the guardian of their temporal as well as spiritual welfare.[172] Under the leadership of their succentor and his council of six senior vicars or 'sex men', the fellows of the Bedern were tenacious defenders of their rights and privileges. Of their many fierce legal battles perhaps the best documented is their successful struggle during the early 1490s to preserve their important rights of pasture on the Vicars' Lees (where the modern York gas-works now stand) against the mayor and commonalty of the city.[173] How far the corporate organization of the vicars choral posed a major constitutional threat to the York chapter itself is as yet a more open and debatable matter. Although individual delinquents were often brought before the auditor of the chapter's peculiar court for correction, in practice the residentiary canons enjoyed little effective control over the internal management of the Bedern. On a number of occasions, and particularly during the course of some especially contentious disputes between vicars and canons in the late 1340s, the former showed themselves quite prepared to appeal against their masters to archbishop, king, or even papal Curia.[174] But it may not be coincidental that what always seems to have perturbed the vicars choral most was the loss of their statutory rights to food at the tables of the residentiary canons. In the last resort the members of the Bedern had no alternative but to accept the patronage of the handful of great ecclesiastical potentates in whose shadow they lived their much more humble and impoverished lives.

It was indeed the state of their economic resources that usually and deservedly gave the vicars choral most cause for alarm. Just because the revenues of the Bedern were almost wholly derived from a large number of very small urban properties, it is exceptionally difficult to generalize with confidence about the vicars' financial position at any one period of time. But in retrospect it seems clear that an institution as elaborate as the Bedern suffered severely from the lack of a sufficiently substantial initial endowment. As it was, a series of financial emergencies during the course of

---

[172] YML, Vm (Succentor's Accounts), 1a–q; Harrison, 'Bedern College and Chapel', 35–9, 42; Harrison, *Medieval College*, pp. 113–47, 300–1; cf. *York Memorandum Book*, iii. (Surtees Soc. clxxxvi, 1973), pp. 67–9.

[173] YML, VC, Box xii; *YCR* ii. 1, 107–12, 116–17.

[174] YML, Vicars Choral Cartulary, fos. 152–235; cf. YML, P 1(1) iii; Harrison, *Medieval College*, pp. 177–93.

the fourteenth century had to be averted by new benefactions, of which perhaps the most important were the advowsons of the churches of Ferry Fryston (1331), Huntington (1353), and St. Sampson's, York (1394). When Richard II licensed the appropriation of this last church to the vicars he did so in order to revive the common life in the Bedern after a period during which financial stringency had compelled many vicars to disperse into separate homes within the city.[175] In the next century, a period during which the contraction of the vicars' rent roll has been used as an index of urban decline in York as a whole, it became increasingly clear that the resources of the Bedern were proving inadequate. Between 1426 and 1456 the latter's income from some 250 York tenements dropped from £160 to £100 a year.[176] The consequence of even graver financial difficulties later in the century was a fall in the number of vicars. Between the 1370s and 1470s the accounts of the vicars' bursar and the Minster chamberlain prove that it was still possible to maintain the Bedern at its full complement of thirty-six fellows. By 1484, when the dean and chapter enlisted Richard III's support in an ultimately vain attempt to secure the appropriation of Cottingham church to the vicars, their numbers had already begun to decline to less than thirty 'because of the growing poverty of their rents and possessions'.[177] In 1509 and thereafter there were rarely more than twenty *vicarii de choro* at the Minster, 'th' occasion whereof is by reason of decaye of landes and revenues of the cytie of York, beyng sore in ruyne and decaye'.[178] This reduction in their total numbers made it possible for each vicar to retain his annual portion of £6 2s. 1d. from the common funds of the Bedern; but what preserved many vicars choral from near penury was their ability to supplement their income by serving one of the Minster chantries. In the late 1540s at least eighteen of the twenty vicars choral served as chaplains of perpetual chantries within the cathedral; and it seems clear that most of their predecessors had done likewise since at least the late thirteenth century.[179] The college of vicars choral at York may have owed its origins to the need to replace a largely absentee body of canons in the

---

[175] *CPatR, 1330–4*, p. 103; *1391–6*, pp. 386, 713; *1399–1401*, p. 172; *Hists. York* ii. 425; Harrison, *Medieval College*, pp. 74–102.

[176] YML, Vp., Vn. (Vicars Choral, Bursar's, Chamberlains' and Rent Rolls), *passim*; J. N. Bartlett, 'The Expansion and Decline of York in the Later Middle Ages', *Econ. Hist. Rev.* 2nd Ser. xii (1959), 28, 30, 32.

[177] BIHR, Reg. Rotherham, i. fo. 100.

[178] *Yorks. Chantry Surveys*, i. 25–30; ii. 438; cf. BM, Harleian MS. 433, fo. 73; *Test. Ebor.* iii. 143; iv. 301–3; Harrison, *Medieval College*, pp. 103–4, 109–11; YML, E1/1–57 (Chamberlains' Accounts, 1370–1489).

[179] *Yorks. Chantry Surveys*, i. 9–42; ii. 431–50; *VCH York*, pp. 146, 347; Purvis, *Mediaeval Act Book*, p. 35.

choir; but to many of their late medieval contemporaries the celebration of obits and masses at the numerous smaller altars in the cathedral was an even more important part of the vicars' *raison d'être*.

Of all the many features of life and worship at the medieval cathedral, the prominent role it afforded to the private chantry is unquestionably the most difficult to recapture. The enthusiasm once felt for what now seems a highly mechanical application of the doctrine of vicarious intercession for souls is almost inconceivable and often positively repugnant to modern eyes. Moreover, at most English cathedrals, and especially at York, the great majority of the once numerous perpetual chantries have left no trace of their previous existence. The two great nineteenth-century fires and subsequent restorations of the Minster swept away what was already a depleted number of physical memorials to a once ubiquitous system. In any case, and rather surprisingly, few of the Minster chantries appear to have taken the form of separate chapels. The only chantry to project outside the walls of the choir was that founded by Archbishop Zouche at a cost of 300 marks in the early 1350s; and even the exceptionally large chantry associated with the tomb of Archbishop Savage (d. 1507) was constructed of wood rather than stone.[180] The great majority of the many York cathedral chantries were comparatively poor. When Edward VI's commissioners visited York in 1548 the only Minster chantries they valued at more than £10 a year were those founded to commemorate the souls of Dean Richard Andrew (1475), Sir Thomas Scrope (1459), Archbishop Bowet (1413), and Archbishop Gray (1241): Gray's chantry in the south transept was the only cathedral chantry to be regularly served by as many as three chaplains.[181] To these generalizations there is only one major, and highly unusual, exception. The chapel of St. Mary and the Holy Angels, usually known as St. Sepulchre's Chapel, had been founded by Archbishop Roger as long ago as the late 1170s in order that 'divine service may be celebrated for ever to the honour and glory of God, and for the remission of the sins of us and our successors'. How far this munificently endowed chapel, situated within the precincts of the archbishop's palace but with a communicating door into the north aisle of the cathedral nave, should be regarded as an early example of a chantry college is, however, open to question. By the late thirteenth century its staff of a sacrist and twelve canons was no more likely to be resident near the Minster than the canons themselves. Those fellows and clerks of St. Sepulchre's College who lived in York, although

---

[180] *Chronica Monasterii de Melsa* (Rolls Ser., 1866–8), iii. 87; *Test. Ebor.* i. 55; *Hists. York* ii. 419, 442; iii. 271–3; Drake, *Ebor.*, pp. 433, 448; Browne, *History*, pp. 267–8; *VCH York*, p. 347.
[181] *Yorks. Chantry Surveys*, i. 9–42; ii. 431–50; YML, M 2(2)c (Repertorium), fo. 20ᵛ; *Fabric Rolls*, p. 297; *Reg. Gray*, pp. 190–1.

constitutionally under the authority of the archbishop and not the chapter, were in practice often assimilated into the general routines of worship at the Minster.[182]

Not long after the foundation of St. Sepulchre's Chapel the new phenomenon of the private chantry began to make its spectacular impact on the cathedral. A *cantaria* of some sort or other existed in the cathedral crypt as early as 1201; and the detailed regulations prescribed by Canon Elias Bernard for the chantry he founded at the altar of St. William of York in 1230 leave no doubt that by that date the concept of the perpetual chantry had reached full maturity.[183] The vagaries of the surviving evidence and the difficulty of distinguishing perpetual chantry foundations from the innumerable obits and anniversaries celebrated in the late medieval Minster make any attempt to estimate their total number a hazardous undertaking.[184] In the course of time some perpetual chantries in the Minster disappeared altogether, others were transferred to different altars, and many more were augmented and re-endowed under a new name. The chantry surveys of 1546 and 1548 record the names of only thirty-eight perpetual chantries in the cathedral (of which slightly more than a quarter were served by two priests);[185] but other evidence raises the total number of Minster chantries to well over sixty, a total unrivalled in England except at the cathedrals of Canterbury, Lincoln, and St. Paul's, London.[186] At least fifty-six perpetual chantries survived from their foundation to the early sixteenth century; and of these, seventeen began their existence before 1300, thirteen were founded between 1300 and 1350, ten between 1350 and 1400, seven between 1400 and 1450, six between 1450 and 1500, and only one or two after 1500.

The chronology of perpetual chantry foundation accordingly displays the same general trends within the cathedral as it did in the parish churches of York. In both cases it seems most probable that the gradual decline of chantry endowments in the fifteenth century was the result of their

[182] *Hists. York* iii. 75–7, 175–81; *VCH Yorks.* iii. 384–6; and the detailed but by no means exhaustive discussion of A. H. Thompson, 'The Chapel of St. Mary and the Holy Angels, otherwise known as St. Sepulchre's Chapel, at York', *YAJ* xxxvi (1944–7), pp. 63–77, 214–48.

[183] Clay, *Fasti* ii. 141; YML, L 2/1 (Magnum Registrum Album), iii. fo. 49; *Hists. York* iii. 138–41.

[184] As the great majority of the Minster obits were administered by the vicars choral, their records (especially Vn. 1–95) provide the most useful evidence on the subject: cf. Harrison, *Medieval College*, pp. 119–20, 164–76.

[185] The most complete lists of Minster chantries are those drawn up by Thomas Water, the chapter's registrar, in the early sixteenth century (YML, M 2(2)c, fos. 19–22); the best published list is that printed by James Raine in *Fabric Rolls*, pp. 274–306, on the basis of James Torre's researches.

[186] G. H. Cook, *Medieval Chantries and Chantry Chapels* (1947), pp. 72–123; cf. R. Hill, 'A Chaunterie for Soules: London Chantries in the Reign of Richard II', *The Reign of Richard II*, ed. F. R. H. Du Boulay and C. M. Barron (1971), pp. 242–55.

increasing cost rather than of any disenchantment with the perpetual chantry as an institution. The detailed foundation statutes of the chantry endowed by Henry Carnebull, archdeacon of York, for the soul of the late Archbishop Rotherham in 1505 reveal a complete commitment to a by now traditional ideal;[187] and the wills of the later medieval canons of York show that the endowment of prayers for their souls, whether within or without a permanent chantry foundation, continued to be their universal aspiration. Indeed the great majority of the cathedral's chantries commemorated the archbishops, deans, and residentiary canons of the Minster. Of the great noble and knightly families of the diocese, the Vavasours, Percies, and Scropes alone founded a perpetual chantry in the cathedral; and the only chantries established there on behalf of York citizens seem to have been those of Richard Tunnock (1328), John de Stayngate (1368), Alan Alnewyke (1377), and the guild of St. Christopher (1426).[188] Even after their deaths the great dignitaries and canons of the cathedral continued to absorb a major share of the spiritual energies of the cathedral clergy in the latter's capacity as chantry priests.

Not all the numerous perpetual chantries in the Minster could be served by vicars choral; and from the late thirteenth century onwards the most important development in the composition of the cathedral clergy was the gradual increase in the number of its chantry chaplains.[189] Almost always and somewhat confusingly known at late medieval York as the *personae* or 'parsons' of the church, the latter were of course the exact equivalent of the cantarists or *custodes altarium* to be found in all the other English secular cathedrals. Although their primary responsibility was the celebration of masses for the founders of their chantries, these chantry priests were firmly brought within the jurisdiction and control of the dean and chapter. Even in the minority of cases where collation to an altar remained in the hands of private individuals, no chaplain could be admitted to a cathedral chantry without the chapter's knowledge and approval. Moreover, from at least the 1290s the York parsons were also obliged to attend divine service in the choir on the major feasts of the year.[190] Although the cantarists enjoyed

---

[187] YML, M 2(4)b; cf. R. B. Dobson, 'The Foundation of Perpetual Chantries by the citizens of medieval York', *Studies in Church History*, iv (ed. G. J. Cuming, Leiden, 1967), 23–5, 33–8.

[188] YCA, G. 70: 33; *Fabric Rolls*, pp. 279, 285, 295, 301; cf. A. H. Thompson, *The English Clergy*, p. 154. In 1472 it was planned to commemorate the recently deceased Earl of Warwick by a 'Neville chantry' in the Minster (*CPatR, 1467–77*, p. 340); for political or other reasons nothing seems to have come of this project. With the important exception of the Scropes of Masham, York undoubtedly conforms to the general rule that 'cathedral churches were not a major burial place for nobles': J. T. Rosenthal, *The Purchase of Paradise* (1972), p. 84.

[189] By the early sixteenth century almost a half of the Minster's sixty or so chantries were served by cantarists: YML, M2(2)c, fos. 19–22.

[190] YML, M 2(4)g, fo. 4; cf. *York Statutes*, pp. 23–4, 36; Edwards, *Secular Cathedrals*, pp. 291–5.

ceremonial precedence over the vicars choral, in practice it would be hard to distinguish between these two groups of clergy in terms of social status, economic wealth, or even their respective contributions to the corporate life of the Minster. By far the most important practical difference was that whereas the vicars were committed to a communal life in the Bedern, the parsons had to find their own private accommodation in the close or city. But as the number of cantarists grew from twelve in the 1370s to over twenty in the 1500s, so it became increasingly desirable to provide residential accommodation for the parsons as well as for the vicars of the Minster.[191]

On 11 May 1461 this aim eventually found fruition in the foundation of 'The College of Persons having Chantries in the Metropolitical church of York', otherwise known as St. William's College. Not only the most important college of cathedral chantry priests ever founded in England, it also proved to be the last major constitutional innovation in the history of the medieval Minster. As early as 1414 Canon Thomas More had been prepared to contemplate leasing part of his prebendal property in Petergate to the use of the Minster cantarists on the grounds that 'they have no common habitation but are dispersed throughout the city of York'.[192] What made the foundation of St. William's College possible half a century later was the prior of Hexham's gift of an ideal site, previously occupied by his own prebendal house, only a few yards from the east end of the cathedral. Royal permission to erect a college under the authority of an annually elected *supervisor* had been obtained as early as 1455; but only after the powerful support of the Neville family had been enlisted five years later did the college finally take shape with a changed constitution which accorded considerably more dignity and power to a long-serving provost. By 1465 the new building, substantial parts of which still survive, was being constructed from magnesian limestone quarried at Huddleston (Plate 9). Two years later the college already possessed its own chapel and by 1479 a library.[193] To judge from the surviving inventory of one chantry priest resident in 1507, the chambers of the fellows of the college were large enough to accommodate a wide range of furniture.[194] By no means as well documented an institution as the Bedern of the vicars choral, St. William's

[191] The numbers of *persone de choro* are regularly recorded in the Minster chamberlains' accounts (E 1/1) from 1370 onwards; and cf. *Test. Ebor.* iii. 84–5, 143; iv. 301.

[192] *CPatR, 1413–16*, p. 368. For the foundation of colleges of chantry priests at other cathedrals towards the end of the Middle Ages see Edwards, *Secular Cathedrals*, pp. 300–1; Jenkins, 'Lichfield Cathedral', i. 113.

[193] *CPatR, 1461–7*, pp. 47, 383; *Yorks. Chantry Surveys*, i. 7–8; ii. 430; *Fabric Rolls*, p. 72; *VCH Yorkshire* iii. 385–6; *Test. Ebor.* iii. 199.

[194] YML, L1(17)33; cf. *Test. Ebor.* iv. 267.

College hardly survived long enough for its full contribution towards the Minster's life to be easily assessed.[195] But its foundation certainly proves, as does Richard III's extraordinarily ambitious but untimely attempt to found a college for a hundred chaplains at York, that even in its last decades the medieval chapter was capable of responding to important new initiatives.[196] Ironically enough, by suppressing the Minster chantries and the college of St. William, Edward VI's commissioners were to destroy not the most antiquated but the most novel features of the late medieval cathedral.

The archbishops and the chapter, 1374–1500

In retrospect, although not of course to contemporaries, the accession of Alexander Neville to the archbishopric of York can be regarded as the last major turning-point in the medieval history of the church of York. After centuries during which the great majority of the archbishops had enjoyed a close and personal relationship with their cathedral and their diocese, there followed a period in which the see was held by equally grand but usually much more distant figures. Of the ten archbishops between 1374 and 1500 not one had been a dignitary of the Minster, not one had ever resided in the close, and only four had ever held a York prebend. One of the ten (Robert Waldby, 1396–7) was an Austin friar in Crown service who died before he could reach York for his enthronement; Alexander Neville (1374–88), Thomas Arundel (1388–96), Richard Scrope (1398–1405), and George Neville (1465–76) represented that group of 'magnate prelates' from whom the see of York had hitherto remained surprisingly immune; while Henry Bowet (1407–23), John Kempe (1425–52), and the half-brothers William and Laurence Booth (1452–64; 1476–80) were central figures in three of those closely knit and well-connected clerical dynasties which amassed so much of the ecclesiastical wealth and power of fifteenth-century England. Only of Thomas Scot (1480–1500), better known by the name of his birthplace at Rotherham, can one be reasonably confident that he owed both the chancellorship of England and the archbishopric of York absolutely to his own abilities (Plate 10). The son of an obscure Yorkshire knight and 'perhaps the most zealous tenant of the see since the time of Thoresby', Rotherham deserves his reputation as an attractive but apparently unusual

---

[195] An early sixteenth-century rental of St. William's College (YML, M2(4)a) reveals the college's dependence on income from urban rents but is otherwise sadly uninformative. The college certainly attracted several bequests from local clergy: see e.g. *Test. Ebor.* iii. 117, 191; iv. 278–9; Harrison, *Medieval College*, pp. 313–14.

[196] For Richard III's plan 'to found a grand college at York on a large scale' to be served by no less than a hundred priests see BM, Harleian MS. 433, fos. 72, 80, 88[v], 90[v], 98; BIHR, Reg. Rotherham, i. fo. 100; *Fabric Rolls*, p. 87; *Test. Ebor.* iv. 79.

example of a late medieval archbishop who made a personal contribution to the quality of religious life in his diocese.[197]

Ever since the disgruntled Thomas Gascoigne of Oxford chose John Kempe and William Booth to exemplify his views on the moral decline of the English episcopate, the late medieval archbishops of York have found few advocates. Yet it is as well to remember that although they undoubtedly visited their diocese less frequently than their predecessors, only Alexander Neville can be judged a seriously incompetent ruler of the see. Five of the ten were holders of university doctorates in theology or law; and the only archbishop (William Booth) who never went to a university at all was subjected to fierce criticism as a 'cupidus legista juris regni' for that reason.[198] Understandably enough, the late medieval archbishops of York were firmly committed to the preservation of the educational patterns which had secured their own promotion. Not themselves men of outstanding scholarship, they were often munificent patrons of learning. It is certainly appropriate that George Neville should now be most often remembered as a Maecenas who fostered the revival of Greek letters, and Thomas Rotherham as the benefactor of Lincoln College, Oxford, and founder of a celebrated school (Jesus College) at Rotherham.[199] It was in any case to their administrative ability and to the pressures of court politics that they owed their promotion to the see of York. The fact that the archbishopric of York was regarded as the appropriate reward for five chancellors of England in this period (Arundel, Kempe, George Neville, Laurence Booth, and Rotherham) marked no very great break with previous tradition. Much more novel was the personal involvement of these prelates in the political faction of later medieval England, an involvement which brought several of them to imprisonment, one to permanent exile, and one to an untimely and much lamented death.[200]

The spiritual welfare of the diocese of York, let alone that of its cathedral church, was therefore always a very minor consideration in the choice of a new archbishop between 1374 and 1500. The chapter's own ability to

---

[197] H. L. Bennett's *Archbishop Rotherham* (Lincoln, 1901) should now be supplemented by Emden, *Cambridge*, pp. 489–91; cf. 'The Fifteenth Century', *Y.M. Hist. Tr.*, pp. 13–14.

[198] T. Gascoigne, *Loci e Libro Veritatum*, ed. J. E. T. Rogers (Oxford, 1881), pp. 52, 194; for William Booth's education at Gray's Inn, see *Hists. York* ii. 435; Emden, *Cambridge*, p. 73. The satirical attacks on his blatant careerism, for which see *Political Poems and Songs* (Rolls Ser., 1859–61), ii. 225–9, seem to be well justified on the evidence of his grasping and unscrupulous activities as a canon of St. Paul's (*History of St. Paul's*, pp. 91, 95–6).

[199] See the excellent survey by G. I. Keir, 'The Ecclesiastical Career of George Neville, 1432–1476' (Oxford B.Litt. thesis 1970), pp. 62–81; R. Weiss, *Humanism in England during the Fifteenth Century* (Oxford, 1967 edn.), pp. 141–8; Emden, *Oxford* ii. 1347–9; Emden, *Cambridge*, 489–91.

[200] 'Considered as a separate rebellion, Scrope's rising simply does not make sense': P. McNiven, 'The Betrayal of Archbishop Scrope', *Bulletin of the John Ryland Library*, liv (1971), 186.

influence the appointment of a particular candidate to the see had long been extremely limited; but in this period it shows all the signs of having reached vanishing-point. Even the traditional ceremony of a supposedly free capitular election withered away in a situation where every single archbishop between Thomas Arundel and Thomas Wolsey was translated to York from another English diocese. The papacy's incontrovertible right to translate bishops from one see to another was now almost always exercised in the interests of the English monarchy. On the only two occasions when a clash of wills between pope and royal government gave the canons of York the opportunity to elect their own archbishop the weakness of their position was cruelly exposed. Although on each occasion the chapter had been careful to elect candidates acceptable to the government (Thomas Langley in 1405 and Bishop Philip Morgan of Worcester in 1423–4), they had to undergo the mortifying experience of seeing both men put aside in favour of two compromise candidates in the persons of Henry Bowet and John Kempe.[201] For the cathedral clergy of York the enthronement of an archbishop was now a much more interesting event than his election. Detailed accounts of the procedure followed at the enthronements of John Kempe and George Neville were carefully preserved among the chapter archives; and the installation of the latter on 22 September 1465 must have been the single most spetacular event in the history of the fifteenth-century Minster. Attended by five bishops, two dukes, four earls, innumerable other lords and knights of the Neville affinity, as well as by the heads of all the important religious houses in the northern province, it was followed by a banquet in the archbishop's palace which was long remembered for its extravagant magnificence.[202]

The Minster clergy could, however, still hope for more substantial benefits from their late medieval archbishops. Admittedly the fact that only four (Scrope, Bowet, George Neville, and Rotherham) of the ten holders of the see between 1374 and 1500 were buried in the cathedral led to some reduction in benefactions to the church. But the Minster was remembered in all the archiepiscopal wills to survive; and Henry Bowet in particular deserved his reputation as a 'pater hospitalis' for his bequests of magnificent vestments as well as 50 marks to the fabric of the cathedral.[203] Such gifts testified to the generally cordial if often physically distant relationship between archbishop and his church. Only in the case of the

---

[201] *CPatR, 1405–8*, pp. 21, 48; *1422–9*, pp. 138, 169; Thompson, *English Clergy*, pp. 18–20.
[202] Cambridge University Library, MS. Ff v 14, fos. 75–80; YML, A 1(2); H 2/3 (Chapter Acts, 1427–1504), fo. 1; *Liber Pontificalis Chr. Bainbridge* (Surtees Soc. lxi, 1875), pp. 373–7; Leland, *Collectanea*, ed. T. Hearne (1774), vi. 1–14; Keir, 'George Neville', pp. 117–21.
[203] *Test. Ebor.* i. 398–402; iii. 82–3; *Hists. York* ii. 433–4; iii. 299–303.

cantankerous Alexander Neville is it possible to find an exception to prove the rule. Also exceptional in that he resided more or less continuously at his palace of Cawood for the first ten years of his pontificate, perhaps no archbishop of York has ever enjoyed a more universally bad press as a 'vir inutilis'; his reputation as 'a predo, a thef, a traytour, bothe to godde and to his Kyng' certainly preceded his political disgrace in 1388 and four last years of exile in Louvain.[204] At York, as at Beverley, Ripon, and Durham, Neville's aggressive assertions of episcopal and metropolitan authority led him into direct conflict with the most firmly entrenched ecclesiastical interests of the north. The residentiary canons, apparently under the leadership of the Minster treasurer, Master John Clifford, were predictably incensed by an archbishop who seems to have threatened their control over both the prebendal estates and those appropriated to the common fund. In the course of a long but obscure dispute, Neville antagonized the York cathedral clergy still further by the unprecedented step of transferring to Beverley not only six vicars choral but the diocesan consistory court.[205] The chapter's appeals for protection to royal government and papal Curia played some part in bringing about Neville's downfall in 1388; and the whole episode was an object lesson in the need to preserve the by now traditional balance of power and interest between archbishop and chapter. No later archbishop was to make Neville's mistakes; and throughout the fifteenth century the canons of York had little to fear from a spiritual leader whose very occasional visits to the city were more likely to be prompted by a desire to see its mystery pageants than to exert his disciplinary authority within the cathedral.[206]

Nor was the exclusion of the archbishops of York from the affairs of the dean and chapter confined to the cathedral itself. After Neville's removal from the scene, the canons' right to exercise ordinary spiritual authority over the parish churches appropriated to their common fund or to individual dignities and prebends was unquestioned. Since at least the thirteenth century the dean and chapter had been the holders of the most extensive ecclesiastical peculiar in the north of England: besides a dozen

[204] W. Illingworth, 'Copy of a Libel against Archbishop Neville, temp. Richard II', *Archaeologia*, xvi (1812), 82–3; cf. *Chronicon Henrici Knighton* (Rolls Ser., 1889–95), ii. 233–4; *Gesta Abbatum Monasterii Sancti Albani* (Rolls Ser., 1867–9), iii. 278. Cf. R. G. Davies, 'Alexander Neville, Archbishop of York, 1374–88', *YAJ* xlvii (1975), pp. 87–101.

[205] *Hists. York* ii. 422–5; cf. *CPatR, 1381–5*, pp. 342, 535; A. F. Leach, 'A Clerical Strike at Beverley Minster in the Fourteenth Century', *Archaeologia*, lv (1896), 1–20; *VCH Yorkshire* iii. 379–80.

[206] In June 1484 Archbishop Rotherham watched the 'ludus Corporis Christi' in the company of the dean and chapter from a room over the gateway of the cathedral close (YML, E 1/47; *Fabric Rolls*, p. 135).

parish churches in the city of York, it comprised at least twenty others in the West Riding, thirty-two in the East Riding, twenty in the North Riding, and six in Nottinghamshire.[207] Over these 'scattered republics of parishes' the canons of York exercised their own visitatorial rights, instituted to vicarages, and punished transgressors. The labyrinthine intricacies of this ecclesiastical franchise (the *iurisdiccio decani et capituli*), complicated as it was by the separate jurisdictional rights enjoyed by individual dignitaries and prebendaries in their own courts over their own spiritualities, defy easy analysis. What is clear is that it gave the York chapter a frequently exercised opportunity to sit as a court of judgement over the moral offences, and particularly the adulteries and slanders, of both clerks and laymen within their jurisdiction. A centralized peculiar court, clearly modelled on the archbishop's own consistory court, had emerged by 1275 under the presidency of an *auditor causarum capituli*. The latter was a professional ecclesiastical lawyer, rewarded by a pension from the chapter's common fund as well as by fees; he might be a canon of the Minster himself.[208] Served by its own advocates and proctors, this court was one in which the residentiary canons often acted as judges in important cases. It was indeed in a judicial capacity that many of the York canons, sitting within the cathedral and often in the chapter-house itself, must have most impressed themselves on the minds of their subjects.[209]

Not surprisingly, the vigilance and authority of the chapter's *auditor causarum* were at their greatest within York itself and in the immediate vicinity of the cathedral. During the course of the thirteenth century the original vague principle that the dean and chapter should enjoy ordinary jurisdiction 'over all staying or living within the close of the church of York and also of all parsons and ministers officiating in that church' was supplemented by an attempt to define the geographical boundaries of St. Peter's liberty within the city. From 1275 (the date of the first surviving survey) onwards these attempts to establish the bounds of the cathedral's liberty led to endless controversy, as was inevitable in the case of a jurisdiction essentially based on tenure rather than territory. But at the least, and possibly preserving the main outlines of the archbishop of York's personal *scyra* as recorded in Domesday Book, the chapter's liberty

---

[207] Lawton, *Collectio Rerum Ecclesiasticarum de Dioecesi Eboracensi*, pp. 1–4; cf. *VCH Yorkshire* iii. 80–8.

[208] YML, M2(1)a, fo. 1; M2(1)f, *passim*; H2/1 (Chapter Acts, 1400–35), fo. 22; E1/1–57 (Chamberlains' Rolls, 1370–1489); L2/1 (Magnum Registrum Album), iv. fo. 37; *Miscellanea*, ii. (Surtees Soc. cxxvii, 1916), p. 241; *CPapR, 1396–1404*, p. 209.

[209] Among the earliest and most important surviving records of the dean and chapter's spiritual Courts are YML, M2(1), a, d, f, g, h; BIHR, D/C. AB. 1 (the latter described by Purvis, *Mediaeval Act Book*).

included most of Petergate, the northern sections of Stonegate and Goodramgate, parts of Grape Lane and Aldwark, as well as the area around the cathedral itself.[210] Within this liberty, not of course strictly identical to the walled close or 'Mynstir Garth' but often confused with it, the chapter's spiritual jurisdiction was accompanied by a rigorous seigniorial control over its tenants. The right of the canons of St. Peter's to hold a secular court 'at the door of the minster' had been acknowledged by the English kings from at least the early twelfth century; and for the rest of the Middle Ages they defended their jurisdictional enclave from a succession of assaults by an increasingly powerful and self-confident city government. After a particularly detailed and informative inquiry in 1275, the king confirmed for ever the chapter's right to its own secular court and its own gaol, 'Peter Prison' on the site of the present Minster Gates.[211] The safeguarding and feeding of the prisoners (of whom there were only four in 1488) was the responsibility of the bailiff of the liberty; but the courts *apud portam* themselves were held by the chapter's steward or seneschal, usually a prominent local landowner. Whether presiding over the regular three-weekly 'Peter Court' or the twice-yearly leet court or sheriff's tourn, the steward heard pleas which testify to the prevalence of debt, wandering animals, and cases of assault in the immediate neighbourhood of the Minster.[212] The records of these courts suggest that the spiritual and temporal franchises enjoyed by the canons did more to enhance their own dignity than to reduce lawlessness in their vicinity: violence and even murder was a not uncommon feature of the close itself.

In the present stage of research any attempt to re-create the physical appearance of the Minster precincts in the later Middle Ages is likely to mislead. York and Lichfield were, however, alone among medieval English cathedrals in lacking a cloister; and there can be no doubt that the Minster was surrounded by a dense jungle of often small and transient urban tenements. Among these, the most important but in many ways the most mysterious, were the prebendal houses of the canons themselves. At York, as perhaps in no other English secular cathedral, it seems highly probable that every one of the five dignitaries and the thirty-six canons had originally had a house assigned to him in the immediate vicinity of the cathedral. As late as 1342 nine of the twelve canons who participated in a

[210] YML, L2/1 (Magnum Registrum Album), iv. 43ᵛ–45ᵛ; cf. L2(3)a, fos. 10ᵛ–11; M2(2)c, fos. 31–2; *Monasticon* vi. 1193–4; Purvis, *Mediaeval Act Book*, pp. 41–4; *VCH York* 21, 38–9.

[211] YML, L2/1, fos. 37–43; Drake, *Ebor.*, pp. 553–6; *Monasticon* vi. 1180–1; *CChR, 1300–26*, pp. 56–8, 184; *1327–41*, p. 47; *VCH York*, p. 496.

[212] YML, F1/3(1); F1/4 (court rolls of 'Peter Court'); F3/1–6 (accounts of bailiff of the liberty, 1487–99).

decanal election possessed a residence at York.[213] Although well over a dozen of such prebendal houses can be identified and approximately located on the basis of charter and other evidence, by the later Middle Ages the practice of non-residence on the part of the canons had inevitably led to a situation which at times confused contemporaries as much as it does the modern historian. In their continual attempts to persuade their non-resident members to maintain their prebendal houses in good repair there can be no doubt that the chapter was fighting a generally losing battle. Statutes issued in 1325 had confirmed the customary right of a prospective residentiary to live in the house of one of his absent colleagues.[214] Several prebendal residences were leased to seculars, others changed their site, and some disappeared without trace. When the inventories of York residentiary canons begin to survive in the fifteenth century it is easy to appreciate precisely how large and well furnished their houses could be without being at all certain of exactly where they were.[215]

It is through their wills and inventories, moreover, that we can hope to know the canons of the fifteenth-century Minster better than any of their predecessors. Conventional though these documents are, they reflect not only the magnificence but also the orthodox piety of their makers. In will after will an alleged distaste for the 'empty and worthless pomp of this world, is accompanied by elaborate directions for the celebration of funeral and requiem masses, for trentals, obits, and prayers.[216] The residentiary canons in particular left behind them at York some of the largest private libraries known to have existed in fifteenth-century England; and all maintained large households which testify to their position as the greatest patrons of the city and surrounding area. Even the comparatively obscure Thomas Parker, residentiary canon and prebendary of Ampleforth, could afford to finance the complete rebuilding of his parish church of Bolton Percy in the most fashionable Perpendicular style shortly before his death in 1423.[217] Northern knights and even bishops were prepared to pay considerable sums to secure the admission of the sons of their relatives and friends to the *familia* of a residentiary canon; and it was in this way that many Yorkshire boys began their own clerical careers. Wealthiest of all the

---

[213] BIHR, Reg. Zouche, fos. 216–17.

[214] *York Statutes*, pp. 38–9; for a helpful but not always convincing map of the close see G. Benson, *Later Medieval York* (York, 1919), p. 113.

[215] The houses of canons were regularly used for the transaction of cathedral and diocesan business: see e.g. BIHR, CP, R VII F, 167, vi; BM, Harleian MS. 669, fo. 21ᵛ.

[216] See e.g. the will made by Treasurer John Barnyngham in 1457 (*Test. Ebor.* ii. 203–7). The copious extracts from the testaments of the fifteenth-century residentiaries to be found in *Test. Ebor.* i.–iv, need, however, to be used with caution in view of their many omissions.

[217] Drake, *Ebor.*, p. 386; YML, L2(3)a, fos. 103, 109.

York canons were the deans, treasurers, and archdeacons of Richmond. Master John Newton, treasurer from 1393 to 1414, owned his own 'ship, called a barge' as well as a large lead-smelting furnace at Poppleton; his colleague, Master Stephen Scrope, archdeacon of Richmond from 1400 to 1418, left bequests to a veritable horde of servants, ranging from chamberlain and esquires to cooks and pages.[218] Even more revealing are the references in canons' wills to their testators' range of acquaintance and experience. Not many residentiaries, like Thomas Walworth who died in 1409, can have visited Christ's tomb at Jerusalem; but many had served on diplomatic missions to Scotland or the Continent while a few had been embroiled in national politics. Thomas Haxey (Plate 11), perhaps the most active residentiary at York in the years immediately before his death in 1425, is now best remembered for his sponsorship of a parliamentary bill to check the extravagance of Richard II's household in 1397.[219] Above all perhaps, the wills of the fifteenth-century canons illuminate the cohesion and close relationship, sometimes one of blood, between the members of the chapter. They gave each other their most precious possessions, served as one another's executors, and even in death often preferred to be buried in carefully chosen and adjoining graves.

Such cohesion was itself a reflection of the very small number of canons who resided at York by the end of the Middle Ages. From the 1370s onwards it is possible to analyse the composition of the chapter in more detail than ever before; and it is immediately obvious that by this period it fell into two main groups—a majority of royal clerks and university scholars who rarely or never visited York at all, and a minority of administrators in archiepiscopal service who spent most of their lives in the diocese. Only a diminishing handful of this second group could afford the initial expenditure of taking up residence at the Minster. The number of residentiaries still stood at seven or eight in the 1370s, but had fallen to four twenty years later and reached its lowest point of only three or even two in the last years of the fifteenth century.[220] Long before Henry VIII complained (in the preamble to the Cathedral Statutes of 1541) that major residence at York cost as much as 1,000 marks, it is clear that only the wealthiest clerks could contemplate so expensive a step. The decision to take up residence was therefore usually reserved to clerks who were

---

[218] *Test. Ebor.* i. 370–1, 385–9: cf. YML, P1(2)ix for the household ordinances of Master Humphrey de Cherleton, archdeacon of Richmond, in 1379.

[219] *Test. Ebor.* i. 354; *Fabric Rolls*, pp. 203–6; M. Aston, *Thomas Arundel* (Oxford, 1967), pp. 311, 364–5.

[220] YML, E1/1–57 (Chamberlains' Accounts, 1370–1489); A1(4); H2/3, fos. 2, 142–3, etc.; BM, Cotton MS. Galba E X, fos. 91, 131.

already well established at York and were prepared to dedicate the remainder of their careers to the archbishop's service there. With the solitary exception of Robert Gilbert, who became bishop of London in 1436, all fifty residentiaries of York between the 1360s and 1500 seem to have died in residence.[221] To put the matter more simply still, the typical York residentiary of the fifteenth century was an elderly ecclesiastical lawyer collated to a York canonry from the household of the archbishop himself. Each archbishop in succession introduced his own most trusted clerks into the chapter; at any moment in time that chapter was consequently the creation of the prelates who had held the see during the previous twenty years. In 1400, for example, the leading residentiaries were Thomas Dalby, John Newton, and Thomas Walworth, all closely associated with Archbishop Arundel; fifty years later the chapter was led by a group of residentiary canons (John Barnyngham, William Duffield, William Felter, and John Marshall) who had earlier served as clerks and chaplains of Archbishop Kempe.[222] Indeed the contraction in the number of canons in residence during the course of the fifteenth century is itself a reflection of the increasing tendency to concentrate administrative authority within the diocese into fewer and fewer hands. Perhaps no canon of York can ever have wielded more power than did William Sheffield during the eight years (1488–96) he was in residence: as treasurer and then dean of the cathedral he dominated the chapter, and as Archbishop Rotherham's vicar-general and official he was the effective governor of the church of York at large.[223]

Throughout all the vicissitudes of the later Middle Ages, the residentiary section of the Minster chapter had therefore retained its essential character. 'It was once more the archbishop's *familia*, but a *familia* whose head was continually absent.'[224] However, the history of a great cathedral is never absolutely identical with that of its governing body; and the cumulative impression left by the voluminous records of the fifteenth century is one of a church which held a place in popular opinion quite unaffected by changes in the composition of its chapter. A medieval cathedral must always have

---

[221] Clerks who were already mature when they took up residence were not of course likely to live for inordinately long periods thereafter: the average term of the 18 canons who took up residence between 1433 and 1500 was 12·5 years: YML, H2/3 (Chapter Acts, 1427–1504), *passim*. In the early fifteenth century the life-expectancy of York residentiaries was lower still (YML, L 2(3)a, fos. 67–103).

[222] YML, E 1/29–34 (Chamberlains' Rolls, 1398–1402); H 2/4, fos. 23, 43ᵛ, 48, 67; cf. Aston, *Thomas Arundel*, pp. 309–19; Emden, *Oxford* i. 601–2; ii. 675–6, 1228.

[223] YML, H 2/4, fo. 198; BIHR, Reg. Rotherham, i. fo. 99; *Test. Ebor.* iv. 118–20; Emden, *Cambridge*, pp. 521–2; Thompson, *The English Clergy*, p. 194; cf. R. L. Storey, *Diocesan Administration in the Fifteenth Century* (St. Anthony's Hall Publications, no. 16, 1959), pp. 22–3.

[224] 'The Medieval Chapter', *Y.M. Hist. Tr.*, p. 15.

9 St. William's College for the chantry priests of the Minster as it survives today. The ground floor, built of magnesian limestone from the Tadcaster area, dates from the original construction of the college in the 1460s.

10 Effigy of the head of Archbishop Rotherham. This badly battered effigy was discovered in Thomas Rotherham's tomb in 1735 and was probably carved from the archbishop's death mask in 1500.

11 'Haxey's Tomb', near the entrance to the west aisle of the north transept. Treasurer Thomas Haxey, who died in January 1425, was buried to the south of this now severely mutilated monument of a cadaver; the iron grating once supported a marble stone upon which rents and offerings were customarily made to the dean and chapter.

been difficult to control; and towards the end of the Middle Ages there are signs that York Minster was subject to increasingly powerful centrifugal pressures. Unruly, turbulent, and at times corrupt, it would be idle to pretend that the late medieval cathedral clergy were able to preserve an oasis of spiritual calm amidst the secular society around them. But at least the Minster responded rapidly to the needs, aspirations, and prejudices of its age. It was by the striking of the cathedral clock that the aldermen of York knew when they were late for council meetings; and it was in the chapter-house that the greatest lords and prelates of the north were asked to give evidence in the *cause célèbre* of Scrope v. Grosvenor in 1386.[225] It was in the Minster too that the visiting magnate, knight, and esquire could find one of the largest repositories of chivalric heraldry and insignia in the north; and it was there that Richard III came to celebrate the investiture as Prince of Wales of his only and ill-fated son in August 1483.[226] At a humbler level many residents of York visited the cathedral as members of St. Christopher's, St. George's, and other city guilds; travellers from further afield came to marvel, then as now, at the antiquity of the great 'temple of York' and to learn something about its legendary history.[227] Countless testamentary bequests to 'Seynt Peter work' from men and women of very obscure as well as distinguished birth testify to a general commitment to the mother church of York. Most dramatically of all, it was popular enthusiasm for the 'glory of York' and 'loyal martyr of Christ', which came near to securing Richard Scrope's canonization in the face of Lancastrian opposition.[228] The 'concourse of people' who came to worship at Scrope's tomb serves as a reminder that the most formally hierarchical church in northern England was at the same time the centre of the most striking manifestations of popular religion and piety. To the argument that the fifteenth century witnessed a withdrawal of lay interest from the institutions of the organized Church, the history of York Minster certainly seems to lend little support. After 1500 it was perhaps never to mean quite so much to so many again.

[225] *YCR* ii. 55; *The Scrope and Grosvenor Controversy*, ed. N. H. Nicolas (1832), i. 91, 129, 135, 141.

[226] Torre 'Minster', p. 109; D. J. Hawke, *The Mediaeval Heraldry of York Minster* (Wakefield, 1971); YML, M2(2)c (Repertorium), fo. 70; *Fabric Rolls*, pp. 210–12.

[227] The historical narratives fastened to the two surviving late medieval folding 'tables' at York are paraphrased in J. S. Purvis, 'The Tables of the York Vicars Choral', *YAJ* xli (1967), 741–8: these tables were almost certainly prepared for the edification of pilgrims and visitors to the Minster (and as such were seen by John Leland in 1534) rather than for the use of the vicars choral of the cathedral.

[228] *Hists. York* ii. 428–33; iii. 291–4, 389–91; *Fabric Rolls*, pp. 193–6; *Test. Ebor.* i. 353; ii. 65–6, 126, 151, 231, 233. For the popular veneration of Henry VI's statue in the Minster by the end of the 1470s see BIHR, Reg. L. Booth, fos. 112ᵛ–13; *Fabric Rolls*, p. 82. Cf. J. W. McKenna, 'Popular canonization as political propaganda: the cult of Archbishop Scrope', *Speculum*, xlv (1970), 608–23; *The Loyal Martyr; or The Life of Richard Scroop* (1722), pp. 37–40.

In addition to the many helpful suggestions made by the authors of other chapters in this volume, I am especially indebted to Dr. David Smith and Miss Katharine Longley for their invaluable advice.

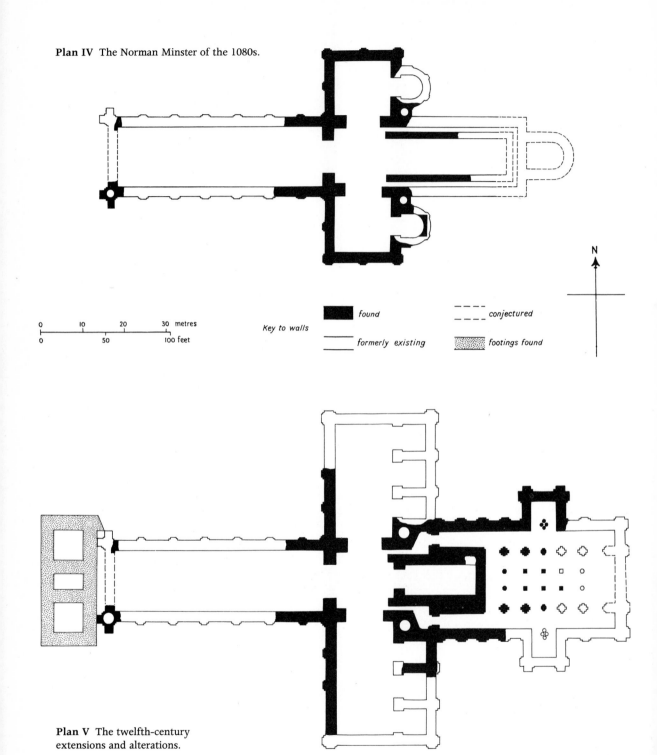

Plan IV The Norman Minster of the 1080s.

Key to walls

■ found — — — conjectured

— formerly existing ▦ footings found

N

0   10   20   30 metres
0   50   100 feet

Plan V The twelfth-century
extensions and alterations.

CHAPTER III

Architectural History until 1290

Eric A. Gee

The pre-Conquest churches

There is still at the time of writing (1976) no positive evidence for the fabric of any Roman or Saxon metropolitan church at York, and as the historical account in Chapter I is very full, this section will only provide a commentary on it. During the Roman occupation emperor worship was popular with the three legions stationed at the fortresses of Caerleon, Chester, and York;[1] it is an easy transition to the statement by Geoffrey of Monmouth that archflamens were replaced by archbishops,[2] and the same idea is embodied in the Abingdon Chronicle under the date 201, that there were archbishops (*archipraesules*) at London, York, and the City of the Legions.[3] Certainly there may have been a Christian community in York for some time when its bishop Eborius attended the Council of Arles in A.D. 314,[4] and it is interesting to consider where the centre of Christianity could have been in Eboracum; it could hardly have been in the fortress only two years after the Edict of Toleration, or even in the 'domus palatina'[5] and would probably consist of a house in the *colonia* or suburbs.

If any of the later Saxon churches represented a pre-Saxon Christian site, their relative dates become important. A sequence can be established for the Saxon churches in the *colonia*, for Holy Trinity Priory, endowed in about 1100 by Ralph Pagnell with lands which had belonged to a Saxon collegiate church called Christ Church, had a precinct wall which carefully allowed for St. Mary Bishophill Junior; so the latter was an earlier foundation. But St. Mary's was invariably called St. Mary 'Bishop' as it had belonged to the archbishop and this was to differentiate it from the other St.

---

[1] C. J. Godfrey, *The Church in Anglo-Saxon England* (Cambridge, 1962), p. 5.

[2] Geoffrey of Monmouth, *History of the Kings of Britain* (Penguin Classics, 1966), p. 125.

[3] *Chronicon Monasterii de Abingdon* (Rolls Ser., 1858), i. 2.

[4] *Councils and Ecclesiastical Documents*, ed. A. W. Haddan and W. Stubbs, (Oxford, 1869–73), i. 9–10.

[5] *Scriptores Historiae Augustae Severus*, pp. 122–7 for references to the 'domus'.

Mary called the Old or Senior, which therefore was the earliest Saxon foundation on that side of the river. If the site were in the suburb outside the fortress on the other side of the river, then St. Peter the Little has a claim, and the legend cited by Camden that at the Reformation a burning lamp was found in a crypt could only refer to that church, which certainly was the only one with a true crypt. Moreover, the fact that the cathedral is called St. Peter the Great[6] could imply a relationship between the two St. Peter's like that between the two St. Mary's.

The opportunity for Roman Christianity to come to the north arrived in 625 or earlier when Paulinus came with Ethelberga, daughter of Ethelbert, king of Kent, as her chaplain. Ethelberga married King Edwin and at Pentecost 626 Paulinus baptized King Edwin's daughter and eleven others.[7] The story of King Edwin's wooden church in which he was baptized and the stone church which succeeded it has been given in Chapter I. On 12 October 632 Edwin was killed at Hatfield Chase and his head was brought to York and put in the *porticus* of St. Gregory.[8] King Oswald who completed the church was himself slain in 641. Torre notes that the feast of dedication took place on 1 October and the seven days following[9] and that this was modified by the dean and chapter on 17 August 1462 to a greater double festival. Kenneth Harrison has argued that Edwin's church could have been like that of SS. Peter and Paul at Canterbury, built by Ethelbert, king of Kent, King Edwin's father-in-law, and could have had the same proportions of 80 feet by 60 feet.

The restoration of the church by St. Wilfrid in A.D. 670 is described in Chapter I and the only interesting fact which might be added is that he glazed windows that previously had contained thin linen cloths, or a fretted slab (*multiforatilis asser*).[10]

When St. Cuthbert was consecrated bishop of Lindisfarne at York in 685 he was granted all that land which lay from the wall of the church of St. Peter to the great west gate and from the wall of the church of St. Peter towards the city wall on the south side.[11] If the present Minster is on or near the site of King Edwin's church, the grant to St. Cuthbert would consist of that part of the Roman fortress bounded by the walls, High Petergate, and the line of Duncombe Place and Museum Street, but there was no continuing Durham interest there to represent the grant. However, if, as

---

[6] *Early Yorkshire Charters*, i.

[7] Anglo-Saxon Chronicle ed. G. N. Garmondsway (1953), p. 25.

[8] Bede, *HE* ii. 20, p. 204.

[9] Torre, 'Minster', p. 1.

[10] Eddi (Eddius Stephanus), *The Life of St. Wilfrid*, ed. B. Cosgrove, (Cambridge, 1927), p. 35.

[11] *Symeonis Monachi Opera Omnia*, ed. T. Arnold (Rolls Ser., 1882–5), i. 199. (Cited elsewhere as Symeon of Durham.)

Bernard Barr has tentatively suggested, the site of the first cathedral was at St. Peter the Little in the civilian suburb to the south-east of the fortress, then All Saints, Pavement, which belonged to Durham, strengthens the identification, and St. Peter's itself belonged to Durham at a later date.

Archbishop Æthelbert (766–82) set up a new altar to St. Paul in the church in which Edwin was baptized and presented to it many costly ornaments.[12] Hitherto all references have been to the church of St. Peter but from this point there is a certain degree of ambiguity as there may have been henceforward no major church; for in 780, with assistance from his disciples Eanbald, who succeeded him as archbishop, and Alcuin, Æthelbert began and completed a new church in honour of Alma Sophia (see Ch. I). It was consecrated by the archbishop ten days before his death,[13] and Professor Willis considered it to be a second church, not necessarily on the same site, and apparently it is not mentioned again. However, the burial-ground found under the south transept would fit Æthelbert's new church in date, and it is remarkable that there are very few early Saxon crosses or stones in the Minster area, which suggests that whereas the burial-ground is near the later church, the present church is not in the vicinity of Edwin's church. In 791 there is a reference to 'ecclesia principalis'[14] which suggests that there was more than one important church at this time. A letter from Alcuin to Æthelred, king of Northumbria, in 793 describes a vision seen in the church of St. Peter, chief of the apostles,[15] and in 796 King Eardulf of Northumbria was crowned at the altar of St. Paul in the church of St. Peter;[16] in the same year Archbishop Eanbald was buried in the church of St. Peter.[17] The altar of St. Paul had been set up in the church of St. Peter by Archbishop Æthelbert, and acquired special significance, and from this period saints Peter and Paul are linked in the cathedral, despite the fact that the church is dedicated to St. Peter only; the great central boss of the tower vault shows them together and their legendary arms are on the doors of the south transept. These references also show that the older church continued to be used.

Alcuin's gift of lead and screens (801) is noted in the historical account, as are the burial of Guthfrith (895), Athelstan's gift of land to the church of St. Peter (934), and King Eadred's gift of two large bells (946). Arguments have been advanced that the early church used Roman buildings in the

[12] Alcuin, *De Pontificibus Ebor.* in *Hists. York* i. 393.

[13] R. Willis, *Architectural History of York Cathedral* (1848), p. 4.

[14] *Symeon of Durham*, ii. 53.

[15] Alcuin, *Epistolae*, ed. E. Dümmler (*Monumenta Germ. Hist., Epistolae Karolini Aevi*, 1895), 43.

[16] *Symeon of Durham*, ii. 57–8.

[17] Ibid. ii. 58.

praetorium, but if this were so a timber church would not have been erected and neither would the timber church have been incorporated in a stone one at a later date. On the other hand, Roman masonry would be utilized, and it certainly was used in a large way in the church of *c.* 1080. The important Saxon cemetery is placed over the Roman buildings and the orientation of the burials suggests that the church would be roughly on the Roman alignment. The large number of pre-Conquest stones in the fabric of *c.* 1080 shows that it was in the vicinity. Kenneth Harrison argues convincingly that Edwin's church should be to the north-east of the junction of Lop Lane and Low Petergate, near the present west front but there is evidence that the church did not own this area until William Rufus gave them permission to use it, and that the late twelfth-century towers were erected on the land concerned.

Canon Addleshaw considered that St. Peter's and the Alma Sophia could have been in tandem, as were the Saxon churches at Canterbury and Hexham. If they were on the oblique Roman alignment they could extend from the west aisle of the present cathedral south transept to the west front. The Saxon churches at Durham and Peterborough were in the south-west angle of the nave and south transept, but in those cases the later churches were on the same alignment. On the other hand, there is a lot to show that a Saxon church at York is in the same relative position, but to the north of the Minster, for the Norman entrance to the precinct, later the base of the chapel of the Holy Sepulchre and roughly on the Roman alignment, could indicate an important building in that position.

The Early Norman church (1075–1100)

The Saxon cathedral would be virtually intact when Archbishop Ealdred, who died on 11 September 1069, was buried in it.[18] On 19 September 1069 the metropolitan church of St. Peter was burnt and many of its charters and fittings were lost, during conflicts between the Danes, rebellious Saxons, and William I and his followers.[19] In 1070 Thomas of Bayeux was consecrated archbishop, and on his arrival began to put the affairs of the establishment in order, restored and reroofed the church, and rebuilt the refectory and dormitory.[20] In 1079 the Danes came to York and destroyed the church of St. Peter.[21] The archbishop then built an entirely new church from the foundations upwards. It is improbable that the Norman church would be on the site of the Saxon one, as that would be kept for continuity

[18] Douglas and Greenaway (eds.), *EHD* ii, *1042–1189* (London, 1953), p. 150.
[19] Hugh the Chanter in *Hists. York* ii. 98.
[20] Ibid. 108, 362.
[21] *EHD*, ii. 157.

of worship, and in any case the Saxon cemetery found in the south transept suggests that the Saxon church was more on the Roman alignment. The early Norman gateway to the precinct on the north sloped in to the north-west angle of the new nave and probably gave access to the Saxon cathedral to the north of the Norman one and on a different alignment. Later, Archbishop Roger put the chapel of the Holy Sepulchre on the gateway, and it was of the same build as two western towers which could only be added to the west front when William II had granted land there in 1089–95.[22]

The date of the early Norman work in the crypt was recognized as long ago as 1912 by Professor Hamilton Thompson, in 1925 Professor Baldwin Brown had no doubt about its Norman date, Sir Alfred Clapham hinted likewise, and the researches of Sidney Melmore and Kenneth Harrison and the present writer have supported this view since 1950.

The Norman church was so homogeneous that it was probably complete by the death of Thomas of Bayeux at Ripon in 1100;[23] he was buried in his new church at York next to his predecessor, Ealdred. It was a remarkable church, not Anglo-Norman except in detail, and this could reflect the archbishop's education at the expense of Odo, bishop of Bayeux, at Liège and in Germany and Spain. It was on the correct orientation, 362 feet long, and consisted of a long eastern arm with an apse to the east and corridors along each side and returning across the face of the apse. The crossing was the width of the central area and the passages and on either side of it was a small transept with, on the east side, an apse on the outer side of a newel stair. A great aisleless nave was of the same width as the crossing. There are aisleless naves at Angers and Fontevrault, and the nave without aisles at Ripon, built by Archbishop Roger (1154–81), must have copied York.

The *footings* of the cathedral were amazingly strong, and throughout they contain great timbers in the Vitruvian tradition, which is not strange, as the use of Vitruvius had been recommended in York as early as a Council in 926.[24] Sir Alfred Clapham had noted the use of timbers as a Norman practice and cited examples at Goodrich and Clifford castles and under the eleventh-century walls at Richmond.[25] In general there were three timbers under the chief walls (Plate 12) and two under the lesser ones and openings, and the wide footings of the choir and central tower had five lines of timbers in two groups. The *walls* are usually seven feet thick, of reused Roman masonry, and include some Saxon carved stones. The dressings are

---

[22] *Early Yorkshire Charters*, i. 117–18.
[23] Anglo-Saxon Chronicle, p. 236.
[24] T. S. R. Boase, *English Art 1100–1216* (Oxford, 1953), pp. 6, 7.
[25] A. W. Clapham, *English Romanesque Architecture after the Conquest* (Oxford, 1934), p. 118.

12 All the wall footings of *c.* 1080 have a lacing of great timbers as seen here in the west wall of the aisleless nave. At the far end the wall abutting the buttress is that of towers added in *c.* 1180.

13 North wall of nave of *c.* 1080, east end, south face. Pitched stones, popular at this time, often produced a herring-bone effect.

14 West wall and buttress of the north transept of *c.* 1080, with a plinth, and rendering lined with red to look like large blocks of stone, which is a rare external finish.

of sandstone or gritstone with no masons' marks, diagonally axed, and at intervals there are buttresses, apparently of two orders, but the walls probably had large round-headed recesses in them with buttresses between, and the inner order is the jamb of such a recess. This treatment is found in the nave aisle wall at the Abbaye aux Hommes at Caen,[26] the nave aisle walls at Santiago de Compostela,[26] and in the south gable wall of the south transept of Romsey Abbey. Round all exterior features and about two feet six inches above the footings is a plain-chamfered plinth. Throughout there were pitched stones, sometimes producing a herring-bone effect (Plate 13) common in *c.* 1080 and found at quite a few Yorkshire castles, including Richmond. Perhaps the most remarkable feature is that the external faces were rendered with hard white plaster and lined in red to look like ashlar (Plate 14), a treatment which may have been found at St. Albans and the White Tower at London. There was internal plaster on the rubble walling.

The eastern arm, 197 feet long, had inner walls nearly five feet wide, as much as ten feet high, not pierced at the undercroft level, and with narrow passages on the outer side. The thicker outer walls ran in to the transepts on the inner side of the archway under the newel stairs and the passage returned across the west side of an apse like the original arrangement at St. Philibert Grandlieu. There may have been small towers on either side of the eastern apse, as originally at Winchester and Hereford, presenting the same appearance as the east end at Morienval. If the passages had barrel vaults and the inner space was filled with earth like the crypts at Chartres,[27] the upper part could have been of the same span as the nave, but with lower walls over those below to back the stalls. Alternatively, there could have been pierced chord walls, the width of the passages below, which could have acted as internal buttresses and could have eased roofing problems. The main apse footings only had two timbers and thus the walls could have been relatively low but would have enclosed an undercroft.

The *transepts* were small (144 feet from north to south internally) and there is evidence for their height in the west wall of the present north transept; each had an apse on the east side and a newel stair between the apse and the crossing (Plate 15). There are newels in this position at St. Benoît-sur-Loire (*c.* 1060), Fontevrault, Leominster (*c.* 1125), and Norwich (1096–1119) and it often implies two-storey transepts as at St. Lorenzo in Verona, Jumièges (1037–66), St. Stephen's Caen, Cerisy, Fécamp, St.

[26] K. J. Conant, *Carolingian and Romanesque Architecture 800–1200* (Harmondsworth, 1959), p. 26, Fig 6. J. H. Harvey, *Cathedrals of Spain* (London, 1957) Pl. 69 and pp. 39–41 (communicated by John H. Harvey).
[27] Observation John Miller.

Georges Boscheville, and Venge Abbey in Denmark. There were galleries of some form, not necessarily over the whole transept, in England at Westminster Abbey (1050–65), Canterbury (1070–7), Lincoln (1072–92), Christchurch (Hampshire), and Winchester. There is no proof of such a transept at York but the apses were two-storeyed and the upper floor was probably reached from the newel stair as perhaps at Norwich.

The *crossing* (Plate 16) had a low tower, for a buttress at its angle which still exists above the water table of the present north transept must have been higher than the adjoining arms of *c.* 1080.

The aisleless *nave* was of abnormal size (162 feet by 45 feet internally). It was of seven bays, and the eastern bay was a little narrower than the others to give abutment. Speyer (1030–65) is of the same width but aisled, and there is a group of naves without aisles in Poitou. The exterior would have had great round-headed recesses between simple pilaster buttresses and below clerestory level, and there were possibly high-set windows at the top of the recesses and clerestory windows each between two blind window forms. The interior elevation may have had a blank wall at the bottom under a bold string course, and then the bays, delineated by shafts, would have a wall passage like a triforium and a clerestory also with wall passage. Ripon nave is probably a direct copy and at Nun Monkton the same effect was produced in *c.* 1210 by adding to walls of *c.*1180. The general effect would have been like the upper parts of St. Albans, Blyth, and Winchester—all of much the same date. There is evidence for newel stairs at each angle of the west end, and between them was probably a giant recess of many orders like those at Tewkesbury, Bath, and Durham. There may have been a south doorway in the fifth bay from the east as at Southwell. There are considerable remains of the early nave above the aisle vaults at the east end of the present nave.

The *decoration* of this church was orthodox, with rolls and scalloped capitals (Plate 17). The most impressive features are two large respond capitals, each for paired shafts (Plates 18 and 19). They have bold volutes at the angles and incised foliage, palmettes at the bottom, cable necking, and traces of red colouration. Crude composite capitals like these are found at Canterbury (*c.* 1075), Durham Castle chapel (1072–*c.* 1080), Lastingham crypt (1078–88), St. John's Chapel in the Tower of London (1080–90), and Blyth Priory nave (begun 1088), A similar capital has recently been found *in situ* of the north respond of the opening to the upper floor of the south transept apse.

Similar capitals at Richmond Castle, together with herring-bone walling on footings with timber reinforcement and other close structural resemblances, suggest that it was by the same school of masoncraft.

15 An arch to carry a newel stair, and the south side of the apse on the east side of the north transept of *c.* 1080.

16 Footings of *c.* 1080 under the present north-west pier of the crossing. A 13th-C. addition has been made to the south side of the west wall.

17 Scalloped capital reused in the footings of the south-west tower pier and probably from the west front of *c*. 1080.

18 A large respond capital of *c*. 1080, found in the footings of a presbytery pier of *c*. 1370 and probably from the entrance to an apse. The volute is found in many early Norman capitals.

19 Respond capital of *c*. 1080 *in situ* on the north side of a first-floor apse of the S. transept. Compare with Plate 18.

The Middle Norman period (1137–54)

On 4 June 1137 York Cathedral was damaged by fire.[28] The worst damage was to the eastern arm and the remainder was patched up or improved as a prelude to the great work undertaken by Archbishop Roger of Pont l'Évêque. The most likely archbishop to have undertaken this is Thurstan, who died on 5 February 1140, for he was a capable administrator, a friend of the Cistercians, and his successors, Henry Murdac and St. William, had troubled tenure of office. It could be argued that William FitzHerbert (d. 1154) would have been buried in the choir if it had been available, and not the nave, which, however, would have been in moderate repair. Joscelin de Bohun, bishop of Salisbury (1142–84), issued an indulgence granting forty days of penance to those who contributed bountifully to the rebuilding of the metropolitan church of York which had suffered badly from a new fire, but this could be a prelude to the erection of a new eastern arm. However, between 1137 and 1154 there were alterations to the cathedral built by Thomas of Bayeux and the walling is characteristic, for not only is magnesian limestone newly quarried for the work, but it has diagonal axeing finer than that of *c.* 1080, but not of the quality of that on the late twelfth-century work, and masons' marks now appear. The wall was rendered and given red lines to represent ashlar as before.

At the east end the *apse* was squared, a regular procedure at this date, but the buttresses are like those associated with the earlier work. The *transepts* were doubled in size by extensions of the same width, as at Coutances, and at the same time two square chapels were constructed on the east face of each transept in a very Cistercian manner, but the transept apses were not altered until after the building of the late Norman choir, for the later ambulatory walls were erected against the apses and small oblique windows were provided to light the aisles. The *newel stairs* were heightened at this time in the characteristic masonry, which suggests that the transepts were heightened. There are remains of the staircase turrets above the choir aisle vaults at the west end.

The Late Norman choir (1154–74)

Even if the eastern arm had not been damaged in the fire of 1137, it would have been antiquated compared with other large churches of the twelfth century, and the indulgence of Bishop Joscelin de Bohun probably indicated a rebuilding. The archbishop with the drive to fulfil such a project was Roger of Pont l'Évêque, who succeeded in 1154, and he is said

---

[28] J. H. Harvey, 'The Fire in York in 1137', *YAJ* xli, pt. 163; *Gervase of Canterbury*, ed. W. Stubbs (Rolls Ser. i, 1879), p. 100.

to have built anew the choir and crypt of the cathedral.[29] The work was probably in hand in 1160 when Henry II held court at York, and the crypt was probably finished in 1166 when a gift by John, son of Alwin de Runton, to Robert de Stutevil was confirmed in it.[30] Before 1173 William de Percy gave Topcliffe church to the fabric, in *c.* 1174–5 a gift by Henry Foliot for the rebuilding of St. Peter's Church was confirmed,[31] and between 1170 and 1190 William, son of Hameline de Ryther, confirmed property to St. Peter's for the rebuilding of the church.[32] In August 1175 William I of Scotland did homage to Henry II and put his breastplate, spear, and saddle on the altar of St. Peter, presumably in the new choir.[33] On 22 November 1180 the archbishop died and was buried in the middle of the church which he had newly constructed.[34] A completion date of *c.* 1175 would suit the earlier character of the York work, compared with Ripon, which was not finished at his death.

The new choir was fully aisled and square-ended, with an ambulatory, and the form of the square end was like that at Old Sarum (1125–30) and Byland (*c.* 1175).

There was an eastern transept, the idea of which may have come from Cluny to Lewes,[35] and it may have been lower than the main choir, as at Canterbury. The footings do not have bond timbers like those of the earlier work and the walling is of wonderful magnesian limestone with numerous masons' marks and very fine diagonal axeing like similar work at Selby, Byland, Roche, Old Malton, and Ripon. Stylistically it is a late example of the Durham School, and suitable analogies are Durham itself, Selby (1097–1123), Kirby Lonsdale (*c.* 1110), Castle Acre (early twelfth-century), Dunfermline (after 1124), Waltham (1125–6), Norwich (1096–1119), and Lindisfarne (1128–50). However, the closest relationship is with St. Mary's Abbey, York, which has similar decorative details.

The new choir was not built on the older walls and its piers and walls were placed outside them. The undercroft was lit from outside and was thus not a true crypt. The herring-bone walls of the earlier undercroft were cased on both sides and the inner casing, two feet six inches thick, including some re-used details of *c.* 1080, may have been plastered but the centre was filled with earth to the west (Plate 20). The outer lining, three feet six inches thick, was of good freestone, as it formed the walls of

[29] *Chronica Monasterii de Melsa* (Rolls Ser. 43) i. 215.
[30] *Early Yorkshire Charters*, ii. 64 (no. 718).
[31] Ibid. ii. 38–9; *Fabric Rolls*, p. 148.
[32] *Early Yorkshire Charters*, iii. 302–3 (no. 1645).
[33] *Chronica Rogeri de Hovedene*, ed. W. Stubbs (Rolls Ser., 1868–71), ii. 79 *et seq.*
[34] Stubbs quoting Browne, *History*, p. 19.
[35] Conant, op. cit., p. 140.

ambulatories. The east end was almost certainly of the full height of the church and its position is known exactly as it was perpetuated by an early parish boundary. The *central part* of the undercroft had two major and two minor arcades, all of six bays, if the double bay at the entrance to the eastern transept is counted as two. The main arcades still exhibit in each case the base of the third pier, a fourth pier with four attached shafts but with post-1200 remodelling, a fifth pier with great central drum with oblique spirals of chevron and detached shafts to each cardinal point, a sixth pier of similar form but with incised lozenge decoration as at Durham and Selby and responds with a round shaft between lesser shafts but in the same plane (Plate 21). The detached shafts may be the earliest example of this form seen to great advantage at Chichester. The minor arcades had round or octagonal shafts and spurs on the bases and seven out of a possible ten were reused in the later crypt.

The *outer walls* consisted in each case of two eastern bays, a square transept, and four full bays to the west, with a fifth one overlapping the earlier transept apse (8–9 bays). The *eastern transepts* projected a bay beyond the main walls and at the centre of the opening from the wall was a pier with four detached shafts. Otherwise each bay of the eastern arm had an elaborate moulded plinth, pilaster buttresses with nook shafts, and at the centre was a window with nook shafts externally and splayed internally. Inside, two of the four western bays were open to the main undercroft and two others formed the side of an ambulatory which led through an exceptionally rich doorway (Plate 22) to a lobby or antechamber at the west end, from which stairs rose to the crossing. In general the bays were separated by half-round shafts with scalloped capitals and bases resting on a wall plinth. At the south-west end the relationship of the choir to other structures there is very clear. Nearly two feet of debris had accumulated outside the plinth of the wall of *c.* 1170 where it was built against the apse of *c.* 1080, before the apse was squared off. Then a wall was built, the footings of which still remain, and although they run in against the central member of the plinth of *c.* 1170, there is a carefully contrived return. The wall has its own plinth and is of re-used ashlar, some of which has plaster and lining on it, but it has no plaster on it like the adjacent walls of *c.* 1140. The later transept wall of *c.* 1220, claw-tooled, is set in about eleven inches west of the wall of *c.* 1180, all the masonry of which has diagonal axeing (Plate 23).

There are large numbers of carved stones from the Norman choir re-used in the footings of the present choir-piers of *c.* 1370, and lesser capitals are re-used in the later crypt. The decoration, which has a profuse use of pellet, enriched scallop forms, a W-shaped chevron (Plate 24) and vaulting ribs

20 Casing of *c.* 1160 on the inner (south) side of a wall of *c.* 1080 by the north-east pier of the crossing. There was an earth infill on this side but the casting on the other side is of good coursed stone as there is an ambulatory there.

21 Respond on the south side where the ambulatory of *c.* 1160 reaches the open part of the undercroft.

22 North jamb of an ornate doorway at the west end of the north ambulatory of the undercroft of *c.* 1160, now removed. The fine mortar joints, diagonal axeing and pellet ornament are characteristic.

with a bobbin-like enrichment as found at St. Mary's Abbey (Plate 25), is of orthodox twelfth-century type, but the presence of keeled rolls and water leaf capitals not *in situ* shows that the main choir was of Transitional character like Byland and Ripon. Large sections of vaulting from this choir are re-used in the vestries to the south of the present eastern arm.

The Norman western towers

The excavations have revealed that in front of the nave of *c.* 1080 the Norman church had two western towers of a remarkable type, for they were so close together as to provide only a ceremonial entrance between them, and they projected a little beyond the line of the aisleless nave, instead of flanking it as at Ripon. They are fairly closely dated because although there is masonry of late twelfth-century date in the footings, yet the quoins and the little masonry above Norman ground level have the fine diagonal axeing of the choir. Moreover, the north wall of the north-west tower was extended to the east in such a way that it was connected with the Holy Sepulchre Chapel, itself built by Archbishop Roger. In no place was there any claw tooling, and thus the towers were not of thirteenth-century date. They could not have been erected before William Rufus had given permission to the Minster authorities to use the land to the west of their church.[36] The collegiate church of Coblenz has western towers, which, as at York, project only a little beyond the central span of the nave and likewise the western doorway is set in a low approach between the close-set towers.[37]

The structure could be called a west work, and west works in various forms were not strange in England. Before the Conquest, Ramsey (*c.* 985) and Durham (999) had towers at the west end which could have needed abutment. After the Conquest, Bury St. Edmunds (finished by 1142) and Ely (*c.* 1170) had a tower at the west end flanked by transepts, and perhaps the latter had a western apse like the Rhineland churches before the present Galilee was built.

At Lincoln the great church built by Remigius (begun in 1072–3 and consecrated in 1092) had a west work with sides too lofty to be mere ends to aisles, but the west towers are a twelfth-century afterthought.[38] It had great round-headed recesses like the one suggested at York, which itself could have had lesser recesses.

The towers at York were of sufficient quality for the designers of the nave of 1291 to consider them worthy of retention, and originally the new aisles

[36] *Early Yorkshire Charters*, i. 117–18.
[37] Observation John Miller, 20 Apr. 1971.
[38] Observation Dr. Peter Kidson, 10 Aug. 1973.

23 South wall of undercroft of *c.* 1160 with on the right side the doorway to the lobby at the west and on the other side the transept wall of *c.* 1220, above the squareing of an apse of *c.* 1080 in *c.* 1180.

24 Piece of chevron ornament of *c.* 1160 re-used in the footings of a choir pier on the south side and also found at St. Mary's Abbey. Note the mason's mark.

25 Section of vaulting rib of *c.* 1160 with annulets and pellet giving a bobbin-like effect, found in the footings of a choir pier; there are similar features at St. Mary's Abbey.

were wrapped round them. Only in *c.* 1310 were they considered an anomaly and then they were removed, but the new towers, set further out, needed modifications to the nave aisles and the penultimate buttresses were enlarged. The corresponding internal responds were made broader to carry chord arches to new piers with an arch between them, and the centre of the west front was rebuilt. The cathedral in 1207 was considered outstanding and the pope in a letter to King John about Stephen Langton refers to the cathedral at York which is so much greater and more dignified than that at Paris.[39]

The south transept

The first building on this site on the same orientation was a transept erected by Archbishop Thomas of Bayeux in *c.* 1080 and over a late Saxon cemetery with the burials roughly on the Roman alignment. Its width from east to west was much the same as that of the central part of the present transept, but its length from north to south was a little over half as long. It had a two-storey apse on the east side and a newel stair between the apse and the crossing. At some time after a great fire in 1137 the transept was doubled in size by an extension of the same width, which had two square chapels against its east face, and between 1180 and 1200 the apse was squared off, providing now three square chapels on the east side in a very Cistercian manner. By 1200, therefore, a transept existed with the same central area as the present one but with the west wall slightly to the east of the present west arcade. It is probable that there was a small tower to the south-west which was the belfry which gave the adjoining parish church of St. Michael its description.

The first part of the present transept to be built was the west aisle (Plate 26), on a virgin ecclesiastical site, on very good footings and placed against the Norman transept of two dates. There is a rumour, for which no contemporary source has been found, that it was started by Geoffrey Plantagenet, archbishop 1191–1207.[40]

Walter de Gray, archbishop in 1216–55, completed the south transept within his lifetime and may have started the great remodelling by adding the west aisle. Certainly King Henry III was interested in the work at York and on 5 July 1223 confirmed the cathedral's privileges.[41] On 22 March 1225 there was a collection of alms for the fabric being constructed[42] and on 18 July 1226 an indulgence was granted to those who would contribute to

---

[39] Communicated by Bishop Douglas Sargent. F. M. Powicke, *Stephen Langton*, Oxford, 1928, p. 31 (quoting *Gervase of Canterbury*, ed. Stubbs, ii, p. lxxiii).
[40] Thomas Gent, *The Antient and Modern History of the famous City of York* (York, 1730), p. 25.
[41] *Hists. York* iii. 117.   [42] *Reg. Gray*, p. 1.

the cost.[43] The most important event in 1226–7 and one which must have been of real value for raising funds was the canonization of St. William of York. On 22 March 1227 officials of the diocese were requested to send a portion of their first fruits for the work on the fabric of the mother church[44] and a little later Walter de Gray published an indulgence of forty days to those benefactors who contributed liberally to the work of the fabric.[45]

Soon afterwards there is evidence of increased activity with the setting-up of various altars, which must mean that the building of the transept was well advanced. In 1230 an altar of *St. William* 'quod in majori ecclesia dinoscitur esse fundari' was ordained by Elias Bernard[46] and on 25 January 1230–1 a bull of Gregory IX sanctioned the foundation of the same altar.[47] The altar of St. William was probably in the north chapel of the east aisle, for John Shelford (d. 1409), parson at St. William's altar, is said to have been buried there, and Samuel Gale in 1699 put St. William's Chapel in that position.[48]

The chapel at the south end of the east aisle was that of *St. John the Baptist*; a roof boss there has his emblem on it, and there is a fifteenth-century figure of St. John in the glass of an adjacent window.[49] William de Langton, dean of York (d. 1279), was buried there in his chantry at the altar of St. John the Baptist.[50]

The most important altar, however, was that of *St. Michael* in the centre of the east aisle as it was connected with the archbishop himself. In May 1228 Archbishop Gray reserved his right to half of Millom church in Cumberland[51] and on 13 November 1230 his intention to found a chantry in the Minster was mentioned in connection with this arrangement.[52] On 5 February 1231–2 he leased to Furness Abbey the reserved portion of Millom church, which he had assigned for chaplains in the church of York.[53]

On 22 March 1241 Archbishop Gray ordained his chantry at the altar of St. Michael, in the middle of the east aisle of the south transept.[54] There is a boss of St. Michael in the roof above and also a fifteenth-century central figure of the archangel in a window there. The archbishop was to be buried

---

[43] Ibid., p. 10.
[44] Browne, *History*, pp. 54–5.
[45] *Accurate Description* (1755), 62. Britton, *York Cathedral* (1819), 79.
[46] *Hists. York* iii. 138.
[47] Ibid. 141.
[48] YML, MS. Add. 43, p. 50 (plan).
[49] Browne, *History*, pp. 71–2.
[50] W. Page, *Chantry Surveys* (Surtees soc. xci, 1892), i. 79.
[51] *Reg. Gray*, pp. 160–2.
[52] Ibid., pp. 47–8.
[53] Ibid., p. 191.
[54] Ibid., pp. 190–1.

before the altar and mass was to be said daily for his soul by three priests and one clerk. The fabric fund had been mentioned in 1240[55] and there is little doubt that the transept was complete by 1241 when the chantry was founded.

There were, however, important structural changes in the thirteenth century, for which there are so far no recorded dates, but a lot of evidence in the fabric. As stated above, the west aisle may have been added to the Norman fabric. Then Walter de Gray replaced the chapels to the east by an eastern aisle, built the east arcade triforium and clerestory and the main south wall, and these items are tied together externally as they all have blind arcading with trefoiled heads in contrast to the sharply pointed blind arcading of the earlier west aisle. The east arcade could be slightly later in date than the east aisle even within this bracket, as the south respond is not bonded in with the south wall of the east aisle but courses through with the south front at the bottom.

It is possible that the west side was not immediately rebuilt, or if it was, it collapsed, for the Norman walls, which proved adequate footings to the east arcade, were not suitable on the west and they were strengthened, and then the arcade triforium and clerestory were built further west, which meant that the west aisle now became narrower than any of the other transept aisles. The moving of the west side can be demonstrated in quite a few ways. The interior blind arcading of the main south wall was designed to fit a wall further east than the present west side and when the latter was moved, the two western bays of blind arcading were widened unobtrusively. Likewise in the stage above the blind arcading there are two lancets on either side of the central feature, and they were designed to have broader rere-arches to the inner lancets than the outer ones. When the west side was moved, the outer rere-arch in that position was made the same width as the wide ones and again the move is skilfully disguised. The respond of the west arcade is not bonded in on the east side at the bottom, but courses through to the jambs of the widened lancet rere-arch and must be of the later date. On the north side of the transept the move of the west arcade is clearly visible. The tower arch was originally in the middle, presumably as late as 1234 when timber was given for the central tower,[56] but when the west side was moved it became east of centre and there is as much as three feet of masonry extra to the west of the crossing arch, again disguised, this time by panelling.

The present plain vault relates to the moving of the west side, for it fits the present width. The earlier vault had moulded ribs like that of the

---

[55] *Yorkshire Deeds* (YAS Rec. Ser. v, 1926), no. 465.
[56] *CClR, 1231–4*, 403.

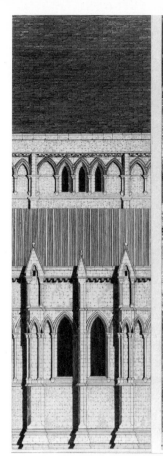

26 Scale drawing by John Browne (1840) of a bay of the west side of the south transept. The aisle buttresses project above the parapet and there is a blind area over the lancets; the clerestory has buttresses also.

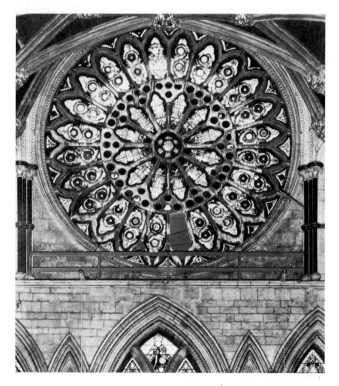

27 Rose Window of the south transept (*c.* 1250) from the inside. There are few mouldings and the centre of the window is to the west of the window below and both of them have been inserted.

eastern aisle, and pieces of it were found under the floor during the recent excavations.

Even after this operation the main south front may have been like the north face of the north transept with orthodox lancets, but it was decided to make it more impressive in the French style and the upper part was altered and provided with a large two-light lancet between two large lancets and above it a great rose window (Plate 27). The upper features are symmetrically disposed to the interior widening and thus do not line up with the bottom detail. There is ample evidence, both inside and out, for these modifications which could have all taken place before Archbishop Gray's death on 1 May 1255, when he was buried in St. Michael's Chapel under a monument which could be the best of its date in the country.

It is possible that both north and south transepts were finished by 22 July 1244 when Henry III ordered that tapers should be placed round the church ready for his forthcoming visit[57] and on 27 July he ordered wax candles to be placed round St. William's shrine.[58] The shrine at this time could have been a large oblong structure which was found in the centre of the south transept under the south tower arch, and the visit of the king could have been associated with the completion of the work.

At some time after 24 June 1245 Lawrence of Lincoln was murdered in Minster Yard and his will asked that he should be buried 'in ingressu magni ostij majoris ecclesie'; he left 5 marks to the fabric and arranged for a chantry 'in majori ecclesia ad altare Sancti Laurentij Martyris'.[59]

There are very few references to materials or craftsmen. Between 25 May and 27 December 1233 Robert le Vavasour granted rights in his stone quarry at Tadcaster to the Minster.[60] He had confirmed the right of the Minster to pass over his land to obtain stone from Thevesdale 'for as often as they shall have occasion to repair, rebuild, or enlarge the said church'.[61] On 11 July 1233 the archbishop was given thirteen oaks for building a certain chapel at York[62] but although this could refer to his own chantry of St. Michael, it is more likely that it means the chapel of the Archbishop's Palace, now the Minster library.

Whereas the master mason is not yet known, the name of the master carpenter is fairly certain. On 29 December 1226 Archbishop Gray granted lands by the Tyne in Northumberland to Gilbert, son of William the

---

[57] *Calendar of Liberate Rolls, 1240–5*, 254.
[58] Ibid. 256.
[59] *Hists. York* iii. 165–7; Clay, *Fasti* i. 34–5.
[60] *Fabric Rolls*, p. 147.
[61] *Monasticon* vi, pt. iii, p. 1198, quoted Browne, *History*, pp. 47 *et seq.*
[62] *CClR, 1231–4*, 238.

Carpenter,[63] doubtless for services rendered, and in 1248 the archbishop granted land at Milford to Gilbert de Corbrig, carpenter, almost certainly the same man. In the confirmation by the dean and chapter he is mentioned as a man who had remained for a long time in the archbishop's service, working well both on the archbishop's own work (Bishopthorpe) and on the Minster.

The thirteenth-century south transept, as completed, had three normal bays with related triforium and clerestory, and on the north side there were narrow blind bays, the one on the east cloaking the Norman newel stair and that on the west embodying a large Norman buttress in the angle of the transept and the aisleless nave.

At the end of the thirteenth century when the new nave was built and with aisles, the arches at the north end of the west arcade were interchanged so that there was now a wide one to the nave aisle and a narrow one to its south. At the end of the fourteenth century the east side was altered to the north when the new larger choir was built, but at first was too daring, for Hugh de Hedon replaced both narrow and broad arches by one great span, perhaps retaining the newel stair. When the tower collapsed in 1407 William Colchester inserted a pier and two arches under the large one, and cut away the base of the newel stair; as a precaution he put the screen at the entrance to the choir aisles, which acts as an extra support. The tower may have collapsed to the south-west, for William Colchester rebuilt the northern bay of the transept's west side, re-using a capital of *c.* 1390 from the previous work, and here the narrow bay was also blocked whereas the other narrow bays were only blocked in *c.* 1730.

The north transept

The whole transept and crossing were all rebuilt after 1220, but whereas Archbishop Gray is associated with the erection of the south transept, his colleague John le Romeyn is specifically connected with the north transept and the crossing, and he is said to have begun it while 'he was chaunter'.[64] Between 1220 and 1233 John le Romeyn gave a grant to the vicars for keeping his obit.[65] On 1 March 1226 he was given a papal dispensation 'super defectu natalium'[66] and on 22 June 1228 he was mentioned as subdean of York,[67] an office to which he was officially collated on 9 November 1228.[68]

[63] *Reg. Gray*, p. 225.
[64] Willis, *Survey*, i. (1742), pp. 15, 16.
[65] *Hists. York* iii. 152–3.
[66] Ibid. 125.
[67] *CPatR, 1225–32*, 191.
[68] *Reg. Gray*, p. 27.

The erection of the transept must have been well advanced in 1234 when John le Romeyn was allowed forty oaks for the belfry in which to hang great bells,[69] for there is little doubt that this means the central tower, which he is known to have built and which would need the abutment of the transepts. Between 1246 and 1251 a confirmation by Peter de Bolton and his wife, Ymeyna, of a warranty made by them at York Assizes in 1246 about a bovate of land in East Bolton to Rievaulx Abbey, mentions a mark of silver 'ad opus fabrice maioris ecclesie Ebor'.[70] On 27 December 1251 Geoffrey de Langley, justiciar, was told to allow the chapter of York to have thirty oaks from the Forest of Galtres for its church,[71] which could be for the roof of the north transept, and the whole transept could have been finished when Alexander of Scotland was married in the Minster to Margaret, daughter of Henry III; and on 6 July 1253 the king referred to the various and immense expenses incurred by the dean and chapter. When John le Romeyn died in 1255 the Chronicle of Meaux said of him that he erected at his own expense that part of the cross of the church which extended north towards the Archbishop's Palace and the famous bell-tower which stood in the middle of the cross.[72]

Like the south transept, the northern one was of three bays (Plate 28) and had the same relationship to the central tower and other arms. In c. 1290–1300 when a new aisled nave was erected, the south end of the west aisle of the transept was broken through to give access to the north aisle of the nave and at this time the narrow and broad bays of the west arcade were interchanged. Also at this time a grand new doorway of strange design was inserted into the north wall of the east aisle to lead to the new chapter-house vestibule, finished in 1280–90. The doorway was fitted into walls added on both sides of the existing wall but as it is built against features in the vestibule walls, it is later than them also (Plate 29).

In 1380–1400 the east side was modified when the choir north aisle was rebuilt, and after the collapse of the tower in 1407 further work consisted of the insertion of a pier, two arches, and a screen in the one large arch which had been built in c. 1390.

At some time in the early fifteenth century there was trouble in the west arcade, for the first pier from the north was wholly rebuilt but it re-used the Purbeck marble abacus of the earlier pier.

The north transept must have been started at much the same time as the south transept, but may have benefited by the various mishaps and

[69] *CClR, 1231–4*, 403.
[70] YML, MS. Add. 285.
[71] *CClR, 1251–3*, 29.
[72] *Chronica Monasterii de Melsa* (Rolls Ser. 43) ii. 238–9; *Hists. York* ii. 409.

modifications there, as it is much more of a homogeneous design.

There is remarkably little interchange of masons between the two, as is demonstrated by lack of relationship between the numerous masons' marks from both.

The obvious comparisons stylistically are with the choir of Rievaulx (*c.* 1210), the choir and transepts at Whitby (*c.* 1220), the east transept at Fountains (1210–40), Beverley Minster (begun in 1232), the choir of Southwell (building in 1233), and the east transept at Durham (begun 1242).

The ashlar at Rievaulx is of Hollins stone brought by a canal, the ground for which was acquired in 1193–1203.[73] The outer walls of Rievaulx choir have a vertical axeing like some at Corfe Castle, Dorset, and the connection will be with the Yorkshire baron, Peter de Mauley, who was constable at Corfe in 1215–21.[74] This suggests a date of *c.* 1210–20. But only the west bay at Rievaulx is like all those at Whitby in that the triforium arches are all enclosed under one round arch in each bay, and Whitby is usually dated *c.* 1220. Geoffrey Webb remarked that York transept was a more sumptuous version of Whitby, with marble shafts and plenty of leaf carving.[75] The choir at Southwell, being built for Archbishop Walter Gray in 1233, has a plinth like that of the south transept of York but necessarily on a smaller scale.

It is often said that the York transepts are inspired by Lincoln, and although St. Hugh's choir of 1186–1200 could be the prototype for an aisle arrangement as at York, with lancets on either side of a subsidiary buttress and blind arches on their outer sides, and all set between main buttresses, this is only found at Lincoln in the nave aisles of 1240–53. Otherwise there are few analogies, none of the piers has the same plan, and plinths at Lincoln are much more complicated. There is good double-wall construction at Lincoln in the Angel Choir (1256–80) and in the central tower (after 1239) but all is later than the work at York.

In many ways relationship established through masons' marks is safer than stylistic comparison, but the study is still rather backward. The south transept at York has a rare mark in the responds to the south, which occurs on the eastern tower arch at Rievaulx but has very few outside connections. On the other hand, the north transept has seventeen or more marks common to the later work at Byland, which is not strange when the similarity between the highly individual west doorway at Byland and that in the north aisle at York are perceived. Over ten marks from both occur at Roche Abbey, which could be expected, and twelve marks in the north transept at

[73] F. Bond, *Gothic Architecture* (1905), p. 652.
[74] *History of the King's Works*, ed. H. M. Colvin (1963), ii. 833. 833.
[75] Geoffrey Webb, *Architecture of Britain in the Middle Ages* (1956), pp. 102–3.

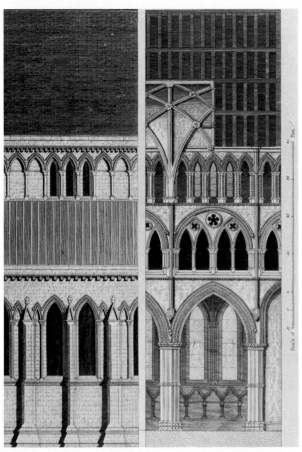

28 Drawing by John Browne (1840) of a bay on the east side of the north transept. Here the aisle buttresses are not so high as those of the south transept, the lancets are larger and there are no buttresses to the clerestory.

29 The vault of the east aisle of the north transept with blocked lancets in the north wall (c. 1250) and the head of the vestibule doorway of c. 1300.

York occur in the south transept at Hexham. It will be noticed here and in chapter IV that York has close relationships with Cumberland and Northumberland.

The thirteenth-century crossing and central tower

The central tower was rebuilt in the thirteenth century as part of the remodelling of the transepts by Archbishop Walter Gray and John le Romeyn senior, the treasurer, and must have been quite well advanced by 12 April 1234, when Peter de Rivallis was ordered by the king to allow John le Romeyn, canon of York, to have forty oaks from the forests of Knaresborough and 'Ockendon' for the construction of a bell-tower to hold the great bells of the cathedral.[76] John le Romeyn senior, father of the archbishop, is said in the Meaux Chronicle to have erected the famous (*egregius*) central tower for bells.[77]

The thirteenth-century tower was probably higher and heavier than the present one for it had a bell-chamber as well as a lantern, on piers not so heavy as the present ones; Browne noted in 1847 that vertical shafts of thirteenth-century date were seen inside the later casing.[78] Thirteenth-century crossings of this period with relatively slender piers and a lavish use of Purbeck marble shafts remain at Lincoln, Beverley, Westminster, and Salisbury, all built between 1240–50. Purbeck shafts used in the presbytery and choir at York Minster and quite out of context in the late fourteenth and early fifteenth centuries, probably came from the piers of the thirteenth-century central tower, which were remodelled just before the rebuilding of the eastern arm.

The tower probably had a timber spire like that at Long Sutton in Lincolnshire, for early seals show such a spire and an agreement of 1370 between the dean and chapter and John, son of Adam le Plummer of Beverley, refers to that part of the belfry called the spire (*vocatam Broche*).[79] Casting pits for bells were found in the north transept area by H. G. Ramm. Access to the upper stages would be by the Norman newel stairs to the north-east and south-east which existed until 1410. It is noteworthy that the pressure on the transepts was produced more by the weighty thirteenth-century tower than the later one.

The chapter-house

The octagonal chapter-house at York (Plate 30) is the largest in England and

[76] *CClR, 1231–4*, 403.

[77] *Chron. Mon. de Melsa*, ii. 238–9; *Hists. York* ii. 209.

[78] Browne, *History*, p. 9.

[79] John Britton, *History and Antiquities of the Metropolitical Church of York* (London, 1819), p. 80.

its stiff-leaf and naturalistic foliage carving is outstanding. It is the culmination of all previous lines of development of the polygonal chapter-house from Lincoln (1220–30) and Westminster (1245–53) to Salisbury (1263–84), and all these had stone vaults with a central column. Chapter-houses at Evesham (1282–1316) and Thornton (1282–1308) probably did not have a central column thus resembling that at Southwell (1287–93) which provides the closest analogy to York, but all are later than York and may have benefited by its experimentation. All these chapter-houses had roofs of flattish pitch and York also may have had the earliest flying buttresses in *c.* 1260.

Archbishop Roger of Pont l'Évêque may have erected a chapter-house when he built the grand new eastern arm, since a parish boundary, which indicated the east end of the late twelfth-century church, ran obliquely thence to the north, touching the main face of the chapter-house but ignoring the buttresses. Thus an earlier chapter-house may have stood on the site of the present one.

The present chapter-house may have been started as early as *c.* 1260, for masons who had worked on the north transept (finished by *c.* 1255) moved from there to work on it. It has a lavish use of Purbeck marble shafts. Some shafts are found in the northern province at Durham Galilee (*c.* 1170), Jervaulx chapter-house (*c.* 1190), St. Cuthbert's, Darlington (building in 1192), Fountains presbytery (1220), York north transept (begun *c.* 1230), and the eastern chapels at Durham (begun 1242). But the use of marble was not popular and was not used in sophisticated work at Hexham (*c.* 1180–1230), Rievaulx choir (*c.* 1220), Whitby (*c.* 1230), and Southwell choir. Though the naves of Lichfield (began in 1258) and Bridlington have a late form of stiff-leaf also found in the York chapter-house, they do not use marble. Thus in the north marble is associated with costly and rather alien work and detached shafts of it are not fashionable after 1242. In polygonal chapter-houses small shafts of marble are found at Lincoln (*c.* 1220), Westminster (1245), and Salisbury (1263) but not much later, and thus they are unfashionable after *c.* 1265. In the York area marble is not used at St. Mary's Abbey (1270–94), the cathedral chapter-house vestibule (finished by *c.* 1290), and the nave (begun in 1291). Thus the Purbeck marble shafts will be not much later than *c.* 1265 if judged by southern standards, or *c.* 1250 if judged by standards in the northern province.

Just over a fifth of all the foliage carving is of the conventional form called stiff-leaf, which is found fully developed as early as *c.* 1210 at Wells and lingers on until *c.* 1270.[80] Most of the stiff-leaf in York chapter-house is

[80] Lawrence Stone, *Sculpture in Britain, The Middle Ages* (1955), pp. 103, 140.

of orthodox form, but some with rosette shapes is moving towards naturalistic foliage and is found at Bridlington associated with ordinary stiff-leaf and at Lichfield nave (begun 1258).

There is more stiff-leaf on the south side, and on the inner parts of the seats; these capitals are the only ones with blue colour, which suggests that the south side was built first and perhaps in a different form, but there is still stiff-leaf in the upper parts, which are therefore not very much later in date.

The first design, associated with these earlier characteristics, had a stone vault at a lower level than the present one, probably with a central pier, and abutment was provided with boldly projecting flying buttresses and large pinnacles.

The chapter-house was remodelled soon afterwards and was completed by *c.* 1285, perhaps when Edward I and Queen Eleanor came for the Translation of St. William in 1284. Certainly on 1 July 1286 Archbishop John le Romeyn announced his intention of holding a visitation in it,[81] and was considering the appointment of a prebendary on 22 April 1295 in the new chapter-house;[82] parliamentary affairs were transacted there in the next year.[83]

Stylistic features confirm these dates. In the second half of the thirteenth century Geometrical windows show experiments with soffit cusps; blunt-ended ones are earlier and in the north are supplanted by pointed cusps with open spandrels. Blunt-ended soffit cusps are found at the east end of Rheims in the clerestory and aisles as early as 1211–41, and in England at Binham, Norfolk, and at Netley, Hampshire. They are at their best in the east front of Lincoln (begun after 1256 and consecrated 1280), and there are other blunt-ended cusps at St. Albans presbytery (begun in 1257), Salisbury cloister (begun 1263), the choir at Tintern (begun 1269 and completed 1287–8),[84] and in the choir aisles at Selby. This type of cusp was not popular in the north and the pointed cusp superseded it at St. Mary's Abbey, York (1270–94), York Minster nave (begun in 1291), and Guisborough east window (built after a fire in 1289). Thus the York chapter-house windows (Plate 31), although advanced in design, need be no later than *c.* 1285. There is insufficient evidence for the form of the earlier windows, which could have been lancets under a segmental containing arch as at Lincoln or the chapel of the Archbishop of York's Palace (now the Minster library). On the other hand the existing tracery may have been at a lower level and could have been reset later.

[81] *Reg. Romeyn*, pt. i (Surtees Soc., vol. 123, 1913), p. 355 (no. 1017).

[82] Ibid., pt. ii (Surtees Soc., vol. 128, 1917), p. 23 (no. 1166).

[83] *CClR, 1288–96*, 517.

[84] *William Worcestre*, ed. J. H. Harvey (Oxford, 1969), p. 61; communicated by J. H. Harvey.

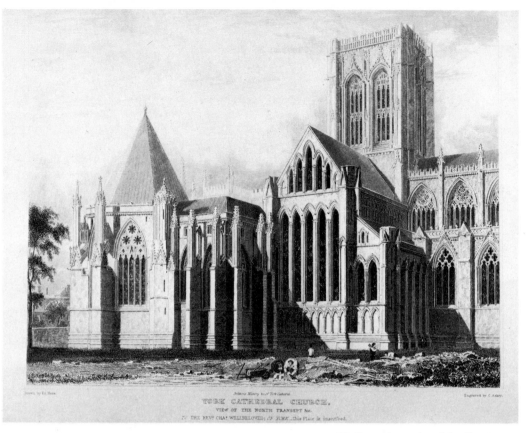

YORK CATHEDRAL CHURCH.
VIEW OF THE NORTH TRANSEPT &c.
TO THE REVᴰ CHAˢ WELLBELOVED; OF YORK This Plate is inscribed.

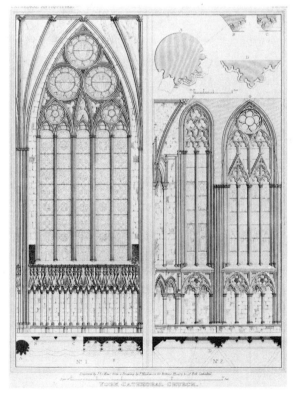

YORK CATHEDRAL CHURCH.

30 General exterior of the Chapter House by John Britton (1819) from the east. The flyers of the buttresses abutted a stone vault inside and when it was replaced the horizontal members were added to abut a wooden vault put at a higher level.

31 Scale drawing by John Britton (1819) showing one bay of the Chapter House (finished 1285) and 2 bays of the west wall of the vestibule (finished 1290). Note in the latter a buttress of *c.* 1250, and the windows, the right hand one of which is like one at St. Urbain at Troyes.

32 A wooden boss of the Chapter House vault (*c.* 1285) showing a rare representation of the Yellow Water Lily with its seeds popularly called brandy bottles.

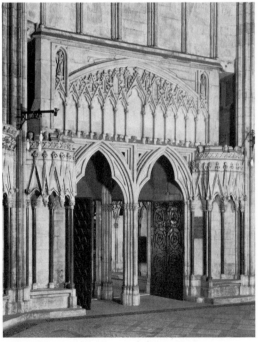

33 The Chapter House doorway in the west bay with 13th-C. door and an inscription on the north side.

34 General view of the Chapter House showing the sense of space. The window form over the entrance was always blind and the niches over the doorway held figures of Christ and the apostles, said to have been of silver.

All the foliage other than the stiff-leaf is naturalistic, found on the Continent at the Sainte Chapelle (1243–8) and Rheims Cathedral triforium (1250–6) in France and at Bamberg and Naumburg in Germany. It appears at Westminster and there are good examples in the Angel Choir at Lincoln (1256–80), while Exeter has excellent naturalistic foliage (1258–1303) and there are good examples on the shrines of St. Thomas Cantilupe at Hereford (1282) and St. Frideswides at Oxford (perhaps 1289). The closest analogies are in the chapter-house at Southwell (1287–93) and it seems possible that the York masons moved from York chapter-house to the one at Southwell and then back again to York chapter-house vestibule.

When the stone vault was replaced by the present wooden vault, the buttresses were provided with trabeation to counteract the thrust at a higher level. Two bosses in the vault show the yellow water lily, with the flask-like seed boxes, that give it the popular name of brandy bottle (Plate 32). It is only found elsewhere, to my knowledge, in the vault of the Angel Choir at Lincoln (finished in 1280) which helps to confirm the completion date of York chapter-house to *c.* 1285.

There was an important restoration under the direction of Sydney Smirke in 1845, when the canopies were restored, some new heads carved by George Peter White (1808–86), and the outer line of Purbeck marble shafts renewed. The floor of Minton tiles and the iron heating grilles are of this date.

Inside, the western bay has niches over the entrance doorway, said to have contained silver statues of the Saviour and Apostles, and the window form above was always blind (Plate 33). There are, in each of the outer bays, six seats under a great window with a wall-walk at its base (Plate 34). The capitals and pendants of the seat canopies are richly carved with foliage and figures and as well as stiff-leaf, there are representations of hawthorn, oak, maple, ivy, buttercup, vine, hop, rose, strawberry, bryony, and other plants. They were originally painted in red or blue and enhanced with gold leaf, and remnants of colour prove that at least five-sixths of the whole are original. On the outer faces of the canopies is a fine series of heads, several of which are of 1845, but all of excellent quality. (Plate 35). The vaulting shafts, standing the full height of the walls, have very fine foliated capitals; the wooden vault has large oak bosses (Plate 36) and above it is a medieval framed oak roof of great complexity.[85]

The chapter-house vestibule

The vestibule or some similar building was planned as early as *c.* 1250. The evidence is that on the north face of the north wall of the east aisle of the

---

[85] See J. Quentin Hughes, 'The Timber Roofs of York Minster', *YAJ*, pt. 152, xxxviii (1955).

35 An oblique view of the 5th bay showing the wealth of carving on the canopies of the seats, with naturalistic leaves on the capitals and pendants (finished by 1285) and the Purbeck marble shafts some of which are of *c.* 1260 and others of *c.* 1840.

36 The Chapter House vault finished by 1285 and with painting by Thomas Willement of *c.* 1840. The plaster web of the vault was fitted in *c.* 1780 and the whole has now (1976) been repainted.

north transept is a high-set round-headed blind arch of that date and designed for a special purpose. The lower part of the north wall of the vestibule courses through with the adjacent chapter-house buttress and wall, and can therefore be of *c.* 1260. At the east end of the vestibule the blind window over the doorway has blunt-ended cusps like a window form at the other end by the transept, which shows that they are related to the second period of the chapter-house (completed *c.* 1285).

However, the upper part of the vestibule is built against the chapter-house, and the windows have pointed soffit cusps like those at St. Mary's Abbey (1270–94). The wall arcading (Plate 37) is like that of the Angel Choir at Lincoln (1256–80) and the bosses of foliage in circles are found at Thornton chapter-house in Lincolnshire (begun 1282). The three large windows are like some at Old St. Paul's (*c.* 1260), at the east end of Ripon (started by Archbishop John le Romeyn in 1286), and the cloister at Lincoln (*c.* 1290). Dr. Peter Kidson has pointed out that the peculiar window, the tracery of which includes an arch and gable (Plate 31), is like one in the transept at S. Urbain Troyes (1260–70) and the cut circles are found in the choir there. The trilobes in another window, like some in the Minster nave (begun 1291) and in the vestibule at Westminster, are some of the earliest in England.[86]

The vestibule was completed by *c.* 1290 and then some of the masons moved to the nave (begun 1291), where their marks are also found.

The doorway from the transept (*c.* 1290) in a section of walling added on both sides of the earlier thirteenth-century one is built against vaulting shafts of the vestibule. The doorway itself would fit nicely under the string course of *c.* 1250 but the upper part blocks the wall passage of that date and could be later. The vestibule is not well laid out, as can be seen at the north-west angle, and whereas the windows are accurately fitted, the buttresses are misplaced.[86]

The bays vary in width and the windows differ, but in general each interior bay has a wall bench, blind arcading, and a geometrical window. The carving is even better than that of the chapter-house, is by the same sculptors as that at Southwell, and is naturalistic, with some stiff-leaf, but there is none of the undulating foliage found in the nave. The entrance from the transept has elaborate fifteenth-century doors, and that to the chapter-house has doors with excellent thirteenth-century ironwork. The stone vault has moulded ribs and good bosses, and the medieval colouration has

---

[86] For details see Nicola Coldstream, 'York Chapter House', *JBAA*, 3rd Ser. xxxv (1972).
[87] Sidney Melmore, 1971 for 1969–70 York Minster, 'Notes on the Construction of the Chapter House and Vestibule,' *YAJ*, pt. 167, xlii, 345–8.

37 Arcading of the south wall of the Chapter House vestibule of *c.* 1290 with excellent capitals and boss like forms in the tracery.

38 The stone vault of the vestibule looking east (*c.* 1290) with original painting.

recently been touched up (Plate 38). In the late fourteenth century the walls were decorated with heraldry, only a shadow of which remains.

A room was put over the vestibule in the early fourteenth century and although a timber roof immediately above the vestibule vaulting was removed, holes for the tie-beams still remain (Plate 39). The walls were heightened, and extra abutment was provided by window-forms added to the exterior pinnacles and acting as flying buttresses; the tops of the pinnacles are crocketted with 'sea weed' foliage and could be of the same date as the early fourteenth-century scissors roof inside. The room is well lit, has a fireplace and a garderobe, and was used as a masons' drawing office perhaps as early as *c.* 1365.[88] Otherwise it could have been a library, for in 1410 a new masons' lodge was planned and the new library was built on the south side of the nave in 1414–19. It could never have been a masons' lodge for the limited access would not allow for the movement of large blocks of stone, but it certainly was a drawing office and its gypsum floor illustrates the procedure of masoncraft. The master of the masons drew a full-scale moulding on the gypsum, and then a template, called the mould, was made from it. The work of each mason could be tested by the template and his mark on the stone proved his identity. There are still some late eighteenth- and nineteenth-century templates hanging on the walls, and at the south end is the head of one of the lancets in the early thirteenth-century east aisle of the north transept, perfectly preserved (Plate 40).

Monuments
York Minster has very few monuments of the period before 1290, but three burials of archbishops in the south transept are noteworthy. The transept is always associated with *Walter de Gray*, son of John de Gray of Rotherfield, Oxfordshire, nephew of John, bishop of Norwich (d. 1214) and archbishop of York (1216–55). In 1241 he directed that he should be buried in front of an altar which he had founded and dedicated to St. Michael, the site of which, in the central bay of the east aisle, is confirmed by a boss of St. Michael in the vault above the monument.

His fine thirteenth-century tomb (Plate 41) has, on a low chest, a Purbeck marble effigy (Plate 42) from the same shop as that of William de Kilkenny, bishop of Ely (d. 1256), for both have lateral shafts held by sprays of stiff-leaf. The canopy, held by nine shafts of marble with stiff-leaf capitals and water-holding bases, has a series of deeply moulded trefoiled arches with excellent carving in the spandrels. So far the monument is a complete production of the Purbeck workshop and the effigy has none of the

---

[88] *FAR*, 40 (1968) J. H. Harvey 'The Tracing Floor in York Minster'.

39 The south arm of the masons' drawing office (*c.* 1330) above the vestibule, with a scissors roof and showing at the end the pent roof of the east aisle of the north transept (*c.* 1250).

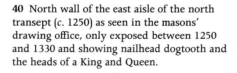

40 North wall of the east aisle of the north transept (*c.* 1250) as seen in the masons' drawing office, only exposed between 1250 and 1330 and showing nailhead dogtooth and the heads of a King and Queen.

41 The tomb of Archbishop Walter de Gray (d. 1255) in the east aisle of the south transept, with effigy under a Purbeck marble canopy, freestone top and finials of 18th-C. date by Bernasconi.

42 (below left). Purbeck marble effigy of Walter de Gray. The stock figure of a Bishop, as there is no pallium or cross. **43** (below right). The Archbishop's coffin *in situ* with on the lid the full length painted figure with pallium and archiepiscopal cross, painted soon after death but before the effigy had arrived from Purbeck.

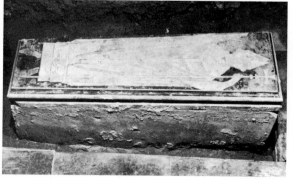

distinctive marks of an archbishop. Above are blind arches on short shafts, with good head stops and under crocketted gables, but here the material is Huddleston limestone. The local addition turns an excellent Purbeck tomb into the finest monument of its date. There are traces of colour and gold, and the bird finials were added in plaster, by Francis Bernasconi, in 1803–5.

When the tomb was being dismantled in January 1968 for restoration, the removal of the effigy revealed that, prior to the arrival of an order from Purbeck, the coffin lid had been decorated with the life-size painting of the archbishop, this time with both pallium and cross-shaft (Plate 43). However, the order was executed promptly, and when mortar was put on the lid to take the effigy, moisture attracted some of the colour, not yet properly set, up into it. The coffin was opened on 3 May 1968 and, with the body, was the largest and most important ring yet found with a bishop, which had a large uncut sapphire set in a bezel adorned with minute rubies and emeralds, each set separately; there was a silver parcel-gilt chalice and paten, and a pastoral staff (perhaps as early as 1214) with a head of walrus ivory.

To the south of Walter de Gray, the coffin of his successor *Sewal de Bovil* (1256–8), already opened and the chalice and paten removed in the eighteenth century, was found in November 1974 to be in its original position. The tomb itself, like the existing one of Godfrey de Ludham but higher, was moved into the presbytery in 1735–6, badly damaged in the fire of 1839, and its plinth was moved back into the south transept in 1883.

On 4 February 1969 the tomb of *Godfrey de Ludham*, archbishop 1258–65, to the north of that of Gray and retaining its original Purbeck marble slab with a cross on it and supported on low arcading, was opened. The archbishop had an intact pallium, a ring with uncut sapphire, a silver chalice and paten, and a staff with elegant head of stiff-leaf in wood.[89]

I have derived much benefit from discussions with Dr. John Harvey and Mr. John Miller and with Mr. T. W. French, whose observation of detail and masons' marks beyond my reach has been invaluable. Without the excavations, ably directed by Mr. Derek Phillips, much of the early part of this chapter could not have been written. Mr. Bernard Barr and his staff at the Minster library have constantly aided my researches.

[89] H. G. Ramm *et al.*, *The Tombs of Archbishop of Walter de Gray . . . and Godfrey de Ludham* (Soc. of Antiquaries, Oxford, 1971).

CHAPTER IV

Architectural History from 1291 to 1558

John H. Harvey

It was on 6 April 1291 that the archbishop, John le Romeyn, laid the foundation-stone for the new nave, at the east end on the south side.[1] The laying of this stone was a formal function and must have taken place some time after the real start of work; that in turn was necessarily subsequent to the official approval of a design already formulated. Though no records have survived of the steps taken to obtain the design there is evidence that it must have been settled in principle before the end of the year 1289. On 26 December houses belonging to the prebend of Dunnington were assigned to the cathedral school in place of the old school which had been wholly made over to the fabric of the church.[2] The old school was evidently in the angle between the Norman nave and the south transept, and its site was essential for the widening of the nave called for by the new plan.

The decision to replace the old nave with its wide span and solid walls by an orthodox design including both arcades and aisles was a fundamental one. While the great transept of two generations before seems to have been built on its own merits, the fresh design for the nave certainly implied the later rebuilding of the eastern arm in Gothic style. Hence the design, which was doubtless recorded on a large sheet of parchment, will have been preserved in the master mason's tracing-house until the completion of the Minster as we know it. Revised designs and details for the successive parts doubtless accumulated to form a large collection of drawings, comparable to those which have survived at Vienna.[3] While the precise forms of each part of the building differed according to the individual styles of each architect, the general character and proportions of the new church were laid down by the master who prepared the plans for a fresh start not later than 1289.

[1] *Hists. York* ii. 409.
[2] *Reg. Romeyn*, i. 381–2; cf. A. Raine, *Mediaeval York* (1955), pp. 32, 37.
[3] H. Tietze in *Jahrbuch der kunsthistorischen Sammlungen in Wien*, N.F. iv, v, (1930–1); and in *Österreichische Kunsttopographie*, xxiii (Vienna, 1931); H. Koepf, *Die gotischen Planrisse der Wiener Sammlungen* (Vienna, 1969).

The character of the design was quite different from that of the transept, whose Early English style was outmoded by the Geometrical Decorated. This involved the use of bar-tracery, invented at Rheims Cathedral soon after 1210, and introduced to England at Westminster Abbey in 1245.[4] The new fashion did not merely involve such decorative elements but also a more sophisticated approach to spatial unity and composition. In the design of the bay—each separate section of the building between supports—the long search for a satisfactory solution was at last rewarded. The old scheme of horizontal division into the three stages of arcade, triforium, and clerestory was given up in favour of a united upper storey, the mullions of the windows being prolonged downwards to form a grille in front of the triforium which was visually absorbed.[5] The nave of York marks the point where tentative approaches to this ideal reached maturity (Plate 44).

The design shows a full awareness on the part of its architect of what had been happening in northern France as well as in England. It is not the outcome of pioneering enthusiasm but of slowly acquired knowledge; it marked the culmination of its period before the break from the restraint of the Geometrical into the fluid movement of the Curvilinear. Before the nave had been completed this revolution had been accomplished by its second master, who finished the west front in a manner absolutely distinct from that of the start. Yet, as we shall see, the original architect himself had radically changed the design while the nave was in course of erection to include the new front itself.

The Gothic cathedral was largely conditioned by the size and layout of its Norman predecessor. The Geometrical designer did not have a free hand and the proportions of his work were governed by the old building and by practical and economic considerations. The old foundations of the Norman side walls were accepted as a hidden stylobate for the new piers; and this placing of the arcades on the alignment of the former walls automatically determined the module for the Gothic plan. Everything else was derived from this dimension of about 27 feet, the width of one of the new bays or half the span of the nave from the central axis of the northern arcade to central axis of the southern. The same unit gave the height from the floor to the capitals, and by the proportion of 'ad quadratum' the diagonal of the square erected on this unit, or diagon,[6] was used as half the height to the

---

[4] The front of Binham Priory, Norfolk, built between 1226 and 1244 was not necessarily the surviving west front, which has bar tracery (see F. Bond, *Gothic Architecture in England*, 1906, pp. 469–71).

[5] J. Harvey, *The Gothic World* (1950), p. 78.

[6] K. J. Conant 'The After-life of Vitruvius in the Middle Ages', in *Jour. of the Soc. of Architectural Historians*, xxvii (Philadelphia, 1968), 33–8.

44 Interior of the nave, looking west. Designed 1290, with west window of 1338; the wooden ▷
vault is a copy of that of 1354–60 by Philip Lincoln, master carpenter.

springing of the windows of the clerestory. Though the resulting proportions were taller than those of the transept they still seem wide and low by the standards of France. Notwithstanding some resemblances to French work the essential character of the nave is English.

In spite of this fundamental distinction there is so marked a likeness to Troyes Cathedral, whose works were then in progress, that it has to be asked whether there was any direct link. The York master, presumably English, might have spent his wander-years working in the Troyes lodge. This could be mere chance, but the background of political history affords another possibility. The younger brother of Edward I, Edmund of Lancaster (1245–96), in 1275 married Blanche of Artois, the widow of Henri III of Navarre and Champagne, and in right of his wife had the custody of Champagne *de jure* until 1284 and *de facto* even later. Troyes, as the capital of Champagne, was thus bound to England by the closest links of kinship and diplomacy, and tension between the courts of London and Paris meant, at that particular time, that English craftsmen in search of French architectural experience would be particularly likely to visit Champagne.[7]

It has been pointed out that several tracery designs used in the later work of the York chapter-house vestibule appear to be derived from the church of S. Urbain at Troyes (choir, 1262–6), rather than from the cathedral.[8] Yet the details of the chapter-house are clearly not by the same hand as those of the nave, in spite of the transfer of some working masons from the one job to the other, as shown by their marks.[9] The conclusion of the chapter-house and its vestibule was perhaps roughly simultaneous with the beginning of the nave, whose foundations were probably dug in 1290, and the works establishment could thus have maintained continuity. On the other hand, there seems to have been a change of architect. Who the earlier and later architects were will be discussed after considering further the origin of the nave design.

Although obviously under strong influence from Troyes Cathedral, the unity of bay treatment derived also from a line of English development of which the latest example was the choir of York's suffragan cathedral at Southwell. This series of English attempts to produce unity in bay design began earlier than the version achieved at Troyes after 1228. Elimination of the triforium, or its absorption into the clerestory, had occurred at Llanthony Priory as far back as *c.* 1180–1210, was carried by a Bristol master to Dublin for the nave of Christ Church Cathedral (begun 1213), and

[7] J. Harvey, *The Mediaeval Architect* (1972), p. 157.

[8] N. Coldstream, 'York Chapter House', in *JBAA*, 3rd Ser. xxxv (1972), 21, quoting Dr. Peter Kidson.

[9] Information from Dr. E. A. Gee, to whom I am indebted for access to his collection of masons' marks.

is found in the new choir of Pershore Abbey built between 1223 and 1239.[10] There, and at Southwell between 1234 and 1250, the motive reached maturity, but had not yet been applied to a church of grand scale such as York. The effect of the York bays would have been of pronounced verticality had it not been for the immense span dictated by the Norman foundations.

In another respect the nave was, as at first designed, much more markedly French. The aisles were perhaps to be roofed, not longitudinally, but with gabled roofs transversely, bay by bay (Plate 171, below). The gables were later incorporated into a horizontal parapet, but their sloping bed-joints, not bonded to the level coursing, betray the original scheme.[11] Since this method of construction applies throughout to both north and south aisles, the change of idea must have come rather late in the period of construction, perhaps about 1320. Another change had been decided upon earlier, when the walls had reached the first stringcourse, beneath the windows. The responds carrying the stone vaults of the north aisle appear to be later insertions up to this level, though coursed with the wall higher up; this seems to imply that it was not at first intended that the aisles should be vaulted in stone.

Far more radical was the alteration to the original proposals demanded by the decision to incorporate lateral towers in the new west front (Plate 45). Both aisles were set out to run in equal bays to the present line of the front, and it seems that they had actually been built, together with their western returns and windows, with the intention of retaining the pair of towers that had been added in the late twelfth century to the Norman west end.[12] It was then, *c*. 1315–20, determined that the old towers should be pulled down, with the result that two afterthoughts can be detected in the building as it stands. The wider lateral buttresses of the present towers swallow up part of the aisle wall so as to produce an apparently narrow bay; and internally the responds between the tower-bay and the rest of the aisles were enlarged so as to cut off a half-bay of wall arcading which had been designed, and probably actually built, from end to end. The second afterthought resulted in the great central west window of the Minster, a substantially later insertion of 1338, designed by another architect.

The architects of York Minster, from the start of the nave onwards, were

[10] Above, n. 5; also J. Harvey, *The Master Builders* (1971), p. 66 and Figs. 47–9; *Dublin: a Study in Environment* (1949; rev. and enlarged Wakefield, 1972), p. 103 and Fig. 154.

[11] This important fact was, I believe, first observed by Dr. E. A. Gee.

[12] Foundations of these towers were discovered in recent excavations; see B. Hope-Taylor, *Under York Minster* (Dean and Chapter of York, 1971), pp. 20–1.

the master masons who are known to us by name.[13] Surviving records are not explicit, however, as to the share that each had in the work, and it is necessary to compare the historical evidence with that of the building. Individual styles can be made out and have to be linked to the architects responsible. Notwithstanding the changes outlined above, there is unity of design throughout both north and south aisles as far as, and including, their western returns and windows. Designed by 1289–90 and begun in 1291, the eastern bays must have been roofed by 1310 and probably earlier, to permit the glazing of the two eastern windows. That on the north, the Heraldic or Peter de Dene window, is regarded by Mr. T. W. French as almost certainly of 1307–8; that on the south not very much later.[14] These windows are important for the use by the glaziers of the new secret of yellow stain, here first found in England, and probably introduced from Spain, though ultimately of Arab origin.[15] Their dating is important for us in another way, since it helps to establish continuous activity for some twenty years on the first phase of the work of the nave.

There was in fact, during the latter half at any rate of that period, one very distinguished master mason, Simon by name, associated with the Minster. In 1301 he paid £1 6s. 8d. in tax, as compared with 1s. 4d. and 11d. from two other York masons. When he made his will on 24 June 1322 he desired to be buried in the nave, and the will was proved in the peculiar court of the dean and chapter, thus showing that he lived in the precincts. He had taken up the freedom of the city in 1315 so as to be able to trade in York, and made marble tombs, as did other noted cathedral masters of the time. This Master Simon of York must be distinguished from several other masters of the same name who flourished in the second half of the thirteenth century. Simon de Tresk (Thirsk, Yorks.) worked on Lincoln Minster from about 1255 and soon afterwards was called 'Magister', having charge of the building of the Angel Choir (*c*. 1256–80) and holding the office of master of the work of Lincoln Cathedral until January 1291. At York the new church of St. Mary's Abbey was begun at the east end in 1270 and was finished in 1294. The start of the work was under a Master Simon the mason (*Cementarius*) who is also described as Simon de Papinham and whose death on 13 May was commemorated by the monks. The year of his death may

---

[13] References are not given for those masters included in J. Harvey, *English Mediaeval Architects* (1954).

[14] Personal communication from Mr. T. W. French, who has made a fresh study of the heraldic and other evidence; see also n. 25 below.

[15] On yellow (silver) stain see L. Williams, *The Arts and Crafts of Older Spain* (1907), ii. 225–7; N. Heaton in *Jour. of the Brit. Soc. of Master Glass-Painters*, x, no. 1 (1947–8), 9–16; *History of Technology*, ed. C. Singer, E. J. Holmyard, A. R. Hall, and T. I. Williams (5 vols., 1954–8), ii. 12.

◁ **45** West front. The central gable and great window of *c*. 1335–38 are here attributed to Ivo de Raghton. The western towers were built 1432–72 to a design probably by William Waddeswyk.

have been 1280 or within a few years earlier.[16] The place 'Papinham' is certainly Pavenham in Bedfordshire, also spelt 'Pabenham', and it seems significant that there was another Simon de Pabenham who had an important career as a mason working for the Crown and for the City of London from 1282, and died in 1334. A close relationship to the York master who also was presumably born at Pavenham would explain the manifest influence of the Court style upon St. Mary's Abbey and upon the design of the chapter-house of York Minster.

The nave, as has been said, differs in character from the chapter-house, but it is by no means unlikely that the architect of the nave was a son of the master of St. Mary's Abbey, who may well have been the designer of the Minster chapter-house vestibule too. Chronologically it is at least possible that Simon de Papinham was uncle of the London Simon; who in that case could have been the first cousin of Master Simon of York who died in 1322. Although this pedigree remains hypothetical, it would go far to explain the up-to-date design at York, preceding by some years the arrival of Edward I and the Law Courts at the time of the Scottish war.[17] Although the work was 'modern' for 1289, it has to be emphasized that it remained strictly Geometrical until the west front was being closed after removal of the twelfth-century towers somewhere about 1320 (Plate 46). Everything suggests that the oversight of the works remained essentially in the hands of the same architect, Master Simon, until his death in 1322. There remains, however, the problem of a minor intrusion of a different style above the central west doorway in the front. The arch of the opening has a moulding enriched with vine-scroll in Curvilinear fashion, the oculus above the doors has trefoils with markedly ogee curves, and there is some use of pellets in the manner of ball-flower; in the small gable or pediment above the doors the ball-flower enrichment itself is used (Plate 47), the only occurrence on the outside of the Minster.

These stylistic discrepancies can be linked directly to the mention of one Hugh de Boudon as 'master of the work of masonry of the greater church of St. Peter of York' about 1310, when he paid visits to the royal works of Knaresborough Castle to take charge at times when the London master, Hugh Titchmarsh, was absent.[18] It is highly significant, as Dr. Eric Gee has pointed out, that ball-flower enrichment is used on the work of this period

---

[16] *The Ordinal and Customary of the Abbey of St. Mary, York* (Henry Bradshaw Soc. lxxxiv, 1949–50), iii. (1951), 370; YML, MS. XVI A.2, fo. 86.

[17] The courts of law were settled in York from 1298 to 1304, as well as for many years later in the fourteenth century; see below, n. 51, also *VCH York*, pp. 29, 522; *YAJ* xlii. 199.

[18] H. M. Colvin (ed.), *The History of the King's Works* (1963), ii. 689. 'Boudon' is not necessarily one of the many places called Bowden or Bowdon; it is more probably a variant of the local Bootham (Bouthom, Boudom).

(1307–12) at Knaresborough, but is rare in York. Boudon, whose name may well represent the York suburb of Bootham, was probably undermaster at the Minster where, perhaps because of the grand scale of the works, two masters were concurrently in charge for much of the fourteenth century. This is specifically evidenced in 1345 and 1352, when rules for the workmen were to be administered by 'the chief mason and second mason, who are called their masters, and the carpenter of the fabric.'[19] Boudon's appearance as designer may have been due to Master Simon's absence or illness, or to his having undertaken a heavy burden of other work.

The completion of the nave and front was long delayed, and several masters were successively concerned. William Worsall, who seems already to have been a mason of standing in 1327 and who took up the freedom of York ten years later, was undermaster in 1345 when an inquiry was held into the serious defects in the (nave) roof, the unfinished state of the buttresses, and losses of materials. The master, not then named, was probably the Thomas de Pacenham who was in charge by 1348 and had an official residence, but died about a year later, probably of the Black Death. Before Pacenham's time, about 1338, the great west window had been inserted in a remarkable Curvilinear style approaching the Flamboyant, undoubtedly designed by an outstanding architect who was not involved on the Minster except for part of the west front. An impressive body of circumstantial and stylistic evidence suggests that this designer was Ivo de Raghton, the master in charge of Archbishop Melton's work in York in 1331.[20] Ivo, from Raughton in Cumberland, had taken up the freedom of York in 1317 and ten years later was by far the wealthiest mason in the city. On stylistic grounds he appears to have originated the richly flowing form of Curvilinear employed on the whole series of works patronized by Melton: the east front at Carlisle, designed soon after 1318; the reredos at Beverley in progress in 1324–34, the great east window of Selby Abbey of *c.* 1330, and the carved base for St. William's shrine at York.[21]

From the contracts for the stained glass and Melton's payments it is known that the western windows of the aisles were ready for glazing by 1338 and the central window within the same twelve months.[22] A change in detail (Plate 48) just below the apex of the great window internally implies

[19] *Fabric Rolls*, pp. 163, 171.

[20] Harvey, *Mediaeval Architect*, pp. 79–80 and refs. (p. 282).

[21] The substantial remains of the freestone base for St. William's shrine, as well as those of its Frosterley marble successor of 1471, are in the Yorkshire Museum.

[22] Dixon and Raine, *Fasti Ebor.*, pp. 432 (reading 1331 for '1332'; see BIHR, R.I.9, fo. 46), 434; YML, Torre MS. L 1(2), pt. ii, p. 56 (abstract of lost Chapter Act-Book, 1314–93, fo. 69), a volume rediscovered by Mr. C. B. L. Barr, to whom I am indebted for pointing out this, the best surviving version of the glazing contracts; cf. Browne, *Fabric Rolls*, p. 38.

that a new master took over before it was finished, and probably that Ivo de Raghton had died about 1338–9.[23] Though responsible only for a small part of the Minster, Master Ivo was certainly one of the most distinguished and original of the architects concerned in its erection. The magnificent sweep of his handling of the great west window puts into the shade the mediocre detail of the other Curvilinear windows in the middle stage of the towers. These are obviously by another master, probably by two different men, of whom one was doubtless Pacenham and the other perhaps his successor William Hoton senior, or else the undermaster Worsall. The fourth stage of niches on the tower buttresses, immediately below the springing of the west window, with 'nodding ogee' canopies (Plate 49), and the gable above the window, belong to the work of Ivo de Raghton somewhere between 1322 and 1338.

At the inquiry of 1345 it was stated that the carpenter was one W., an old man no longer able to work at a height, and decreed that a young man should take over; this was Philip de Lincoln, appointed on 1 August 1346. He continued in charge of the timberwork of the Minster until 1375 at least, and was responsible for the whole of the original timber vaulting of the nave, now replaced by a replica made after the fire of 1840. The outer roofs, in such a bad state that there were deep pools of water in the nave in 1345, must have been erected by 1338 when it was decided to glaze the west window, a work which would not be undertaken until the central span had been covered. It was no doubt arranged for the glazing to be done from the last bay of the scaffolding of the interior used for roofing. Probably because of the great pestilence of 1348–9, the vaulting was not completed for many years, and additional timber for it was being sought from Archbishop Thoresby in January 1356.[24] The work must then have been pushed on to reach substantial completion of the whole nave by about 1360, in time for operations to be transferred to the eastern arm in the next season.

The whole building of the nave therefore occupied some seventy years, two generations or the extent of a lifetime. Begun in the Geometrical style, it was not finished until after the appearance of Perpendicular characteristics, yet its most distinguished feature is the Curvilinear west window with its glass of 1339. The earlier glass in the aisles displays, as has been said, the first known yellow stain produced by the silver process, a cardinal landmark in the history of glass-painting. Furthermore, the date for the glass in the clerestory windows suggested by Mr. French, around 1320–30—stylistically intermediate between the eastern aisle windows and

[23] I am indebted to the dean and chapter for permission to inspect the details of the window when it was scaffolded in March 1967.
[24] *Fabric Rolls*, pp. 170–1.

46 Nave clerestory window; the tracery design is here attributed to Master Simon.

47 West front: detail of gablet over central doorway, showing ballflower ornament, *c.* 1310; here attributed to Master Hugh de Boudon.

48 West window of nave, interior. Detail of bases of nichework near head, 1338, showing (left) the typical design throughout most of the window, here attributed to Ivo de Raghton; and (right) a base marking the transition towards Perpendicular, possibly by Thomas Pacenham.

the west windows—indicates that the nave had been roofed only some thirty years from the start.[25] The long gap, a whole generation, between the building of the outer roof and the completion of the inner wooden vault, bears striking witness to the difficulties, financial even more than technical, which faced the builders.

The eastern arm of the church

While it is possible that the grand design of Master Simon already envisaged the rebuilding of the old choir, this project certainly existed before 1348. One of the canons, Thomas Sampson, then bequeathed £20 to the fabric of the new choir provided it were begun within a year of his death.[26] The will was proved on 4 July 1349 and the size of the legacy seems to have secured prompt action, for the Zouche Chapel, already begun by 1350, shows by its precise alignment that the new choir must already have been set out on the ground. The start of work on the chapel was apparently on 23 April 1350 and if this means that setting-out was then possible, a still earlier date for marking out the new walls of the choir is implied.[27] By superimposition of the plan of the existing Minster upon that of the twelfth-century choir it can be seen that the foundations of the Zouche Chapel were so arranged as to be built around the south-eastern transept of the old work, which was no doubt to be left undisturbed as long as possible. The foundations for the outer walls of the new choir could be dug and laid throughout the rest of their length quite clear of the earlier work.

The Zouche Chapel, together with the two vestries between it and the east wall of the great south transept, is in a style quite distinct from any other part of the Minster (Plate 53). The details are unusual but the general character, and particularly that of the vault of the chapel, belongs to the middle of the fourteenth century. The stones for the vault were probably prepared well before the date of erection, which would have had to wait for demolition of the old south-east transept at a much later stage. The vestries, even though their walls could have been erected at any time, were vaulted with re-used materials of late Romanesque type undoubtedly from the demolished choir. Their completion may, therefore, have been delayed for thirty years or more. They must have been roofed before 8 December 1394 when the 'new vestry' began to be used for services after the abandonment of Roger's choir.[28]

---

[25] T. W. French in *AntJ*, li (1971), 87, revised in personal communication, 21 Dec. 1973. I am grateful to Mr. French for much help over matters of dating.

[26] *Testamenta Eboracensia*, i (Surtees Soc. iv, 1836), 54.

[27] Dixon and Raine, *Fasti Ebor.*, pp. 447–8, n. v.

[28] *Hists. York* ii. 426.

50 Nave pier. Capitals of *c.* 1305, here attributed to Master Simon.

49 West front, exterior. Niche-head with nodding ogee, *c.* 1335, here attributed to Ivo de Raghton.

51 Nave, interior. Triforium arcade, showing continuity of design beneath clerestory windows, *c.* 1315; here attributed to Master Simon.

52 Nave, interior. Detail in north-west angle, *c.* 1325.

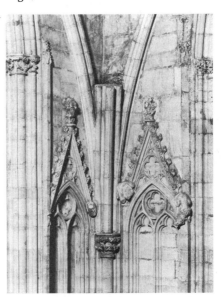

53 Zouche Chapel, begun 1350 under William Hoton senior, completed before 1394.

54 Choir, exterior. South side, showing the eastern work of the Lady Chapel (right); the aisles begun in 1361 under William Hoton junior, the clerestory designed after 1368 by Robert Patrington. To the west is the choir, built between 1385 and 1400 by Hugh Hedon. In the foreground are the Vestries and Zouche Chapel.

Apart from the Zouche Chapel, paid for by the archbishop's funds and very likely designed by his own master rather than by the Minster architect William Hoton the elder who supervised the work, the eastern arm was built in two main campaigns (Plate 54). As was normal, it was the east end that came first, for that could be erected to full height without taking down any part of the existing choir. The plan involved an eastward lengthening for three bays beyond the old front, but the line of the new east wall had to be kept back (as shown by the narrow end bay) to clear the west end of the little church of St. Mary ad Valvas, not pulled down until a date later than August 1365.[29] In the meantime Archbishop Thoresby had laid the first stone on 29 July 1361, and the Lady Chapel was substantially complete at his death, on 6 November 1373.[30] That is to say that the four easternmost bays of the present Minster, built around the old east end, were finished as regards the outer walls, though the tracery of the great east window had not been inserted. At least the two eastern bays must have been roofed, for Thoresby was buried in the new chapel in front of the altar. But it seems more probable that the eastern bays of the old choir had been demolished, so that the whole Lady Chapel of three standard bays and the narrower eastern bay, could have been structurally complete (Plate 55).

The Lady Chapel is not to a single design, but consists of three separate elements. The first of these includes both aisle walls with their windows, including those to the east, and must be due to the master mason, William Hoton the younger, who had succeeded his father on 1 October 1351. He died during the course of the works and was succeeded by master Robert de Patryngton, appointed on 5 January 1369. Hoton's full-size setting-out for the early Perpendicular tracery of the aisle windows survives on the plaster floor (Plate 56) of the tracing-house above the chapter-house vestibule.[31] As the earliest recognizable drawing there it proves that the tracing-house had been brought into use by about 1360 at the latest. The design is uninspired, but was accepted in principle for the aisle windows of the later western bays (Plate 57); this tends to confirm an original intention to build the whole of the Lady Chapel and choir to a single design.

The main arcades and clerestory tell a different story and bear the stamp of a designer of markedly higher rank, evidently Robert de Patryngton. Patryngton's imaginative design for the clerestory, with external

---

[29] YML, L 1(2), pt. ii. p. 74 (from lost Chapter Act-Book, 1353–76, fo. 52); also BM, Harleian MS. 6971, fo. 119.

[30] *Hists. York* ii. 420; cf. the indenture of 20 July 1361 providing for the materials of the destroyed hall of the archbishop at Sherburn-in-Elmet to be given to the new choir (Browne, *Fabric Rolls*, pp. 51–6).

[31] J. Harvey in 40th *Report of the Friends of York Minster for 1968* (1969), 11.

screenwork and window traceries including Flamboyant elements, combined with Perpendicular detail of fine quality, is another high-water mark. An interesting feature, found both on the internal niches of the Lady Chapel and on the outside of the clerestory screenwork, is the use of mouldings intersecting at right-angles. Patryngton's style is sharp and crisp, and highly recognizable, and markedly different from the earlier work of Hoton. The third element in the design of the work consists of the tracery of the great east window (Plate 58). It was certainly inserted long after the structural completion of the east front, which must have been boarded up from about 1373 until shortly before the glass was made in 1405–8.[32] On the exterior the mouldings change at the level of the springing, from which an enriched casement runs up to the apex, belonging with the inserted tracery. The design may have been by Patryngton, but was perhaps modified after his disappearance from the scene in or after 1385.

After Thoresby's death there is little evidence of active work for some ten or twelve years. The delay was probably due to shortage of funds, for steps were taken in 1377 to appropriate the church of Misterton to the completion of the choir for a period of ten years. In 1385 an eighty-year lease of a stone quarry at Huddleston was taken, but in 1390 there was a complaint at the archbishop's visitation that the income of the fabric had been diverted and the work delayed.[33] Active demolition of Roger's choir probably started soon after this although, as already mentioned, it was not until December 1394 that services began to be performed in the new vestry.[34] Active prosecution of the work on the five western bays (the choir and presbytery) then began, and was assisted by the king's gift of 100 marks (£66 13s. 4d.) early in 1395.[35] Later in the year Richard II made the still more valuable gift of a relic of one of the Holy Innocents, which was enclosed in a silver and gilt shrine and carried into the Minster on 28 December 1395, apparently in the king's presence.[36]

The royal gifts were marked by the carving of the king's badge of a white hart, crowned and chained, on the capital at the springing of the main arcade on the south-east crossing pier, facing the south choir aisle. The eastern crossing piers of the thirteenth-century central tower were cased in new masonry and at the springing of the crossing arches, 40 feet higher up,

[32] The best surviving version of the contract for the glass (from lost Chapter Act-Book, 1390–1410, fo. 90) is in YML, L 1(2), pt. ii, p. 34, but this can be supplemented from BM, Harleian MS. 6971, fo. 141[v].

[33] Browne, *History*, p. 248; *Fabric Rolls*, p. 13; Willis, *York Cathedral*, p. 43.

[34] See above, n. 28.

[35] J. Harvey in F. R. H. DuBoulay and C. M. Barron (eds.), *The Reign of Richard II* (1971), p. 207.

[36] *Hists. York* ii. 426.

◁ **55** Choir, interior looking east. The four eastern bays forming the Lady Chapel of 1361–72, by William Hoton junior and Robert Patringon; the western bays of 1385–1400 by Hugh Hedon. The altar-screen, now a copy of that of *c.* 1425, is here attributed to John Long.

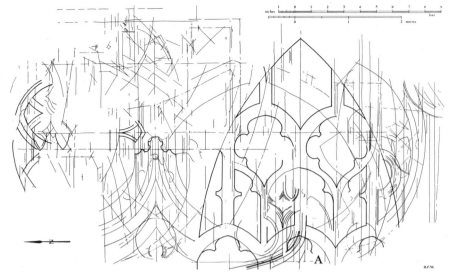

56 A. Tracing floor, above vestibule of Chapter House. Superimposed drawings on plaster, dating from *c.* 1360 to *c.* 1500. Above A is the full-size setting-out of the window tracery for the aisles of the Lady Chapel, begun in 1361 under Master William Hoton junior.

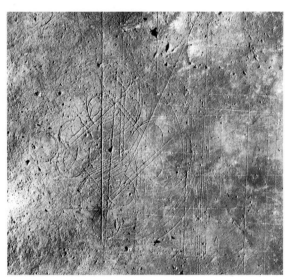

56 B. Tracing floor, above vestibule of Chapter House. Detail of setting-out on plaster, second half of the fourteenth century.

57 Choir. Window of north aisle, *c.* 1395, here attributed to Hugh Hedon, adapting the earlier design of William Hoton junior.

there is a carved head of an emperor, apparently alluding to Richard's negotiations for the imperial throne, public by the autumn of 1397 (Plate 60). These allusive enrichments give some indication of the progress of work, also marked by various substantial bequests of funds and by an exemption from tolls on the River Aire for stone carried to the works, granted in 1400 by the new king, Henry IV, as duke of Lancaster.[37] Another crowned head on the south side of the south-east crossing pier at a high level may well be Henry's portrait.

The details and mouldings employed show that the five western bays, linking the new Lady Chapel to the crossing, and the recasing of the crossing piers and arches, were all by the same designer (Plate 61). This was Hugh de Hedon, who took up the freedom of York in 1394 and was certainly master mason in 1399 and 1404. Though Hedon accepted the earlier design for the aisles, his arcades and clerestory are manifestly distinct from the precedents set by Hoton and by Patryngton. The clerestory in particular reversed the position of the screenwork, placing it internally and the tracery on the outer face of the wall. Hedon's tracery is by now fully developed Perpendicular tending towards the gridiron type and devoid of Curvilinear elements.

The recasing of the eastern crossing arch was necessary in order to provide an adequate opening into the new eastern arm, and symmetry demanded that the other three arches should be treated likewise. Structural evidence shows that there was a break in the work at this point, but that remodelling was resumed on the western piers and southern, northern, and western arches, to the same design and therefore still in the period when Hedon was master. The thirteenth-century belfry was being underpinned, but was not at this stage to be rebuilt. It was 'lofty and delectable to see' and must have been a famous landmark comparable to the central tower of Lincoln. In 1407, however, some part of the tower fell, 'stricken by a horrible tempest' according to a petition to the pope, but 'by the carelessness of the masons' in the appeal sent to Henry IV.[38] There may be truth in both statements, and Hedon was superseded by Master William Colchester, sent from London by the king. Colchester's appointment was on 14 December 1407 and Hedon died in the summer of the following year.

Colchester, who was already master mason to Westminster Abbey, was trained in the Court School of Perpendicular and his work closely reflects the style of Henry Yeveley and his immediate pupils, men such as Walter Walton. At York this intrusive southern style, in sharp contrast to the

---

[37] Browne, *History*, p. 200.
[38] *CPatR, 1405–8*, p. 383; *CPapR, Letters, 1404–15*, pp. 137–8, 304–5.

58 East front. Begun in 1361 by William Hoton junior; the east window completed in 1405 under Hugh Hedon.

59 East front: detail of external niche-head.

adjacent northern detail, is seen in the two screen-arches which abut the eastern crossing piers on north and south, providing gateways to the choir aisles (Plate 64). Bonded into the aisle wall, they are provided with a sliding unbonded joint against the shafts of the great piers, to allow for subsidence of the latter. In this way Colchester displayed considerable skill as an engineer, and provided lateral abutment to the crossing to increase rigidity and reduce sway from wind-pressure or such accidents as earth tremors.

It was observed as long ago as 1848 by Robert Willis, in his fundamental study of the architectural history of the Minster, that extensive structural alterations had been made to the arcades of the transepts.[39] To accommodate the old arches to the new widened aisles of the choir and to the new aisles of the nave, it was necessary to take down four piers of the transept arcades, nearest to the crossing, and to rebuild them further out. A complex interchange of architectural elements from the thirteenth-century work was carried out with great ingenuity, and probably in the period when Hugh de Hedon was master. Further rebuilding was done, especially in the west arcade of the south transept, after 1407, as a consequence of the partial collapse of the old tower. The northernmost pier of the western arcade in the north transept was also taken down and rebuilt by shoring the upper part of the transept wall, a remarkable technical achievement (Plate 65).

The eastern arm was by no means completed at the time that the old tower fell and Colchester was sent to York by Henry IV. The glass for some of the aisle windows had been made a few years earlier, and that for the east window, by John Thornton of Coventry, in the three years 1405–8, but the stone and brick vaults of the aisles (Plates 66, 67) were still in progress after 1420.[40] The glazing of the clerestory windows of the western bays, and of the transeptal bays, was going on between about 1405 and 1430. The wooden vault beneath the central span of the roof was probably not inserted until fairly late in this period. Most of these subsidiary parts of the work were continuing through the time when William Colchester was master mason and went on under his successor, and assistant in former years at Westminster, John Long. Long became master at Colchester's death late in 1420, when he also took up the freedom of York, indicating permanent settlement in the city. The new library, a building attached to the west side of the south transept, was also in course of construction from about 1414 and lead was laid on its roof in 1419 (Plate 68); the books were labelled and chained in 1422.[41]

---

[39] Willis, *York Cathedral*, pp. 47–50.
[40] *Fabric Rolls*, pp. 47–8.
[41] Ibid., pp. 36, 38, 39, 46.

Just how much of the old lantern tower fell in 1407 is uncertain, but Colchester decided to build an entirely new tower above the strengthened arches of the crossing (Plate 69). Shortly before his death a great wheel was set up above the great tower, to hoist materials, and it is to be presumed that by this time, 1420, all major structural works on the eastern arm and upon the crossing had been brought to a conclusion.[42] Colchester's design, which must have existed on a large sheet of parchment for fifty years or more after his death, was for a tall tower of two main stages; but after long delays only the lower stage was actually built.

The completion of the towers

It is likely that the project approved by 1290 included both a new nave and a complete new eastern arm consisting of choir and presbytery, but that the splendid central tower which had then been finished for only thirty or forty years was meant to stand. We have seen, too, that the nave was first planned to include also the twelfth-century towers which had been built about a century earlier against the Norman west front. By about 1315–20 it had been decided to pull down these old towers and to transform the front by incorporating new towers in the western bays of the aisles. These, separated by the whole width of the broad nave, necessarily involved the addition to the scheme of a great west window in a front with panels and niches both inside and out, in the place where the closely coupled old towers had stood. The fact that the main feature of the west end is an afterthought, and was completed in sections under several architects, accounts for the unsatisfactory and somewhat disjointed effect made by the Minster front.

At the death of William Colchester in 1420 the whole length of the church from east to west was structurally complete, but the central lantern had not emerged from the roofs, nor had either of the western towers above the main parapet of the front. References in the accounts of 1419, mentioned above, to the great hoisting wheel, describe the central tower as the great 'campanile', and there can be no doubt of the intention to hang the bells in the proposed upper stage, above the lantern. Scaffolding of the tower was in progress in 1422 under John Long, but it is likely that the work done consisted only in placing a temporary roof over the crossing.[43] In 1423 there is no sign of work on the tower in the surviving account.[44] Ten years later, when the next roll shows work beginning on the bell-tower (*campanile*), this can be identified with certainty as the south-west tower (Plate 70).

[42] Ibid., pp. 40–1.
[43] Ibid., p. 44.
[44] YML, E 3/11.

60 South-east crossing
pier. Capitals, and head of
Richard II wearing
Imperial Crown, c. 1397.

61 Choir. Capitals,
c. 1395, belonging to the
work of Hugh Hedon.

62 Crossing pier. Bases of
c. 1395, here attributed to
Hugh Hedon.

Certainly a major change of plan must have taken place by 1430, to give time for the setting of stones to begin on the new tower by 1433.[45] Presumably the defects and distortions found at the crossing and in the transepts during the twenty years following the collapse of 1407, and the difficult works of underpinning involved in their repair, caused the master to have doubts or the dean and chapter to take fright. Instead of proceeding with a great central tower provided with a bell-chamber above the open lantern, the bells were to be hung elsewhere, and a design was prepared for the south-west tower above the parapet of the west front. The design, which is in stylistic agreement with a date near to 1430, can bear no resemblance to any drawings for the new towers first proposed more than a century earlier. The details, which were accurately followed in the later north-west tower, closely resemble those of the stone screen behind the high altar. As will be seen, this was probably designed by William Colchester, and the less assured proportions of the tower are likely to be the work of Colchester's assistant William Waddeswyk, who was appointed chief mason in January 1426 and died late in 1431.[46]

Funds to proceed with the new belfry were given by the treasurer, John Berningham, but the work went on slowly so that the tower cannot have been finished in less than fifteen years. The surviving fabric rolls are uninformative and merely show that, between 1433 and 1473, all three towers were carried up and structurally completed. Even then, a ring of four small bells for the north-west tower was not made until 1475, and metal vanes for the pinnacles were being added in 1485 and 1498.[47] In 1471 the carved bosses were being made for the vault of the great lantern (Plate 71) and payments were made for iron bars and glass for its windows.[48] The painting of the vault and bosses was finished by 1473 at latest, and it would seem that the whole fabric of the Minster was regarded as complete by the time of the consecration on 3 July 1472.[49]

Though the historical evidence makes it difficult to distinguish precisely the years in which each of the towers was built, the architectural evidence is clear. Whereas both of the western towers were built to the design—none too brilliant—of about 1430 attributed to William Waddeswyk, the central lantern was both earlier and later. After the collapse of 1407 and the arrival of William Colchester, there was undoubtedly a grand design for a central tower of the largest scale. Had it been completed, with an upper

[45] Browne, *Fabric Rolls*, p. 28, checked with YML, E 3/12.
[46] YML, M 2(5), fo. 222; BIHR, York Wills, Reg. 2, fo. 655.
[47] *Fabric Rolls*, pp. 80–1, 88, 90.
[48] Ibid., pp. 74–7.
[49] Ibid., p. 77; Browne, *Fabric Rolls*, pp. 12–13; Browne, *History*, p. 253.

◁ **63** Choir. North-east transept, by Hugh Hedon, designed *c.* 1390–1400.

64 Stone screen across north choir aisle, inserted *c.* 1415 by William Colchester as a stiffener to the central tower.

65 North transept, looking west. Pier inserted by underpinning early in the 15th C.

stage analogous to that at Durham but considerably larger and, quite possibly, with a tall spire as well, it would have outdone the steeples of Old St. Paul's and of Lincoln. On its far wider base, and with the newly strengthened piers and arches of the crossing, it would have rivalled even the most magnificent of the continental towers. As we have seen, however, the dream was abandoned and the design followed only as far as the decorative parapet crowning the lower stage, with its truncated pinnacles at the four corners.

Masons' marks found on all parts of the stonework suggest that the central lantern was mostly built before the middle of the fifteenth century. An alternative possibility is that the stones were worked in the yard and stored for a long period before being used. The tracery of the eight tall windows is later, and resembles that of the school of East Anglia and Lincolnshire. This is easily explained by the fact that John Porter, a Lincoln mason, was called to York to give advice about 1450 and had become master by 1452.[50] Moreover, upon his death in 1466 he was succeeded by Robert Spillesby, probably from Spilsby in Lincolnshire, who died in 1473 and was buried in the nave.

Fittings and lesser works

It has been necessary, in giving a consecutive account of the building of the fabric of the Minster, to omit a great deal. So large a cathedral has a story bristling with side issues, and the building itself includes subordinate parts, monuments, and fittings which are relevant to its architectural history. There were in addition some minor works which continued after the consecration of 1472 and until the period of the Reformation. At least brief mention must be made of the tombs of archbishops William Greenfield (d. 1315) and Henry Bowet, made about 1413–15; of the chapel of St. Mary and the Holy Angels, of the rood screen and the altar screen, of the carved base made for the shrine of St. William of Frosterley marble in 1471; and finally of the whole parish church of St. Michael le Belfrey, designed by the Minster mason and built at the charge of the fabric fund.

Before discussing these lesser architectural works, we have to consider a remarkable and almost unique piece of graphic evidence relating to the Minster. It was long ago pointed out that a manuscript of the *Histories* of Geoffrey of Monmouth (BM, Royal MS. 13 A.iii) contained drawings of English cities which appeared to preserve actual information of their

---

[50] YML, E 3/21, which shows that by 1456 Porter had held the house in Lop Lane granted to him by the chapter for five years inclusive of the then current year.

67 South choir aisle. Brick web of vault, *c.* 1420.

66 South choir aisle. Carved boss,
c. 1420.

68 Old Library. Roof of 1415–18, by
John Askham, master carpenter.

topography.[51] Since the date of the drawings lies somewhere near 1320, and in any case within the first quarter of the fourteenth century, such direct observation by an artist is most unusual. The view, labelled as 'Ebrauc' (York), shows amid houses and minor steeples two large churches seen from the west, the larger on the right of the smaller which corresponds in position and type to St. Mary's Abbey. The greater church, in the middle of the view, is remarkable for having a ground storey of crocketted gables above doorways and niches, surmounted at each side by flying buttresses abutting a partially erased area of the drawing. What can still be seen of the drawing seems to show a pair of tall slender towers rising three more stages above the canopies and with parapets and low pyramidal roofs, contrasting with the tall spire covered in herring-bone leadwork on the central tower of the smaller church to the left. What can be seen of the erased front bears no resemblance to that of the existing Minster, but could very well be intended for the pair of twelfth-century towers now known to have been built before the Norman front. Accepting the view as a somewhat diagrammatic but real picture of *c.* 1320 implies that the artist sketched the western aspect of the Minster after both nave aisles had been built and provided with their pinnacled flying buttresses, abutting the new nave completed to clerestory height but hidden by the old towers. The front itself had been built only to the top of the main doorway. Slightly later, discovering that the old towers were after all to be demolished, the artist erased this part of the finished drawing, presumably with the intention of inserting the new front.

The great interest of this drawing lies, firstly, in the fact that it can be closely dated by costume and armour shown in other drawings in the manuscript from the same hand; secondly, that it shows or clearly implies the completion of the nave with both its aisles and with their buttresses, while the old towers still stood. It must be remembered that the very existence of these towers was quite unknown until their recent discovery in excavation. The towers are indicated as having tall windows or arcading, and the low spires that might be expected at a period well before 1200. The style of the flying buttresses and of the lower part of the west front is Geometrical, without any trace of the Curvilinear detail seen in the present west window and upper levels. We have therefore in this picture an independent control on the story deduced from the succession of styles.

The tomb of Archbishop Greenfield was probably designed not much

---

[51] C. Caine in *JBAA*, N.S. iv (1898), 319–21; the view of York is reproduced also in C. Caine (ed.), *Analecta Eboracensia* (1897), p. 7, from Royal MS. 13 A.iii, fo. 16ᵛ. The draughtsman was probably a clerk attached to the royal household or to the courts of law, which were again settled in York in 1319 and 1320, 1322 and 1323 (see above, n. 17).

earlier than 1315, the year of his death, and very probably soon afterwards (Plate 72). Its details closely resemble on a small scale those of the nave; its pinnacles and tracery panels are essentially the same. The general design is like that of the tomb in Westminster Abbey of Aveline, Countess of Lancaster, who died in 1273 but whose monument is probably of *c.* 1290–1300; but it has the double cusping of that of her husband Edmund, Earl of Lancaster (d. 1296), without the latter's introduction of ogee curves. The Greenfield tomb can be confidently assigned to Master Simon, and shows that, though fully aware of the Court School, he was firmly grounded in the style of the end of the old century, and remained a traditionalist to the end of his career.

The monument of Archbishop Bowet, a century later, is an eccentricity bearing little resemblance to the main body of work of its time (Plate 73).[52] It was projected by 1413 and finished by 1415, but its detail in no way suggests the metropolitan style brought to York by William Colchester. In the curious fashion of its 'everted' canopy and in some other respects the tomb resembles that of Catherine Swynford at Lincoln, and both belong stylistically to the Midland School practised by the alabaster workers of Nottingham and Derbyshire.[53] This connection is probably to be accounted for by a close personal friendship between Bowet and Henry Beaufort, the later cardinal and son of Catherine, bishop of Lincoln at the time of his mother's death. The eastern bay of the south aisle, next to the monument, formed the archbishop's chantry chapel. The vault was built of brick ('waltiell') in 1423, the year of Bowet's death, and his arms were painted on the central boss.

One later monument is of decidedly architectural character, that of Archbishop Thomas Savage, who died in September 1507. Together with a wooden chantry chapel above it, the tomb had been built after Savage's death but before 1518 for Thomas Dalby, archdeacon of Richmond from 1506.[54] The style of the work is not distinguished, but the quality of execution is high, and the designer was probably Christopher Horner, master mason of the Minster from 1505 until his death in 1523. The well-carved angels and heraldic shields may have been by Robert Waterton, 'enteiler', who occurs in the fabric rolls at the time.[55]

The chapel of St. Mary and the Holy Angels, also known as St. Sepulchre's Chapel, stood to the north of the Minster nave. It had been founded by Archbishop Roger in the third quarter of the twelfth century,

[52] Dr. Gee points out that there is a net vault below the gallery walk across the great east window.
[53] J. Harvey, *Catherine Swynford's Chantry* (Friends of Lincoln Cathedral, 1971), pp. 13–15.
[54] J. B. Morrell, *York Monuments* (n.d. [1944]), p. 5 and Pl. vi; Browne, *History*, pp. 267–8.
[55] *Fabric Rolls*, pp. 96 n., 97.

69 Central tower from west. Completed in 1472 to a design of *c.* 1415 by William Colchester; the ▷
details probably by John Porter, *c.* 1452–65.

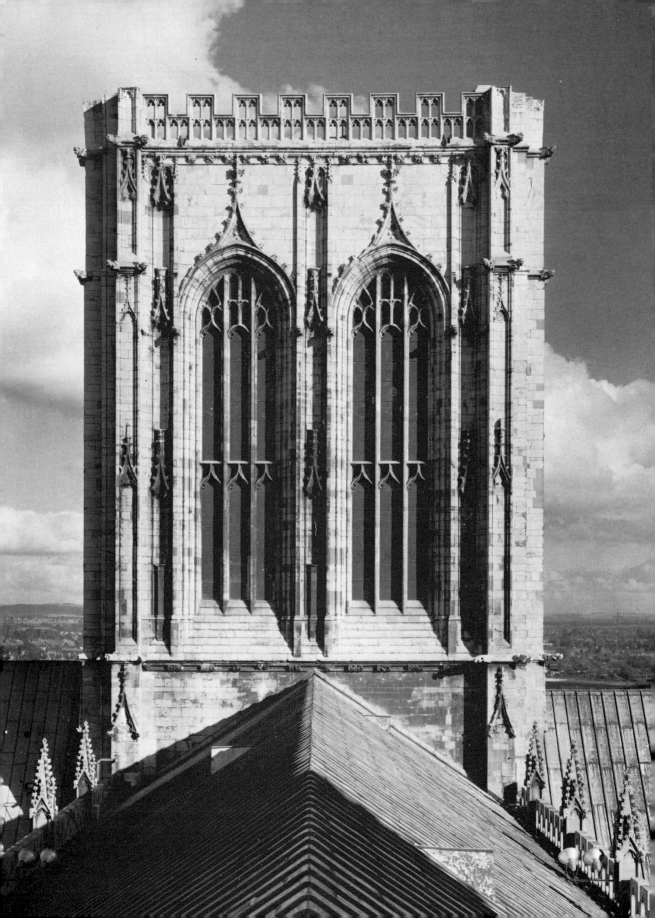

but was enlarged under a licence granted by Archbishop Melton in 1333.[56] To this period would seem to belong the communicating doorway leading from the north nave aisle, now the only surviving part of the chapel apart from a blocked staircase. The doorway itself is an unobtrusive alteration of the wall arcading, but above it is a carved figure of the Virgin under a canopy bearing ball-flower ornament. Two shields, of France Ancient and of England, probably refer to the moment when Edward III claimed the throne of France on 7 October 1337; the quartering of the arms followed only in 1340. The completion of the enlargement of the chapel and its linking to the new nave seem then to belong to the same phase of work as the great west window, also paid for by Archbishop Melton.

The two principal screens within the Minster: the pulpitum between the eastern piers of the crossing, and the altar screen (renewed after the fire of 1829), present difficult problems of dating. No unambiguous documentary evidence has so far been found which shows precisely when either of the screens, or the old choir stalls (burnt in 1829) were made. The high altar existed by 1416 and a great beam for the rood was bought then.[57] In 1428 a great 'table' or altarpiece for the high altar was begun, but as late as 1458 a bequest was made to the new altar table, perhaps still the same work.[58] Another bequest in 1471, for the marble base for the shrine of St. William, confirms the meaning of an entry in the roll for 1470.[59] The master mason, Robert Spillesby, spent twenty-eight days with his servant riding to find marblers. The shrine-base, of which many large fragments are now in the Yorkshire Museum, was placed in the feretory behind the high altar, which until 1726 stood one bay to the west of its present position. The stone altar screen (replaced after the fire of 1829 by a reasonably faithful copy) dates probably from before 1428, and its Westminster style suggests that the drawings were made by Colchester or his successor John Long. The details of the western towers resemble this screen but their composition is less competent; probably their designer was the third of the trio from Westminster, William Waddeswyk, master in 1426–31.

It would similarly be expected that the choir stalls, and the stone screen against which the western return stalls stood, would have been made soon after the completion of the new structural choir, early in the fifteenth century. From the existing replicas of the stalls, made after 1829, and from engravings of details of the old stalls before the fire, they would seem in fact to have been of relatively early date. It is difficult to suppose that some

[56] A. Hamilton Thompson in *YAJ*, xxxvi (1944–7), 67.
[57] *Fabric Rolls*, pp. 35, 36.
[58] Willis, *York Cathedral*, p. 45; J. S. Purvis, Classified Subject Index (BIHR, 1962), p. 83.
[59] Purvis, op. cit., p. 81; *Fabric Rolls*, p. 73.

◁ **70** South-west tower. Built 1432–56, probably to a design of *c.* 1430 by William Waddeswyk.

substantial part of the pulpitum or rood screen had not been built by, say, 1425. This argument may be buttressed by another, drawn from the design and arrangement of the screen as it exists. The design is extraordinary in that the doorway is not central, having seven niches for statues on the north and eight on the south (Plate 74). This asymmetry is very noticeable and can hardly have been intended originally. The probable explanation is that the outline of the design was first drawn up by William Colchester, and that the extremely thick screen was intended to play a part in stiffening the eastern arch of the crossing. Very likely the eastern wall, against which the stalls were to be fixed, was built by 1420. The design for the western face would, at that time, have had a central archway between seven niches on each side. The total of fourteen allowed for statues of all the Kings of England from the Conquest down to the reigning sovereign, namely Henry V. Henry's short reign, from 1413 to 1422, must surely be that of the design.

Execution must have been delayed, and by the time that the work was set out it had to be modified so as to permit of the inclusion of a fifteenth statue, of Henry VI. An injunction of 1479 against the improper reverence shown to an image of the murdered king, already removed from its position, shows that there had been a statue of Henry VI in the Minster. Though this was not necessarily the statue on the rood screen, it is extremely likely that it was, and in that case the screen must be dated before the triumph of Edward IV in March 1461. In 1516 an image of King Henry was painted, or repainted; this was almost certainly of Henry VI, probably in the last niche of the screen. If so, it may have been the original statue brought out of some hiding-place after 1485, or else a new statue to replace the old. It was presumably regarded as the object of superstitious worship at the Reformation and again removed, since the niche remained empty, then filled by James I, before the present statue was carved by Michael Taylor in 1810.[60]

Turning from historical to stylistic evidence, the screen and its original details (for there was much tinkering by Francis Bernasconi in 1803–5) do not indicate the late period of c. 1475–1500, or even to 1515, generally assigned to it. The doorway with its vault and panelwork is derived fairly closely from the 'welcoming porch' type of the last years of Henry Yeveley: particularly the north porch and screen of Westminster Hall (1397–9) and other rood screens such as that of Canterbury (before 1411) (Plate 75). A closer parallel is to the north porch doorway and west door of Beverley Minster, both parts of the final build of the early fifteenth century. Undoubtedly later than these examples at Beverley, the York screen may

[60] G. W. O. Addleshaw, *Four Hundred Years* (published by the Friends of York Minster, 1962), 21.

71 Central tower, interior looking up. Wooden vault of 1471–3 by John Forster, master carpenter. ▷

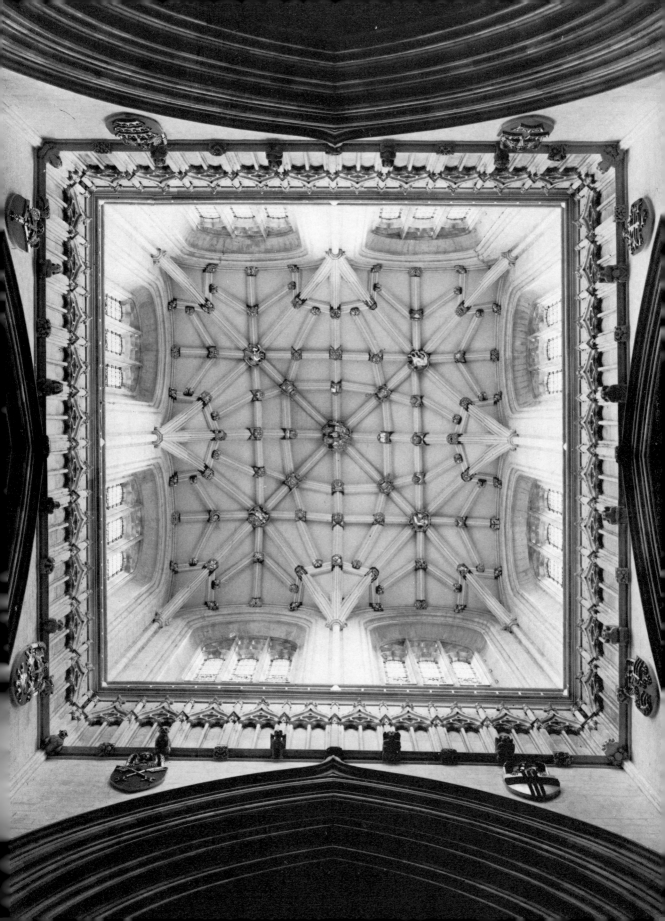

72 Tomb of Archbishop Greenfield, died 1315; here attributed to Master Simon.

73 Tomb of Archbishop Bowet, made in 1413–15.

well have been executed in the time of Richard Andrew, dean of York from 1452 and secretary to Henry VI from 1443 to 1455.[61]

To sum up: the design for the rood screen must have been made by 1422 at the latest, and the eastern wall towards the choir was probably built about that time; if earlier, then there must have been subsequent alteration to move the central opening northwards. The western face with its niches, after revision of the design, must have been built after 1422 and very likely between 1452 and 1461. In that case it seems probable that the whole series of statues, including one of Henry VI, was carved *c.* 1455–60. The last statue would not have been removed until after Henry's death in 1471 and his alleged miracles. This dating tends to be confirmed by two entries in the fabric rolls: in 1456 a reward was paid to carpenters and other workmen at the time of erecting the scaffolds within the Church ('tempore ereccionis les scafald infra Ecclesiam'), and in the next year a painter received 3s. 4d. for cleaning the 'reredoses' of the high altar and before the gates of the choir.[62] The latter can only refer to *a* rood screen, though regarded by Raine as meaning an earlier one on the present site. The cleaning might well be that undertaken immediately after erection and while the scaffolding was being removed.

It will be seen that there are certain residual problems. Why is there no record of the costs of the screen? The most obvious answer is that the fabric rolls, besides being kept in brief and uninformative fashion, are an extremely defective series. Between 1415 and 1515 the rolls are missing for consecutive periods of three years and more for 1424–32, 1436–41, 1450–1, 1459–69, 1476–8, 1486–97, 1500–4, and 1511–15, besides the loss of single years and pairs of years: the survivors number only 30 out of one hundred. Another possibility is that the screen was paid for from a special fund, for which no accounts at all survive. Secondly, there is the question of what work it was that required the carving of 175 crockets in 1479 and, in 1485, 240 crockets and 32 gargoyles. It seems probable that these were the decorative part of structural works or renewals on the building, and there is nothing to suggest that they belonged to the rood screen. The services of carvers may also have been required in connection with the marble base for the feretory begun in 1471 (Plates 77, 78). Thirdly, what are we to make of the much-discussed rebus, said to be a hind couchant for (William) Hyndeley ('hind lay'), the master mason brought from Norwich in 1472 and in charge at the Minster until his death on 1 November 1505? The facts seem doubtful and, in any case, there were other masons of the

---

[61] James Raine in *Fabric Rolls*, pp. 79 n., 80 n., 82 n.
[62] *Fabric Rolls*, pp. 67, 70.

same surname: John Hyndelay of York (d. 1407) and Thomas Hyndeley of Durham, who worked there from 1401 until 1433, as master after 1416, but whose later career is unknown.

Yet another possibility is that some parts of the screen may be substantially later than the rest, or the result of a major repair. Some colour is lent to this by the 'vaults' of the canopies over the statues. Not all are of the same design, and some look decidedly later in character than others. Be this as it may, the question arises of the extent of the damage done by the great fire of 1464. The fire, serious enough to be mentioned in several annals, broke out on 11 March 1463–4 at the feretory of R. Scrope, that is the 'shrine' of the martyred archbishop in the north-east bay of the Lady Chapel.[63] As long afterwards as 1519 a visitation recorded that there was in the crypt 'a goodly well', then disused but 'whiche hath bene used in old tyme & dyde grete goode what tyme as the churche was borned'.[64] This well in the crypt is close to the northern staircase leading up to the Lady Chapel and was nearest to the Scrope chapel in the east end of the north aisle. It is not easy to see how a fire at the extreme east end could affect the rood screen, but such records as there are remain silent both as to the extent of the fire and as to the repairs which may have been necessary.

The fact is that, after the consecration of 1472, there remained a great deal to do on the fabric. We get a glimpse of this from the mention in the fabric roll of 1475 of the large payment of £24 13s. 5d. over and above a bequest of 100 marks from Dean Andrew (£66 13s. 4d.) for the making of the upper and lower battlements, with finials ('cum finyall') on the south side of the choir.[65] Other battlements, general maintenance, and work on other buildings in the charge of the fabric fund, could well account for the busy lives led by Hyndeley and his successors, and the masons working under them. Hyndeley, together with Christopher Horner who succeeded him as master mason to the Minster, was imprisoned in 1491 as suspect of the murder of John Partrik or Patrik, a tiler, in the course of a dispute as to which trade should build the brick Red Tower of the city defences.[66] It is not now possible to point to any work as being certainly to the design of either Hyndeley or Horner.

Horner's successor, John Forman, the last of the Gothic masters from 1523 until his death in 1558, was undoubtedly an architect of distinction.

---

[63] Bodl., MS. Laud Misc. 84, fo. 164, a contemporary entry in a service calendar; cf. Sir Richard Baker, *A Chronicle of the Kings of England* (1679), p. 217.

[64] *Fabric Rolls*, p. 268.

[65] Ibid., p. 80.

[66] R. M. Butler in *An Inventory of the Historical Monuments in the City of York* (Royal Commission on Historical Monuments, England), ii: *The Defences* ('1972'; 1973), pp. 20, 139.

74 Choir Screen. West side, showing asymmetrical arrangement with seven niches to north and eight to south. Probably after a design by William Colchester, but built *c.* 1452–6 under John Porter.

76 Choir Screen: detail and statue of 'King John.'

75 Choir Screen: detail of doorway.

From 1525 until 1537 he was in charge of building the new church of St. Michael le Belfrey, beside the Minster, out of fabric funds. As a fine example of the Tudor town church, as well as an appendage of York Minster, St. Michael's is of outstanding importance. It shows us amply the personal style of the last of York's medieval architects. Had there been any comparable addition to the Minster itself at that time, it would have been of like character; and we can tell that, far from decadence, the Gothic practised by Forman was a living style of great beauty and spaciousness. It is a strange commentary upon the period that the church was finished a year after the suppression of the smaller monasteries, and a year before the start upon the dissolution of the greater: St. Michael le Belfrey is the swansong of English Gothic architecture. Yet its architect lived on, through the last ten years of the reign of Henry VIII, all of that of Edward VI, with its iconoclastic excesses and demolition of less fortunate churches. Forman continued to have charge of the giant fabric of the Minster, long enough to supervise the redecoration under Mary's Catholic revival, in 1557. Perhaps supremely happy in the moment of his death, John Forman remained 'the maister of the maysons in the Cathedrall churche of Yorke' until his end in the summer of 1558, a few months before the death of Queen Mary and accession of Elizabeth. No new master was appointed. The Minster was launched on its second career, as the greatest ancient monument in England.

This account of the architectural development of York Minster owes much to discussions over a period of years with Dr. Eric A. Gee, who has generously placed at my disposal his unrivalled knowledge of the fabric; and to Mr. T. W. French in regard to the dating of the stained glass and the evidence of heraldry and mouldings. In reconsideration of the documentary sources I am grateful for the very great assistance given to me by Miss K. M. Longley, Mr. C. B. L. Barr, and Mr. Denis Hunt; and again to Dr. Gee for access to his collections of dating evidence and of masons' marks, and his transcripts of the fabric rolls.

APPENDIX: The Architects of York Minster from 1290 to 1558

The following brief careers are mostly of the master masons in charge of the Minster works, appointed by the dean and chapter. Those who designed important parts of the building are shown in **bold**; other master craftsmen of distinction, who never held the office of master mason, are shown indented from the margin. Abbreviations used are *c.* (about); *d.* (died); *free* (took up the freedom of the City of York).[67]

[67] References will be found above in the notes to the text, supplementing *English Mediaeval Architects*; working careers at the Minster are from unpublished fabric rolls in YML. I am grateful to Dr. E. A. Gee for allowing me to use his full transcripts of these rolls, of which only extracts were printed by Raine in *Fabric Rolls*.

77 Base for St. William's Shrine. Carved in Frosterley Marble and begun in 1471 (fragments in the Yorkshire Museum).

78 Base for St. William's Shrine (fragments in the Yorkshire Museum).

Simon le Mason, the original architect of the late Gothic cathedral *c.* 1289; a wealthy man by 1301; free 1315; d. 1322.

Hugh de Boudon (? Bootham), second master *c.* 1310, when he acted as deputy master for the royal works of the new tower at Knaresborough Castle.

Ivo de Raghton, from Raughton near Carlisle; free 1317; a wealthy man by 1327; mason of Archbishop Melton 1331 and probably designer of the great west window of the Minster and other works in a rich Curvilinear style at Carlisle, Beverley and Selby; ? d. *c.* 1339.

Thomas de Pacenham, master mason *c.* 1339–*c.* 1348.

Philip de Lincoln, appointed master carpenter 1346, still in office 1375; erected, and probably designed, the original timber vaulting of the nave.

William de Hoton senior, succeeded Pacenham *c.* 1348 and had charge of the building of the Zouche Chapel; d. 1351.

William de Hoton junior, succeeded his father 1351; the designer of the choir aisles and presumably draughtsman of the full-size setting-out of an aisle window on the plaster floor of the tracing house; d. 1368.

Robert de Patryngton, free 1352; appointed master 1369; designer of the high work of the Lady Chapel and of tombs for the archbishops made in 1368–73, as well as work at Cawood Castle in 1369 and monuments elsewhere; living 1385.

Hugh de Hedon, free 1394; designer of the choir and of the new crossing arches, but the old tower collapsed during the work of underpinning in 1407; d. 1408.

William Colchester, a leading mason at Westminster Abbey 1395; succeeded Henry Yeveley as master mason there 1400; sent to York by Henry IV to rebuild the fallen belfry and to supervise all other works of the church 1407; in 1408, with his assistant William Waddeswyk, was injured by a conspiracy of York masons; recalled to Westminster 1410; came back to York by 1415. Colchester designed the new central lantern tower, which was to have an upper stage for the bells, and the stone screens which stiffen the eastern piers of the crossing; perhaps also the stone altar screen; King's Master Mason to Henry V from July 1418; d. 1420.

John Long, a mason at Westminster Abbey 1394–1401; master in succession to Colchester, and free 1420; d. *c.* 1425.

William Waddeswyk, a mason at Westminster Abbey in 1398–9 and at York Minster for part of 1402; returned to York in 1408 as assistant to William Colchester, and injured by conspiracy of York masons, but granted wages for life by the chapter; warden of the masons by 1415 and continuing under Long;

appointed master January 1426; free 1427; d. 1431. Probably designed the western towers.

John Askham, carpenter, free 1387; master carpenter at the Minster by 1415, and probably designer of the wooden high vault of the choir and of the old choir stalls; joined Corpus Christi Guild 1429; d. late 1436.

Thomas Pak, a working mason at the Minster by 1418 and until 1421; free 1421; master 1432 in succession to Waddeswyk; occupied the house over Monk Bar; d. *c.* 1435.

John Bowde or Bolde, a working mason by 1418; paid as a setter from 1419; master *c.* 1436 in succession to Pak; d. 1443.

John Barton, a working mason at the Minster by 1415 and until 1421 or later; free 1427; a working mason on York Guildhall 1448, though he had succeeded Bowde as master at the Minster by 1444. About 1450 John Porter (below) was called from Lincoln to advise on the works.

John Porter, mason of Lincoln, in 1450 twice called to York to advise on the works of the Minster; later appointed master; free 1454; d. late 1465. Porter was probably the designer of tracery and other details of the central tower.

Robert Spillesby, who had been a working mason at Eton College in 1445–6, was appointed master at York Minster in December 1466 in succession to Porter, and became free the same year. Under Spillesby the central tower approached completion, and he found marblers to carve the new base for the shrine of St. William; d. in spring 1473.

William Hyndeley, mason of Norwich, where he was free 1466; warden of the masons' lodge at York Minster *c.* 1471 and promoted master at the death of Spillesby in spring 1473; free 1474. Hyndeley was in charge of the building of battlements on the Minster and of the great marble shrine-base begun in 1471; he may also have completed the rood screen or repaired it after damage. With his assistant Christopher Horner (below) he was imprisoned in 1490 on suspicion of murdering John Patrik, a tiler, during a trade dispute; carried on trade as an engraver of monumental brasses; d. 1 November 1505.

James Dam, carver, free 1457; in 1470 worked with his servant for nine weeks and in 1479 for thirteen weeks, as well as carving 175 crockets; his son John Dam, a goldsmith, was free 1483. David Dam, possibly another son, was a carver of the bosses for the vault of the central tower 1471, still working for the Minster in 1485.

Christopher Horner, apprentice mason under Hyndeley 1478–82; free 1489; imprisoned with Hyndeley on suspicion of murder 1490; working mason 1495; succeeded Hyndeley as master 1505; again imprisoned twice in 1504; d. 1523.

John Forman, last master mason of York Minster, succeeded Horner 1523; designed and built the church of St. Michael le Belfrey 1525–37; also master mason to the archbishop for works at Cawood and Southwell; in charge of the Catholic redecoration of the Minster 1557; d. 1558.

Forman was the last master mason in the architectural sense and had no successor. Later leading masons at the Minster formed a more or less regular series from c. 1630 to 1869.

CHAPTER V

From the Reformation to the Restoration

Claire Cross

The years between the accession of Henry VIII and the restoration of Charles II saw many drastic changes in English religious life which affected York Minster in common with all other English cathedrals. Already in the early sixteenth century the dean and chapter, by their very nature a conservative body, appeared at least to radicals as a fossilized relic from an age long past. In the mid-sixteenth century contemporaries faced the new problem of trying to adapt an essentially medieval institution to the needs of a national Protestant Church. The central government imposed change upon the dean and chapter; first there came a century of relatively moderate and sporadic change, then two decades of revolutionary reorganization, all in an ultimately vain endeavour to find a fresh purpose for a cathedral corporation in a reformed Church. Unlike the chapters of Wells or Durham, the dean and chapter at York themselves rarely initiated change, and only in the reaction of 1662 do they seem to have acted with positive enthusiasm. They succeeded in preserving their institution remarkably unscathed in a century and a half of violent political and religious upheavals. Whether their achievement served the best interests of the city or the diocese of York is a matter more open to question.

At the beginning of the reign of Henry VIII the Minster seemed to be set in an immemorial routine, and the prospect of any change appeared remote. In 1514 the king had Thomas Wolsey promoted to be archbishop of York; like his immediate predecessors, Thomas Savage and Christopher Bainbridge, Wolsey never resided and performed all his archiepiscopal duties in the north through deputies. The new dean of York, Brian Higden, appointed in 1516, differed from many of his predecessors and successors in that he did live in York and attended chapter meetings fairly regularly during the twenty-three years he held his office. The dean, together with only two or three residentiaries, carried the burden of the administration of the cathedral; the remainder of the chapter of thirty-six prebendaries never resided and apparently rarely visited the Minster. The vicars choral performed the regular round of services; originally there may have been thirty-six vicars choral, one for each prebendary, but by the early sixteenth century the revenues of the vicars would not stretch to maintain so many. Often a vicar choral combined his duties with the office of chantry priest at one of the many chantries established in the Minster. A small choir of boys supplemented the singing, and other boys served at the altars. The dean and chapter as a body, in addition to the dean and canons as individuals, employed a very considerable number of servants, ranging from the professional accountant and surveyors and builders who supervised the chapter's lands and the fabric of the Minster, to the vergers, doorkeepers, and washerwomen. The Minster remained, as it had for centuries, an independent, rich, self-sufficient institution which could function fairly efficiently with a minimum of guidance from its chief dignitaries.

A report made in 1519 by the vicars and chantry priests in response to an inquiry from the dean and chapter reveals the Minster in all its tarnished splendour. These conservative-minded priests uncovered no great scandals; indeed, they mentioned no defects at all which they felt that a thorough spring-cleaning could not put to rights. Dust and cobwebs festooned the walls and pillars, and particularly the reredos, which they feared might fall to pieces unless it was cleaned and looked after better than it had been in the past. The ragged and torn coverings of the little altars, they thought, would have disgraced an upland village, let alone a great cathedral. The hangings of the choir lay neglected in the presbytery, fouled by dogs and the wax dropped from candles; the lectern needed scouring and setting up in the middle of the choir. The vicars noticed a general slackness in the performance of the services and ceremonies, as well as in the upkeep of the church. A clerk of the vestry did not always supply a torch at the renewing of the sacrament or regularly light candles before the statue of the Virgin as he ought to have done. The choir books were not looked after properly, and so the vicars often sang out of tune. At the high altar the priests made no distinction between the nine lessons and the double feast days and allowed the children to come around the altar in dirty albs, some wearing one colour, some another, and took no account of the colour of the liturgical season. Many of the albs for the priests were torn, and so skimpy that they had a struggle to get them on. No one had decided whether the clerk of the works or the chamberlain had the responsibility for mending vestments, so copes, tunicles, and chasubles had not been repaired. The priests often found the door of the vestry locked, and not kept open from matins till eleven in the morning, as it used to be, and this had prevented them from getting their bread, wine, and water when they wanted to say mass. Then, after mass, there were difficulties in the vestry, as the sink was stopped up and the priests had to wash their mass vessels in a bucket, when all that needed doing was for the pulley to be mended and the sink unblocked. Throughout the return the vicars continued their recital of petty abuses; clearly their corporate pride had been wounded. In future they wanted their church to compare favourably with any other church in the land, and services to be as seemly and uniform as those of other cathedral foundations. They concerned themselves only with the regular performance of the daily offices; the administration of the Minster as an ecclesiastical corporation did not lie within their responsibility and they made no comments upon it.[1]

A more critical assessment of the way in which the dean and chapter carried out their duties on the eve of the Reformation appears in the visitation made in 1534 by Archbishop Edward Lee. The archbishop most wished to see the non-residence of the canons remedied. In fact, although he did not allude to this in his injunctions, the only canons in residence in the last decade had been Dean Higden and the treasurer, Lancelot Collins; the two of them had shared the very considerable income of the common fund. The archbishop wanted all the non-resident canons, whenever they happened to be in York, to be present at matins, the procession, and the major masses, and especially to attend at the double feasts and principal feasts. He felt it necessary to admonish the canons against permitting women of bad character to go into hospices, houses, or anywhere else in the close. He also commented on some economic anomalies. The canons were not giving rich copes worth £10 to the Minster in their lifetimes or, failing that, 20 marks and their best palfrey at their deaths, as the Minster statutes bound them to do. The archbishop ordered those canons who drew tithes from parish churches, which formed part of the endowment of their prebends, to provide pensions for the vicars who served their cures.[2] Lee confined himself to issuing brief injunctions; he obviously did not believe that the York chapter needed a thorough-going reformation, but he was a conservative churchman, reluctant to alter any of the old ways. Already Thomas Cranmer had the king's ear, and in 1539 he confided to Thomas Cromwell his scorn of the 'sect of prebendaries' who 'spent their time in much idleness, and their substance in superfluous belly cheer'. At least in the new cathedral foundations then being set up Cranmer hoped there would be no prebendaries at all, and that the revenues which would have maintained them would be used instead to support students at the

[1] *Fabric Rolls*, pp. 267–9.
[2] 'Visitations in the Diocese of York holden by Archbishop Edward Lee', *YAJ* xvi (1902), pp. 433–5.

universities.[3] York was a cathedral of the old foundation and wealthy : with a reformer as archbishop of Canterbury it seemed probable that the dean and chapter of York, together with the chapters of all cathedrals of the old foundation, would be compelled to undergo drastic change.

In fact the cathedrals never had to withstand an onslaught from the Henrician government; they were made to surrender much of their treasure but they were not made to reduce the size of their establishment significantly. When Henry VIII re-endowed the former monastic cathedrals in 1541 he allowed the most important—Canterbury, Durham, and Winchester—to have a dean and 12 prebendaries. Most refoundations and new foundations, like Norwich, Rochester, Bristol, Chester, Gloucester, and Peterborough, were only given a dean and 6 prebendaries, while indigent Carlisle had to operate with a dean and 4 prebendaries. The cathedrals of the old foundation presented a great contrast with those of the new. Even after the Henrician and Edwardian purges, Lincoln still retained a dean and 52 prebendaries, Bath and Wells a dean and 50 prebendaries, Salisbury a dean and 45 prebendaries. York had never possessed a chapter of this magnitude but, when the value of its individual prebends is taken into account, it was among the richest of the cathedrals of the old foundation.

In 1530 York had 36 prebends; in 1550 it had 30, and it kept this number until the nation-wide reorganization of cathedral chapters in the reign of Queen Victoria. The chapter lost two of its prebends, it seems, almost by accident and there is little evidence of any concerted attack by the government on its establishment. Two of its prebends were annexed to northern religious houses, and when the Crown dissolved them, it automatically confiscated the prebends together with all their other lands and revenues. The prebend of Bramham, valued in the *Valor Ecclesiasticus* at £55 a year, had long been associated with Nostell Priory and came to the Crown in 1540 on the priory's dissolution. Similarly, it had been customary for the prior of Hexham to hold the prebend of Salton worth £53 13s. 4d. a year; this also was confiscated by the king when he dissolved Hexham in the same year. Two of York's prebends came temporarily or permanently into the hands of royal servants. The richest prebend in the church of York, and one of the richest in the whole of England, Masham, recorded at £136 in the *Valor Ecclesiasticus*, was first leased to John Gostwick, the treasurer of First Fruits and Tenths in 1536, and then finally resigned to the Crown by Robert Peterson in 1546. A few weeks before he died, Henry VIII included the former prebend of Masham among the endowments of Trinity College,

[3] J. E. Cox (ed.), *Cranmer's Miscellaneous Writings* (Parker Soc., Cambridge, 1846), pp. 396–7.

Cambridge.[4] John Wilson, the last prebendary of South Cave, another very valuable prebend worth £87 a year, alienated the prebend to Sir Michael Stanhope and his heirs in 1549; Archbishop Robert Holgate and the dean and chapter subsequently ratified the secularization. Finally, the Crown forced the dean and chapter to surrender their richest office, that of the treasurer, to which the prebends of Newthorpe and Wilton were attached. Although of the four dignitaries of the church the treasurer came last in precedence, his office, valued in 1535 at £220, was second only to that of the dean, being worth more than the offices of the precentor and chancellor combined. The government excused the abolition of the office by saying, as it did also at Lincoln, that now the church's treasure had gone to the Crown the office of the treasurer had become redundant, but there can be no real doubt that the Crown took the office because of its endowment. What is more surprising is that royal confiscation of prebends stopped at this point. At a time when the archbishop of York, in common with many other Edwardian bishops, had to make disadvantageous exchanges of lands with the Crown, a further attack on the still generous provision of prebends at York might well have been expected, but it did not come. It may be that prebends were still looked upon as a useful source of remuneration for royal servants, and so they were spared, though ironically the Crown used this form of reward for services rendered less and less in the sixteenth century as the numbers of laymen in the royal administration increased.

Apart from the loss of six prebends and a dignity in the last years of Henry VIII and first years of Edward VI, the other most important change to be imposed upon the dean and chapter of York was the revision of the cathedral statutes, again a relatively moderate, not a radical, change. Richard Layton, one of the Crown's chief agents in the dissolution of the monasteries, had been given the deanery of York in 1539 on the death of Brian Higden, and he seems to have been the moving spirit behind the drafting of the new statutes which the king granted in 1541. These statutes set out to remedy the lack of residentiary canons in the church about which Archbishop Lee had earlier complained. They abolished the old custom that a residentiary had to spend the huge sum of a thousand marks on banquets in his first year of residence which not surprisingly had deterred many from taking up residence at all. Now any canon who had a prebendal house in the close and an income of £100 a year could petition to reside. The statutes laid down that all canons, whether resident or not, should be

---

[4] YML, Torre, 'Minster' p. 1124; C. H. Cooper, *Annals of Cambridge* (Cambridge, 1842), i. p. 450. All the sixteenth-century valuations of prebends are taken from *Val. Ecc.* v. p. 1–2, 63, except for Salton, Masham, South Cave, and the treasurership which do not appear there. Torre gives these in 'Minster' vol. pp. 1119, 1123, 1185, 611.

summoned to chapter meetings. The administrative section of the Henrician statutes modified the constitution of the Minster, but did not greatly alter it.[5] The number of residentiaries rose a little, from one or two in any given year to three or four. The only section of the statutes which showed any sign of new religious thinking was the one concerning preaching. The statutes required every canon with a prebend worth £8 a year or more to give the chancellor 6s. 8d. annually, in order that he might commission sermons in the Minster. 'And the chancellor shall at his own discretion provide, nominate and assign pious and learned preachers who shall sincerely preach the word of God in the church or chapter house on rogation days and Sundays, and other seasons of the year.'[6] This new provision did not excuse the dean, chancellor, and other canons from preaching as they had been expected to do under the old statutes, but now it was intended that preaching should be more frequent.

While Lee remained archbishop, on the prompting of the privy council the chapter took its first steps in pulling down monuments associated with the papal supremacy. Directed by Layton they authorized the breaking-up of the jewelled portable shrine of St. William in October 1541, and applied a little of the £64 they raised from its sale to buy bibles for some of their York churches.[7] There was as yet little evidence of Protestant thinking in the Minster. Perhaps the injunctions which Lee gave to the dean and chapter concerning the parish churches in their care reflect his theological caution. He required the dean and chapter to see that in the parish churches appropriated to the Minster the priests taught their people the Pater Noster, the Salutation of our Lady, and the Creed in English, and to repeat prayers in English after the curate; and he expected the curates themselves to buy a bible in English, and to read and compare it with the Latin Vulgate. The only one of Lee's injunctions which could not have been devised by a reforming Catholic was that ordering ministers publicly to deny the authority of the bishop of Rome, and to proclaim the king supreme head of the Church under God.[8] Not until Lee died in 1544, and Robert Holgate replaced him, did an active Protestant archbishop appear in the church of York.

Holgate held his first visitation of the Minster in March 1547, and turned immediately to the lack of frequent preaching. Individual canons or their

---

[5] *York Statutes*, pp. 41–9; G. Austen, *The Statutes of the Church* (*Y.M. Hist. Tr.*, no. 18, 1927); *VCH Yorkshire* iii. p. 380.

[6] YML, Torre, 'Minster' p. 766.

[7] H. Nicolas (ed.), *Proceedings and Ordinances of the Privy Council of England*, vii (London 1837), p. 247; Browne, *History* i. p. 293; BIHR, D/C R. Reg. fo. 117ᵛ.

[8] YML, MS. M. 1. 7 1 (23 Sept. 1538).

deputies were not preaching their sermons as laid down in the recent statutes. They, the four dignitaries, and the vicars choral did not even perform their duties in attending divine service and, when they did attend, used too much 'confabulation'. Neglect of the Minster fabric and ornaments continued; copes and vestments needed repair, while parts of the Minster itself had fallen into decay. The archbishop saw the Minster establishment as something of a parasite upon the diocese, and admonished prebendaries who had benefices in the country for spending all their time in the city of York and for not living on their cures as was their bounden duty.[9] Yet, despite Holgate's attempts at innovation, much of the old order remained; chantry chaplains still thronged the Minster, saying their masses, and the vicars choral, though their numbers had decreased much below the nominal thirty-six, still carried on the round of services in the choir.

The government of Edward VI fully perceived the dangers of allowing these reminders of the Catholic past to persist in the new State Church, and it acted swiftly in ordering a royal visitation of all English cathedrals. In common with the clergy of other cathedrals, it required the ministers of York to abstain from drinking, dicing, carding, hunting, hawking, and all unlawful games and, once service had ended, to devote themselves to reading and studying the Scriptures. Whenever sermons were preached, all other services in the Minster should cease, and all clergy present should attend on the preacher. As well as providing two bibles in the choir for the ministers' use, and two others in the body of the church to be available for the laity, the government instructed all cathedrals to set up libraries and to stock them with the works of the early fathers—Augustine, Basil, Gregory, Nazianzen, Jerome, Ambrose, Crysostom, Cyprian, Theophylact—and 'good' modern writers like Erasmus.[10]

When the royal visitors reached York in October 1547, they did not restrict themselves to tendering these general injunctions, but devised particular injunctions appropriate for the archbishop, the dean and chapter, and all other ecclesiastical ministers of the cathedral church of York. They directed the greater part of their efforts towards simplifying the Minster services. On those days when the nine lessons had been appointed to be sung, now the visitors instructed the cathedral clergy only to sing matins of six lessons and six psalms. They ordered them to sing only one mass a day, at 9 a.m., and to abandon the singing of any hours, prime, and dirge, and even prescribed the two anthems they should sing. The time

[9] YML, MS. H. 3. 3. fo. 36^r.
[10] YML, MS. H. 3. 3. fos. 46^r–47^r (printed in W. H. Frere and W. P. M. Kennedy (eds.), *Visitation Articles and Injunctions of the Period of the Reformation* (1910), ii. pp. 135–9).

which the clergy saved in performing the round of services the visitors wanted spent in the study and contemplation of God's Word.[11]

The Act of 1547, which abolished chantry foundations and annexed their revenues to the Crown, caused perhaps the greatest alteration in the Minster in the Edwardian period. At one stroke some fifty or so chantries disappeared and the chantry priests who had lived corporately in St. William's College lost their living.[12] The number of relatively uneducated priests in the Minster was thus considerably cut down. The abolition of chantries also affected the vicars choral, for many of the vicars had combined their office with that of a chantry priest in the Minster. It seemed at one stage that they might lose their corporate dwellings in the Bedern as well. Although this did not happen, as the dean and chapter prevailed upon the government to confirm the vicars choral in their estates, the number of vicars which these lands could support continued to fall. There had been twenty-one vicars in 1530; in 1558 there were ten.[13]

Royal confiscation of plate and vestments, begun under Henry VIII, went on throughout the reign of his son. The Edwardian government did its best to ensure that no valuables were diverted from the royal coffers; and chalices of gold and silver, boxes for singing bread, censers, gold and silver basins, sconces, cruets, paxes, pectoral crosses of gold and silver set with precious stones, candlesticks, superaltars, standing cups, bowls, and holy water pots all left York for London. Not even the residentiaries' plate, silver gilt basins, ewers, goblets, and ale pots escaped the commissioners' notice. At the same time the government took practically all of the immense number of vestments possessed by the Minster; nearly fifty red and purple copes, dozens of green, blue, white, and black copes and sets of vestments, altar cloths and curtains, fringes, hangings, canopies, cloths of tissue, turkey carpets, and mitres decorated with diamonds, sapphires, and pearls. When, in 1552, Holgate ordered the place above the high altar where the images had stood to be painted with Scripture texts, the transformation of the Minster from a resplendent, if somewhat shabby, edifice of late medieval Catholicism to a sombre temple of the new Protestantism must have been practically complete.[14]

Holgate's second series of injunctions breathe a new urgency for the spreading of Protestantism. He required the dean and chapter to appoint a theologian to read a theology lecture in addition to the lectures which the chancellor had customarily been expected to deliver. He wished the vicars,

---

[11] YML, MS. H. 3. 3. fos. 47ᵛ–48ʳ (printed in part in Frere and Kennedy, op. cit. ii. pp. 153–7).
[12] D. M. Palliser, *The Reformation in York 1534–1553* (Borthwick Papers, no. 40, York, 1971), p. 4.
[13] YML, F. Harrison, MS. 'List of Vicars Choral Documents', p. 3.
[14] *Fabric Rolls*, pp. 306–14.

deacons, and all inferior ministers to be present daily at the lectures, and gave the reader himself, or a prebendary, the duty of examining them. The instruction of the clergy came first, followed by that of the laity. The archbishop imposed upon all prebendaries the responsibility of preaching in person or by proxy on one Sunday in the year; by placing an extra burden upon the dignitaries of the cathedral, he succeeded in arranging for a sermon on every Sunday. Under the 1552 Prayer Book the set services in the Minster had been further curtailed; the vicars now sang morning and evening prayer and the communion service, and, moreover, were instructed to sing so that the words might be heard distinctly. The archbishop banished the playing of organs during divine service, exhorting the organist who combined the office with that of master of the choristers to serve God in such other ways as he could conveniently do.[15]

Holgate's zeal for religious education underlay the greater part of his injunctions. He required the vicars choral under 40 years old and the deacons to learn by heart every week a chapter of St. Paul's Epistles, starting with Romans, allowing those over 40 merely to read the chapter, but with sufficient concentration as to be able to repeat its contents in detail; he wished the choir-boys to learn a chapter of the Gospels weekly, beginning with St. Matthew. The examination of the choir-boys he left to their master, but proposed to examine the vicars himself. He further ordered that a deacon who did not daily attend the grammar school after due warning should be expelled. He had devised a scheme which, if it had ever been set in full operation, could have turned the Minster into an institution for educating young men for the Protestant ministry. Yet of the whole scheme only the archbishop's grammar school in the York parish of St. John-del-Pyke which he had founded in 1546 survived the upheavals of Mary's reign.[16]

Until 1553 no York prebendary or other ecclesiastic serving in the Minster seems to have opposed the religious changes of the reigns of Henry VIII and Edward VI so strongly that he resigned his office. For most clergy—and this would probably have been particularly true of the vicars choral and the deacons—their office was their livelihood and in return for this they seem to have been ready to accept whatever changes the royal government or their archbishop might impose. With the restoration of Catholicism by Mary, some of these men found that they no longer had this freedom to drift with the tide. Archbishop Holgate, for one, could not choose between conforming and retaining his office, or remaining loyal to

[15] Frere and Kennedy, *Visitation Articles* ii. pp. 310–21.
[16] *Deed of Foundation of the Free School of Robert Holgate, York* (Archbishop Holgate Soc. Record Ser. no. 1, n. d. [1948?]).

Protestantism. He was deprived at once on account of his marriage and replaced by Nicholas Heath who, although a largely absentee archbishop, did much to secure the return of the pillaged archiepiscopal lands to the see. On the other hand, Nicholas Wotton, who had succeeded Layton in 1544, continued as dean without a murmur. The rest of the cathedral chapter came under scrutiny and a minor purge took place, something that the two previous reigns had not seen. On the issue of marriage again, seven canons (Thomas Cottesford, prebendary of Apesthorpe, Robert Watson of Strensall, Miles Wilson of Ulleskelf, Thomas Wilson of Bilton, William Clayborough of Ampleforth, William Perepointe of Husthwaite, and Henry Williams of Fridaythorpe) all lost their prebends. Three vicars choral (Robert Cragges, Walter Lancaster, and Peter Walker) were also deprived on account of their marriage, but Walker later regained his office in the Minster after doing penance. At least some of these men seem to have been convinced Protestants, and most had come to their offices in the reign of Edward VI. Cottesford, at least, believed sufficiently strongly in Protestantism to join the Marian exiles, while Thomas Wilson received a prebend at York again in 1560 and went on to enjoy an active career in the Elizabethan Church.[17]

Little information remains concerning the restoration of Catholic services and ceremonial in the Minster. The majority of prebendaries and vicars seem merely to have accepted the change, though some citizens of York positively welcomed the return to the old forms of religion. In his will made in 1556 George Gale, alderman of York, left to the high altar of the cathedral in return for prayers a front cloth of purple, red, and blue velvet with the Resurrection wrought on it in gold; a year later Sir Leonard Beckwith gave the Minster a canopy of green and red sarsenet under which the blessed sacrament used to be carried. In 1557 somewhat belatedly the accountant of the fabric fund paid for the repainting of the high altar and for setting up again a statue of Our Lady and St. John.[18] Very gradually the Minster built up a new stock of vestments and ornaments necessary for Catholic ceremonial, for in 1559 the chapter could order the sale of a pair of censers and five years later agreed to the sale of 'all such plate as was used for the furniture of the old services in the choir'.[19] Nevertheless, this return to the old forms of worship does not seem to have aroused any deep enthusiasm. As had happened before the Henrician changes, deputies still conducted the services since the dean and most of the prebendaries did not reside, some

[17] *VCH York* 148; A. G. Dickens, *The Marian Reaction in the Diocese of York* (St Anthony's Papers, no. 11, York, 1957), pp. 23, 25, 28.
[18] *Fabric Rolls*, p. 306 n.; YML, MS. E.3. 48, Fabric Rolls, 1556/7–1557/8.
[19] Browne, *History* i. 300–1; BM, Harl. MS. 6971 fo. 156.

of the prebendal houses in the close needed urgent repair, and pigeons still fouled the Minster building.[20]

Yet not quite all of the Marian restoration of Catholicism at York can be dismissed as a blind reaction; something of the spirit of the Catholic Reformation touched the dean and chapter when they decided to refound the Minster school. Whether this school had survived the Reformation in York is extremely difficult to determine; it had lost a boarding house for fifty boys on the dissolution of St. Mary's Abbey and, even if it struggled on, it may well have been outclassed by Archbishop Holgate's new grammar school. In 1557, inspired by Cardinal Pole's recent decrees at the Synod of Westminster, Dean Wotton and the chapter set up a grammar school for fifty boys in the former hospital in the Horsefair, for the express object of propagating Catholicism and combating Protestantism. The school, they considered, could help militant shepherds

put to flight the rapacious wolves, that is devilish men, ill-understanding the Catholic faith, from the sheepfolds of the sheep entrusted to them; which object we hope may be more easily attained if the giddy and ignorant youth is kept in tight reins by the work of schoolmasters, and having been exercised alike in letters and learning as in sound morality, may afterwards pass into the broad field of sacred and canonical literature and emerge learned.[21]

The Marian dean and chapter, however, had no more success in their scheme for religious indoctrination than Archbishop Holgate had done, though their school survived to serve a subsequently Protestant city. Within a year of the school's refoundation Mary had died, and the York dean and chapter were expected to turn Protestant again.

In 1559 the prebendaries of York, like the other cathedral chapters throughout the country, had to make a decision which they had not been required to make so explicitly earlier in the century. The seven prebendaries had been deprived under Mary because they had married in Edward's reign; they had not been asked in the first instance whether they would accept the pope as the head of the Church and the restoration of Catholic liturgy. In 1559 there was no longer any blurring of the issue; the prebendaries had now to face the theological and moral problem, whether they could accept the royal supremacy and the re-establishment of a Protestant English Church. For the first time the episcopal hierarchy led the way, and Nicholas Heath in common with the rest of the English bishops refused to recognize Elizabeth as head of the English Church. Apart from

---

[20] J. C. H. Aveling, *Catholic Recusancy in the City of York, 1558–1791* (Catholic Record Soc., 1970), pp. 17–18; PRO S.P. 12/10/244–5.
[21] A. F. Leach, *Early Yorkshire Schools* (YAS Rec. Ser. xxvii, 1899), p. xxxv.

the example of their absentee archbishop, the prebendaries at York did not receive much guidance about the way they should act when the royal commissioners reached York in September 1559. Nicholas Wotton, their non-resident dean, did not appear before the visitors at York; but he accepted the royal supremacy as dean of Canterbury and so contrived to hold the deanery of York without a break from his appointment in 1544 through all the changes of the reigns of Henry VIII, Edward VI, Mary, and Elizabeth until he died in 1567. More significantly—for he had been active in carrying through the restoration of Catholicism in the York diocese between 1553 and 1558 and had served frequently as a canon residentiary—John Rokeby, the precentor, headed the band of prebendaries who agreed to recognize the royal supremacy and accept a Protestant prayer book. Robert Babthorpe, the subdean, together with George Williamson asked for time to think, but subscribed within a week. Some prebendaries, and not all of these had been appointed under Mary, did not hesitate to refuse the oath. Robert Pursglove, suffragan bishop of Hull, who had been prebendary of Wistow since 1541, a regular attender at chapter meetings, and occasionally a residentiary, had already refused the oath when the royal commissioners had visited Southwell the previous month. He went away to live for a time at Ugthorpe in the North Riding where in 1561 he was described as being 'very wealthy, stiff in papistry and of estimation in the county'. He subsequently retired to Derbyshire where he died at Tideswell in 1579. Geoffrey Downes, a prebendary of York since 1533 and chancellor of York since 1537, who like Pursglove had taken a prominent part in Minster activities in the Marian period, had also refused to take the oath at Southwell, though he may have compromised later since Archbishop Young consented to his being granted a pension a few months before his death in 1562. Two prebendaries, Dr. Palmes and Dr. Marshall, openly defied the royal commissioners in York in September. Roger Marshall, once prior of Sempringham, had become succentor of York in 1546; after his deprivation he went south to Newmarket. A hostile observer reported that he was wealthy and not unlearned. George Palmes, who since 1539 had held in succession the prebends of Givendale, Langtoft, and Wetwang, and had also been archdeacon of York and a frequent residentiary, withdrew to his family home of Naburn near York, where his relatives remained recusants until late in the eighteenth century. Two eminent Marian clerics, though never resident in York, John Boxall, secretary to the queen, and Thomas Reynold, one of her chaplains and bishop elect of Hereford at the time of her death, lost the prebends of Stillington and North Newbald respectively among the mass of their other ecclesiastical preferments when they refused to swear to the royal supremacy in 1559. The royal commissioners definitely deprived five other prebendaries in 1559 for refusing the oath of supremacy—John Seaton of Ulleskelf, Thomas Arden of Weighton, Alban Langdale of Ampleforth, Arthur Lowe of Fridaythorpe, and William Taylor of Fenton—while two others, Baldwin Norton of Langtoft and Richard Petre of Knaresborough, conformed in 1559 but became recusants soon after. When other doubtful cases are considered it seems that around half the members of the chapter lost their prebends at the beginning of Elizabeth's reign, a displacement of canons such as the chapter had never experienced before.[22]

The lack of leadership from its senior members from which the chapter suffered in 1559 continued during the first years of Elizabeth's rule. Because of the death of her first candidate, Elizabeth did not appoint an archbishop of York until the beginning of 1561. While there was no archbishop, Ralph Rokeby, himself closely related to some of the Yorkshire gentry hostile to the religious settlement, carried on the administration. When he came to York, Thomas Young consciously tried to work with the conservative clergy he had inherited; and with such loyal government servants as Wotton and Rokeby remaining prebendaries the chapter seemed scarcely capable of initiating change, though slow change there was, as the conservative canons died or withdrew. In 1561 Richard Barnes replaced Downes as chancellor and soon began preaching energetically in the Minster against the 'absurd doings' of the popes. When in 1567 Wotton died and was buried at Canterbury, the Crown appointed Matthew Hutton dean. The chapter at last had at its head a comparatively young man—active, resident, and a committed Protestant.[23]

One innovation did take place at the Minster very early in Elizabeth's reign; the appearance of the wives of the married prebendaries. It was by no means universally welcomed in the city. Some Edwardian clerics had indeed married. Archbishop Holgate had made a none too wise venture into matrimony in 1549, only to find in 1551 that a suit had been brought against him in the ecclesiastical courts on the ground that his presumed wife, Barbara, daughter of Roger Wentworth, had been pre-contracted to another. This suit against Holgate failed, but four years later the Marian government both deprived Holgate of his see and forced him to renounce his marriage.[24] Since she was Holgate's legal wife for so short a time, Barbara

[22] H. N. Birt, *The Elizabethan Religious Settlement* (1907), pp. 151–2: *VCH York* p. 149; Aveling, *Catholic Recusancy in York*, pp. 20–1, 294, 305–6; PRO S.P. 12/10/29–40; H. Gee, *The Elizabethan Clergy and the Settlement of Religion, 1558–1564* (Oxford, 1898), p. 179; T. B. Trappes-Lomax, 'The Palmes Family of Naburn', *YAJ* xi (1962), 444; BIHR, A.B. 1. fo. 63.
[23] *CSPDom, 1566–79*, pp. 72–3; Aveling, op. cit., pp. 21–2.
[24] A. G. Dickens, 'The Marriage and Character of Archbishop Holgate', *EHR* lii (1937), 428–42.

Holgate can hardly have made much impression upon the Minster clergy, while there is no evidence that any of the Edwardian prebendaries who married (Clayborough, Cottesford, Perepoint, Watson, Henry Williams, Miles, and Thomas Wilson) ever lived in York. The first decade of Elizabeth's reign in consequence saw the continued presence of clergy wives in Minster society for the first time, and among these ladies there were some of considerable interest. Archbishop Young gave a lead. He had married first in Edward's reign, a daughter of the registrar of St. David's where he held the office of precentor. On the death of this wife, he married Jane, daughter of Thomas Kynaston of Staffordshire, by whom he had at least two sons. Jane Young accompanied Archbishop Young to York in 1561; she survived him for upwards of forty years and then, dying in 1614, was buried in the Minster.[25] Richard Barnes had already married Fredesmund, daughter of Ralph Gifford of Buckinghamshire, when he became chancellor in 1561; they had a large family of five sons and four daughters.[26] Since Matthew Hutton resided regularly after he took up his appointment as dean in 1567, his second wife, Beatrice, daughter of Sir Thomas Fincham, must have been a familiar figure in York. They had several children. After Beatrice's death in 1582, Hutton married Frances, widow of Martin Bowes, and this was the Mrs. Hutton with whom Lady Margaret Hoby enjoyed talking of religion at Bishopthorpe in the 1590s.[27] Perhaps the lady in the close who had the most irreproachably Protestant ancestry was Mrs. Palmer, wife of William Palmer whom Grindal made chancellor in 1571 and who held the office till 1605. She had been born Anna Taylor, the daughter of Dr. Rowland Taylor, the Marian martyr, as she proudly recorded on the monument which she erected to her husband's memory. The Palmers had seven children.[28] At least some of the citizens of York shared the queen's hostility to married clergy, and reacted to the presence of clergy wives in the same way as Elizabeth tended to do. In 1570 Alderman Allen appeared in court for objecting to a sermon preached by Prebendary Tunstall, in which the latter had defended clerical marriage, arguing that the apostles themselves had been married men.[29]

Despite the appearance of clergy wives in the close, the dean and chapter remained essentially medieval in constitution as Young's successor, Edmund Grindal, found in 1572 when he attempted to continue with Protestant reformation. Now that the Puritans had begun to attack

[25] *DNB* xxi. 1305–6; Willis, *Survey* i. 47.
[26] *DNB* i. 1172–3.
[27] *DNB* xxviii. 257–8; D. M. Meads (ed.), *Diary of Lady Margaret Hoby* (1930), p. 73.
[28] *DNB* xv. 164–5; YML, Torre, 'Minster' p. 250.
[29] Aveling, op. cit., p. 169.

cathedral foundations, Elizabethan higher ecclesiastics no longer had the freedom to question fundamentally the value of such institutions, as Cranmer had done earlier. In these difficult circumstances Grindal perhaps achieved as much as he could have hoped to achieve, working within the conventions of an ancient corporation. He returned to the educational scheme of Holgate, exhorting the dean and chapter again to provide a reader in divinity apart from the chancellor. He required this reader to lecture twice a week in the cathedral and all the vicars choral and inferior ministers to attend his lectures. He had the weekly preaching schedule renewed, and ordered the precentor to see that the choristers were virtuously brought up in the principles of religion. Grindal made a further contribution to Protestant uniformity by his attack upon Catholicism, still apparently latent within the Minster, as elsewhere in the diocese. On all major feast days and on the first Sunday of every month in which a major feast did not fall, he wished holy communion to be celebrated, if not more frequently, and all dignitaries, other prebendaries, and all inferior ministers in the cathedral, all excuses apart, to prepare themselves to communicate. This would have made any token conformity in the future extremely difficult.[30] Yet Grindal's admonition does not seem to have banished all suspicion of Catholic sympathies among some of the Minster clergy, for five years later Archbishop Sandys still felt it necessary to ask the dean and chapter whether they knew of any of their officers who had spoken against the Word of God or were known in their hearts to be against the religion publicly received and to provide their names, and also the names of those who used to say popish mass, or favour popish religion, or who relieved those who did so. Sandys, like many of his fervent Protestant contemporaries, may have exaggerated the extent of Catholicism in York. Some, though not very many, of the laymen who served the dean and chapter as registrars or accountants and some of the ecclesiastical lawyers who lived chiefly in St. Michael-le-Belfrey's parish were conservative in religion, and others had family connections with the recusant community based on Holy Trinity parish, King's Court. John Fletcher, who had previously been master of the Minster school, was imprisoned in 1575 in St. Peter's prison for recusancy. Religious conservatism, a state of mind very different from deliberate recusancy, lingered long in a body as traditional as a cathedral chapter, and an archbishop on his own could do little to alter it.[31]

The man who could influence the chapter far more than the archbishop was the dean, at least one who resided, and it may be no accident that in the

---

[30] Frere and Kennedy, *Visitation Articles* iii. 345–54; Aveling, op. cit., pp. 30–40.
[31] YML, MS. Coll. 1906; Aveling, op. cit., pp. 309–19.

year of Hutton's appointment the Minster accountant commissioned workmen to whiten places in the cathedral where the altars had been and began buying Geneva psalm-books and an English bible. Fairly regularly after 1567 he purchased more copies of Geneva psalms.[32] Yet not even Hutton, despite his undoubted zeal, could make much headway against the chapter's inertia. Grindal wanted to have the Minster statutes revised, so that superstitious and unnecessary statutes could be removed and new statutes substituted which would accord with the spirit of a Protestant cathedral. He nominated Hutton, the precentor and the chancellor, and three other prebendaries to go through the old statutes and to suggest a revision; but nothing came of the scheme, and the dean and chapter continued to operate under such of the statutes of 1221, modified in 1542, as were 'not repugnant to the word of God'. In his attempt to make chapter meetings more representative of the whole capitular body and not merely of the canons residentiary, Grindal seems to have had rather more success. He proposed that henceforth chapter meetings should be summoned regularly on the Wednesday mornings immediately following the feasts of St. Martin, the Purification, Whitsun, and St. Matthew, and that all canons living in the diocese of York be given twenty days advance warning of the meeting; all prebendaries who lived more than twenty miles from York had the right to appoint a proctor. Particularly towards the end of the sixteenth century more than the customary three or four did attend some chapter meetings but the trend did not last. By the middle of the reign of James I the number declined again, and until the Civil War did not normally rise above three or four at a meeting.[33]

Grindal was the last archbishop to try to make the Elizabethan dean and chapter participate more actively in the life of the diocese. He did not remain long enough in York to bring the chapter to reform its statutes; no other archbishop even attempted constitutional reform, partly perhaps because cathedrals as institutions were coming increasingly under attack from Puritans. In 1572 the writers of the Admonition to the Parliament castigated cathedral churches as 'dens . . . of all loitering lubbers', adding ominously, 'the church of God never knew them, neither doth any reformed church in the world know them'. They went on to urge that cathedral endowments should be used to redeem impropriate livings, so that all parish minsters might receive a sufficient maintenance.[34] In the next decade the propaganda directed against cathedrals became even more strident. Advanced Puritans attacked prebendaries for being 'unprofitable

[32] YML, Fabric Rolls, E. 3. 50, 1567/8–1568/9; E. 3. 51, 1568/9–1569/70.
[33] Frere and Kennedy, *Visitation Articles* iii. 345–54.
[34] W. H. Frere and C. E. Douglas (eds.), *Puritan Manifestoes* (1954), pp. 32, 95.

members, for the most part dumb dogs, unskilful sacrificing priests, destroying drones, or rather caterpillars of the word, they consume yearly, some £2,500, some £3,000, some more, some less, whereof no profit, but rather great hurt cometh to the church of God and this commonwealth'.[35]

It would be less than fair to maintain that no profit, even by the standard of these Elizabethan Puritans, came to the diocese of York from the continuing existence of the dean and chapter. Occasionally an exceptional prebendary like Edmund Bunny, who had been brought north by Grindal, used his prebends in the cathedrals of York, St. Paul's, and Carlisle to finance his itinerant preaching throughout the north of England. The Minster itself provided sermons which the townspeople of York could come to hear, and fairly often in the 1570s the York High Commission bound over recusants to hear sermons there.[36] Yet whether townsmen did attend the Minster regularly is doubtful. In 1570 the corporation of York ordered two representatives of every household in the city to go to sermons in the Minster on Sundays and holidays; but by 1580 the city, under pressure from the President of the Council in the North, began financing its own civic preachers based on the city churches, which it continued to support with growing enthusiasm until the Civil War. The mayor and corporation attended the Minster on special occasions, to give thanks for the victory over the Turks in 1571, or for the escape of the queen from an attempt on her life in 1586, but they did not come in a body week in, week out, as the corporation of Winchester apparently did to its cathedral.[37] Rather the Minster remained more a concern of the Yorkshire gentry, as it may well have been in the Middle Ages. Lady Margaret Hoby, on a visit to York from Hackness in 1599, went as a matter of course to service in the Minster where she heard the chancellor, William Palmer, preach, 'but to small profit to any'. The following year she found Mr. Smith, who was not a prebendary, more tolerable; in his sermon he upheld 'the truth against the papist, the question being whether the regenerate do sin'.[38]

The impression grows of the Minster as an island of privilege, isolated from the city of York, even isolated from the civic clergy, and the archbishops now seem to have lost the inclination to interfere. Sandys inquired into possible recusancy among members of the Minster staff, but otherwise contented himself at his visitation with repeating the inquiries Grindal had made. Because of his quarrels with Dean Hutton and the

---

[35] A. Peel (ed.), *The Seconde Parte of a Register* (Cambridge, 1915), ii. p. 211.

[36] Aveling, op. cit., pp. 172, 176, 202.

[37] A. Raine (ed.), *YCR*, YAS Rec. Ser. vii. 13, 40–1; viii. 123; Winchester City Record Office, First Book of Ordinances, fo. 15; I owe this reference to the kindness of Dr. R. Houlbrooke.

[38] Meads (ed.), *Diary of Lady Margaret Hoby*, pp. 73, 113.

President of the Council in the North, he chose to live not at Bishopthorpe but Southwell. Archbishop Piers, his successor, held office for less than five years and, although he visited his diocese twice in this time, he seems to have made little impact upon the cathedral. Since, earlier in his career, he had been simultaneously dean of Chester, dean of Salisbury, and dean of Christ Church, he was scarcely the archbishop to overhaul the York chapter. Hutton, between 1567 and 1589, had gained considerable respect as a resident dean, but for part of the decade when he came back to York as archbishop he had also to act as President of the Council in the North, and civil administration demanded much of his energy. During his long tenure of office Archbishop Matthew interested himself in frequent preaching throughout the diocese rather than in influencing chapter affairs; he did no more than summarize Sandys's articles when he visited the Minster in 1615. Whatever his innovating tendencies in theology and church government, Archbishop Neile at his visitation of the chapter in 1632 merely reissued Matthew's visitation articles word for word. Any impetus which there had been for Protestant change in the chapter had quite died away by the early years of the reign of Charles I.[39]

The deans of York must surely bear some responsibility for the stagnation into which the Minster had declined after the mid-Elizabethan period. When Matthew Hutton left the deanery of York for the bishopric of Durham in 1589 York lost the only active, resident dean it had had since Brian Higden, or was to have again for almost a century. John Thornborough, the new dean, rapidly joined the ranks of the clerical pluralists. From 1594 he combined the office of dean of York, first with the bishopric of Limerick and then with that of Bristol, and only relinquished the deanery when in 1617 he obtained the relatively wealthy see of Worcester. George Meriton, who succeeded him, seems to have been a far more conscientious dean, but he only lived until 1624. The next dean, John Scott, soon acquired a notorious reputation for gambling; because of the debts he accumulated he spent the latter period of his office in the King's Bench prison in London where he died in 1644.[40]

The ladies of the close seem to have striven far more than their husbands in the early seventeenth century to keep the Elizabethan tradition of Protestant piety alive. Frances Matthew, wife of Archbishop Matthew, could indeed be described as the living embodiment of this tradition. The daughter of the Edwardian Bishop Barlow, she had married as her first

[39] YML, MS. Coll. 1906, Sandys's Visitation Articles, 1577; M. 1. 7. 4, Matthew's Visitation Articles, 1615; Coll. 1906, Neile's Visitation Articles, 1632.

[40] YML, Act Book H. 4. fos. 261ʳ–519ʳ; *DNB* xix. 766–7, Thornborough; J. and J. A. Venn, *Alumni Cantabrigienses*, part I, iv (Cambridge, 1922) p. 32, Scott.

husband Matthew, the second son of Archbishop Parker, and so had 'a bishop to her father, an archbishop to her father-in-law, four bishops to her brethren and an archbishop to her husband'. She came to York with Archbishop Matthew in 1606 and, outliving him by a year, died in York in 1629. Perhaps from disappointment at the conduct of her sons (Sir Tobie Matthew, their eldest son, to his parents' great grief had announced his conversion to Rome some years previously) Mrs. Matthew left her husband's magnificent library of over three thousand learned volumes to the cathedral, and these books form the nucleus of the present Minster library.[41] Much younger than Mrs. Matthew, but it seems of a similar temperament, Jane Hodson, wife of Chancellor Hodson, was accounted 'pious, modest, benovolent'. She died in 1636, aged 38, a 'fecund mother', as her husband without any exaggeration described her on the memorial he erected in the Minster; she had born him twenty-four children. It has been suggested that Phineas Hodson could not afford not to co-operate in the Arminian changes of Archbishop Neile because of the claims of his huge family.[42] Prudential considerations of this nature for the requirements of her family weighed little with Mrs. Scott. Her husband's delinquencies deterred her not at all from setting her face against Archbishop Neile's policies. She and her daughters openly disregarded the Church's ruling over receiving sacraments in their own parish and crossed York to take holy communion at the hands of John Birchill, the Puritan incumbent of St. Martin's Micklegate. One of her daughters married Thomas Squire, a public preacher at the Minster, alleged as early as 1627 to have held theological opinions apparently too Protestant for the party in power.[43]

When Richard Neile, a close supporter of Laud, became archbishop in 1632, he encouraged the spread of Arminianism among members of the chapter. This brought a fresh element into the antagonism between the mayor and corporation of York and the Minster which was partly jurisdictional, partly theological. Until the accession of Charles I the corporation seems to have been apathetic towards the Minster, showing no particular interest in its services or organization, but also no clear hostility; after about 1625 a distinct change occurred. The first clash over jurisdiction came in 1627, in connection with the immunity of the liberty of St. Peter. The dean and chapter claimed the right to arrest York citizens misbehaving in the Minster Yard and elsewhere in the liberty, and to bring them before special capitular sessions of the peace, but the corporation increasingly

---

[41] *DNB* xiii. pp. 60–3, 63–8.
[42] Venn, *Al. Cant.*, part I, ii. p. 386; YML, Torre, 'Minster' p. 251; R. A. Marchant, *The Puritans and the Church Courts in the Diocese of York, 1560–1642* (1960), pp. 50–1.
[43] Marchant, op. cit., pp. 44, 87, 227–9, 280–1.

began to encourage its citizens to defy the Minster's jurisdiction. Matters grew worse when the city obtained a new charter from the Crown in 1632 under which the city seemed to be in a position to annex villages previously in the liberty of St. Peter, though ultimately the city failed to make good its claim. The quarrel reached its height in an unedifying dispute over seating in the Minster. The aldermanic body was already on the alert for any ecclesiastical slights to its dignity, and when in 1633 Archdeacon Wickham sat in a stall in the Minster choir higher than that of the lord mayor, the corporation's indignation knew no bounds. It decided to boycott the Minster entirely until Wickham apologized for his disrespect which, after the intervention of the central government, he had no choice but to do.

Doctrinally, too, in this period, the chapter and the city governors drew farther and farther apart. By the early seventeenth century the city government had become enthusiastically Protestant. Those of the citizens of York who made bequests to religion now left money to supplement the preaching in their parish churches; the Minster, apparently, did not enter into their consideration. They lined up solidly behind those of their city clergy who were being prosecuted in the archiepiscopal courts for not observing the whole of the Book of Common Prayer, and for holding religious conventicles. Archbishop Neile and the two members of the chapter on whom he chiefly relied, Phineas Hodson and Henry Wickham, failed completely to convey the spiritual attractions of Arminianism to the leading citizens. At a time when the dean and chapter were making an exceptional effort to beautify the Minster, no member of the corporation made a gift. The money for setting up the great organ, buying new plate and frontal cloths, for colouring and gilding the screen behind the altar, all came from a thousand pounds' fine imposed by the York High Commission court which the king granted to the dean and chapter. The king took a personal interest in the cathedral and ordered unsightly pews to be cleared away and houses built against the Minster walls to be demolished on his visit to York in 1633, but the citizens of York did not share his concern.[44] It proved even more difficult for the laity to understand the spiritual self-abnegation which formed a part of Arminianism. When Timothy Thurscross, who had succeeded his father, Henry, as prebendary of Langtoft, underwent a conversion from Puritanism to Arminianism and in 1638 resigned the archdeaconry of Cleveland and his vicarage of Kirkby Moorside, being 'much troubled in his conscience for having obtained them through simony', Sir Henry Slingsby could only describe Thurscross's scruples and the spiritual and bodily austerities he imposed upon himself and his wife

---

[44] Ibid., pp. 74–96, 125–7; *Fabric Rolls*, pp. 319, 325–8.

with a wondering incomprehension.[45] Among the rulers of the city a positive desire to change both the Minster's liturgical elaboration and institutional exclusiveness was beginning to develop.

The two glowing reports of the Laudian services in the Minster, the one written by some Norwich gentlemen inspecting the antiquities of York, the other composed over thirty years after the event by a nostalgic and highly enthusiastic musician, from all the evidence did not reflect the feelings of the inhabitants of York. They did not appreciate the 'fair, large, high organ, newly built, richly gilt, carved and painted', or 'a deep and sweet snowy robe of choristers', though the attendance in state of 'the lord mayor in his gold chain, with his twelve grave brethren, two sheriffs, two esquires, vizt. the sword bearer, and his left-hand marcher with the great mace, the recorder, many serjeants with small maces' accorded more fully with the tastes of the citizens. The crowds who flocked to the Minster at the time of the siege of York in 1644, made up partly, as Mace concedes, of royalist 'lords, knights and gentlemen of the countries round about' who had taken refuge in the city, seem to have been even less representative of Minster congregations in normal times. Mace greatly admired the custom at York 'which I hear not of in any other cathedral, which was that always, before the sermon, the whole congregation sang a psalm, together with the choir and the organ: and you must also know, that there was then a most excellent-large-plump-lusty-full-speaking organ which cost . . . a thousand pounds'.[46] The citizens of York, as their subsequent actions showed, displayed little reluctance in dispensing with the organ and the choir, though they kept their communal psalm-singing. With the parliamentary victory over the royalists at Marston Moor, and the consequent surrender of the royalist garrison in York in July 1644, the Puritan aldermen and clergy of the city at last could make their true feelings about the Minster known. Through the York committee of the Northern Association the city now established a control over the city's religious life for which it had striven for decades.[47]

In many respects the Minster had been left wide open for a Puritan take-over. John Williams, the newly appointed archbishop, had indeed come to York to be enthroned in the summer of 1642 but then had been frightened by threats from parliamentarian troops and fled from Cawood in October to his ancestral home in Wales. Dean Scott had long been imprisoned in London for debt. Parliament ordered Richard Marsh, the Laudian

[45] D. Parsons (ed.), *The Diary of Sir Henry Slingsby* (1836), pp. 7–9.
[46] *Fabric Rolls*, p. 319 n.; T. Mace, *Musick's Monument* (1676), pp. 18–20.
[47] The Minute Book for the York Committee of the Northern Association 1645–50 is now preserved in YCA, E. 63 (extracts have been published in YAS Rec. Ser., *Miscellanea*, vi (1953), pp. 1–22).

archdeacon of York, and future dean, to be taken into custody in 1642 for his known allegiance to the Crown. Henry Wickham had died in 1641, George Stanhope in 1644, while the other well-known Laudian, Timothy Thurscross, seems already to have gone south to London. Phineas Hodson appears to have been the only important member of the chapter in York after July 1644. He lost his office of chancellor but the Yorkshire committee did not order his sequestration and allowed him a pension of £75 a year to maintain his family. Henry Mace, one of the vicars choral and vicar of St. Mary Bishophill junior, proved more adaptable and until 1647 found a new outlet for his talents in leading the psalm-singing in the Minster.[48]

With a speed which indicated its eagerness for reform, York corporation drew up a scheme to convert the Minster into a preaching centre for the whole city, and successfully petitioned Parliament for a grant of £600 a year out of the lands of deans and chapters to maintain four ministers based on the Minster, who would also preach in the city churches. From late in 1645 the Minster ministers began to receive their stipends of £150 a year.[49] They could in no way be seen as intellectual, religious, or social outsiders; indeed, one of the ministers, Thomas Calvert, had been born in the city. Calvert, a renowned Hebrew scholar, had held the living of Holy Trinity, King's Court, since 1638, but the three other ministers, Edward Bowles, Nathanial Rathband, and Theodore Herring, had not previously been closely associated with the city, though Bowles had married Archbishop Hutton's granddaughter. Bowles accompanied Fairfax to York as his chaplain, and soon became the leader of the parliamentarian clergy in the area, and dean of York in all but name. So highly did the corporation esteem him that in 1656 it gave him a permanent annuity of £50 and a little later offered him the freedom of the city without fee. Rathband, an Edinburgh graduate, only remained in York till 1650 when he moved to Prestwich and Peter Williams replaced him. Williams had been educated at Emmanuel College, Cambridge; his ministry in York was described as being 'painful and pious'. Herring, the other original minister appointed to the Minster, had also graduated from Emmanuel and he served in York till he died in 1658. On his death Richard Perrot left Cambridge to take up his work.[50]

Under the direction of these ministers the city's old suspicion of the Minster melted away, indeed for the first time the Minster seems to have been fully integrated in the life of the city. All its old isolation disappeared and the city took advantage of the times to obtain the abolition of the liberty of St. Peter. In 1654 the lord mayor sent representatives to London

[48] YCA, E. 63 fo. 84; A. G. Matthews, *Walker Revised* (Oxford, 1948), p. 394.
[49] YCA, E. 63 fos. 19, 24.
[50] YCA, Housebook 1650–63, fos. 52, 59, 84, 125.

to negotiate for the purchase of the liberty and by 1660 the city had taken over the jurisdiction of St. Peter's court. By 1654 Alderman Sir William Allanson had bought the deanery and lived in it as a private dwelling-house.[51] The fabric of the Minster also came under the city's control. Now that it belonged in a novel way to York, the corporation showed a new concern about its preservation and certainly there was no outburst of iconoclasm to mark this change of possession. Even in 1645 when the committee of the Northern Association ordered the great brass reading desk in the choir, the brass about the shrine called Thomas Becket's, and the silver candlesticks to be sold, it provided that the money raised by their sale should be used for the repair of the Minster fabric. The following year when the much disliked organ was taken down, together with the little altars in the side aisles, the corporation acted firmly against any possible looting of Minster goods. The city governors did not concern themselves exclusively with destroying what they considered to be monuments of superstition; they allowed new seating to be constructed in the Minster and repeatedly authorized minor restoration.[52]

Perhaps it would not be too much to claim that most members of the ruling class of the city found the form of religion established in York between 1644 and 1660 and directed by the four Minster ministers more congenial than any which they had enjoyed since the Reformation or were to enjoy again after the Restoration. With the return of the king in 1660 when all the signs indicated the imminent re-imposition of Anglicanism, they made one last attempt to retain some of the godly practices they had fostered in the past decade. They tried, though in vain, to keep the Minster ministers and formally approved a scheme to raise voluntary subscriptions to pay their stipends. Bowles, rumoured to have been offered the deanery of York, Calvert, Williams, and Perrot all chose to be ejected rather than conform, though Bowles died in 1662 before his ejection could be carried out. The city had no alternative but to accept the full restoration of the old religious order.[53]

Richard Marsh, the former archdeacon of York, appointed dean during the Civil War, returned to the city with haste to take up his office in 1660; on 7 August he held his first chapter meeting aided by Anthony Elcock, the new prebendary of Dunnington, and John Neile, nephew of the former archbishop, who had held the prebend of North Newbald since 1634 which he now exchanged for the much richer one of Strensall. With these two prebendaries, with Tobias Swinden, prebendary of Wistow, and Tobias

[51] Ibid., fos. 54, 72; Will of Sir William Allanson, BIHR, Reg. Test. lvi. 90.
[52] YCA, E. 63 fos. 20, 62, 64, 76–7, 84; Housebook 1650–63, fos. 48, 59.
[53] YCA, Housebook 1650–63, fo. 147.

Wickham, son of Archdeacon Wickham and now in his turn prebendary of Bilton and precentor, Marsh worked tirelessly to restore Anglicanism and to recover the lands of the church, determined that all at the Minster should be exactly as it used to be. The self-governing religious corporation, the liberty of St. Peter, the separation of the Minster from the civic churches, were re-established. When Archbishop Frewen came to carry out his visitation of the dean and chapter in February 1663 he expressed his uneasiness (subsequently fully justified) that the canons in their enthusiasm might have misappropriated the funds of the cathedral. He wanted to ensure that a due portion of the Minster's revenues should be set aside for the church's needs as in time past. He also ordered the chapter to see that none but grave, orthodox men and licensed preachers officiated in the cathedral, and that communicants received the sacrament kneeling. That there could be any change in the organization of the Minster which would enable it to serve the city and the diocese better in the future obviously occurred neither to him nor to the dean and chapter. The Commonwealth experiment might never have been tried; the Minster and the city became two exclusive corporations again, and each was the poorer for being so.[54]

In legal terminology the dean and chapter of York did indeed together constitute a corporation, yet historically the name may be misleading. It is doubtful whether between 1520 and 1670 a majority of prebendaries, who appear never to have set foot in the Minster, felt any particular corporate loyalty either towards the institution which provided their stipends or towards each other. A prebend need be no more than a sinecure, and a great many prebendaries treated it as such and spent their lives on Church or State business outside the diocese; some prebendaries, though a small minority, were not even ecclesiastics. The archbishop of York possessed the right of appointment to all the thirty York prebends, a right which fell to the Crown during vacancies of the see. In a period like the sixteenth and seventeenth centuries when Church and State were so closely linked the archbishop naturally came under considerable influence from the government, from interested laymen, and from his fellow bishops, in making his appointments, while the largely undisturbed wealth of the York chapter meant that men from all over the British Isles sought prebends at York. Generalizations about the type of men who obtained York prebends, their attachment to the Minster, and the value to them of prebends in furthering their careers can be made with some accuracy. These generalizations, nevertheless, are limited by the nature of the records kept by the dean and

[54] YML, Act Book H. 5, pt. ii, fo. 15^r; M. 1. 7. 6. (a) & (b), Frewen's visitation.

chapter, for these records are almost exclusively administrative and financial. Consequently, a great deal can be known about the Minster as a corporation, singularly little about its spiritual life or the religious activities of the prebendaries.[55]

The chapter act-books span most of the period from 1520 to 1670. The first act-book for the sixteenth century, which runs from 1504 to 1543, was very carefully kept. Perhaps political uncertainties affected record-keeping in York during the troubled reigns of Edward VI and Mary; at all events, the next act-book from 1543 to 1558 is not very full for the reign of Edward VI and fragmentary for the reign of Mary. The seventeenth-century York antiquaries, Hutton and Torre, saw and independently made notes on an act-book which covered the latter years of Henry VIII and continued into the first years of Elizabeth; this has since disappeared and there is a gap in the records until 1565. From 1565 to 1641 and from 1660 onwards the act-books are complete. With rare exceptions these continued to record routine business which had scarcely changed over the centuries, the admission of new prebendaries, the taking-up of residence, confirmation of leases of capitular lands or of leases made by the archbishop, the institution of clerics to livings in the possession of the dean and chapter. Little in the act-books hints at the great religious changes of the sixteenth and seventeenth centuries, but these records do yield some information on the relationship between the individual prebendaries and the Minster. The early-sixteenth-century act-books regularly indicate whether the dean did or did not attend chapter meetings and, particularly in the absence of the dean, give the names of the prebendaries who were present. From 1565 onwards the attendance of all prebendaries is systematically recorded, and so for this period at least fairly precise deductions can be made.[56]

It is not possible to know how many prebendaries attended services in the Minster, or how frequently they came to the city, but from the act-books it is fairly clear how often they were present at chapter meetings, and it seems improbable that a prebendary would participate in Minster services and not in chapter meetings, since decisions taken in chapter

---

[55] Except when there is a special footnote with additional information, all biographical details of York prebendaries mentioned in this section are taken from the *DNB* (when there is an entry) and Venn, *Al. Cant.*, or J. Foster, *Alumni Oxonienses*, pt. I (Oxford, 1892–2).

[56] The act-books referred to in this section on which all the following generalizations are based are in the Minster library: H. 3. 1, Act Book 1504–43; H. 3. 3, Act Book 1543–58; H. 4, Act Book 1565–1634; H. 5, Act Book 1634–1700. The missing act-book is referred to by Torre in his MS. 'Minster' volume, also in the Minster library. Somewhat earlier in the seventeenth century Matthew Hutton also made extracts from the act-book which is now missing and his notes are in BM Harl. MS. 6971 fos. 148–56. These notes are useful for admission to prebends, etc. but do not give attendance at chapter meetings.

would directly involve his financial interests. Of approximately 280 prebendaries admitted to prebends between 1520 and 1670 only a little under half of them are definitely known ever to have attended any chapter meetings. Half of these again only made a token appearance, perhaps coming to York to be admitted to their prebend in person and some perhaps attending once or twice more during their clerical careers, but in no case ever being present at as many as ten meetings. Quite clearly a small inner ring within the thirty prebendaries at any one time administered the chapter business. About 40 or so prebendaries came to more than 40 chapter meetings, while 26 of these attended more than 70 meetings.

To a certain extent the burden of work lay upon the great dignitaries of the church, whom the statutes bound to continuous residence, though by no means all observed this obligation. Brian Higden, dean from 1515 to 1539, certainly attended just over 300 chapter meetings, a figure not attained by any other dean in this period except Matthew Hutton who attended about 380 meetings between 1567 and 1589. Two chancellors were exceptionally active, William Palmer who held office from 1571 to 1605 and Phineas Hodson who followed soon after him and held the office from 1611 until the Civil War; Palmer appeared at almost 400 meetings, Hodson at 450. Precentors and subdeans treated the obligation of constant residence rather less seriously than some of the chancellors seem to have done. John Rokeby, precentor from 1545 to 1574, spent a great deal of time in York but Sir John Gibson, the lay lawyer, who succeeded him, only attended some 200 meetings in thirty-eight years, and at this period the chapter met about twenty times a year. John Favour, precentor from 1617 to 1624, had a no higher rate of attendance while Richard Palmer, precentor from 1624 to 1631, came to one chapter meeting. As subdean, Henry Wright, who held office from 1576 to 1606, was present at some 20 chapter meetings and Andrew Byng, subdean from 1606 to 1644, absorbed in his academic work in Cambridge, appeared in York only once.

While not all the great dignitaries nominally bound to continuous attendance did in fact attend the Minster with any sort of regularity, some canons, upon whom this obligation did not fall, did occasionally take a very full part in chapter administration. William Thomas, prebendary of Bilton from 1591 to 1614, attended almost 300 chapter meetings; he also held the post of master of the Minster school and so for this reason lived in the city. Ralph Coulton, prebendary of Holme Archiepiscopi and archdeacon of Cleveland from 1570 to 1582, Christopher Gregory, prebendary of Ampleforth and archdeacon of York from 1577 to 1600, George Slater, prebendary of Barnby from 1574 to 1590, and John Neile, prebendary first of North Newbald and then of Strensall between 1634 and 1675, all came to more than 100 chapter meetings. Slater had married Matthew Hutton's daughter and it may have suited his domestic arrangements to be in York frequently while his father-in-law was archbishop, but the examples of these men still show that a canon who did not hold one of the four great offices could sometimes play a major part in chapter business, while some of the dignitaries succeeded in evading their responsibilities entirely.

Whether active or inactive in Minster affairs, some men found a canonry at York to be a stepping-stone to high office in the English Church. Two prebendaries of York rose to be archbishops of Canterbury in the sixteenth and seventeenth centuries. Reginald Pole's attachment to York must have been minimal. His prebend of Knaresborough which he held for ten years from 1527 can have been no more than a pension and only helped in the most indirect way his advancement to Canterbury in 1555. William Sancroft, however, did briefly take up his appointment as dean of York in 1664 before moving on to be dean of St. Paul's and ultimately primate of all England. From the Reformation to 1670 only one man followed the examples of Christopher Bainbridge and Thomas Wolsey and progressed from dean to archbishop of York. Matthew Hutton, the energetic dean of York from 1567 to 1589, went from York to Durham as bishop and returned to York as archbishop in 1595. His advancement apart, in every other respect he differed from Bainbridge and Wolsey; he was no civil servant or diplomatist but first and foremost a theologian, and he confined his career largely to the Church and to administration in the north of England. No other men who held prebends at York at this time achieved an archbishopric, but several became bishops. Of the Elizabethan bishops, Richard Barnes had been very active as chancellor at York and suffragan bishop of Nottingham before he became bishop of Carlisle in 1570 and then in 1577 bishop of Durham. The connection of four other bishops with York seem to have been much less close. Edmund Scambler was prebendary of Wistow from 1560 to 1575, William Day prebendary of Ampleforth from 1560 to 1566, William Blethyn prebendary of Osbaldwick in 1567, and William Chaderton archdeacon of York from 1568 to 1575 and prebendary of Fenton from 1573 to 1579, before they became respectively bishops of Peterborough, Winchester, Llandaff, and Chester. Scambler in fact held a prebend at York for the first four years he was bishop of Peterborough but is not known to have ever visited the north, and neither is William Blethyn who held Osbaldwick for a year before becoming bishop of Llandaff. John Thornborough, dean from 1589 to 1617, tried to fulfil his duties as dean and bishop simultaneously. From 1594 he was bishop of Limerick until in 1603 he exchanged that see for Bristol, holding on to his deanery till he secured the see of Worcester in 1617. He did not visit York much more than once a year, and not always as frequently as that, but refused to allow the chapter to transact important business in his absence.[57] Of the seventeenth century York ecclesiastics who attained to bishoprics none participated at all actively in York ecclesiastical life. Thomas Morton, presented to Husthwaite in 1610, retained the prebend when he became bishop of Chester in 1616 and then bishop of Coventry and Lichfield in 1619, but resigned it after obtaining the wealthy see of Durham in 1632. John Bramhall very briefly held the prebend of Husthwaite before becoming bishop of Derry in 1634 and later archbishop of Armagh. Gilbert Ironside was prebendary of Tockerington for some of the time he was bishop of Bristol between 1661 and 1671. John Wilkins, for eight years prebendary of South Newbald, gave up the prebend when he accepted the bishopric of Chester in 1668. Henry Bridgeman was bishop of Sodor and Man from 1671 and at the same time prebendary of Stillington. When Humphrey Lloyd received the bishopric of Bangor in 1673 he continued to hold the prebend of Ampleforth to which he had been appointed in 1644. Lastly there were the episcopal brothers John and Benjamin Parry. John Parry, presented to Bugthorpe in 1663, resigned the prebend when he became precentor of St. Patrick's Cathedral, Dublin, in 1666 and then bishop of Ossory in 1672. Benjamin Parry, prebendary of Knaresborough for ten years from 1664, succeeded his brother as bishop of Ossory on his death in 1677, but only lived to enjoy the see for a year.

Proportionately few York prebendaries obtained episcopal sees, and those sees tended to be the lesser ones. Rather more typical of York canons were those who left York to be dignitaries of other chapters, like William Goodwin who, after fifteen years as prebendary of Bole and a further five as chancellor, from 1605 to 1611, finished his career back in an academic environment as dean of Christ Church. Throughout the time he was dean of Winchester in the first part of the seventeenth century John Young retained the prebend of Riccall. Arthur Williams, who held Fenton from 1579 to 1602, seems to have moved from a prebend at York to the poorly endowed precentorship of Bangor which he held with other Welsh livings. Thomas Triplett, prebendary of Fenton half a century later, contrived to retain this prebend in addition to prebends in various other cathedrals when he became subdean of Westminster in 1662. Henry Thurscross, prebendary of Osbaldwick from 1608 to 1614, of Langtoft from 1614 to 1622, and archdeacon of Cleveland from 1619 to 1635, fairly represents those eleven York prebendaries whose highest preferment proved to be an archdeaconry, either in the diocese of York or elsewhere.

[57] A considerable number of his letters deferring business till he could be present in York are in YML, Chapter Files, 1591–9; 1600–9; 1610–14; 1615–19.

In fact the majority of prebendaries who lived within the diocese of York did not get high preferment outside the diocese. A prebend for them was a useful supplement to their parochial living to which they gave their main, if not their exclusive, attention. Melchior Smith, the decidedly Protestant vicar of Hessle in the East Riding from 1561 to 1591, combined his living from 1564 with the fairly lucrative prebend of Ampleforth but only appeared four times at chapter meetings in a quarter of a century. Richard Perrot, another vicar of Hessle from 1615 to 1641 and prebendary of Osbaldwick from 1626, showed a similar lack of interest in chapter affairs. Not many Yorkshire incumbents who held prebends seem to have participated much in the life of the Minster, though a cleric like Christopher Lindley, prebendary of Husthwaite and rector of Laughton from 1570 to 1610, attended over thirty chapter meetings. All the evidence suggests that incumbents prized their canonries above all for their financial advantages and the movement between prebends at York further confirms this. Few prebendaries were as fortunate as George Palmes, who went from Givendale, which he obtained at the end of the reign of Henry VIII, to the prebend of Langtoft and lastly, in 1558, acquired that of Wetwang, one of the richest prebends in the cathedral. Most prebendaries only had a chance of changing their prebends once, but even so over thirty at this period succeeded in exchanging an inferior York prebend for a wealthier one.

From an analysis of York prebendaries it becomes clear that for many not even on the most mundane level did the York dean and chapter have first claim on their allegiance. Besides those ecclesiastics who combined their York prebend with a bishopric or a dignity in another cathedral, a significant number held one or more canonries in other cathedrals. Over the century and a half a hundred York prebendaries had at least one prebend in another chapter. Anthony Bellasis who died in 1552 in possession of the prebend of Knaresborough also held prebends at Durham, Westminster, Lincoln, Wells, and Ripon. After the accession of Elizabeth it remained common for a York prebendary also to hold a prebend at Southwell or, after the restoration of the chapter there in the early seventeenth century, at Ripon, but the simultaneous holding of several prebends in different dioceses declined. The practice seems to have increased again after the restoration of Charles II. Thomas Triplett, who was admitted to the prebend of Fenton in 1641, regained possession of it in 1660, and held it till his death in 1670, was also installed as canon of Salisbury and canon of Durham in 1660, and two years later obtained the dignity of subdean and canon of Westminster.

Since the right of appointment to the thirty prebends at York, and to the prebends at Ripon and Southwell, remained throughout the period vested in the archbishop of York, not surprisingly a considerable number of men who began their careers as chaplains in the archbishop's household went on to secure prebends in the church of York. Wolsey, though never in York, made extensive use of his patronage in this way, and an Italian, Peter Vannes, a Latin secretary to Henry VIII, Edward Fox, William Franklyn, Robert Shorten, and William Clayton, to name but a few, were all attached to Wolsey's household and gained prebends by this means. Wolsey appears to have regarded prebends exclusively as a form of financial reward, few if any of his protégés seem ever to have visited York, but Grindal deliberately used his patronage to strengthen Protestantism in the north. At the end of his life, ill, half-blind, in disgrace with the queen, the archbishop of Canterbury remembered with affection his old chaplains whom he had placed in the cathedral at York.[58] William Palmer, one of these chaplains, went on to serve the Minster diligently as chancellor for more than a quarter of a century; Ralph Tunstall, another of Grindal's chaplains who held the prebend of Knaresborough, while only making infrequent appearances at York chapter meetings, was active as a canon of Durham and archdeacon of Northumberland from 1583 to 1610. Often a cleric who benefited from receiving a prebend also received further patronage in the shape of a benefice in the archbishop's gift. Thomas Lakin, who became prebendary of Wistow in 1564, had already been given the archiepiscopal living of Bolton Percy in 1560. Henry Coppinger, the rector of Laneham since 1578, got the prebend of Apesthorpe in 1591; Philip Forde, rector of Nunburnholme in 1601, obtained the prebend of Stillington four years later. The examples could be multiplied. A cleric who held a good archiespiscopal living could reasonably hope to obtain a prebend at York, or vice versa. This was a system which tended to give further emoluments to clerics already reasonably provided for, but it could to some extent be justified as a way of attracting educated men to a diocese where impropriations, and consequently impoverished livings, were very numerous. Throughout the period, whether he lived in the diocese or not, it was exceedingly rare for a man who had not graduated at least as a bachelor of arts to receive a prebend.

Nepotism, both clerical and lay, undoubtedly helped many men to prebends at York. A notorious case was that of Thomas Wynter, Cardinal Wolsey's son. The mass of benefices he accumulated through his father's influence included the prebend of Fridaythorpe to which he was appointed in 1522, but exchanged the following year for the much richer prebend of Strensall and the archdeaconry of York. From the time the clergy could

---

[58] *Hutton Correspondence* (Surtees Soc. xvii, 1843), p. 57.

legally marry, legitimate archiepiscopal children became a noticeable charge upon York prebends. Thomas Young, son of Archbishop Thomas Young, obtained the prebend of Barnby as early as 1561 when he was about 16 years old.[59] Edwin Sandys had so many sons that his plans for their promotion seriously worried the members of the chapter; they thwarted his attempt to grant offices to Thomas and Henry Sandys but could not avoid confirming the grant of prebends to Edwin and Miles while both were still students at Oxford.[60] Neither young man went on to enter the Church; Miles, however, did attend chapter meetings diligently between 1585 and 1596, and he seems to have shared his father's dislike of elaborate ecclesiastical ceremony. After Archbishop Sandys's death Thornborough, the new dean, tried to enforce the wearing of hood and surplice in chapter, but Miles Sandys refused to conform, protesting 'that there were many other things amiss and forth of order in this church and more needful to be reformed than that'—a unique comment by a prebendary upon the body to which he belonged.[61] When an archbishop had no sons to promote he advanced sons-in-law or nephews. Samuel Hutton, prebendary of Ulleskelf, was nephew to Archbishop Hutton, John Neile, prebendary of Strensall, nephew to Archbishop Neile, while Henry Wickham, prebendary of Fenton, was the nephew of Archbishop Matthew's wife. George Slater, prebendary of Barnby, and Richard Remington, prebendary of North Newbald, both married daughters of Archbishop Hutton. Holders of other sees obviously exerted influence upon the archbishop of York to gain prebends for their relations, Theophilus Aylmer, son of Bishop John Aylmer of London, obtained a York prebend when Sandys was archbishop, and Hutton advanced Emmanuel Barnes, the son of his former colleague in the York chapter and later bishop of Durham, to the prebend of Fenton. Richard Neile, a consistent promoter of Laud, did him a further kindness when archbishop by presenting Laud's half-brother, William Robinson, to the prebend of Weighton.

Archbishops did not act in any way out of the ordinary when they promoted their own and their colleagues' relations to prebends; they had probably been doing this from time immemorial. Nevertheless, with the authorization of clerical marriage and the growth of clerical dynasties nepotism in the early seventeenth century seems to have been increasing. There are signs that some Yorkshire clergy were beginning to regard not

---

[59] After his father's death he was deprived in 1573 for not being in orders and for being a pluralist, BIHR, CP. G. 2437.
[60] YML, H. 4. fo. 225ʳ. In BM, Lans. MS. 50 fos. 72–4 Archbishop Sandys lists some twenty-six leases, etc. he granted to his six sons, and writes defending his actions.
[61] YML, H. 4. fo. 269ᵛ.

only their livings but also their prebends as family possessions. In 1622 William Banks followed Henry Banks as prebendary of Bugthorpe; a few years later he also obtained his livings of Settrington and Scrayingham. Walter Bennett came to Langtoft after Sir John Bennett had resigned it in 1608. Thomas Blakiston replaced his father, Marmaduke Blakiston, as prebendary of Wistow in 1623 while two years later John Cosin, who was Marmaduke Blakiston's son-in-law, succeeded him as archdeacon of the East Riding. Timothy Thurscross took over from his father in 1622 as prebendary of Langtoft, and later as archdeacon of Cleveland and vicar of Kirkby Moorside. He was unusual only in that he developed a conscience about having done so. Occasionally archbishops would make over the right of presenting to a prebend when it next fell vacant to a layman, and in this way in 1588 Thomas Cancefield presented Robert Cancefield to Grindale, in 1615 Edward Lister presented William Lister to Holme Archiepiscopi, presumably relatives in both instances. National politicians interfered in the church of York less openly than this, but it can be no accident that William Turner appears as prebendary of Botevant in 1549 a few months after William Cecil, then secretary of state to Edward VI, and later Queen Elizabeth's chief minister, had promised him a prebend at York.[62] Richard Barnes, Richard Bird, Matthew Hutton, Robert Ramsden, and Edward Stanhope were all also connected with Cecil and all received prebends or other offices at York. The Earl of Leicester presented Robert Dudley to Wetwang in 1569, the richest prebend at York, and William Chaderton, who received Fenton in 1574, also enjoyed his protection. The layman, Richard Swale, prebendary of South Newbald from 1589 to 1608, was an intimate friend of Sir Christopher Hatton.

Some sort of pattern can also be discerned in the type of men appointed to prebends at York between 1520 and 1670. From about the beginning of the reign of Edward VI the Crown no longer used the most lucrative ecclesiastical offices at York to reward its leading civil servants to anything like the same extent as it had previously done. Wolsey, Bainbridge, Pace, Fox, Vannes, Layton, Sydnor can all be regarded as men who received compensation for eminent services rendered to the State with prebends and other offices at York. Nicholas Wotton, who lived till 1567 and had been appointed dean in 1544, was the last of the line of English ambassadors whose public employment was paid at least partly by the church of York. After about 1550 the number of prebendaries with degrees in law markedly decreased, while the number of those with degrees in theology noticeably

---

[62] *DNB* xix. 1290–3.

increased until the seventeenth century when it was unusual for a prebendary not to hold a doctorate of divinity.

At almost the exact time when leading civil servants were tending to disappear from among the members of the York chapter, a new phenomenon arose, the lay canon. It had been acceptable since the later Middle Ages for a scholar to be maintained at the university by a prebend. Colet's holding of the prebend of Botevant while studying at Oxford could be justified on these grounds, and Archbishop Young when he gave William Jack, a 'mere boy', the prebend of Husthwaite, or Archbishop Sandys when he presented his intellectually better qualified sons to Wetwang and Weighton could claim to be acting in accordance with this tradition. They could not have known that the young men would not eventually enter the Church. Some prebends, however, began to be given to mature laymen who had no intention of being ordained. Queen Mary in 1554 made Thomas Clement, the son of Dr. John Clement, a member of More's household, prebendary of Apesthorpe. Clement was not in orders— indeed he was a married man—and, though for a time he contrived to retain his prebend under Elizabeth, he lost it when it became known that he and his family had joined the Catholic exiles at Louvain.[63] In 1560, during the next vacancy of the see, Elizabeth gave Wetwang to her former tutor, Roger Ascham, who, it is quite clear, looked on it merely as a pension: he never came to York. In 1563 the queen rewarded her physician, Richard Masters, with the prebend of Fridaythorpe. Gilbert Wakering presented another layman, William Wilkinson, a Cambridge schoolmaster, to this prebend in 1588. Whitgift in 1602 dispensed James Eveleigh, M.A., prebendary of Wetwang, from the obligation of ordination.[64] So it came about, though whether from accident or design it is impossible to say, that laymen held Wetwang almost continuously from the accession of Elizabeth until the Civil War, and Wetwang was the most valuable of the prebends at York.

With the exception of Miles Sandys, these laymen showed no interest at all in chapter administration, but there was now also a little group of laymen with legal qualifications who rose to considerable influence within the chapter. Sir John Gibson, prebendary first of Botevant and then North Newbald, and precentor from 1574 until 1609, was never ordained. Successive archbishops rewarded him liberally with ecclesiastical offices for his services in their courts, though in 1582 Matthew Hutton made a stand against an unlimited diversion of Minster funds. On behalf of the dean and chapter he successfully challenged Gibson's right to receive the

---

[63] Aveling, *Catholic Recusancy in York*, p. 299.
[64] J. A. Giles (ed.), *The Whole Works of Roger Ascham* (1864–5), i. xc.

revenues of a canon residentiary though non-resident and appealed to Grindal who persuaded Gibson to promise to reside, a promise he never fulfilled.[65] Sir John Bennett, disgraced in 1622 for misappropriating funds in the prerogative court of Canterbury, had an identical background to that of Gibson. He was the archbishop's vicar-general, and prebendary of Langtoft from 1591 to 1608, though he ended his career by concentrating his practice in the southern province. Two other lay ecclesiastical lawyers who both held York prebends at the end of Elizabeth's reign, Richard Swale, chancellor of the diocese of Ely from 1588 to 1606, and Edward Stanhope, vicar general of the province of Canterbury, did not even perform legal duties for the York diocese. An analysis of the Elizabethan chapter of Lincoln has shown that there, too, a considerable number of prebends came into the hands of lay ecclesiastical lawyers.[66] It was against this practice of permitting prosperous laymen to hold prebends and other offices without cure of souls that Puritans so strongly protested.

Even so, laymen never at any one time formed more than a very small proportion of the York chapter and they seem to have disappeared at York after the Restoration, presumably because there was a large supply of royalist clergy demanding prebends from the Crown to recompense them for their sufferings during the Civil War. Until the king had filled the bench of bishops he had in 1660 a very large number of prebends in all the cathedrals of England, Wales, and Ireland to which he could appoint, and some ecclesiastics proceeded then to accumulate prebends on a scale which had not been possible since the reign of Henry VIII. More than ever before, apart from the inner ring of Dean Marsh and his helpers, Swinden, Soresby, Elcock, and Stone, the connection of most prebendaries with York was tenuous in the extreme. The chapter indeed came back in 1660 in exactly the same form as it had been in 1641 and the prebendaries had no intention whatever of imposing a new burden of residence upon themselves; their prime concern was about their emoluments.

The eagerness of men in the sixteenth and seventeenth centuries to obtain a prebend at York can largely be explained by the continuing wealth of the dean and chapter. Even after the loss of the prebends of Masham, Salton, Bramham, South Cave, and the treasurership, to which the two other prebends of Newthorpe and Wilton were annexed, the church of York still retained thirty prebends of a total value on the *Valor* estimates of a little under £1,000 a year. In addition the dean and chapter enjoyed a corporate endowment considered in the mid-sixteenth century to be worth just under £450 annually. This constituted a very considerable amount of economic patronage, as contemporaries fully realized. The enthusiasm of men otherwise uninterested in York to acquire prebends there can, in most cases, only be understood on financial grounds.

After 1547 the dean and chapter of York still managed to keep some very valuable prebends; Wetwang, rated at a little over £80, was now apparently the richest prebend, though the canons always spoke of Strensall, named at £67 in the king's book, as 'the golden prebend'. A further fifteen prebends stood at over £30 a year, while only four were set down at under £10 in 1535. These assessments had been supplied for taxation purposes and may even in the 1530s be undervaluations. What little evidence there is points to a slow rise in the value of prebends throughout the sixteenth and seventeenth centuries. Browne Willis, when he compiled his *Survey of Cathedrals* in the early eighteenth century, gave £6 as the nominal valuation of Warthill, next to Tockerington the lowest prebend in the church, but added that actually the endowments of Warthill brought in nearly £20 a year. Any York prebend, whatever its value, could usefully supplement a cleric's income, quite apart from the fact that a prebend at York entitled its possessor to take up residence. A prebendary when he resided for the first time undertook to serve in the Minster for twenty-six weeks without a break; in subsequent years when he was in residence he had to be in York, not necessarily continuously, for twenty-four weeks. This residence brought financial benefits in some cases ten times the value of a prebend.[67]

Most York prebendaries, however, when they accepted their prebends in the sixteenth and seventeenth centuries seem to have had no intention of taking up residence or indeed of performing any more than token services in the Minster. They looked upon their prebends exclusively as pensions. Reginald Pole, for example, received over £42 a year from the prebend of Knaresborough for ten years from 1527 and used this to help subsidize his studies in Italy where he maintained a large household. Roger Ascham regarded his prebend of Wetwang, worth over £80 a year, as a proper reward for the services he performed as Queen Elizabeth's Greek tutor and tried, unsuccessfully, to persuade Archbishop Young to pass on the prebend as a kind of endowment policy for his son.[68] For Samuel Ward, an early fellow of Sidney Sussex College, Cambridge, and from 1610 its master, one of the translators of the Authorized Version of the Bible and Lady

[67] Willis, *Survey* i. 173–4.
[68] Giles, *The Whole Works of Roger Ascham*, ii. 124–32.

Margaret professor of divinity, his prebend of Ampleforth, worth £35 a year, which he held from 1618 to 1643, merely contributed to financing his Cambridge career. Similarly, ecclesiastics who worked chiefly or exclusively outside the York diocese supplemented their main stipend by holding York prebends. Theophilus Aylmer, who devoted himself to his duties in the south as rector of Shoreditch and archdeacon of London, drew nearly £20 annually from the prebend of Botevant from 1591 to 1626. George Boleyn, a distant relation of Queen Elizabeth, chose to reside in Canterbury where he also held a prebend, but still had over £34 a year from Ulleskelf plus the benefits he would have received as a residentiary at York, since he was dispensed to be non-resident.[69] At the same time as he was dean of Winchester from 1616 to 1644, John Young kept his prebend of Riccall, and so added more than £33 a year to his income. That already wealthy clerics should augment their fortunes in this way was perfectly in harmony with the conventions of the ecclesiastical establishment, though Puritan reformers could justifiably protest that they drew revenues from York but gave little to the cathedral or the diocese in return.

Puritans constantly complained about the inadequacies of impropriate livings to maintain a well-educated clergy. Impropriations abounded in Yorkshire and therefore, at least in theory, the use of a prebend to subsidize the stipend of a parochial living could more easily be defended. In practice, however, York prebends tended to go to clerics already fairly well beneficed. From 1564 Thomas Lakin as rector of Bolton Percy, valued at £39 in the king's books, prebendary of Wistow, worth £65 a year, and also a prebendary of Southwell, must have been getting over £100 annually. George Rowe, from 1571 rector of Wheldrake, worth £25, and prebendary of Stillington, worth £47, cannot have received much under £75 a year. Other Yorkshire incumbents who held prebends had to content themselves with rather lower incomes. From 1582 until his death in 1614 Thomas Cole held the living of Kirkby in Cleveland, worth £21 a year, the prebend of Holme Archiepiscopi, worth £11 a year, and the mastership of St. John's Hospital, Ripon. Barnaby Barlow in 1640 had a formal £19 from his living of Barton in the Beans in Nottinghamshire (in practice the living had probably appreciated considerably by this date) and a further £19 from the prebend of Dunnington in addition to his Southwell prebend. For the fortunate few who went on to become residentiaries yet more income could be derived from the Minster.

The York statutes obliged the four great officials to reside, though they often evaded this obligation, and they also permitted any prebendary to

[69] YML, H. 4. fo. 14[r].

take up residence. Since the dean and chapter held in common lands valued in the early sixteenth century at a little under £450 a year a prebendary who did reside could receive very substantial financial compensation. The account rolls which the Minster chamberlain produced twice a year at Martinmas and Whitsun have survived sporadically for the sixteenth and the first part of the seventeenth centuries. Sufficient remain to give an impression of the chapter's corporate finances, but not sufficient for a strict statistical survey. The income of the dean and chapter fluctuated fairly sharply during this period, as any income did which was derived chiefly from rents and tithes. In 1550 they had an income of £587; in 1585 their income rose to £615 and again to £622 in 1607; it fell to around £550 in both 1619 and 1634. Whatever the variations in income it seems that they enjoyed well over the figure of £450 at which their estates had been valued by the king's commissioners in 1535. Out of the rents which came in twice a year the chamberlain paid fees to Minster servants, and other sums to churches appropriated to the dean and chapter, to the vicars, the choristers, the sextons, and others who were employed by the Minster. The surplus, once these payments had been made, remained to be divided twice a year among the canons residentiary. The surplus was always substantial; £259 in 1550, as much as £308 in 1585, about £279 in 1607, £268 in 1619, though merely £183 in 1634. As there were normally not more than four residentiaries at any one time, and usually not more than three between 1520 and 1640, the rewards to individual residentiaries could be great.[70]

Some idea of the value of a residentiary's place can be gained by considering the income of individual canons. In 1540 Richard Layton alone resided. He drew £150 in this one year from the common fund over and above his income as dean. It was exceptional for there to be only one residentiary: from Whitsun 1578 to Whitsun 1579 there were three; Dean Hutton and the chancellor, William Palmer, from Whitsun to Martinmas 1578, Hutton, Palmer, and George Slater from Martinmas 1578 to Whitsun 1579. Hutton in this year benefited from the common fund to the extent of £115 which brought his income up to at least £456 since he also received £308 as dean and £35 as prebendary of Osbaldwick, and this figure does not include his stipend as rector of Settrington. Palmer in the same year had over £100 from the common fund, that is, more than his stipend as chancellor which was formally £85 a year. Usually between 1520 and 1670

[70] YML, Chamberlains' Account Rolls, E. I VI 84, 1549–50; E. I VI 85, 1550; E. I VII 97, 1584–5; E. I VII 99, 1585; E. I VIII 108, 1606–7; E. I VIII 109, 1607; E. I IX 125, 1618–19; E. I IX 126, 1619; E. I X 134 2, 1633–4; E. I X 136, 1634. In the matter of residence, York closely resembles Lincoln where by the end of the sixteenth century the number of residentiaries had become established at four; Walker, 'Lincoln Cathedral in the Reign of Elizabeth'.

the residentiaries were drawn from the dean, the chancellor, the precentor, or the subdean but, as with George Slater in 1579, any prebendary could, in theory, take up residence, and occasionally an ordinary prebendary did so. For his residence in the half-year from Martinmas 1578 to Whitsun 1579 George Slater had over £52, very considerably more than his prebend of Barnby, rated at £14, was worth for a whole year. In 1562 Anthony Blake, the holder of the poorest prebend in the church, Tockerington, only valued at £2 17s. 1d., gained a share of over £40 from the common fund for half a year's residence. Fifty years later Emmanuel Barnes, prebendary of Fenton, rated at a little over £37, had more than £85 for a whole year's residence.[71]

Residentiaries could enjoy such substantial shares of the common fund because at York other separate funds existed for the upkeep of the cathedral buildings and for the provision of religious services. The Minster fabric fund, which stood at £294 in the financial year 1530–1, fell in the second half of the sixteenth century to about £150 a year at which figure it remained until the Restoration. The great period of building at the Minster had ended by 1530; in most years the dean and chapter seem to have found £150 sufficient to carry out necessary repairs to the Minster. In 1578, for example, even though they had involved themselves in quite heavy expenses over glazing and repairs to the Minster glass and in repairs to their school they managed to balance their accounts, receiving just over £147 in the fabric fund and spending a little over £140. Occasionally the dean and chapter made payments to musicians out of the fund, once to the Lord President's musicians, for setting songs to be sung in the choir, and sometimes invited the waits of York to play. The vicars choral, however, remained responsible for the main charges of the music of the services and had their own estates, valued at £136 in 1535, to provide for them. The number of vicars choral fell as this fund proved increasingly to be too small to maintain the original establishment, and the vicars themselves brought in lay vicars and boy choristers to help them in their work; but except on extraordinary occasions the dean and chapter did not have to make heavy payments to the vicars.[72]

The dean and chapter administered one other fund on behalf of the Minster which, by Elizabeth's reign, had developed into a general purpose fund. Twice a year when they divided the common fund among the

---

[71] YML, Chamberlains' Account Rolls, E. I VI 76, 1540; E. I VI 77, 1540–1; E. I VII 93 b, 1578; E. I VII 93, 1578–9; E. I VI 81 2, 1562; E. I IX 115, 1611–12; E. I IX 117, 1612.

[72] YML, Fabric Rolls, E. 3 41, 1530–1; E. 3 55, 1577/8–1578/9; E. 3 58, 1580/1–1581/2; E 3 63A, 1623/4–1624/5. For the establishment of the vicars in the sixteenth century see Aveling, *Catholic Recusancy in York*, pp. 306–9.

residentiaries they set aside one share for the use of the Minster and called this share St. Peter's portion. Like the dividends of the individual residentiaries, St. Peter's portion varied from year to year: in 1576 it stood at the high figure of £197 for the full year; in 1597, a more typical year, it only received £84 over the whole year. The dean and chapter spent the fund on miscellaneous fees, on law suits in which the church might be involved, on repairs to appropriated churches, and indeed, it seems, on any purpose for which a special fund did not exist. They paid for furred gowns and short clothes for the Minster choir-boys out of St. Peter's portion and made occasional contributions of £6 or £9 to the poor of York. When George Slater and George Rowe read lectures in the Minster, the dean and chapter rewarded them with payments from the fund. Like the chapter at Chester, they even continued the pre-Reformation custom of making payments to strolling players on a fairly grand scale; scarcely a year passed between 1576 and 1600 without the Minster accountant recording a reward of £1 or £2 to the Queen's players, the Earl of Essex's players, Lord Stafford's players, Lord Strange's players, or to those of Lord Scudamore.[73] Had John Field and his Puritan helpers in London known of this item of York clerical indulgence they could hardly have refrained from using it in their propaganda campaign against cathedral churches where

twenty or thirty prebendaries . . . live of spoil of twenty or thirty of the best benefices in that or some other near dioceses, loitering either in the church unprofitably, or employed in any other place far from regard, sometime from knowledge of the place and persons from whence their stipend is answered . . ., the vicarages for the most part left bare and, therefore, basely supplied, the revenues of the common residence or chapter consisting of the like number of impropriations, thirty or forty miles compass together in some dangerous shires, yielding their whole tithes towards their chapter dividends, [the impropriated livings] furnished most pitifully, without preaching or catechising . . .[74]

Archbishop Frewen at his visitation of the dean and chapter in February 1663 particularly emphasized in his injunctions the administration of the common revenues of the Minster. Fearing with good cause that the profits from the renewal of the leases of the dean and chapter lands had been going into the prebendaries' pockets, he instructed the chapter to see that fines on the renewal of leases of fabric lands should be given as before to the fund for the upkeep of the Minster and that a share of the common fund should

---

[73] YML, Accounts of St. Peter's Portion, E. 2 21 fos. 17–19, 50–52. These accounts only cover the period 1572–1600; R. V. H. Burne, 'Chester Cathedral in the reigns of Mary and Elizabeth', *Jour. of Chester and North Wales Architectural, Archaeological, and Historical Soc.* XXXVIII (1951), 49–94.
[74] Peel, *The Seconde Parte of a Register*, ii. 17–18.

be set aside for St. Peter's portion as in times past.[75] In financial matters, as in others, all was to be as it used to be. At the Restoration no York ecclesiastics gave any indication of new thinking about the purposes to which the very large revenues of the Minster should be put, just as they gave no indication of new thinking about the purpose of the Minster in the religious life of York. In matters of religious practice and of administration the Minster was in the all too successful process of being put back not only to where it was in 1641 but even to where it had been in 1553. Once again in 1662 the Minster stood aloof from some of the prime religious concerns of the leading citizens of York. On the passing of the Act of Uniformity without hesitation certain aldermen's widows extended their protection to clandestine Nonconformist meetings. The Toleration Act of 1689 enabled these groups to unite and in 1693 the St. Saviourgate chapel opened for worship, a new outward and visible sign of the separation of the Minster and the City.[76]

I should like to thank Professor G. E. Aylmer, Professor A. G. Dickens, Professor Barrie Dobson, and Dr. David Smith for their most helpful criticism, and Mr. Bernard Barr and Miss K. M. Longley of the Minster library for their kind assistance in interpreting the documents in their care.

[75] YML, M. 1 7 6(b); see *York Statutes*, pp. 94–8. In January 1663, in reply to Frewen's visitation articles, John Neile alleged that the dean and Anthony Elcock had misappropriated revenues from dean and chapter leases. Certainly rivalries were already dividing the newly formed chapter; BIHR, V. 1662/3, D./C./A.E.

[76] Aveling, op. cit., pp. 252, 253; *VCH York*, pp. 205, 404.

CHAPTER VI

From the Restoration until 1822

Dorothy M. Owen

In a distinguished study of the restoration of the Anglican Church in 1660 Dr. Robert Bosher has demonstrated how the 'Laudian' party, eager to re-establish episcopacy before Parliament, which might well be hostile to it, could meet, had hastened, with the co-operation of the lord chancellor, Clarendon, to re-constitute the cathedral chapters, as the first step to the election or translation of bishops.[1] York was early in the field. By June Richard Marsh was seeking confirmation of the grant of the deanery of York which he had received in 1644; he was duly nominated on 25 July, and was installed at York on 14 August. From this point the dignitaries surviving from the past, and the newly appointed, followed very quickly, and as soon as the election of the new archbishop, Accepted Frewen, was confirmed on 4 October, the remaining prebends could be, and were, filled.[2]

On 26 August Edward Gower wrote to Sir Richard Leveson: 'Dean Marsh, Dean of York, has carried things in order to a settlement of the church very high; the singing men and organs are preparing. Prayers, I mean Common Prayers, are settled in the Minster, as formerly, twice a day.'[3] The prebendal sermons were reintroduced at the same time; the fines levied on defaulting preachers were fixed as early as 20 August, and the 'preaching ministers' appointed by Parliament in 1654 to 'preach in the cathedral and other churches in York' had been displaced and were already seeking compensation from the Crown. The dean and three prebendaries (John Neile, Toby Swindon, and Anthony Elcocke) protested residence on 24 October, and at Martinmas, in accordance with the Henrician statutes, the terms of their residence were fixed for the following year. The first leases of chapter property were sealed on 2 October, but it was Christmas

[1] R. S. Bosher, *The Making of the Restoration Settlement* (1951), pp. 143–218, *passim*.
[2] *CSPDom, 1660–1*, pp. 83, 87, 110, 119, 225–6; YML, Chapter Acts, 1634–1701, fos. 14–17.
[3] *HMCR* V, Sutherland MSS., p. 199.

before locks and keys were provided for the common chest, and resumption of the common life was slow and painful.

The building of which they now resumed occupation had been relatively little harmed during the Interregnum, and the corporation of York had, on the whole, treated it well. The great organ which had been installed on the north side of the choir had been dismantled, and some of the plate and altar furniture had disappeared. John Evelyn, visiting the cathedral in 1654, saw 'A Bible and Prayer Book covered with crimson velvet and richly embossed with silver gilt; also a service for the altar of gilt wrought plate, flagons, basin, ewer, chalices, patins etc., with a gorgeous covering for the altar and pulpit.'[4] James Scruton, who had become a verger in 1634, and was now clerk of the vestry, reported to the archbishop at the visitation of 1662 how much more there had been:

There were fower guilt bowles with covers, two guilt flagons, one guilt bason, one single guilt plate, two guilt candlestickes and three little white plates . . . sold by Mr. Dossey, by order from My Lord Mayor. There were three copes taken away by the Committee of Sequestrators . . . for all the rest cusshions, canapies, cloths, linen and silkes . . . are remaineing in the churche . . . For the silver candlestickes, the brasse deske, the brasse taken of the graves, a statue of brasse lying where six of clocke prayer used to be read . . . was sold by Mr. Dossey, with order from My Lord Mayor.[5]

Regular use and occupation of the Minster had continued throughout the Interregnum: the people of York had accompanied the civic authorities, who occupied the stalls on the north side of the choir once assigned to the archdeacons, to all services. As late as November 1665 it was necessary to rail in the reading desk from which the scriptures and litany were read, 'Ut legentes populi multitudine seu turba non opprimerentur',[6] and as they had appropriated the choir, so they had continued to use the empty nave for the idle noisy promenades of which Archbishop Neile had complained in 1632. The city houses pressed close to the Minster too, for building had long been permitted on each side of the great south door (Plate 79), and on the north-west, where some of the ground formerly occupied by the Archbishop's Palace had been occupied since 1616 by a great house built by Sir Arthur Ingram. All the houses of dignitaries and prebendaries, except the deanery, had now been alienated on long leases, and many of the occupants had made considerable encroachments on the Minster Yard, while the returning residentiaries were obliged to find lodgings elsewhere in the town.[7]

[4] *John Evelyn, Diary and Letters*, ed. E. S. de Beer (1955), iii. 128–9.
[5] BIHR, V. 1662–3.
[6] YML, Chapter Acts, 1634–1701, fo. 55.
[7] BIHR, V. 1662–3.

Some repairs to the fabric were of course needed, and these were increased by the great storm of December 1660, which badly damaged the south west tower and the nearby roof.[8] Yet no such wholesale restoration was called for as some other cathedrals needed. John Neile reported at the 1662 visitation that above a thousand pounds had been spent since 1660 on roofs and windows, and when, in December of that year, a list of 'needfull repairs' was drawn up a further thousand pounds was thought necessary, chiefly for the roofs.[9]

There is no further mention of the resumed services until 26 April 1661, when the draft minutes record an order 'That he that reads six o'clocke prayers shall doe it in his gowne and surplisse.' Apart from these instances, it seems from these laconic mentions that the pre-revolutionary services were restored, at least in intention, yet the visitation evidence of 1662 shows clearly how half-hearted the changes really were, and how little the residentiaries agreed on the form which they should take. John Neile, who had been archdeacon of Cleveland, and a residentiary since 1638, had much to say on the subject:

The dean hath not preached this long time but finds others . . . and some young men, strangers, have been suffered to preach here formerly . . . They are wont to omitt the morning prayer in the Quire on Wednesday and Friday in Advent and Lent when we have sermons . . . The precentor forbade the Quire to sing an anthem or the organist to play it . . . before the prayer for the King, as the rubricke appointes it in Quires. And the last time he administred communion he kneeled at the canon or prayer of consecration, though admonished that he ought to stande. And in the very form of consecration he omitted a principall word, viz. 'eate', saying 'Take, this is my bodye', when he should have said 'Take, eate'.

The precentor and future dean, Toby Wickham, had nothing to say about the services, but Robert Hitch, archdeacon of the East Riding and also now a residentiary, had complaints about the management of sermons:

He hath had only three courses; for the first, he preacht a sermon the second Sunday in the Lent Assizes last before the Judges, the second course Mr. Sikes, rector of Spofford, the respondent being then att London, came to Yorke to preache, but was refused, and for the third course this respondent preacht a sermon the second Sunday in Lamas Assizes last at the earnest request of one of the residentiaries, when no man else could be got. And to prevent all neglect he sent his curat Mr. Foyle, a learned and orthodox man to preache that course, but he was refused also.

---

[8] Drake, *Ebor.*, p. 485.
[9] BIHR, V. 1662–3.
[10] *CSPDom, 1660–1*, p. 300; YML, Chapter Acts, 1634–1701, fo. 14.

In the services, as in every other branch of the corporate life, it was clear that there were clashes of personality among members of the chapter. The trouble arose not only from genuine doctrinal differences, and the natural distrust felt by those like Neile who had suffered most during the Interregnum, but also from the difficulty of recovering necessary sources of income and the failure of inexperienced men to re-establish a workable financial administration. Neile's evidence of 1662 enlarged on the gaps in fabric revenue: 'There is also more designed for the church, Mr. Dickenson's and Sikes' arrears and all other for the fabric as soon as they can be recovered, which will amount to about £1200 as I believe.' Even worse was the failure of the chapter to set aside a large enough portion for St. Peter, and to ensure that the vicars were receiving all the income to which they were entitled. John Neile, it seems, like his contemporary at Lincoln, John Fairclough or Featley, and other 'old hands' in similar situations, only antagonized his fellows by his attempts to enforce regularity and observance of the statutes:

[when he remonstrated] they have angrily told me that I hindr'd the business of the church and stood upon these things more than was needed and ever after took their time to let leases when I was out of towne as I was often forced to be by my place at Durham . . . [as to the precentor] I beseach your Grace privately if you please, to admonish him, for he cares not to hear the admonition of his bretheren.

There were other members of the chapter, certainly, who had some concern for the statutes, and for the financial integrity of the body. Robert Hitch and William Davison both referred to the absence of audit and the habit of clandestine leasing; there are accusations of improper leases of the Langwith woods, which were intended to supply the needs of the fabric, and of concealment of lease fines by the subdean Elcocke. Neile's comment on this accusation is illuminating about the rather hand-to-mouth methods of the chapter: 'Dr. Elcocke, belike thinking this a competent sum to stop a patient man's mouth sent also £20 to my wife in my absence at London for the fourth parte of a lease which I am tolde hath been lett out for £59 per annum . . . but hath not given one penny to St. Peter.' Davison said that 'I have been present at passing many leases in the chapter, but they were let clandestinely betweene two or three of them in some parlour or the like . . .' and Neile again repeats a story that

One evening itt being somewhat darke the dean came to Dr. Stone in the churche, taking him for Dr. Elcocke, as Dr. Stone himself saith he believeth, said to him 'You have received such a rent, of which you gave me not my share'. Also that the

---

[11] YML, Draft Chapter Acts, 1661–3, fo. 1.

registrar's patent was sealed in private, by Dr. Elcocke calling Dr. Stone privily out of the chapterhouse, the dean not being present at the sealing, and so I thinke it voyd nor the officer sworn, nor the patent read in the chapterhouse.[12]

The first genuine attempts to re-establish a proper financial administration and enforce the statutes came in the injunctions with which Archbishop Frewen concluded his visitation in 1662–3. The archbishop ordered that chests should be provided for the fabric fund, St. Peter's portion, the common fund, and the vicars choral, with appropriate safeguards on expenditure from each. Annual public audits, and regular terms for the declaring of dividends were re-instituted, leases were to be granted only in accordance with the statutes, and the usual tenths were to be paid regularly to the choir.[13] There was certainly greater precision in record-keeping after this, and, presumably, in administration, though as late as 1665 there was difficulty about some of the fabric accounts, and disputes about the uses of St. Peter's portion continued until much later. On the other hand, both funds seem to have been solvent by 1670, and to have repaid advances made to them by the dean and other prebendaries.[14]

The restoration of the cathedral services and the provision of suitable furniture also quickened in pace after this visitation. In December 1662 'it was ordered by the chapter that upon Wednesdays and Fridays in Advent and Lent the whole morning prayer with Latin only is to be used, and the prayer for the militant church and another before and after sermon are to be sunge not said', and this was an important step towards seemly observance.[15] Some of the difficulties were no doubt due to the defects of the organ and choir, and until these were remedied little real improvement could be effected in the services. Meanwhile, the best possible was done, and two sackbuts and two cornets were provided in May 1663 for the service of the choir, 'Mr. Girdler and his company to have £5 for one half year and forty shillings to provide themselves with instruments for the purpose'.[16] The bells, too, were restored by this time and on Sundays and feasts the little or sermon bell rang from eight o'clock for half an hour, after which the big bell rang from half past eight to nine, at which time the vicar choral was to read matins in the choir.[17] Improvement in the services continued, especially after Thomas Comber became precentor in 1683. It

[12] BIHR, V. 1662–3.
[13] *Fabric Rolls*, pp. 94–8.
[14] YML, Chapter Acts, 1634–1701, fos. 55ᵛ, 86; *The autobiographies and letters of Thomas Comber*, ed. C. E. Whiting (Surtees Soc., vols. 156–7, 1946–7), i. 62.
[15] YML, Draft Chapter Acts, fo. 12.
[16] Ibid., fo. 19ᵛ.
[17] YML, Chapter Acts, 1634–1701, fos. 53ᵛ, 57ᵛ.

was characteristic of his activities that he should insist on sitting, not in the
usual residentiary's stall, but in the seat of the precentor 'because he cannot
from his prebendal stall inspect the whole quire, whereof the more especiall
charge belongeth to him' and it is equally characteristic of him that he
should describe his part at the consecration of a suffragan bishop as 'master
of ceremonies'.[18] Archbishop Dolben's injunction of 1685 restoring the
weekly celebration of communion, and ordering all priests belonging to the
church 'to prepare themselves devoutly to accept it', coincided with
Comber's own practices before he came to York, and greatly strengthened
the hands of the cathedral authorities.[19] By the time of Archbishop
Lamplugh's visitation in 1690 great improvements had undoubtedly been
made, though it was still necessary for the visitor to order that all
prebendaries and dignitaries who were resident in York should attend
service regularly, that the vicar choral reading the service should be on
time, and waiting to begin, that no vicar should leave before the end of the
service, that there should be a celebrant, epistler, and gospeller, as in the
chapels royal, for the celebration of communion, that the vergers should
escort the dean and residentiary to and from their seats, and prevent people
from walking and talking in the choir.[20]

Suitable ornaments and furniture was steadily acquired or restored
during the thirty years after the Restoration, although the theft of some of
the plate in 1676 was a serious set-back.[21] The 'great candlesticks' (the
chandeliers) were refurbished and given new chains in 1680, and in 1686
by Comber's orders the great Bible in the choir was 'mendyd, bossed and
pasted'.[22] When Nicholas Proctor became vestry clerk in 1681 an inventory
was made of the goods for which he was responsible and this included no
plate except one little silver plate gilt, and two silver candlesticks.[23] In
1683, however, Archbishop Sterne bequeathed 'all my gilt plate commonly
used in the said chapell . . . that is to say one gilt bason, two gilt flagons, one
gilt paten, one gilt chalice with cover together with the cases wherein they
are commonly laid up'.[24] The brass lectern still in use in the cathedral was
presented by Thomas Cracroft, one of the prebendaries, in 1686,[25] and in
the next four years, between the solicitations of Precentor Comber and the

[18] Ibid., fo. 171[v]; *Comber* i. 14.
[19] *Fabric Rolls*, p. 100.
[20] YML, Lamplugh Visitation, Injunctions.
[21] Drake, *Ebor.*, p. 482.
[22] YML, Chamberlains' Accounts, 1677–1707, s.a. 1678, 1680, 1686.
[23] *Fabric Rolls*, p. 317. Miss Longley has subsequently provided me with a transcript of this
document from the earliest register of burials, marriages, and baptisms in the Minster.
[24] YML, Chapter Acts, 1634–1701, fo. 159[v].
[25] Ibid., fo. 184[v].

generosity of Archbishop Lamplugh, a great deal more was done.[26] The effect of all these gifts is to be seen in the vestry clerk's inventory of 1691:

Imprimis one piece of crimson velvet fringed with gold placed at the back of the altar, one covering or cloth for the table, of crimson velvet imbroidered and fringed with gold, two crimson velvet quishions on Bible and one Common Prayer Book embossed with silver guilded, another Bible . . . with silver clasps . . .[27]

The furnishing of the altar and the choir had thus taken on the form which so much appealed to Celia Fiennes when she saw it in 1697, and which it retained when Drake's *Eboracum* was first published in 1736 (Plates 80, 81).[28]

Some of the difficulties and quarrels which beset the restored chapter were inherent in the statutes, and particularly those which concerned residence. The 'new' statutes of 1541 had laid down that those wishing to become residentiaries must protest their intention to reside immediately upon a vacancy, but had not stated explicitly how many could reside, and whether the dean's residence was to be included in the total number, nor what the period of residence was to be.[29] The usual number, including the dean, seems to have been five between 1660 and 1683, with three in full residence for twenty-four weeks at a time. There were a good many opportunities of conflict in such an arrangement, but when James II began to press for the admission of a sixth residentiary, the system came near to breaking. As Comber, who was deeply concerned about the matter, explained:

St. Peter's part can be no more than the part of one residentiary and it is the only fund to pay all the salarys and charges of the cathedrall and its attendants etc. And when I came Dr. Lake showed me an account of divers years wherin St. Peter's part was not able to pay this and mony was yeerly taken up of the Residentiary to make out the salarys etc. and for these summs St. Peter was yeerly returned debtor to the church which was then got to a very great sum yet we were then but five residentiaries. But if there be six or more it will so miserably lessen St. Peter's part that it can never bear half the charges incumbent on that share, and must in time silence the choir or ruin the prebend residentiaries. I never knew St. Peter's part able to defray its charge all my time. . . .

Disapproval of the royal action must have aggravated the chapter's dislike for James II's toleration proposals, and added fuel to the heat of the opposition which Comber led.[30]

---

[26] Drake, *Ebor.*, p. 522; *Comber* i. 22–3.

[27] YML, Inventory 1691.

[28] *The journeys of Celia Fiennes*, ed. C. Morris (1949), p. 77; Drake, *Ebor.*, Pl. 50; see Pl. 80.

[29] *Appendix to the first report of the Cathedrals Commission* (1854), pp. 17–18.

[30] *Comber* i. 62.

Reform of the statutes had been mooted as early as the 1662 visitation but the chapter failed to agree on it, and the minutes of 11 November 1663 allow us to sense the deep divergences among its members:

Mr. Precentor did not approve of the said draught but humbly desires that there might first be a deane for the further considering and perfecting of the same. Dr. Elcocke the same in all things. Dr. Hitch not consenting for that he had not compared the said draught with the original statutes of the church. Mr. Chauncellor that they be presented to my lord Archbishop as now drawne and exhibited but desired that they be again reviewed and perfected when there was a deane. Doctor Neale the like. Dr. Parrish did approve of the said draught soe as to be presented to the Archbishop. Mr. Wickham the like in all thinges. Mr. Davison that he had read part of the said draught exhibited and did find them soe imperfect as not fitt to be presented to the Archbishop and therefore voted against it. Mr. Boninge that whereas there is a former chapter and Injunctions touching this matter he desired that according to the litteral sense thereof the same might be disposed of and none otherwise.[31]

No more was heard of that particular proposal, but disputes continued, as Comber recorded: for example in 1683 when 'Dr. Cook's lady rail'd at the Body for not admitting her husband Residentiary'.[32] Finally, in 1698, with Archbishop Sharp's help, and after considerable negotiation, in which the lead was taken by the precentor James Fall, a petition to the Crown sought a reinterpretation of the statutes, asking that the dean might be allowed to protest residence, though no canon, and that no more than five residentiaries be allowed, so that St. Peter's part should never be less than one-sixth of the dividend. Dean Gale fortified the petition by notes for the archbishop on the claims on St. Peter: organist £30, singing boys £24, master of boys £8, library keeper £6, six choristers' gowns £6, sweeping the church £1 6s. 8d., in all £75 6s. 8d., besides several contingencies for law suits, the clock, music, and prayer books and some lights, whereas the yearly sum received had rarely been more than £60. The Crown acceded to the petition and there were now no more than five residentiaries but the length of residence continued to be twenty-four weeks, during which the residentiary lived in a canonical house and was present each day at matins and vespers.[33] From 1660 only the dean could keep his residence in his own house, and at times, as in 1730, disputes arose as to what constituted a canonical house for the rest, until, in the eighteenth century, a residence was built in the south-east corner of Minster Yard which served for all.[34]

---

[31] YML, Chapter Acts, 1634–1701, fo. 35[v].
[32] *Comber* i. 59.
[33] YML, Chamberlains' Accounts, 1677–1707, s.d. 11 Oct. 1697; BIHR, Bp. C & P XIX.
[34] This house is still standing: *VCH York*, p. 341 and plan on p. 340; YML, Chapter Acts, 1728–47, fos. 40[v]–41.

During the period of residence the two or more residentiaries transacted all the business of the church, acted as fabric masters, wrote the chapter letters, and held the keys of the chest. In 1730 an obstructive residentiary, Edward Finch, brother of the late dean, proved how much trouble this could cause: on 9 December he was asked to come to chapter and bring with him his key of the chest where the common seal was locked up. He refused, unless he was asked by a prebendary, and though Sterne and Breary went to him he again declined. Finally the chest was broken, and the seal applied without him. On 14 December Finch was cited to the chapter for contempt, and for failure to make payments due to the vergers and songmen, and replied 'that he was now undrest and could not come, but would appear on 17 December'.[35] The chapter seems to have postponed action after this and there was only one more instance of opposition from Finch, but it is clear that at times when the dean was in York, but not in residence, as in this case, trouble might well arise. Dean Osbaldeston certainly found in this same year, when he attempted to impose on the chapter a new practice about the Nicene Creed, that a question arose as to his 'right to collect the debates of such as have a right to be present', and two years before there had been trouble between the dean and the residentiaries about responsibility for bell-ringing. In this case Osbaldeston had triumphed, and in most matters he was rarely opposed, except by the most abrasive of personalities, and residence continued to be a relatively untroubled affair.[36] It was attended by an agreeable degree of pomp, as the poet Gray reported in 1762, when his friend William Mason became precentor: 'We went twice a day to church with our vergers and all our pomp', and a young ordinand, seeing Mason leave the church in 1769 'in his surplice, cap, hood and scarf', 'thought what a happy man he was to have such a dignified station in such a cathedral, where he might gratify his taste for music in the injoyment of such a heavenly mode of worship'.[37] Yet Mason himself was anything but happy in York as 'the pupil of a bell', in 'residentiary imprisonment', exiled from all his friends, from books and company, and his letters to his friends Hurd and Walpole are full of complaints of the demands of business and visiting tourists.[38] He succeeded as early as 1768, with the help of his influential patron Lord Holderness, and Archbishop Drummond, in

[35] YML, Chapter Acts, 1728–47, fos. 61–63.
[36] Ibid., fos. 9ᵛ, 51ᵛ.
[37] *Correspondence of Thomas Gray*, ed. P. Toynbee and L. Whibley (3 vols., Oxford, 1971), iii. 361; *Papers and diaries of a York family*, ed. Almira Gray (1927), p. 13.
[38] *Horace Walpole's correspondence with William Mason*, ed. W. S. Lewis, G. Cronin, and C. R. Bennett (2 vols., Yale Univ. Press, 1955), i. 23, 83; *The correspondence of Richard Hurd and William Mason*, ed. E. H. Pearce and L. Whibley (Cambridge, 1932), p. 116; cf. *A candidate for praise, William Mason, 1725–97, precentor of York*, compiled by C. B. L. Barr and J. A. S. Ingamells (York, 1973).

effecting the reduction of the residence to twelve weeks. At the same time the statutes were changed to allow the dean six months to deliberate before choosing among would-be residentiaries when a vacancy occurred, instead of his previous obligation to take the first man who came to York and protested.[39] The dean was thus confirmed in the power to nominate, which seems usually to have been implicit: Mason himself was Dean Fountayne's nominee, through the influence of a friend who was Fountayne's brother-in-law.[40] It was obviously the dean who really took the lead in chapter affairs after the rather ineffectual period of Dean Wickham, when he was undoubtedly obscured by Comber's greater talents. No doubt the long tenure, forceful characters, and genuine distinction of Gale, Finch, Osbaldeston, and Fountayne, who ruled the church from 1697 to 1802, and the support they received from successive archbishops ensured their dominance. Osbaldeston, it is true, suffered at first from difficult colleagues whom he had inherited from his predecessor, but Fountayne, who owed his own elevation to his uncle, Thomas Sherlocke, bishop of Salisbury,[41] was able to promote a series of congenial colleagues as residentiaries.

The deanery was a Crown appointment, but the choice was often influenced by the archbishop's wishes, especially after Finch's elevation in 1702. There can, for instance, have been little desire to see Jacques Sterne as dean, in 1747, despite his strong support by Lord Irwin, and in 1802 George Markham was obviously the nominee of his brother the archbishop.[42] The archbishop's influence was also felt in the nomination to prebends, which were in his gift. It was said by his contemporary Browne Willis that Sharpe deliberately recruited the prebendaries 'from such as had lived in his diocese and had recommended themselves by doing their duties in their parochial cures', although the memoirs of his patronage secretary and son-in-law Heneage Dering suggest that not all the nominees to the chapter were quite of this character.[43] The successive archbishops were certainly much beset by applicants for prebends, though not all were quite such deserving objects as William Herring, whose letter to Archbishop Drummond is a model of its kind:

I do not complain but as my Family is large and daily growing more expensive, any Addition Your Grace may presume would not be unacceptable to Me. I take the Liberty of solliciting for myself, because if I may be obliged, I should desire to owe

[39] YML, Misc. Documents, 1700–1821, letter from Mason; BIHR, Bp. C & P XIX.
[40] *Gray Corr.*, p. 353.
[41] *HMCR Various Collections*, viii, papers of Hon. F. L. Wood, p. 171.
[42] Ibid.
[43] A. T. Hart, *Life and times of John Sharp archbishop of York* (1949), p. 15; 'Autobiographical memoranda by dean Dering', ed. C. Jackson, in *Yorkshire Diaries* (Surtees Soc. 65, 1875).

that Obligation immediately to Your Grace. . . . I am constantly resident in my Parish and it is matter of Comfort to Me, though not of boasting, to find myself as well respected and to have as great an influence among my Parishioners as any Clergyman can desire to have. If my Request is impertinent or cannot at any time be conveniently complied with, I beg Your Grace will take no Other Notice of it than to pardon it. . . .[44]

There were certainly many relatives of former archbishops and dignitaries among the prebendaries throughout the period, but they were on the whole a dignified and even distinguished body, very well represented in the *Dictionary of National Biography*, and including many antiquarians, book-collectors, musicians, and theologians. On the whole, unless they resided in York, and could thereby claim to be summoned to chapter meetings, the prebendaries were of relatively little importance to the cathedral community, and only during Osbaldeston's time was any attempt made to disturb them in their prebendal estates and peculiar jurisdictions.[45]

The archdeacons and subdean rarely came to the Minster, unless, like Jacques Sterne, they were also residentiaries, or held another dignity, and the chancellors had been dispensed from residence apparently by Sharpe, despite their duty of oversight of the preaching table. The precentors, however, were almost all residentiaries, and played an important part, from Comber's time onwards, in the regulation not only of the cathedral music, but also of most of its other activities. Mason's long tenure of the dignity (from 1762 to 1797), his distinguished early career, and important political and literary connections, gave him many chances of activity, and his letters reveal him writing the inscription for a monument to a local physician, or refurbishing Prince William of Hatfield's statue, writing fast-sermons, acting as a justice of the peace, entertaining visitors of quality, reforming the conduct of the service ('when I was well with the Dean of York and a kind of Prime Minister to him'), reorganizing a local mental hospital, and dabbling in the agitation for parliamentary reform.[46]

The chapter meetings are rarely recorded in much detail, unless there was wide divergences of opinion. The quarrels about statute reform in 1663–4, a dispute about nominations to a chapter church in 1686, Dean Osbaldeston's prolonged wrangles about bell-ringing, and the narrative of Edward Finch's contumacy, are all recorded in full, but for the most part the chapter acts are a bald and incomplete list of decisions taken in chapter meetings. It is clear that many matters, even those involving expenditure,

---

[44] BIHR, Bp. C & P VII. I am grateful to Dr. David Smith for bringing this to my notice.
[45] YML, Chapter Acts, 1728–47, fo. 54ᵛ: injunctions after visitation of prebendal peculiars, 1730.
[46] For sources for Mason's life, see nn. 37 and 38 above.

or raising questions of principle, were decided by the deans or individual residentiaries, and not *capitulariter*.

The matters discussed in chapter between 1670 and 1730 rarely rise above the domestic detail of alms to wandering Greek churchmen, an index for the muniments, or authority to transmit chapter accounts to London for a lawsuit. There was little attention, it seems, to property management, or to threats to the status of the cathedral body in York or in a wider field until Osbaldeston's time. Much time and energy were spent in the early 1730s on recovering and releasing the chapter property in Serjeants Inn, Fleet Street, and exploiting it with building leases;[47] the threat presented by the Aire and Calder Navigation to chapter mills at Brotherton was averted only by long negotiation in 1757–8;[48] the survey and drainage of Misterton Carr (Co. Nottingham) in 1788[49] was a profitable venture for the common fund, though costly in the initial stages, and every parliamentary enclosure involving chapter land received careful scrutiny.[50] Some proposals for legislation were also discussed and petitioned against by the chapter, notably the playhouses bill of 1735, which was held to threaten the Liberty of St. Peter, and a bill for tithe recovery from Quakers, of the following year.[51]

Much more chapter time was taken up, especially before 1700, by oversight of the vicars choral and of the choir. The vicars' property was mismanaged at the beginning of the period, the Bedern was allowed to fall into disuse, and the succentor Henry Mace (who survived from before the Interregnum) and his fellow vicars were lax about paying the songmen's wages, and were often contumacious. In 1662 the registrar noted in his draft minutes: '10 june memorandum that Mr. Mace called me knave in the chapter where I am in the presence of Mr. Dean'.[52] Even as late as Osbaldeston's time there was trouble with the vicars, and the dean sought the archbishop's advice on the best way 'to humble the insolence of a saucy vicar'.[53] On the whole, however, after this time the vicars gave little trouble; they read early prayers and served the various chapter churches in York in a relatively seemly manner, and many of them regularly preached the prebendaries' courses. By the end of the eighteenth century their body was adorned, and their tone much elevated, by the long service as succentor of the pioneer evangelical William Richardson, whose sermons in the

[47] YML, Chapter Acts, 1728–47, fos. 90, 110–11, 124; St. Peter's Account, 1720–69, s.a. 1732–3.
[48] YML, Chapter Acts, 1756–71, fo. 17; St. Peter's Account, 1720–69, s.d. 15 May 1758.
[49] YML, Chapter Acts, 1784–1807, p. 70.
[50] YML, Chapter Acts, 1756–71, and 1784–1807, *passim*.
[51] YML, Chapter Acts, 1728–47, fos. 107, 132ᵛ.
[52] YML, Draft Chapter Acts, 1661–3, fo. 11; BIHR, V. 1662–3.
[53] BIHR, Bp. C & P XIX.

Minster and St. Michael-le-Belfrey, as Faith Gray recorded, were of great influence in the close and the city.

There were also various crises of discipline and morals involving songmen, upon which the chapter took action, perhaps the most outrageous occurring in 1816, when Matthew Huby was dismissed by the chapter 'for being married a second time and having also suffered banns to be published in St. Sampson's church for his being married a third time, his first wife being now living, all which he confessed to be true'.[54]

With the ministers of the chapter, the vestry clerk, and vergers, as might be expected, there were occasional disputes about their fees and privileges, which probably arose from the way in which they were paid, by a very small stipend supplemented by fees and gratuities. Between 1696 and 1705 there were bitter disputes about the vergers' claim to dine daily, as of right, with the residentiary or to receive a daily payment for food. In 1691 the vestry clerk Nicholas Proctor abused his trust 'in charging the church with candles when none such were boughte . . . for a whole yeare and a halfe', and was removed from office.[55] Temptations of this sort were removed by improved supervision as time went on, and no more is heard of them, especially after 1749, when the perquisites of the dean and the vestry clerk were finally settled:

All mourning put up in the church, all fees for ladys seats or stalls, belongs to the Dean. The clerk is to have one shilling from every wedding fee, and to divide one quarter of the rest of the fee with the three vergers. He is also to have one quarter of the money given for showing the church, and one quarter of the fee given for renewing [i.e. sealing] leases and patents. The vergers now have fees for ringing the great bell, and money paid for the gentlemens seats; they are further to receive the money given by the Sheriff or Judges for their seats during assize weeks.[56]

The early days of the Restoration were attended by financial uncertainty and difficulty which were only partly to be attributed to losses of property during the Interregnum. It was clearly some time before any systematic supervision of receipts and payments was established, and although the central accounts of the church, those of the chamberlain, survive from 1667, they are ill arranged and uninformative before the appointment of Robert Squire as chamberlain and registrar in 1677. There are fabric accounts for routine payments, from 1661, but none for St. Peter's portion before 1720, and other subsidiary and special accounts for sealing fees, lighting funds, court fines, and library expenses appear only in the early eighteenth century.

[54] YML, Chapter Acts, 1807–30, fo. 127.
[55] YML, Chapter Acts, 1634–1701, fo. 223ᵛ.
[56] YML, Misc. Documents, 1700–1821.

The chamberlain's receipts came almost entirely from rents of leasehold properties, including the rectories of appropriated churches; they brought in about £300 between 1667 and 1740, but had almost doubled in yield by 1806. Out of this sum were met the regular daily commons to the residentiaries (£11 each year), the wages of vergers and vestry clerk, the fees of officers (auditor, steward, registrar, chamberlain, and clerk of courts), the chapter contribution to the vicars' stipends, the cost of communion bread and wine, fees for sermons, and additional lighting in the choir. Besides there were at first a variety of non-recurring payments, charitable gifts, restoration of chapter churches, organ repairs, book purchases, bell-ringing, and bonfire materials, and entertainments such as £1 'to the town waits for music in the quire the first day that the Archbishop came to visit the cathedral' in 1683. The accountant also found money for gilding and painting the new dyall plate, in 1687, and paid a writing master for copying letters to Lord Falconbridge, the lessee of some chapter properties. When at Martinmas the chamberlain's accounts were audited the residue was divided among the residentiaries and St. Peter. Between 1667 and 1681 the total sum for division varied between £101 and £175; in 1747 it was £136 19s.; in 1806 £174 19s. 7d.[57]

In addition to this dividend the residentiaries shared the fines for renewals of leases, the installation and collation fees, the profits of the seal, and of chapter jurisdiction, and of the archiepiscopal *sede vacante* administration. The sums involved here were, apart from the lease fines, which were irregular in occurrence, and subject to negotiation, fairly small. They amounted in all, during the eighteenth century, to an annual average of £21, and were regularly presented at the Martinmas audit in a composite account, which included various special funds. There is no account for lease fines, and the amounts involved can rarely be discovered: the one case mentioned in the records, because it led to controversy, was the unusually large profit from the Serjeants Inn renewal in 1735, when £2,600 were thus divided:

> £31.10 to Mr. Osbaldeston (counsel) for his time and trouble
> £21 to Thomas Jubb (chamberlain)
> £10.10 to Mr. Cruwys (junior counsel)
> £418.3.8 to each of six residentiaries, St. Peter being one.[58]

During the eighteenth century, or at least between 1720 and 1769, St. Peter's part increased as the residentiaries' shares grew, but the receipts still fluctuated widely (1721, £256 15s. 3d.; 1722, £129 15s.; 1723,

[57] YML, Chamberlains' Accounts, 1677–1707, 1705–67, 1767–1821, *passim*.
[58] YML, Chapter Acts, 1728–47, fo. 111[v].

£196 13s. 4d.) and it is obvious from the accounts that the authorities aimed at accumulating money in hand, and even used the interest from other temporary funds to supply St. Peter's needs. In 1747–8, for example, the fund for a time held £2,500 collected for the fabric. At the same time many expenses still met from the common fund before 1700 were now borne by St. Peter, which paid for sermons and special bell-ringing:

> 1759
>
> 21 August paid the ringers on victory gained by our forces over the French near Minden
>
> 24 August on a (false) reported victory gained by the Prussians over the Russians
>
> 11 September for a victory gained at sea by Admiral Boscawen
>
> 22 October for the taking of Quebec by our forces

the drawing of maps and plans, and work on the cathedral plate:

> 1743
>
> Mr. Buckle for mending the vergers' maces, £3.2.2.
>
> Mr. Paul de Lamerie, for gilding some more of the plate, £10.8.

gifts and donations:

> 1744
>
> Mr. Buckle for six silver spoons and two salts for Mr. Warwick as a present for repairing the organ, £6.11.

Various charges about a fire of 1753, and the subsequent purchases of fire-fighting equipment, were also met by St. Peter:

> 1 December 1754 Paid the Venerable the Dean for a fire engine and buckets bought at London for the use of the Minster, £24.17. and for freight and crane dues for the fire engine, £1.2.6.

At times it is difficult to know whether the fund is not paying for things which might have come on the fabric fund, like the £3 paid for packing-cases for plate glass for the altar screen, in 1761.[59]

The fabric fund was financed, like the common, from rents and lease fines, with some casual sources such as the sale of building materials, and fees for graves and monuments in the Minster. There were continued attempts, especially during the later eighteenth century, to increase the yield from rents, which between 1757 and 1790 rose from £182 to £639, very largely as a result of the improvement of the Misterton Carr estate. Out of the income the clerk, glazier, and plumber received their salaries, timber, lead, glass, and stone were bought, and the running repairs of the Minster fabric and the various properties in the precinct paid for. Some large-scale restoration, like the repaving of the choir, in keeping with that of the nave,

[59] YML, St. Peter's Account, 1720–69, *passim.*

in 1735, was also met from the fabric fund, but special efforts were usually made to raise the cost of bigger projects. Throughout the eighteenth century the dean and chapter were trying to raise money for the use of the fabric, either by mortgage as in 1729, when £1,000 was raised on property at Aldborough, or by short-term loans, on the collateral security of the Serjeants Inn fine, from merchants in Hull and York. Small sums coming in from bequests, or as trust funds, were also invested in 4 per cent mortgages and after 1780 money raised evidently on appeal from the public was invested in consols. In all this financial activity the responsible agent was always the clerk of the fabric, who was also often registrar and chamberlain, and whose legal and financial connections were plainly of the utmost importance. A good example was Thomas Jubb, who held these offices during Osbaldeston's time, whose operations are recorded in some detail, and who was evidently an object of deep suspicion to the more traditionalist canons like Finch.[60]

The fabric repairs of the early Restoration, most of which concerned the roof, have already been described. They cannot have been very thorough, for in 1685 a survey of all the leads was thought necessary, and Comber, who took the lead in promoting it, estimated the cost of needful repairs at £3,500. An attempt was made to raise the money for this by a parliamentary levy on the coal trade of the north-east, but the plan was lost in the constitutional upsets of these years; a little additional money was somehow raised for extensive purchases of lead. For the next four years the plumbers were busy on the south transept, the surrounds of the central tower, and the chapter-house.[61] The external walls of the Minster had little attention in this period, apart from the demolition of houses on the eastern side of the south door, as the leases ran out, which, as Drake records, 'cleaned this part of the church from the scurff it had contracted by the smoke proceeding from these dwellings'.[62] Drake gave the credit for this operation to Dean Gale, but his successor, Finch, continued the good work by a thorough external cleaning of the walls. A tourist who visited York in 1725 described the work going on in a sort of bo'sun's chair: 'there is at this time a man employed for cleaning the walls on the outside, who has contrived a chair for that purpose which he fixes on any part he has a mind to and sits in it for the performance of his business'.[63]

[60] YML, Fabric Accounts, 1661–1827, and Fabric Day Book, 1678–1747, *passim*.
[61] *Comber* i. 16; YML, Chamberlains' Accounts, 1677–1707, s.d. 8 Dec. 1685; Fabric Accounts 1661–1827, fos. 18ᵛ–20ᵛ; cf. *The beautifullest church, York Minster, 1472–1972*, K. M. Longley and John Ingamells (York, 1972).
[62] Drake, *Ebor.*, p. 486; YML, Chapter Acts, 1634–1701, fo. 107ᵛ; Chamberlains' Accounts, 1677–1707, s.a. 1700.
[63] *HMCR Portland*, VI, 93.

More work on the roof was soon necessary: in 1732–3 the top of the central tower was repaired at a cost of £600, with additional timber taken out when the revestry was demolished in 1726. In 1744 the chapter-house roof was new leaded, for about £500, and when in 1751 the north-west tower pinnacles were blown down, the whole of the west end of the nave roof was renewed when the pinnacles were restored. Work on the roof was a continual drain and in 1753 it led to a fire which might have been disastrous and which certainly destroyed the roof on the west side of the south transept:

By the carelessness of the workmen a chafing dish of coals used in fixing the lead on the roof was left in one of the lead gutters and by the heat of the coals the wood under the lead, which was extremely dry, took fire and blazed out with great rapidity before it was discovered. So soon as it was observed, about eight o'clock in the evening the inhabitants of the city were in the utmost consternation and ran from all quarters to assist in extinguishing the flames; which by means of a number of engines was happily effected, after burning a considerable part of the roof over the low aisle in the South cross. The damage occasioned by this fire was with great diligence repaired by the active care of the present dean.[64]

After a survey made at the chapter's request by the York architect John Carr in 1770, fundamental repairs to the choir roof were called for in the spring of 1773, and to make this possible the services were entirely discontinued from 7 May to Whit Sunday (30 May). In fact there were almost continuous repairs in the years 1770–88, subscription lists were opened, and Archbishop Drummond, who himself contributed two hundred guineas, was active with Dean Fountayne in interesting wealthy tourists in the work. In 1775, for example, Drummond wrote to thank Fountayne for civilities to a Mr. Toll, who had wished to see the cathedral, and added: 'I suppose that he will give a proportionate subscription to the repair of the cathedral'.[65] In 1793 the whole interior was cleaned and painted: 'the gilded key knots in the vaults and gilded ribs, with every other decorated part of the vaults and walls, even the marble columns, imposts and string courses were painted with a body of terra and ochre, and all the remnants of the former embellishments totally obliterated'.

While the scaffolding was in place Halfpenny made drawings, for his work on Gothic ornaments, of features of the roof which were completely obliterated by the fire of 1829, and a painter fell from the scaffold.[66] In the next year, 1794, more serious trouble was discovered in the nave roof: a

---

[64] Drake, *Ebor.* (2nd edn. 1788), p. 295; Browne, *History* i. 314.

[65] YML, Fabric Accounts, 1661–1827, fo. 68; *Walpole–Mason* i. 84; Browne, *History* i. 317; YML, Misc. Documents, 1700–1821.

[66] YML, Add. MS. 93/2, Hornby small MS., p. 179; Fabric Accounts, 1661–1827, fo. 83ᵛ.

further survey was required from Carr of 'the canopy of the middle aisle', on 24 February, and before the end of April he had reported that the lead on the south side of the middle aisle of the nave was so perished as to make a completely new covering necessary. At his suggestion the chapter resolved to remove the lead and put it to other uses while covering the entire nave with 'the best blue Westmoreland slates'. The work was put in hand during 1795: a chapter order of 11 May in that year shows that the entire labour force of mason, plumber, carpenter, and painter, with an unspecified number of assistants for each, was intended to be employed on 'the present extraordinary works' for which detailed arrangements were now made. The opportunity was taken to stucco the nave ceiling, and services were again discontinued, at least on week-days, for the whole three-month term of William Mason's residence (August to October).[67]

The two decades of George Markham's tenure of the deanery saw the final clearance of the external buildings from the Minster walls, with the purchase and demolition, between 1809 and 1814, of the Irwin house which since 1616 had abutted on the north-west corner of the Minster. This facilitated the clearing and restoration of the west front, with a substantial lowering of the pavement level before it, which was carried out at leisure in the decade after 1802. At the same time, the derelict chapel of the archiepiscopal palace, was repaired at the dean's expense, and adapted for use as a cathedral library. Finally, in 1803, as the last step in the clearing of the fabric, the small beacon turret built on the roof of the central tower in 1666, at the instance of the commander of the royal forces in the north, the Duke of Buckingham, was demolished.[68]

After the enormous cost of lead, by far the largest items in fabric expenditure were undoubtedly the maintenance and repair of the windows, and the care of the bells. During a whole century and a half after the Restoration, glasswork of some kind was always going on. In 1663 two glaziers named Crossley and Giles were replacing and supplementing the existing glass, and for the rest of the century purchases of blue, green, or painted glass are continually made. The nature and extent of the work done in the late seventeenth century is admirably set out in these scraps of memoranda preserved in the muniments:

2 January, 1692/3 articles of agreement between Charles Crosby, glazier, and Robert Oates, clerk of the fabric, to take down a certain decayed window to the south of one recently set up, having five lights and tracery, well and truly amend and sett it anew, and assist the painter in setting up and taking down ladders, the

---

[67] YML, Chapter Acts, 1784–1807, pp. 144, 149, 163; *Hurd–Mason*, p. 116.
[68] Browne, *History* i. 319; YML, Chapter Acts, 1807–30, pp. 90–2; Hornby small MS., p. 179.

work to be completed before Lady Day. 17 June to 7 October, 1695, work done by the glaziers on the chapter house windows and elsewhere: memorandum that there was three of pigges marked TR used by the glaziers this year, 25 foot of new glass, 8 tables of glass, 4 foot of painted glass; also for another window they used $11\frac{1}{2}$ tables of white glass at 18d. per table and 17 foot of painted glass at 6d. per foot.[69]

At this period Ralph Thoresby's friend Henry Giles, 'the famousest painter of glass perhaps in the world' and one of a distinguished group of York artists working in and around the Minster, undoubtedly supplied much of the new painted glass, but it is certain that medieval glass from the Minster and elsewhere must sometimes have been re-used. Twice at least there is evidence of deliberate acquisition of medieval glass by the Minster authorities: in 1723 the plumber was ordered to repair the dilapidation of the east window of St. Martin Coney Street and remove the old glass for the use of the cathedral, and in 1818 the fabric clerk was paying the charges of removing painted glass to the Minster from the windows of the Bedern chapel.[70]

Work on the windows in the second half of the eighteenth century was dominated by William Peckett, who from 1753 onwards was supplying painted glass (sometimes as much as £100 was paid to him in a single year) and who was intermittently employed on the cathedral windows for the next forty years. A nineteenth-century account of this work, which seems to have been written by John Browne, recorded that in 1757

the great eastern window was extensively repaired in the stone work and the ornamental glass was at the same time repaired, not very skilfully by the glaziers of the church, but the most important part was performed by a young artist of York, Peckett, who was employed in restoring the heads of the bishops and other eminent persons represented in the windows. Shortly afterwards he was engaged in the reparation of the west window of the south aisle of the nave, in which he placed new figures of St. Peter and St. John. He also repaired the large crucifix in the same window and inserted two new faces. He had previously painted and stained a figure of St. Peter and the arms of the see for a south window in the south transept. In 1768, having attained a great excellence in his art, he was dissatisfied with the figure of St. Peter he had supplied, and presented another far superior, which now occupies the window.

Before his death in October 1795 Peckett communicated to the dean his desire to see placed in the Minster 'the most improved and masterly part of my works in that art after forty years experience'. This was a window of

[69] YML, Draft Chapter Acts, 1661–3, fo. 19; Fabric Accounts, 1661–1827, fos. 8, 19[v], 21; Misc. Fabric Papers.
[70] YML, Chapter Acts, 1701–28, s.d. 4 Nov. 1723; Fabric Accounts, 1661–1827, fo. 107[v].

three figures, which he proposed to give to the Minster at half its estimated cost, with the further suggestion that the old glass which it would replace, should be kept for use elsewhere in the church. Peckett died before the scheme could be put into effect, and the terms of his will slightly altered the original proposals, so that his widow gave two figures without charge, and received £24 18s. for the third.[71] A final addition to the glass was made by the Earl of Carlisle, who in 1804 gave a window depicting the Visitation of St. Elizabeth, which came from the church of St. Nicholas at Rouen, and which was now installed in the easternmost window in the south choir aisle.[72]

Work on the bells was less continual, but equally costly, and their importance, like that of the clock, in the life of the city, concentrated much attention on them, and attracted funds for their repair. The parties in a duel fought in 1675 arranged to be 'at Penley's croft at the ringing of the Minster prayer bell' and no doubt life in shops and workshops was always regulated by the bells.[73] Certain rearrangements of the bells had been made during the Interregnum, and from 1655 the peal hung in the south-west tower, with the little prayer or sermon bell in a small turret over the south door, where it stayed until Dean Finch had it removed to the top of the central tower. Routine care and maintenance of the bells were the business of the clerk of the fabric, but neglect or age had brought them into disrepair by 1728, when there was a dispute involving the clerk and the clock-keeper. Soon after this date, in 1733, a good deal of work was done to the bell frame and the tower itself, and Drake suggests that it was undertaken on the insistence and at the expense of the ringers themselves:

. . . the frames of all these bells were renewed and they re-hung in a manner much more commodious for ringing than before; towards the expense of which a set of public-spirited citizens, admirers of this kind of music and exercise, contributed £20. They also at their own expense, built a new floor, twenty-one feet higher than the old one, for their greater convenience in ringing.

Thirty years later the bells themselves were held not to be tunable, and the five treble bells were given to St. Michael Spurriergate, in exchange for three others which with the residue of the cathedral peal were traded in as old metal to Messrs. Lester and Paul of London, who cast a new peal of ten bells. This did not please the citizens, as the local chronicler, Beckwith, recorded:

[71] YML, Fabric Accounts, 1661–1827, fos. 60–61ᵛ, 85; Misc. Documents; Chapter Acts, 1784–1807, p. 174; Hornby small MS., p. 179.
[72] YML, Chapter Acts, 1784–1807, p. 321.
[73] G. Benson, *An account of the city and county of York from the Reformation to the year 1925* (York, 1925), p. 50.

This year the Dean disposed of the old bells in the Minster and got a new peal of worse bells; before there were twelve, but now they are reduced to ten. The inhabitants of York thought they had no reason to thank the Dean for meddling with 'em, for the old bells were much better, as well as the former Dean.[74]

The great medieval clock, which covered the wall between the south door and the southernmost chapel, and blocked one of the windows there, survived without much alteration, with chimes playing tunes at set hours. A new gilt and painted dial was put up in 1687, a fresh set of chimes was supplied by John Wragg in 1706, and Dean Finch installed a new dial, perhaps on the outside wall, with two images striking the hours. Despite this the clock itself was by 1749 'very ruinous and bad' and the dean and three residentiaries were empowered to arrange for a new one to be made. 'The celebrated artist Mr. Hindley of York, supplied an elegant and excellent clock' at a cost of almost £300, but the chimes, and Dean Finch's dial, vanished completely. Here, too, Drake says, many of the citizens were willing to contribute to the cost 'As the minster clock is that by which the inhabitants of the city chiefly regulate their hours, they were considerable contributors towards the expense of this work'.[75]

The remaining major item of expenditure on the fabric in the eighteenth century was the great re-paving of the entire church, which took place between 1731 and 1738, and which was supplemented by the re-making of the steps at the south door. The floor design, which can be seen in Drake's Plate, along with the muddle of grave slabs which it replaced, seems to have been the work of the well-known virtuoso Lord Burlington and his associate William Kent, and the cost was borne by a subscription from local peers, gentry, and clergy, the lord mayor and commonalty of York, and many private citizens: the total cost was estimated at over £1,600 (Drake says in the end it reached £2,500), and this despite Sir Edward Gascoign's gift of stone from his quarry at Huddleston, the re-use, wherever possible, of marble grave-stones, and a remission of sixpence in the ton of tunnage on the shipments of marble. The four-inch-thick stone blocks were hewn in the quarry, the old floor completely lifted, and three courses of brick set edgewise in mortar as a foundation for the new work. All this, and the laying of the new floor, was executed by four masons—John Watson of Hothroyd, Robert Stout of Helmsley, William Ellis of Malton, and John Rushworth of Beverley—at 1¾d. per square foot for brick, 12d. for marble, and 8½d. for stone. The blue marble used came in part from St. Martin Coney Street, where the churchwardens agreed to exchange it for some of

[74] Drake, *Ebor* (2nd edn.), pp. 273–4, 276; Browne, *History* i. 317.
[75] YML, Chamberlains' Accounts, 1677–1707, s.d. 17 Jan. 1687; Fabric Accounts, 1661–1827, fo. 31; Chapter Acts, 1747–56, fo. 32ᵛ; Drake, *Ebor*. (2nd edn.), p. 274.

the old floor materials, which were intended for the building of a new porch. The rest was bought through Hull, from a Mr. Wilberforce, in fifty-four cases. It was estimated that there were in all, in the nave, 34,797 feet 9 inches of brick, 10,589 feet 3 inches of marble, and 23,708 feet 6 inches of stone.[76] Once the work was completed it remained a matter of care and pride throughout the century. Torrington, it is true, visiting York in 1792, called it 'the invention of *that great architect* Lord Burlington, and might be invented by a schoolboy for his kite', but it was in general much admired, and various attempts were made by the chapter to prevent its disturbance by fresh graves. In 1735 it was ordered 'to preserve it in its beauty and strength, that no new graves be opened, or corpses put in, except behind the communion table', but disturbance plainly continued until in 1795, and 1803 a series of stringent sanitary decrees required all future burials to be in lead coffins, in graves lined and arched with brick, and sealed above 'with a large stone or black marble ledger to lay over the body, even with the surface of the pavement of the church'.[77] The laying of the pavement was followed by the construction of a handsome flight of steps outside the south door, in 1735–6. The plan proposed had a 'nosing or Welsh ogee' on the steps themselves, and plain work or flagging above and on the half pace, and the resultant flight, which was replaced in the nineteenth century, is shown in many of the contemporary engravings of the south door. The entire plan of paving and steps was part of a great refurbishing initiated by Dean Osbaldeston, in which, as we shall see, the restoration of the choir was carried to great lengths.[78]

The provision of lighting for the services was always a matter of concern, and very costly, for the fund provided for this purpose by Sir Arthur Ingram, before the Civil War, was almost all lost, and as the chamberlain's account for 1695–6 showed there was a good deal to make up:

> small candles for the use of the body of the church this half year, besides sir A. Ingrams, £2.11.3
>
> candles for the branches formerly found by sir A.I. £3.12.3
>
> small wax candles or sizes for the quire and residentiaries £6.12.2 waxing (coating tallow with beeswax) the candles for the branches, formerly paid by sir A.I. £3.16[79]

In 1722 the town clerk of York, Mr. Darcy Preston, gave a sum of £80 to the chapter to improve the lighting, and the interest of this fund enabled a wax

[76] YML, Misc. Fabric Papers; Chapter Acts, 1728–47, fo. 109; Drake, *Ebor.* (2nd edn.), p. 279.
[77] *The Torrington Diaries*, ed. C. B. Andrews (reprint of 1970), iii. 36; YML, Chapter Acts, 1728–47, p. 109; Chapter Acts, 1784–1807, pp. 163, 302.
[78] YML, Misc. Fabric Papers; Drake, *Ebor.*, p. 486.
[79] YML, Chamberlains' Accounts, 1677–1707, s.a. 1696.

candle to be put at every other stall in the choir. In 1724 a further £100 was made available by the archbishop's gift to the dean and chapter of wax commutation money, which provided four further candelabra, and in 1749 John Allen, gent., 'formerly an eminent dancing master of York', bequeathed £200 to permit the candles to be lit earlier for afternoon service during the winter season. The arrangements now made seem to have continued without much change for the next seventy years, as Drake's continuator described them:

In winter, from All Saints to Candlemas the choir is illuminated at evening service by several large branches, besides a small wax candle fixed at every other stall. Three of these branches were the gift of Sir A. Ingram, anno 1638, as appears by an inscription on each, who also settled £4 per annum on the church for finding them with lights, two more were given by Ralph Lowther esq., of Ackworth, the last unknown. These, with two large tapers for the altar, are all the light commonly made use of, but on the vigils of particular holidays, the four great dignitaries of the church have each a branch of seven candles placed before them at their stalls.[80]

The brief archiepiscopate of Thomas Lamplugh (1688–91), coinciding as it did with the last years of Thomas Comber's vigorous tenure of the precentorship, was of great importance in the internal arrangement and furnishing of the Minster. It was in this brief space that a new organ, to purchase which Lamplugh, at Comber's instance, contributed £200, and for which he provided fitting, casing, and painting, was placed in its present position on the choir screen. It was the Archbishop, too, who re-fitted and furnished the altar in so complete a manner that it was thirty years before more changes were made. The list of Lamplugh's benefactions, as given by Drake, and shown in his illustration, sets the scene admirably:

Archbishop Lamplugh gave the covering of antependium of the table of crimson velvet, richly adorned with a deep embroidery of gold and fringe with the velvet for the back of the altar. He gave also three pieces of tapestry for the same use (this tapestry in the middle represents Moses found by Pharaoh's daughter, on the north side God sending manna from heaven to the Israelites and on the south side of the altar is Moses again smiting the rock Horeb from which comes a pouring of waters that seem gently to glide in delightful streams). He likewise erected the innermost rails and paved the space with black and white marble. And lastly, he gave three large Common Prayer Books and a Bible for the use of the altar.[81]

From this time on the dean and chapter concentrated on further enrichment and embellishment, and on increased comfort; crimson velvet, silk fringe, and lustring, with curtains for the pew doors, gave some semblance of

[80] Drake, *Ebor.*, p. 524.
[81] *Comber* i. lv, 23; Drake, *Ebor.*, pp. 284, 287–8.

79 A view of the south door of the Minster, taken before the Restoration. The houses built against the eastern side of the door were demolished before 1725, and the rest had gone before the steps were rebuilt in 1735–6.

The South Crosse of the Cathedrall Church of St Peter of Yorke.

80 A view of the choir and high altar showing the tapestries and rails presented by Archbishop Lamplugh, as they were re-arranged by Dean Finch.

An internal perspective view of the Choir-end of the Cathedral church of York.

comfort, though Mason fifty years later was still complaining bitterly of the autumn cold of the unheated building. Yet the choir, at least when the sun shone, must have presented a rich picture of contrasting dark wood and crimson silk and velvet.[82]

It was 'the very worthy Dean, Dr. Finch' who in his later years conceived plans for more fundamental alterations to the interior, while he was also engaged in the outward tidying of the walls, and whose activities, in the opinion of one tourist at least, made the Minster 'preserved both of the inside and outside in the best order of any cathedral church I have yet seen'.[83] It was Finch who resurrected the old pulpit and put it in its present position on the north side, facing the archbishop's throne, so replacing the unseemly and ineffectual arrangement by which a movable pulpit was brought out on preaching days to the lowest step below the altar. He also began the stripping of woodwork from the choir chapels (which was continued by his successor) and not long before his death successfully carried out a major scheme of demolition and rearrangement behind the altar. The medieval revestry, a wooden chamber between the altar and the stone screen behind it, was now demolished, and the altar and its rails moved back to stand directly before the screen, thus lengthening the choir by a whole bay. The Lamplugh tapestry was hung against the stone screen, and the general effect produced was that shown in Drake's Plate 50. There is no doubt that Finch and others meant this arrangement to be only temporary, for a drawing made by Hawksmoor for a canopy and high altar in a severe classical style has survived in the Bodleian Library. Evidently this plan met with little favour, and Dean Finch's death in 1728 seems to have prevented its execution.[84]

Osbaldeston's energies were absorbed for his first ten years by the re-paving, but the involvement of Burlington and Kent in that scheme seems to have led to Kent's further employment in the embellishment of the choir. In 1738 he designed a new throne and pulpit, and three years later refashioned the 'ladies' pews' which lay before the pulpit, and devised doors which would restrict public access to the stalls of dignitaries, residentiaries, and prebendaries. All the pew fronts were raised, in 1746, and the choir had thus assumed the appearance it was to have until the fire of 1829. The last touch was given by Dean Fountayne's removal of the altar tapestry in 1761, and glazing of the altar screen to the spring of the arches. Fountayne's other major contribution to the furnishing of the choir was the restoration of the

---

[82] *Walpole–Mason* i. 369; ii. 275–6.
[83] *HMCR Portland*, VI, 93.
[84] Drake, *Ebor.*, p. 523; YML, Chapter Acts, 1701–28, fo. 128; Browne, *History* i. 313; Bodl., K45.7, fo. 2.

two southern chapels of the south transept as a morning chapel in 1753–4. For at least fifty years the six o'clock prayers seem to have been said in the choir itself, but a chapel close to the clock was apparently the traditional place for them, and the tasteful refurbishing, with 'sixteen yards of rich crimson Genoa velvet at 27s. a yard' gave great satisfaction.[85]

'By the curious this [the glazing of the altar screen] is esteemed one of the greatest beauties of the church' and certainly it seemed to be the start of a much more seriously antiquarian and 'conservationist' attitude on the part of the cathedral authorities. It is true that Thoresby and his friends, and Archbishop Sharp, seemed to have something of the same attitude, and there had been a constant trickle of curious tourists to be gratified by the sight of Ulphus's horn and St. Mary's well. From Thomas Baskerville in Charles II's reign, Celia Fiennes and Defoe at the end of the century, Nicholas Blundell visiting his daughter at school and calling to see the tombs, all of William Mason's literary and genteel connections making summer expeditions, and John Wesley climbing the central tower when in York on a preaching tour, to George III's brother the Duke of York making a ceremonial visit in 1766, there was never any lack of tourists. For the northern gentry who frequented York for race week, or 'to learne qualitye' as Mrs. Thornton expressed it, the curiosities of the Minster fitted in very well with the 'puppy show' seen by Blundell and the 'exhibition of a stuffed zebra and other animals at the Blue Boar' in 1773, so much despised by Mason.[86] The beginnings of tourist literature, with Thomas Gent's *History of the Great East Window* which appeared in 1761, the visits of Horace Walpole to his friend Mason, their projected restoration of the tomb of Prince William of Hatfield, and the employment by Walpole of artist-craftsmen to make casts of the figures on the choir screen, are symbolic of the new attitude to the past.[87] It was not, however, until the 1790s that much more was done in the Minster. Even then, as Browne recorded, some wholesale destruction of inscriptions and decoration was allowed, and as late as 1806 Dean Markham renewed the furnishings of the altar in a completely conservative spirit with 'new velvet coverings with suitable enrichments for the communion table, pulpit and throne'. Nevertheless,

[85] YML, Chapter Acts, 1756–71, fo. 35ᵛ; Fabric Accounts, 1661–1827, fo. 53ᵛ; Fabric Day Book, 1678–1747, s.a. 1740, 1742; St. Peter's Account, 1720–69, loose account of 28 Apr. 1740, 1735–6, 1737–8, 1752–3; Drake, *Ebor.* (2nd edn.), p. 288.

[86] *HMCR Portland*, II, 311; *Fiennes*, ed. Morris; D. Defoe, *A tour through the whole island of Great Britain*, ed. G. D. H. Cole and D. C. Browning (2 vols., Everyman, 1962), ii. 228–31; *Great diurnall of Nicholas Blundell*, ed. J. J. Bagley (Record Soc. of Lancs. and Cheshire, 1968, etc.) iii. 19–20; *Correspondence of Gray*, p. 90; *Y. Cour.* 26 Aug. 1766; *Walpole–Mason* i. 91, 147–50; *The autobiography of Mrs. Alice Thornton*, ed. C. Jackson (Surtees Soc. 62, 1873), p. 222.

[87] *Walpole–Mason* i. 42, 100, 254–60.

81 A view of the choir published just before the great fire, showing the Burlington pavement ▷
and the new furnishings introduced by Dean Osbaldeston in 1746.

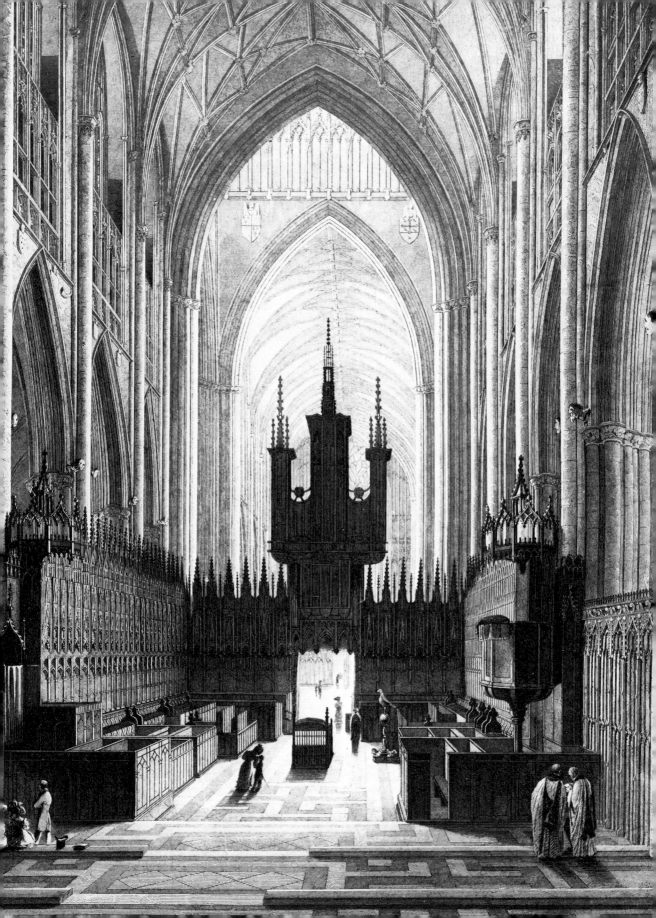

efforts were being made, according to the best lights of the time, to repair and restore, and Markham played his part in them. The plasterer Bernasconi and the statuary Michael Taylor of York were both employed from 1803 onwards in the restoration, and unfortunately the replacement, in some cases, of the statues of the west front and choir screen (Browne said that Bernasconi's work 'crowded together a profusion of small images and cement') and Gray's tomb was repaired and surrounded with bronze rails. This newly antiquarian attitude of the church authorities is reflected at once in their purchase of old oak for use in repairs, and their willingness to accept the gift of a silver bowl given by Archbishop Scrope to the York cordwainers; it was to be the forerunner of the nineteenth-century rebuilding and restoration.[88]

The Restoration chapter and its successors introduced few real innovations in the nature of cathedral worship, once order and decency were restored, and by 1700 the services had taken the form they were to retain until well into the nineteenth century. Early prayers were said by one of the vicars choral (a deacon), in gown and surplice, at six o'clock in summer and seven in winter, daily matins were sung at nine, heralded by a bell, and evensong at five; the Minster was evidently closed at six. On Sundays and festivals, and on certain state occasions, there was a sermon after matins; after the archbishop's visitation in 1685 there was also a weekly celebration on Sunday morning, and after Lamplugh's visitation of 1690 this was conducted by three priests, celebrant, epistler, and gospeller, 'as in the King's chapel and other cathedrals'. For Advent and Lent matins were said and in Latin, and additional sermons were preached on Wednesdays and Fridays. Before 1700 various efforts to omit matins on the sermon days, or to hurry or shorten them at other times, and to allow the preacher to come into the choir only just before his sermon was due, were rigorously repressed. The vergers were to escort the dean and residentiaries to their seats, fetch the preacher to the pulpit, and escort him back to his stall, and to keep order in the choir and prevent walking and talking there in service time.[89] After 1700 the only variations in worship were slight modifications to the communion service. Dean Osbaldeston seems to have tried in 1730 to introduce a said Nicene Creed, with the celebrant remaining meanwhile at the altar, but this was resisted by the two most conservative of the residentiaries. Lamplugh and Finch, and was apparently discontinued until Mason, soon after he became precentor, reintroduced the practice. He told a correspondent that at the same time he replaced the

[88] YML, Hornby small MS.; Browne, *History* i. 116; YML, Fabric Accounts, 1661–1827, fos. 89, 98[v], 104[v]; Chapter Acts, 1807–30, p. 39.
[89] Drawn from YML, Lamplugh Visitation; Draft Chapter Acts, 1661–3; BIHR, V 1662–3.

'unmeaning voluntary' which had been played while the celebrant moved to the altar, with a 'fine Sanctus of Dr. Boyce's', quoting in both cases the authority of the royal chapels.[90]

Throughout the whole of this period, as everywhere in England, there was a succession of fast-days with sermons, in time of national peril and distress (for example in plague time in 1665, and after the great storm of 1702), and thanksgivings, with sermons and bell-ringing, for victories, on coronation days, or for 'delivery by the Prince of Orange'. On such days the city authorities attended, the sermons were of some distinction and were often published, like the two preached in 1706 by Samuel Terrick and William Stainforth, both residentiaries of the church, on 'the day of thanksgiving for the late signal and glorious victory' on 27 June, and 'for successes vouchsafed this year to the arms of Her Majesty' on 31 December. The citizens of York attended in large numbers, especially in times of national hysteria, as for example in 1689, when Comber had a great congregation for his improvised sermon after the proclamation of William and Mary, and on Accession Day 1795, when both services, though it was a Saturday, were widely attended:

The Duke of Norfolk, Earl of Scarborough and Sir Thomas Gascoyne were at the Minster here yesterday. Mr. James Richardson preached. His text was 1 Peter, c.1, v.1, a good sermon. The tune of God save the King was played in honour of the day. The appointed service was used. Afternoon Mr. R.'s text 2 Chron., c.36, v.15, a very excellent and striking sermon on the state of affairs, of our national privileges and the abuse of them, on the contempt for religion showed by the highest and lowest classes of people, on the judgment of God which was upon us and hung over our heads and the necessity of repentance in order to avert our utter destruction . . . etc. The tune of God save the King was again played in honour of the day. The bells rang both morning and evening.[91]

Distinguished visitors such as the Duke and Duchess of York in 1665, the Duke of Buckingham and Sir John Reresby in 1666–7, attended the Minster escorted by the city authorities. The judges of assize adjourned their courts to hear a fast-day sermon in 1692, and Thoresby, who recorded this fact, and was a regular hearer of both daily services whenever he was in York, tells of a fast-day on 19 December 1701 when he came in from Bishopthorpe to the Minster with the Archbishop and his entire household.[92] The civic authorities and their ladies, and most of the genteel residents of the city, had continued their attendance at the Minster throughout the Interregnum, and the Restoration at first made little difference. The 'ladies' of the ladies'

[90] YML, Chapter Acts, 1728–47, fos. 40^v–41, 51^v; *Hurd–Mason*, p. 120.
[91] R. Davies, *Memoirs of the York Press* (1868), p. 125; *Comber* i. 21; *Correspondence of Gray*, p. 89.
[92] Benson, *Account*, p. 49; *Diary of Ralph Thoresby*, ed. J. Hunter (2 vols., 1830), i. 225–349.

pews had keys to their seats, and paid fees to the dean for their privileges.[93] Other members of the congregation, called by the registrar and chapter 'mob' or 'rabble', crowded into empty prebendal stalls or wherever they could gain a footing, until Dean Osbaldeston caused doors to be fixed to the entrances of the stalls, to restrict their use to 'the dignitaries, gentlemen, and better sort of citizens who attend divine service'. An unseemly dispute about the seats occupied by the civic authorities marred the years after the Restoration and was seen by some in the early days after the Yorkshire Plot as a serious threat to civic peace and public order. It had originated early in 1664 in the chapter's decision to reserve for the archdeacons their former stalls on the north side, which had been, and still were, used by the lord mayor and his company. Labels announcing this fact were affixed to the stalls, and gave great offence. Even when the chapter declared that the stalls could be occupied by the civic party, they retained the labels, and an uneasy peace was disturbed by further disputes, in 1667 and in 1681. Order was only restored by the intervention of Lord Chief Justice Jeffreys during the assizes of 1684, acting, it seems, at Comber's suggestion. Royal authority was invoked, the lord mayor and his party were ordered to come to church and to occupy stalls on the south side, near the throne, while Jeffreys himself, and his suite, sat facing them on the north side. This, and the resolution of other differences with the city, ended the trouble, and the civic party continued to sit on the south side.[94]

In general the week-day congregation was small enough. Laurence Sterne once recorded that he had preached on All Saints' Day 1756, to 'one bellows blower, three singing men, one vicar and one residentiary', and Mason later said that the regular attenders were 'ancient maiden gentlewomen and decayed tradesmen of this town'. Yet the citizens continued to frequent the Minster in times of national upheaval and rejoicing, and for their own specific festivals, and perhaps the most agreeable of these is that of the York Female Friendly Society, founded in 1788:

On 15 May once in two years when the whole society, Honorary as well as General members, should attend divine service at the cathedral in this city, distinguished by a green ribband placed in their hats, and afterwards to be regaled with tea and cakes, in a room engaged for the purpose, the whole expense to be paid by the Honorary members from the 'Private Fund'.[95]

[93] YML, Misc. Documents; Draft Chapter Acts, 1661–3, fo. 18[v].
[94] YML, Chapter Acts, 1634–1701, fos. 68, 145[v]; BIHR, Draft Chapter Acts, 1663–8, fo. 8[v]; *CSPDom, 1663–4*, pp. 447, 466, 501; *1667*, pp. 291, 511.
[95] *The letters of Laurence Sterne*, ed. L. P. Curtis (Oxford, 1935), p. 29 n. 8; *Walpole–Mason* i. 181; *Correspondence of Gray*, p. 54.

Thoresby thought the regular service without sermon 'unintelligible to country auditors', and quoted his son Richard's dislike of 'the singing service, because, he said, he understood not what they said'. Fifty years later the future succentor William Richardson found the music and lights deeply moving, and his words are worth quoting:

In my return through York I strayed into the Minster. The evening service was then performed by candlelight. I had never before been in the Minster but in the middle of a summer's day. The gloom of the evening, the rows of candles fixed upon the pillars in the nave and transept, the lighting of the chancel, the two distant candles glimmering like stars at a distance upon the altar, the sound of the organ, the voices of the choir raised up with the pealing organ in the chaunts, service, and anthem had an amazing effect upon my spirits as I walked to and from in the nave. The varied tones, sometimes low, sometimes swelling into a great volume of harmonious sound, seemed to anticipate the songs of the blessed and the chorus of praise round the Throne of God and the Lamb. I was greatly affected.[96]

For most Minster congregations of the time, however, it was undoubtedly the sermons which were the chief attraction, and which were most often discussed and remarked on by contemporary writers. When one takes into account the apparently casual nature of the arrangements, and the large numbers of sermons preached, this seems rather remarkable. It must be attributed to the enduring spirit of the age, when sermon-tasting of a type enjoyed by Pepys, or by the American Loyalist Samuel Curwen, was universal. Ralph Thoresby, for example, went from the Minster fast-sermon on 13 September 1692 to the New Meeting in St. Saviourgate, where the sermon left him 'much disappointed and disgusted', the Gray family a century later discussed and recorded the many sermons they heard, and purchasers were evidently found for all the sermons which were printed.[97] The arrangements by which all dignitaries and prebendaries were required to preach on Sundays and festivals, according to a regular rotation, had been first laid down in 1552 by Archbishop Holgate, and the plan was elaborated in 1571 by Grindal. The chancellor supervised the rota, and provided substitutes where necessary. After 1660, as we have seen, there were difficulties about the supply of preachers, and about their opinions; twenty-five years later the complaints were about the conduct of the preachers, who waited 'in the vestry or elsewhere, not coming into the quire untill that are called to the pulpitt'. There were still some troubles about the supply of preachers for certain feasts (St. Barnabas and the Conversion of St. Paul) and for the 'new' occasions of 29 May, 5 November,

[96] *Thoresby* ii. 162, 266; *Correspondence of Gray*, p. 13.
[97] *The journal of Samuel Curwen, loyalist,* ed. A. Oliver (2 vols., Harvard University Press, for the Essex Institute, 1972); *Thoresby* i. 244.

and 30 January, but these were resolved by Archbishop Dolben, who ordered the amended table of preachers to be displayed in a frame hung in the vestry, and enjoined the chancellor to find preachers for the Wednesday and Friday Lent sermons.[98] Besides these regularly recurring courses sermons were required for assizes, fast-days, and thanksgivings and it is hardly surprising that even those responsible for a regular course occasionally defaulted, and did not always find substitutes, and that the vicars choral, or ready preachers among the many clergymen in and near York, were able to supplement their stipends by many preaching fees. Sterne referred in two well-known letters to Archdeacon Blackburne, to the sermon agency run by the York bookseller Hilyard:

Being last Thursday at York to preach the Dean's turn, Hilyard the bookseller who had spoke to me last week about preaching yours in case you should not come yourself, told me he had just got a letter from you directing him to get it supplied. . . .

Now as to the future supply of any of your vacant turns you may be assured I should be willing to undertake them whenever you want a proxy. My daughter will be twenty pounds a better fortune by the favours I have received from the Dean and Residentiaries this year, and as so much at least is annually to be picked up in our pulpit by any man who cares to make the sermons, you, who are a father will easily guess. . . .[99]

Sterne's attitude to preaching does not suggest that the level of the usual Minster sermons can have been very high, or the amount of trouble bestowed by the preachers on their sermons very great; nor does it seem likely that the chapter was particularly solicitous about the standards and conduct of the preachers. It is salutary, therefore, to learn of the outcry of December 1730, when a preacher called Annesley was accused of omitting the bidding prayer required by the fifty-fifth canon, and exculpated himself (in the registrar's words) rather lamely: 'He did not remember any particular reason why he omitted it, but believed it was on account of the coldness of the season, the length of the service that day and considering the sacrament was to administer after the sermon was ended, or words to that effect.'[100] There is no record that Annesley was even admonished, but grounds for uneasiness about the sermons continued, and in 1760 it became necessary for the chapter to take action about the inconveniences and irregularities inherent in the system. The chapter acts record the matter thus:

[98] *Fabric Rolls*, pp. 100, 102.
[99] *Sterne*, pp. 25, 31.
[100] YML, Chapter Acts, 1728–47, fos. 67ᵛ–68.

1 March 1760: a conference held about the inconveniences and irregularities occasioned by the mistakes and forgetfulness of some of the dignitaries and prebendaries of the church, or those whom they appoint to preach or take care of their turns in this cathedral, in omitting to give timely notice to the Dean, or in his absence to the senior Residentiary in residence, of their intention to preach, and sometimes entirely omitting either to preach their turns or to appoint one, the said Dean and Chapter unanimously ordered and decreed that all and singular the dignitaries and prebendaries of the said cathedral and those who are nominated by them . . . do each of them give notice or order notice to be given to the Dean or Senior Residentiary not later than immediately after evening service upon the Friday preceding each Sunday . . . or if upon a festival two days before . . . if no notice is given the Dean or Senior Residentiary is to appoint a suitable person.[101]

After this revision, it seems the system worked smoothly enough, and it is clear that the standard of preaching, and of the conduct of preachers, rose considerably during the last decades of the eighteenth century. William Mason and others undoubtedly composed their sermons with a view to publication and the influencing of public opinion. Like Subdean Tully, who was suspended by royal mandate in 1686 for preaching sermons hostile to the Crown, Mason preached at least one sermon of a political cast, in 1781, in support of the clerical members of the Yorkshire Reform Association, who had been censured by the archbishop. No doubt some of the routine sermons remained as insipid as the effusion of Dr. Kaye which was described rather maliciously by Mason to Horace Walpole in 1780: 'I remember some years ago Dr. Kaye preached a sermon in York Minster in which he praised the excellency of our ecclesiastical constitution its purity simplicity etc. so highly that I whispered the Residentiary that sat next to me "Almost thou persuadest me to be a Presbyterian".'[102] On the other hand, William Richardson and his brother James expounded evangelical doctrine in sermons which were plainly found both moving and satisfying by the large congregations which flocked to hear them, and which must have helped to raise the general level of preaching; something of the effect they created can be felt in the passage quoted above about Accession Day 1795.

If the more respectable citizens of York were regularly summoned by the sermon bell to hear their favourite preachers, the entire population, 'too many of them of the looser sort', seem, at least until about 1750, to have frequented the cathedral nave as a public lounge, especially in service time. There were many complaints about this nuisance at the 1662 visitation, especially from the vicars:

[101] YML, Chapter Acts, 1756–71, fo. 31.
[102] YML, Chapter Acts, 1634–1701, fo. 185; *Walpole–Mason* i. 361–2; ii. 40, 153–4.

commonly in time of divine service there is such a noise in all parts of the church excepting the Quire, by walking and talking and shouting with boyes, especially upon Sundayes and Holydays, that those who read the prayers and chapters can scarcely be heard though they streine their voices to the uttermost.[103]

There were many reports to government, during and after the Yorkshire Plot of 1663, of the bad relations between the cathedral and city authorities. No doubt the delicate state of public order was reflected in the impossibility of suppressing the nuisance in the nave, and in continual minor outbreaks. One of the worst of these, in February 1673, ended in serious rioting in Minster Yard, as the canon in residence, John Lake, recounted to Joseph Williamson:

Since I left London I have continued above two years here as a canon residentiary and a Justice of the Peace for the Liberty of St. Peter, during which I have endeavoured to restrain some unparalleled disorders in the cathedral where on Sundays and holidays when the younger people of the town were afloat, four or five hundred would walk and do much worse things to the disturbance of divine service (not to mention other aggravations) that nothing could be heard; though I have used such temper and moderation that nothing has been done against any of them further than to cause them either to go to prayers or to go out of the church, unless sometimes I have caught at a rude boy's hat and kept it to the end of prayers, and given it to him again with a chiding. This so exasperated the youth of the town that yesterday, being Shrove Tuesday, they during divine service broke open the church doors which I had caused to be shut, and when after service ended I was going to my house, they so affronted and abused me that Captain Honeywood and other officers of the garrison, who were walking in the church, were forced not only to come, but to send for two files of musketeers to my rescue. Hereby I obtained a free passage to my house, but the soldiers retiring shortly to their guard, the rout came together again and assaulted my house with such violence that they broke all the windows, pulled down their frames, plucked up and broke fifty seven yards of pales etc. to the damage of about £40. Their wild rage might have proceeded to fire the house, to which they often incited one another and so have made this day indeed *Diem cinerum* or by entring at some of the breaches they made, to do further violence to my person, if they had not been happily restrained at last by the return of the soldiers, some of whom they knocked down, and when they were driven out of the Minster Yard, they embodied themselves before the gates and there braved the guard for nearly an hour, and sought to break in again.

The city authorities refused to intervene and disperse or punish the rioters, even when they came into the city's jurisdiction, and the trouble between them and the cathedral chapter was only pacified by judicious intervention

103 BIHR, V 1662–3.

from a specially despatched judge of assize.[104] The continuing presence of a large garrison in the city, and increasing suspicions of the king's intentions after James II came to the throne, inevitably led to fresh explosions. Sir John Reresby, who had become governor of the town in 1682, and who thought it 'more remarkable than most for height of faction', recorded many ugly incidents, including a dispute in the Minster in October 1683 which reflects clearly the difficulties of the situation:

The Sunday following, being in the Minster, I found the cussin which used to be in my seat removed into the next, wher Sir John Brook was to sit (a person that I had thought fitt with other deputy lieutenants to disarm in our late search for arms). This gentleman riseing at the psalmes, I took up the cussin and replaced it in my seat. Service being ended, Sir John asked me if I had the same commission to take his cussin that I had to take his arms. I said I took it as my own, as I should always doe when I saw it misplaced, and if he took his being disarmed ill from me he made choice of an ill place to quarrell in . . .[105]

Some of the ill-feeling was undoubtedly exacerbated by the insistence of the 'cathedral doctors' on their jurisdictional liberty, and by the difficulties they experienced in maintaining it without military help. After Reresby's coming the garrison was continually strengthened, in view of the growing unpopularity of royal policy. At first he had believed that he had the support of clergy, gentry, militia officers and soldiers, and about a quarter of the citizens, in maintaining order and enforcing government commands. He was ready enough to provide troops to suppress the ugly scramble for souvenirs which attended the funeral of the Countess of Strafford, in 1686:

As the said herse came to the west end of the Minster and the corps was taken down there was a rabble or route of ordinary people that pressed very rudely upon this informant and his souldiers and wold needs take the escocheons from the herse by force . . . at the quire door the said rabble did then presse and croud very rudely to come in and follow the said corps . . .[106]

The cathedral people themselves sometimes provoked the mob: bell-ringing and bonfire-lighting went on without restriction, and was increasingly hostile to the royal party. It is clear from the chapter accounts that the ringers were paid, and the firing provided, from cathedral funds, at least during the last two years of James II's reign, but by this time the role of the chapter had changed, and the stand of its two most influential members, Thomas Comber and George Tully, against the king's attempts to repeal the

[104] *CSFDom, 1672–3*, pp. 546–7; *1673*, pp. 36–7.
[105] *Memoirs of Sir John Reresby*, ed. A. Browning (Glasgow, 1936), pp. 283, 317.
[106] Ibid., p. 408; *Comber* i. 17–19; *Depositions from the Castle of York*, ed. J. Raine (Surtees Soc. 40, 1861), pp. 278–81.

Test Act and Penal Laws, had attracted the support of the citizens of York. Comber's determined resistance to the king's attempt to intrude Roman Catholic nominees into the chapter, which was in marked contrast to the vacillations of Dean Wickham, suited the mood not only of the citizens, but of the neighbouring gentry, and he emerged before the accession of William and Mary as their undoubted leader in a time of uncertainty and dismay.[107]

Troubles with the unruly mob virtually ceased with the end of James II's reign, and the cathedral was no longer a battle-ground. Archbishop Lamplugh's injunction of 1690 ordering that a verger, bell-ringer, or bedell should be in the nave at all times between 8 a.m. and 6 p.m. 'to prevent the tumultuous playing of boyes in the bodye of the churche' helped in the restoration of seemliness, and when Celia Fiennes visited York in 1697 the nave was frequented only by the gentry: 'on that account its much pity they keep it not cleaner'.[108] Thirty years later the Earl of Oxford saw the nave parade in its most developed form:

In the main aisle of the inside betwixt the western gate and the choir the gentlemen and ladies walk after evening service in the summer time for want of the convenience of a park and gardens, and it seems some people take as much delight in sitting here and a liberal gentleman has for that purpose covered some of the stone seats on the north side with wood above which is a brass plate with his effigies and an inscription underneath signifying his kind contribution to the health of such as were inclined to rest themselves on that bench.[109]

Soon after Oxford's visit the New Walk was laid out and no doubt its attractions diminished those of the Minster nave, which was now left to the curious visitor and to the Minster congregation.

No more is heard for many years of differences with the city but the Minster authorities continued to be sensitive about the maintenance of their liberty. In 1703, for example, they successfully petitioned Parliament against a bill to set up 'courts of conscience' for the recovery of small debts in York, on the grounds that such courts would harm those of their liberty. In 1735, with equal success, they petitioned against a bill about play-house licensing, in the belief that it might hand over the power of licensing all such houses in the city to the civic authorities. The practical grounds of their objections were set out in the chapter minutes:

which [the bill] seems to allow the continuance of a play house in Minster Yard. Six months ago a play house was set up in Minster Yard by Thomas Kerregan without

[107] YML, Chamberlains' Accounts, 1677–1707, s.a. 1679, 1685, 1688; Comber, i. 19–22; G. Duckett, 'King James II's proposed repeal of the penal laws', *Yorks. Arch. and Top. Jour.* v (1877–8), 433–69.
[108] YML, Lamplugh Visitation.
[109] *HMCR Portland*, VI, 93.

consent and he and his players have performed plays there ever since, are reputed papists and have no settlement.[110]

These cases apart there was no more trouble except in 1786 about a hairdresser living within the liberty. The lord mayor and corporation,

requiring him to take his freedom of the city on account of his waiting upon and dressing Ladies hair within the city liberty, the said Dean and Chapter unanimously resolved to support their jurisdiction and privileges and defend the said Clint., or any other person to be prosecuted by the said Mayor and Corporation for exercising his trade within the city liberty without taking his freedom.[111]

On the whole, however, the liberty functioned normally, like any other jurisdiction, with the occasional bastardy scandal, with regular sessions, and with some attention in the last years of the century to the state of the prison and the welfare of the prisoners.[112]

At the proclamation of peace in 1802 there was a slight dispute with the civic authorities, who ignored the correct behaviour of the chapter officials in unlocking the chain at the south-west gate of the liberty, and came in, unheralded, at the south door of the Minster, to read the royal proclamation. No action was taken then, but it seems that the dean and chapter were undoubtedly more sensitive about their liberties at this time, while at the same time more alive to their responsibilities. The national climate of opinion undoubtedly inspired such activities as the fund set up for the relief of felons and debtors in St. Peter's Prison, in 1792, and the continued improvements made in the prison buildings, just as the fear of riots and disturbances caused them to employ extra security forces during race week.[113]

There may have been causes for friction here, but a much more powerful irritant was the stand taken by the dean and chapter against some of the 'improvements' attempted by the city. During the eighteenth century the dean and chapter were, it seems, ready to give benevolent assistance to improvement schemes which affected the vicinity of Minster Yard, such as the Lighting Act of 1762, to which the dean, residentiaries, and St. Peter subscribed, the Lop Lane alterations of 1785, which were helped on the ground that they would 'make a more commodious approach to the Minster', and the improvements of 1800 to College Street or Little Alice Lane. They also, at considerable cost, themselves cleared and improved the

---

[110] YML, Chapter Acts, 1701–28, fo. 14; ibid., 1728–47, p. 109.
[111] Ibid., 1784–1807, p. 37.
[112] Ibid., 1756–71, fo. 32^v; Jursidiction Accounts, 1716–1813, *passim*.
[113] YML, Chapter Acts, 1784–1807, pp. 258–9; Jurisdiction Accounts, fos. 99, 121, 131–2.

west end of Minster Yard by the promotion in 1813 of a private act which empowered them to buy the Irwin properties and to open up the space before the Minster.[114] Yet in the same period they memorialized the government in 1807 and 1809 against dilapidation of the city walls and gates by the corporation, and in the latter year they petitioned Parliament against the corporation's bill to take down, widen, and improve the Ouse bridge, unless it could be altered to '*altering* and widening, but not taking down'.[115] Despite this friction the last three decades of the eighteenth century were marked by a more genuine participation of the cathedral body in city affairs. Even residentiaries like William Mason, who were in York for no more than three months each year, played their part in this. Precentor Sterne's sordid intrigues and pamphlet war on the Bar Convent, and Dean Fountayne's squabble with Dr. Topham, did nothing to enhance the reputation of 'the cathedral doctors' in their own city, but Mason's bold Whig stand in support of the Yorkshire Reform Petition of 1780, his association in that affair with William Gray and other prominent citizens, and his share in attempts to reform the management of the York Asylum, inevitably recommended him to the sober philanthropic liberal citizens who were by this time dominating local affairs.[116] The relationship thus created foreshadowed the part to be played in York and Yorkshire by the dean and chapter in the next century.

The period covered by this section has been depressingly characterized as 'one of the most unsatisfactory in the history of the English church',[117] and it is easy to see the Minster's history in this light. The quite unwarranted influence of Sterne's frivolous comments, and the unsavoury quarrels of a minority of prebendaries in the mid-eighteenth century have tended to obscure the part played at York, and in the whole country, by a man like Comber, the academic distinction of the chapter in Dean Gale's time, the dignified and seemly appearance gradually assumed by the Minster in the eighteenth century, and the re-establishment of a powerful connection between the Minster and the laity of the city. At the outset the Minster nave was sometimes a battle-ground for the mob, and always a place of disorderly resort. The services were conducted in a state of siege, and the citizens felt no responsibilities towards the Minster, but only claims against it. By 1753 this was entirely altered, for when in that year fire

---

[114] YML, St. Peter's Account, 1720–69, s.d. 29 Apr. 1762; Chapter Acts, 1784–1807, pp. 10, 220; Chapter Acts, 1807–30, pp. 90, 92.
[115] YML, Chapter Acts, 1807–30, p. 40; Misc. Documents, 1700–1821.
[116] A. H. Cash, 'Sterne as a judge in the spiritual courts', in *English Writers of the eighteenth century*, ed. J. H. Middendorf (Columbia University Press, 1971); Davies, *Memoirs*, pp. 255–7, 282, 323.
[117] 'The eighteenth century', *Y.M. Hist. Tr.*, no. 26.

broke out in the roof timbers, the entire population of the city turned out to fight it, and by 1800 orderly crowds frequented the services on each Sunday and feast day. The hundred and fifty years after 1660 were in fact years of restoration and consolidation for the Minster, after the political and religious upheavals which had threatened to overthrow it entirely. There were few violent incidents, but many small modifications which, taken together, brought about a seemly and workable compromise. Minor personal frictions loom disproportionately large in such an uneventful history, and articulate critics are able to pose as victims, yet in fact, allowing for the part played by political and personal influence in the selection of members of the chapter, the Minster at York was well and faithfully administered in this period.

I should like to thank all my friends at the Borthwick Institute and York Minster library for much help in the preparation of this chapter. It owes a great deal to the advice of Katharine Longley, Bernard Barr, and David Smith.

CHAPTER VII

From 1822 until 1916

Owen Chadwick

Dean Cockburn, 1822–58

The Victorian age was a high age for cathedrals. Railway lines made them the centre of their diocese as never before, and enabled them to satisfy all who travelled in search of history, or art, or music, in their relations to Christian worship. They had the beauty of the old ruined abbeys of the countryside, and were still a place where people said their prayers. England had money to spend, and all over England public-spirited men spent their money on restoring, building, decorating, cleaning, adding. York was no exception. Probably it was pre-eminent. The item *Restoration of York Minster* appeared in the newspapers as frequently as, or more frequently than, such an item about any other cathedral.

Calamity was in part responsible. During the thirteen years after 1828 the Minster suffered the three greatest disasters of its history. These trials were not caused by the negligence of the dean and chapter; they were afflictions which no skill in business could avert. But the dean and chapter, faced with these afflictions, needed extraordinary prudence in dealing with the consequences. By a further misfortune few of the canons were equipped with ability in business. That was not why they had been chosen. They were men of old ways, and floundered in unaccustomed seas. All might have been well if their dean had possessed the qualities which they lacked. But by a still further misfortune Dean Cockburn had less skill in business than his canons. He had not been chosen for worldly prudence, his ways were even more old-fashioned than those of his canons. That he was imprudent was not all that might be said against the dean. York Minster met its worst crisis under the care of its worst dean.

William Cockburn (1773–1858), of a family of very ancient Scottish lineage, was the youngest of three brothers to inherit, each in turn, a baronetcy from their father, Sir James Cockburn. That was, however, many years ahead of him at his installation as dean on 10 May 1823. His wife was the sister of Robert Peel, but Peel was home secretary, and not yet prime minister. His brother, Sir George Cockburn, G.C.B., as a rear-admiral, conveyed Napoleon Bonaparte to St. Helena.[1]

Cockburn's first sermon as dean, preached in the Minster on Whit Sunday 1823, was greeted as 'a display of eloquence seldom equalled'.[2] Within five months of his installation, plans were well advanced[3] for a radical improvement of 'the public view of the cathedral' by further demolition, the planting and fencing-off of the immediate surroundings of the Minster, and the creation of a 'broad circular road'[4] from the west end to Ogleforth. And a cultural event of unprecedented size and splendour had already been arranged.

Dean Markham had always opposed Archbishop Vernon's desire to hold another musical festival in the Minster, but Dean Cockburn agreed enthusiastically.[5] The first of a series of festivals (to benefit four Yorkshire hospitals) took place in September 1823. 'Galleries' of tiered seating, the fronts camouflaged with a form of Gothic stage-scenery, were erected in the Minster, where sacred music was performed, with enormous choirs and orchestras and soloists of star quality.[6] Secular music was played in the Assembly Rooms, which were also the scene of two balls, but for the next festival, in 1825, a new concert room[7] was erected, communicating with the Assembly Rooms through bronze folding doors, leaving the 'Egyptian Hall' free for an all-night fancy-dress ball, attended by many of the clergy, the county nobility and gentry, and the officers of the Yorkshire regiments with their wives and daughters. The third festival, in 1828, was even more

---

[1] T. H. Cockburn-Hood, *The House of Cockburn* (Edinburgh, 1888); *DNB*.

[2] *York Chronicle*, 22 May 1823.

[3] YML, Chapter Act, 27 Sept. 1823.

[4] This road was completed in 1839.

[5] A Handel commemoration had been held in the Minster in 1791. Canon W. H. Dixon was chairman of the festival in 1825 and 1828.

[6] The actor Macready, performing at the Theatre Royal during the festival, attended the Minster and recorded: 'On no occasion that I can remember have I listened with more enrapt delight to the strains of Handel and Haydn, with which the grandeur and beauty of this majestic edifice seemed so perfectly to harmonise. By some it may be deemed a species of heresy to regard these noble temples, our cathedrals, as ill-calculated for the service of Protestant worship. It is, however, indisputable that the voice of the preacher or reader can rarely reach without violent effort through their vast expanse, and in consequence only a portion of them, the chancel, is reserved for divine service; but in this performance of sacred music every note of the vocalist and the finest tone of the instruments are distinctly heard at the furthest extremity of the galleries, that raise the auditor nearly to the roof of the building at its most distant range.' (W. C. Macready, *Reminiscences*, ed. Sir F. Pollock, i (1875), 286.)

[7] Canon W. V. Vernon was active in the purchase of the site. The concert room was vested in the archbishop, the dean, and the lord mayor of York.

splendid, the results of amicable co-operation between church and city that seemed to augur well for the future.[8]

Jonathan Martin was a tanner of Hexham in Northumberland. He was seized by a press-gang to serve in the navy and fought in the war against Bonaparte. After the wars he felt a vocation like that of the old Ranters, to warn England of the wrath to come—which he identified with a French conquest under a returned Bonaparte—and especially to warn the clergy of the Church of England against their sins, in particular the formality of their services, their card-playing and wine-drinking and deception of the people, dragging millions down to hell. He came to York in January 1829, hawked copies of an autobiography, attended Methodist or Ranter services, and on Sunday evenings attended the Minster evensong, where the sexton Job Knowles came to know him well by sight.

On Sunday, 1 February 1829, Martin attended a Methodist chapel in the morning, then evensong in the Minster at 4 p.m. After the service he hid himself by lying down behind the tomb of Archbishop Greenfield in the north transept. At 6.30 p.m. Job Knowles locked the north-west door after the bell-ringers and went home, leaving Martin alone in the dark.

He felt his way up the stairs to the bell chamber, cut off the long rope of the prayer bell, and knotted it, seamanlike, into a 'ladder'. Then he went down the nave, climbed over the iron gate into the north choir aisle, and used the rope to climb over a high wooden door which divided the choir aisle from the choir.

Once in the choir he set to work. He noticed crimson velvet hangings round the archbishop's throne and the pulpit and at the end of the north or ladies' stalls. He cut them down with a razor, slashed off the gold tassels of the pulpit cushion, and decided to take them all away to make a cloak. Then he assembled two piles of prayer books and cushions from the choir, each pile against the woodwork of the stalls, north and south. He knelt down and cried 'Glory be to God' so loud that he was afraid of being heard outside. He lit one pile with two candles from the eagle lectern, the other with a whole box of matches. Then he left the choir as he had entered, carrying in a bundle his crimson velvet, and a little bible which he had found. He saw in the north transept the 'Fleet', the platform on wheels used to clean and repair the interior of the building. He wheeled it against a window in the west aisle of the transept[9] (next to the Five Sisters) and used pincers to cut out enough glass and leading to enable his body to pass, tied the rope ladder

---

[8] J. Crosse, *An Account of the musical festival held in September 1823 . . .* (York, 1825); YML, COLL 1926 (archives of the musical festivals).

[9] The west aisle was partitioned off in 1925 to form St. John's Chapel (K.O.Y.L.I. memorial chapel).

to the Fleet and passed it through the window, then climbed down outside. As he knelt and thanked God, the clock struck three.

About 7 a.m. a choir-boy named Robert Swinbank came early to choir practice, and started sliding on the ice. He fell on his back, and in that position 'saw a great smoke coming out of one of the doors at the side of the west tower'. A mason and the sexton arrived, and when they fetched the keys and stepped inside they were almost suffocated and stepped out again. However, by the vestry door the smoke was less dense. They found most of the south stalls ablaze, and the archbishop's throne—for one of Martin's incendiary piles burnt so much more merrily than the other that the workmen were even now able to salvage the prayer books and curtains from the north side of the choir. They rescued the altar and eagle lectern and the ancient chair used for the enthronement of the archbishops. The city fire-engine arrived with an aged and incompetent crew. Slowly the flames moved along the southern stalls, until at about 8 a.m. they reached the organ screen—and suddenly flames swallowed the organ, which gave out a weird sound, alarming the crowd gathered outside. From the organ the flames shot up to the roof, and caught the maplewood bosses; and from the organ they started to catch the north stalls. Molten lead began to pour from the roof, then pieces of burning timber. Fire-engine after fire-engine arrived, but one stream of water stopped after a time because the tap in the Minster Yard became choked. Now the whole choir was ablaze from organ screen to east window, birds and bats came flitting out to escape, and about 9 a.m. part of the roof crashed down to the pavement of the choir. Rafters went on dropping until by 10.30 a.m. all the choir had fallen. By mid-afternoon twelve fire-engines, including the Tadcaster engine and four from Leeds, were playing on the fire and beginning to win. The fire spread no further. By the evening they knew that they had saved the nave, the central tower, and the great east window. The Minster had lost a marvellous fourteenth-century carved oak roof, sixty-six carved stalls with seats, archbishop's throne, pulpit, and not only an entire organ but a valuable collection of music in manuscript. The east window had come within a few feet of destruction, but stood, still glorious though blackened.

That evening the magistrates of the liberty—headed by Archdeacon Markham, for Dean Cockburn was elsewhere—met in the Residence and examined witnesses. Job Knowles had seen the piles of books and cushions in the early stages of the fire, one of the masons produced the rope ladder from the broken window of the transept, and the pincers were found on the window-ledge. The pincers were identified by Tuesday evening (3 February 1829) as the property of the shoemaker with whom Jonathan Martin lodged. Archdeacon Markham issued a warrant for Martin's arrest.

Wm Cockburn DD of York — preached 1st time in Cathedral 18 May 1823 — 11 chap John 25&26V.

82 Dean Cockburn.

83 The Fire of 1829.

Unable to find him in York, the dean and chapter advertised in the newspapers with a description and a reward of one hundred pounds. As a direct result, Martin was arrested at a house near Hexham on Friday, 6 February. He had on his person the tassels, the crimson velvet lined with silk, the little bible, and a few bits of stained glass from the transept window. He was content, and believed that he had done right. He was tried at York Castle on 31 March (no less a man than Henry Brougham defending), found guilty but insane, and died in a London lunatic asylum after nine years of confinement. The prosecution took pains to exculpate Methodism, for men rumoured that Methodist ranting caused such madness.[10]

On 6 March 1829 the chapter decreed 'that henceforward a watchman shall be employed to keep watch every night in and about the cathedral'. (It was unfortunate that the previous watchman had recently been discharged.)[11]

Ten days after the fire the lord mayor presided at a large meeting in the Guildhall, to send an address of condolence to the dean and chapter. He announced a subscription list, to which he personally gave £50; the corporation contributed £500. Archbishop Vernon gave a munificent £2,000 and a replacement of communion plate, Dean Cockburn £300, the four residentiary canons £250 each. The Roman Catholic Sir Edward Vavasour gave £25 and 'an offer of stone from the quarries from which the church was built'. The architect Robert Smirke was asked to prepare a report on the restoration, and gave an estimate of not less than £60,000, excluding the organ. Canon W. V. Vernon said that the chapter could not give more than £1,500, and would need to postpone all other repairs or improvements which they had planned. On 5 March the Earl of Harewood presided at a meeting of the nobility and gentry of the county of York in the Festival Concert Room, which received Smirke's report and created an appeal committee. On 19 March a London committee was formed. By 31 March £40,000 had been subscribed.

Robert Smirke, soon afterwards knighted, was chosen to be the architect. Elliot and Hill of London were appointed to rebuild the organ. Lumley Savile, one of the York prebendaries (afterwards Earl of Scarborough), who thought Jonathan Martin pretended madness and wanted him 'hanged out of the way',[12] promised £3,000 to build the new organ. All was set in hand, and on 6 May 1832, though the organ was not quite finished, the Minster was reopened for services.

[10] T. Balston, *The Life of Jonathan Martin* . . . (1945); YML, Hailstone collection BB12 (York Lent Assizes 1829: *The King against Jonathan Martin* . . . Brief for the prosecution).

[11] Browne, *History* i. 320.

[12] Lumley Savile to Elliot and Hill, 23 Oct. 1831 (in Jonathan Gray, *Letters to the editor of the Musical World* (1837), p. 11).

This work restored the choir and organ screen as we know them. Vexation and a law suit accompanied and followed the result. A long dispute developed on whether the screen should be built precisely in its old place, or should be moved several feet to the east to uncover the noble bases of the pillars of the lantern tower. Canon Vernon was the prime mover in this suggestion,[13] for which he fought with zeal and 'an unwearied and unabated perseverance'. Subscribers' meetings in London and in York considered the proposal, voting went this way and that, the Press joined in and a pamphlet war of considerable rancour developed; for the beauty of the Minster concerned good men deeply, and those good men were not all citizens of York nor even members of the established Church. Although Dean Cockburn agreed with Vernon he was forced to bow to the storm. The archbishop (Vernon's father) sent for him and recommended him to cultivate 'peace and goodwill, rather than to gratify taste'.[14]

The organ suffered a series of changes in plan. Should it be rebuilt on the screen? If on the screen, should it be made lower, and concealed from view, that eyes in the nave might see a vista to the great east window? Should the organ be built in two halves, each against a wall, with the same idea of opening a vista? All these plans were at one time on the drawing-board, and favoured by architect and dean; and the organ-builders chased the changes of plan, while expenses mounted though they had accepted a contract at fixed price. 'Confound that east window,' said the organ-builders with feeling, 'what a bother it is to us all.'[15] Finally they sued the dean and chapter for extra expenses, and were awarded (8 December 1836) a miserable £200 (costs divided between the parties), the arbitrator holding that the organ-builders exaggerated the extra expenses they had suffered. But their lawyer published letters tending to show Dean Cockburn as one who stood on the letter of the law and refused a higher obligation of fair dealing. Elliot had died, and the sufferers were his three daughters, including an idiot whose plight brought sympathy. 'The cries of females and orphans', declared the idiot's guardian, 'will ascend to heaven with the sounds and peals of this majestic organ.'[16] The fault did not lie with the dean, except in so far as he wanted nothing less than the best for the Minster, and pursued that best through changes of plan, hardly aware that

[13] Canon Vernon was president of the Yorkshire Philosophical Society when it built its headquarters and museum, in classical style, upon the site of the domestic buildings of St. Mary's Abbey.

[14] J. S. Kerr, *Improvers and preservers: a dissertation* [for the diploma of conservation at the Institute of Advanced Architectural Studies, York] *on some aspects of cathedral restoration 1770–1830, and in particular on the great screen squabble of York Minster from 1829 to 1831* . . . (York, 1973). (Copy in YML.)

[15] Hill to Camidge, 15 Aug. 1829 (in Gray, op. cit., p. 24).

[16] A. Maxwell, *A Letter to Jonathan Gray, gentleman* (1837). Gray was attorney to the dean and chapter.

he added to the cost. He consoled himself and others by saying 'we should not be pinched for a hundred or two.'[17]

When the state of the Minster and the nature of its services between 1832 and 1858 are considered, let us not lay all the blame upon Dean Cockburn. Because he was inclined to trust the experts, the Minster was saddled with an instrument which made the best of music impossible, an ineffective monster of an organ, which had to be vastly reconstructed in 1859.[18] The fire of the incendiary Martin helped to bring about the slow decline in the numbers attending the Minster on Sundays. A prebendary who arrived in 1847 remembered the services during his early years as 'dull, cold and thinly attended.'[19] 'The choral music in this cathedral', wrote Canon W. V. Harcourt in 1857, 'is sunk below the level of religious impressiveness.'[20]

Now the dean and chapter started on a course which might have impoverished the Minster had it not been in the process of impoverishment by another route. When the fire was lit, they were already in debt, through continuing the improvement of Minster Yard, pulling down the old deanery which partly obscured the Minster on the south side, and building a new deanery on the north side.[21] Their debts were now increased because the subscriptions, however generous, failed to meet the huge cost of restoration. In spite of subscriptions amounting to £49,619, the gift of £3,000 from Lumley Savile, a gift of teak from the government dockyards to the value of £4,216, the return of the duty on timber, lead, and glass (£1,165), which was also the government's gift, half the profits of the 1835 musical festival[22] (£1,783), and the interest on exchequer bills (£683), there was still a deficiency in January 1837 of £1,419.[23] The dean and chapter

---

[17] Ibid., p. 13.

[18] The organ was drastically renovated in 1901–3, and partially reconstructed in 1917.

[19] George Trevor, in *Parliamentary Papers* (1884), xxi. 444.

[20] W. V. Harcourt to the secretary of the Ecclesiastical Commissioners, 9 Apr. 1857 (*Ecclesiastical Commissioners' Papers*, 11778). W. V. Harcourt was formerly W. V. Vernon.

[21] Ten months before it needed all the fabric fund to restore the Minster, the chapter had decided to reduce repairs to the fabric to a maximum of £800 a year, in order to pay off the debt incurred in building the new deanery. (YML, Chapter Act Apr. 1828 (H 8/7). No day recorded.)

[22] During this festival Princess Victoria and her mother attended a performance of the *Messiah* in the Minster.

[23] Account in Gray, op. cit., p. 12. For the further improvement of Minster Yard the chapter obtained a private Act of Parliament in 1825 (it had already obtained one in 1814); in 1827 the High Petergate gateway and a house at the south side were taken down, and by 1831 seven more houses had been demolished. A new Residence for the residentiary canon on duty was built in 1824. The new deanery was completed in 1831. In 1833 a new building (which the chapter had decided to erect as early as 1824) was completed for St. Peter's School (moved in 1828 from St. Andrewgate into a large upper room adjoining the Old Residence); in 1844 the dean and chapter acquired a struggling proprietary school at Clifton and transferred the school there. Dean Cockburn may be credited with infusing new life into the school, though the connection was not always a happy one.

began to live on capital. The most interesting, and potentially the most profitable, of their estates was Serjeants Inn, Fleet Street. In 1837 the dean and chapter obtained a private Act of Parliament to sell Serjeants Inn.

The troubles of the dean and chapter were only beginning.

On the evening of 20 May 1840, at about 9 p.m., two or three boys saw a light in the belfry of the Minster. They shouted to passers-by, one of whom was a bell-ringer. The cry ran through the city, 'the Minster on fire'. Three engines were quick upon the scene, and a special train left for Leeds to fetch more. A meeting of fifteen hundred members of the York Operative Protestants Association, gathered in the Festival Concert Room, refused to credit the report and at first suspected it to be a Roman Catholic hoax. Within an hour the belfry in the south-west tower was a shell, and the famous peal of bells of 1765 fell, carrying down woodwork and floors. The nave roof was soon alight, inhabitants of nearby houses removed their furniture, birds fluttered in and out of the flames. The watchers were afraid that the lantern tower must catch from the nave. But the engines saved the lantern tower, the new organ, and the screen. By 8 a.m. the nave was a smouldering ruin, open to the sky, windows broken.[24]

That afternoon the lord mayor and the magistrates of the city—for the dean and chapter had just allowed their jursidiction as magistrates to lapse—held an inquiry in the Guildhall, together with three of the residentiaries, canons W. V. Harcourt, W. H. Dixon, and C. Hawkins. Dean Cockburn arrived from the south of England before the end, but too late to examine witnesses. The clockmaker had been working in the belfry, using candle and matches; the floor was covered in dry sticks and straws dropped by nest-making jackdaws; the clockmaker was known as an honest man— and the meeting decided that the fire was an accident.[25]

The following Sunday the services were held in St. Michael-le-Belfry. But the ruins were opened to thousands of sightseers.

In two fires within eleven years York Minster lost all its roof and interior ornaments, except in the lantern tower and the transepts, one of which was almost undamaged by either fire. 'It can never be again' were the words heard.

[24] In 1899 Dean Purey-Cust recorded that 'persons still living remember the terrifying incidents of that awful night, how as children they were carried from their beds out of the surrounding houses lest the blazing towers should fall upon them, and how, when the great roof fell and a sudden glare of fire lit up the smoke and darkness within, the great crucifix in the west window of the south aisle shone out distinct and beautiful, and the cordon of soldiers, which surrounded the building to keep back the crowds, involuntarily raised their right hands and saluted'. (*The Restoration of York Minster* (Feb. 1899), 14.)

[25] At a second inquiry (reported at great length in *Y. Gaz.* 20 June 1840) the clockmaker confessed to having lied at the first. He had disobeyed the dean's orders and taken a naked candle into the tower.

So a second great appeal was made for money, after only eleven years. But the climate of opinion was different. The unedifying squabble over the restoration or removal of the screen had left its mark, for the rights of subscribers to vote on the proposals had not found favour with the dean, who had offered to return their money to the dissatisfied. Moreover, it was now revealed that the accounts of the previous subscription had never been made public. Now men asked whether dean and chapter might be charged with negligence, thus twice to suffer ruin.

On 15 June 1840 the chapter resolved to insure the Minster against fire.

The inquiries of the new reforming governments after 1832 shed an excess of light upon the endowments of cathedrals, and the endowment of York did not escape notice. Men said that they would never subscribe unless dean and chapter gave more from their own abundant coffers. So the dean and chapter, with no feigned reluctance, sold a second estate from the corporate revenues, and mortgaged still a third estate; and concentrated much of the revenue from the fabric fund on paying the interest on money which they needed to borrow. Perforce they committed the fabric fund for many years—and how should they be able to make the 'normal' repairs during the next ten or twenty years?

By 1854 the total cost of restoration (that is, two restorations) was £105,560; of this sum, £71,590[26] was given in donations—which means that the second appeal only achieved the sum of £22,000, less than half the product of the first appeal.

They were not only in debt to the bank. The second estate which they sold was used for repair of the fabric, but as part of the corporate revenue its true destination should have been the canons. If the canons had still had their old undefined powers, all might have stood. But the government had lately (1836) constituted the Ecclesiastical Commission; and so York Minster found itself paying to the Commissioners, for the next forty years, £362 16s. a year, to compensate for the 'misuse' of money from the estate. They paid the last instalment in 1883—by which time they minded less.

Here is a contrast which shows their plight. In 1835 the government inquiry reported the fabric to be in good order, and the fabric fund equal to the likely needs. Nineteen years later the fabric fund came nowhere near to covering the cost of necessary repairs, and about half of it went to pay interest and principal on money borrowed after the fires.[27]

Thus the second, accidental, fire was a greater calamity than the first,

---

[26] *PP* (1854), xxv. 53. The architect of the second restoration was Sydney Smirke, brother of the architect of the first. While the works in the nave were in progress, three sides of the central crossing were bricked up to prevent disturbance and to protect the organ.

[27] *PP* (1854), xxv. 231 ff. (22 ff.).

intentional, fire. And meanwhile the building began to decay. 'There is no decay more to be regretted', wrote Canon W. V. Harcourt on 9 April 1857, 'than that of the magnificent painted glass, the Glory of Ancient Art, for which York Minster is conspicuous, now fast perishing, and never likely to be replaced.'[28]

When crisis looms, men usually divide, sometimes bitterly. The chapter was no exception. One or two of the residentiary canons could hardly bear, at such a time, the unbusinesslike nonchalance of the dean. The most articulate, and soon the leader, of the dean's critics was the residentiary William Vernon (who had in 1831 followed his father's example in taking the extra surname Harcourt). His father was the archbishop of York. William Vernon Harcourt (1789–1871) was one of the ablest, though not one of the wisest, prebendaries in the history of York. His character had been formed by five years' service in the Royal Navy from the age of twelve years; he is said to have possessed 'a directness, even a rashness of action, some insensitivity, a certain naivety and a thorough and tenacious dedication to the job in hand'[29] which led him into a number of unfortunate episodes. He was general secretary of the first meeting (in 1831) of the British Association for the Advancement of Science (a meeting held in York), and the nearest thing to a founder which that famous body possesses. In 1839 he was elected its president, for the considerable services which he had rendered to physics and chemistry. He was an exemplary parish priest; but something about his conduct in chapter reminds us that he was also the father of the most truculent statesman of the later nineteenth century.

Harcourt found Cockburn's habits, or oddities, irritating. In December 1836 he wrote Cockburn a letter which shows that his patience would soon be exhausted:

I must here make my stand; I have in vain remonstrated with you privately on the manner in which you transact chapter business. I feel a settled conviction that it can end in nothing but ruin and disgrace; you appear to me to consider the cathedral property as a wreck which may be torn up and shared among us . . .[30]

When the second fire occurred to what Harcourt called 'a mortgaged Minster', the breach came.[31] The fabric fund was in deficit. The dean had

---

[28] *EC* 11778.

[29] Kerr, op. cit., p. 16.

[30] *A Report of the proceedings in the visitatorial court of His Grace the archbishop of York, which was opened on Monday, the eighteenth day of January . . . 1841* (1841), 122 (9th day's session).

[31] Dean Cockburn behaved irresponsibly after the fire, countermanding the chapter's instructions for dealing with the emergency. He soon fell foul of the restoration committee, telling his brother-in-law Canon Charles Hawkins that he was keeping 'clear and independent' until he saw upon what plan they intended to proceed. (YML, copy letter of 4 Sept. 1840 in M 1/7/11 xi.)

treated the fabric fund with a cavalier freedom. The conflict within the chapter over the rights and wrongs of the fabric fund at last forced the archbishop of York to intervene. He gave notice that early in the year 1841 he would *visit* the Minster.

To *visit* the Minster lay within an archbishop's power. Records of old visitations, between 1343 and 1715, lay in the archives. But chapters, inheriting ancient privileges, and still the institutions of the Church of England nearest in constitution and ethos to a medieval monastery, never liked to be visited. And the practice appeared to be obsolete. No archbishop had visited the Minster for a century and a quarter. It must look like public criticism, if not public insult, that gentle old Archbishop Vernon Harcourt should now decide to visit. Before he even came to the chapter-house, the mere fact of visitation announced to the world that all was not well, or was suspected of not being well, with York Minster.

Meanwhile, York Minster was grievously touched by the national plans for reforming the Church of England.

The reformers of the age after the Reform Act turned their minds to the Church. They saw all sorts of 'abuses', some imaginary and some real; some things, which by the standards of dissenters were abuses, were to conservatives hallowed institutions of the past. As the storm of criticism passed over, it left behind it one widespread agreement about the pastoral system of the established Church. That system was ill adapted to a land of growing industry and of flight to towns. The new urban areas, ill served perhaps by a single ancient parish church, must be given churches and clergy, and for this money must be found. That meant (it was widely agreed in both political parties) that bishops and deans and chapters must lose endowments, because nowhere else could money be found once it was ruefully accepted that the government would give no money.

By 1836 this plan was imminent: the Ecclesiastical Commission, to receive these endowments and transfer their use, was founded; and various more or less wild proposals were made for the mulcting of cathedrals to find the free money that men needed. These proposals were known to deans and canons, most of whom saw them as robbery, as 'the church spoliation bill'. The chapters had the duty of caring for churches which were the glory of England. They usually maintained their fabrics on the endowment but were afraid of ruin, in more than one sense, if the endowment were given instead to slums in Manchester or Sheffield. Moreover, anyone who cared for trusteeship was nervous. Benefactors left their money to benefit York. Why should government suddenly take the money to benefit Manchester?

Four among Dean Cockburn's prebendaries at York held other deaneries themselves (Norwich, Lichfield, Gloucester, Wells). All resented the 'church spoliation bill'. Dean Cockburn was undecanal enough to write letters against it to the York newspapers. Naturally, as the threat moved nearer, deans and chapters wondered how to use their money to advantage before the state confiscated. They considered how to unload if they could, as the richest of all cathedrals, Durham, had unloaded to found a university.

But no other dean spoke so loud about his intention to unload as Dean Cockburn of York. He was perfectly open, perilously frank. 'When I found,' he wrote to the chapter clerk, 'that the bishops[32] were plotting to gain possession of all our preferments, I offered the next presentation of every living I had for sale, which was then a legal transaction, and requiring no concealment. . . . I beg that you will make no mysteries of these things, if any one makes inquiries about my private arrangements, you may tell them that if I had one hundred livings, since the spoliation bill was talked of, I resolved to sell them all.'[33] The dean himself made no mystery of his intention. He wrote in this sense to the *York Courant*.

Dean Cockburn, already charged with being dangerously cavalier about Minster money, was being provoked by politicians in London to act still more recklessly—so that almost he walked with the air, give it away before the enemy can rob.

Dean Cockburn was austere in manner and formidable to approach. He possessed a love of the Minster and a sensitive taste in art and architecture, which were no mean qualities in an age when the interior of the Minster must almost totally be rebuilt. He had no inquiring mind, was inclined to shrink from asking for information which he needed to form a judgement, and was too apt to trust the last speaker who gave information. In the city of York, where the office of dean was always eminent, he was popular for his kindness and his oddities; and this though he invariably lived half the year in Somerset. The people of York liked to have as their dean a character, an eccentric. He had a very dry wit, and could be caustic, and did not mind what he said. If men were rude, or crossed him, he could flare into towering passion. And now, by the calamity of Archbishop Harcourt's visitation, the oddness and the over-frankness and the passion were exposed to the fascinated eyes of all England.

The archbishop opened his visitation in the chapter-house[34] on 18 January 1841, with the civilian lawyer Dr. Phillimore as his commissary. The dean plainly regarded himself as the victim of an onslaught by other

[32] Under the 1840 Act (3 & 4 Vict. c. 113, s. lxxviii) all the bishops of England and Wales were added to the number of the Ecclesiastical Commissioners, also fifteen other dignitaries, including the deans of Canterbury, St. Paul's, and Westminster, but not the dean of York.

[33] W. Cockburn to C. A. Thiselton, Oct. 1840 (evidence in adjourned visitation, 23 Mar. 1841; *Report*, 87).

[34] The visitation continued from the second day in the ecclesiastical court room in the Minster.

members of the chapter. He publicly described himself as surrounded by hosts of enemies, and seemed to think that every clergyman in the chapter-house came for the express purpose of injuring him. The next day he challenged the court's jurisdiction, and walked out dramatically, followed by his wife. Though the archbishop issued tickets to admit, hardly a tenth of those who wished to be spectators could henceforth be accommodated in court.

At first the inquiry proceeded amicably. The dean appeared again, two days later, and spoke in praise of the archbishop. But near the end of February, at a time when the dean had retired to Somerset, an inquiry into the fabric fund and how to get it into order was changed into something far more sinister. In an answer to one of the archbishop's written questions one of the prebendaries, William Henry Dixon, made a charge wholly irrelevant to the question. He accused the dean of selling livings—accepting money in return for a promise to appoint to a parish in his patronage.

Simony!—for the dean of York to be accused before his archbishop of one of the worst of Church offences was suddenly a national scandal. Dr. Phillimore, the sitting commissary, who ought to have known better, henceforth behaved with an incompetence exceptional among civil lawyers. He began to hear evidence about the dean's 'simony', a strange and misty mixture of the dean's too frank letters to the *York Courant*, his threats to unload, and queer roadside meetings between curates and the dean's agent, Singleton, who was alleged to have told the curate that he could have a living for a cash payment. The dean came to the court on 23 March and created a tremendous uproar, interrupting Phillimore, denying his authority, bidding 'defiance to all sneaking and roguery', and coming very near to being ejected from the court by force, an event which he obviously would have preferred. Phillimore declared the dean in contempt of court, and then (2 April 1841) guilty of simony; whereat he deprived him of his deanery, its title and emoluments. The archbishop, who should also have known better but who perhaps at 83 years of age could do no other, confirmed the sentence. York was torn asunder. The parish meetings, with resolutions for and against the dean, reminded observers of the atmosphere of a general election.

The dean went straight to the court of Queen's Bench. On 20 June 1841 (*Queen v. the Archbishop of York*) the court, consisting of lords Denman, Coleridge, and Patteson, found almost contemptuously for the dean. The archbishop had no power whatever to deprive the dean of his office without due process of law. This process had lately been determined in an Act of Parliament,[35] and the judges found it extraordinary that Dr. Phillimore was

[35] 3 & 4 Vict. c. 86.

not aware of the Act. (Dr. Phillimore also held the Regius Professorship of Civil Law at Oxford University.) The judges even animadverted severely on the declaration that the dean stood in contempt of court. By the time the judges finished, nothing was left of the deprivation of Dean Cockburn from the deanery of York.

To understand Dean Cockburn, we must distinguish between the selling of a living, the selling of an advowson (that is, the right of appointment to a living), and the selling of the 'next presentation', that is, the use of the advowson the next time the living was vacant. To sell the next presentation was perfectly legal, for it merely handed over the right to appoint. The next presentation might not be sold if the living was vacant, otherwise it was equivalent to selling the living, which was the crime of simony.

The dean was foolishly frank; muddled his accounts; used the fabric fund for purposes unconnected with the fabric; was intolerable to clear-headed accountants; took solitary decisions, like selling the melted lead and bells after the fire, which the chapter should have taken; used an unscrupulous agent who said what he should not have said. The dean was culpably careless, but nothing else that we know about him suggests that he was criminal. When we think of the damage that this *cause célèbre* wrought to York Minster, we should remember that four other people contributed more than the dean—the able and truculent William Vernon Harcourt, who persuaded his father the archbishop that he must visit; the archbishop who agreed to visit; Canon Dixon, for making the gravest of charges at an unsuitable place and time; and Dr. Phillimore, a professor of law who turned out not to know the only law relevant to the case. Blameless, good-natured Archbishop Harcourt had been so complaisant that he hurt the most glorious church of his diocese.[36]

[36] The injunctions given by the archbishop to the Minster on 22 Feb. 1841 are printed in *York Statutes*, pp. 104 ff. (The 9th, 19th, and 22nd injunctions were, however, amended, and the amended injunctions (YML, M 1/7/11 vi) were signed and sealed on 18 Mar. 1841 and received and accepted by the chapter on 1 Apr. 1841. Additional injunctions (YML, M 1/7/11 viii) were made on 20 July 1841, and received and accepted on 24 July 1841). Their most important act was to order the weekly celebration of holy communion, which Cockburn had reduced to a monthly celebration in 1824 because the numbers attending were so often below the minimum required by the rubric. They sought also to limit the power of the dean in relation to chapter and residentiaries; and to clarify the rules for handling the trust funds.

The visitation had a further side-effect, of making the non-residentiaries more aware of their essential part in the constitution of the Minster. Between 1841 and 1843 the dean challenged the rights of the non-residentiaries to vote in chapter; this dispute came to a head in 1843–4 when the chapter, but not the dean, wished to dismiss the Rev. William Hewson, the inefficient headmaster of St. Peter's School. (In 1845 he sued the dean and chapter in Chancery. The case was settled out of court. He resigned in exchange for a pension from the dean and chapter.) It was eventually accepted that the Cathedral Act had not, as Cockburn assumed, affected the rights and privileges of the non-residentiaries.

Dean Cockburn was still the dean. On the whole the city of York was pleased. Well-wishers started raising a penny subscription to give him a token of their respect, until the dean heard of the plan and stopped the collection because, however good in intention, it would keep unpleasant memories in the public mind. The subscribers nevertheless bought him a piece of silver with the money already collected—a sugar bowl in the shape of the great Minster bell, nine inches in diameter, mounted on a four-wheeled carriage of silver, and engraved with a view of the Minster and a tribute of esteem.

The deprivation vanished in the Queen's Bench. But the consequences did not vanish. Cockburn never cleared himself. The archbishop appeared to agree that he was guiltless, for if the dean were really guilty of simony, he must now prosecute him under the Act of Parliament—but he did not prosecute. Cockburn was acquitted by silence, or inaction. But the charge had been made and never disproved. In the nation it was often believed that the dean of York had been proved guilty and acquitted only on a technicality. The reputation of the Minster suffered because the reputation of its head lay under a cloud—and not for a short time, because Cockburn lived for another seventeen years. The appeal for money after the second fire did not prosper. Charity was tired after the first fire. But that was not all. York Minster could not prosper so long as Cockburn remained dean.

Nor could the internal politics of the chapter be healthy. Both sides had spoken the unforgivable. No relations but the most formal were possible between the dean and his friends Canon Charles Hawkins (his brother-in-law) and Canon Henry Spencer Markham on one side, and Canons Harcourt and Dixon. The chapter must meet to govern the cathedral. In the nature of the case, the temperature at meetings could seldom rise above freezing-point.

Meanwhile, the great 1840 Act of Parliament, which reconstructed the Church of England more radically than any Act since the seventeenth century, and made possible the prosperity of Victorian parishes, began to work. York Minster must lose for the sake of others' gain.

York was far less affected by the Act than many cathedrals. The Act had a preference for tidiness and ordered that the majority of the chapters should consist of a dean and four residentiary canons. York had had its number fixed at five residentiaries (including the dean) during the reign of William III, and was therefore untouched by the Act of 1840. Moreover, the corporate revenue of the dean and chapter was small: £1,352 for the chapter and £569 for the college of vicars choral; contrast Durham with £27,933, or Canterbury with £15,982. No English (as opposed to Welsh) cathedrals except Lichfield and Chester had a smaller corporate endowment. The wealth of York lay in endowments which were not corporate, that is, which endowed the individual prebend: in 1830–1, £1,953 a year divided among thirty people unequally, and a proportion of the leases which fell in (in the three years to 1830–1, £12,915 divided unequally among ten people).[37] The difference made to the five people chiefly concerned was significant only for the dean. (The dean's stipend before the Act was well over £2,000; after Cockburn's death it was to be £1,000. A residentiary's stipend before the Act was calculated at £461; future residentiaries were to receive £500.)[38] The Act abolished the stipends of all the other prebendaries (as each prebend fell vacant). A small part of this money went to increase the stipends of future residentiaries, the rest away from York. The Act changed the mode of appointment to the residentiary canonries, ordering that the archbishop (as soon as Cockburn died or resigned) should have the right to appoint. It removed all the fifty benefices the patronage of which was attached to individual offices (but not the nineteen benefices in the corporate patronage of the dean and chapter) and transferred the patronage to the archbishop.

The change of 1840 from the old constitution to the new was not therefore marked, and its extent was hidden for many years because it could not take full effect while the dean and prebendaries of 1840 still lived. William Vernon Harcourt did not die till 1871, T. H. Croft (prebendary of Stillington) not till 1873, Archdeacon Charles Musgrave not until 17 April 1875. The last relic of the old constitution in York survived for thirty-five years after the Act of Parliament.

Certain differences were obvious.

In 1840 the thirty prebendaries held also (some in plurality): four other deaneries (Lichfield, Wells, Norwich, Gloucester); two other residentiary canonries (Exeter, Carlisle); a canonry at Oxford; two prebends in other cathedrals (Exeter, Durham); one Yorkshire sinecure; eighteen parishes in

---

[37] *PP* (1835), xxxii. 103–5; (1837), xli. 116–17. The old exempt precinct, St. Peter's liberty, faded away. (The Peter Prison still held one prisoner in 1832, but was pulled down in 1837.) The Commission of Peace granted by William IV was extended to 4 June 1838, but the dean and chapter decided not to seek its renewal, and their jurisdiction as justices of the peace lapsed. (Chapter clerk's replies to a questionnaire of the Ordnance Survey, 1845 (YML, D 2/1845/4/1).) The jurisdiction account continued until the death of the last steward, C. J. Newstead (1857); when his pension was no longer payable, the account was wound up. The dean and chapter's Peculiar jurisdiction was abolished by Order in Council dated 27 Aug. 1846.

In 1914 an eighteenth- or late seventeenth-century seal matrix, evidently of the dean and chapter's Court of Audience, was purchased from a collector in Liverpool by Dean Purey-Cust, and despite its bearing the inscription '. . . ad causas et negocia', and despite the chapter clerk's doubts, the chapter decided on 1 April 1914 (a significant date) to adopt it as its common seal in place of the 'comparatively modern' one then in use.

[38] *PP* (1840), xxxix. 1.

Yorkshire; two parishes in Cumberland; one parish each in Somerset, Berkshire, Cheshire, Norfolk, Essex, London, Cambridgeshire, Kent, the Isle of Wight, Northamptonshire; they included one squire who lived in Suffolk, and one gentleman who lived in London, both of whom had no other preferment but the prebend. In 1857 the twenty-three new prebendaries appointed since 1840 included twenty-two Yorkshire incumbents, one of whom also held a living in Suffolk, and the rector of a parish near Newcastle upon Tyne. These new prebendaries were all unpaid for their prebends.

The inference is possible that the Minster lost the support of weighty persons throughout England. Certainly the Minster lost money by the abolition of the stipends, because endowed prebendaries were in the habit of generosity. But the inference is also possible that the diocese gained as the chapter of its cathedral became diocesan, and that a stipend could be far better used than in giving extra pay to the dean of Wells. The Act of 1840 brought the world of Barchester to a lingering death. But these figures show that the difference between Barchester and its successor must not be exaggerated. Even before the 1840 Act, the Minster was diocesan.

Were the new men different in kind from the old? Dean Cockburn's successor was less learned than Dean Cockburn, but Cockburn's learning was not of the type to win national credit, for he regarded the new geologists as fools, and defended the literal truth of Genesis with intemperate contempt for scientists who doubted; he became absurd in the eyes of intelligent men, even though he took the trouble to walk through new railway tunnels while they were dug (once with the engineer Brunel in person) to examine the strata before the sides were bricked. One of the prebendaries appointed before 1840, William Vernon Harcourt, was a leading scientist. Though no one chosen after 1840 could emulate him, this should be attributed not to the making of cathedral prebends less attractive, but to the sciences outrunning the amateur.

In the year 1841 two men became prebendaries under the new constitution who adorned learning more eminently than any of the old prebendaries. Robert Isaac Wilberforce, formerly a tutor at Oriel College with Newman, and son of the slave-emancipator, became prebendary of Apesthorpe and archdeacon of the East Riding; his first duty was to attend that miserable visitation of the Minster. Quiet and scholarly, he had a subtle and original mind which led him to examine the idea of Church authority in a growing mood of criticism. He resigned the prebend in 1847 and the archdeaconry in 1854, shortly before he was received into the Roman Catholic Church.

Edward Churton became prebendary of Knaresborough in 1841, and archdeacon of Cleveland in 1846. (He died in 1874.) Those were days when country clergymen still had leisure and libraries to rank among the leading scholars of England. Churton became recognized as an authority upon Spanish literature and language, though he only once visited Spain.

Other names, of less weight, might be cited. These are sufficient to show that, unexpectedly, the new chapter gained rather than lost in learning. But this was nothing to do with the new constitution and happened because learning and books and historical method were more freely available in mid-Victorian England.

Two of the prebendaries of 1840 had the prefix Hon. before their names. Two of the prebendaries of 1857, appointed after 1840, had the same prefix. We cannot detect any sudden lowering of social station by the decline of Barchester. And one change pointed in the opposite direction. The Act lowered the dean's stipend from over £2,000 for Cockburn to £1,000 for any future dean. But the dean was expected to be the lion of York city, generous, hospitable, patron of all good causes, and living in a house to match. Dean Cockburn could supplement his dean's stipend by being rector of Kelston in Somerset. His successor would not have that resource. The 1840 Act forbade a dean to hold livings, except in the cathedral city and then of no greater value than £500. The prospects of finding a new dean of York after Cockburn already looked slim. In a stiff letter to the Ecclesiastical Commissioners[39] Archbishop Vernon Harcourt pointed out that unless something were done when Cockburn died, no one but a rich man could become dean of York—which was not what the Act intended.

The Act also compelled deans to reside for eight months. As we shall see, this had another unexpected consequence in the deanery.

The Act provided that none of the existing holders of deaneries or canonries or prebends should suffer. But one man at York suffered grievously from the act: the chapter clerk, C. A. Thiselton. His stipend was small, much of his income came from managing the estates of the dean and chapter. But now the Ecclesiastical Commissioners managed more and more from London. Only four years after the Act fourteen prebends had already fallen in by vacancy.[40] In 1844 Thiselton applied for compensation and was refused. He applied again and again, each time (according to himself) nearer to ruin. Cockburn told him that he was treated unjustly, and soon afterwards the Commissioners agreed to make him a small payment 'for services'.[41] The Act protected the sitting clergy but failed to protect their servants.

[39] *EC* 19107/3955/46 (14 Nov. 1846).

[40] *PP* (1846), xxiv. 199. Two more prebends fell in during 1846.

[41] *EC* 8083/2024/51 (Cockburn to Thiselton, York Deanery, 11 July 1851); compensation 1 Apr. 1852.

With these exceptions the radical Act of 1840 made little difference to York. Yet afterwards men blamed it for a robbery which cast the Minster into its toils. This is understandable, because until 1840 the chapter mostly paid for repairs out of endowment, and after 1840 always needed to appeal for money. Forty years later a sad prebendary of York, asked for his opinions about the Minster, wrote thus:

The enquiry appears to me to take on the character of a post-mortem examination, as the blood, which is the life of these corporations, I mean their endowments, has been so let out of them, that little but an exhausted carcase remains . . . The nut has been cracked and the kernel removed . . .[42]

We shall see that so far as this gloom had any truth, it happened not directly through the 1840 Act, but through events resulting from powers granted by the Act.

Dean Cockburn was one of the first to see the possibility of private advantage. He garnered his stipend after endless bother with an agent, Singleton, whom he even sued, unsuccessfully, during the autumn of 1841[43]—his name again appearing in the national Press among complicated circumstances. He realized that he could be rid of the problem if the Ecclesiastical Commissioners would take his estates now—for they must take them at his death—and grant him an annual payment. Like all Dean Cockburn's financial arrangements, this went wildly awry. Several years elapsed, the files were fat, his letters grew more urgent, his appeals more piteous, his handwriting doddered, before the lawyers finally settled.[44]

Prebendaries began to follow the example with less harassment: prebendary of Givendale, 1847 (£4,000 down); of Weighton, 1847 (W. H. Dixon of ill memory, £481 a year); of Barnby, 1847; subdean, 1852; succentor, 1853 (he was also dean of Lichfield); precentor, 1853 (he was also dean of Gloucester). Commutation had advantages on both sides. And quite

---

[42] *PP* (1884–5), xxi. 450 (Landon, Ledham Vicarage, 2 Jan. 1880).

[43] Judgement in the Vice-Chancellor's Court, 11 Jan. 1842; cf. *The Times*, 12 Jan. 1842. (A very complex affair of leases; and although the vice-chancellor held for Singleton, he markedly refused to grant him costs.)

[44] For the prolonged negotiations, *EC* 7854 (a bulky file); agreement at £2,468 per annum, sealed 27 Feb. 1844; gazetted 19 July 1844 (*PP* (1845), xxxv. 86); found not to be fully in order, first because the dean's affairs with Singleton were so complex as to give Singleton certain rights, and then because of strong argument (especially with W. V. Harcourt) over the exchanges of 1828, made without any legal agreements, between dean and dean and chapter when the old deanery was pulled down and the new built. The Commissioners only paid Cockburn certain sums on account. He wrote heart-rending letters, appeared in person before the estates committee (4 Feb. 1845), assigned his still unsettled annuity to a third party for £9,000, appealed to the archbishop of Canterbury (19 Aug. 1846); the secretary of the Commission, a worse culprit himself than any dean, showed a flinty face by advising the archbishop, 'He has committed so many irregularities at York'. The administrators in London observed what one described as 'so much conflict, and almost collision, between the dean of York and the chapter' (White to Murray, 25 Feb. 1847).

early in the process the members of the chapter realized that what was good for them as individuals must be (if legal) good for them as a corporate body. They therefore proposed to the Ecclesiastical Commissioners that they should hand over all their corporate estates in return for an annual payment. After due legal advice the Commissioners accepted, and on 18 August 1852 commuted the York estates for £4,410 a year—until such time as the Commissioners should convey to the chapter landed property sufficient to produce an equivalent revenue.[45]

In this act of commutation York and Carlisle were the pioneers. Other cathedrals slowly followed their example. Some of these cathedrals prospered by the arrangement, and founded their Victorian prosperity on a steady income which reached them without effort. For other cathedrals the act proved almost fatal.

The chapter felt poor; did not see how to mend the great west window when two mullions were near collapse in 1853; lamented that the marvellous stained glass must soon perish; had no high morale about music or choir. As Dean Cockburn grew older, he came less and less from his Somerset rectory, until the 'new' deanery, which he had built himself, fell into disrepair and, somewhat to the scandal of the city, was hired to wealthy race-goers for the races, or advertised as suitable accommodation for the hunting season. The city churches had full congregations because the Minster drew few worshippers.

Though dean and chapter were sad, and found it hard to adjust to a new world, the life of the Minster continued. Dr. Stephen Beckwith, a physician of York, left £5,000 for a new peal of bells and the restoration of the chapter-house,[46] and these bells pealed on 7 July 1844 when the Minster was solemnly reopened (with a sermon from Cockburn) after the second fire. (At first the belfry was found to alarm the city on stormy nights by producing weird sounds like the howling of a demon.) That the Minster had not lost the pride of the city was shown when churchwardens of city churches went round their parishes collecting money for a Great Peter bell in the Minster, a clock bell 'of surpassing size', the largest in the country (until Big Ben in 1856), weighing ten tons fifteen hundredweight, with a deep mellow voice.[47] The two lengthy closures partly broke the habit by which the city

---

[45] Order in Council, 18 Aug. 1852. *London Gazette* (1852), 2436.

[46] The bells were repaired in 1914, recast in 1925. The restoration of the chapter-house included the entire repainting of the ceiling (restored in 1976), destroying the last vestiges of the medieval design, which the artist, Thomas Willement, had originally hoped to retain in part.

[47] Great Peter was first rung on 14 Aug. 1845, recast in 1926. The people of York had a real love for their bell. It was at first allowed to strike the hour only at 12 noon, but in 1849 the subscribers begged that the clock might strike on that bell, assuring the dean and chapter that it would not be an 'annoyance' (YML, Chapter Act 29 Sept. 1849).

used the nave as a place of public promenade or gossip, with the result that services in the choir were less disturbed by movement or conversation, but the Minster felt colder. Under Dr. Camidge the choir continued to sing its two services daily, on special days might be heard by up to two thousand people, but had not the highest repute among musicians. Camidge persuaded the chapter to reduce the full-time songmen from eight to six and with the money saved to engage eight 'supernumeraries' at £10 each a year. In 1850 he was stricken with paralysis while playing the organ, and continued as organist, but all the duties were performed by his son Thomas Simpson Camidge, the fourth generation in succession. By ancient custom the offertory was still distributed among the poor old people who attended service. The three vergers were still paid only £11 odd a year and maintained themselves by tips from visitors. The library began to suffer from the abolition of the endowed prebends because by custom the prebendaries at their installation paid to the library a fee which constituted its income.

To chronicle a decline is not easy. But here are two memories of the Minster, one from the beginning of Cockburn's time, the other from near the end:

As a boy Harvey Goodwin attended a service of the early 1820s, and never forgot. It was

like the opening of a new world. I do not pretend that at that early age such worship as I could offer would be very intelligent, but I do think that it is a striking result of the choral service in a beautiful building . . . that during more than forty years the childish recollection of the service in York Minster has not faded away, but has ever been mingled with the most inspiring thoughts of the public worship of God.

James Raine, the future historian, went to a service of the early 1850s, and never forgot.

We well remember being among the worshippers on a Sunday, chilled to the bone with piercing damp; pigeons were flying about the choir during the service; and there were only six communicants, including the officiating clergy![48]

Dean Cockburn died on 30 April 1858. In his reign the Minster rather continued than prospered. But the chapter had to face the greatest double disaster ever suffered by an English cathedral, and twice restored it with courage and taste. It also had to accept the loss to cathedrals by the measure through which Parliament tried to bring the Church of England into the

---

[48] Goodwin in *Church Congress Report* (1866), 199; James Raine, *A Memorial to the Hon. and Very Revd. Augustus Duncombe D.D.* (London and York, 1880), viii.

modern world, and adapted itself with dignity, and attracted new men of distinction. And the dean served posterity by clearing the clutter from the south side of the Minster. If the dean and chapter were sad, that was not because they neglected their duty.

Dean Duncombe, 1858–80

A month after Cockburn's death, the name of the new dean was announced (a Conservative prime minister, Lord Derby, was responsible). The prime minister, said Disraeli in the House of Commons with some lack of tact, had encountered 'very grave difficulties in ultimately fixing upon this selection'.

The chief difficulty was obvious. The dean of York needed to entertain in the city. He must inhabit a house with more than thirty rooms. During the last years of Cockburn this house was so dilapidated that any dean must spend several thousand pounds before he resided. The Act of 1840 prohibited a new dean from holding another living outside York. Dean Cockburn felt poor though he had more than £2,000 a year from York as well as his parish stipend. The money available for his successor was £750 a year and the Ecclesiastical Commissioners had a scheme for raising the stipend to the statutory £1,000. No man with £1,000 a year could repair the deanery, or live in the deanery, or behave as deans of York always behaved—unless he had money of his own, lots of money. The prime minister chose the Hon. Augustus Duncombe because he was rich.

The wealth did not escape public notice. Even in the House of Commons a rude questioner argued that deans were chosen either for learning or for distinction as parish priests, and asked pointedly, why Duncombe?[49] 'The fact was', answered Disraeli frankly, 'that the income bore no proportion whatever to the expenses in which the gentleman was involved who happened to fill the office . . . The range of selection was much limited by that fact. . . . Whatever the other recommendations of Mr. Duncombe for the office, he certainly had the advantage of possessing ample means.'

So they chose Duncombe for the wrong reasons. And in time York found that the Earl of Derby had given them one of the great deans of Victorian England.

Duncombe was the third surviving son of the Earl of Feversham, and therefore a member of a family eminent in the county. He was married to Lady Harriet, sister of the Marquis of Queensberry. For a short time he had ministered in the family parish of Kirby Misperton. When his father died he inherited money, and retired to an estate at Calwich Abbey on the Dove in

---

[49] *Hansard*, cl. 1522 (4 June 1858, Ewart).

Staffordshire, where he lived as a layman. He held a prebend in York Minster from 1841 but, as this was after the Act of 1840, was unpaid. He had very little parish experience, and manifestly was not eminent for learning. The archbishop of York, now Thomas Musgrave, recommended him for dean—'a most amiable and respectable man, of sound and reasonable opinions, of irreproachable conduct, and an excellent clergyman'.[50] Lord Hotham said the same in the House of Commons. But the argument that he was blameless provoked various retorts. An unpleasant correspondent wrote anonymously to *The Times* asking whether a blameless character was so rare in the Church of England that it made a special ground for promotion.[51] Nothing could hide the awkward truth that he had not ministered as an active clergyman for sixteen years.

Duncombe came to York and preached in the Minster his first sermon, which impressed by its conciliatory manner while it depressed by its feeble delivery, and began to spend money to make the deanery habitable.

His seat was not yet comfortable. The public airing of his wealth, and the poverty of the official stipend, made good men ashamed that the dean of York should be so shabbily treated compared with deans in London or Canterbury or Durham. York city was vexed; the bishop of London, and especially the archbishop of York, thought it discreditable. From November 1858 onwards, while Duncombe was paid no money whatever, the Ecclesiastical Commissioners argued the size of the stipend. When the law officers of the Crown told them that it was legal to raise the stipend, though 'contrary to the spirit' of the Act, they decided (12 January 1860) to raise Duncombe's stipend to £2,000. This £2,000 became absurdly magnified in the Press. The dean of York's salary was a national controversy. What madness did the Commissioners commit handing out an extra thousand pounds to a man chosen specially because he needed no pay?[52]

Duncombe acted with perfect propriety. He never asked for more money, only for his stipend. He refrained from stopping the discussion of the stipend. Moreover, when he finally received his first two years' stipend, he gave half the sum—£2,000—to St. Peter's fund for investment to improve the songmen's salaries.[53] 'He may not be a great man,' said an M.P. in the House of Commons, 'but he is undoubtedly a good man.'[54]

In April 1858 York had a dean aged 84; his successor two months later was aged 43. The Minster felt a vigorous hand. For one thing, he was always

[50] Ibid. 1526 (T. Ebor to Earl of Derby, 41 Belgrave Square, 4 May 1858).
[51] *The Times*, 7 June 1858 ('Theophrastus').
[52] All the papers were collected in *PP* (1860), liii. 237 ff.; cf. *Hansard*, clix. 1946 (16 July 1860).
[53] YML, Chapter Act, 9 Aug. 1860.
[54] *Hansard*, clx. 1825 (25 Aug. 1860).

there. He had no other parish—the law forbade a parish outside York. Instead of the chapter acting on decisions made by the canon or canons who happened to be present at meetings, the dean remained in the chair. The chapter began to have a policy. What critics sometimes called 'the reign of slumber' was past.

Duncombe collected power. The four canons-in-residence still resided in turn, three months at a time, in the Residence. They came and went in rotation, he stayed. In the cathedrals of the Old Foundation (unlike the cathedrals of the New) the office of precentor was important, often next in rank to the office of dean. The precentor was in charge of the services. But from near the beginning of the century the York precentorship had been held by the dean of Gloucester, who said five years before that he was too old to do his duty as precentor of York. Therefore the office, though theoretically occupied, was practically vacant. Duncome ordered services, choir, worship, as he thought fit. In 1862 when the dean of Gloucester died and the precentorship was vacant, Duncombe persuaded a friendly archbishop of York (now Longley) to make him precentor. Some prebendaries wondered whether the dean might legally be also the precentor. Moreover, at York the chancellor had the duty of appointing the preachers according to a rota laid down in ancient statute. When Duncombe came, the chancellor was Leveson Venables Harcourt, who lived in London and seldom came to York. He died in 1860; and all later chancellors found when they arrived that their chancellor's work lay in the hands of the dean, and they did not like to raise questions. The dean possessed the broad and partly undefined powers of his office in ordering the affairs of the Minster, controlled its services because he was precentor, and its preachers because he acted as chancellor. It says much for his quality that these powers were acquired without a battle and to everyone's contentment—until the next archbishop (Thomson) was enthroned. When a canon was asked why he had not done his duty as chancellor, he said that he found when he arrived that the dean discharged the duties, and so he 'shrank from unsettling'. 'The truth is,' wrote the new archbishop, who disliked what he found, '. . . the duties of dean, precentor and chancellor were all centred in one person. . . . These duties comprehend nearly all that the Minster has to do; and it is not wonderful that the work of the chapter shrank in to very narrow compass.'[55] After a time the members did not even receive an agenda paper before the quarterly meeting of the chapter. 'This democratic constitution', wrote Archbishop Thomson with disapproval, 'has been turned into an absolute monarchy'.[56] Duncombe became the Minster.

[55] *PP* (1884–5), xxi. 442–3.
[56] Ibid. 442.

He once explained his idea of the duty of a dean—that he must not go round the diocese performing sacred duties, for his place was within the walls of the cathedral. 'If they turned their dean into a mere roaming animal, and converted him into a locomotive . . . what became of the cathedral?'[57] What is clear from various utterances is the experience which he found when he came to York as dean. Previously they had had a dean old and ill and usually absent; and Duncombe saw the church officers to be slack, the services 'flagging', the organization in danger of 'collapse', small congregations.

From public exhortation to the new dean we scent the musty atmosphere of the Minster that summer of 1858. 'Too long has vergerdom sat like a dark dragon at the porch of God's house in the obscure watch for sixpences.'[58] The nave gave no sense whatever of worship—it was 'without life or meaning—a lounge for idle citizens—a raree-show for cheap excursionists, for whom seedy vergers darkly lie in wait'. The same acid leader-writer described it as 'a hollow shell', and 'a scandal to the city and to the Church'.[59] A few years later Duncombe looked back. The cathedral of the past did no work, exercised no influence; was regarded with little interest; its walls mouldering; its services 'cold, flat, meaningless, and without life'.[60] He had not eloquence, nor intellectual ability; his aesthetic and architectural taste could not rival Cockburn's; his piping voice prevented him being a powerful preacher in a big space; he had not ministerial experience—but he was always there, sensible and courteous, looking at every detail, caring for the people, with high ideals of worship, wanting a cathedral service to be a model for parish services, and the Minster to be a mother church in its diocese.

One of his earliest acts was to give the vergers fixed salaries and forbid them to receive any other 'fees and perquisites' on pain of dismissal; that dragon at least was soon dispatched.[61] He had already offered to restore the exterior of the chapter-house at his own expense—estimate £1,000, or his whole stipend as then planned. Indeed Duncombe's munificence,[62] whether to the Minster or to the city of York, silenced the critics of his

---

[57] *Guardian* (1868), 179 (York Convocation, Oct. 1868).

[58] *Yorkshireman*, 29 May 1858.

[59] Ibid., 3 July 1858.

[60] Duncombe at Church Congress, 1866 (*Guardian* (1866), 1077); cf. James Raine's epithets about the Minster under Cockburn: 'lifeless and desolate' (*A Memorial to . . . Augustus Duncombe*, printed at the request of the family.)

[61] YML, Chapter Act, 6 Oct. 1858.

[62] His three daughters, the Misses Florence, Eleanor, and Evelyn Duncombe, continued his benefactions to the Minster; the Duncombe fabric fund was formed in 1908 from their bequests, totalling £52,078.

choice or his stipend. Another first need was a new organist. John Camidge, though paralysed, still held the post; his son acted. But the son had not the same gifts as the father and the grandfather, and Duncombe refused to make his appointment permanent, to the grief of some among the public who thought that to appoint the fourth Camidge was now just. In 1859 E. G. Monk was appointed organist and started to reconstruct the organ.

Duncombe was a moderate high churchman who believed deeply in an ordered and ceremonious form of worship, and in liberty for others to do within the Prayer Book tradition as they thought fit. His was the age when 'ritualism' became a controversy in the nation. Though Duncombe was not a ritualist, as the public understood the term, he always acted and voted for liberty,[63] not to repress confession for those who wished to practise, nor to alter the ornaments rubric which sanctioned vestments. An undergraduate at Oxford during the high age of J. H. Newman, he was touched by that inheritance, and had a vision of the Church of England as part of a Catholic tradition wider than that of Roman Catholicism. He strenuously disapproved the Public Worship Regulation Act of 1874, by which Queen Victoria and Disraeli tried vainly to end 'ritualism'. He once defined the principles of the Church of England as 'reasonable liberty and comprehension—liberty without licence, sincerity without bigotry, and seriousness without superstition'.[64] In the general life of the Church he wanted to free her worship from the control of Parliament, and hand it over to the two Convocations, if possible meeting together. He was the mainstay of the York Convocation when after 1860 it began to meet in Archbishop Zouche's chapel in the Minster.[65] The Lower House (1863) elected Duncombe its prolocutor (speaker). In 1864 he persuaded the Lower House to allow common sittings with the bishops, though each house continued to vote separately. Nearly all those who experienced both the Convocations, of Canterbury and York, were at first agreed that the York system was the better. He was indeed an admirable chairman,[66] conscientious, firm, master of the business. In York and the nation he cared most for the causes of temperance and better housing for the poor.

He helped the archbishops to invite good men into the chapter; for example, an eminent Victorian, Dr. Charles John Vaughan (vicar of

[63] Cf. his speeches (*Journal of the York Convocation* (1878), 60, 105–6; (1879), 95–6, 101).

[64] Ibid. (1875), 84; for his moderate Catholic outlook, see esp. the sermon preached in Durham Cathedral 19 Oct. 1876, printed in W. C. Lake (ed.), *Sermons at the reopening of Durham cathedral* (1877).

[65] They met ceremonially in the chapter-house and then, because no one could hear a word there and it was icy cold, adjourned to Archbishop Zouche's chapel.

[66] See e.g. dean of Durham's tribute to his chairmanship (*Journal* (1880), 7–8) and minutes of debates, *passim*.

Doncaster, former headmaster of Harrow, later to be master of the Temple and dean of Llandaff) was chancellor of the Minster 1860–71; W. B. Jones (later a well-known bishop of St. David's) was a prebendary 1863–71 and chancellor 1871–4; C. P. Eden (formerly a fellow of Oriel and Newman's successor as vicar of St. Mary's, Oxford) prebendary of Riccall 1870; Dr. Alfred Gatty (an incumbent in Sheffield, well known as a divine and local historian in South Yorkshire) subdean 1862; James Raine (prebendary of Langtoft 1866) became the historian of York, and at every excavation or renovation, as of a gas main, was always to be seen standing by the workmen in case they uncovered evidence important to archaeology. He loved every stone of the Minster and, because he could remember what it was like before Duncombe, came almost to worship the ground on which Duncombe walked.[67]

In the eighteenth century the Minster had been a city church, its clock the time-keeper of the city, its nave a place of fashionable promenade or gossip, its choir the chief place of worship. Between the fire of 1829 and the coming of Duncombe it lost or partly lost all three characteristics. The railway, opened in 1840, brought ever more tourists. Duncombe used the chance to recover the sense of such noble services as could only be achieved by the presence of hundreds of people. When the fires broke the promenade in the nave, and Victorian propriety found gossip in church irreverent, the nave became a nothing, a cold desert. Duncombe brought it into the worshipping area of the Minster. In 1863 he installed another organ[68] in the north aisle of the nave, for the purpose of accompanying great nave services during the winter months. In the same year he gave full lights to the nave, with gas jets clustered round the capitals of the columns. These services were so successful that one of the incumbents of a parish in York resigned because he lost his congregation to the Minster. The nave services were not filled with tourists, but attracted vast numbers of labourers. That was the intention, for Duncombe provided benches, not chairs, as seats.[69] The services must have been more popular for the worship than for the sermons, since evidence was afterwards given that not one preacher in a

---

[67] See Raine's address in *Memorial*.

[68] This organ was sold in 1904 to the parish of St. Thomas, Radcliffe, Manchester.

[69] Replaced by chairs, 1879 (*Y. Gaz.* 31 Jan. 1880); improved gas in the choir, 1861 (ibid. 13 Apr., 31 Aug., 12 Oct. 1861). When in 1867 it was feared that the nave services would not be resumed, about 1,200 working men signed a petition (which survives) requesting their continuance. (YML, Chapter Act 16 Oct. 1867.) The *Yorkshireman*, at the outset of Duncombe's reign (3 July 1858), had appealed to him to follow the example of Westminster Abbey in instituting such services in the nave for the benefit of the poorer classes 'and of all those whom the want of a black coat prevents from now attending any kind of religious worship'.

hundred could make himself properly heard throughout the nave.[70] The Minster was warmed with new Gurney (1861) stoves.[71]

When the nave organ was opened in 1863 a festival of parochial choirs was held, which excited much interest in the musical world and led to the establishment of a triennial festival of music performed by various church choral associations.

The climax of this recovery was reached in 1866, when the dean and chapter invited the Church Congress to York, and erected a large wooden temporary hall just by the Minster for its meetings. The Church Congress was an annual forum for most of the eminent speakers, clergy and lay, in the Church of England. Duncombe spoke upon 'Cathedrals—their proper work and influence', and was greeted with prolonged and repeated cheering as the author of a revival. Dean Hook of Chichester described Duncombe to the audience as a model dean. During 1866, before the congress, Duncombe instituted choral celebrations of holy communion, the first in any cathedral since the Reformation. Every week-day morning during the congress between 400 and 700 people attended a choral celebration in the Minster, and the event was widely discussed throughout the Church of England. The table of communicants in the Minster tells its story:

1863	1614	*1866*	2205
1864	1639	*1867*	2240
1865	2198	*1868*	2645[72]

Meanwhile restoration and improvement continued steadily. In 1862 Duncombe shocked the aesthetic world by 'protecting' some of the stained glass with plate glass outside; so that the Five Sisters and the east window appeared with a melancholy greenish hue; and the plan was publicly denounced as an error of glaring bad taste and judgement.[73] In his first

---

[70] *Journal* (1883), 5 (Purey-Cust).

[71] Unheated till 1830; stove in crypt—considered dangerous after the fire of 1840; hot water pipes in crypt, 1845 (Browne, *History*, p. 328); Gurney stoves, 1861 (*Y. Gaz*, 31 Aug. 1861); central heating, 1928 (YML, Chapter Minutes, 1927–9 *passim*)

The preachers in the nave still conformed to the old table of preaching in this sense at least, that with the archbishop's leave the sermons, preached by ancient usage on saints' days, were abandoned, and the turns transferred to the nave services. (*York Statutes*, pp. 137–8). But under Duncombe first began the custom by which the dean or canon in residence invited 'strange preachers' to various services.

[72] *The Times*, 15 Feb. 1869. These choral celebrations were discontinued for a time because of Archbishop Thomson's opposition, except for being partly sung monthly; but renewed in 1874 with Merbecke and became permanent (*VCH York* 354–5).

[73] *Builder* (1852), 700. The west window also was double-glazed in 1862. One of the chapter house windows was double-glazed in 1876 at the expense of Canon Thorold (YML: Chapter Act 3 Nov. 1875).

84 The West Front in 1828. ▷

years as dean, Duncombe was fiercely attacked for destruction by means of restoration, when masons were found creating new and thinner pinnacles, or shutting the mouths of gargoyles, without any guidance from an architect—'we tries to compress the pinnacles', a York mason told a reporter.[74] Like his two predecessors, Duncombe continued to clear the cathedral from the clutter of unsightly buildings, joining the civic authorities in the 1860s in pulling down the tumbled houses in Little Blake Street (himself subscribing £1,000) and two houses[75] at the east end to make College Green,[76] so that both west front and east end gained much beauty when seen in better perspective from outside. In honour of this clearance, the new wide street to the west was called Duncombe Street (later Duncombe Place), even while he was alive.

When he arrived, five boys sang on each side in the choir. He soon increased the numbers to seven a side.[77] The choristers were hitherto taught in the ancient chapel in the Minster which was the archbishop's court. The inspectors of schools frequently complained. In autumn 1873 Duncombe persuaded the Ecclesiastical Commissioners to make over a vacant house in Minster Yard for a choristers' school.[78] In services they began to use *Hymns ancient and modern*, first published in 1861. In 1871 he changed the old costume of the choristers—coats trimmed with fur, in Lent black gowns— for cassocks and surplices; and from the following year the songmen, who had worn surplices, also wore cassocks. Meanwhile, he helped the salaries of the songmen. He found them at very low stipends of £15, and augmented the income from his own pocket so that they received between £50 and £100. In 1865 he persuaded the college of subchanter and vicars choral to commute their endowment.

The south transept was the only part of the Minster undamaged by two fires. Duncombe asked the architect Street to report and received a gloomy answer, especially about the clerestory. He issued an appeal, to which he gave £500. The restored transept was reopened in November 1874, and

---

[74] *Builder* (1859), 302, 743; taken up by *YH* that June.

[75] These houses stood on the site of the Wistow prebendal house.

[76] College Green extended 1955; pavement much widened and road laid with setts 1972 (connection with south side of Minster then stopped up by making of the Queen's Path).

[77] *PP* (1867), xx. 44.

[78] Purey-Cust, July 1880, persuaded the Commissioners to exchange this house for another house to the north-east of the Minster. The school was closed in 1887 but revived in 1903.

A chorister of 1868–74 (R. Lambert Fearby) records an informal memory of Dean Duncombe's reaction when, in testing the boys' knowledge of the Psalms, he received an appropriate but amusingly jumbled reply: he 'shook with laughter . . . and patting me on the head said I should live to be the editor of "Punch" '. (in C. C. Bell (ed.), *Us and our song-school* (York [1927]).)

appropriately contains the beautiful monument to Duncombe.[79]

His last years were troubled by two constitutional conflicts. The lesser concerned the method of appointing to chapter livings. Until 1864 the dean and residentiaries often chose men for livings at their 'individual option', but this appeared to be a custom rather than a right.[80] In 1864 Archbishop Thomson pointed out that the choice must be the choice of the whole chapter, but further and more serious complications arose in 1875 and 1879, the non-residentiaries once again having cause to fear that their rights were endangered.

The other dispute concerned the appointment of residentiary canons under the new Act. The first signs of this difficulty arose when Canon W. V. Harcourt, at the end of 1863, resigned from the position of residentiary canon but remained a member of the chapter. The law of 1840 ruled that the archbishop should appoint a new residentiary canon. The old statutes of the Minster ruled that only a prebendary was eligible for a residentiary canonry. There was a conflict here, at first hardly perceived. Under York custom, the residentiary was only a prebendary called for special duty, and the chapter consisted of all the prebendaries. The Act, which assimilated all the cathedrals of England in a common condition, expected—though (so far as concerned the Old Foundations) it did not quite declare—the residentiary canons to be the chapter and the honorary canons not to be part of the chapter.

In 1864 Archbishop Thomson was new, and Duncombe, after taking the legal advice of Dr. Phillimore (the son of Dean Cockburn's enemy), behaved according to the old ways: an existing prebendary (William Hey) became a residentiary.[81] If this was well founded in law, the archbishop's power was limited; for he could only make a residentiary canon out of someone who was already a prebendary; whereas his fellow bishops could make a residentiary out of any priest whom they chose.

This could have worked happily. The archbishop only had to make a new prebendary and almost simultaneously make him residentiary. But from time to time Archbishop Thomson was afflicted with sudden folly. He seems to have felt a personal resentment against the independence of the

---

[79] Flower vases first on altar, 1863 (J. W. Knowles, *Historic notes of York Minster*, n.d. (YCL), 39); stone sanctuary rails removed to Lady Chapel and replaced by (longer) brass and iron rails, 1866 (ibid); extra communion service (8.30 a.m.) on first Sunday in month, 1868 (YML, Chapter Act, 1 Jan. 1868); extended to every Sunday, 1873 (*Y. Gaz.* 11 Jan. 1873); new frontal for altar, gift of congregation, 1869 (YML, Chapter Act 7 Apr. 1869); new reredos, 1876 (*Y. Gaz.* 15 Feb. 1879).

[80] Cf. *York statutes*, pp. 133–4.

[81] The archbishop was much vexed because Canon Hey protested his residence (in order to complete the statutable residence which had been protested by Canon Harcourt but subsequently vacated by his resignation) five days before his collation by the archbishop on 15 Aug. 1864.

dean and chapter, and thereby lost any sane idea of how to cope with a legal tangle. As no archbishop before or after, he plagued the dean and chapter. Duncombe once said that the plight into which they now fell was more grievous to him than any other event of his career as dean. Under the same archbishop's pressure Duncombe's successor came within distance of nervous breakdown.

The affair was made far more complex by the quality of the York canons. For the Crown started to make them bishops. And by old custom the Crown claimed the right to appoint a clergyman to the vacancy created when a man became a bishop. The prime minister happened to be Benjamin Disraeli, who had no desire to hurt the dean and chapter but had no patience with the intricacies of church law and felt contempt for the whole business. In this way an easily soluble problem became ever more insoluble, until it was a scandal in York, the talk of the country, and matter for debate in Parliament.

In 1874 Disraeli made Basil Jones bishop of St. David's and chose the Hon. Orlando Forester to succeed to the residentiary canonry. Duncombe (22 July 1874) asked that Forester be first made a prebendary. Archbishop Thomson asked that nothing be done to seem to limit the powers of the Crown. The chapter held a meeting (29 December 1874) and was unanimous in asking that the dispute might go to arbitration. It only wanted a mandate to fill two offices simultaneously.[82] It was afraid of a mandate to fill only the canonry, as this would mean that the rights of the prebendaries to be the chapter would little by little be weakened.

Disraeli's advisers thought it an argument over nothing—which on one view was right. To read the voluminous papers of this affair is to be reminded of the litigiousness of medieval monastic chapters standing on corporate rights. 'The position shortly is this,' wrote one of Disraeli's secretaries to another. 'There is a quarrel between the archbishop and the dean and chapter and the crown is not interested. . . .'[83] The dean and chapter got their two mandates but swallowed their point of principle, for by Archbishop Thomson's advice the mandates were made out, first to the canonry, secondly to the prebend, instead of the other way round.

Into the head of Archbishop Thomson now dropped a more mischievous notion. In August 1875 he realized that the Crown had only power to appoint to a stipendiary office, not to an unpaid office. If that was right, the Crown had no power to make a prebendary, only power to make a residentiary canon. He asked Disraeli whether he agreed.[84] The prime

---

[82] Archdeacon Hey to Forester, 31 Dec. 1874 (Hughenden Papers, C/III/b/iii/21).
[83] Turner to Corry, 5 Jan. 1875 (ibid. 25).
[84] Thomson's letter of 11 Aug. 1876 (ibid. 49a).

minister's office took the opinion of the solicitor to the Treasury, who said that the archbishop was right but it was unwise to tell him so. Disraeli's men therefore failed to answer letter after letter from the archbishop, and even a personal interview between Corry (one of the prime minister's secretaries) and the archbishop ended fruitlessly; until finally on 8 January 1877 Disraeli accepted defeat and sent a message to the archbishop that he was 'disposed to coincide in the view taken by Your Grace'.

The Crown that summer made a bishop out of another residentiary canon of York—A. W. Thorold to the see of Rochester. In June 1877 Disraeli offered the canonry to a popular preacher and favourite of Queen Victoria, James Fleming, vicar of St. Michael's Chester Square in London. The archbishop offered the vacant prebend to a different man; and thus came the battle feared by the dean and chapter. If the canonry need not be held by a prebendary, the archbishop could add not one but four extra persons to the chapter and end by destroying the ancient constitution of the Minster. Fleming himself, and Canon Randolph as a representative of the chapter, begged the Crown to appoint Fleming both to the canonry and the prebend. Disraeli was busy with higher matters.

At Fleming's institution in August 1877 the ceremony in the chapter-house went ill. No stall existed, for 'his' stall was already occupied by the archbishop's new prebendary. The dean, who treated him with much kindness, led him to a stall 'by courtesy'; but Canon Randolph made public protest, and Fleming felt 'somewhat humiliated'. And now began a long series of vexations: if Fleming attended chapter meetings, someone protested; if he voted, someone protested; as he was not a prebendary he had no occasion to preach in the Minster pulpit, though he was a famous preacher. The dean and chapter kept applying that the conflict—between this interpretation of the law of 1840 and their old statutes—might be settled by a test case in the courts. Disraeli's advisers held that since Fleming had his stipend and his canonry, and these were admitted by the dean and chapter, no ground for a suit at law existed. The archbishop of York demanded that the Crown use its might to force the dean and chapter into submission. Fleming, who blamed the archbishop and not the dean, made speeches in York denouncing his treatment; trying to acquit the dean in the critical eyes of the citizens of York; and from January 1878 threatening ever more insistently to resign his canonry. Since the Crown would not, or could not, prosecute the chapter, and the chapter continued its protests, the dean begged Fleming to accept the situation—which Disraeli also would have preferred. On and on dragged the affair, not good for Fleming, bad for the Minster, worst for the reputation of the archbishop. In January 1879 the case attained the celebrity of a comic fourth leader in

The Times.[85] On 16 June 1879 it was debated in the House of Lords, when Disraeli belaboured the dean and chapter, and Archbishop Thomson lost the sympathies of all Yorkshire by describing the atmosphere of the city as 'cold and suspicious'.[86] In December appeared a printed correspondence between archbishop and dean.

By then Duncombe lay on his death-bed. On 16 December 1879 the chapter met under an acting chairman (Archdeacon Hey) and by a majority of one voted to allow Fleming to move a motion; and then carried his motion (by eleven votes to five) which asked for the deletion of the statement, in an answer to the Cathedral Commissioners, that none but prebendaries were qualified to be members of the chapter. Disraeli's men waxed ecstatic and published the news that the chapter gave way. They were wrong. The moment a new dean was installed, the same argument continued. In 1881 the archbishop partially conceded defeat by collating Fleming to the succentorship; in 1883 he became precentor[87] and prebendary of Driffield. All was not yet regular. At the very meeting of the chapter where Fleming was installed as precentor in January 1883, Archdeacon Blunt was installed as canon residentiary though he had resigned his prebend—and the dean and two other canons read protests and went out of the chapter-house, leaving Fleming to install the new canon. The rub between York statutes and one interpretation of the 1840 Act did not make for happiness. Yet we cannot imagine Duncombe walking out of a chapter meeting.

As Duncombe lay dying, a priest at his bedside talked gratefully of his work. Duncombe said, 'Say nothing of that. When you are where I am now, you will see nothing will bear looking at, of one's own. There is only one trust then, the infinite mercies of the Saviour.'[88] He died on 26 January 1880.[89] He found a Minster still backward like a cathedral of the eighteenth century and turned it into the Minster that we know. His name stands high in any list of benefactors to York and the Church of England. Everyone wanted him buried inside the Minster. But the home secretary refused, so he was buried in the churchyard at Helmsley near the home of his childhood.

---

[85] 27 Jan. 1879 (not by its chief leader-writer on church affairs, Henry Wace, though Wace had been asked to collect information).

[86] *Hansard*, ccxlvi. 1887 ff.

[87] In 1908 the dean again became precentor. The chapter made a coherent statement to the Cathedral Commissioners of its point of view, adopting on 9 May 1881 a report of a committee on the statutes (printed in *York Statutes*, pp. 110 ff.).

[88] *Memorial*, 52 (George Body, then rector of Duncombe's old parish of Kirby Misperton).

[89] On the very day of his death he sent a message to the members of the chapter, thanking them for their sympathy in his illness and for the good relations that had prevailed among them (YML, Chapter Act Book, entry 26 Jan. 1880).

Dean Purey-Cust, 1880–1916

Duncombe's death produced a strong desire in York to have a successor as like him as possible. Duncombe's brother, Lord Feversham, first suggested to Disraeli the name of Purey-Cust, archdeacon of Buckingham.[90] Certainly he was like Duncombe; of a noble family, married into a noble family, a man with private means, a strong but moderate high churchman, and a kindly host, with far more experience of the Church than had Duncombe on appointment. Disraeli was urgently warned by a friend that he should take care, for Purey-Cust (he alleged) was 'an out-and-out high churchman, smooth as butter as his master Samuel Wilberforce'.[91]

Purey-Cust accepted the deanery on 18 February 1880. He turned out not to be quite a Duncombe. In a conflict with Archbishop Thomson over the workings of Convocation, he once said publicly that he knew how in the eyes of the archbishop the dean of York was a doormat;[92] and we cannot imagine Duncombe saying this privately, let alone publicly. The time when Purey-Cust was prolocutor of the Lower House in the York Convocation (1884–8) produced unhappiness for everyone and was well ended by his sudden and emotional resignation from that office. More artistic than Duncombe, he was a little more absent-minded. In a letter about drains he once spelt the Deanery the Drainery.[93] We find complaints that he had not the right touch in staging great occasions, which sometimes were ill organized, and sometimes a little theatrical. And like Duncombe he was no more than moderate as a preacher—in his case because of an absence of cutting edge.[94] But though he was not a Duncombe, he was excellent as a continuer of Duncombe's work; always in the Minster, never away, caring about every stone and every service, generous with his money and his affections, much liked and often revered in the city, artistic, an antiquarian by taste who wrote of the Minster heraldry and of its history and monuments. The long reign of Purey-Cust was a quiet and steady time, continuing and developing what Duncombe made.[95]

[90] Feversham to Disraeli, 9 Feb. 1880 (Hughenden Papers C/III/b/iii/102). Disraeli had briefly met Purey-Cust at Buckingham.

[91] Ibid. 107–8.

[92] *Journal* (1888), 28.

[93] EC 661001/1 (1892).

[94] e.g. John Morley, *Recollections* (1917), i. 316: 'York: went to morning service at the Minster: lovely music, but little edified by 40 minutes of sermon from the dean, who among other naïvetés admitted that if he had had the ordering of things in this universe, he would have ordered them very differently.' [1892] For the charge that he lacked a sense of occasion, see e.g. *Church Times* (1881), 467; J. G. Lockhart, *Cosmo Gordon Lang* (1949), 193–4 (but by then Purey-Cust was ageing fast). The organist responsible for the lovely music that Morley heard was John Naylor (1883–97) who succeeded Monk.

[95] The Cathedral Commission published in 1885 the draft of a proposed supplement of statutes for York, but they never received the force of law (Common Paper, *c.* 4378).

85 Dean Duncombe.

86 Dean Purey-Cust.

Since the canons continued to serve in rotation in the Residence, for three months at a time, the dean remained the effective maker of policy. This was further fostered because deans remained longer in office than many canons, and because the residentiary's stipend failed to keep pace with the value of money. In 1862 the Ecclesiastical Commissioners handed back to the Minster lands (the 'capitular estate') calculated to produce the (commuted) revenue; but the Commissioners handed back to cathedrals agricultural land not likely to be capable of improvement. Therefore, when the agricultural slump of the 1880s hit England, several cathedrals were nearly bankrupt. York suffered less than most. Still, three-quarters of a century after an Act of Parliament took away the money of York Minster, and decreed that its four canons should receive £500 a year, its four canons in fact received about £370 a year;[96] and during those decades the value of money declined. This meant that a canon of York must have either private means or more important work elsewhere, as James Fleming who could not but regard the precentorship of York Minster as an extra to his real work as a London vicar. The dean was still the only officer *committed* to the cathedral—except for those like the historian James Raine, who was committed by his deep affection for the place and its past. Just before Purey-Cust died Archbishop Lang was successfully persuading the Commission to a new arrangement.[97]

During his first autumn of 1880 Purey-Cust made innovations in the prayers, not warranted by the Prayer Book, until the archbishop sternly protested—so sternly that on 22 October 1880 the dean proved that he had not quite Duncombe's stature by reading a public protest in the Minster against the interference of the archbishop.[98] (That these battles between dean and archbishop were not the sole fault of the dean was proved when Maclagan succeeded Thomson as archbishop and all was harmony.) In the following year he started a harvest festival in the Minster, and four years later (19 April 1885) a service called the Military Service, originally a memorial to the murdered General Gordon, but later one of the events of

---

[96] The average income of a canonry in Purey-Cust's last five years was £365 to £375.

[97] *EC* 13794 (1851). Lang was disturbed to find how difficult it was in the circumstances to find the right men for York canonries; see his letter, 25 Sept. 1916.

[98] H. Kirk-Smith, *William Thomson* (1958), 85 ff. The two came into further disagreement, high churchman versus low churchman, over the proposed celebration of a Luther commemoration in Nov. 1883. (cf. E. H. Thomson, *Life and letters of Archbishop Thomson* (1919), 336 ff.) The innovations in the prayers were tiny. They were based on the injunctions of the 1547 visitors; had a versicle and response, a collect of unexceptionable language, and the peace. They were printed with the original spelling on a card (two packets of these cards remain among the archives in mint condition); for the text see *Notes and queries*, 6th Ser. ii (1880), 305. Archbishop Thomson invoked the Act of Uniformity and in law was correct.

Yorkshire. The garrison of York had always close links with the Minster, and the general in command attended matins in uniform, sitting next to the dean. A woman remembered from her childhood how her father always took his top hat, and her mother put on her best clothes, and that matins in the Minster had 'a certain sartorial magnificence'.[99] To the Military Service paraded regulars and territorials from all parts of Yorkshire, and when it was fully established, crowds came long distances by special train to see the sights. At the Military Service of 1909 the Minster is said to have contained two thousand troops and ten thousand people. In the age of the armament race before the First World War these services could stimulate martial sermons. A pacifist group appealed to Purey-Cust to abolish this liturgy. He refused and the Military Service continued until 1939. Though he was suspected of high churchmanship, candles were not lit at holy communion till 1896, and copes not used until after his death.

The life of the Minster continued steadily. Among the canons appointed to the chapter during this period, mention must be made of John Julian (prebendary of Fenton, 1902), who, as vicar of Wincobank, Sheffield, had already produced the *Dictionary of hymnology* which remains the standard work.

The spirit of reform had by now spread to charities, and in 1898 St. Peter's School was given a new constitution which removed it from the control of the dean and chapter, though they were to elect four of the representative governors and the dean remained a governor *ex officio*. (Several of the other charities with which the dean and chapter had been closely connected received new schemes from the Charity Commissioners.) In 1902 the chapter purchased from St. Peter's School the building in Minster Yard which they had originally erected for the school; the Song school was then revived and given this building (1903).

Stone and glass were now endangered by the pollution of the atmosphere with smoke (one result of the achievements of Cockburn's old enemy George Hudson, the 'railway king'). The St. Cuthbert window, the St. William window, the nave roof, the pinnacles on the south side were restored, but in February 1899 the dean was obliged to appeal for £50,000. Under the guidance of the architect Bodley, the east end was restored, pinnacles were added to the buttresses on the north side, and flying buttresses, which the architectural newspapers denounced as a useless absurdity,[100] but which were claimed as a restoration of those shown in old engravings. Ketton stone, harder than Tadcaster, was now used for the first

[99] Ethel Thomson, *Clifton Lodge* (1955), 83.
[100] *The Times* correspondence columns, June 1905; *Builder* (1905), 382, 617, 648. The flying buttresses were constructed partly in order to keep the masons employed.

time. The west window had its glass and mullions repaired, and the glass of the chapter-house and the Five Sisters window was preserved. The parapet of the central tower was restored. The restoration of the entire west front (1907) was the superb building achievement of Purey-Cust's time. The dean gave a fine reredos for the Lady Chapel in memory of Queen Victoria, and caused a life-sized statue of King Edward VII in his coronation robes to be erected in a niche.

Dean Purey-Cust continued and expanded the work of Dean Duncombe in organizing the staff of the Minster and developing a certain *esprit de corps* among them. The benevolent paternalism of Duncombe towards the workmen was extended by his successor with 'substantial' tea-parties to celebrate the end of a repair or some domestic event. A week's annual holiday for the workmen was introduced in the late 1880s.

In the Edwardian age the dean became an institution, and York expressed its gratitude in May 1911 by making him a freeman of the city. After buying the old subdeanery house in Precentor's Court from the Ecclesiastical Commissioners he leased the site for a nursing home, and so (like Duncombe) had the rare honour of seeing a place in the city called by his name during his life. 'A s'pose', a workman was overheard saying as the dean passed him in the street, 'it taakes about three hundred years to make *that*.'[101]

In one matter his memory was ill served. Because the new road constructed in 1902 from Goodramgate to Minster Yard was given the name Deangate, men believed, as an official Minster publication has expressed it, that Dean Purey-Cust thereby 'thought to confer a benefit upon the citizens of York'.[102] On the contrary, his strong and repeated protests, not only in chapter and in meetings with the corporation committee, but in the local Press, that such a road would imperil the fabric by the vibration of heavy traffic, were eventually overriden by a chapter which had now learned the rights of non-residentiaries; an amendment approving the scheme (provided the traffic were restricted to 'vehicles on springs and to loads of under one ton in weight') was carried by 14 votes to 4.[103]

Deangate once built, the Minster stoneyard was moved there in 1913, its old site being incorporated in the grounds of the new nursing home.

[101] Lockhart, op. cit. 200.

[102] *York Minster News*, spring 1974.

[103] The construction of Deangate came at the end of a long period of encroachment upon the privacy of Minster Yard, resulting from the city's taking over the powers of the improvement commissioners for the Liberty of St. Peter, which faded out by about 1850. In 1843 it was feared that by carelessness after the demolition of the old gateway and the houses to the west of Belfrey church, a public right of way had been created, but after a meeting with the town clerk Minster Yard was closed once more with gates (shown on the 1st edition 6-inch Ordnance Survey map, surveyed in 1851). C. W.

The war of 1914 found Purey-Cust old and decrepit. The dean was able to read the lesson at the occasion in 1916 when the Marquis of Zetland unveiled a memorial to Admiral Sir Christopher Cradock who perished at the Battle of Coronel. But the same year zeppelins floated across York, dropping a bomb within a few hundred yards of the Minster. Archbishop Lang went to the dean and insisted that the glass be removed from the Minster windows and buried for safety. With tears running down his face the dean pleaded that he was too old to oversee such a work;[104] and it led to his death, for he caught a fatal chill while surveying the windows. He died at Christmas 1916 at the age of 88. Everyone wanted what they failed to get for Duncombe, burial in the Minster; the home secretary was agreeable, at least as far as the precincts, and Purey-Cust was interred[105] outside the wall just below the Five Sisters window. *The Times* gave its obituary a rare headline: 'A charming personality'.

The author wishes to record his indebtedness to Miss Katharine M. Longley, Minster archivist, for indispensable help in preparing this chapter.

Thiselton told his successor as chapter clerk, 6 Dec. 1889: '. . . there were gates across the carriage way which were closed once or more than once in every year in order to preserve to the dean and chapter the right of way—during the time that the railings [at the west end of the Minster] were standing, heavy carts and waggons were stopped and turned back by the dean and chapter's policeman'. Thiselton thought it was then 'nearer thirty than twenty years since the Minster Yard was thrown open to the public' by the removal of the railings. (YML, Misc. Papers.)

In 1870 a deputation from the city corporation asked the chapter to grant them a permanent right of carriage way through the Minster Yard (YML, Chapter Act, 5 Jan. 1870). This was not granted until 1891 (and then very reluctantly), when the corporation offered to make and maintain a proper roadway through Minster Yard from Petergate to Chapter House Street. The city surveyor then demanded the destruction of the ancient gateway in College Street, the fate of which hung in the balance until Deangate was constructed (YML, Chapter Act, 21 Feb. 1891).

In 1899 the corporation proposed to widen College Street; the dean thought this a so-called improvement' very objectionable (YML, Chapter Act, 3 Jan. 1900).

A long correspondence on the subject of the proposed new road appeared in the local Press in March and April 1901 and was printed as a pamphlet.

[104] Lockhart, op. cit. 253.

[105] Seven months later his wife was laid in the same grave. In modern times the difficulty was solved by cremation. The ashes of deans Milner-White (1963) and Richardson (1975) were interred within the Minster. For this and other help, my thanks to Bernard Barr.

CHAPTER VIII

The Stained and Painted Glass

David E. O'Connor and Jeremy Haselock

Introduction

The stained glass plays an important role in making York Minster one of the major Gothic cathedrals in Europe.

That over half the medieval glass in England can be found in the Minster is a myth. Nevertheless, no single building in the country can approach it for sheer quantity of material, and few churches in Europe have retained their original glazing on such a scale. Taken in conjunction with the wealth of material in the parish churches of the city, York may be considered one of the major centres in Europe for the study of glass-painting.

The range of the glass also sets the Minster apart. Without leaving this one building it is possible to obtain a fair survey of virtually the whole history of English glass-painting from the last quarter of the twelfth century down to the present day. Moreover, the Minster examples will more often than not be amongst the finest of their date. The late-twelfth-century glass from the nave, the thirteenth-century grisaille in the Five Sisters window, the west window of 1339, and the east window, completed in 1408, are just a few examples which are major monuments of English medieval art. In the post-medieval period, too, the Minster has much to offer: Renaissance and seventeenth-century glass of English and French origins, much work by the eighteenth-century York glass-painter William Peckitt, and, if no major examples of nineteenth- and twentieth-century windows, then at least something representative of these most recent periods.

When we consider the enormous losses sustained by English medieval glass, then the survival of so much in the Minster becomes something of a miracle. Although most of the rich works of art which once adorned the cathedral were ruthlessly destroyed at the Reformation, the glass escaped the iconoclasts, doubtless because of its functional value. It also somehow survived the other major era of destruction, the Civil War, even though for

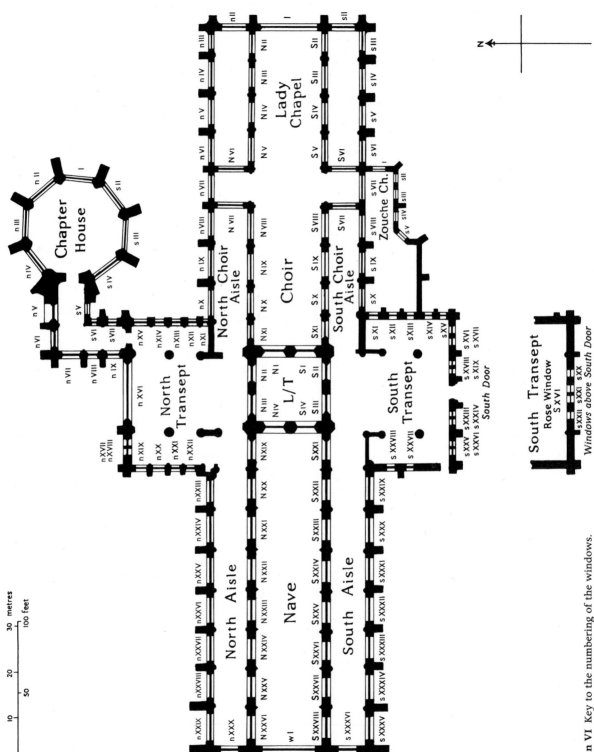

Plan VI Key to the numbering of the windows.

a time York was at the centre of the action.[1] One of the articles signed by the captors of the city agreed to protect churches from desecration.[2] A story is told that Sir Thomas Fairfax, the Parliamentarian general, actually took down the windows to protect them from 'the ungovernable Fury of an enraged Rabble'.[3] Torre mentions the loss of a window in the nave, 'taken down and sold in the time of the late Troubles'.[4]

Although deliberate vandalism may have been held at bay, the glass did suffer enormously through neglect from the Reformation onwards. With the decline of craftsmanship in York, the windows were repaired by local plumbers and glaziers. Much of the patchy nature of many of the Minster panels can be attributed to centuries of attention from this quarter. Broken or decayed pieces were repaired with whatever was at hand, until what had once been an aesthetically and iconographically pleasing unit was reduced to a heap of fragments. The basic problem was that post-medieval glass-painting was out of sympathy with the pot-metal techniques of the Middle Ages. William Peckitt, who carried out much repair work and replacement in the Minster between 1753 and his death in 1795,[5] made some attempt to improve the quality of his coloured glass, but in general the raw material at his disposal was inadequate and his Italianate style hopelessly at odds with the ancient glass.

The windows emerged from two disasters in the nineteenth century, the fires in the choir in 1829 and the nave in 1840, reasonably intact. There were some losses in the choir clerestory, where fire-crazed glass still bears witness to the force of the conflagration. In the nave most of the damaged glass was plain (sXXXV, SXXVIII, and NXXVI) except for some figure and heraldic panels in the clerestory, restored by William Wailes.[6]

By this time, the revival of interest in medieval glass was well under way and the true principles of glass-painting firmly restored. This new awareness of the beauty of old glass did not necessarily mean that it was treated with greater care. In their zeal for restoration the Victorians often discarded even slightly damaged glass, so that whole panels could become mere copies. This was the case with John Barnett's restoration of the east window in the chapter-house (C/H I) in 1845, and, on a lesser scale, Burlison and Grylls's work on the Mauley window (sXXXII) in 1903.

In the present century two world wars have posed major threats. After a

---

[1] See Chapter V by Dr. M. C. Cross, above p. 213, citing Mace, *Musick's Monument* (1676), 20.
[2] Drake, *Ebor.*, p. 170.
[3] T. Gent, *The Antient and Modern History of the Famous City of York* (York, 1730), p. 49 n.
[4] Torre, 'Minster', p. 25.
[5] YML, E4a, Fabric Accounts and E3/123ᵛ–162ᶜ, Vouchers.
[6] YML, B3, Restoration 1840–5.

zeppelin had loomed over the cathedral in 1916, a plan to remove the windows was put into action. This drew attention to the decayed state of much of the glass, and an appeal was launched for a large programme of restoration. The Society for the Protection of Ancient Buildings advised on how this should be conducted. The distinguished committee, reporting on the work, could not 'suggest any improvement on the method adopted at York, namely to re-lead the glass in the exact arrangement in which it is found, and where pieces are actually missing, to fill the holes with plain glass'.[7]

When war struck again in 1939, the enormous task of removing the windows had to commence afresh. Another opportunity for major restoration presented itself. It was carried out by the Minster glaziers under the guidance of the dean, Eric Milner-White. The strictly preservationist approach of the 1920s was abandoned for an attempt to improve the panels by reconstructing them into something approaching their original design. Occasional misreading of their subject-matter has led to iconographic problems. This is further hampered by the lack of full documentation of alterations.[8] This must be borne in mind when looking at the glass.

The problems of preserving the Minster's great treasury of medieval glass are far from over. By its very nature, glass is prone to attack from moisture, which can cause severe corrosion and weathering. This is the case with some of the Minster glass. Founded in 1967, the York Glaziers Trust, a team of craftsmen backed by specialist advisers, exists primarily to care for the glass in the Minster. Research is being conducted by the Department of Physics at the University of York into the causes and possible solutions of the decay of the glass.[9] As a result it is hoped that the life of the windows can be extended.

There survives a considerable amount of documentary evidence relating to the Minster glass. Apart from a few earlier references, this occurs principally in the fabric rolls, which survive with gaps from the second half of the fourteenth century onwards.[10] Entries are mainly concerned with repairs rather than original glazing, usually paid for by individual donors. Further information occurs in the chapter act-books, in some cases only in copies made by Torre and other antiquarians. The contracts for the west

[7] YML, D10/FAB/G, S.P.A.B., *Report on York Minster Windows* (1921).

[8] *The Friends of York Minster Annual Reports* (1945–63) contain short accounts by Dean Milner-White.

[9] R. G. Newton, *The Deterioration and Conservation of Painted Glass: A Critical Bibliography and Three Research Papers* (Corpus Vitrearum Medii Aevi Great Britain, Occasional Papers 1, 1974) includes results of experiments on Minster glass.

[10] Raine, *Fabric Rolls*.

end glazing by Robert and his associates and the east window by John Thornton, survive only in this way. Besides these windows, the only others which can be attributed to particular glass-painters and their workshops on documentary evidence are those in the central tower (L/T SI-SIV and L/T NI-NIV), the work of Matthew Petty and others in 1471. Attribution of other windows must largely rest on style, notably less reliable than documentation.

'The indefatigable Mr. Torre' not only preserved the contents of lost medieval documents for posterity, he also wrote a description of the Minster of vital importance to the history of the glass.[11] In it he described virtually every figure and heraldic panel in the windows, with diagrams to show their locations. Since he wrote, whole windows have disappeared, and inscriptions, vital to our knowledge of the donors and the subject-matter, have vanished or been reduced to fragments. Eighteenth-century writers like Gent[12] and Drake,[13] heavily indebted to Torre, mention the windows briefly. The former wrote a little book on the east window with a suitably stirring title which looks forward to the Romantic descriptions of the glass in early nineteenth-century guide-books.[14]

It was left to the Victorians to begin an examination of the glass in detail. Writing for the Archaeological Institute meeting at York in 1846, Charles Winston, who pioneered the study of medieval glass in England, expressed the need for a catalogue of the glass in the Minster and parish churches.[15] Various people rose to the challenge. John Browne, who had reproduced colour plates of some panels in his history of the Minster,[16] went on to produce a long description of the windows, completed in 1859 but not published for over fifty years.[17] Water-colour drawings by Browne are valuable records of the state of York glass in the middle of the nineteenth century.[18] Winston himself was the joint author of an important article on the Heraldic window (nXXIII).[19] This was followed by panel by panel accounts of the St. William and St. Cuthbert windows (nVII and sVII) by

---

[11] Torre, 'Minster'.

[12] *History*.

[13] *Ebor*.

[14] T. Gent, *The Most Delectable, Scriptural and Pious History of the Famous and Magnificent Great Eastern Window (According to Beautiful Portraitures) in St. Peter's Cathedral, York* (York, 1762).

[15] C. Winston, 'On the Painted Glass in the Cathedral and Churches of York', *Proc. Arch. Inst.* (1846), reprinted in *Memoirs Illustrative of the Art of Glass-Painting* (1865), 75–6.

[16] Browne, *History* ii.

[17] J. Browne, *A Description of the Representations and Arms on the Glass in the Windows of York Minster* (Leeds, 1915).

[18] YCL, Knowles Collection, and YML.

[19] C. Winston and W. S. Walford, 'On a Heraldic Window in the North Aisle of the Nave of York Cathedral', *Arch J* xvii (1860), 22–34, reprinted in *Memoirs*, 256–84.

James Fowler and his brother.[20] In the 1880s Westlake discussed much of the glass in his monumental survey of European glass-painting.[21] The York glass-painter John Ward Knowles began his description of the windows about this time.[22] It contains useful information on the state of the windows prior to twentieth-century restorations. His photographs of the glass are amongst the earliest to survive.[23]

Writers on the glass in this century have been numerous. Two general books by George Benson and Canon F. Harrison contain large sections on the Minster.[24] J. A. Knowles, the most prolific writer on the York glass, and author of an extensive book on the subject,[25] wrote many articles on various aspects of the windows. Besides his accounts of restoration already referred to, Dean Milner-White and the Friends of York Minster produced two lists of the windows.[26] A more recent list has appeared in the Minster entry for The Buildings of England series,[27] and a more extensive, illustrated account can be found in a volume produced for the nineteen-hundredth anniversary of the city.[28] Winston's catalogue has yet to appear. The Corpus Vitrearum and Royal Commission volumes, when they are published, will remedy this. They should provide a permanent record of the windows and a foundation on which future scholarship can build.

Pre-Conquest glass

Glass functions primarily as a translucent wall against the elements. The earliest reference to the glazing of the Minster in about 670 brings this graphically home. St. Wilfrid, we are told, 'prevented the entry of birds and rain through the windows by means of glass, through which, however, the light shone within'.[29] The Saxon cathedral, and any glass which still survives, still await discovery. Wilfrid no doubt had to send to Gaul for glaziers like his contemporary Benedict Biscop, founder of the monastery at

---

[20] J. Fowler, 'On a Window representing the Life and Miracles of St. William of York, at the North End of the Eastern Transept, York Minster', *YAJ* iii (1873–4), 193–348, and J. T. Fowler, 'On the St. Cuthbert Window in York Minster', *YAJ* iv (1877), 249–376.

[21] N. A. J. Westlake, *A History of Design in Painted Glass* (3 vols., 1881–94).

[22] J. W. Knowles, *The Stained Glass of York Minster* (3 MS. vols., YCL, Y478 19561).

[23] YCL, Knowles Collection.

[24] G. Benson, *The Ancient Painted Glass Windows in the Minster and Churches of the City of York* (York, 1915); F. Harrison, *The Painted Glass of York* (1927).

[25] J. A. Knowles, *Essays in the History of the York School of Glass-Painting* (1936).

[26] *An Index and Guide to the Ancient Windows of the Nave* (York, 1959) and *An Index and Guide to the Windows of the Transepts and Choir* (York, 1967).

[27] Ben Johnson in N. Pevsner, *Yorkshire: York and the East Riding* (1972), 96–105.

[28] P. Gibson, 'The Stained and Painted Glass of York', in *The Noble City of York*, ed. A. Stacpoole *et al.* (York, 1972), 79–162 for the Minster.

[29] Eddi (Eddius Stephanus), *The Life of St. Wilfrid*, ed. B. Colgrave (Cambridge, 1927), 35.

Monkwearmouth in 674, as the art had been lost in this country.[30] Excavations at Monkwearmouth itself and other pre-Conquest sites at Jarrow and Escomb in Northumbria, have produced fragments of cylinder-blown window-glass[31] which exhibit a wide range of colours, but are unpainted, and must have been leaded into patterns. It is possible that the earliest glass in the Minster was of this type.

Romanesque glass

The earliest surviving glass in the Minster comprises the substantial remains of twenty-seven figure scenes, fifteen more fragmentary portions of similar scenes, and the remains of fifteen different border designs. This important early glass owes its survival to the decision of the fourteenth-century glaziers to re-set it in the nave clerestory windows.[32] Examples of the re-use of early glass in later glazing schemes are rare[33] and it is unfortunate that at York, where examples of re-used twelfth-century sculpture have also come to light,[34] the decision to whiten the nave vault during the recent restoration has resulted in the removal of most of the tracery lights into store.

The figure panels have suffered much in earlier restorations, a high proportion of the original glass has been lost and the missing portions made up with either alien pieces of medieval glass or poor quality modern coloured glass. In 1927 Canon Harrison concluded that 'most of these panels are so hard to read that, though the groups can be described as Torre described them, it is impossible to identify many of them with any well-known scenes from Biblical history or the lives of the Saints'.[35] It was indeed an impossible task to read these panels when they were in the clerestory windows. Recently, however, they were removed for restoration and conservation and have been available for close study since 1971–2. Even so the problems of identification are formidable. It is probable that originally the panels had inscriptions referring to the scenes illustrated but none has survived. Although much of the original glass has perished, in

[30] Bede, *Historia Abbatum*, ed. C. Plummer (1896), 368.

[31] R. Cramp, 'Decorated Window-Glass and Millefiori from Monkwearmouth', *Ant J* l (1970), 327–35, and 'The Window Glass', Appendix I in M. Pocock and H. Wheeler, 'Excavations at Escomb Church, County Durham, 1968', *JBAA* xxxiv (1971), 26–8. The precise dating of the fragments is problematical, but both Monkwearmouth and Jarrow were founded late in the seventh century and were abandoned by the middle of the ninth.

[32] See T. W. French, 'Observations on some Mediaeval Glass in York Minster' *Ant J* li (1971), 86–93, for the present distribution of the glass which he suggests was removed from the Norman choir *c.* 1335.

[33] Other examples are listed by J. Lafond, *Le Vitrail* (Paris, 1966), 57–8.

[34] G. Zarnecki, 'Deux reliefs de la fin du XIIe à la cathédrale d'York', *Revue de l'art*, xxx (1975), 17–20.

[35] Harrison, *Painted Glass*, 36.

many cases later re-leadings have retained the original lead-line compositions much disfigured and confused by the repair work. Reconstruction of these original compositions enables comparisons with other works to be made and by this method identifications are possible. Owing to the incomplete nature of the material, however, many of the identifications must be regarded as tentative.

It appears that the panels are the remains of an extensive series of windows with subjects including scenes from the Old Testament, the genealogy and Passion of Christ, legends of saints Benedict, Nicholas, Martin, and possibly Richarius, as well as the Last Judgement.

There is one Old Testament scene of Daniel in the lions' den, combined with the apocryphal account of his being fed by Habakkuk, now in the centre lancet of the Five Sisters window (nXVI).[36] Lethaby suggested that this panel came from a window of Old and New Testament types and anti-types, as it is a type of the Annunciation to the Virgin Mary.[37] A panel of a King from a Tree of Jesse has been placed in the nave aisle (nXXVIII).[38] Westlake[39] first noted that the formal pose of the king, seated against the vertical stem of the vine and grasping its branches with both hands, is closely related to the Jesse Tree window design found first in France at St. Denis, *c.* 1142–4, and then at Chartres, *c.* 1150–5.[40] It is certainly the first extant, and probably the earliest, example of this iconography in English glass-painting. A somewhat later example at Canterbury Cathedral is also derived from the St. Denis model.[41]

Lethaby suggested that the Jesse window was probably in the central eastern chapel of the choir rebuilt by Roger of Pont l'Évêque, archbishop of York 1154–81.[42] He also suggested that it would have been flanked on either side by typological windows of the Infancy and Passion of Christ. At least four panels depict events after the Crucifixion and may have come from such a window. These are: the Three Maries at the Tomb (SXXVI), the Supper at Emmaus (SXXVI), Christ and the Disciples (SXXVI), and the Miraculous Draught of Fishes (SXXVI). There is no doubt about the identification of the first two scenes but the third panel is less certain. There are Old Testament types for each of these events[43] but there is no evidence

[36] Benson, *Ancient Painted Glass*, 5, Fig. 2.

[37] W. R. Lethaby, 'Archbishop Roger's Cathedral at York and its Stained Glass', *ArchJ* xxii (1915), 42.

[38] Browne, *History*, Pl. CXXIII; Benson, *Ancient Painted Glass*, 6, Fig. 4.

[39] Westlake, *History of Design* i. 43–4.

[40] M. Aubert, *Le Vitrail français* (Paris, 1958), 105–7, Pl. 65.

[41] M. Caviness, 'The Canterbury Jesse', *The Year 1200. A Symposium* (New York, 1971).

[42] Lethaby, op. cit. 44–5.

[43] See M. R. James, 'Pictor in Carmine', *Archaeologia*, xciv (1951), and L. F. Sandler, *The Peterborough Psalter and other Fenland Manuscripts* (1974).

extant to show that they were represented in the York window. The fourth scene is not found in typological series but in narrative cycles of Christ's Passion[44] so the possibility is raised of all four panels having come from a Passion sequence and not from linking typological scenes.

The next series of related panels, however, would form a logical pendant to such a typological series as they depict the Last Judgement.[45] One panel shows St. Peter and St. Paul standing at the Gate of Heaven and two show angels sounding trumpets (SXXIII). There are six panels depicting the torments of the souls in Hell (all in window SXXIV), the four most complete of which suggest a narrative sequence. First the souls are led in procession by attendant devils; they are thrust into the mouth of Hell, conventionally represented by the gaping jaws of a large dragon's head with pointed teeth and staring eyes; two scenes show them being boiled in cauldrons over a fire. Although incomplete and much disturbed, the compositions have great vivacity and powerful appeal. One particular detail, a devil with a crook pole holding down a soul in a cauldron, has a close parallel in the contemporary sculptured slab in the crypt of the Minster.[46]

A number of panels can be identified as scenes from the lives of at least four saints. The most important shows a tonsured monk lowering a basket to a seated figure. The two figures are placed on different levels and there is an undulating boundary-line between them (SXXV) (Plate 87). This composition is virtually the same, though reversed, as an illustration in the eleventh-century Monte Cassino Life of St. Benedict, now in the Vatican Library.[47] The Life relates how St. Benedict made his hermitage in a cave and was daily brought provisions by the monk Romanus who lowered them to him in a basket. Attached to the end of the rope was a bell, used to summon the saint's attention. On one occasion the devil appeared and threw a stone which broke the bell.[48] Nothing comparable has been found in the legends of other saints so the identification of this panel as part of a St. Benedict window is reasonably certain. There are two other panels that may have come from the same window. One (SXXV) shows a monk seated at a table holding a drinking vessel, before him stands a woman and behind her a large grotesque devil is going off to the left. This can be related to the legend of the two monks who disobeyed St. Benedict's rule that they should

[44] See e.g. M. R. James, 'Four Leaves of an English Psalter 12th cent.', *Walpole Soc.* xxv (1936–7), 15, Pl. VIII.

[45] M. R. James, 'Pictor in Carmine', 166.

[46] F. Harrison, *York Minster: its story* (1955), 67.

[47] Vatican Library, Cod. Lat. 1202. Published D. M. Inguanez and M. Avery. *Miniature Cassiniense del secolo XI Illustrante la Vita di San Benedetto* (1934).

[48] *Golden Legend* (Caxton version) (1900) iii. 81. Illustrated in the Vatican MS. fo. 2^r.

not break their fast outside the monastery.[49] The other scene shows a nimbed monk accompanied by monastic and lay persons, one of whom is a youth. This could represent St. Benedict receiving either St. Placitus or St. Maurus into the monastery.[50]

Two scenes can be associated with the life of St. Nicholas. Both are of miracles brought about by invoking the saint's intercession. The first is the often represented miracle of St. Nicholas appearing to sailors at sea and calming the storm. The second scene is rarely represented but appears again in the Minster in glass of *c.* 1430 in the Wolveden window (nVIII). It shows a man being run over by a cart and horses while behind stands a man (with a staff over his left shoulder) (Plates 88, 89). This is probably the legend of the Jew who invoked St. Nicholas to recover a debt from a Christian who had falsely sworn that he had repaid it. The Christian was run down, the money recovered, and the Jew converted.[51] While there is a similar legend associated with St. Bavo of Ghent,[52] the rarity of his cult in England makes the St. Nicholas interpretation more likely.

Two panels may be identified as scenes from a St. Martin window. Both are very incomplete but the identification of one is virtually certain as it has the standard iconography of the equestrian figure of the saint dividing his cloak with a beggar (NXXV).[53] The other fragment shows a man hanging from a gallows (NXXV) and may relate to the legend of St. Martin having brought to life a man who had been hanged.[54] As, however, other saints effected similar miracles, for example St. James the Great, the precise identification of this scene cannot be established.

A seated figure of a bishop (NXXIV) has been identified as St. Richarius, founder of the abbey of St. Riquier in the seventh century.[55] The identification is based on an incomplete inscription shown in Browne's engraving[56] but now lost. Benson interpreted the panel as 'the forerunner of the figure and canopy treatment'[57] and Lethaby thought that it came from a clerestory window.[58] The engraving, however, suggests that it is a fragment of a narrative scene and not a self-contained design.

These panels are amongst the earliest extant English examples of

[49] Vatican Library, Cod. Lat. 1202. fo. 44^r.
[50] Ibid., fo. 30^v.
[51] *Golden Legend*, ii. 117.
[52] L. Réau, *Iconographie de l'art chrétien*, iii, pt. I (Paris, 1958), 189.
[53] *Golden Legend*, vi. 142.
[54] Ibid. 145.
[55] Benson, *Ancient Painted Glass* 7.
[56] Browne, *History* ii, Pl. CXIX.
[57] Benson, *Ancient Painted Glass* 7.
[58] Lethaby, op. cit. 45.

87 SXXV South nave clerestory, 12th C. St. Benedict in a cave, fed by his disciple Romanus. This composition conforms closely to an illustration in the 11th-C. life of the saint from Monte Cassino now in the Vatican Library.

88 (*below left*) ex SXXV South nave clerestory, 12th C. A miracle of St. Nicholas. The first of the 12th-C. panels to be completely restored. The strong, clear composition is typical of the surviving romanesque glass. The detail in **89** (*below right*), one of the best preserved heads in the series, shows the bold and expressive style of the 12th-C. glass-painter.

windows depicting the lives and legends of the saints. The identification of the Benedict, Nicholas, and Martin scenes is a welcome addition to our knowledge of twelfth-century iconography.

The ornamental border strips, which from their number and variety of design[59] must have been a striking feature of the twelfth-century glass (Plate 90), are at the time of writing in store. In general feel they closely resemble the richly decorated borders of windows at St. Denis and Le Mans but the extensive use of painted grisaille, which dominates the design and subordinates the coloured foliage, makes the York borders distinctive in style.[60]

In spite of the significant early use of white glass in the borders, the overall impression created by the twelfth-century glass in the Minster is of deep and intense colour. Dark greens, purples, and blues abound, rendered even darker by the application of thin coats of vitreous paint on the outside. Roger's church must have borne eloquent testimony to the threefold properties of glass enumerated by Abbot Suger of St. Denis.[61] His glass was the bearer of sacred images, an intrinsically rich material with the appearance of precious stones, and mysterious because it glowed without fire.

It is possible to draw convincing stylistic parallels between the surviving York panels and examples of Romanesque glass in France, notably that at Le Mans,[62] in order to stress the influence of French craftsmen working for Archbishop Roger.[63] Comparison, however, with works in other media produces strong arguments for important local traditions. Madeline Caviness[64] has drawn attention to the connection between the York Jesse Tree fragment and the figure of St. Sigismund on the reliquary head of St. Oswald, made in England *c.* 1170[65] and now at Hildesheim, as well as to the style of the Master of the Apocrypha Drawings of the Winchester Bible.[66] George Zarnecki[67] finds Mosan elements mixed equally with a strong local style exemplified by the Copenhagen Psalter[68] and fragments of sculpture now in the Yorkshire Museum. The study of the glass being made during

[59] Surveyed by C. Wardale for York Glaziers' Trust, Nave Clerestory Glass (unpubl. report 1972).
[60] See *The Year 1200*. Exhibition New York 1970. Catalogue ed. K. Hoffmann, Cat. nos. 222 and 223.
[61] Suger's ideas are succinctly related to twelfth-century glass by O. Von Simson, *The Gothic Cathedral* (New York, 1956).
[62] Cat. *The Year 1200*. Cat. no. 224.
[63] Lethaby, op. cit. 41–7.
[64] 'Canterbury Jesse' 384.
[65] Illustrated in H. Swarzenski, *Monuments of Romanesque Art* (1967), Fig. 484.
[66] Illustrated in W. Oakeshott, *The Artists of the Winchester Bible* (1945), Pl. XII.
[67] 'Deux reliefs' 19.
[68] Copenhagen, Royal Library, MS. Thott, 143 20.

the present (1975–6) restoration will contribute considerably to our knowledge of this style and perhaps confirm the views of Lethaby[69] and Lafond[70] that this glass all formed part of the glazing of Roger's choir of 1170–80 and was completed some years after his death in 1181.

The transepts and lantern tower

The earliest glass *in situ* is to be found in the transepts, the oldest parts of the present structure above ground. On the south the windows were presumably glazed by 1241, when Archbishop Walter de Gray founded his chantry in the east aisle, and it is possible that some windows were already in place by 1230 when the altar of St. William was founded.[71] The north transept glazing must have been completed shortly afterwards, by *c.* 1250. Of this original glazing only a portion survives: the heads of two small lancets in the south wall (sXXV and sXXVI)—though according to Browne they were only placed in their present position *c.* 1847[72]—and the five tall lancets opposite, known collectively as the Five Sisters window (nXVI). The remaining windows have been reglazed at various intervals from at least the 1430s onwards, which accounts for the rather uneven lighting in this part of the church. The legacy of sharply contrasting styles has been increased in more recent times by using the transepts as a home for panels from other areas of the building as well as from other city churches.[73]

The thirteenth-century glass, with its emphasis on grisaille, represents a major change in the lighting of the church. The Romanesque glass-painters had relied on dark, glowing colours to create a highly charged atmosphere of mysterious luminosity. White glass was used sparingly. With the new work the reverse was the case and the contrast between the sombre choir and nave and the brilliantly lit new transepts must have been very striking. The influence of Cistercian ideals has been seen as the major factor in this new approach,[74] but it may simply have been an aesthetic response to stylistic changes in architecture. New demands were made of the glass-painter to create a bright and harmonious interior for the transepts with their Purbeck marble columns, deep mouldings, and richly carved ornament. Although the new system had the added advantage of

---

[69] Lethaby, op. cit. 145.
[70] Lafond, Review of Woodforde, *English Stained and Painted Glass*, in *ArchJ* cxi (1954), 240.
[71] See Dr. Gee above, p. 128 and Ch. III, nn. 46–48. His suggestion that the altar was in the north chapel of the east aisle is reinforced by a figure of St. William of *c.* 1434 in the glass here (sXI).
[72] Browne, *Description* 257. No references to this appear to have survived in the Minster accounts.
[73] For the glass from St. Martin-le-Grand, Coney Street (sXXVII and sXXVIII) and from St. John's Micklegate (nXVII–nXXII) see respectively *The Friends of York Minster Annual Report* (1946), 29–30 and *Royal Commission on Historical Monuments, York* iii (1972), 19.
[74] Knowles, *York School* 137–57.

cheapness—coloured glass had to be imported and was far more costly than white—the general effect was of rich patterning. No doubt figure panels once existed as at Salisbury and Lincoln, where grisaille formed an important element of the glazing.[75] The wealth of altars in the transepts would have demanded some imagery and may have suggested the subject-matter as was the case later. The remnants of such a combination of grisaille and coloured medallions dating from the first half of the thirteenth century can still be seen in St. Denys Church, York.[76]

The two small panels in the south transept (sXXV and sXXVI) (Plate 91) consist of stiff-leaf foliage, the latter with fruit, very boldly painted in thick outline against a more delicate cross-hatched background. Originally this would have formed a balanced design. Coloured glass is reduced to a minimum, mainly to reinforce the geometric designs boldly leaded against the white glass.[77] The panels are much simpler in design than those in the north transept and, apart from the plain modern surround, have no borders.

The Five Sisters window (nXVI) confronts the visitor entering through the south door and the general effect of architecture and glass is impressive. For sheer scale the grisaille in these lancets has no rivals, but on closer inspection it is apparent that the window is a shadow of its former self. Over the years much of the original glass has been replaced or suffered severe paint loss. The medallion at the base of the centre light is an intrusion of long standing.[78] Vast numbers of breaks require an inordinate amount of leading so what must have originally been a series of very bold, clear patterns is now confused and difficult to follow. The external quarry glazing, which protects so many of the Minster windows, cuts down the light and further confuses the design.

Conventional foliage is again the principal feature of the ornament, mainly a trefoil leaf with fruit, the glass-painters equivalent of the carver's stiff-leaf foliage which adorns the transepts. However, more naturalistic forms make their first appearance in York glass, notably in the centre light,

[75] For Salisbury see Winston, *Memoirs* 106–29, and for Lincoln, where the glass often exhibits close affinities with York, J. Lafond, 'The Stained Glass Decoration of Lincoln Cathedral in the thirteenth century', *ArchJ* ciii (1946), 119–56. An illustration of this grisaille appears in J. Baker, *English Stained Glass*, (1960), Pl. 19. For the parallel use of grisaille in French glass see L. Grodecki in *Le Vitrail français* (Paris, 1958), 157.

[76] Window nV. See Knowles, *York School* 149–51. Lafond, 'Stained Glass Decoration', n.5, 133, identifies the subject as the Theophilus legend, though his 'man in white tunic and red mantle' appears to be the Virgin Mary with crown, as in the other medallion.

[77] For close parallels in French glass of this date see *Cathédrales* exhibition cat. Louvre Museum (Paris, 1962) nos. 153–4.

[78] See above, p. 320.

where forms akin to ivy and maple can be seen (Plate 92). This is paralleled in some sculptured capitals in the north transept and presages developments in the second half of the century, notably in the chapter-house. Bold geometrical patterns, more complex than those in the south transepts, are set on the grisaille. The designs change from light to light, consisting of variations on circular forms, foils, and star-shapes. Broad borders, accounting for almost a third of the width of each light, contain various foliage patterns interspersed with small areas of colour. A thin coloured strip runs up the outer edge of the light within a plain modern surround.

Apart from those windows lost with the rebuilding of the nave and choir, the original transept glazing may well have remained intact for nearly two centuries. The first windows to be replaced were those in the eastern aisles (sXI—sXV and nXI—nXV) for which some documentation survives. In the fabric rolls for 1434 there are payments to Robert Johanson for making iron bars for two newly glazed windows at the altars of St. William and St. Nicholas (sXI and nXI).[79] The same year a glazier called John was paid for repairing windows.[80] He was almost certainly John Chamber the Elder who had been paid the previous year for glazing work.[81] It may well be that these transept windows are products of Chamber's workshop.

The decision to replace the old glass may have reflected a desire to honour with large figures the saints to whom the altars beneath were dedicated. Certainly the choice of subject-matter was planned to a greater degree than usual in the Minster.

On the south side much of the original glass survives, if a little jumbled and patched. The panels beneath the figures belong to the early fourteenth-century glazing of the nave clerestory and were only set up here in 1960.[82] Their small-scale figures and brilliant colouring clash violently with the glass above. In the north transept much of the glass is by Charles Eamer Kempe whose firm restored the windows between 1899 and 1903.[83] The figures of St. Lawrence (nXIII), St. Paul (nXIV), and St. Peter (nXV) are entirely modern and replace lost figures recorded by Torre.[84] Apart from the shields above the figures and a few quarry and border pieces most of the remainder of this glass is modern. The shield above St. Peter again comes from the nave clerestory. Much more original glass survives in the St.

[79] Raine, *Fabric Rolls*, p. 53.
[80] Ibid., p. 54.
[81] Free of the city 1400, d. 1437. See J. A. Knowles, 'Glass-painters of York. 1. The Chamber Family', *Notes and Queries*, 12th Ser. viii (1921), 127.
[82] *Friends (of York Minster) Annual Report (FAR)* (1960), 16 and Pls. IV–VIII.
[83] YML, D10/FAB/G, transept windows 1902–3.
[84] Torre, 'Minster', p. 48.

90 Two examples of recently restored 12th-C. border panels. These panels, in common with much of the romanesque glass in the Minster, owe their survival to their re-use by 14th-C. glaziers in the nave clerestory.

91 sXXVI South transept, *c.* 1240. A remnant of the simple grisaille glass ornamented with 'stiff leaf' foliage which once filled the transept windows.

92 nXVI Five Sisters Window, *c.* 1250. The original design of the grisaille in the centre light of this window can best be seen in Browne's reconstruction. (Browne, *History*, Vol II, pl. 65).

Nicholas and St. Stephen windows (nXI and nXII) though even here the heads are replacements by Kempe.

The general design of each window is simple. Life-size figures stand in the middle of each lancet filling half the height. Instead of diapered grounds and architectural canopies the figures are set on quarry glazing, ornamented for the most part with a standard cross motif. The areas of quarry glass are broken up by heraldry. Borders with a central stem, crowns, leaves, and occasionally scrolls, surround each light. The thirteenth-century emphasis on white glass is retained, perhaps as a conscious aesthetic decision, perhaps for reasons of economy. Beside the quarry panels most of the figure work is white enriched with yellow stain. Coloured glass is obligatory for the shields, with its use elsewhere restricted to small amounts of drapery and the border backgrounds. Ruby glass is used for the dragon slain by St. Michael (sXII) and a very thin flashed ruby is used to good effect for the bloody stones held by the protomartyr St. Stephen (nXII).

Although much broken, the Archangel Gabriel (sXIII) is one of the best-preserved figures (Plate 93). He stands on a tiled plinth, robed in feathered tights and ermine mantle. A scroll on the right bears the Annunciation greeting. Considerable care has gone into the drawing of the facial features, finely delineated and carefully shaded, the lively cork-screw hair, elegant hands, and firmly modelled feet. Although the influence of John Thornton's soft style is still apparent—notably from his work in the western choir aisles where projecting plinths and border scrolls also appear—the transept style is harder and coarser.[85] John the Baptist (sXIV) (Plate 94) wears a camel robe painted with bold brush strokes—the head and leg bone portrayed graphically—and a mantle with simple strong ornament. The head of the saint is an unfortunate replacement using mid-fourteenth-century glass totally out of scale with the figure. The small-scale work is more delicate, particularly the painting of the donors who are members of the Saxton family.[86]

Though much of the ornamentation is simple, the figures of St. William and St. Nicholas (sXI and nXI) have exotic chasubles ornamented with birds. These two windows, fixed at the same time and executed from the same cartoons, contain the arms of Robert Wolveden, treasurer of the Minster 1426–32, as well as borders with scrolls bearing his name. Wolveden is associated with several Minster windows, notably one in the

---

[85] See below, p. 373.

[86] The donors may well have been members of the Guild of John the Baptist. According to Browne, *History* i, a chantry dedicated to the saint existed here in the 1430s. The Minster possessed several relics of the saint. Raine, *Fabric Rolls*, pp. 150–2, 299.

93 sXIII South transept, *c.* 1440. The Archangel
Gabriel. The scroll on the right bears the
Annunciation greeting.

94 sXIV South transept, *c.* 1440. St. John the
Baptist with donors. The head of the saint,
totally out of scale, is a restoration using mid-
14th-C. glass.

north choir aisle.[87] It has been suggested that a donor panel, placed in nVIII after the war, came originally from one of the transept windows.[88] St. William appears once more in a fourth Wolveden window (SVII). The inclusion of Archbishop Scrope's arms in one of the transept windows (nXIII) is one of several examples of the dean and chapter's desire to honour this archbishop.[89]

Important documentation survives for the glazing of the eight windows of the lantern tower (L/T SI–SIV and L/T NI–NIV), one of the rare occasions when new windows were paid for by the dean and chapter out of their own funds. In the fabric roll for 1471 payments occur to a team of eight glaziers. They are headed by Matthew Petty, one of the leading York glass-painters of the day, who appears several times in the fabric rolls between 1447 and 1472.[90] A large quantity of glass, purchased from various sources,[91] heads the account. Petty received payment for making forty-four panels as well as for time spent on the site. He produced a scheme for two bands of heraldic panels (Plate 95)—variations on the cross-keys of the Minster—surrounded by wreaths and set on plain quarry glazing. The glass is nearly all white as is to be expected in a tower giving light to the crossing and screen. The work is crude and so great the desire for economy that fake leaded quarries are painted on the heraldic panels. From ground level this glass is in any case little more than a faint blur of colour in the distance.

The replacement of the early transept glass continued into the first years of the sixteenth century and the reglazing of the central section of the south wall formed the last major work of the medieval glass-painters in the Minster. This wall, with its three levels of glazing, presents an odd mixture of styles today as the lower lancets contain eighteenth-century figures by William Peckitt.[92]

The Rose window and the upper levels were clearly glazed at the same time. The Rose (SXVI) (Plate 96), although less spectacular than many of its continental counterparts, is, with its elegant stonework and bright glass, one of the most impressive sights in the Minster. The sunflower at the

---

[87] See below, p. 373.

[88] *FAR* (1952), 32. This seems unlikely as it would spoil the unified design of this group of windows.

[89] See below, p. 378.

[90] Raine, *Fabric Rolls*, p. 76. For Petty see J. A. Knowles, 'Glass-painters of York. 7. The Petty Family', *N. and Q.* 12th Ser. ix (1921), 21–2.

[91] The rolls refer to *Vitri Anglicani* which must have been white glass. Coloured glass was not manufactured in England during the Middle Ages and had to be imported from the Continent. Records show that glass for York windows was imported from both the Normandy and Rhineland glass-houses. See Knowles, *York School* 196–203. For recently excavated raw material see D. E. O'Connor, 'Debris from a Mediaeval Glazier's workshop', *Interim. Bull. of the York Archaeological Trust*, 3, no. 3 (Aug. 1975), 11–17.

[92] See below, p. 388.

centre dates from Peckitt's restoration in 1793.[93] Yellow rays burst from the conventional blue clouds around it and, in the outer section, alternate pairs of white and red roses symbolize the union of the houses of York and Lancaster in 1486. The small rayed roundels were inserted in the latest restoration in 1970.

The lancets beneath (sXX–sXXII) occupy an important position in this axis wall, and full advantage was taken to proclaim saints of special importance to the Minster. In the tracery is a somewhat reconstructed half-length figure of God the Father. Beneath, in the centre, St. Peter and St. Paul (Plate 97) stand under canopies holding their usual attributes. Flanking them are the heavily restored figures of St. William, with head and mitre from Peckitt's restoration of 1790,[94] and St. Wilfrid who possesses a tiny mid-fourteenth-century head. The arms attributed to these saints are placed beneath them. To some extent the subject-matter summarizes the more elaborate programme of the west window (wI), by juxtaposing apostles and patrons of the church with two of the most prominent local saints connected with it. In addition to the shrine of St. William, relics of the other three saints were preserved in the Minster.[95]

Dean Milner-White suggested that the upper lancets were a memorial to Archbishop Savage, who reigned from 1502 until his death in 1507. Accordingly, he dated the glass between 1504 and 1510.[96] This argument was based on part of a mitre and a fragment he interpreted as a piece from the shield of Archbishop Savage's arms. Both pieces are now placed above the head of St. Wilfred. This evidence is very fragmentary and far from convincing but the dean brought forward more evidence to corroborate his dating. In one of the lower lancets (sXVII) there was once a portrait of John Petty, who had worked with his father Matthew on the lantern tower glazing in 1471, and who died in 1508[97] when lord mayor of the city. He was shown kneeling at a prayer-desk, in the robes of his office, with an inscription recording his death. This memorial would almost certainly have been carried out by the Petty workshop under John's brother, Robert.[98] As Dean Milner-White points out, there is a strong possibility that the Petty firm also glazed the upper windows in this wall. Robert Petty was paid for work in the Minster in 1510,[99] though once again probably for repairs.

---

[93] His bill survives. YML, E3/159^v.

[94] YML E3/156^v.

[95] Raine, *Fabric Rolls*, pp. 150, 221.

[96] *FAR* (1948), 28–30, and E. Milner-White, *Sixteenth-Century Glass in York Minster and the church of St. Michael-le-Belfrey* (St. Anthony's Hall Publications, no. 17, York, 1960), 4–7.

[97] J. A. Knowles, 'Glass-painters of York. Sir John Petty', *N. and Q.* 12th Ser. ix (1921), 61–4.

[98] J. A. Knowles, 'Glass-painters of York. Robert Petty', *N. and Q.* 12th Ser. ix (1921), 103–4.

[99] Raine, *Fabric Rolls*, p. 95.

96 SXVI The Rose Window, *c.* 1515. Pairs of white and red roses commemorate the union of the Houses of York and Lancaster in 1486.

95 L/T NI Lantern Tower, 1471. By Matthew Petty and atelier. A panel from one of the two bands of heraldic devices in the windows of the central tower. Both design and execution are poor.

Much has been made of the influence on these windows of the Anglo-Flemish glass-painters based at Southwark.[100] Such features as the curtains draped behind the figures, the little round-headed quarry windows behind the heads of the saints, the design of the canopies, and the smooth, stipple-shaded head and drapery painting, suggest that the artist was aware of developments elsewhere. However, these are general stylistic features which became characteristic of much English glass-painting in the early sixteenth century. It is quite clear from the details that the glass is the product of a York workshop, probably that of Robert Petty, as there is a considerable amount of glass in a similar style in York and the north. Besides glass now in the nave of the Minster (nXXIX),[101] there is extensive sixteenth-century glazing in St. Michael-le-Belfrey[102] and a panel in St. Helen's Church, York.[103] The south transept style can be seen further afield at Greystoke and Cartmel Fell in Cumbria. Reliable evidence for dates *c.* 1520 for the last-named sites,[104] and a dating in the 1530s for the Belfrey glass, suggests that the south transept glass in the Minster should be dated rather later than has been hitherto suggested—perhaps to the end of the second decade of the sixteenth century.

The chapter-house

The survival of the seven windows of the chapter-house gives us for the first time a comprehensive and unified glazing scheme. It is particularly significant in a building which has the minimum of wall area, and thus provides vast spaces for the glazier to demonstrate his art both in tall lights and complex traceries. It is still possible to get some idea of the intended effect both as regards general design and iconographic programme. Also for the first time in the church there is a whole series of narrative panels, the earliest surviving *in situ*, which in most cases present the earliest examples of subjects which were to become the standard themes in the Minster windows throughout the later Middle Ages. Unfortunately, time and the restorer have not treated the windows well and severe corrosion has necessitated much replacement over the years. In 1845, for example, a

---

[100] Milner-White, op. cit.

[101] Panels of the Ascension and Pentecost. The made-up canopies above include work in the south transept style. Dated 1508 by Milner-White in *FAR* (1954), 24, but attributed to Matthew Petty who died in 1478.

[102] E. Milner-White, op. cit.

[103] Donor panel in west window.

[104] Greystoke, east window, figures of the Virgin Annunciate and a bishop saint dated 1520 by D. J. Chadwick, The Ancient Glass in the East Window of the Church of St. Andrew, Greystoke, Cumbria (unpubl. B. Phil. diss., Univ. of York, 1974), 69. Cartmel Fell Chapel, whole glazing scheme *c.* 1516–20

legacy made money available for a restoration which had disastrous results for the east window (C/H I).[105] This in turn fell victim to yet another restorer under whose direction the glass was removed in 1959 to make way for the present motley collection. This decision destroyed at a stroke both the iconographic integrity and the aesthetic harmony of the building which the Victorian restorers had at least preserved.[106]

The windows also mark a new approach to lighting, which achieved a compromise between the dark colours of the Romanesque choir and nave and the bright grisaille of the transepts. By setting the figure panels on the grisaille to form four bands of colour across the lights, quite large narrative sequences could be depicted while plenty of light was admitted for the roof, the carvings, and the tiles. The same principles were extended to the tracery, where shields of arms were set on white foliage.

The grisaille is leaded into geometrical patterns, crossed in turn by plain coloured shapes and painted strapwork (Plate 98). The final result is a complex design, the clarity of which has been destroyed by breakages and thickly leaded repairs.[107] From a central stem, painted on the grisaille, spring symmetrically arranged branches of foliage with recognizably naturalistic leaf forms. This takes up an idea barely present among the mainly stylized stiff-leaf patterns of the Five Sisters window,[108] (Plate 92) but which forms the most important element in the carved ornament of the chapter-house.

The figure panels are enclosed in firmly outlined geometrical shapes often with an inner or outer border of simple patterning (Plates 99 and 133). This design feature is maintained throughout except for the first light of the south-west window (C/H sIV) (Plate 101) where a new feature breaks the regular pattern. Here the figures are depicted under architectural canopies of very simple form. The appearance of the crocketted gable introduces an element which becomes one of the major features of glass design.

The simplicity of both design and execution can be seen in the panel of St. Peter in Prison (C/H sII) (Plate 99), rather better preserved than most. The angel's wings fill the frame, St. Peter sits under a very basic piece of architecture with but the slightest hint of landscape in the foreground. His head and robe well illustrate the linear quality of the drawing. The heads of the two apostles in the Burial of the Virgin panel (C/H nII) (Plate 100) are both painted on the same piece of glass. Though not of great quality, they

---

[105] See below, and Pl. 133.
[106] For a rather different point of view see *FAR* (1960), 31, and Gibson in *Noble City*, 82–5.
[107] For reconstructions of these panels see Browne, *History* ii, Pls. LXXVIII, LXXIX, LXXXIII, and LXXXV, and Benson, *Ancient Painted Glass*, Figs. 11–13 and 15–20.
[108] See above, p. 326.

97 sXXI South transept façade, *c.* 1515. St. Peter and St. Paul. The last glass to be inserted before the Reformation shows clearly how York glaziers were aware of the new Flemish style popular in the south.

98 C/H nIII Chapter House, *c.* 1285. Grisaille, decorated with markedly naturalistic leaf forms, leaded into geometrical patterns.

have a spontaneity and liveliness which characterizes much of this glass. That there are slightly different head types—a fact which emerges from a comparison of these two panels—hints at the number and variety of hands to be detected in the glass.

As with the dating of the architecture, there has been much speculation in the dating of the glass in the chapter-house. Knowles, following Westlake's suggestion of 'a strong tincture of thirteenth-century character' in the head drawing, went on to conclude that the medallions dated from 'some time in the thirteenth century'.[109] Believing that, if this were the case, formalized stiff-leaf ornament of the Five Sisters type should have accompanied the medallions, he went on to suggest that the grisaille was fourteenth-century and the medallions re-used, perhaps from an earlier chapter-house.[110] Naturalistic forms, however, appear in carvings in the Sainte-Chapelle, Paris, consecrated in 1248, and in various other sites in the second half of the century.[111] Indeed the parallel chosen by Knowles for the chapter-house grisaille, a panel from Merton College, Oxford, can probably be dated *c.* 1289–96.[112] A look at the medallions themselves shows that naturalistic forms are in fact common to both figure and grisaille panels. In the Assumption of the Virgin scene (C/H nII), for example, both ivy and oak leaf can be found. This, together with the integrated nature of the design, seems to confirm that the chapter-house glazing was planned as a unity.

Dr. Gee has proposed a date of *c.* 1285 for the completion of the chapter-house,[113] and a date of this order would not be unreasonable for the glass. Comparative material of this date in English glass is not extensive but there are figures under canopies of the type found in the south-west window (C/H sIV) at Merton College which can be dated, like the grisaille mentioned above, to *c.* 1289–96. As the Merton canopies are slightly more developed than those at York they provide a convincing *terminus ante quem* for the chapter-house glass. Continental parallels with heavily outlined medallions in conjunction with naturalistic leaf forms are common from the period 1270–80[114] and a similar, slightly awkward, stance for the figures can be

[109] J. A. Knowles, 'An Inquiry into the date of the Stained Glass in the Chapter House at York', *YAJ* clix (1961), 451–61. See 452.

[110] Ibid. 460–1.

[111] E. A. Gee, above, p. 141.

[112] P. A. Newton, 'Stained Glass at Oxford', in J. Sherwood and N. Pevsner, *The Buildings of England. Oxfordshire* (1974), 81. See also H. W. Garrod, *Ancient Painted Glass in Merton College, Oxford* (1931), and H. Read and J. Baker, *English Stained Glass* (1960), Pl. XI.

[113] E. A. Gee, above, p. 136.

[114] In e.g. German Bible windows of Wimpfen im Tal, now at Darmstadt, *c.* 1275. S. Beeh-Lustenberger, *Glasmalerei um 800–1900 im Hessischen Landesmuseum in Darmstadt* (Frankfurt-on-Main, 1967), Pls. 15–37. See also Cologne Cathedral, from the Dominican Church *c.* 1280: H. Rode, *Die Mittelalterlichen Glasmalereien des Kölner Domes*, CVMA Deutschland IV (Berlin, 1974), Pls. 53–67.

99 C/H sII Chapter House, *c.* 1285. St. Peter in Prison. The simplicity both of design and execution of the figure panels is shown by this well preserved example.

100 C/H nII Chapter House, *c.* 1285. Detail from the Funeral of the Virgin. Heads with a spontaneity and liveliness characteristic of the Chapter House glass.

seen in a window in La Trinité, Fécamp, in Normandy. These panels, illustrating the life of St. Katherine, are enclosed in similar barbed quatrefoils with beaded frames.[115] These admittedly general parallels cannot be taken as definitive dating evidence but together they place the York chapter-house glass in the thirteenth century.

It is difficult to ascertain from the confused and mutilated state of some one hundred and forty narrative panels, whether the consistent plan, which is such a feature of the design of the glass, extends to the iconographic scheme. The window opposite the entrance (C/H I) contains none of its original subject-matter. Nevertheless, its theme can still be clearly seen from Barnett's carefully traced copies and confirmed from Browne.[116] It is an axis window and so appropriately illustrated the events of the Passion, Death, and Resurrection of Christ in twenty scenes. The window immediately to the north (C/H nII) has scenes from the Nativity and Ministry of Christ, while the two adjacent to the south (C/H sII and sIII) each contain twenty scenes from the lives of St. Peter and St. Paul respectively. Despite the depredations of time and men these windows have retained much of their internal inconographic integrity. Many panels, however, are patched almost out of recognition, and the order of scenes may not be exactly that intended by the designers.

The window to the north of the doorway (C/H nIV) is again dedicated to the legend of one saint, not, as Browne suggested with considerable ingenuity, St. Agnes,[117] but clearly St. Katherine. Her deliverance from torture on the wheels can still be made out in the top panel of the central light.[118]

The pattern of one theme to one window is broken by that to the south of the door (C/H sIV) where each light commemorates a different saint. Saints Margaret, Nicholas, John the Baptist, and Edmund are each represented by four scenes from their legends.[119] The first light contains four scenes listed by Benson as from the life of St. Denys.[120] This identification has been followed without question ever since, but is clearly wrong.[121] The topmost

[115] J. Lafond, 'Le Vitrail en Normandie de 1250 à 1300', *Bulletin monumental*, cxi (1953), 317–57. Illustrated p. 343.

[116] Browne, *Description* 53–62.

[117] Ibid. 33–6.

[118] St. Katherine was also chosen by one of the first chapter donors of nave windows, Peter de Dene. See below, p. 349.

[119] St. Edmund also appears on the contemporary roof paintings, seen by Drake in 1736 (*Ebor.*, p. 476) and taken down in 1798 (Browne, *History*, p. 99). The surviving painted boards are at present not on display.

[120] Benson, *Ancient Painted Glass*, 26.

[121] Wrongly listed as recently as 1972. N. Pevsner, *Buildings of England. York and the East Riding* (1972), 104.

scene (Plate 101) represents the martyrdom of St. Thomas Becket. On the left of the panel are two men in chain-mail, brandishing swords, one of whom cleaves through the skull of the saint as he kneels in the centre with hands clasped in prayer. On the right stands the eyewitness Grim, holding the primatial cross. The panels below confirm this identification as they depict three key incidents in Becket's life. The bottom panel represents his enthronement as archbishop, the second his defence of the criminous clerk before Henry II,[122] and the third his departure into exile.

The reason why the identification of these panels with St. Denys and not with St. Thomas Becket persisted was probably that all previous commentators on the glass were convinced that the remaining window in the building (C/H nIII) depicts the life and miracles of the same Thomas Becket.[123] Once again this is not borne out by the visual evidence. The window has been severely tampered with, there are several intruded panels of no relevance to the iconographic scheme, and the original panels themselves are very hard to read. Nevertheless, it is possible to see that, with the exception of several quite obvious representations of a shrine, there is nothing to connect the glass with Becket or his cult. Many of the incidents, however, are far more comprehensible in the context of the life and miracles of St. William of York. Incidents depicted include the Ouse Bridge Miracle,[124] the Ralph and Besing story,[125] the rescue of a drowning boy,[126] and several cures at the shrine. It is perhaps significant that the cult of St. William received added impetus by the solemn translation of his relics from the nave to the choir at about the time of the insertion of this window.[127] The dedication of a large window to St. William seems more likely than one to the rival miracle-worker at Canterbury, particularly when the latter saint was dealt with in a number of panels more fittingly representative of his relative importance.[128]

The five windows which confront the visitor as he enters the building thus commemorate the five most significant figures in the devotional life of the Minster. The central position is occupied by Christ, who is flanked by the Virgin and St. William on one side and St. Peter and St. Paul on the other. The six saints depicted in the other two windows are all important

[122] This scene is also depicted in the sixteenth-century Becket panels intruded into C/H I. *FAR* (1963), 16.
[123] Browne, *Description* 37; Benson, *Ancient Painted Glass* 17; and Harrison, *Painted Glass* 51.
[124] Fowler, 'Life and Miracles', 240.
[125] Ibid. 265–70.
[126] Ibid. 224.
[127] The translation took place in 1284. Dixon and Raine, *Fasti Ebor.*, p. 228.
[128] Harrison (*Painted Glass* 51) was clearly aware of the incongruity of a Becket window but he failed to make the obvious deduction.

figures and represented either in the Minster relic collection[129] or by altars in the church. This suggests a planned iconographic scheme.

It appears from the evidence of the glass that the windows of the chapter-house vestibule were glazed within a few years of the completion of the chapter-house. Taking their cue from the south-west window of the chapter-house itself (C/H sIV), the glass-painters solved the problem of the tall, narrow lights by providing a series of figures standing under canopies. These, though necessarily taller and thinner, take basically the same simple form as before (Plates 101 and 102). The figure styles are identical, with the same awkwardness of pose and gesture and similar linear drapery. It is interesting to note, in view of the architectural links between the vestibule and S. Urbain at Troyes, some general similarities with the style of the glass-painting there.[130]

The design preserves the scheme of alternating bands of white and coloured panels established in the chapter-house, thus geometric grisaille again forms an important part in the glazing. Amongst the coloured panels there are no narrative scenes, with the exception, if indeed it is, of a Crucifixion in C/H nVI. The various figures who appear beneath the new tall canopies are listed by Benson;[131] particularly interesting are the rare figures of the Fall of the Synagogue and the Triumph of the Church in the third light of C/H sVI. These two personifications often appear in association with the Crucifixion in the thirteenth century.[132] At York they seem to have figured twice in the chapter-house iconography, for the blindfolded figure of the Synagogue, with her broken pennant, appears amongst the remains of the old painted vault.[133]

The nave

The impressive scale and rich ornament of the nave create an atmosphere of splendour and the stained glass gives brilliant colour to the interior. While the nave was being built the Scottish wars were in progress and the consequent presence of the royal court in York is reflected in the sculpture and heraldry, and in the style and scale of the building. The glazing, which dates from a period between 1291, when the foundation-stone was laid in the south-east corner,[134] and 1339, when the windows of the west wall were

[129] Raine, *Fabric Rolls*, pp. 150–2, 219–22.
[130] e.g. the prophets illustrated in *Le Vitrail français*, Pls. 50, VIII.
[131] Benson, *Ancient Painted Glass* 55–62.
[132] E. Mâle, *The Gothic Image* (1913), 189.
[133] See n. 119 above.
[134] J. Harvey, above, p. 149.

commissioned,[135] is the most important scheme of this time to survive in England.

Unity is given to both upper and lower levels by the adoption of aesthetic principles previously observed in the chapter-house. Horizontal bands of colour, in the form of figure panels, canopies, and shields, are set on white glass and run virtually the whole length of the building. These principles were largely maintained except in the west wall and the Jesse window (sXXXIII). With the latter a compromise was reached by setting the stem and the figures on a background of white foliage.

The less sophisticated figure styles of the clerestory, coupled with a complete absence of yellow stain in the original glass at this level, suggest that these windows are for the most part earlier than those in the aisles below, and should perhaps be dated to the second decade of the fourteenth century. Evidence from the heraldry and the identification of donors in the few instances possible tends to support this proposition. Although losses have been sustained, the scheme is basically intact but it has been weakened by the redistribution of several panels to various windows on lower levels. Towards the end of the 1967–72 restoration, re-used twelfth-century glass, an important feature of the clerestory glazing, was removed from the tracery lights and replaced by light-toned modern glass in order to brighten the roof.[136] No doubt there were economic reasons behind the decision to preserve this old glass—high up its antiquated style would not be very apparent—but equally there can be little doubt that the original intention was to concentrate a wide area of dark colour into the tracery openings.[137]

The white glass in the clerestory is unpainted but is leaded into a variety of patterns consisting mainly of chevron and interlace motifs.[138] These designs are remarkably old-fashioned for the fourteenth century and suggest that an earlier pattern was being followed. The closest parallels are with French Cistercian glazing of the second half of the twelfth century, though there are English and German comparisons nearer in date.[139]

---

[135] For the contracts see T. W. French, 'The West Windows of York Minster', *YAJ* xlvii (1975), 81–5.

[136] See above, p. 319, for this re-used glass.

[137] As e.g. in the choir clerestory at Sées Cathedral (Orne, France) in the 1270s. J. Lafond, 'Les Vitraux de la cathédrale de Sées', *Congrès archéologique* (Paris, 1955), 59–83.

[138] Illustrated in Knowles, *York School*, Fig. 62.

[139] French examples include La Benissons-Dieu (Loire) and Pontigny (Yonne). E. von Witzleben, *French Stained Glass* (1968), Ill. 3. For mid-thirteenth-century pattern glazing from the north transept of Salisbury Cathedral see Winston, *Memoirs*, Pl. IV opp. p. 121. An extensive use of such pattern glazing occurs in the choir clerestory of Cologne Cathedral, *c.* 1304–15. This and comparative material is discussed and illustrated in detail in Rode, *Die Mittelalterlichen Glasmalereien des Kölner Domes*, 103 and 115 ff.

Across the plain pattern glazing of the clerestory run two bands of colour. The lower consists of a series of heraldic shields, set on richly diapered grounds and enclosed in barbed quatrefoils. These shields, together with the series carved in stone in the spandrels of the arcade and the carved figures of standing knights in the triforium, constitute a *locus classicus* for the use of heraldry in fourteenth-century decorative schemes. Originally the royal arms of England occupied the central light of each window and were flanked by the arms of northern magnates, many of whom, like the Percys and Vavasours, were intimately connected with the building of the Minster.[140]

One window (SXXIII) contains the arms of members of the de Mauley family of Mulgrave Castle, Yorkshire, above carved stone shields of the same family. A recently restored panel displays the arms of Sir Edmund de Mauley, who fell at Bannockburn in 1314, *or on a bend sable a wyvern argent* (Plate 103).[141] In much restored form he appears holding this shield with five other members of the family, in the Mauley window in the aisle below (sXXXII). In the centre light of this window but in rather better state of preservation kneels the figure of Stephen de Mauley, archdeacon of Cleveland and prebendary of Bugthorpe, who died in 1317.[142] His connection with the Minster suggests that he was the principal figure behind the erection of these windows. Torre records his name beneath his portrait in the Mauley window where one of the panels illustrates the Martyrdom of St. Stephen.[143]

A series of figure panels running across the upper part of the main clerestory lights provides the second band of colour. No clear iconographic programme seems to have been envisaged, indeed one feature is the rather haphazard survival of panels from various twelfth-century windows.[144] Some windows present a sequence of narrative panels such as those removed from one clerestory window (NXXI) to the south transept (sXI–sXV). They illustrate the Joys of the Virgin: the Annunciation, Nativity, Resurrection, Ascension, and Coronation.[145] Viewed from close to, their simple design and bold execution lend them an air of naïvety. The way the head of the ass rises above the Virgin in the Nativity panel (sXIV)

---

[140] For a list of the shields, not entirely correct, see Harrison, *Painted Glass* 202–4.

[141] In the Parliamentary Roll *c.* 1312 his arms are tricked as *de or, a une bende de sable, en la bende iij wyvres de argent.* N. H. Nicholas, *A Roll of Arms of the Reign of Edward the Second* (1829), 61.

[142] He is the only one of the six donors to retain his original head. Four survived until the restoration of 1903. Photograph, YCL, Knowles Coll. For some details of his career see Clay, *Fasti* i. 40 and ii. 18.

[143] Torre, 'Minster', p. 31.

[144] See above, pp. 319 ff.

[145] See above, n. 82.

101 C/H sIV Chapter House, *c.* 1285. The Martyrdom of St. Thomas Becket. Figure subjects under canopies, a design feature which dominates the 14th-C. glass of the Minster, appear here for the first time.

102 C/H nVIII Chapter House Vestibule, *c.* 1290. A king beneath a canopy. The glaziers solved the problem of tall narrow lights by developing the canopy forms first used in C/H sIV (Plate 101).

103 SXXIII South nave clerestory, early 14th-C. Arms of Sir Edmund de Mauley, died 1314. A recently restored shield from the important series in the upper levels of the nave.

and the massive hands given to Christ in the Resurrection (sXIII) may even appear clumsy, but they were intended to be seen from a considerable distance and clarity was essential. The style certainly appears archaic when compared with the work in the aisles below and the iconography harks back to older traditions.[146] Colours are simple and strong with dark reds, blues, greens, pot-yellows, and only a little white.

Two more clerestory panels can be seen in the transept (sXXIII and sXXIV). According to Dean Milner-White they represent the donation of barrels of money to the Minster funds.[147] It is apparent, however, from one panel (sXXIII) (Plate 104) that less pious activities are being depicted. The man on the left holds a scroll PUR:CINK:MARS (For five marks) and a measuring rod and is clearly offering the contents of the barrels on the right to the man behind them who holds out a coin. Some trading scene is obviously intended, probably wine-selling. The companion panel shows the wine merchant seated at a table counting coins, having just sold another barrel.[148] Representations of such trade scenes are rare in English medieval glass but numerous examples occur on the Continent, the most extensive series being at Chartres.[149]

Two panels removed from the north clerestory (NXXI) and now in the south transept (sXVIII and sXIX) show male and female donors kneeling at a shrine. Dean Milner-White suggested that they represented Fitz Urse[150]—presumably Francis Orsini—treasurer of the Minster in 1335, and his wife, although no medieval treasurer would have been represented in lay costume with a wife. Torre described the shield held by the man as *Or a lion passant murrey*,[151] but the present leading does suggest the outline of a bear, though it is patched with modern blue glass.[152] If the shrine is connected with the Minster then it must be that of St. William, but the figure of St. James the Great from this window (Plate 105), dressed as a pilgrim and displaying his scallop badge, suggests the famous shrine at Compostella as an alternative.[153] St. James forms one of a number of

---

[146] In the Nativity the Christ-child is raised up in the crib, well away from contact with his mother.

[147] *FAR* (1961), 17–18.

[148] ibid., Pl. IV.

[149] T. Legge, 'Trade Guild Windows', *Jour. of the Brit. Soc. of Master Glass-Painters*, iv (1931), 51–64. The most obvious parallel is the St. Lubin window in Chartres Cathedral given by the wine-carriers, where a similar hooped cask is depicted. P. Popesco, *La Cathédrale de Chartres* (Chef-d'œuvre du vitrail européen, Paris, 1970), Fig. 39.

[150] *FAR* (1961), 18. But see Le Neve–Jones, vi. 13.

[151] Torre, 'Minster', p. 38.

[152] It might be a patched shield of Percy, *or a lion rampant azure*.

[153] In 1361 one Agnes de Holme left as much money as would be spent by one man on a pilgrimage to Compostella towards the construction of a window which was to have an image of St. James painted in it. Browne, *History*, pp. 149–50.

standing figures of saints in the clerestory, many of them set on similar grounds diapered with naturalistic foliage and surrounded by quatrefoil frames. The figure style is doll-like in its proportions, with bold head painting and drapery folds.[154]

Another window with standing saints (NXXIV) is by a different hand. The style of the heads, draper folds, and diapers is cruder. The panels show St. Peter enthroned, holding his keys, and a church; St. Edmund, crowned and flanked by two massive arrows; a king being blessed by a bishop, possibly Edwin and Paulinus; and two archbishop saints, painted from the same cartoon, representing possibly St. Wilfrid and St. William. Across the base of the window an inscription in leaded letters confirms that it was caused to be made by Robert de Waynflete, abbot of Bardney, Lincolnshire. His abbacy extended from 1280 to 1318 so the glass can be dated with fair certainty to before the latter date.[155]

Some losses have occured in the nave aisle windows,[156] but much of the original glazing has been preserved. The windows on the north side are generally in a better state of preservation than those on the south. However, some of the glass suffers from severe corrosion.

Once again white glass has been used in abundance, though now, as in the chapter-house, in the form of grisaille. Springing from a central stem are balanced designs of naturalistic foliage with recognizable oak and maple leaves. Across the grisaille run two rows of coloured figure panels under canopies and colour is also concentrated into the tracery lights, where some windows preserve their original figures.[157] Coloured glass is also used to relieve the monotony of the white in the borders, where little figures under canopies appear as well as heraldry, leaf ornament, and animal motifs.[158] The emphasis on heraldry, already seen in the clerestory, is maintained by setting brilliantly coloured shields on the grisaille. Little medallions with figures and grotesques are also used.

Though the over-all approach to the glazing was carefully controlled, once again there was no planned iconographic scheme. Subject-matter was left to the individual interests of the donors of each window. As elsewhere

---

[154] This style can be paralleled to some extent in the late-thirteenth-century 'Westminster Bestiary' (Westminster Abbey Library MS. 23), which belonged to the Franciscan Friary in York. (J. Armitage-Robinson and M. R. James, *The Manuscripts of Westminster Abbey* (Cambridge, 1909), 77–81) see e.g. fo. 32.

[155] For Waynflete see *Monasticon* i (1846), 625.

[156] See above, p. 315.

[157] For Peckitt's contribution to the tracery see below, pp. 387–389.

[158] This use of border figures in niches is paralleled in manuscript painting, e.g. the Queen Mary Psalter. G. Warner, *The Queen Mary Psalter* (1912). For subsequent developments in Minster glass see below, pp. 356–357.

104 sXXIII South transept (ex NXXIII), early 14th-C. This panel, shown in its pre-restoration state, is one of a pair of trade scenes probably connected with wine selling.

105 ex NXXI North nave clerestory, early 14th-C. St. James the Great. Although not nimbed this figure probably represents the saint robed as a pilgrim to his shrine at Compostella. The squat proportions and extremely bold painting are typical of the clerestory figures designed to be seen from a distance.

106 nXXIII Heraldic Window, north nave aisle,
c. 1310–20. Head of the donor, Peter de Dene. In
spite of corrosion this remains a good example of
the simple painting style of the nave aisles.

107 nXXIII Heraldic Window, north nave aisle,
c. 1310–20. St. Katherine, visited by an angel, is
adored in prison by Porphyry and the Empress
Faustina. In the borders are heraldic lions and
eagles.

in the Minster these were mainly clerics connected with the foundation, though laymen also made contributions.

The importance of the donor is well demonstrated in the Heraldic window (nXXIII). This was given by Peter de Dene shown kneeling under a canopy at the base of the centre light (Plate 106) and whose name is recorded in an inscription beneath. De Dene was an important Minster cleric. He attended Parliament and enjoyed the patronage of Archbishop Greenfield, becoming his vicar-general in 1309 and again in 1313.[159] His choice of subject for the window was St. Katherine, a saint of international importance, relics of whom were kept in the Minster.[160] Her legend, which has the flavour of a romance, begins in the window with her appearance before the Emperor Maxentius and continues with scenes of her torture on the wheels, imprisonment, and martyrdom. Maxentius, a thoroughly evil character, is shown seated on a splendid throne with a little green devil perched on his shoulder. The panel of the saint in prison (Plate 107) shows Maxentius's queen and his general Porphyry, who were converted by St. Katherine, kneeling before her cell. The elaborate turrets, battlements, and roofs of the prison show for the first time in York glass some feeling of perspective. The artist, possibly more used to drawing Annunciation scenes, has included an angel with an *Ave Maria* scroll.[161] The series culminates in the tracery with panels, unfortunately poorly preserved, of the saint's burial on Mount Sinai.[162]

It is the heraldic aspect of the window which has justly claimed most attention. A set of eight shields, set on the grisaille panels, proclaim the arms of England and the monarch's connections with other royal houses in Europe.[163] This emphasis is continued in the borders with heraldic eagles and lions and a series of small figures under canopies. These latter commence with armed knights in chain-mail and heraldic surcoats,[164] who are followed by members of the royal families of England and France (Plate 108 and frontispiece). At the top are figures possibly of a Knight Hospitaller and Templar, and censing and musician angels.

---

[159] Winston, *Memoirs* 265–72, sketches his colourful career.

[160] Raine, *Fabric Rolls*, pp. 151–2.

[161] The angel should be attending to the wounds of the saint—see *Golden Legend*, vii. 22.

[162] For the St. Katherine panels at Fécamp see above, p. 339. Panels with iconographic details in common are illustrated by Lafond, 'Les Vitraux de l'abbaye de la Trinité de Fécamp'. L'Abbaye bénédictine de Fécamp. Ouvrage scientifique du XIIIe centenaire, 658–1953 (Fécamp, 1958). Three St. Katherine panels from the Bedern Chapel are described by Torre, 'Minster', pp. 1227–30, and F. Harrison, 'The Bedern Chapel, York', *YAJ* xxvii (1924), 197–209. This glass was removed in 1816 to the Minster but its present whereabouts is unknown. W. Hargrove, *History and Description of the Ancient City of York*, ii (1818), 150–1.

[163] The shields are identified in Winston, *Memoirs* 263.

[164] Clifford, Percy, Ros, Mowbray, Warrin, Beauchamp, and Clare (ibid. 264–5).

The brilliant colouring of the window is partly achieved by the use of yellow stain to highlight some of the white glass. It is used on only one main head, that of Porphyry (Plate 107), but is used with great skill in the canopies and borders to colour small details such as sword hilts and spurs (Frontispiece).[165]

On the basis of the heraldry, Winston judged the probable date of the window to be *c.* 1306–7.[166] The heraldry may, however, be retrospective, as in the earliest documented use of armorial glass in England.[167] If Winston's date is accepted the window predates the earliest firmly dated example of the use of yellow stain which is 1313.[168] Peter de Dene's prebendal stall of Grindale was not reallocated until 1322[169] so that a date perhaps as late as the 1320s is possible. The window opposite, which has many features in common with the Heraldic window, is probably a memorial to Archbishop William de Greenfield, who died in December 1315.[170] Perhaps Peter de Dene looked back to the courtly world with which he had been associated and wished to be permanently identified with it. If this were so, a date based on the heraldry would be misleading.

The adjacent window (nXXIV) presents a very different world view which again reflects the concerns of the donor, Richard Tunnoc. He occupies the lower half of the subject panels, kneeling in the centre and presenting a model of the window to St. William (Plate 109). Tunnoc, clearly a man of considerable wealth and influence, was a goldsmith and bellfounder who lived in Stonegate close to the Minster.[171] In 1328 he became one of only three York citizens to found a perpetual chantry in the

---

[165] For yellow stain see Ch. IV, n. 15 above, and also J. Lafond, *Trois études sur la technique du vitrail* (Rouen, 1943), 39–116.

[166] Winston, *Memoirs* 277.

[167] In 1247 Henry III ordered his own arms and those of 'the late Count of Provence' for the Hall of Rochester Castle. P. A. Newton, 'Three Panels of Heraldic Glass in the Burrell Collection', *Scottish Art Review*, viii, no. 4 (1962), 13–29, quoting *Cal. Lib. Rolls*, 1245–51, p. 113.

[168] At Le Mesnil-Villeman (Manche France); J. Lafond, 'Un Vitrail du Mesnil-Villeman', *Bulletin de la société nationale des antiquaires de France* (1954), 93–5. This glass is presumably the product of a Rouen workshop and not the first time stain had been used.

[169] Le Neve–Jones, vi. 54.

[170] Since Browne's misreading of the inscription (*Description* 86) the window has been described as a memorial to Archbishop Walter de Gray who died in 1255. Enough survives, albeit fragmentarily, at least to show that this is incorrect and to suggest, more appropriately, that it commemorates Archbishop William de Greenfield, who died in 1315. The inscription appears to run: *Priez pur l[e tres reverent] mestre Wil . . . ercevesk' d[e] . . . eglise.* A shield at present at the top of the centre light shows an odd combination of colour on colour, *vert a cross gules*, but Torre recorded it ('Minster', p. 29) as *vert a cross argent* on which appear to be *five mitres gules*. This could well be the arms of Greenfield containing a punning reference to his name.

[171] For his career as bailiff 1320–21 and M.P. 1327 see YCL, MS. R. M. Skaife, Civic Officials of York, iii. 782.

108 nXXIII Heraldic window, north nave aisle, *c.* 1310–20. Canopy with figures of
the kings of France and England. The heraldic emphasis of this window makes it one
of the outstanding monuments of the period.

109 nXXIV Bell Founders Window, north nave aisle, *c.* 1325. The donor, Richard Tunnoc, presents a model of the window to St. William of York. The canopy is of bells and in the borders are the remnants of ape musicians.

Minster.[172] The chantry was attached to the altar of St. Thomas the Martyr, before which Tunnoc was buried in 1330. According to Raine this was situated to the north-west of the lantern pillar[173] so it is quite possible that the window was erected in connection with the chantry.

The panels flanking the donor are interesting examples of the trade scenes already encountered in the clerestory.[174] On the right (Plate 110) a bell is being cast, the molten metal flowing into a mould. One figure, possibly female to judge by the chaplet, operates a pair of bellows with her hands, while another figure—originally with a similar headdress—treads them vigorously up and down. In the panel on the left[175] the finished bell is being tuned by filing the metal.[176] Bells dominate the whole composition. They hang from the main arches of the canopies which themselves become niches filled with bells. They are also set on the grisaille, in the borders of the outer lights, and in the tracery, flanking the figures of saints Peter, Paul, and Andrew.

The St. William theme of the window is continued in the upper band of subject panels which, though severely mutilated, clearly represent the principal miracle associated with his cult. When Ouse Bridge collapsed in 1154, under the weight of the throng of people who had arrived to greet him, St. William miraculously saved all those who had been thrown into the river. The scene of disaster and the saint on his horse are still discernible in the confusion of these panels. St. William's shrine, one of the focal points of the Minster, once stood in the nave near the south-west lantern pillar and may well have influenced Tunnoc in his choice of subject.

In Tunnoc's window and that of Peter de Dene, local saint contrasts with international saint, and trade scene with heraldic display, and in the border decoration of the centre lights the counterpart of de Dene's courtly figures are ape musicians (Plate 109). The complete absence of yellow stain in the Bellfounder's window suggests that it came from a more conservative workshop. Certainly the figure style is stiffer and the heads, with their very distinctive eyes and ears, appear rather more hieratic than in the Heraldic window. The same head types, heraldic grounds, and grisaille designs can be seen further down the aisle in the Penancers' window (nXXVII) (Plate

---

[172] *CPatR, 1327–30*, p. 309. R. B. Dobson, 'The Foundation of Perpetual Chantries by the Citizens of Mediaeval York', *Studies in Church History*, iv (Ecclesiastical Hist. Soc., Leiden, 1967), 22–38.
[173] Raine, *Fabric Rolls*, pp. 302–4.
[174] See above, p. 345.
[175] Illustrated in Gibson, *Noble City*, Pl. 9.
[176] For a twelfth-century description of these processes see Theophilus, *De Diversis Artibus*, ed. C. R. Dodwell (1961), pp. 150–9.

111), probably also from the third decade of the century.[177] Here, however, there is a slight use of yellow stain in the archbishop medallions[178] and on the coins collected, presumably as fines, by some of the seated penancers in the borders. The scenes in which they brandish scourges over the heads of the unfortunate sinners provide an interesting variant on the trade window idea.

In another north aisle window (nXXV) male and female donors dressed as pilgrims appear with their horses on either side of a figure of St. Peter (Plate 112).[179] As in the clerestory and west window he holds a key and a model of a church. This designer's eye for detail can be seen in the little profile heads, which appear with fleurs-de-lis on the cushion, and the lion's-head mask which decorates the end of St. Peter's pallium. Even though yellow stain is again absent, a greater use of white glass and lighter tones of colour, coupled with the good state of preservation of the glass, make this window particularly bright and brilliant in effect. The glass's natural brilliance is enhanced by the merciful lack of quarry back-glazing in this window. This type of protective glazing cuts down the amount of light coming through the window and, in the case of the Heraldic and Bellfounder's windows, makes dark glass even darker.

The upper row of panels in the Pilgrimage window depicts the scene on Calvary, spread across all three lights. A suffering Christ hangs on a green cross in the central panel, flanked by Longinus and Stephaton. The left-hand panel contains the swooning figure of the Virgin while that on the right shows St. John the Evangelist, the Centurion, and a Jew.[180] The Passion imagery is continued in the tracery where Christ sits in majesty, flanked by angels holding Passion emblems.

Perhaps the major interest of this window is the way in which it so clearly demonstrates the close interaction between different art forms in the Middle Ages, especially the influence which manuscript-painting had on the more monumental art of glass-painting. In some respects the window is very nearly the page of a manuscript transformed into glass. The border

[177] The west window of the north aisle in Patrick Brompton Church, N. Yorks., contains fragments of glass by the Bellfounder's workshop. The naked figures suggest a 'Doom' probably from the east window. The architecture is dated 1310–30 in *VCH Yorkshire* i. 337.

[178] One archbishop has wandered into nXXV.

[179] The saint's head and tiara are replacements. It is possible the window was given in place of a pilgrimage to Rome on the lines of that given by Agnes de Holme—see above, n. 153.

[180] As a result of a wrong identification of these scenes by Milner-White (*FAR*(1948), p. 36), a fifteenth-century head of Christ with crown of thorns was inserted into the panel with the Virgin. A similar arrangement across three lights of a Calvary *c.* 1300 can be seen at Evreux Cathedral, chapel XII on the south side of the ambulatory. The Evreux glass offers some general parallels to the Minster nave glazing—see M. Baudot, 'Les Verrières de la cathédrale d'Evreux', *Nouvelles de l'Eure*, no. 27 (Paris, 1966), 26–43.

111 nXXVII Penancers Window, north nave aisle, *c.* 1325. Men and women before a Penancer. The very distinctive head types are common to this and the Bell Founders Window.

110 nXXIV Bell Founders Window, north nave aisle, *c.* 1325. Casting a bell. One of the two bell founding scenes which flank the donor.

running across the base of the window is clearly derived from the *bas-de-page* scenes which are such a prominent feature of contemporary manuscripts, particularly those of the so-called East Anglian style. In the first light (Plate 113) a fox reads from a lectern to a cock who gazes upwards oblivious of his fate. This theme, extremely popular in medieval art, was treated in a variety of modes and media.[181] Next comes a monkey funeral cortège led by a hand-bell ringer and crucifer. Four apes carry the draped bier on their shoulders, while a smaller one pushes against the base of the coffin. The iconography of this lively and amusing scene is derived from representations of the Funeral of the Virgin. In this apocryphal story the Apostles carrying the coffin were attacked by a Jew who tried to push the bier to the ground. Instead his hands stuck fast to the coffin until he agreed to become a Christian.[182] The theme also appears in the glass of the chapter-house and Lady Chapel clerestory (Plates 100 and 129).[183] On the right of the panel the interest in *babewyns* continues with a scene in which they play one of their most frequent roles, that of the doctor. A reclining patient is ministered to by one monkey, while another examines a urine sample in a flask (Plate 114). The same idea is carried over into the main borders, where delightful monkey doctors, monkeys with owls on their wrists aping falconers, and squirrels eating nuts can be seen.[184] At the bottom of the centre light Reynard the Fox reappears, this time with a goose in his mouth. He is hotly pursued by a woman armed with a distaff, again a popular *bas-de-page* theme.[185] Finally, at the foot of the third light, an archer and hounds hunt a stag. The animals are not in their original order, and, rather inappropriately, a heraldic lion from an adjacent window has been intruded into the scene.[186]

These fancies and drolleries are also evident in the medallions which occupy the middle of the grisaille panels. Here a series of whimsical monsters, griffins, and centaurs[187] mingle with genre scenes which include

---

[181] K. Varty, *Reynard the Fox* (Leicester, 1967), 51–9 and illustrations.

[182] M. R. James, *The Apocryphal New Testament* (1924), 214.

[183] The incident formed one of the plays in the York Mystery Cycle where the characters represented four apostles carrying the shrine, Fergus hanging beneath it, two other Jews, and an angel (*York Plays*, ed. L. T. Smith (New York, 1885), xxvii). The play was abolished in 1485 and no text survives. Manuscript illustrations of animal funerals are common in this period; e.g. Gorleston Psalter, BL, Add. MS. 49622 illustrated in J. Evans, *English Art 1307–1461* (Oxford, 1949), Pl. 24b.

[184] See H. W. Janson, *Apes and Ape Lore in the Middle Ages and Renaissance* (1952).

[185] Varty, *Reynard*, pp. 31–42.

[186] Cf. Peterborough Psalter, Brussels, Bib. Roy. MS. 9961–2. fo. 14. Illustrated in L. F. Sandler, *The Peterborough Psalter in Brussels and other Fenland MSS* (1974), p. 89, Pl. 296.

[187] For parallels in glass see J. Lafond, *Les Vitraux de l'église St. Ouen de Rouen* (CVMA France, vol. iv–2, Tome 1 1970), Pl. 1. For the same themes in sculpture see Mâle, *Gothic Image*, pp. 59–61, illustrating the Portail des Libraires in Rouen. See also the fragments of St. William's shrine in Yorkshire Museum.

◁ **112** nXXV Pilgrimage Window, north nave aisle, *c.* 1320–30. St. Peter, unfortunately with an over-small restored head and tiara, enthroned as patron of the Minster and holding the key of heaven and a model of his church.

a woman seizing a man by the ear and two men wrestling. It is only necessary to look at the fine series of carvings flanking the windows, together with those along the west wall and on the roof bosses, to realize that in their love of the fanciful or grotesque the glass-painters of the nave were expressing something typical of their age.[188]

Although poorly preserved the window in the penultimate bay of the north aisle (nXXVIII) forms an interesting link between the earlier glass to the east and the new style which appeared with the west-window glazing in 1339. Only two panels in the bottom three rows are original and these are very fragmentary. They represent the Virgin and Child and an unidentified figure with the inserted head of a female saint.[189] The figures in the Annunciation, Nativity, and Adoration of the Magi panels higher up are somewhat better preserved. In the tracery the subject panels are completed by a Coronation of the Virgin, flanked by censing angels.

Something of the greater elegance of the figures compared with those further east can be seen in the better-preserved Annunciation panel. The original lead line preserves the gently curving stance of the Virgin, and more subtle washes of paint for the modelling of the heads produces softer features and flowing hair. Dark tones are combined with a greater use of white and stain to give a distinctive colour effect. One unusual technical feature is the application of stain to the inside of the glass in several panels. This conveniently preserves it from exterior corrosion.

Glass very close in style and design, again using some stain on the inner surface, clearly by the same workshop can be seen in St. Martin-cum-Gregory church, York.[190] It can be dated on chantry evidence to *c.* 1335.[191] A similar date, a few years before the glazing of the west wall, would be appropriate for the Minster window.

The west window (wI), with its superb curvilinear tracery, is one of the most imposing examples of medieval glass-painting in the country. Its monumental figures and carefully balanced colouring render it more successful as a piece of design than the east window.

Archbishop Melton's register records his donation of 100 marks for the glazing of the west wall windows on 4 February 1338–9.[192] A contract was subsequently drawn up between the Custos of the Fabric and a glass-painter called Robert, possibly, as Knowles suggested, the Robert Ketelbarn

[188] Note particularly the contemporary carving over the north-west door of the Minster where Reynard appears pursued by a hunter, also two men wrestling and a man and woman quarrelling.
[189] Milner-White's suggestion (*FAR* (1950), pp. 28–9), that the Virgin and Child were in the centre, and that the other figure may be a donor, is probably correct.
[190] e.g. sII and nVI. See *RCHM York* iii. 21 and 24, Pls. 29, 31, 114, and 116.
[191] Ibid. 21, quoting *CPatR, 1330–4*, pp. 370–1.
[192] French, 'West Windows', quoting BIHR, R1 9 fo. 81.

who was free of the city in 1325.[193] The contract survives in transcripts by Torre.[194] A similar document referring to the west windows of the aisles (sXXXVI and nXXX) has caused much speculation.[195] A convincing solution proposed by T. W. French transforms the vicar choral (*vicarii*), who was supposed to have been one party to the agreement, into a glass-painter (*vitrarii*), Thomas de Bouesden.[196]

If two masters were at work on the west-wall glazing, as this interpretation suggests, they were clearly working in close co-operation and from the same designs. No technical or stylistic peculiarities differentiate the one from the other. Use of pot-yellow for some crockets and yellow stain for others, if that can be claimed as an inconsistency, occurs within the same window (nXXX).[197] Though the whole scheme may be the labour of many hands, the final impression is one of harmony and unity.

When drawing up the iconographic scheme Archbishop Melton appropriately chose to commemorate in the main window eight of his predecessors. They stand in full pontificals with their hands raised in blessing. There are basically four figure designs arranged in the sequence ab ab cd cd. Lost inscriptions, recorded by Torre, enable some of the figures to be identified. They include saints John of Beverley, Thomas of Bayeux, Wilfrid, Oswald, William, and Sewall de Bovill.[198] Gent, presumably following Widdrington's seventeenth-century manuscript, omitted Thomas, but inserted Paulinus, Bosa, and Egbert alongside the others mentioned by Torre.[199] Of the four doubtful attributions, Paulinus, founder of the Church in York and a properly canonized saint, must have been included. St. Bosa and St. Egbert are represented elsewhere in York glass but, as builder of the Norman cathedral, Thomas of Bayeux could justly claim a place among the other founders.[200]

In the central row stand apostles, originally twelve in number, forming a balanced series with pairs placed in the first and last two lights. In the

---

[193] Knowles, *York School* p. 31. For possible identification of these Roberts with Robert le Glazenwright, Robert the Glazier, and Robert le Verreour mentioned in York documents of the 1320s and 1330s see French, 'West Windows' 82–3.

[194] French, 'West Windows', pp. 81–2, quoting Torre, 'Minster'.

[195] Knowles, *York School*, pp. 31–2.

[196] French, 'West Windows', pp. 83–5.

[197] The variation in colour of crockets was noted by Knowles, *York School*, p. 71, who claimed that the aisle windows were later in date than the main west window.

[198] Torre, 'Minster', p. 23.

[199] Gent, *History*, p. 144. Sir T. Widdrington, *Analecta Eboracensia*, ed. C. Caine (1897).

[200] Bosa appears in Minster NXIV, first light with inscription; *San Bosa archieps*. Egbert appears in St. Martin-cum-Gregory sV tracery.

113 nXXV Pilgrimage Window, north nave aisle, *c.* 1320–30. The cock and the fox, the monkey's funeral, and monkey doctors. A love of humour and the grotesque pervades much of the art of the nave. The monkey's funeral, derived from the iconography of the Funeral of the Virgin, is perhaps the most outstanding example. A further example from the borders of the window is the monkey doctor (plate 114, left).

114 nXXV Pilgrimage Window, north nave aisle. *c.* 1320–30. Monkey Doctor holding up a urine flask. Such *babewyns* were very popular.

115 wI Great West Window, *c.* 1339. By Master Robert and atelier. St. John the Evangelist, upper part. Amongst the best preserved panels in the Minster, this well illustrates the Parisian elegance of Master Robert's style.

seventh light, where Torre recorded 'two old apostles'[201], the upper panel is replaced by part of a deacon saint of similar style and date.[202] The presence of St. Paul alongside St. Peter in the centre of the group means that one apostle, probably Matthias, is excluded. Not all the saints hold attributes which would clearly identify them.

The idea of proclaiming the saints of the Minster beneath the row of Apostles was a particularly effective piece of religious propaganda, well suited to one of the major windows of the church. Variations on it can be seen in the bottom row of the east window (I) and in the glazing of the south axis wall (sXX–sXXII).[203] To honour one's predecessors is an idea which requires very little prompting, but in view of the close stylistic parallels which exist between Master Robert's glass and that of the Rouen-Paris area, it is possible that the choice may have been influenced by two similar series of *c.* 1310–20 in the Lady Chapel at Rouen Cathedral and the south transept of Meaux Cathedral.[204]

Higher up the west window are five scenes, again forming a Joys of the Virgin sequence: the Annunciation, Nativity, Resurrection, Ascension, and, at the top of the central lights, the Coronation of the Virgin. The disposition of the scenes in pairs across the lights, ignoring the stonework, though more common on the Continent is seldom seen in England at this date.[205] This element in the design no doubt influenced the iconography in which several ideas are introduced into York glass for the first time. In the Annunciation, Gabriel, unlike his counterpart in the aisles, goes down on bended knee before the Virgin. In the Nativity panels the Christ-child is held by the Virgin who is now seated and offering her breast to her son. This more maternal representation is paralleled in the adjacent window to the north (nXXX), where the standing Virgin gives suck to the child.[206] In this window the canopy figures of kings and prophets, which culminate at the top in a small figure of the Virgin, suggests a relationship with the Tree of Jesse motif. The companion window in the south aisle (sXXXVI) also

[201] Torre, 'Minster', p. 23.

[202] This figure, perhaps connected with the other deacon saints which may have come from the nave (see below, p. 387), was probably inserted in Peckitt's restoration of 1757. It was certainly there in 1859 when it was seen by Browne: *Description*, p. 92.

[203] See above, p. 332.

[204] For Rouen see J. Lafond, 'Le Vitrail du XIVᵉ siècle en France' in L. Lefrançois-Pillion, *L'Art du XIVᵉ siècle en France* (Paris, 1954), pp. 187–238, and F. Perrot, *Le Vitrail à Rouen* (Rouen, 1972), pp. 18–20 and Pl. 4. The Meaux glass, nearly all restoration, is mentioned by Lafond, in Lefrançois-Pillion, 210.

[205] Other examples in the nave include the Crucifixion (sXXVI and nXXV) and St. William crossing Ouse Bridge (nXXIV).

[206] It was also depicted in a roof boss in the nave, slightly later in date. The original is illustrated in Browne, *History* ii. Pl. CI. The Victorian copy has replaced this aspect by substituting a feeding-bottle.

shows evidence of this growing tenderness. Mourning angels in attitudes of extreme sorrow are depicted flying about the crucified Christ.[207]

The archbishops and apostles shown in the west window, standing on plinths and beneath canopies, are conceived in terms of sculpture. Flanking the window are architectural niches once presumably adorned with statuary so that the window may once have formed the centrepiece of an elaborate composition in glass and stone.

The high quality of Master Robert's work is best illustrated by those figures least touched by Peckitt. Finest of all is that of St. John the Evangelist, who retains his original head. It is one of the best preserved medieval figures in the Minster (Plate 115). The bold painting of the head, softened by washes of paint, develops a type already present in one of the aisle windows (nXXVIII). The drapery style, with its deeply curving folds reinforced by the original lead lines, is almost tactile in quality, especially where the deep folds hang from the left hand beneath the mantle.[208] The illusion of depth created in the drapery is also a feature of the plinths and canopies, especially those over the archbishops where the underside of a ribbed vault can be seen (Plate 116). These simple attempts at perspective continue with the battlements surmounting some of the canopies, and in architectural features such as crib and tomb in the narrative panels.

One of the most impressive features of the window is the great wealth of carefully executed ornament, none of which interferes with the legibility of the design from a distance. The Evangelist's mantle has a hem decorated with a band of quatrefoils scratched out of the paint and highlighted with yellow stain. This motif recurs time and time again both in the drapery and architecture. The vestments of the archbishops, richly ornamented, often with heraldic motifs, become vehicles for brilliant effects in yellow stain which is used on blue glass as well as white. The richly coloured grounds against which the figures stand leave the naturalistic ornament of the earlier nave glass behind for tightly curling arabesques with frond, trefoil, quatrefoil, and kidney diapers.[209] This change may also be seen in the bottom-row panels of the window. These panels raise the archbishops up from the sill[210] and form a lattice work of frond-like foliage.

[207] This is perhaps one aspect of Italianate influence on Master Robert's work—sorrowing angels appear in the Crucifixion panel of Duccio's *Maesta* illustrated in Schiller, *Iconography of Christian Art*, 2 (1972), Pl. 511. Cf. pp. 379 ff. below.

[208] See, e.g. the deep folds at the bottom of the Virgin's robe carved over the entrance to St. Sepulchre's Chapel.

[209] For detailed illustrations see French, 'Observations', Pls. XVb and XVIIa from the Lady Chapel clerestory. Also *RCHM York* iii, Pl. 29 from St. John's Micklegate now Minster (nXXI–nXXII) which has all the hallmarks of Master Robert's style reduced to a smaller scale.

[210] For coloured drawings of three foliage panels see Bell and Gould, 'Selections of Painted and Stained Glass from York', *Quarterly Papers on Architecture*, ii, ed. J. Weale (1844).

In the tracery the vast majority of lights are filled with white trefoil foliage. The increased use of white glass and yellow stain is one of the more obvious features of the west-wall glazing. From the contract it is clear that Master Robert was paid 12d. per foot for coloured glass and only half that amount for white.[211] The decision to fill the tracery openings with foliage, rather than a complex scheme of figure subjects like the 'Dooms' at Selby and Carlisle, meant that besides allowing the main body of the church to be brightly lit, the over-all cost could be kept down.

The stylistic sources of the west-end glazing, as so often with the Minster glass, lie in northern France. A series of windows of the first quarter of the fourteenth century survives in Normandy, products of workshops in Rouen. In Rouen itself, besides glass in the Lady Chapel and south transept of the cathedral of *c.* 1310–20, there is an extensive set of windows, completed before 1334, in the choir of the abbey church of St. Ouen.[212] Further afield are important windows in the choir clerestory of Evreux Cathedral and at La Mailleraye, which was made originally for Jumièges Abbey.[213] As M. Aubert has pointed out, in style this glass is very representative of the art of Paris where unfortunately so little glass of this date survives. At Rouen the elegant figures, with deeply modelled drapery folds, the lightly constructed canopies, and the greater use of white glass and yellow stain set the tone which Master Robert was to follow at York. At times the parallels between the St. Ouen glass and the west window come very close. Scenes such as the Annunciation[214] are very similar in design, although in the French version Gabriel is standing. Both occupy two lights. Details such as the head types, drapery, and frond diaper confirm the general similarities.[215] At Evreux, in a window of *c.* 1325, the donor Canon Raoul de Ferrières is seen kneeling before a standing figure of the Virgin who gives suck to the Christ-child very much like her slightly later counterpart in the west wall of the Minster (nXXX).

Master Robert introduced the latest Parisian styles into the Minster glass. These were to be developed in a number of windows now for the most part in the Lady Chapel.[216] He was also to carry the style outwards to those areas of the north of England traditionally dependent on York for their stained glass. In the east window at Acaster Malbis is what almost amounts to a

---

[211] See n. 135 above.

[212] For the cathedral see n. 204 above. For St. Ouen see J. Lafond, *Les Vitraux de l'église Saint-Ouen de Rouen.*

[213] For Evreux see n. 180 above. For the glass formerly at Jumièges see J. Lafond, 'La Peinture sur verre à Jumièges', *Jumièges congrès scientifique du XIIIe centenaire* (Rouen, 1954), pp. 529–36.

[214] Illustrated in Lafond, *Saint-Ouen*, Pls. 2 and III.

[215] French, 'Observations', p. 89, points out other close parallels between Rouen and the Minster.

[216] See below, pp. 370 ff.

Minster window reduced in scale.[217] At Selby Abbey the east window was filled with a Tree of Jesse by Master Robert probably shortly after the Minster west window. In the curvilinear tracery so reminiscent of the Minster design was placed a 'Doom'.[218] Further afield in St. Cuthbert's, Carlisle, Cumbria, is a large-scale head and some canopy work again of west window type, which may have been removed from the cathedral close by.

The choir and Lady Chapel

It is hardly an exaggeration to say that the choir of York Minster is dominated by the great east window. The contract for glazing this vast area was drawn up in 1405 between the dean and chapter and one John Thornton of Coventry, glazier. The original document does not survive but there are two copies, one by Torre[219] and one by Matthew Hutton.[220] It stipulates that the work was to be finished in three years and Thornton was required 'to portraiture the said window with historical images and other painted work in the best manner and form that he possibly could. And likewise paynt the same where need required according to the ordination of the Dean and Chapter'.[221] Two tracery lights bear Thornton's monogram and the date 1408, a rare example of an English glazier signing his work.

It is the largest window in the Minster, being 76 feet high and 32 feet wide, containing about 1,680 square feet of glass. It was an immense project to carry out in the space of three years and the fact that it was accomplished on time suggests that Thornton had a considerable number of assistant glaziers working under his direction.

The general condition of the glass is extremely good. The main light panels are the best preserved, there being very little replacement glass except in the blue- and ruby-coloured backgrounds. The tracery lights are more disturbed and less complete. The last restoration of the window took place between 1942 and 1952 when mistakes made in earlier restorations were corrected and alien intrusions removed.

The over-all design of the window is unusual and combines four different series of scenes into a unified composition. The iconographic programme

[217] The window includes the remains of an aspostle series and a Christ in Majesty under canopies. There is also a panel from the base of the window reminiscent of the lowest row in the Minster west window. The ornamental panel is illustrated in Bell and Gould, 'Selections', Pl. VI.

[218] See J. T. Fowler, 'The Great East Window, Selby Abbey', *YAJ* v (1879), 331–49. Following the fire of 1906 the glass seems to have been virtually if not entirely replaced. Portions including some original glass are now in the sacristy.

[219] YML, L.I.2.

[220] BM, Harleian MS. 6971 fo. 141[v].

[221] The full text is available in Benson, *Ancient Painted Glass*, pp. 86–7.

has to be read from the top of the window down to the bottom, a reversal of the usual order. In the apex tracery light God is seated holding a book inscribed with the initials A and Ω for 'Ego sum alpha et omega'.[222] The tracery lights contain, in descending order, the Nine Orders of Angels, the Patriarchs, the Israelite worthies, the Prophets, and Christian Saints. A great cloud of witnesses to the power of God.

The narrative panels in the main lights illustrate the words Alpha and Omega, 'the beginning and the end'. The first three rows contain twenty-seven scenes from the Old Testament, beginning with the Days of Creation and continuing down to the Death of Absalom. The next nine rows contain eighty-one scenes from the Revelation of St. John.

The bottom row of panels depicts legendary and historical figures associated with the history of Christianity in the north of England and the see of York. In the centre light, kneeling before an altar and identified by his coat of arms on the frontal, is the figure of Walter Skirlaw, bishop of Durham from 1388 until his death in 1406. In January 1398 Skirlaw, a Yorkshireman and one time archdeacon of the East Riding, was elected archbishop of York only to find, a month later, his election set aside in favour of Richard Scrope.[223] However, the execution of Scrope in 1405 may have tempted Skirlaw to press his candidature again, this time considerably reinforced by the vast gift of the east window. The York vacancy led to the by now familiar contest between king and pope and Skirlaw died before the matter was resolved. Nevertheless, the contract for the east window had been signed and the work was under way.[224]

The window is a masterpiece of design and invention, a major monument not only of English, but also of European glass-painting at the time.

Thornton's style and techniques are consistent throughout the whole window. In the figures there is a predominance of white glass and yellow stain which makes a striking contrast with the rich blue or ruby backgrounds. The compositions display much originality, for example the panel of St. John writing to the Seven Churches (Rev. 1–3) (Plate 117). The seven churches are represented as seven archbishops standing in niches in the walls of one great church. The design shows much interest in three-dimensional representation and empirical perspective. The north wall of the church is set along a diagonal line so that the west wall is also shown. The central tower is similarly set. The architectural niches of the

---

[222] Rev. 21:6.

[223] Le Neve–Jones, vi.4.

[224] The chronology of Skirlaw's donation is reviewed by Knowles, *York School*, pp. 219–20, and more recently by T. W. French, 'The Dating of the Lady Chapel in York Minster', *AntJ* lii (1972), 317.

116 wI Great West Window, *c.* 1339. By Master Robert and atelier. Two Archbishops of York. These life-size figures stand like statuary in three dimensional niches.

117 I Great East Window, 1405–8. By John Thornton and atelier. St. John's vision of the Seven Churches. (Rev. 2 and 3). The unity of the early church expressed in terms of seven niches on a single building.

archbishops are carefully modelled so that there is an interaction of light and dark to stimulate the eye.

Thornton's powerful sense of design is also apparent in the way he presents the narrative of the twenty-four elders, first seated on their thrones and then casting down their crowns before the Throne of God (Rev. 4). His unified composition spreads over three lights. In the central panel is God ringed by the symbols of the Evangelists and attendant angels. To the left the Elders sit enthroned and then, in the right-hand panel, kneel and offer their crowns (Plate 118). All attention is focused on God. Again the diagonal line plays an important part in the organization of the composition. The Elders are disposed along two diverging diagonals, enabling Thornton to show the figures at various different angles, frontal, three-quarters, profile, and back views.

While the individual panels are masterpieces of design, the over-all effect is perhaps not quite a success. Modern leaded repair work and the shadows cast on the glass by the exterior protective glazing make it difficult to appreciate the original impact of the glass. Moreover, the panels are so remote from the eye that all the fine detailed painting cannot be seen and the power of the compositions is diminished by the distance. Here the fault lies not perhaps with Thornton but with whoever formulated such an extensive iconographic programme to be contained in a single window.

The east window is dated 1405–8;[225] the indenture for the glazing states that Thornton, the master glazier responsible, came from Coventry. The design and execution are extremely sophisticated and evidently the work of an experienced artist. It has been assumed that this style of painting and design were personal to Thornton and that with the east window he established a 'York style'. In consequence much glass in various parts of England produced in the first quarter of the fifteenth century is considered to be indebted to this 'York style'.[226] It does not in any way diminish Thornton's stature as a great artist to suggest that this hypothesis is something of a distortion of the truth. Coventry is at the centre of the Midland counties where there can be found the remains of a number of glazing schemes, datable *c.* 1398–*c.* 1430, that have many affinities with Thornton's work.[227] It would, however, be equally misleading to replace the York label with a Coventry one as the origins of this style are diverse and restricted neither to England nor to glass-painting.

[225] Thornton's monogram and the date is illustrated in Benson, *Ancient Painted Glass*, p. 87.
[226] See E. A. Gee, 'The Painted Glass of All Saints' Church, North Street, York', *Archaeologia*, cii (1969), 178–85.
[227] P. A. Newton, Schools of Glass Painting in the Midlands 1275–1430 (unpubl. Ph.D. thesis, Univ. of London, 1961), pp. 98–124.

118 I Great East Window, 1405–8. By John Thornton and atelier. The Elders before the Throne (Rev. 4:10).

Two panels from a group of three which spread the scene across three lights of the window.

A great deal of light could be shed on this problem by a detailed examination of an important but hitherto undervalued group of Transitional windows in the Minster together with that welcome guest amongst so much local glass, the Oxford Jesse. The group of Transitional windows (sII, sV, SV, NIV, and NV) is to be found in Archbishop Thoresby's Lady Chapel, in the south aisle, and the north and south clerestories. This glass, most probably *in situ*, dates from after 1373[228] and seems to be typical of the kind of work being produced in York in the years before Thornton's arrival. Window sV contains figures of St. James, St. Edward the Confessor, and St. John the Evangelist under architectural canopies of a type not previously seen in York (Plate 119). This interest in elaborate architectural detail, treated with a more developed concern for perspective, is found in glass extremely close in style in the west window of All Saints, Pavement, York[229] and in Wycliffe church in the North Riding. There are close affinities between the style of this group of windows and an Anglo-Italian style of manuscript-painting to be found in the Fitzwarin Psalter[230] and the M. R. James Memorial Psalter.[231] In the Minster fragments of similar canopies can be seen in window sII but they appear most strikingly, combined with elaborately ribbed vaulting, over the remains of a set of Apostles and Prophets holding, respectively, Creed and Prophecy scrolls in windows SV, NIV, and NV of the clerestory.[232]

Westlake first drew attention to the strong similarity between the Transitional work in the Minster and glass at Winchester and Oxford,[233] and Knowles puzzled over what he saw as the evident influence of William of Wykeham being brought to bear in York,[234] but neither appreciated the true significance of this glass in bridging the gap between the style of the west window and that of the east. However, Knowles did quite plausibly link the Transitional work with the name of a York glazier, one John Burgh.[235] From the fabric rolls it is quite clear that Burgh was the principal glazier employed in the Minster in the period 1399–1419[236] and as he was free of the city in 1375,[237] shortly after the completion of phase one of the

[228] The completion date of the first phase of the eastern arm of the Minster. See French, *AntJ* lii, 315.

[229] Originally the east window of St. Saviour's, York. Benson, *Ancient Painted Glass*, p. 175.

[230] Paris Bib. Nat. lat 765. See F. Wormald, 'The Fitzwarin Psalter and its Allies', *J. Courtauld and Warburg Insts.* vi (1943), 71–9.

[231] BM, Add. MS. 44949. Calendar and Litany evidence point to Durham.

[232] A full set of Apostles in the clerestory is recorded by Gent, *History*, p. 159.

[233] Westlake, *History of Design* iii. 26.

[234] Knowles, *York School*, pp. 108–9.

[235] Ibid. 211. See also *N. and Q.* 12th ser. x (1922), 88–9.

[236] *Fabric Rolls*, pp. 13–40.

[237] Surtees Soc. xcvi (1897), 74.

119 sV South choir aisle, *c.* 1373. This canopy from the Transitional window shows a new interest in elaborate architectural detail and developed perspective which is closely paralleled in contemporary manuscripts.

eastern arm, he may well have been responsible for much of the Transitional work in the Lady Chapel. Despite his evident activity he was not given the commission for the great east window and in consequence his work has been labelled as 'old fashioned'.[238] Contemporary work in York, claimed Knowles, was far behind that which was being done at Oxford.[239] From the point of view of design this can be argued, but a comparison of Burgh's mature painting style with that of his Oxford contemporaries reveals a remarkable similarity.

By a strange accident of history it is possible to make this comparison without leaving the Minster. In 1765 William Peckitt[240] somewhat reluctantly accepted the remains of the medieval glass from the west window of New College, Oxford, in part-payment for a window of his own painting which was to be erected in its place.[241] Surrounded by borders of Peckitt's design a number of the Oxford panels now occupy a window in the south choir aisle (sVIII) of the Minster.

A comparison of the head of the prophet Amos (Plate 120), from Burgh's work in the clerestory (NIV), with that of King Manasses (Plate 121) from the Oxford Jesse (sVIII) cannot but demonstrate the former artist's command of the new 'soft' style.

Burgh is thus a figure of some importance. Knowles, in addition to listing some of his appearances in the fabric rolls,[242] speculates on his relationship with a William Burgh who in 1399 filled the great window of Westminster Hall with 'flourished glass' for the king.[243] This same William Burgh worked extensively for the Crown at Eltham Palace between 1399 and 1404,[244] and it is interesting to note that in this latter year a John Burgh, glazier, is also recorded as having worked at Eltham.[245] Were the two John Burghs the same person, and the John Burgh of York not only related to one of the king's glaziers but himself in the king's employ, then his familiarity with the latest stylistic developments would be easy to understand.

The Oxford Jesse itself presents many internal stylistic problems, not least the very obvious difference between the styles of the main light figures, surrounded by the tendrils of the genealogical vine, and the remains of the 'Doom' scene in the lower tracery lights. The slightly later version of the same scheme painted by the same workshop for Winchester

[238] Knowles, *York School*, p. 40.

[239] Ibid. 211.

[240] Peckitt's work in the Minster is surveyed below, p. 387.

[241] C. Woodforde, *The Stained Glass of New College, Oxford* (1951), p. 20–1.

[242] Knowles, *York School*, p. 27.

[243] H. M. Colvin, *History of the King's Works* (1963), i. 203, 532.

[244] PRO, E101/502/15 m4, E101/502/25 m4.

[245] PRO, E101/502/26 m6.

College chapel[246] seems not to have these internal inconsistencies.[247] The period of glass-painting is aptly named Transitional and similar variations in style and technique can be detected throughout the York work of these years.[248]

John Thornton remained in York after the completion of the east window and was made a freeman of the city in 1410.[249] He was still alive in 1433 when the dean and chapter made a payment to him.[250] While there is no documentary evidence relating to any later work by him in York, a number of windows are so closely related in style to the east window that an attribution to Thornton and his workshop can be justified.

Within the Minster sufficient of Thornton's work remains to suggest that he was responsible for glazing the whole of the choir area west of and including the choir transepts. Three windows in the north choir aisle (nVIII, nIX, and nX) of uniform design were originally balanced by three on the south side, of which one remains intact (sIX). The seventy-five-foot high St. William window in the north choir transept (nVII) is balanced by one to the south dedicated to St. Cuthbert (sVII) which though arguably not by Thornton bears considerable evidence of the influence of his work. Finally, the entire western choir clerestory of eight windows, four on each side (NVIII–NXI, SVIII–SXI), all of uniform design and using, with but minor variations, the same standard cartoons throughout, appears to be from his workshop.

The three windows in the north aisle were probably painted at the end of the pontificate of Henry Bowet, archbishop from 1407 to 1423. They were given by Bowet himself, Thomas Parker, prebendary of Ampleforth 1410–23, and Robert Wolveden, treasurer from 1426 to 1432.[251] Each window has three registers of narrative scenes surmounted by large, full-length figures under canopies. The choice of saints and scenes is interesting and can be seen to reflect both the careers and the private devotion of the donors.[252] The figure of St. Chad from Wolveden's window (nVIII) (Plate 122) is one of the best preserved of this set. Comparison of the saint's head with those of the angels in the Four Winds panel of the east window (Plate 123) provides a clear illustration of the continuity of Thornton's workshop style. St. Chad is also a fine example of Thornton's lively treatment of the

[246] J. D. Le Couteur, *Ancient Glass in Winchester* (Winchester, 1920), pp. 62–83.

[247] J. H. Harvey and D. G. King, 'Winchester College Stained Glass', *Archaeologia*, ciii (1971), 149–53, attempt to shed some light on the international origins of this style.

[248] Knowles, *York School*, pp. 74–5, Pl. XXIII.

[249] Ibid. 217, citing Surtees Soc. xcvi (1897), 115.

[250] Ibid. 217, citing *Fabric Rolls*.

[251] Harrison, *Painted Glass*, p. 89. Le Neve–Jones, vi. 4, 28, 14.

[252] The subjects are described in Benson, *Ancient Painted Glass*, pp. 92–7.

figure and canopy theme. The background is broken up by regularly placed fleur-de-lis-type insets, the shafting is populated by beautifully drawn prophet figures in grisaille, and an interplay of diagonals leads the eye inwards thereby creating the illusion of recession.

The narrative panels were severely damaged by the holocaust of 1829 and are difficult to read in spite of a skilled restoration.[253] Nevertheless, from an iconographic point of view, they are of absorbing interest and include a scene from the life of St. Thomas Becket unique in English art,[254] a posthumous miracle of St. Nicholas represented also in the Romanesque glass,[255] rare scenes from the lives of St. John of Beverley and St. Chad,[256] and, in a panel of the Annunciation, an example of the lily crucifix whereby it is recalled that the Annunciation to the Virgin and the Crucifixion took place on the same date—25 March.[257]

The surviving member of the Thornton trio in the south choir aisle (sIX) depicts the Holy Kindred[258] and in design varies only slightly from the scheme adopted on the opposite side. There are only two registers of narrative scenes and the main subjects above are not single figures but family groups.[259] The head of the priest from the scene of the marriage of Joachim and Anna (Plate 124) is a superb example of the variety of techniques employed by Thornton on a single piece of glass—fine-line modelling, stipple shading, stickwork, varying intensities of painted line, and silver stain. It is interesting to compare this head with that of Eve from the panel illustrating the Fall in the east window (Plate 125). The soft flow of the line-modelling around the eyes can be seen as a characteristic of this style.

The problem of legibility noted before in connection with the east window applies with equal validity to the St. William and St. Cuthbert windows (nVII sVII). Twenty-one registers of five narrative panels each tower above the spectator, and all but the lowest scenes defy identification from ground level. Nevertheless, the St. William window contains panels which combine excellence of design with draughtsmanship equal to the

---

[253] *FAR* (1952, 1953, 1956).

[254] P. A. Newton, 'Some New Material for the Study of the Iconography of St. Thomas Becket', *Actes du Colloque International de Sedières* (Paris, 1975), p. 257.

[255] See above, p. 322.

[256] Wolveden was also dean of Lichfield where the relics of St. Chad were enshrined (H. Wharton, *Anglia Sacra*, London, 1691, i. 452). Chad's legendary association with King Wulfhere, reputed builder of Peterborough Abbey, was commemorated in the windows of the cloister at Peterborough (T. Gunton, *History of the Church of Peterborough* (1685), p. 103).

[257] C. Woodforde, *The Norwich School of Glass Painting in the 15th Century* (Oxford, 1950), p. 92.

[258] Subjects listed in full by Benson, *Ancient Painted Glass*, p. 89.

[259] cf. east window, Holy Trinity Goodramgate, York.

120 NIV North Lady Chapel clerestory, *c.* 1380. The Prophet Amos from the 'Creed' series. This figure bridges the stylistic gap between the transitional work and the 'soft' style of Thornton.

121 sVIII The 'Oxford' Jesse, south choir aisle, *c.* 1380. King Manasses. Originally from New College, Oxford, and presented to the Minster by William Peckitt in 1765, this window is valuable comparative material in examining pre-Thornton 'soft' style glass at York.

122 nVIII North choir aisle, *c.* 1423. St. Chad. This window was given by Treasurer Robert Wolveden and was probably produced in the workshop of John Thornton.

123 I Great East Window, 1405–8. By
John Thornton and atelier. The Angels
with the Four winds. (Rev 7:1). Facial
types characteristic of Thornton's
workshop and an amusing solution to the
iconographic problem of the text.

124 sIX Holy Kindred Window, south choir aisle,
c. 1425. The head of a priest. This detail, clearly
Thornton's work, is from the Marriage of Joachim
and Anna.

125 I Great East Window, 1405–8. By John Thornton
and atelier. Head of Eve. This head, a detail from the
panel illustrating the Fall, makes an interesting
comparison with that in plate 124.

finest in the east window. A particularly good example of the best in this window is a panel which shows St. William received by the King of Sicily (Plate 126). The iconography of both windows was surveyed in some detail by the brothers Fowler[260] who provided much information of use when the opportunity arose in 1955 to reorder the St. William panels into a more coherent narrative sequence. Certain elements in the St. William window have given rise to the suggestion that the panels originally formed two windows, one on each side of the choir.[261] Upon an offer from Cardinal Langley of Durham to donate a window in honour of St. Cuthbert the choir transepts were raised to their present height, the St. William panels gathered together on the north side, and the new window inserted opposite. This theory is certainly plausible. The St. Cuthbert window is undoubtedly later than the St. William and shows a marked decline in the standard of design and draughtsmanship. It does contain, however, examples of a technique which is rarely employed in the windows of the Minster. Small 'jewels' of pot-metal glass are set into the ornamental borders of clothes or vestments in hollows drilled into the parent glass. These coloured insets are not leaded into place but fused in during the firing.[262] The technique is found, used to very rich effect, in the windows of the Beauchamp chapel at Warwick, the work of John Prudde, the king's glazier, dated 1447,[263] and, nearer at hand, in St. Michael Spurriergate, York, possibly by Thornton.[264]

The western choir clerestory windows contain representations of kings, popes, and bishops connected with the conversion of the north of England to Christianity.[265] The glass can be dated by reference to the arms of Minster clergy set in the lowest visible register of panels in each window and would seem to be contemporary with the work in the aisles below.[266] The connection between these two groups of windows extends to the use of the same cartoon for the bishop saints.[267]

The clerestory of the south choir transept, consisting of an east and a west window of five lights each (SVI and SVII), contains representations of two figures of importance in the history of the Minster which, because of

---

[260] See n. 20.

[261] J. A. Knowles, 'Technical Notes on the St. William Window in York Minster', *YAJ* xxxvii (1949), 150.

[262] Described by Theophilus, *De Diversis Artibus*, pp. 57–8.

[263] C. Woodforde, *English Stained and Painted Glass* (Oxford, 1954), p. 22.

[264] Illustrated by Gibson, *Noble City of York*, p. 202.

[265] F. Harrison, 'The West Choir Clerestory Windows in York Minster', *YAJ* xxvi (1922), 353.

[266] Ibid. 372.

[267] The same cartoon is used yet again for an archbishop saint in the east window of Cartmel Priory, Cumbria.

their deliberate juxtaposition, are of great iconographic interest. That on the eastern side shows Archbishop Scrope identified by a scroll reading *Dns Ricard Scrope* and distinguished by the nimbus of a saint. Below his feet kneels Stephen Scrope, archdeacon of Richmond 1402–18,[268] with a prayer-scroll which reads *O Ricarde pastor bone tui famili miserere Steph.* Opposite, in the central light of the west window, is the figure of St. William, holding a book and similarly identified—*Scs Willmus.* Below his feet kneels Robert Wolveden, again with a prayer-scroll and similar formula, *Sce Willme ora p. tui famili aia roberti.* Both windows have a row of armorials including Scrope of Masham, Scrope, Wolveden, and the dean and chapter. In portraying Scrope as a saint and associating him with St. William, whose bona fide sanctity was not then in doubt, Wolveden and his chapter colleagues were endeavouring to foster the cult of the martyred archbishop which had grown up around his tomb in the Minster. *Semen ecclesiae est sanguis Christianorum*; and the example of Becket at Canterbury shows how much financial benefit such seed could yield. Scrope's execution was bitterly resented in York and his cult was popular, but the unofficial canonization of a man executed for treason not unnaturally infuriated the government and royal attempts to end the cult were eventually successful.

Amongst the remainder of the eastern-arm glazing is a corpus of panels the study of which presents more problems than any other glass in the Minster. None of the glass is *in situ* and what appears to be a stylistically and iconographically homogeneous group has been split up and inserted into five windows. Two of these are in the Lady Chapel clerestory (SIII and SIV) and thus virtually impossible to see clearly, a third group forms a window in the north aisle (nV),[269] and single figures from the series are intruded into the east windows of each aisle (sII and nII). On grounds of style and subject, two panels in the nave (sXXXV) must also be included.[270] One of them, depicting Joachim in the Wilderness (Plate 127),[271] illustrates clearly the superb quality of design and execution to be found throughout the group.[272] Both paint and stain are handled with great skill in the delicate background diaper in reserve on ruby glass and in yellows which vary from a pale lemon to a fierce orange. The other nave panel (Plate 128) is of the Annunciation and in the boldness of its composition illustrates how clearly the master glass-painter responsible for the whole series was aware of

---

[268] Le Neve–Jones vi. 26.

[269] Moved by Milner-White from sXI—*FAR* (1953), p. 26.

[270] Moved by Milner-White from the chapter-house and described by him in 'The Resurrection of a Fourteenth-century Window', *Burlington Mag.* (Apr. 1952), pp. 108–12.

[271] Dr. P. A. Newton suggests this panel may represent the Annunciation to the Shepherds.

[272] The panel was exhibited in Paris in *L'Europe gothique XII–XIV siècles* (Musée du Louvre, 1968) cat. no. 219.

developments in design and iconography on the Continent. The Virgin is shown standing before her lectern and framed by an arch which forms part of a larger structure. This architectural setting is an important element in the composition, locating the two main figures in the picture space and allowing the artist to experiment with perspective. God the Father is also given access to the scene through the medium of the architecture, appearing as a face in the small window in the top left of the building. The composition is derived from a panel of the Annunciation of the Virgin's Death, painted by Duccio as part of the great *Maestà* altar-piece completed in 1311 for Siena Cathedral.[273] It is not easy to see how a York glazier came into contact with the new ideas of the Italian *Trecento* save through the medium of more portable works of art. Duccio's composition was introduced into northern Europe by the French manuscript-painter Jean Pucelle, who used the design for the Annunciation of the Birth of Christ in his Hours of Jeanne D'Evreux[274] of *c.* 1325. The same composition, using Duccio's architectural setting and lectern but also introducing the head of God the Father in the small window, was again used by Pucelle in the Belleville Breviary[275] of *c.* 1326. It is in this version that the design was transmitted to York and used with very little alteration for the same scene in glass.

The Joachim and Annunciation panels are detached narrative panels but the rest of the group to which they belong preserve the original, somewhat unusual, scheme of full-length figures under canopies which rise to form flat plinths on which the narrative scenes rest. The two clerestory windows each contain five such pairs of figures and scenes, the north aisle window contains six arranged in two tiers of three, and the two east windows of the aisles each contain a figure and canopy but lack narrative panels. Thus there survive sixteen pairs of figures and scenes and two each of detached figure and scene panels.

In his attempt to solve some of the mysteries surrounding this glass[276] J. W. Knowles made an analysis of the iconography which, though not wholly accurate, leads to the nevertheless valid conclusion that originally there must have been at least seven more figure and scene combinations. Of the eighteen surviving figures ten are apostles, six are prophets, and two female saints. The Apostles can be identified by their attributes and the series includes both saints Paul and Matthias[277] but lacks saints Peter,

[273] E. Panofsky, *Early Netherlandish Painting* (Harvard, 1953), i. 30–2.

[274] Paris, Coll. Rothschild. L. Delisle, *Les Heures dites de Jean Pucelle* (Paris, 1910).

[275] Paris, Bib Nat. MSS. lat. 10483–4.

[276] J. A. Knowles, 'Notes on some Windows in the Choir and Lady Chapel of York Minster', *YAJ* xxxix (1956).

[277] Matthias is usually omitted when Twelve Apostles series include Paul.

126 nVII St. William Window, north choir transept, *c.* 1423. St. William in exile, received by the King of Sicily. Probably from Thornton's workshop.

127 sXXXV South nave aisle, *c.* 1350. Joachim in the wilderness. This panel, using only white and ruby glass and yellow stain, best illustrates the skill and elegant style of Master Robert's group of glaziers.

128 sXXXV South nave aisle, *c.* 1350. The Annunciation. An iconographic form originating with Duccio's Maestà of 1311 appears in York glass some forty years later.

Philip, and James the Less. Of the six prophets, four face right and two face left, moreover, they all hold scrolls with prophecies foretelling the coming of Christ and identifying the bearer—the two most important authors of such prophecies, Isaiah and Ezekiel, are lacking. The two female saints, Margaret and Helen, would be inexplicable in this context unless accompanied by others to form a series. As they both face right it is likely that at least two facing left are missing. Similarly, the narrative panels form a continuous series from the Annunciation to Joachim[278] to the Coronation of the Virgin but several vital scenes, such as the Nativity, Crucifixion, and Resurrection, do not exist.

The original location of what must thus have been at least twenty-five figure and subject pairs has proved impossible to establish. Each combination measures approximately 11 ft. 6 ins. by 2 ft. 6 ins. so, grouped together, all twenty-five would form a window of about the same size as the St. William window.[279] There is no single window or group of window-openings in the present building into which this glass could have fitted. If a site in an earlier structure has to be found then the precise date of the glass becomes a crucial factor in establishing whether the series was made in an attempt to smarten up Archbishop Roger's choir in the years shortly before the decision was taken to replace it.

This problem has been studied by T. W. French who has concluded, on the basis of a comparison of the styles of this glass and the west window, that the series belongs to the decade 1330–9 and, he suggests, was inserted into the Norman choir as part of a campaign to focus greater attention on the shrine of St. William.[280] Such an explanation seems unlikely for a number of reasons. John Harvey has suggested that the decision to replace the Norman nave implied, as early as 1289, the later rebuilding of the eastern arm in the Gothic style.[281] Moreover, this project seems to have existed in a fully considered form from before 1348.[282] Given the strain imposed on the fabric fund by the demolition of the old western towers and the re-thinking of the west end—which itself necessitated a huge injection of funds from Archbishop Melton before it could be completed and glazed[283]—it is unlikely that a large sum of money would be diverted into refurbishing a

[278] The Marian emphasis of the narrative panels suggests this is the correct identification of this panel, however, with the exception of a spurious Marriage of Joachim and Anna concocted by Milner-White in nXXXV, there is no evidence of other early scenes from the Protoevangelium Life of the Virgin.

[279] Knowles, 'Notes' p. 111.

[280] French, 'Observations' p. 91.

[281] See above, p. 149.

[282] Above, p. 160.

[283] French, 'West Windows', p. 82.

choir whose future was very much in question. The forward-looking style of the glass would have served only to highlight the antiquity of the surrounding architecture and its subject-matter would have provided no iconographic context for a focusing of interest on the shrine of St. William.

The most important determining factor is the style of the glass. French asserts that ogee forms are common in the architectural and decorative details of the west window glass but are completely lacking in the Lady Chapel panels.[284] A close examination of both fails to bear this out. On the contrary, there are no ogee forms at all in the west window glass but three clearly defined ogee canopies survive above the narrative scenes in the Lady Chapel north aisle group (nV).[285] The architectural details of the canopies in the two clerestory windows show a far more advanced interest in perspective for balconies, cornices, window-openings, arcades, and corbels[286] than can be found in the west window. Small windows with open wooden shutters, identical to those found in the Selby Abbey east window, are found in the Lady Chapel glass but not in the west window. These factors all indicate a date after the completion of the west window, somewhere in the decade 1340–50, but it is possible to be more precise still. The clerestory panels are distinguished from the others by superbly executed figures in niches in the side-shaftings.[287] These, as French points out, are closely paralleled in monumental brasses, particularly that of Sir Henry Hastings at Elsing in Norfolk, dated 1347.[288] In this brass the shafting figures are set against richly diapered backgrounds as in the York glass. Closer still are the shafting figures from the glass of St. Stephen's chapel, Westminster,[289] which can be dated precisely to the years between 1349 and 1352.[290] A date for the York glass of *c.* 1350 would thus seem not unlikely but would rule out any possibility of the series having been made for the Norman choir.

There remains as yet unexplored one last possible Minster location for these homeless panels. The chapel of St. Mary and the Holy Angels, known popularly as St. Sepulchre's, which had been built by Archbishop Roger on an awkward site off the north-west corner of the nave,[291] had, in consequence of the rebuilding of the nave, to be considerably altered in the

---

[284] French, 'Observations', p. 91.
[285] That originally there were more can be seen from identical side-shafting and corbels in the panels below—Knowles, 'Notes', pp. 94–5
[286] Illustrated in Knowles, 'Notes' 94–5
[287] Illustrated in French, 'Observations', Pl. XX.
[288] *Cat. of Rubbings of Brasses and Incised Slabs*, V. & A. Museum (1929), Pl. 4.
[289] Illustrated in J. T. Smith, *Antiquities of Westminster* (1807), Pl. XXXI.
[290] Colvin, *King's Works* i. 518.
[291] Browne, *History*, p. 180.

second quarter of the fourteenth century.[292] Archbishop Melton granted a licence for the enlargement of the chapel buildings in 1333, and by 1340 the work had proceeded as far as the door, still to be seen in the north aisle of the nave, which linked the chapel to the Minster.[293] St. Sepulchre's was an important archiepiscopal foundation, with a staff of nineteen supposedly resident clergy,[294] and it is possible that the quite major alterations and enlargements occasioned by the work on the west end provided an opportunity for a sumptuous reglazing. The building, redundant after 1547, fell into decay and had disappeared entirely by 1816, leaving no record of its appearance or fenestration. The pronounced Marian emphasis of the narrative panels in the Lady Chapel glass, which include such rare scenes as the Funeral of the Virgin (Plate 129), combined with an important Passion sequence, would be appropriate in a building known both as St. Mary's and St. Sepulchre's, so the scale and distinctive design of this fascinating glass may provide a valuable clue in reconstructing the chapel's appearance.

Closely related in style to the mid-fourteenth-century glass and only marginally less problematic are the three large figures of saints Stephen, Christopher, and Lawrence in the north aisle of the Lady Chapel (nIV) and the figure of St. Vincent two windows further west (nVI). The figures, though much travelled within the Minster,[295] have latterly come to be regarded as belonging to the Lady Chapel clerestory (NII) largely through an incorrect dating of *c.* 1380.[296] The glass, however, is clearly of the same style as the west window as a comparison of St. Christopher from nIV (Plate 130) and St. John from the west window (Plate 115) amply demonstrates. The two saints are evidently from the same workshop and very close in date. Treatment of hair, articulation of facial features, and design of the ornamental borders to the drapery are all exactly the same. Moreover, the furry trefoil diaper in the Christopher panels is also common in the west window and the canopy design is paralleled in the group of windows at the west end (sXXXVI, nXXVIII, and nXXX).

A solution to the problem of the original position of these saints is suggested by their close stylistic affinity with the west-end glazing. Torre records the two westernmost windows of the nave aisles (sXXXV and nXXIX) as glazed with plain white glass only.[297] Given the change in the

---

[292] Ibid., p. 181.

[293] See above, p. 125.

[294] A. Hamilton Thompson, 'The Chapel of St. Mary and the Holy Angels, otherwise known as St. Sepulchre's Chapel at York', *YAJ* xxxvi (1944), 63–77.

[295] Their travels are chronicled by Milner-White in *FAR* (1958), pp. 34–5.

[296] Ibid.

[297] Torre, 'Minster', p. 25.

129 SIV South choir clerestory, *c.* 1350. The Funeral of the Virgin. A panel from the fine collection of 'homeless' 14th-C. glass now displayed in the choir. This scene is parodied by 'babewyns' in nXXV (see plate 113).

130 nIV St. Stephen's Chapel, *c.* 1340. St. Christopher. Close in style to Master Robert's work in the West Window, this figure may have originally been at the west end of the nave.

original nave design occasioned by the decision to demolish the Norman towers[298] it is possible that the glazing scheme was also slightly altered. Tall figures under canopies could have been inserted in the windows of the last bay rather than the smaller scene and canopy groups which characterize the others. The figures fit happily into the nave window-openings[299] and, with grisaille or trellised foliage panels above and below, would have interfered far less with the over-all aesthetic of the nave glass than the Jesse window (sXXXIII). The iconography also lends support to this theory as the three deacon saints, Stephen, Lawrence, and Vincent, form a neat group for the north window (nXXIX), where they would complement the figures of Stephen and Lawrence in the west window of the aisle (nXXX). St. Christopher, and two other saints now lost,[300] would occupy the south window (sXXXV), near the door, a traditional position for representations of this saint.[301]

Post-medieval glass

York's position as a great regional centre of glass-painting had been maintained for many centuries, but from 1421 standards, it has been claimed, steadily declined. The glass in St. Michael-le-Belfrey, dating from the 1530s, was described by Knowles as 'coarse in character and brutal in execution'.[302] On the contrary, this glass shows the glass-painters of the time to have been still open to new styles and techniques and to have been competent practitioners of their art. The Reformation, however, was a severe blow. Suddenly demand for religious imagery was cut off and, with the destruction of monasteries and the amalgamation of parishes, even repair work became hard to come by. Glass-painters were forced to turn to less exalted tasks: plain and domestic glazing and heraldry, still in constant demand.

The craft itself was also undergoing change in the middle of the sixteenth century. Traditional pot-metal techniques were now having to compete with coloured enamels which were eventually to destroy the role of leading in the design and to make possible all sorts of painterly effects.[303] They appear on the Continent *c.* 1538 and reached York soon after, the earliest

[298] See above, p. 170.
[299] Barnett restored them there (see below, p. 392).
[300] Torre, 'Minster', suggests they were sold during the Civil War.
[301] F. Bond, *Dedications and Patron Saints of English Churches* (1914), p. 167.
[302] Knowles, *York School*, p. 14.
[303] See J. A. Knowles, 'The Transition from the Mosaic to the Enamel System of Painting on Glass', *AntJ* vi (1926), 26–35.

example being in St. Michael-le-Belfrey, *c.* 1540.[304] By 1585, when Bernard Dininckhoff executed the heraldic glass at Gilling Castle, Yorkshire, enamel techniques were firmly established.[305]

It is not possible to follow the full impact of the Renaissance on English glass in the Minster but the church is extremely fortunate in possessing a number of fine examples of French sixteenth-century glass (sIII, sVI, nIII, and nXXIX).[306] These were purchased or given to the Minster at various dates but most of them arrived in England early in the nineteenth century, when the English, their interest in old glass renewed, were buying up the contents of demolished French churches. It is perhaps fitting, given the long connections between the medieval glass-painters of York and Normandy, that the majority of this glass should come from churches in Rouen.

Also from Rouen, the church of St. Nicholas, comes a seventeenth-century window of the Visitation, presented by the Earl of Carlisle in 1804.[307] Based on a print by Raphael Sadeler, it is for its date, 1625, a rare example of monumental glass-painting in the technique which still for the most part makes use of pot-metal glass.[308]

Glass-painting in England was perhaps at its lowest ebb during the seventeenth century. Apart from a revival of religious imagery under Archbishop Laud, work was mainly restricted to pagan subjects and heraldry. Inserted into fourteenth-century grisaille in the nave (nXXVIII) are three small shields, shockingly leaded, with the arms of Ingram and Greville, dated 1623. They are probably to be associated with the memorial to William Ingram (d. 1623) in the north aisle of the Lady Chapel.[309] From the end of the century comes another heraldic panel (sVI) (Plate 131) displaying the arms of Archbishop Lamplugh. His monument lies a little to the east of the window and the glass again formed part of his memorial. The archbishop's arms impale those of the see. A bold inscription beneath records his death in 1691 and suggests the date of the glass. Borders with the same design reversed feature a central stem with roses, laurels, and putti.

---

[304] Blue enamel is used at Antwerp in 1538 and Montfort l'Amaury in France in 1543; Lafond, *Trois études*, 135. It is used for the jewels on a crown in St. Michael-le-Belfrey, York (sIII). Prior to the post-war restoration the crown was to be found above the head of St. James in sIV. Its original position is unknown but it clearly forms part of the original glazing scheme and must date from *c.* 1540.

[305] Knowles, *York School*, Pl. VII. Dininckhoff, probably a Fleming, was free of the city in 1586. Surtees Soc. cii (1900), 28.

[306] *FAR* (1947), 18–21, Pl. XI; (1952), 12–13; (1953), Pl. VII; (1955), 21–25; (1954), 23–26 illustrated in Gibson, *Noble City*, Pl. 39.

[307] Payments to James Pearson for setting it up and painting the arms of the Earl of Carlisle occur in YML, E4a Fabric Accounts 1805, 1806, and 1810.

[308] Lafond, *Le Vitrail français*, p. 267 and Fig. 204.

[309] Presumably executed locally but by whom?

This panel, carried out in white glass with yellow stain and a variety of coloured enamels, is by Henry Gyles of York (1645–1709).[310] Gyles was 'the famousest painter of glass perhaps in the world' according to the antiquary Ralph Thoresby, who described one of his windows at Denton-in-Wharfedale as 'the noblest painted glass in the North of England'.[311] The ornament is typical of the secular spirit of his work.[312] Much of his inspiration was drawn from Italian art, reproduced in prints and maps, as well as Mannerist glass-painting of the previous century.[313]

In William Peckitt (1731–95) York produced yet another glass-painter of national importance.[314] His career began in 1751 with heraldic glass for John Fountayne, dean of York.[315] This connection with the Minster and its officials was to last until his death. Between 1753 and 1795 he supplied the dean and chapter with a great deal of glass, much of it unpainted, for the repair of the windows.[316]

In 1757 Peckitt provided glass for the restoration of the west window (wI). Besides canopy and border pieces, he painted '$7\frac{1}{2}$ Heads, Faces, Miters etc'.[317] The heads, mainly for the archbishops in the lower register of the window, are grotesque in appearance. His work the following year on the two side windows of the west wall (sXXXVI and nXXX) shows no improvement. Clumsily painted patches in the Christ figure of the former window add a touch of bathos to what was originally a tender and moving representation of the Crucifixion.[318] New panels depicting kneeling figures of St. John and St. Peter were introduced at the base of the centre lights of each window where Torre had seen defaced images of a man and a boy, possibly remnants of donor figures of Archbishop Melton.[319] The figure-

---

[310] J. A. Knowles, 'Henry Gyles, Glass-painter of York', *Walpole Soc.* xi (1923), 47–72. J. T. Brighton, 'Cartoons for York Glass—Henry Gyles', *Preview, City of York Art Gallery Quarterly*, xxi, 84 (1968), 772–5. More heraldic glass can be seen at Bishopthorpe Palace, illustrated in Gibson, *Noble City*, Pl. 22A.

[311] *The Diary of Ralph Thoresby F.R.S.*, ed. The Rev. J. Hunter (1830), i. 366 and ii. 435. This window of 1702 is illustrated in Knowles, 'Henry Gyles', Pl. XXVIIIb.

[312] e.g. Staveley, Derbyshire 1672: J. T. Brighton, 'The Heraldic Window in the Frecheville Chapel of Staveley Church', *Derbyshire Archaeological Jour.* (1960)/98–104, Pl. XI. Also York, Merchant Taylors' Hall, south window, 1679. Goldsborough, N. Yorks, south aisle east window, 1696.

[313] e.g. the glass by a Master of Vasari's Circle in the Biblioteca Laurenziana, Florence, illustrated in G. Marchini, *Italian Stained Glass Windows* (1957), Fig. XXXIV.

[314] J. A. Knowles, 'William Peckitt, Glass-painter', *Walpole Soc.* xvii (1927), 45–59. J. T. Brighton, 'William Peckitt, the greatest of the Georgian Glass-painters', *York Georgian Soc. Annual Report* (1967–8), 14–24 and 'Cartoons for York Glass', *Preview, CYAGQ* xxii, 85 (1969), 779–83.

[315] York City Art Gallery, MS. Peckitt Commission Book, 1.

[316] YML, E4a Fabric Accounts and E3 Vouchers.

[317] YML, E3/123v Voucher.

[318] For documentation on these two windows see Commission Book, 9 and YML, E3/124v.

[319] Torre, 'Minster', pp. 21–2.

drawing is lamentable and the painting extremely coarse. Pot-metal blue and green are used, but to overcome his lack of ruby Peckitt had to apply several coats of yellow stain to white glass to achieve a reddish colour.[320] Though the work is very poor in quality these two panels are of great interest as Peckitt has clearly tried, albeit unsuccessfully, to copy the diapered grounds and canopy work of the original fourteenth-century glass. This fumbling attempt is amongst the earliest efforts to capture something of the medieval style. Peckitt worked for Horace Walpole at Strawberry Hill[321] and 'Gothick' motifs, perhaps inspired by what he saw around him in York, became an important element in his style. According to William Warrington, one of the leading exponents of the Gothic Revival in glass, Peckitt 'perhaps incorporated more ancient feeling into his work than any other contemporary artist'.[322]

Several nave windows possess ornamental traceries carried out by Peckitt in mosaics of coloured glass.[323] In comparison with the medieval glass below they stand out loudly but they are amongst the best colours available in Europe at this date. One tracery panel must be amongst the most unusual pieces of glass in the Minster (sXXX). A pair of chubby, naked female legs stand on a plinth. Behind coils a serpent, biting an apple. The glass is white, with yellow stain and enamels for colouring. The date 1782 is leaded above. This curious panel is a portion of a copy of the Eve which Peckitt painted in 1774 to designs by Biagio Rebecca for New College, Oxford.[324] Cut down to fill a quatrefoil opening it was set high up where few would notice it. The York fragment has acquired added interest since Victorian censorship, frowning on Eve's scanty clothing, provided the Oxford figure with a more substantial purple mantle.[325]

Mention has already been made of Peckitt's restoration work in the south transept in 1791 and 1793.[326] His earliest work in the Minster was a figure of St. Peter, painted in 1754,[327] replaced by the present figure (sXXIV), which

---

[320] York City Art Gallery MS. Peckitt, The Principles of Introduction into that rare but fine and elegant art of painting and staining of glass (1793), 6, gives a recipe 'to stain a deep yellow one one side of the glass; or a red, when laid on both sides'.

[321] Commission Book, 15 (1761), 16 (1762), and 46 (1772). Some of the work for Walpole is illustrated by A. C. Sewter, *The Stained Glass of William Morris and his Circle*, i (1974), Pl. I.

[322] W. Warrington, *The History of Stained Glass from the Earliest Period of the Art to the Present Time* (1848), p. 68.

[323] They are dated in large leaded figures, 1779 (nXXVI), 1782 (sXXIX and sXXX), and 1789 (sXXXIII).

[324] For Peckitt's extensive work here see Woodforde, *New College*, pp. 20–38. See also above, p. 372. The Oxford Eve is illustrated in Knowles, 'William Peckitt', Pl. XXIX.

[325] Woodforde, *New College*, p. 62.

[326] See above, p. 331.

[327] Commission Book, 3.

he presented to the church in 1768.[328] This saint is based on a design by Sir James Thornhill and had been used by Peckitt as the central figure in the west window of Exeter Cathedral, painted the previous year.[329] The other three figures in this group, Abraham (sXVIII), Solomon (sXIX), and Moses (sXXIII) were painted in 1793, once again to designs by Rebecca,[330] and set up after Peckitt's death, two of them as a bequest to the Minster and probably replacing earlier Peckitt figures.[331] They are executed in mixed enamel and pot-metal techniques, the leading, mostly in squares, weakening the design. Although they suffer by comparison with the medieval glass around them, these figures are Peckitt's best work in the Minster. Brilliance of effect is sought for and the turbanned figure of Abraham (Plate 132) has all the splendour of an eastern potentate from the pages of a Gothic novel. Standing under a Gothic canopy, he well captures the eccentricities of English taste in the second half of the eighteenth century.

Peckitt's transept windows are the last of major importance in the Minster. For the most part, more recent work has been restricted to restoration or the filling of gaps. The next generation, led by men like Thomas Willement, Augustus Welby Pugin, and Charles Winston, brought about a major revival of the art of glass-painting by a more thorough analysis of medieval styles and techniques. When the history of this movement comes to be written it is unlikely that York Minster will feature prominently except as a constant source of inspiration.[332] There was little room for large glazing projects in a building retaining so much of its original glass but one such rare Victorian scheme, by Clayton and Bell (nXIX–nXXII), was installed in 1863. Apart from the inscriptions, it was replaced by medieval glass from St. John's Micklegate in 1945.[333]

After the fire of 1840 two of the leading Victorian glass-painters were considered for the restoration of the damaged glass in the nave. Sydney

[328] Ibid. 30. See Knowles, 'William Peckitt', Pl. XXVIIa.

[329] Knowles, 'William Peckitt', Pl. XXVIII for Pranker's engraving of the Exeter window removed in 1904.

[330] Abraham and Moses appear among the New College figures.

[331] J. A. Knowles, *N. and Q.* 12th Ser. ix (1921), 443–4. In 1780 Peckitt presented life-size figures of Abraham and Solomon to the Minster: Commission Book, 79.

[332] See Sewter, *William Morris* i. 1–16, and 'The Place of Charles Winston in the Victorian Revival of the Art of Stained Glass', *JBAA* xxiv (1961), 80–91. Amongst designs based closely on Minster windows are Willement's east window at St. Paulinus', Brough, Yorks. (1837) from designs of Browne based on the Five Sisters window, and John Ward Knowles's south chancel window at Kirkby Wharfe, Yorks. (1865), incorporating panels of fifteenth-century Austrian glass in foliage based on the Minster west window.

[333] Harrison, *Painted Glass*, p. 20.

Smirke, the Minster architect, wrote that William Wailes of Newcastle was 'perfectly competent to do this work well; he is largely employed (Pugin, I believe, employs no one else) and may be regarded as the second artist we have in this line. Mr. Willement is far more eminent than Wailes, and ranks as the first in England.'[334] Wailes wrote a long self-advertisement in the form of a letter to the committee in which he offered to make good the damage at cost price. He regretted that 'circumstances do not permit greater liberality to an edifice, to which above all others I not only venerate and admire, but am professionally indebted to'.[335] His offer was accepted but his work was restricted to patching or plain glazing apart from a few copies of shields in the clerestory (SXII and NXIX).

When the Minster authorities turned their attention to the restoration of the chapter-house, work on the windows was entrusted to the local firm of John Barnett and Son.[336] Rumours obviously circulated about the nature of the work as Smirke had to send a reassuring letter to the subcommittee explaining the conservative approach adopted. He pointed out, however, that 'other windows are more damaged and it will be necessary to insert many small pieces with portions of faces and hands painted on them . . . You may rely on our doing nothing at all counts that will discredit us.'[337] Tracings were made of the original panels and John Browne undertook to account for the archaeological accuracy of the work.[338] Unfortunately, one window (C/H I) was almost restored away and virtually reduced to a facsimile. Although a great tragedy the skill of Barnett's work is apparent. The *Ecclesiologist* wrote that

upon the closest scrutiny of both the old and new glass (we admit with some degree of prejudice against the apparent rashness of so inexperienced an artist); we are bound in justice to say that his work appears quite unexceptionable, nor do we believe that it could have been more truthfully or closely restored. Contrasted with some late attempts by Mr. Wailes of the windows in the nave, Mr. Barnett's success is incomparably greater, and we feel no apprehension whatever of the result.[339]

The quality of Barnett's work can be seen in the panel illustrating the Harrowing of Hell (Plate 133), an extremely able copy of the thirteenth-century original. Barnett, making no attempt to 'improve' on what he found, manages to convey much of the life and humour of the original. The

[334] YML, B3 Restoration 1840–5. Letter, 19 Oct. 1842.

[335] Ibid., Letter, 2 Oct. 1842.

[336] J. A. Knowles, 'Glass-painters of York. The Barnett Family'. *N. and Q.* 12th Ser. ix (1921), 483–5 and 523.

[337] YML, B3 Restoration 1840–5. Letter, 4 Sept. 1844.

[338] Browne, *History* i. 329 and *Description*, p. 53.

[339] *Ecclesiologist*, iv, no. 4 (1845), 190.

131 sVI All Saints' Chapel, *c.* 1691. By Henry Gyles. Arms of Thomas Lamplugh, Archbishop of York. This is entirely of white glass coloured with yellow stain and enamels. The Italianate ornament is typical of the secular spirit of much of Gyles' work.

132 sXVIII South transept, 1793. William Peckitt from designs by Biagio Rebecca. This gothick figure of Abraham bearing the sacrificial knife is one of Peckitt's best works in the Minster. use of both pot-metals and enamel creates an effect of great brilliancy in colour.

133 ex C/H I Chapter House, 1845. By John Barnett. The Harrowing of Hell. A faithful facsimile of glass of *c.* 1285. Such 'restorations' were to play an important part in the 19th-C. revival of stained glass.

Ecclesiologist's approval was not shared by Dean Milner-White, who removed the figure panels after the war to make room for medieval glass from other parts of the Minster.

Barnett's firm was also responsible for the restoration—fortunately much less severe—of the figures of St. Stephen, St. Christopher, and St. Lawrence (nIV), in 1846, when in their former position in the nave (sXXXIV).

In 1903 another Minster window suffered severely at the hands of restorers. The Mauley window (sXXXII) was sent to London, to the firm of Burlison and Grylls, who replaced large amounts of the original glass. While regretting the principles behind this kind of restoration, the skill with which the work was carried out must be admired.[340] It was a rare venture for this firm into a style far removed from the pseudo-sixteenth-century one which they favoured for so much of their original work.

Kempe and Company's work in the transepts (sXVI, sXVII, sXXV, sXXVI, nXI–nXV) between 1899 and 1903 is equally skilful.[341] They followed closely the scheme of the fifteenth-century glazing but could not resist the temptation to produce something more splendid than the original. St. Peter and St. Paul are given mantles with jewelled hems formed by leading in small coloured pieces of glass.[342] Abrading techniques, not used in York until the sixteenth century, also add to the splendour.[343] Perhaps more effort should have been made to integrate the figure style more closely with the original, but Kempe's work is not aggressively out of sympathy with the over-all concept of the transept glazing.

Post-war contributions to the Minster glazing, in spite of their fairly conservative styles, have blended in less successfully. What little modern glass there is—Harcourt Doyle's arms of the Worshipful Company of Glaziers (sXXX) dating from 1949[344] and a few simple panels by Harry Stammers (sX, nXIV, and nXV),[345] who worked in York for several years—will arouse few passions. Arguments are sure to be raised, however, by the most recent addition to the Minster glass, a window by Ervin Bossanyi dating from 1944 and erected in 1975 in the Zouche Chapel (Z sII).[346] Its bold

---

[340] For a coloured plate of the St. Andrew panel see J. Betjeman, *A Pictorial History of English Architecture* (1972), p. 37.

[341] See above, pp. 327–9.   [342] ibid.

[343] Abrasion of ruby glass is used in the arms of Thomas Dalby, archdeacon of Richmond (sXXV). He died in 1525 and the glass may have been put up in association with his monument in the north choir aisle; Drake, *Ebor.*, pp. 502–3. Further examples of the technique from the following decade can be seen in St. Michael-le-Belfrey.

[344] Gibson, *Noble City*, Pl. 46.

[345] Ibid., Pl. 47 for Stammers' Passion Emblems in sX. See *JBSMGP* xiv, no. 4 (1968–9), 189–90.

[346] The work of this artist is reviewed with special reference to Canterbury by D. Hayes, *Bossanyi* (Canterbury, 1965).

figure style and powerful colouring are commendable qualities in stained glass, but there will be those who feel these monumental attributes to be out of scale in such a building, and to underline the danger of setting glass in a position for which it was never intended.

We should like to thank Dr. Peter A. Newton, not only for the use of his uniquely important notes on the iconography of the Romanesque glass, but also for inspiration, advice, and encouragement throughout. Our thanks are also due to Mr. Bernard Barr of York Minster library, to Dr. Eric A. Gee and Dr. John H. Harvey for permission to read their chapters in advance of publication, to Mr. T. W. French of the Royal Commission on Historical Monuments (England), to Mr. Peter Gibson of the York Glaziers' Trust, and to Mrs. Enid Hodder for patiently typing and re-typing a much altered manuscript.

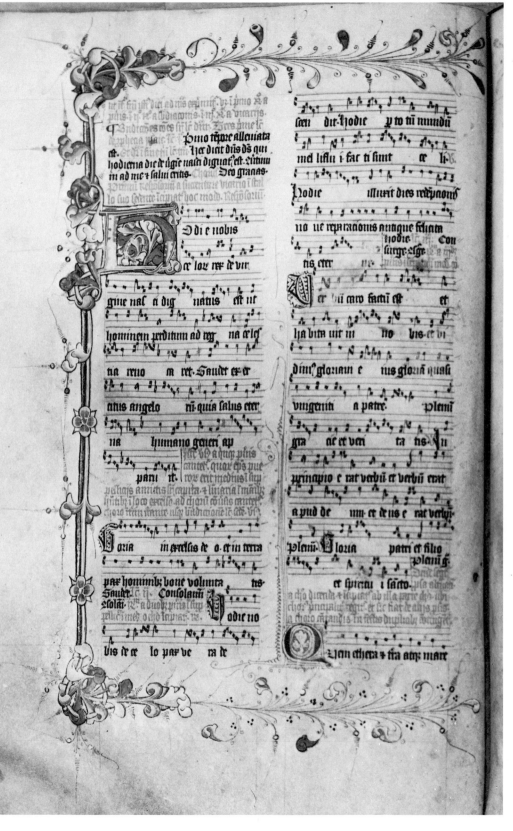

CHAPTER IX

Music since the Reformation

Peter Aston

The first events of the Reformation brought few changes to music or worship in York Minster. Henry VIII's ideal of 'the papacy without the pope' made radical liturgical reform unnecessary, and it was not until the visitation of Edward VI in 1547 that any real attempt was made to impose serious restrictions on musical services. The list of injunctions, issued within a few months of Edward's coronation, included the following directives:

Item, youe shall sing or celebrate in note or song within your said churche but onelie one Masse, that is to say High Masse onelie, and none other;
Item, you shall hereafter omytt and not use the singing of ony Howres, Prime, Deriges or Commendacions, but every man to saie the same as he haith tyme or is disposed.[1]

These instructions, together with an injunction that 'all sermons, collacions and lectures of Divinitie shall not be used in the Latyn tonge but in th'Englishe',[2] are of particular interest for they indicate the determination with which the new Edwardian administration sought to ensure the end of 'popish' practices and ceremonies. Similar orders were issued at, for example, Winchester, Canterbury, and Windsor, while the Lincoln Cathedral Injunctions, dated 14 April 1548, are quite specific in forbidding the singing of any anthems of Our Lady or other saints. The only anthems permitted were songs 'of our Lord', and these were to be sung in English with 'plain and distinct note, for every syllable one'.[3]

It is impossible to form a clear picture of musical life at York during the period immediately before the Reformation, but a certain amount of information is forthcoming concerning the ceremonial, the music which

[1] *York Statutes*, p. 63.
[2] Ibid., p. 65.
[3] *Lincoln Cathedral Statutes*, ed. H. Bradshaw and C. Wordsworth (1897), vol. 2, pp. 584 ff.

◁ **134** Fifteenth-century antiphoner from the Chapel of St. Mary and the Holy Angels, York Minster.

embellished it, the duties of the vicars choral and the instruments which were used. The fabric rolls record various payments during the fifteenth and early sixteenth centuries for installing, repairing, cleaning, and playing the organs;[4] from these notes of payment, dated between 1399 and 1536, it is clear that there were several organs, both positive and portative, in use in various parts of the Minster. There was also at least one great organ,[5] probably situated in the choir.

A post not mentioned in the medieval statutes is that of organist; until the last quarter of the fifteenth century the task of playing the organs seems to have been shared between the vicars choral and was not the responsibility of one man. Shortly before the Reformation this sharing of performing duties was discontinued—a move doubtless necessitated by the special skills required to meet the increasing technical demands of the music. The first vicar to be named as organist was John Austan; in 1475 he was paid 6s. 8d. 'for playing on the organ within the choir this term'.[6] Thereafter, the chamberlains' rolls show regular half-yearly payments of 6s. 8d. to Austan until his death in 1481, and subsequently to John Symson (1484–92),[7] John Usher (1510–24)[8] and Robert Holmes (1527–9).[9] The duties of these vicars are not defined, and it is not clear whether, in addition to playing the organs, they were also responsible for instructing the choristers. A vicar not named as organist was George Gaunt who is described in his will, proved on 26 October 1471, as 'master of the choristers'.[10]

The choir, whose task it was to sing the daily services, was by ancient statute the responsibility of the precentor.[11] Until shortly before the Reformation the adult part of the choir consisted entirely of vicars choral; strict rules governed their behaviour, defined their duties, and laid down conditions for their attendance.[12] The vicars, originally thirty-six in number, were given in the middle of the thirteenth century a residence called Bedern. They were empowered to elect their own head, who was responsible to the precentor for the conduct of the vicars and the management of their affairs.[13] Whether or not it was also the duty of the

[4] For details of these payments see Peter Aston, *The Music of York Minster* (1972), pp. 4–5.
[5] *Fabric Rolls*, p. 74.
[6] YML, Chamberlain's Roll E1/45.
[7] YML, Chamberlains' Rolls E1/47–59.
[8] YML, Chamberlains' Rolls E1/61–2.
[9] YML, Chamberlains' Rolls E1/63–7.
[10] YML, Wills, vol. 1, fo. 326[r].
[11] *York Statutes*, p. 122.
[12] Ibid., pp. 13, 17–18.
[13] Ibid., pp. 141–3. For a detailed account of the life and work of the vicars choral of York Minster see Frederick Harrison, *Medieval College* (1952).

135 A page of a fifteenth-century York Missal, now in the Minster Library (MS Add. 30). ▷

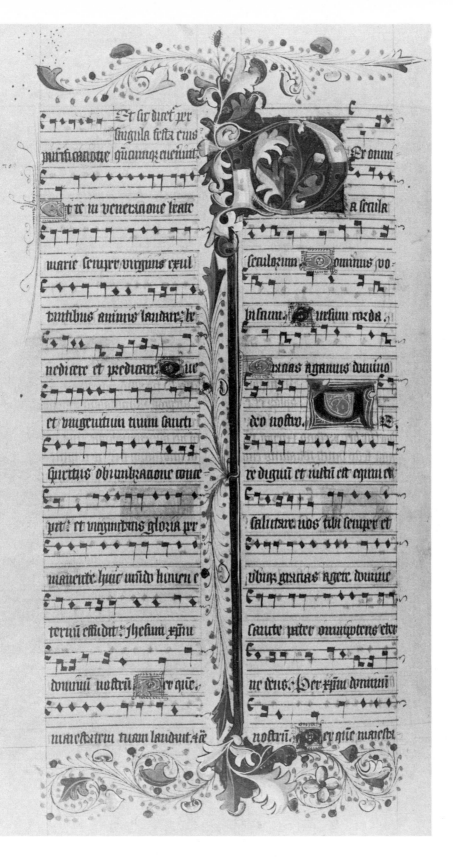

succentor vicariorum to supervise the musical training of the choristers is not clear. During the fifteenth century the bursars' rolls record regular payments of 12d. to the 'controller of the choir', though this may simply refer to the vicar responsible for marking the register. Nevertheless, the post of master of the choristers had become firmly established by the middle of the sixteenth century. In 1531 Thomas Kirkby was admitted at a salary of £13 6s. 8d.,[14] to be succeeded in 1542 by John Thorne.[15] Both these appointments were to the double office of organist and master of the choristers. Later the two posts became quite distinct, and from 1613 until the end of the eighteenth century they were separately paid and frequently were not held by the same man (see Table 1).

In addition to the vicars there were originally in the choir seven boys who normally sang only at obits and chantries. In 1425 the number of choristers was increased to twelve as a result of a gift of money by Thomas Dalby, archdeacon of Richmond.[16] The introduction of lay singing-men (called 'cantores in choro' or simply 'singing-men'—later 'songmen'—in the chapter act-books) probably dates from the end of the fifteenth century; the practice of employing lay singers was certainly well established by 1552 when Archbishop Holgate ordered that the singing-men who made up the number of men's voices to twenty should be paid £8 per annum, and that 'there be the full nombre of xii queresters, according to the aunciente custome of the church of York'.[17] As time went on the proportion of lay singers to vicars choral increased considerably. This was the direct result of the poverty of the vicars, whose estates had become inadequate to support more than a small number; after the Reformation the number of vicars fell rapidly from thirty-six to six.[18]

The first regular *cantor in choro* named in the chapter acts is William Harrys, who was appointed, initially for one year, on 9 August 1567 at a salary of £10.[19] He was succeeded in 1576 by John Wormall, who was granted a pension (i.e. salary) of £10 per annum by the vicars choral 'in place of William Harrys deceased'.[20] There can be little doubt that Wormall is the same man as the John Wyrnal who, according to Drake, lies buried in the Minster 'in the South Cross-Isle'.[21] Evidently, he was a musician of some

[14] YML, Register of Leases etc., Wa, fos. 50[v]–51[r].
[15] Ibid., fos. 157[v]–158[v].
[16] *York Statutes*, p. 144.
[17] Injunctions of Archbishop Holgate, ibid., pp. 72, 76.
[18] Ibid., p. 144.
[19] YML, Chapter Acts, 1565–1634, fo. 22[r].
[20] Ibid., fo. 149[r].
[21] *Ebor.*, p. 496. Wormall's pedigree is shown in *The Visitation of the County of Surrey* (Harleian Soc. 43, 1899), pp. 169–70.

distinction, as can be seen from the inscription quoted by Drake: 'Musicus et logicus Wyrnal hic jacet ecce Johannes, Organa namque quasi fecerat ille loqui' ['Here lies John Wyrnal, so well skilled in the art of Music and Speech that he made the organ almost speak'].[22]

Table 1 List of masters of the choristers, 1531–1799

After 1799 the posts of organist and master of the choristers were always held by the same man. Before that date it may be assumed that the organist undertook the duties of the master of the choristers where no mention of the latter post occurs in the chapter acts or chamberlains' accounts. In the following list the names of York Minster organists who were not separately appointed master of the choristers appear in square brackets; those appointed to both posts appear in *italics*.

1531–1540	*Thomas Kirkby*	1638–1639	James Stevenson
1540–1541	[name illegible]	1639–1640	Richard Marston
1542–1573	*John Thorne*	1640–1645	*John Hutchinson*
1573–1597	*Henry Thorne*		(readmitted)
1598–1604	[Cuthbert Byas]	1666	*Thomas Mudd*
1605–1607	*Henry Farrande*	1666–1675	*Thomas Preston*
1607–1613	[Mr. Browne]	1675–1677	Thomas Tong
1613–1616	George Mason	1677–1682	William Greggs
1616–1618	*Thomas Kingston*	1682–1692	John Blundevile
1618–1619	Christopher Spenceley	1692–1698	*Thomas Wanless*
1619–1637	John Norwood	1698–1742	Thomas Benson
1637–1638	John Goodday	1742–1756	*James Nares*
1638	John Hutchinson	1756–1799	*John Camidge*

The employment of lay singers, whose number by the time of Wormall's death had risen to at least four, was no doubt originally due to the need for expert professional assistance in the performance of polyphonic music. The practice of polyphonic singing, first recorded in 1375,[23] seems to have become standard by the beginning of the sixteenth century. Rule 24 of the statute and minute book of the vicars choral, drawn up in 1507, required that every vicar should 'be competent in music and singing', and that he should learn 'how to sing priksong, faburdon and discant'.[24] By 1531, though probably from a much earlier date, this expertise in part-singing was also demanded of the boy choristers. The terms of Kirkby's

[22] The inscription is also noted by Torre ('Minster', p. 195). Torre gives the date as 1489 and the name as Wymal, while Dodsworth (Bodl., MS. Dods. 157, fo. 27ᵛ) gives the name as Wynnall. These discrepancies are no doubt due to the fact that the stone, lying just inside the south door of the Minster, had become badly worn.

[23] *Fabric Rolls*, p. 243.

[24] The rule is quoted in full by Harrison, op. cit., p. 63.

appointment as organist and 'marster of the quiristers' required not only that he should 'keep and play of the organs within the [Lady] chapell and . . . play of the organs in the quire of the church', but that he should instruct 'the quiristers or children of . . . the church . . . in planesong, prikesong, figuration and descaunt'.[25]

From the early fourteenth century onwards a fairly comprehensive view of the York ceremonial is provided by the service books which have survived. These show that York, like Hereford, had adopted elements of the Sarum Customary, but remained distinct in its calendar of observances and in the antiphons and responds of the Breviary. As W. H. Frere has shown,[26] the most conspicuous differences between the Uses of York and Sarum occur in the sequences, many of which are peculiar to York. Other important differences are to be found in the Ordinary of the mass. Of eight settings of the Gloria given in the York Gradual, only six correspond with Sarum; further discrepancies between the two occur in the settings of the Sanctus and Agnus Dei. Nevertheless, the influence of Sarum on the northern province was considerable, as can be seen from the increasing tendency for the York service books to incorporate extracts from the Sarum ceremonial documents.

No polyphonic settings of the mass peculiar to York have survived. Leaves detached from the bindings of the York Consistory Court Act Book of 1563–4 contain incomplete Mass settings of the late fifteenth century,[27] but the music clearly belongs not to the York Use but to that of Sarum. It has been suggested that the choirbook from which these leaves were taken may have originated at Lincoln, a diocese which followed the Sarum Use during the fifty or so years before the Reformation.[28] The manuscript seems to have been compiled *c.* 1490–1520, and must therefore be more or less contemporary with the Eton Choirbook.[29] It contains parts of a four-part mass by Johannes Cuk (the composer should not be confused with the John Cooke who was *succentor vicariorum* at York between 1452 and 1455), of a Kyrie by Horwood, and of some shorter Mass settings, all of which are anonymous. Cuk's Mass *Venit dilectus meus* is based on the sixth antiphon at matins on the Assumption of the Virgin. The *cantus firmus* is used

[25] YML, Register of Leases etc., Wa, fos. 50[v]–51[r].

[26] 'The Newly-Found York Gradual', *Jour. of Theological Studies* (July 1901); 'York Service Books', *Minster Tracts*, no. 19 (1927). Both papers are reprinted in *W. H. Frere: A Collection of his Papers on Liturgical and Historical Subjects*, ed. J. H. Arnold and E. G. P. Wyatt (Alcuin Club, Collections, 35, 1940).

[27] BIHR, MS. Mus 1.

[28] H. Baillie and P. Oboussier, 'The York Masses', *Music and Letters* (1954), p. 24; see also Frank Ll. Harrison, *Music in Medieval Britain* (1958), pp. 261, 276–7, 291.

[29] A modern edn. is published by Stainer & Bell, *Musica Britannica*, vols. 10–12.

somewhat informally, often appearing in an abbreviated form. The general style of the melodic writing is extremely florid, as is that of many of the anonymous fragments in the collection, and in this respect the music closely resembles some of the pieces in the Eton Choirbook. Further similarities with the Eton manuscript are to be found in the ingenious cross-rhythms and occasional use of imitation, suggesting that the style of the Eton collection was by no means confined to music written for the chapel choir of Eton College. Whether or not the York fragments were ever performed in the Minster is immaterial. The manuscript provides evidence that florid polyphony of this kind was in fairly general use in different parts of the country, and polyphonic settings of the Mass similar in style to the extract from the anonymous 'puzzle' Kyrie[30] would certainly have been performed at York during the early years of the sixteenth century.

With the publication of the 1549 Prayer Book, the York Use finally came

EXAMPLE 1

---

[30] Kyrie I (BIHR, MS. Mus 1, fos. 1–2). The bass part, which is in canon with the soprano, is not written out; a note explains that the performers must puzzle out how it fits into the texture.

to an end. Within three years Puritan reaction to the elaborate ornaments and ceremonial which had persisted throughout the reign of Henry VIII was reflected in the injunctions issued by Archbishop Holgate in 1552. The Minster was to be cleared of all monuments and images, the walls were to be cleansed and Scriptural texts painted upon them. With regard to music, the Archbishop's directives were no less severe. Item 15 ordered that 'there be none other note songe or used in the said churche at any service there to be hadde, savinge square note, playne, so that every sillable may be playnelie and distinctlie pronounced and undrestood, and withoute any reportes or repetinges which may induce any obscurenes to the herers'.[31] Under items 24 and 25 the organs were silenced and the master of the choristers ordered 'to serve God in suche vocacion as he can conveniently and may' by helping 'to singe Divyne service within the quere of the churche'.[32]

It is ironic that these orders should have been issued during the time that John Thorne was in office as organist and master of the choristers, for to judge from contemporary opinion of his work his talent, as a composer was exceptional. Morley considered him the equal of Tallis and Redford, citing his music as a model for the student of counterpoint.[33] In 1571 Thorne's name was included by Nicholas Sanders in a list of musicians who suffered for their adherence to the old faith under Elizabeth,[34] and it says much for the respect he commanded at York that, despite his Catholic sympathies, he was appointed clerk of the fabric when his services as organist were no longer required.[35] His epitaph, recorded by Drake,[36] attests to his great popularity as a man, speaks of him as a musician 'most perfitt in art', and mentions his excellence 'in logick's lore'. This last phrase is presumably a reference to Thorne's ability as a poet. Three of his poems are contained in a manuscript in Redford's hand, now in the British Museum.[37] Although none of these verses can rank as poetry of a very high order, each shows a genuine feeling for language and, despite a certain rhythmic clumsiness, for poetic structure. The best of the three is the charming, if overlong, 'The hunt ys up'.[38] The other two poems, 'In worldlye welthe for man's releafe'[39]

[31] *York Statutes*, p. 74.

[32] Ibid., p. 77.

[33] Thomas Morley, *A Plaine and Easie Introduction to Practicall Musicke* (1597), p. 96; modern edn. by A. Harman (1952), p. 177.

[34] *De Visibili Monarchia* (1571); noted by W. H. Grattan Flood, 'New Light on Late Tudor Composers', *Musical Times* (Jan. 1925), p. 28.

[35] YML, Register of Leases etc., Wb, fos. 124^r–124^v.

[36] *Ebor.*, p. 500.

[37] BM, MS. Add. 15233.

[38] Ibid., fos. 33^r–34^v.

[39] Ibid., fos. 55^r–55^v.

and 'Who shall profoundly pray',[40] are more pedestrian, though not without some occasional points of interest.

Thorne was appointed organist at York on 24 July 1542 at a salary of £13 6s. 8d;[41] in the previous year he had served a probationary term as 'organist within the choir'.[42] As clerk of the works, a position he held between 1567 and 1571, he was responsible to the dean for the upkeep of the fabric, and his account for the year 1567–8 reflects the zeal with which the Marian decorations were swept away under orders from the new dean, Matthew Hutton.[43] We can do no more than imagine the distaste with which Thorne must have complied with Hutton's orders, and with which he entered in his account the words 'for making playne and washyng over with whyte the places where the altar stood'.

Thorne's readiness to respond to the dictates of authority and to adapt to the changing fashions of his day is also reflected in his music, very little of which has survived. His natural inclination as a composer was towards the imitative polyphonic style of the mid-century, or so this would seem from the four-part *In Nomine* preserved in the Bodleian Library, Oxford,[44] and from the organ fantasia, 'Exultabant Sancti'.[45] But to judge from the predominantly syllabic underlay in his setting of the Te Deum (the tenor part only is extant), he was quite prepared to meet Archbishop Holgate's stringent requirement that every word should be 'playnelie and distinctlie pronounced and undrestood'. The only composition by Thorne for which a probable date can be conjectured is the three-part motet *Stella coeli*, included by John Baldwine in his Commonplace Book of *c.* 1600[46] and later printed by Hawkins.[47] This motet, possibly composed in 1551 as a thanksgiving for deliverance from the plague,[48] is hardly comparable with the best work of Tallis or Redford. Nevertheless, its rhythmic subtlety, ingenious cadential harmonic shifts, and assured use of sequence mark it a work of considerable charm.

It is not clear for how long the order forbidding the playing of organs was enforced, but they were certainly in use again in the Minster by the end of 1573. In December of that year Henry Thorne—presumably a relative of

[40] Ibid., fos. 58ᵛ–59ʳ.
[41] YML, Register of Leases etc., Wa, fos. 157ᵛ–158ᵛ.
[42] YML, Chamberlain's Roll E1/79.
[43] *Fabric Rolls*, pp. 113–14.
[44] MS. Mus. Sch. d. 212–16.
[45] BM, MS. Add. 29996, fo. 37ᵛ.
[46] BM, Royal Music MS. 24 d 2, fos. 161ᵛ–163ʳ.
[47] *A General History of Music* (1776), vol. 2, pp. 527–30.
[48] The plague of 1550–1 was particularly severe. A letter from the lord mayor (*YCR*, v, 1946, p. 49) is emphatic in thanking God for the city's deliverance from the pestilence.

EXAMPLE 2

John—was admitted master of the choristers and keeper of the organs for a probationary period of twelve months;[49] his appointment as organist was confirmed the following year at a salary of £19 6s. 8d.[50] Henry Thorne continued in office until his death in 1597, to be succeeded in 1598 by Cuthbert Byas,[51] formerly a chorister at Durham, and in 1605 by Henry Farrande. Farrande, who seems to have been a man of prickly temperament and dubious honesty, was admitted organist and master of the choristers on 22 November.[52] The appointment was not a happy one. Before long, trouble arose between the organist and the vicars choral, and though still named in the list of payments at Pentecost 1607,[53] Farrande was dismissed from both offices on 22 December for quarrelling with the vicars and for 'malconversion', by which is probably meant embezzling the choristers' fees.[54]

There is no record in the chapter acts of an immediate successor to Farrande, and the chamberlains' rolls and account books refer simply to 'the organist'. However, an entry in the fabric rolls for the year 1607–8

[49] YML, Chapter Acts, 1565–1634, fo. 115[v].
[50] YML, St. Peter's Accounts E2(21).
[51] Ibid.
[52] YML, Chapter Acts, 1565–1634, fo. 395[r].
[53] YML, St. Peter's Accounts E2(2).
[54] YML, Chapter Acts, 1565–1634, fo. 422[r].

suggests that, following Farrande's dismissal, the duties of organist may have been undertaken by the junior organist at Durham, William Browne. In that year William Barton, a vicar choral, was paid 20s. 'for playing the organ in the absence of Mr. Browne'.[55] Browne's first name is not given, but an entry in the same roll records a payment of 36s. to Mr. Mor[ley][56] 'for his journey to Duresme for the organist there'.

In view of the unfortunate circumstances in which Farrande's employment at York had been terminated, it is a little surprising that less than ten years later the dean and chapter should have approved the appointment of Thomas Kingston to the post of organist. They can hardly have been ignorant of Kingston's behaviour at Lincoln, where he had been organist since 1599. In 1611 he was admonished by the Lincoln Cathedral authorities 'for beating the boys and calling . . . the Master of the Choristers an ass', and in the following year he was ordered 'never hereafter to meddle with teaching the Quiristers'. In 1615 he was again admonished for being 'verye often drunke', as a result of which his 'unorderlye playing on the organns [had] putt the quire out of time and disordered them'.[57] Despite all this, he was appointed organist of York Minster on 30 August 1616.[58] At first his behaviour must have been exemplary, for less than a month later he was appointed master of the choristers.[59] The latter post he held for little more than two years, and on 4 February 1619 Christopher Spenceley, a songman, was admitted *magister choristarum* in place of Kingston, who had been expelled 'on account of certain failings'.[60] Kingston's fondness for alcohol led finally to his being brought before the dean and chapter, and on 11 August 1629 he was admonished because 'he was lately so inebriated that at evensong he was unable to perform his duties, to the great scandal and disgrace of the church'.[61]

For this misdemeanour Kingston somewhat surprisingly escaped expulsion; he continued as organist until 1633. We can only conclude that his excellence as a musician was considered sufficient compensation for his other failings, and there is ample evidence that during his period of office music at York flourished. Between 1617 and 1624 the choir was at full strength;[62] there was also a certain amount of collaboration between

[55] YML, Fabric Rolls, 1569–1640, E3/62A.
[56] Christopher Morley, songman 1607–33.
[57] Quoted by J. E. West, *Cathedral Organists Past and Present* (1899), pp. 47–8.
[58] YML, Chapter Acts, 1565–1634, fo. 507^v.
[59] Ibid., fo. 514^v.
[60] Ibid., fo. 558^v.
[61] Ibid., fo. 676^r.
[62] YML, Vicars Choral Kitchen Book, fo. 225^r, shows that the total number of vicars and singing-men was twelve.

cathedral and city musicians, and in 1623 33s 4d. was paid to the York waits 'for playing in the quire five services this year'.[63] As to the music which was performed, some indication is given by an incomplete set of part-books now in the Minster Library.[64] The set contains services by Byrd, Parsons, Mundy, Sheppard, and Morley. Occasional performance dates are scribbled into the margins of the Medius Decani book, on the fly-leaf of which appear the names of Kingston and some of his choristers and singing-men (Plate 136).

Perhaps the clearest indication of the healthy state of music at this time was the decision of the dean and residentiaries to raise money for a new organ. In 1631 they petitioned the king for permission to use for this purpose part of a £1,000 fine, imposed by the Court of High Commission at York on Edward Paler of Thoraldby.[65] The request was granted on 28 November 1632, and articles of agreement were drawn up between the dean and chapter and the builder, Robert Dallam of London. The case was made under a separate contract by Christopher Richardson of Durham, who was paid 20s. a week for one year.

The instrument, which was very similar to the one Dallam's father had built twenty years earlier for Worcester Cathedral,[66] consisted of 'a great organ containeinge eight [the specification[67] shows that the number should be nine] stoppes . . . every stopp containeinge fiftie-one pipes' and 'a chaire organ containeinge five stoppes'. It was completed on 24 July 1634 and, in accordance with the wishes of Charles I, was set up on the north side of the choir where it would not obstruct the view from the nave of the east window.[68] It immediately excited much favourable comment. Sir William Brereton, who visited York later that year, remarked on 'the very stately organ lately erected in the minster-quire',[69] while visitors from Norwich commented that at York they had seen and heard 'a faire, large, high organ, newly built, richly gilt, carv'd and painted'.[70]

The last musician to hold the office of organist before the Interregnum was John Hutchinson, who had previously been organist at Southwell Minster. He was appointed on 24 March 1634,[71] and continued to be

[63] YML, Fabric Roll E3/62C.

[64] YML, M 13/1–3(S).

[65] *Fabric Rolls*, p. 319 n.

[66] A description and detailed specification of the Worcester organ is given by R. T. Dart in *Musica Britannica*, vol. 5 (1964), p. xvi.

[67] For details of the specification and costs see *Fabric Rolls*, pp. 319–25.

[68] [Jonathan Gray] *Letters to the Editor of the Musical World Relative to the York Organ* (1837), p. 6.

[69] *Fabric Rolls*, p. 319 n.

[70] 'A Relation of a Short Survey of Twenty-six Counties observ'd in a Seaven Week's Journey, 1634', BM, Lansdowne Collection, MS. 213, fos. 317–48.

[71] YML, Chapter Acts, 1565–1634, fo. 745ʳ.

responsible for music at York throughout the period of growing unrest which culminated in 'the *great* and *close Siege*', as one writer described it,[72] of 1644. As at Worcester, where during the 1630s it had been the custom on Sunday afternoons for organist, choir, and congregation to join in the psalms after the sermon,[73] the civil disturbances threatening the royalist city of York led to large congregations of citizens assembling in the Minster, so that the church was 'even *cramming* or *squeezing full*'. There, during the eleven-week siege, they joined together in 'the most *excellent Singing of Psalms*' while the enemy, 'who had planted their *Great Guns* so *mischievously* against the *Church*', fired on the walls.[74] Recounting this some years after the Restoration, Thomas Mace described his memory of the events in characteristically colourful prose:

Now here you must take notice that they had then a *Custom* in *that Church* (which I hear not of in any other *Cathedral*) which was that always before the *Sermon* the whole *Congregation sang a Psalm*, together with the *Quire and the Organ*; And you must also know that there was then a most *Excellent-large-plump-lusty-full-speaking Organ*, which cost (as I am credibly informed) a *thousand pounds* . . . This *Organ* I say (when the *Psalm* was set before the *Sermon*), being let out into all its *Fulness of Stops*, together with the *Quire* began the *Psalm*. But when *That Vast-Conchording-Unity* of the whole *Congregational Chorus* came (as I may say) *Thundering in* even so as it made the very *Ground shake* under us (*Oh the unutterable ravishing Soul's delight!*); In the which I was so *transported* and *wrapt* up into *High Contemplations* that there was no room left in my *whole Man*, viz. *Body, Soul* and *Spirit*, for any thing below *Divine* and *Heavenly Raptures* . . .[75]

Mace's enthusiastic, and probably exaggerated,[76] description of the events of 1644 was no doubt coloured by his own political views and by his knowledge that the organ which had so impressed him had failed to survive the period of Puritan rule. On 4 August 1645 the Commonwealth Committee ordered that 'Mr. Doctor Hodson be desired to deliver unto Richard Dossy the books and parcells of the organs',[77] an instruction with which Hodson seems not to have complied, for two months later the sequestrators 'with assistance of musketeers' were told 'to repair to the house of the said Dr. Hodson, there to seise and take the organ pipes, books, coaps, surplisses

---

[72] Thomas Mace, *Musick's Monument* (1676); facsimile reprint (Paris, 1958), p. 18.

[73] W. L. Woodfill, *Musicians in English Society from Elizabeth to Charles I* (Princeton, 1953), p. 157.

[74] Mace, op. cit., pp. 18–20.

[75] Ibid., p. 19.

[76] In one respect at least Mace was guilty of gross exaggeration. The cost of the organ was in fact £297, not £1,000 as he reported.

[77] *Proceedings of the Commonwealth Committee for York and Ainsty* (YAS Rec. Ser. cxviii), p. 4. Phineas Hodson, or Hodgson, was chancellor of York Minster from 1611 until his death in 1646. Dossy appears to have been a junior parliamentary/civic official. Cf. p. 440, n. 33.

and the like, and deliver them to Mr. Dossy'.[78] Not content with this, the Committee seems to have been anxious that no visible trace of the organ should remain. Less than a year later fresh orders were issued, and Mr. Dossy was required to 'furthwith cause to be pulled downe the great organ lofte in the Minster and the canopie over the same'.[79]

After the Restoration an immediate attempt was made to return to normal. In April 1660 Edward Gower reported in a letter to Sir Richard Leveson that 'the singing men and organs are preparing at York Minster',[80] and less than three years later Archbishop Frewen ordered that 'the great organ be made and sett up before Michaelmas next'.[81] Some instrument must have been in use by 1666, for in September of that year Thomas Preston was admitted organist[82] in succession to Thomas Mudd. Less than a month earlier, Mudd had been appointed master of the choristers,[83] having previously been organist at Lincoln and Exeter. Though described at his burial at Durham on 2 August 1667 as organist of York Minster, there is no record of Mudd's appointment to this office. It is a fair assumption that the hastily rebuilt Restoration organ would have incorporated whatever had survived of the original Dallam instrument, but this could not have included the pipes which had beeen sold.[84] In any case, the renovated organ seems to have been a makeshift affair, for by 1685 it had deteriorated to such an extent that Archbishop Dolben was obliged to order that 'the great organ . . . be with all convenient speed repaired and made fitt for service'.[85] In 1688 the organ was removed from the north side of the choir and returned to its original position on the screen,[86] and less than three years later plans for a new instrument were in hand. In an agreement dated 22 January 1691 Bernard Smith, court organ-builder to Queen Ann, promised 'to make & set up a new great, chair & eccho organ in the Church of York within the space of twelve months'.[87] There is no positive proof that this organ was ever built. Gray, writing in 1837, makes no mention of it, and talks of his having played forty years earlier 'the old organ of King Charles, the keys of which were deeply hollowed by long use'.[88] However, Gent's

---

[78] Ibid., pp. 5–6.
[79] Ibid., p. 8.
[80] Duke of Sutherland's MSS., *Historical Manuscript Reports*, p. 200.
[81] *York Statutes*, p. 97.
[82] YML, Chapter Acts, 1634–1700, part 2, fo. 59[v].
[83] Ibid., fo. 58[v].
[84] *Fabric Rolls*, pp. 333–4.
[85] *York Statutes*, p. 102.
[86] Drake, *Ebor.*, p. 522.
[87] Bodl., MS. d 11, fo. 336[r]. The full specification of this instrument is given by Peter Aston, 'The Organs of York Minster, 1634–1803', *Musical Times*, no. 1564, vol. 114 (1973), 637–9.
[88] Gray, op. cit., p. 5.

description of the Minster organ in 1730 fits more or less exactly with Smith's specification;[89] furthermore, a comparison between Smith's stop list and that of the organ renovated in 1803 by Green and Blyth leaves little doubt that Smith's organ, not Dallam's, was the instrument to be restored and modernized.

From all this it is clear that, contrary to popular belief, the organ built by Dallam in 1634 did not survive the troubles of the seventeenth century. However, it was not only the organ which had suffered during the upheavals of the Interregnum. In answer to articles proposed to them by the dean and chapter[90] the vicars choral wrote, 'wee have but foure common prayer books . . . for the whole Quire which are in folio; wee have 10 bookes printed in folio of services and anthems which are something rotted and decayed [and] our written bookes are very old and much torne'. More serious was the problem of rebuilding the choir and training a new generation of boy choristers. In 1667 the adult section of the choir was almost back to full strength—there were four vicars choral and seven songmen—but even as late as 1676 there was still an acute shortage of competent boys. Writing of conditions at York and Durham, Roger North reported that wind instruments were used 'to supply the want of [boys'] voices, very notorious there'.[91] The situation cannot have been helped by the policy of the Chapel Royal to obtain singers from provincial cathedral choirs. In November 1670 Mr. James Hart, 'a base from Yorke', was sworn in place of Edmund Slater;[92] Lincoln, Salisbury, and Worcester were among other cathedral churches to lose singers to the service of the king. However, the practice of 'press-ganging' boys from the provinces into the royal choirs in no way affected those cathedrals where standards were poor, and the name of York Minster is conspicuously absent from the list of cathedrals visited by Captain Cooke in his search for 'boyes for the Chappell'.

On 18 April 1691 Thomas Wanless was admitted organist of York Minster in succession to Thomas Preston;[93] he was appointed master of the choristers in the following year.[94] Wanless, himself a prolific composer of church music, was editor of the earliest extant edition of the York Anthem Book, a collection subsequently enlarged, revised, and reprinted no less than fifteen times during the course of the next 250 years. The date of the

---

[89] See Aston, 'Organs of York Minster'. The article also contains a detailed examination of the similarities between Smith's organ and the instrument renovated by Green and Blyth.
[90] The 'humble answers of the Vicars Chorall' are quoted in full by Frederick Harrison, op. cit., pp. 325–7.
[91] John Wilson, *Roger North on Music* (1959), p. 40.
[92] E. F. Rimbault, *The Old Cheque-Book of the Chapel Royal*, Camden Soc. N.S. 3 (1872), pp. 14–15.
[93] YML, Chapter Acts, 1634–1700, part 2, fo. 219[r].
[94] YML, St. Peter's Accounts E2(22).

136 The names of Thomas Kingston and some of his singing-men, as they appear on the fly-leaf of MS M 13/1(S).

137 Opening of the 'York Litany' by Thomas Wanless, as it appears in the Foster collection. The hand is later than Foster's.

first edition is not known, but a second appeared in 1705. It contains the words of seventy-eight anthems, no fewer than seventeen of which are by Wanless himself.

From the few anthems and other sacred settings by Wanless which have survived, it is difficult to understand how he can have earned the reputation he enjoyed during his lifetime. His music, when not incompetent, is often plain to the point of dullness. His funeral anthem, 'I am the Resurrection',[95] suffers from a marked paucity of melodic invention, a weakness made more noticeable by the squareness of the rhythmic structure and the repetitive harmonic patterns. Wanless was also the composer of the four-part 'York Litany', a work which remained popular for more than a century after his death (Plate 137). It was reprinted at least three times during the nineteenth century, and though temporarily dropped from the Minster repertoire was reintroduced in 1941 on the recommendation of Dean Milner-White, from which time it was in regular use at York until the songmen ceased singing at matins in 1955. In 1889 John S. Bumpus reported that the Wanless Litany was regularly performed at Lichfield, where it was considered 'by no means less beautiful and pathetic' than the setting by Tallis.[96] This may seem extravagant praise, and perhaps reveals more about the taste of the late nineteenth century than it does about the ability of Wanless. Nevertheless, he could occasionally come up with an arresting musical idea. The exuberant opening of his anthem 'Awake up my glory' is certainly striking enough despite the somewhat obvious debt to Purcell, though it must be said that the rest of the work falls far short of the level of the first few bars. The only complete version of this anthem to have survived is found in the manuscript collection prepared by Thomas Tudway for Lord Harley,[97] where it is described as 'a verse anthem accompanied with instruments ... compos'd by Mr. Tho. Wanless, organist of York, for his Batchelour of Musick's degree in Cambridge'. For a degree exercise the music is surprisingly undisciplined. Consecutive fifths and octaves between the voice parts abound, the string writing is often clumsily contrived, and some of the harmonic progressions are, to say the least, rather inept.

A third edition of the York Anthem Book was brought out in 1715. It was edited by Charles Murgatroyd, who succeeded Wanless as organist in 1712.[98] Not surprisingly, almost half the anthems by Wanless included in

---

[95] BM, MS. Add. 17820, fos. 107–9.
[96] J. S. Bumpus, *A History of English Cathedral Music, 1549–1889* (1908), i. 11.
[97] BM, MS. Harl. 7341, fos. 129^r–133^r. The anthem is also found in YML, M 117 (incomplete); in YML, M 164–H1–2 (one voice part and both string parts missing); and in YML, M 198 (bass part only).
[98] YML, Chapter Acts, 1701–28, fo. 44^r.

EXAMPLE 3

the earlier edition were now dropped to make room for some of the forty-five anthems appearing for the first time. Subsequent editions of the Anthem Book brought out during the remainder of the eighteenth century reflect the changes of taste under Murgatroyd's successors, William Davies (appointed 1721 and expelled the following March for absence),[99] Charles

[99] Ibid., fos. 98[v], 100[v].

Quarles (1722–7),[100] Edward Salisbury (appointed 13 February 1728[101] and expelled in 1735, having several times been admonished for absence),[102] James Nares, and John Camidge. The Anthem Book of 1736, edited by Thomas Ellway,[103] was much larger than any of its predecessors. Included for the first time were anthems by Steffani and Handel, together with six anthems by the new organist, James Nares.

Nares was born in Stanwell, Middlesex, in 1715. As a chorister at the Chapel Royal, he was educated under Gates, Croft, and, later, Pepusch. He was appointed organist of York Minster on 8 November 1735,[104] having previously been deputy organist at St. George's Chapel, Windsor. There is no record of the date on which he was officially appointed master of the choristers at York, though he appears to have undertaken these duties from some time in 1742 (he was paid £2 per quarter-annum as master of the boys from May 1744, with an additional £10 back pay).[105] In 1756 he was appointed organist and composer to the Chapel Royal in succession to Maurice Greene, becoming master of the children the following year. He died on 10 February 1783, and was buried in St. Margaret's, Westminster.

Such was the career of one of the most prominent church musicians of the eighteenth century, a man renowned in his day both as a choir trainer and as a composer. In addition to his church music, which is somewhat uneven in quality, Nares published a considerable quantity of keyboard music, glees, catches, and songs, as well as treatises on singing and keyboard playing, and a dramatic ode, 'The Royal Pastoral'. Most of his sacred settings are in a watered-down Handelian idiom, the verse anthems consisting of a succession of solo movements followed by a closing chorus, often in semi-fugal style. In the foreword to his collection of anthems published in 1778, Nares wrote:

In my Compositions for the Church, it has been my Endeavour to preserve the true character of Church Music . . . I have been very sparing of Divisions, thinking them too airy for the Church, though proper enough in Oratorios, which seem to hold an intermediate Place between the Church and the Theatre. I have had the greatest Regard to the Words, endeavouring rather to illustrate their Beauties and enforce their Sentiments than to display the Art of Musical Composition.[106]

---

[100] Ibid., fo. 103r.
[101] Ibid., fo. 132r.
[102] YML, Chapter Acts, 1728–47, fos. 67v, 107v, 108r–v.
[103] On the title-page Ellway described himself as 'Master of the Children', a position he did not in fact hold. He was assistant to Thomas Benson, master of the choristers 1698–1742.
[104] YML, Chapter Acts, 1728–47, fo. 116r.
[105] YML, St. Peter's Accounts E2(23)–(24).
[106] *Twenty Anthems in Score . . . by Dr. Nares* (1778).

Despite these remarks, it is difficult to escape the conclusion that Nares designed many of his solo movements, particularly those for bass voice, to show off the vocal skills of the performer. However, it would be wrong to suggest that these solo passages are no more than empty display. At his best, Nares was capable of producing music of great charm and delicacy, and the second section of his anthem 'Rejoice in the Lord, O ye righteous'[107] is typical of the freshness with which he wrote for solo treble.

EXAMPLE 4

A similar feeling for melodic lyricism can be seen in the opening trio of 'O praise the Lord',[108] one of the settings included in his manuscript collection of anthems 'compos'd for the use of the King's Chapel'.[109] Originally written at York in 1746, this setting of passages from various Psalms was revised and shortened twenty-one years later so that it would fit the requirements of George II, who 'never sat during the anthem, & began to be fategued with standing long as usual'.[110]

On his resignation from York in 1756, Nares was succeeded by his pupil, John Camidge, who was appointed organist on 31 January at a salary of £40

[107] Ibid. A modern edn. by Watkins Shaw of the Allegretto movement, 'The voice of joy', is published by Novello (1970).
[108] A modern edn. by Peter Aston is published by Novello (1973).
[109] BM, MS. Add. 19570.
[110] Ibid., from a note in Nares's hand on the title-page.

per annum.[111] Camidge, a native of York, had been a chorister at the Minster in 1735 before going to London to study with Maurice Greene, at the same time taking lessons from Handel. His first professional appointment was as organist of Doncaster Parish Church; while at Doncaster, he occasionally deputized for Nares during the latter's absences from the Minster.

A fairly comprehensive picture of the music which was performed at York under Camidge is provided by the manuscript collection of anthems and services edited by William Foster, subchanter from 1755 until 1768. The collection, dated 1761, was at one time owned by William Knight, subchanter 1722–39, but the catalogue was made by Foster and the preface is in his hand. The eleven volumes, not all of which survive, evidently included the 'five volumes of Church Music in Folio left by the late Mr. Knight's Will for the use of the Subchanter [and] deposited in the Evidence House in Beddern'.[112] The collection[113] contains the music of most of the anthems listed in the printed Anthem Books, together with services by Byrd, Blow, Child, Purcell, Wise, and others.

The next two editions of the Anthem Book, published in 1782 and 1794, were edited by William Mason, who was precentor from 1762 until 1797. Mason, the son of a Hull clergyman, was a man of remarkably diverse talents whose active career in the Church still left him time to cultivate his interests in writing, painting, music, gardening, and politics. As a poet, he was admired by Horace Walpole and Sir Joshua Reynolds; he was also intimate with Thomas Gray, who had first shown interest in his work at Cambridge. His ode for the installation of the Duke of Newcastle as Chancellor of Cambridge University in 1749 was set to music by William Boyce, composer to the Chapel Royal. Later, Thomas Arne provided music for Mason's dramatic entertainment, *Elfrida* (1772), and for the Covent Garden production of *Caractacus* in 1776. The adulation heaped on Mason by his contemporaries was considerable. Burney thought him 'a superior Man to every one except his Friend Mr. Grey',[114] while Walpole considered him the equal of Shakespeare and Milton.[115]

Mason's interest in music was both practical and enthusiastic. As precentor at York he exercised his right to control musical affairs in the Minster, and at the south Yorkshire parish of Aston, where he was rector, he took an active part in training the choir. He was also something of a

[111] YML, Chapter Acts, 1747–56, fo. 128[v].
[112] YML, Subchanter's Book, vol. 2, p. 446.
[113] YML, M 8, M 164/G, H, H2, J, J2, J3, M 14/1, 2.
[114] Letter from Burney to Mrs. Allen, Apr. 1764, quoted by Roger Lonsdale, *Dr. Charles Burney* (1965), p. 70.
[115] Letter from Walpole to Mason, May 1783, quoted by Bernard Barr and John Ingamells, *A Candidate for Praise* (York, 1973), p. iv.

composer. His anthem 'Lord of all power and might' was performed at the Chapel Royal and printed in John Page's *Harmonia Sacra* of 1800, while seven more anthems by him were included in the York Anthem Book of 1809. His views on church music were typical of his age; like many of his contemporaries he was outspoken in his condemnation of the 'complex and artificial style' which did little but 'perplex or bewilder the general congregation'. In the preface to his Anthem Book of 1782 Mason dismissed the work of Elizabethan and early Stuart composers as 'almost entirely unintelligible', arguing that the sole object of music in church should be to convey the sense of the words with utmost clarity. This essay, admired by Burney, was reprinted in abridged form in the seven editions of the Anthem Book brought out between 1794 and 1861. It was also published separately by Mason in 1795 as one of four *Essays, Historical and Critical, on English Church Music.*[116]

Following the resignation of John Camidge in October 1799, his son Matthew was appointed organist and master of the choristers,[117] In this way, responsibility for music at York Minster passed to a second generation of the Camidge family. Eventually, it was to pass to a third, John Camidge the younger, whose son, Thomas Simpson Camidge, was active as deputy organist between 1848 and 1859.

The long reign of the Camidges, lasting for more than one hundred years, saw considerable changes in the musical life of the Minster. Shortly before the appointment of James Nares in 1735, the choir had comprised five vicars choral, seven songmen, and six boys, but by the middle of the century the adult section of the choir had been reduced to six voices.[118] Under John Camidge the situation seems to have deteriorated even more, and in 1822 it was reported that, when Dean Markham first took office at the beginning of the nineteenth century, the choir was scarcely able to perform the ordinary choruses in the anthems, which were therefore omitted.[119] The size of the choir was later increased by John Camidge the younger, who persuaded the dean and chapter to engage six supernumeraries to attend on Sundays and for other special services; later still, Dean Duncombe increased the number of boys from five to fourteen and doubled the number of regular songmen to a total of twelve.[120]

[116] The essays, respectively on instrumental music, on cathedral music, on parochial psalmody, and on the causes of the present imperfect alliance between music and poetry, were reprinted in vol. 3 of Mason's *Works* (1811). A further essay on rhythmical psalmody survives in manuscript (YML, M 94S).

[117] YML, Chapter Acts, 1784–1807, p. 216.

[118] Frederick Harrison, op. cit., p. 277.

[119] *Yorkshire Gazette*, 5 Oct. 1822.

[120] *VCH York*, p. 354, with nn. 98 and 9.

Despite the fluctuating standards in choral singing under the Camidges, the anthem books which appeared between 1753 and 1854 tended to increase in size. (An exception was the edition of 1854 which contained twenty-one anthems fewer than the previous publication.) The changing musical tastes of the period are clearly reflected in the contents of these books. The most popular composers at the end of the eighteenth century were Croft, Greene, and Purcell, who between them contributed almost one-third of the total number of anthems printed in the 1782 edition. However, the rage for oratorio, which Mason complained was spreading 'from the Capital to every Market Town in the Kingdom',[121] was not slow in reaching York, and by 1809 the number of anthems adapted from oratorios by Handel had risen from two to nineteen. The trend was to continue. During the next fifty years anthems by Boyce and Greene were gradually replaced by extracts from works by Handel, Mozart, and Haydn, arranged and 'improved' by Matthew Camidge and others.

The Camidges themselves were also represented in the Minster repertoire, though not to the extent that might be expected. The elder John Camidge contributed only two anthems to the 1782 Anthem Book (three more were included in the Foster collection), and Matthew only four to the edition of 1809. The next three editions, published in 1831, 1834, and 1854, included several arrangements by Matthew Camidge, but no additional anthems of his own. This seems surprising in view of his reputation as a composer. Like his father, he had studied in London (he received his early musical education at the Chapel Royal under Nares), and later he published a number of sonatas and other instrumental pieces, a collection of psalm tunes, and *A Method of Instruction in Musick by Questions and Answers*. Even more surprising is the fact that the printed collections contain very few anthems by the younger John Camidge, who succeeded his father as organist in October 1842.[122] From the quantity of church music he published, John Camidge seems to have been considerably more prolific than either his father or grandfather. His neglect at York may possibly be due to the fact that his active participation in music came to an abrupt halt in 1850. In that year he was stricken with paralysis, and for the remainder of his period of office was incapable of playing the organ or directing the choir. He was eventually forced to resign on 10 September 1858, and was granted a pension of £100 per annum.[123]

The first half of the nineteenth century was an eventful period in the history of the Minster organs. In 1803 the instrument which had been in use

[121] Essay on parochial psalmody, *Works*, vol. 3, p. 388.
[122] YML, Chapter Acts, 1830–42, pp. 371–2.
[123] YML, Chapter Acts, 1842–73, p. 450; YML, P 236, p. 139.

since the end of the seventeenth century was renovated and enlarged by Green and Blyth at a cost of about £800. The original case and some of the old pipes were retained, but the finished instrument, which included a pedalboard and almost twice the former number of stops, bore little further resemblance to the earlier organ. Jonathan Gray, who had played both instruments, was severely critical of the changes which had been made. Though ready to praise the improved 'sweetness and mellowness of tone', he thought the full organ 'scarcely more powerful than before'. He also complained that the treble of the great organ was 'feeble and thin', that there was 'a muddy breathing articulation in most of the stops', and that the swell was 'neither so distinct nor so elegant as formerly'. He continued: 'We were wont to observe a marked contrast between the boldness of the full organ, the softness of the choir and the richness of the swell. Now the character of each . . . is so indeterminate . . . that the different transitions from one to another lose their effect'.[124]

In 1815 improvements to the organ were carried out by Ward of York. The wind pressure was increased, the pipes revoiced, and new sound-boards were added.[125] So successful were these improvements that in 1820 Ward was given the contract for a major rebuild, carried out to the specification of Matthew Camidge.[126] The work was completed in 1823, and the new instrument (to which Ward had added a detached console) was used in the 'Grand Musical Festival' held in that year. Though generally held to be one of the finest instruments in the country[127]—one observer described it as 'the largest and most complete in Great Britain'[128]—this organ lasted for less than six years. On the night of February 2 1829 an anti-clerical maniac, Jonathan Martin, set fire to the choir, completely destroying the organ and stalls. At his trial Martin declared: 'While I was at prayers that afternoon I thought it was merely deceiving the people that the organ made such a noise of buzz, buzz. Says I to myself, I'll have thee down tonight. Thou shalt buzz no more'.[129]

Plans for a new organ were immediately drawn up, the contract being given to the London firm of Elliot and Hill. After considerable delay, caused by a series of petty disagreements between the autocratic and quarrelsome

---

[124] Gray, op. cit., pp. 6–7.

[125] Ibid., p. 8.

[126] For details of the specification, see Andrew Freeman, 'The Organs of York Minster', *The Organ*, vol. 5, no. 26 (1926).

[127] G. A. Poole and J. W. Hugall, *An Historical Guide to York Cathedral and its Antiquities* (York, 1850), p. 208.

[128] John Crosse, *An Account of the Grand Musical Festival held in the Cathedral Church of York* (York, 1825).

[129] Quoted by Gray, op. cit., p. 10.

Dean Cockburn and the organist, Matthew Camidge, the work was eventually completed in September 1833. The finished instrument proved far from satisfactory. Writing in 1863, a later Minster organist, E. G. Monk, was at pains to point out its faults, commenting that 'the prevalence of false and vague theories upon the nature and disposition of stops' had led to 'many grave errors of design'.[130] Immediately after its completion steps were taken to improve the organ, and by 1850 twenty-six more stops had been added, including a tuba mirabilis given by George Hudson, the 'Railway King'. Monk remained unimpressed. 'The faults of the first arrangements', he wrote, 'were still not only uncorrected but made more prominent by the useless system of multiplication of stops of a calibre of tone already existing'. As for the restricted lower compass of the manuals, it 'converted the whole into a discordant mass, destitute of order, system or effect'.[131]

Table 2 List of York Minster organists, 1475 to the present day

1475–1481	John Austan	1691–1712	Thomas Wanless
1484–1492	John Symson	1712–1721	William Davies
1510–1524	John Usher	1722–1727	Charles Quarles
1527–1529	Robert Holmes	1728–1735	Edward Salisbury
1531–1540	Thomas Kirkby	1735–1756	James Nares
1541–1573	John Thorne	1756–1799	John Camidge the elder
1573–1597	Henry Thorne	1799–1842	Matthew Camidge
1598–1604	Cuthbert Byas	1842–1858	John Camidge the younger
1605–1607	Henry Farrande		
1607–1616	[?William] Browne	1859–1883	Edwin George Monk
1616–1633	Thomas Kingston	1883–1897	John Naylor
1634–1645	John Hutchinson	1897–1913	Thomas Tertius Noble
c. 1663–1666	Thomas Mudd	1913–1946	Sir Edward Bairstow
1666–1691	Thomas Preston	1946–	Francis Jackson

Monk's outspoken criticism of the 1833 organ was evidently intended to draw attention to his own superior design, and to justify the cost of the alterations. Immediately on his appointment in 1859[132] he had recommended an entire reconstruction of the organ, 'introducing those modern mechanical appliances so indispensable to the comfort of the organist and the control of so large an instrument'.[133] The work, carried out by Hill and

[130] 'A Descriptive Account of the York Minster Organs', reprinted by A. P. Purey-Cust, *Organs and Organists of York Minster* (York, 1899), pp. 18–30.
[131] Ibid., p. 24.
[132] YML, Chapter Acts, 1842–73, p. 459.
[133] Purey-Cust, op. cit., p. 25.

Son, was completed in 1863. Although smaller than the previous organ, Monk considered it 'an undoubted improvement', adding, 'its increased depth, richness and beauty of tone are manifest to any one conversant with organ effects'.[134]

In the same year a separate three-manual organ designed by Monk was built by Hill and Son. Its purpose was to accompany choral services in the nave, a measure introduced by Dean Duncombe 'to induce the working classes to attend divine worship'.[135] On special occasions the organ was used to support 'very large bodies of singers'; accordingly, it had been 'designed, scaled, voiced and winded with reference to this purpose', the aim being for 'fullness, breadth and vigour of tone'.[136] At the 1903 rebuild of the screen organ, the console was placed so that the organist could accompany services in the nave. Consequently, the nave organ, which had been built into a dark wooden case of the plainest design, was no longer required. It was sold to St. Thomas's Church in Radcliffe, Manchester, where it was reopened on 29 June 1904.

The appointment of Monk was by no means entirely popular with the citizens of York. For the past ten years the organist's duties had been taken over by Thomas Camidge, acting in place of his crippled father. Many expected that, on John Camidge's resignation, the post would be offered to his son, so continuing the tradition established at the end of the previous century. Instead the Minster authorities decided to look further afield for a man of greater experience and more widely acknowledged ability. Monk, who had studied with Macfarren and Henry Field, was nine years Thomas Camidge's senior. He had been admitted to the degree of D.Mus. at Oxford in 1856, by which time he had already published a considerable quantity of church music and had held a variety of appointments both in his native country and in Ireland. These achievements were impressive—certainly more so than Camidge's—and it is not altogether surprising that Monk was preferred to the younger man. However, news of the decision was greeted with certain hostility from the public, who saw the appointment as a slight to the former assistant organist. To make matters worse, Monk promptly dropped from the repertoire all music by members of the Camidge family. The Anthem Book of 1861 contained not a single Camidge anthem, and though Monk himself was not the compiler of this edition,[137] two anthems by him were included in the appendix published in 1864.

The contents of the 1861 Anthem Book clearly reflect the interest of the

---

[134] Ibid., p. 26.
[135] *Yorkshire Gazette*, 8 Dec. 1866.
[136] Purey-Cust, op. cit., pp. 31–2.
[137] The collection was edited by Samuel Shepherd, precentor of Rochester.

Victorians in second-hand (and often second-rate) continental music. Handel, now represented by no less than forty-one pieces adapted from various sources, remained the most popular composer, but also included in the repertoire were several arrangements of pieces by Mendelssohn and Spohr. More such arrangements appeared in the anthem books of 1868 and 1883, together with a host of English imitations of the feeblest kind. Nevertheless, a few composers were able to preserve an individual identity in the face of the current vogue for imitating modish but insignificant examples imported from abroad, and despite his indebtedness to Mendelssohn, a composer such as S. S. Wesley could occasionally produce music of real conviction and originality. But Wesley's work was exceptional, and for every composition by him included in the anthem books brought out during Monk's period of office there were six or more by composers of little or no real talent.

From 1881 a complete record of the music performed in the Minster is provided by the weekly service sheets. These show a number of interesting changes in repertoire under Monk's successors, Naylor and Noble. By 1900 anthems and services by Elizabethan and Jacobean composers were beginning to find their way back into use after a century or more of neglect, though it must be emphasized that anthems by Byrd and Gibbons had been reprinted several times during the eighteenth and nineteenth centuries. These works were now performed with increasing frequency, and the growing attention paid to the music of Tudor and early Stuart composers was soon to be followed by a revival of interest in the music of Purcell and his contemporaries. A random selection of service sheets from the years 1891 to 1911 gives some indication of the general repertoire at that time and the changes which were taking place. The lists for the week beginning the second Sunday in Advent, taken at five-yearly intervals, show a gradual decrease in the amount of Victorian music being performed and a corresponding increase in the number of anthems and services by, for example, Tallis, Tye, Byrd, Gibbons, and Purcell. Under Bairstow, who succeeded Noble in 1913, this trend was to continue. More and more anthems by Victorian composers were dropped in favour of music by pre-Restoration composers and by some of Bairstow's contemporaries such as Vaughan Williams, Charles Wood, and Walford Davies.

On his resignation from the Minster in 1883, E. G. Monk was granted a pension of £150 per annum.[138] Five months later his successor, John Naylor, was appointed at a salary of £300, to be raised to £400 on Monk's death.[139]

---

[138] YML, Chapter Acts, 1873–90, p. 298.
[139] Ibid.

Naylor was never to receive the promised increase. He resigned on 7 April 1897,[140] and died the following month on a voyage to Australia, so predeceasing Monk by almost twelve years. Naylor, one of a distinguished family of composers and church musicians,[141] was born in Stanningly, near Leeds, in 1838. As a boy he had been a chorister at Leeds parish church, and at the age of eighteen was appointed organist of Scarborough parish church where, in spite of his youth, 'he soon began to promote a taste for good music in the town'.[142] Later he became organist at All Saints', Scarborough, where 'he raised the musical services to a pitch of great excellence'.[143] On moving to York, he was appointed conductor of the York Musical Society, for which he wrote a number of large-scale cantatas, including *Jeremiah* (1884), *The Brazen Serpent* (1887), *Meribah* (1890), and *Manna* (1893). These were all performed with great success in the Minster, and together with Naylor's other professional activities earned him the respect of many of his contemporaries, one of whom described him as 'an excellent cathedral organist, a musician of catholic tastes, and a composer of no mean merit'.[144]

Eight months after his resignation from the Minster, Naylor was succeeded by Thomas Tertius Noble,[145] a former pupil of Bridge and Stanford, and, immediately prior to his appointment at York, organist and choir-master at Ely Cathedral. Like Naylor, Noble devoted much energy to musical activities outside the Minster: in 1899 he founded the York Symphony Orchestra, an amateur body still active in the city today, and in 1901 he became conductor of the York Musical Society. Five years later he was made principal conductor of the Hovingham Festival, where his 'Birthday Greeting to Joachim' was performed. Together with Sir Walter Parratt, Noble drew up the specification for a new organ built by Walker and Sons and set up in the Minster in 1903 at a total cost of £4,835. In this rebuild little of the old instrument was retained apart from the case and the best of the pipe work. A new blowing plant was put in, the swell box was lowered so that it could not be seen from below, and the console was moved from the east front to the south side to enable the organist to accompany services in either the nave or the choir.[146] In 1917 a partial reconstruction of this instrument was carried out by Harrison and Harrison of Durham for the

---

[140] YML, Chapter Acts, 1890–1914, pp. 254–5.
[141] His son, Edward Woodall (1867–1934), was a prominent composer and writer on music, and his grandson, Bernard (b. 1907), a composer, scholar, and conductor of international repute. Both have at some time held appointments as church organists.
[142] *Grove's Dictionary of Music and Musicians* (2nd edn 1907).
[143] Ibid.
[144] Ibid.
[145] YML, Chapter Acts, 1890–1914, p. 266.
[146] For details of this instrument see Freeman, op. cit.

new organist, Edward C. Bairstow. Several extra stops were added to the great, the swell and choir organs were revoiced, and the entire mechanism of the instrument was overhauled, electric motors being installed in place of the old blowing apparatus.

Bairstow, born in Huddersfield on 22 August 1874, was appointed to the Minster in 1913, having previously been organist at Leeds parish church. In 1893 he was articled to Sir Frederick Bridge, remaining with him for nearly six years as his pupil and amanuensis. Bairstow's reputation as a choir trainer was almost legendary in the north of England: by 1929 he had conducted choral societies at Petworth, Southport, Blackburn, Preston, Barnsley, and York, as well as the more celebrated Leeds Philharmonic Society and Bradford Festival Choral Society. Not surprisingly, the standard of choral singing in the Minster reached a high level during Bairstow's period of office; in the years following the 1914–18 War the choir quickly established a considerable reputation, and by 1930 was considered one of the best cathedral choirs in the country.

As a composer, Bairstow devoted himself almost entirely to church music, much of which is still performed today. In addition to his organ works, he published a large number of anthems and services; he also composed the introit for the coronation service of George VI in 1937. Many of these works are indebted to the influence of Brahms, though the best of them reveal a strong individual indentity, as can be seen in the dramatic opening of his justly celebrated anthem 'Let all mortal flesh keep silence'.

EXAMPLE 5

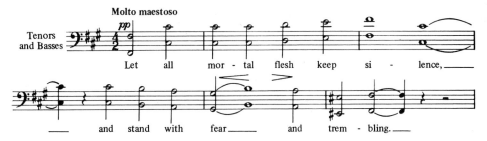

Hardly less impressive is the imaginative and colourful setting of the Creed in his D major Communion Service, or, in a different vein, the mystical and more introspective 'I sat down under his shadow', one of *Three Introits or Short Anthems* composed in 1925. The latter is remarkable for the almost total absence of harmonic chromaticism. However, it is by no means the only work by Bairstow to depart from the harmonic language of late

German Romanticism, and not the least of the composer's gifts was his ability to write a memorable and wholly engaging diatonic tune such as the one taken from the Benedictus of his Morning Service in E flat. Bairstow was knighted for his services to music in 1932; twenty-one years later the Friends of York Minster gave as a memorial to him a single-manual chamber organ, built in 1802 by Henry Lincoln of London and restored by Mander.[147]

EXAMPLE 6

Bles-sed be the Lord God of Is - rael,— for he hath vi - si -ted and re - deem-ed his peo-ple; and hath rai -sed up a migh-ty sal -va - tion for us in the house of his ser - vant Da -vid.

In 1928 a new specification for the Minster organ was drawn up by Bairstow in consultation with Arthur Harrison. Amongst other improvements Bairstow recommended a complete remodelling of the solo and pedal organs. The work, carried out by Harrison and Harrison, was completed in 1931, and the instrument, which included a new console and new electro-pneumatic action, was opened on 29 April.[148] For nearly thirty years this organ was in almost constant daily use, and apart from minor repairs it received little attention. Towards the end of the 1950s it was in obvious need of an overhaul: dust was affecting some of the smaller pipes, and the pitch 'had sunk so low as to make combined performance with an orchestra a practical impossibility, especially in cold weather'.[149] Accordingly, a new scheme was drawn up by the present Minster organist, Francis Jackson, and the renovations, carried out by Walker and Sons, were completed in May 1960. Further repair work was begun in 1967, and completed in 1972. An important addition in 1960 was a detached nave console, a duplicate of that on the screen. Originally occupying a fixed position only a yard or so

[147] *25th Annual Report of The Friends of York Minster* (1953), pp. 9–11.
[148] For an assessment of this instrument, see Reginald Whitworth, 'The Rebuilt Organ in York Minster', *The Organ*, vol. 11, no. 32 (1931), pp. 65–70.
[149] Francis Jackson, 'York Minster 1960 and Schweitzer', *The Organ*, vol. 40, no. 157 (1960), pp. 23–30. The article includes a detailed specification of the instrument.

Table 3 List of major organs

Date	Builder	Great	Swell	Choir	Solo	Pedal	Couplers	Tremulants	Total	Accessories
1634	Dallam	9	—	5	—	—	—	—	14	—
1691	Smith	10	1 (echo)	6	—	—	—	—	17	—
1803	Green & Blyth	13	8	6	—	1	—	—	28	—
1823	Ward	23	8	8	—	13	6	—	58	—
1833	Elliot & Hill	24	13	9	—	9	9	—	64	—
1850	Elliot & Hill	40	18	11	2	8	9	—	88	—
1863	Hill & Son	24	14	9	3	19	6	2	77	8
1903	Walker & Sons	20	16	10	8	16	15	2	87	39
1917	Harrison & Harrison	20	16	10	9	16	15	2	88	39
1931	Harrison & Harrison	20	16	10	11	16	20	2	95	43
1960	Walker & Sons	22	16	12	11	17	18	3	99	46
1972	Walker & Sons	22	16	12	11	17	18	3	99	46

from the place where the nave organ once stood, the console has now been made movable so that it can be used for a greater variety of purposes.

Shortly after his death on 1 May 1946 Sir Edward Bairstow was succeeded by his former pupil, Francis Jackson, who was appointed organist of York Minster on 8 October in that year. As a boy, Jackson had been a chorister in the Minster choir. He later became organist of Malton parish church, returning to the Minster as assistant organist in April 1946 to deputize for the ailing Bairstow, who was to live for only ten more days. The affection felt by Jackson for his old teacher is reflected in the large amount of Bairstow's music still sung by the Minster choir. During the past few years only two composers, Byrd and Stanford, have been more frequently performed. Also included in the current repertoire are works by other former York Minster organists, notably Nares and Noble, and by a growing number of living composers including Jackson himself.

In addition to his organ music, chamber and orchestral works, Jackson has written a large quantity of anthems and services, most of which have become a standard part of the modern English cathedral repertoire. The style of his church music is somewhat eclectic, and it is possible to recognize a number of influences ranging from Debussy to Vaughan Williams and Walton. However, these influences have become fully absorbed into a characteristically individual idiom, and much of Jackson's recent music reveals a high degree of originality within the restrictions imposed by the composer's strong sense of tradition. Almost every work demonstrates a remarkable technical assurance, whether in quiet, reflective pieces such as

EXAMPLE 7

the early *St. Patrick's Even-Song* (1949), the deservedly popular Evening Service in G (1952), or in more extrovert settings such as 'Blow ye the trumpet in Zion', composed in 1963 for the St. Cecilia Day Festival Service at the Church of the Holy Sepulchre in Holborn. The dance-like syncopations in the voice parts of the extract quoted in Example 7 are carried a stage further in a number of more recent settings. The passage from the G major Te Deum (1964) set out in Example 8 is typical of the energetic thrust the composer manages to achieve by the simplest means; it is also reminiscent of the rhythmic brilliance of much of Jackson's organ writing.

EXAMPLE 8

That Jackson is equally well known as a composer of organ music is hardly surprising in view of his outstanding ability as a performer. Since returning to York in 1946, he has established an international reputation as one of Britain's foremost recitalists. Despite his frequent engagements abroad and his many recitals and recordings in England, Jackson has still found time to involve himself in local music-making outside the Minster, writing several works for amateur musicians in the city and conducting the York Musical Society and Symphony Orchestra.

In 1974 the Minster choir consisted of some thirty voices. Apart from a period immediately after the war when songmen were difficult to recruit, the numbers have remained little changed since 1930. At that time there were twenty choristers and nine songmen (a tenth has since been added), who together sang full daily services except on Mondays and Wednesdays. However, the choir has been differently constituted since 1964 when the dean and chapter and the University of York introduced a scheme of choral scholarships, tenable by students at the University or St. John's College. There are now four songmen and six choral scholars who sing the full Sunday services and daily evensong except on Wednesdays. Matins has not been sung since 1967, when the recent repairs to the fabric of the Minster were begun; before that, matins had been sung since 1955 by the boys only. Though there are now fewer sung services, the repertoire of the choir is no less extensive or varied than at any time since 1881 when printed service sheets were first introduced. Each year nearly four hundred separate anthems and services are performed, and visitors to the Minster are able to hear music of all periods from the fifteenth century and earlier to the present day.

As for music from the more distant past, little has survived, though there is evidence that York's musical traditions go back at least as far as the seventh century. The few contemporary accounts of musical practices at York during the Saxon period[150] show that, from the earliest times, music had played an important part in the ecclesiastical life of the diocese. The traditions established in the seventh century continued to flourish for some time, and though they may not have survived the Viking period, new and stronger traditions were established under the Normans. Almost five centuries later radical liturgical reform brought fundamental changes to the established order and severe restrictions in the use of music. Despite these reforms, the musical tradition revived, and though itself undergoing fundamental changes was eventually revitalized.

The course of music at York since the first Edwardian Act of Uniformity in 1549 has not always been smooth, and compared with some other great English cathedrals the musical achievements of the Minster have not been spectacular. No composer of real stature has ever held the office of organist, as did Byrd at Lincoln, Weelkes at Chichester, or Tomkins at Worcester. But it would be wrong to judge the vigour of a musical tradition by the

---

[150] Bede, *HE*, Bk. 2, Ch. 20, p. 126; Bk. 4, Ch. 2, p. 205; *Hists. York* i. 22; for Alcuin's description of music under Archbishops Egbert and Albert, see *Hists. York* i. 386, 391.

achievements of one or two men. During more than four centuries of worship in the Minster the contribution of the choir and organist has been a vital one. There is every sign that it will continue to be so for many years to come.

For permission to quote a passage from Edward Bairstow's 'Let all mortal flesh keep silence' and from the Benedictus of his Morning Service in E flat, grateful acknowledgment is made to the publisher, Messrs. Stainer & Bell. For permission to reproduce the opening bars of 'Blow ye the trumpet in Zion' by Francis Jackson, and to quote a short extract from his G major Te Deum, grateful acknowledgment is made to the Oxford University Press.

CHAPTER X

Funeral Monuments and other Post-Medieval Sculpture

G. E. Aylmer

To know who has been buried in a church will tell us something about its history. When we consider the importance of burial in Christian churches, be they cathedrals, abbeys, parish churches, or private chapels, from the earliest times to our own, this may seem obvious. But we need to know who was allowed to be buried where, as well as who was in fact buried in, under, or outside a church at different dates.[1] We are fortunate in having a reasonably full record of burials in York Minster from the time of Charles I until their cessation almost exactly 200 years later.[2] Before 1634 we are dependent on evidence of a different kind, mainly that relating to the actual tombs or other visible remains of burial. Taken together, these sources show that far more people, and of more varied types, were once buried in the Minster than is revealed by the tombs or other monuments that are still there today.

In the eighteenth century, almost exactly half-way through the time-span covered by the burial register, the cathedral authorities decided to restrict burials to the extreme eastern end of the church. But the rate of burials, at least as recorded, had already slowed down.[3] At the same time an ambitious plan to re-pave the floor of the nave and its aisles led to the removal of many existing tombstones and brasses. Far more were removed

---

[1] White Kennett, *Parochial Antiquities* . . . (1695), esp. pp. 592–3; Richard Gough, *Sepulchral Monuments in Great Britain* . . . i (1786), Intro.; Richard Burn, *Ecclesiastical Law* . . . (7th edn., 4 vols., 1809), i. 255–73, 372–4; Sir Robert Phillimore, *The Ecclesiastical Law of the Church of England*, 2nd edn., ed. W. G. F. Phillimore and C. F. Jemmett (2 vols., 1895), i. 650–701; H. W. Cripps, *A Practical Treatise of the Law relating to the Church and the Clergy* (7th edn., ed. A. T. Lawrence and R. Stafford Cripps, 1921).

[2] Robert H. Skaife, 'The Register of Burials in York Minster, accompanied by Monumental Inscriptions and Illustrated with biographical notices', *YAJ* i (1870), 226–330.

[3] YML, H7, Chapter Acts 1728–47, fo. 109, 21 Apr. 1735. From Skaife's edn. of the register and the items which he added from other sources, the rate of known burials was as follows: 1634–70 about 4 a year average; 1671–81 1·4; 1682–91 3; 1692–1730 1·6; 1731–80 1·01; 1780–93 1·3; 1793–1836 0·93.

in this way than in the iconoclastic outbursts associated with the Protestant Reformation of the sixteenth century, or with the Puritan Revolution of the seventeenth. So for all burials before the register begins in 1634, unless the tombs or monuments have themselves survived, we are dependent on the antiquarian scholars of the seventeenth and early eighteenth centuries who recorded them.[4] There are very few still visible in the main body of the church, west of the great crossing tower and the transepts. Further disturbances of existing tombs and monuments, and additional restrictions on the placing of new ones, followed the severe fire damage of 1829 and 1840.[5] And in 1854 a ban was imposed on all burials in cathedrals, on grounds of public health.[6] As a result relatively few tombs and inscriptions are visible today for a great metropolitan church, and these are mostly limited to a narrow range of the social and ecclesiastical hierarchy. A large proportion commemorate individuals who were closely associated with the Minster, members of their immediate families, or of very prominent Yorkshire landowning families, usually aristocratic. There are exceptions, some of which will be mentioned in the pages which follow, while in the nineteenth and twentieth centuries many individual and collective memorials were erected to persons not actually buried there. Even in earlier times a surprisingly large number of people connected in one way or other with the cathedral were buried instead in the parish church of St. Michael-le-Belfry which stands close by, under the shadow of the south-western tower.[7] Nor was the cathedral ever the main burying-place for the civic dignitaries and other worthies of York; there had always been at least four parish churches in which more lord mayors, sheriffs, aldermen, and so on had been interred and commemorated.[8] None the less, if the re-flooring of the 1730s had not taken place, the cathedral would contain many more tombs and inscriptions than it does today. Moreover, several have been

[4] Esp. Roger Dodsworth in 1619 (Bodl., MS. 27, 693 = Dodsworth MS. 161); Nathaniel Johnston in 1669–70 (Bodl., MS. Top. Yorks. c. 14, fos. 24–75: YML, microfilm); James Torre in 1685–6 (Torre, 'Minster', pp. 134–274); John Le Neve in the 1710s (*Monumenta Anglicana* . . . (5 vols. 1717–19), York refs. scattered, esp. in vols. 3 and 4); Browne Willis in the 1720s (*Survey*. . .)(1727)); Thomas Gent (*The Antient and Modern History of the Famous City of York* . . . (York and London, 1730), esp. pp. 84–142); and Francis Drake (*Ebor.*, pp. 494–519).

[5] Particularly the former which affected the east end of the cathedral very badly (see Ch. VII above).

[6] Orders in Council, 18 Oct. and 11 Dec. 1854, copies in YML, Dean & Chapter Muniments, D2/1854/12/18a–c (I am grateful to Mr. Barr for this reference).

[7] Skaife, 'Burial Reg.'; Yorkshire Parish Register Soc. i, ii (1899, 1901), *Register of St. Michael-le-Belfry*, pts. 1 and 2.

[8] All Saints, Pavement; St. Crux (parish hall only surviving); St. Martin's Coney Street (largely destroyed by bombing, 1942); and St. Michael's Spurriergate. See Yorks. Par. Reg. Soc., 36, 70 (1909, 1922), *St. Martin's Coney St.*, and *St. Crux*, pt. 1, and monuments and inscriptions where these survive. I am grateful to Dr. David M. Smith, director of the Borthwick Institute, who has re-listed many of these, for his generous help.

moved once and some even twice or more times. Only some of even the most famous medieval archbishops' tombs are definitely in their original positions.[9]

Two of the four last pre-Reformation archbishops are commemorated by tombs in the Minster.[10] Thomas Rotherham, alias Scot (1423–1500), had a long and active political career after a brilliant academic start at Cambridge: twice keeper of the privy seal and for nine years lord chancellor of England, he is the archetype of the medieval prelate cum man of affairs. Translated from Rochester to York in 1483, he held no high political office after that, apparently being regarded with some mistrust by both Richard III and Henry VII. His large, plain chest-tomb was moved to the extreme east end, and in consequence nearly destroyed in 1829.[11] Thomas Savage (c. 1450–1507), by contrast, of superior social origins to his predecessor, was more of a scholar, studying at Bologna and Padua as well as Oxford. He did, however, enjoy royal favour under the new dynasty, and was employed as diplomatic envoy to Spain in connection with the ill-starred marriage alliance, first of Prince Arthur and then of the future Henry VIII to Catherine of Aragon, which was to be—indirectly—the occasion of the English Schism. His tomb, erected by his chaplain Thomas Danby, on the inner side of the north choir aisle, is notable for having had a small chantry chapel over it. The tomb was restored in 1813, and the wooden chantry rebuilt and the tomb again restored under the direction of the late Sir Albert Richardson by a firm of craftsmen from Kilburn, Yorks., in the mid-twentieth century.[12]

The last pre-Reformation dean, Brian Higden, or Hygdon (?1460s–1539), whose monument—less the brass by which it could be identified—may be on the outer wall of the north choir aisle, was likewise typical in his career of many later medieval churchmen. His university degrees were in law, but

[9] See Chs. III and IV above.
[10] But not Christopher Bainbridge, 1508–14, or Thomas Wolsey, 1514–30.
[11] *DNB*; A. B. Emden, *A Biographical Register of the University of Cambridge to 1500* (Cambridge, 1963), pp. 489–91; J. B. Morrell, *York Monuments* ('The Arts and Crafts in York', n.d. [1944]), p. 5, misplacing it in the north transept; E. A. Gee, Notes, quoting the Chapter Acts for 1862 (I am extremely grateful to Dr. Gee for allowing me to consult and to cite his unpublished notes on some of the monuments, compiled for his forthcoming inventory volume on the Minster to be published by the Royal Commission on Historical Monuments (England)).
[12] *DNB*; A. B. Emden, *A Biographical Register of the University of Oxford to 1500* (3 vols., Oxford, 1958), iii. 1646–7; Morrell, *York Mons.*, p. 5; G. W. O. Addleshaw, *Four Hundred Years: Architects, Painters, Sculptors, Craftsmen, 1560–1960, whose work is to be seen in York Minster* (York, 1962), under 'Richardson'; also References compiled by Canon Addleshaw for his Booklet *400 Years* (1962), TS. in YCL and YML; and G. W. O. Addleshaw, 'Architects, sculptors, painters, craftsmen, 1660–1960, whose work is to be seen in York Minster', *Architectural History*, x (1967), 89–119 (with annotations). I am grateful to Dean Addleshaw for kindly giving me a copy of his Monuments not mentioned in '400 Years', Additional TS. (1962), and for other generous help.

concurrently with obtaining them he took orders and began to acquire livings. He was an officially licensed pluralist from 1511, and became dean of York in 1515, additionally also becoming a canon of St. Paul's in 1536. He served on the council of Henry VIII's illegitimate son, the Duke of Richmond, as his chancellor from 1525 to 30; and then was on the King's Council for the Northern Parts from 1530. But by the time of the critical challenge to the royal religious policies, the Piligrimage of Grace in 1536-7, Higden was lapsing into senility, and he took no discoverable part in the great events of the 1530s.[13]

So far from the social and ecclesiastical changes of the sixteenth century having led to any drop in the number and quality of funeral monuments erected, at York, as in the country generally, the reverse was the case. The development of English monumental sculpture, replacing the plainer chest- or coffin-type tombs and the recumbent effigies and the brasses of earlier centuries, has been admirably described and illustrated by several authors over the last forty years or so.[14] Early in the reign of Elizabeth I a solemn proclamation was issued in the queen's name, prohibiting the desecration or defacement of tombs and memorials on ostensibly theological or doctrinal grounds.[15] That there are so few tombs or monuments in the Minster surviving from the sixteenth century, indeed before the second decade of the seventeenth century, may be a matter of chance, and partly due to the subsequent damage and removals in the eighteenth and nineteenth centuries; partly perhaps to an element of Puritan disapproval

---

[13] *DNB*, 'Hygdon'; Emden, *Oxford* ii. 930-1; R. R. Reid, *The King's Council in the North* (1921), pp. 103, 113, 137-40, 490; J. F. Williams, 'The Brasses of York Minster', *Transactions of the Monumental Brass Soc.* 7 and 8 (1942-3), 342-53 and 1-8.

[14] Katharine A. Esdaile, *English Monumental Sculpture since the Renaissance* (1927); and *English Church Monuments 1510 to 1840*, with an Introduction by Sacheverell Sitwell (1946); 'Sculpture and Sculptors in Yorkshire', *YAJ* xxxv (1943), 362-88, pts. ii-iii; 'Sculptors and Sculpture' and 'Additions and Corrections', *YAJ* xxxvi (1947), 78-108, 137-63, 390; also 'Some Annotations on John Le Neve's "Monumenta Anglicana" (1717-19)', *AntJ* xxii (1942), 176-97; J. G. Mann, 'English Church Monuments, 1536-1625', *The Walpole Society*, 21 (1932-3), 1-22 and 26 Plates; Margaret Whinney and Oliver Millar, *English Art 1625-1714* (Oxford History of English Art, ed. T. S. R. Boase, viii, Oxford, 1957), Chs. VI and X; E. Mercer, *English Art 1553-1625* (O.H.E.A. vii, Oxford, 1962), Ch. VI; Frank Burgess, *English Churchyard Memorials* (1963); Margaret Whinney, *Sculpture in Britain 1530 to 1830* (Pelican History of Art, ed. N. Pevsner, Z23, Harmondsworth, 1964). For the late medieval background and the changes in the early sixteenth century see: F. H. Crossley, *English Church Monuments A.D. 1150-1550: An Introduction to the Study of Tombs and Effigies of the Medieval Period* (1921); A. C. Fryer, *Wooden Monumental Effigies in England and Wales* (rev. edn. 1924); A. Gardner, *Alabaster Tombs of the Pre-Reformation Period in England* (Cambridge, 1940); and *English Medieval Sculpture* (Cambridge, 1951); Lawrence Stone, *Sculpture in Britain: The Middle Ages* (Pel. Hist. Art, Z9, Harmondsworth, 1955).

[15] At Windsor, 19 Sept. 1560. Paul L. Hughes and James F. Larkin (eds.), *Tudor Royal Proclamations*, ii, *The Later Tudors (1553-1587)* (New Haven, Conn., and London, 1969), no. 469, pp. 146-8. It was cited in J. Weever, *Ancient Funerall Monuments* (1631; 2nd edn. 1767).

of the whole practice of erecting human images in God's house. After Higden, there seem to be none surviving until we come to three from the late Elizabethan period. Elizabeth Eynnes, Eynnis, or Eymes (d. 1585) was a lady of the privy chamber to the queen. Her husband, Thomas (d. 1578), whose monument (also once in the south transept) no longer exists, was deputy secretary of the Council in the North from 1542, and secretary from 1550 to his death—a striking case of bureaucratic continuity through all the religious changes of the times; partly or wholly out of the profits of his office, he built the original Heslington Hall in the later 1560s.[16] Another Councillor of the North, Ranulph Hurlestone, a professional lawyer of Cheshire origin (d. 1587), has a monument under the great east window which is curious rather than beautiful, with a carving of what might equally well be a dog or a fox and his arms above the inscription.[17] A Dubliner who died in York in 1595 is commemorated by a brass—one of the very few still in the nave aisles.[18] While in the extreme south-east corner of the church (now All Saints' Chapel) one of the least-known Elizabethan archbishops, John Piers (1523–94; at York 1589–94), has a remarkably modest monument: an inscribed tablet with two columns and strapwork, erected by his chancellor, Dr. John Bennett, a leading ecclesiastical lawyer of his time. Described by his Calvinist contemporaries as an ideally 'primitive' bishop, and by his nineteenth-century biographer as 'learned and liberal', Piers none the less conformed sufficiently to pre-Reformation stereotypes to have been for much of his career an officially licensed pluralist. At the same time he was far enough removed from any taint of Puritanism to have attained the post of lord high almoner to Elizabeth I; no doubt his life-long celibacy also helped commend him to the Virgin Queen.[19] Dr. Bennett's wife, Anne, is among the group of Jacobeans commemorated from the 1610s.[20] She did not live to see her husband

---

[16] Now at extreme east end of south choir aisle (or south aisle of presbytery). *DNB*, 'Sir Edward Neville'; Harleian Soc., xvi, *Visitation of Yorkshire 1563–4*, p. 359; Reid, *King's Council*, pp. 170–1, 257, 488; Williams, 'Brasses of Y.M.'; Nikolaus Pevsner, with contributions by J. Hutchinson, *Yorkshire: York and the East Riding* (The Buildings of England, ed. N. Pevsner and Judy Nairn, Harmondsworth, 1972), pp. 32, 106, 251.

[17] *Students admitted to the Inner Temple 1547–1660* (1877), pp. 17, 102; Harl. Soc. lix, *Pedigrees at the Visitation of Cheshire 1613*, p. 133; Reid, *King's Council*, p. 495.

[18] J. or R. Coteril, alias Cotterel or Cotrel. See Torre, 'Minster'; Willis, *Survey*, pp. 4, 6; Williams, 'Brasses'; Pevsner, *York and E.R.*, p. 108.

[19] *DNB*; Reid, *King's Council*, p. 495; Morrell, *York Mons.*, p. 14 and Pl. VII; Pevsner, *York and E.R.*, p. 106.

[20] *DNB*, 'John Bennett'. She actually died in 1602, but the monument is 1615 (W. Hargrove, *History and Description of the Ancient City of York* (2 vols. in 3, York, 1818), ii. 98; Addleshaw, *400 Years*, 'Stone'; also Ronald A. Marchant, *The Church under the Law: Justice, Administration and Discipline in the Diocese of York 1560–1640* (Cambridge, 1969), p. 44 *et seq.*; Brian P. Levack, *The Civil Lawyers in England 1603–1641: A Political Study* (Oxford, 1973), pp. 209–10.

attacked in the Parliament of 1621 for corruption and other malpractices.

Surviving monuments become more numerous from the reigns of James and Charles I (in fact from *c.* 1610 to 1640). They include the next archbishops, both of which suffered severe fire damage in the nineteenth century and have been much altered and restored. Matthew Hutton (1529–1606: dean of York 1567–89; archbishop 1596–1606) is portrayed lying on his side, with his head to the west looking east; three of his children kneel below, also facing east (Plate 138). In the late seventeenth century a lady visitor to York found his effigy looking 'more like a soldier or Beau than a Bishop'. A self-made man, Hutton was accused posthumously of having granted favourable leases of church lands to members of his family; however, he also founded a school and alms-houses at his birthplace in north Lancashire. He was a scholar of distinction whose strong doctrinal Protestantism and middle-of-the-road position on church government led to his being accused of being pro-Puritan, and his preferment being delayed. Certainly he advocated conciliation rather than repression of the Puritans, and he belongs in the tradition of Edmund Grindal (archbishop of York 1570–6, then of Canterbury; buried in Croydon), rather than to that of the more courtly Edwin Sandys (1577–88; buried in Southwell).[21] Up to a point the same is true of his more pliant, circumspect successor, Tobie or Tobias Matthew (1546–1628), son of a west country merchant, who moved from a highly successful academic career at Oxford to be dean of Durham in 1583, and followed Hutton both in that see and at York. Until his last years Matthew was an exceptionally active preacher as well as administrator; his own records show that he delivered no less than 1,992 sermons from the time that he went north until the early 1620s, an average of 50 a year for nearly forty years! In 1624, too old to come south again for attendance on parliamentary or other duties, he surrendered the London residence of the archbishops, York House, to the Crown, in exchange for former church lands in the north of England; and James I at once handed it over as a gift to his favourite George Villiers, Duke of Buckingham. Matthew's much restored effigy rests on a nineteenth-century chest-tomb by Sydney, younger brother of Sir Robert Smirke, the architect.[22] Others dating from

[21] Outer wall of south choir aisle. *DNB*; Surtees Soc. xvii (1843), *The Correspondence of Dr. Matthew Hutton . . .*, ed. J. Raine; Morrell, *York Mons.*, Pl. IX; Addleshaw, *400 Years*, quoting C. Morris (ed.), *The Journeys of Celia Fiennes* (1949), p. 78; J. T. Cliffe, *The Yorkshire Gentry From the Reformation to the Civil War* (1969), pp. 100, 274, 372–3; Ronald A. Marchant, *The Puritans and the Church Courts in the Diocese of York, 1560–1642* (1960), pp. 19, 22–4, 140, 149; Marchant, *Church under the Law*, pp. 49, 239.

[22] North side of Lady Chapel, set into the railings. *DNB*, also 'Smirke, Robert' and 'Edward'; Morrell, *York Mons.*, pp. 17–18, Pl. XIII (b); Addleshaw, *400 Years*; Marchant, *Puritans and the Church Courts*, pp. 29–30, 38–9, 43–4, 66, 155–66; *Church under the Law*, pp. 132–4, 140; E. A. Gee, *Notes*.

138 Matthew Hutton (1529–1606), Dean of York 1567–89, Lord President of the North 1595–1600, and the last Elizabethan archbishop of York. By an unknown sculptor; restored after damage in the Fire of 1829; an example of the 'wooden', lifeless work of local craftsmen. S. choir aisle.

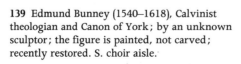

139 Edmund Bunney (1540–1618), Calvinist theologian and Canon of York; by an unknown sculptor; the figure is painted, not carved; recently restored. S. choir aisle.

early in the century include two Anglican controversialists (Plate 139);[23] a young child of Sir Arthur Ingram, of York, Temple Newsam, and Sheriff Hutton, one of the most ruthless and successful business magnates of early Stuart times;[24] Ingram's brother, Sir William, who was his deputy as secretary to the Council in the North, with his wife (Plate 140); Ingram's predecessor as secretary, Sir William Gee, whose monument is described by Sir Nikolaus Pevsner as 'large and bad'—perhaps a posthumous punishment for his Puritan sympathies (Plate 141);[25] and a distinguished ecclesiastical lawyer, whose professional writings have recently been studied.[26] Besides Mrs. Bennett, three ladies are commemorated from this time in addition to those who, like Catherine Lady Ingram, have joint memorials with their husbands. Annabella, the wife of Archdeacon Henry Wickham, himself a nephew of Archbishop Matthew, has a simple alabaster and slate tablet (north choir aisle). On the opposite side is a handsome tablet with columns, figures, and armorial shield, to Mrs. Jane, wife of Dr. Phineas Hodson or Hodgson, chancellor of the Minster from 1625 to 1641; she died at the age of 38, having given birth to twenty-four children, fourteen of whom had been baptised in St. Michael-le-Belfry.[27] But pride of place should go to Frances Matthew, widow of the archbishop, who was daughter, daughter-in-law, wife, and sister-in-law of members of the episcopate, and is renowned as the principal benefactress of the Minster library. This monument (Plate 142) was one of those in the east end of the

[23] *DNB*, 'William Palmer (1539–1605)'; 'Edmund Bunney (1540–1618)'.

[24] Lionel, died age 6 years 3 months, son of Sir Arthur and his wife Mary, née Greville (St. Stephen's Chapel, extreme north-east corner of the church). *DNB*; A. F. Upton, *Sir Arthur Ingram. The Making of an English Landed Fortune, c. 1575–1642* (Oxford, 1960); G. E. Cockayne, *The Complete Peerage* (ed. and rev. V. Gibbs, H. A. Doubleday, D. Warrand, Lord Howard de Walden, G. H. White, R. S. Lea; 13 vols. in 14 parts, 1910–59), 'Irvine, alias Irwin' (none of the extant Ingram pedigrees shows the child Lionel).

[25] For Sir William Ingram *c.* 1560–1623 (north choir aisle), see *Students admitted to the Inner Temple*, p. 106; Surtees Soc. xxxvi (1859), *Dugdale's Visitation of Yorkshire*, p. 146; J. and J. A. Venn, *Alumni Cantabrigienses* (2 parts in 10 vols., Cambridge, 1922–54), I. ii. 449; Reid, *King's Council*, pp. 381, 391, 489, 497; Marchant, *Church under the Law*, pp. 46–7, 251; Levack, *Civil Lawyers*, pp. 41, 243; Upton, *Sir Arthur Ingram*. And for Sir William Gee (*c.* 1550–1611; south choir aisle): *Records of Lincoln's Inn*, i (1896), *Admission Register*, p. 90; Venn, *Al. Cant.* I. i. 205; Reid, *op. cit.*, pp. 384, 489, 497; J. W. Clay (ed.), *Dugdale's Visitation of Yorkshire* (3 vols. in 10 parts, Exeter, 1894–1912), ix. 20–3; Cliffe, *Yorks. Gentry*, pp. 269, 280; Pevsner, *York and E.R.*, p. 107; Dr. Gee (Notes, 1966) compares it to Thomas Hesketh's monument in Westminster Abbey.

[26] Henry Swinburne, B.C.L. (1551 or 55–1624; north choir aisle): *DNB*; J. D. M. Derrett, *Henry Swinburne Ecclesiastical Lawyer* (Borthwick Booklets, no. 47, York, 1974); Marchant, *Church under the Law*, pp. 43, 45 n., 49–50, 58, 110 n., 249; Cliffe, *Yorks. Gentry*, p. 71.

[27] Mrs. Wickham: north choir aisle; Le Neve, *Fasti* iii. 134; Venn, *Al. Cant.* I. iv. 398; Morrell, *York Mons.*, Pl. XXIV (c); Marchant, *Church under the Law*, pp. 49, 101. Mrs. Hodson: south choir aisle (inscription now virtually illegible); Skaife, 'Burial Res.', no. 3; Venn, *Al. Cant.* I. ii. 386; Reid, *King's Council*, p. 498; Marchant, *Church under the Law*, pp. 49–50, 101.

140 Sir William Ingram (c. 1560–1623), Secretary of the Council in the North, with his wife. In painted stone, by an unknown sculptor. Sir William's brother, Sir Arthur Ingram the elder, was one of the greatest financiers of his time, whose 'palace' was built near the west front of the Minster. N. choir aisle.

141 Sir William Gee (c. 1550–1611), Secretary of the Council in the North, with his first wife, Archbishop Hutton's daughter, on his right. Presumably by a local craftsman; recently repainted. S. choir aisle.

church which had to be restored after the fire of 1829.[28] The work of one of early Stuart England's finest and best-known sculptors, Nicholas Stone (1586–1647), is represented by the modest memorial to Mrs. Bennett, also by another wall monument with life figures (Plate 143). This is to Sir Henry Belasyse of Newburgh Priory and Murton Grange and his wife, by birth a Fairfax of Denton; their son was raised to the peerage as Lord Fauconberg and their grandson married Oliver Cromwell's youngest daughter. Belasyse was one of the richest landowners in the whole of Yorkshire, and his estate could well bear the cost of employing Stone, who seems to have executed the monument and ornamented a chimney-piece as well for £150.[29] To Stone is also ascribed a large inscribed polished tablet set into a floor-tombstone to Frances Clifford, Countess of Cumberland (*c.* 1594–1644), a daughter of James I's chief minister, Robert Cecil, first Earl of Salisbury.[30] Excluding Stone's work the figure sculpture of this date is extraordinarily awkward and often technically incompetent; the carvers seem unable to render movement or perspective. Dr. Henry Swinburne is either kneeling very upright or standing in a curious dwarf-like posture; Sir William Gee's knees have got lost altogether. Even Nicholas Stone's figures here are static compared with his best work.[31] Nothing in the Minster from the pre-Civil War period can equal the two Slingsby monuments, perhaps by Epiphanius Evesham, twenty miles away in Knaresborough parish church.

'As with the Protestant Reformation, so too the notion that Puritan iconoclasm in the 1640s led to an orgy of destruction has been grossly exaggerated. Deliberate damage to churches and their fittings—we can hardly call it 'vandalism' when committed by sincere Christians—was mainly limited to glass and sculptural representations of the Persons of the Trinity, the Virgin Mary, saints, and angels. In 1643 and again in 1644 the Long Parliament legislated in favour of this iconoclasm, but each time forbade the defacement of funeral monuments, in terms remarkably reminiscent of the Elizabethan government just over eighty years earlier.[32] Despite this and the orders of the Parliamentarian commander, Sir Thomas

[28] Sources as for Archbishop Matthew; Morrell, *York Mons.*, Pl. XVIII; Pevsner, *York and E.R.*, p. 105.

[29] North choir aisle. *Complete Peerage*, 'Fauconberg'; Reid, *King's Council*, pp. 375, 497; Cliffe, *Yorks. Gentry*, pp. 96, 110, 112, 381, 385, shows that Belasyse employed fifty-one servants in 1609, was worth nearly £4,000 a year at his death, and left £8,000 personal estate; *Walpole Soc.* vii (1918–19), 'Note Book and Account Book of Nicholas Stone', pp. 41–2 (for Anne Bennett's monument, see ibid., pp. 39, 42).

[30] *Complete Peerage*, 'Cumberland' and 'Salisbury'; Addleshaw, *400 Years*, 'Stone'; to be compared with his monument to the Countess of Cumberland in Londesborough church (E. A. Gee, Notes).

[31] See M. Whinney, *Sculpture in Britain*, Ch. 4. Some fine pieces by Stone saved from redundant churches can now be seen to excellent advantage in the Victoria and Albert Museum.

[32] C. H. Firth and R. S. Rait (eds.), *Acts and Ordinances of the Interregnum* (3 vols., 1911), i. 266, 426.

Fairfax, for the Minster's protection when the city was captured in July 1644, some brasses certainly were removed and sold, though on whose orders and for whose financial advantage is not clear.[33] Moreover, the social and ecclesiastical changes of the Interregnum led to a slower rate of burials in the Minster and to a virtual cessation of monumental sculpture.[34]

With the return of an episcopalian church at the Restoration in 1660, a new phase opened. From the time of Charles II to the late eighteenth century the surviving monuments and tablets are far more numerous, and the best are of much greater artistic merit than earlier, even if relatively few of the country's leading sculptors are represented in the Minster. Compared with the work done before the Civil War, there is a great advance in sheer technical accomplishment: Renaissance standards in stone figure-carving had at last reached York. Perhaps we should distinguish between work done by local craftsmen and by London sculptors, commissioned or brought to York specially. According to Mrs. Esdaile all the monuments down to and including the first post-Restoration archbishop's were by northerners, apart from those by Stone. Plausible as this may seem, Dean Addleshaw and Dr. Gee have noted stylistic likenesses between some pre-Civil War monuments in the Minster and in Westminster Abbey; nor was all the best work done during the following hundred years or so by southerners.

The succession of monuments commemorating the later Stuart archbishops are fittingly impressive: visible evidence of *ecclesia anglicana restaurata*. The career of Accepted Frewen (1588–1664; at York 1660–4) was more than half spent before the Civil War broke out. His father, a Sussex parson, is said to have been a Puritan, suspected of nonconformity, but Accepted interrupted his academic career at Oxford to become chaplain to Sir John Digby, later first Earl of Bristol, and through the embassy postings which resulted he came to enjoy the favour of Charles I. Already president of Magdalen College, Oxford, and dean of Gloucester, Frewen was made bishop of Lichfield and Coventry during the Civil War, but spent the latter part of the Interregnum in exile. His appointment to York at the age of 71 may have represented the influence of the old Cavalier interest and principles within the restored Church; but like Juxon's archiepiscopate at

---

[33] *Fabric Rolls*, App. LXII, refers to sale by one Mr. Dossy; Richard Dossie or Dossey was employed by the Parliamentarian Committee as clerk of the Works for the Minster fabric (PRO, State Papers Domestic, Charles I, SP16/511/105).

[34] See Ch. V above. Minster burials included the son of the Rev. Edward Bowles, one of the salaried Puritan preachers who replaced the dean and canons from 1646 to 1660, in September 1654, and the following March the daughter of Colonel Robert Lilburne, brother of John Lilburne the Leveller leader and himself garrison commander at York, shortly to become deputy major-general for Yorkshire and Durham (Skaife, 'Burial Reg.', nos. 58 and 61).

142 Frances Matthew (d. 1629), daughter of
Bishop Barlow, married successively to the
young son of Archbishop Parker, and to
Tobie Matthew, archbishop of York; she was
the real foundress of the Minster Library (see
Ch. XI). By an unknown sculptor; restored
after Fire of 1829. Lady Chapel (under N.
corner of great East Window).

143 Sir Henry Belasyse (d. 1624), with his
wife, a Fairfax of Denton. By Nicholas Stone
(1586–1647), who charged £150 for this and a
chimney-piece, 1615. N. choir aisle.

Canterbury it could only be a brief postscript prolonged into the new reign. The monument with a recumbent effigy was almost destroyed in 1829, and a collateral descendant replaced it in 1840 (Plate 144). In the 1740s another descendant of Frewen's brother and heir wrote a pamphlet refuting the popular belief that his lifelong celibacy arose from the archbishop's horror at learning that his own birth had been by Caesarean operation while his mother was fully conscious.[35] Apart from one or two of Frewen's relatives,[36] and a tombstone to a senior ecclesiastical lawyer who was killed in a duel, relatively little survives until we reach the 1680s. George Aislabie (1617 or 1618–75), official principal of the diocese from 1660, died defending a lady's honour. He was of humble origin, according to one hostile account having served as clerk to Archbishop Matthew's legal secretary (though this cannot have been in the archbishop's lifetime), and then by marrying his master's widow having acquired the books and the fortune which enabled him to buy his office at the Restoration. His second wife was the elder daughter and co-heiress of the Mallory family of Studley Royal, near Ripon, and she inherited this estate in 1666. Such were the foundations for the political and architectural careers of his son, John Aislabie (1670–1742), chancellor of the exchequer at the time of the South Sea Bubble, who retained £119,000 out of a total fortune of £164,000 when he was forced out of public life and then proceeded to rebuild and landscape Studley.[37]

From the last years of Charles II's reign until the middle of George II's there is an almost continuous sequence of major monuments including some of the most striking, if not also the most beautiful, of all those in the cathedral. Whereas Frewen had lived into his seventy-seventh year, his successor Richard Sterne, born only about eight years after, survived to his later eighties. A chaplain to Archbishop Laud himself, and a leader of the defeated High-Church and Royalist party in Cambridge, he was actually imprisoned by the Long Parliament for some months, but finally escaped with no worse than sequestration and apparently lived out the rest of the 1640s and 1650s as a local schoolmaster in Hertfordshire, in the role of an 'internal refugee'—a well-known phenomenon in other revolutions. He

---

[35] Lady Chapel. *DNB*, also under 'John Frewen (1558–1628)'; Morrell, *York Mons.*, Pl. XXIII; Pevsner, *York and E.R.*, p. 105.

[36] Judith Frewen, his niece by marriage, d. 1666, St. Stephen's Chapel; Joseph Foster, *Alumni Oxonienses 1500–1714* (4 vols., continuous pagination, Oxford and London, 1891–2), p. 536.

[37] Monumental Inscription (= M.I.), floor of presbytery; *DNB*, 'John Aislabie'; *The History of Parliament*, R. Sedgwick (ed.), *The House of Commons 1715–1754* (2 vols., 1970), i. 409–11; Skaife, 'Burial Reg.', no. 81c; Marchant, *Church under the Law*, p. 83, n. 3; Torre 'Minster', p. 264, no. 1; J. R. Walbran, 'A Genealogical and Biographical Memoir of the Lords of Studley in Yorkshire', in *Memorials of the Abbey of St. Mary of Fountains*, ii, pt. I, (Surtees Soc. lxvii, for 1876, 1878), App. XI.

came to York from Carlisle. Gilbert Burnet later criticized his excessive concern with material provision for himself and his family, and his dependence on the political backing of James, Duke of York. But despite his thirteen children, one of whom was the grandfather of Laurence Sterne, he left legacies to the rebuilding fund of St. Paul's and to each of his colleges at both universities. The monument (now on the inner side of the north choir aisle) has been moved, reassembled, and in the process deprived of its surrounding iron railings. It is dominated by the recumbent figure with his head resting on his arm. Art historians have for long disputed whether this was the work of the famous wood-carver, Grinling Gibbons, or by either of two minor sculptors of the time: Caius Cibber and Francis Bird. Gibbons and Bird, as we shall see, may each be credited with an archbishop's monument apiece; and it has now been suggested that Sterne's, if not by Gibbons himself, is by a member of his studio or workshop team.[38] The iron railings or palisade round this and other monuments were presumably intended to prevent damage or desecration. Other monuments were put to practical, if not sacrilegious, use: the flat top of Thomas Haxey's tomb (canon and treasurer of the Minster, 1418–25) was used for rental payments by tenants of the dean and chapter until well into the nineteenth century.[39] As if to make assurance doubly sure, in the early eighteenth century the east ends of the north and south choir aisles were closed off by partition doors or other barriers.[40]

With John Dolben (1624–86; at York 1683–6) we jump forward a generation. He had interrupted his student career at Oxford to fight for the king, surviving wounds sustained at Marston Moor. Deprived of his fellowship in 1648, he was ordained in 1656, and helped to keep Anglican

[38] *DNB*; Esdaile, *English Monumental Sculpture*, p. 45 (Cibber); *English Church Mons.*, p. 104 (Bird); *YAJ* xxxvi (Gibbons); Morrell, *York Mons.*, p. 38 and Pl. XXV; Addleshaw, *400 Years*; Rupert Gunnis, *Dictionary of British Sculptors 1660–1851* (1953; rev. edn. 1964), pp. 53–5, 101–3, 167–70; E. A. Gee, quoting Todd, *York Guide* (1798) on the iron palisade. J. Douglas Stewart, 'New Light on the Early Career of Grinling Gibbons', in *Burlington Magazine*, cxviii, no. 880 (July 1976), 508–13, showing the probable connection with the Sterne family, but provisionally ascribing the actual monument to the Flemish-born sculptor Arnold Quellin (1653–86), on the grounds of its superiority to all Gibbons's known works in stone—emphatically not his medium. I am grateful to Professor Stewart for giving me the reference, to BL, MSS. Whitley Papers, Notes on Artists, F–G, copy of a letter sold by Sothebys in 1916, from Gibbons to John Etty, 10 July 1684, where he writes of receiving a 'Mr. Stavnes' letter' about some work which Gibbons was doing for him; this must surely be, as Prof. Stewart argues, a modern misreading or a contemporary miswriting of 'Sterne's'. I am grateful to Mr. John Ingamells, Curator of York City Art Gallery, for his generous help over this, as in numerous other respects.

[39] *DNB*; Crossley, *English Church Mons.*, pp. 79, 182–3, 249; one of the earliest known 'cadaver' tombs; Pevsner, *York and E.R.*, p. 107, 'grim' (quoting J. Hutchinson); for the rents, see BIHR, Yarborough Muniments, Langwith Deeds.

[40] Willis, *Survey*, ground-plan, between p. viii and p. 1.

144 Accepted Frewen (1588–1664), the first post-Restoration archbishop and an active royalist during the Civil War in Oxford. Sculptor unknown, largely restored after 1829. Lady Chapel (against E. wall of cathedral).

145 John Dolben (1624–86), wounded at the battle of Marston Moor in 1644, Charles II's 3rd and last archbishop of York. Probably by Jasper Latham (d. 1693); the urn is a modern replacement. S. choir aisle (inner wall).

ministrations alive until the Restoration. His start in life had been helped by his mother being a niece of James I's last lord keeper, John Williams, later bishop of Lincoln and then archbishop of York (1641–50); his career was further advanced by his own marriage to the niece of Gilbert Sheldon (archbishop of Canterbury, 1664–77). Dean of Westminster from 1662 and bishop of Rochester from 1666, it is perhaps surprising that Dolben was not rewarded earlier with a more important and lucrative see. In his brief time at York he was remembered for having reformed the services in the Minster, and as a benefactor of the cathedral and its library. His monument too (on the inner side of the south choir aisle; Plate 145) has been ascribed to Gibbons, but seems more likely to be by Jasper Latham, who was responsible for Sheldon's monument at Croydon (1678; since destroyed by fire). His head faces eastward, with angels above, and he is half-rising, as if waking to the Last Trump.[41]

Dolben's successor is a less attractive figure, or perhaps history has been unkind to him. Actually older by eight or nine years, Thomas Lamplugh (1615–91; at York 1688–91) was a young don when Oxford was visited by the Long Parliament's Puritan commissioners in the later 1640s. Unlike many royalists and episcopalians, he survived the purge by taking the Solemn League and Covenant—as he afterwards maintained—to uphold the principles of the Church in bad times as well as in good, and to protect those whose stricter consciences forbade them to do the same. At the Restoration Lamplugh was forward in renouncing the Covenant and took part in the Anglican counter-purge of the University; the most constructive part of his career, and the least disfigured by persecution or careerism, was his twelve years (1676–88) as bishop of Exeter. Having cautiously refused to join the growing opposition to James II and his policies, he protested his loyalty to the doomed king at an interview in the autumn of 1688 and was instantly rewarded with the vacant archbishopric of York, being elected and installed in a matter of weeks. Yet within five months he was officiating at the coronation of James's joint successors—his nephew and son-in-law King William III and his daughter Queen Mary II. Unless he was a 'trimmer' by genuine conviction, it is hard to escape a hint of the 'Vicar of Bray' in Lamplugh's career. His wife too was a bishop's niece; but before concluding from such evidence that seventeenth-century Anglican prelates rose through nepotism, the dates must be carefully checked. Intermarriage within a particular group may as often be the consequence of membership as the cause of rising within it. There is no doubt that his monument is by

---

[41] *DNB*; Esdaile, *English Church Mons.*, p. 104; Addleshaw, *400 Years*; Gunnis, *Dictionary*, pp. 169–70, 234; E. A. Gee, Notes.

146 Thomas Lamplugh (1615–91), the Archbishop who changed sides in 1688–9. This is the only authentic monument in the cathedral by Grinling Gibbons (1648–1720), the famous wood-carver, and the earliest representation of a fully standing figure. S. choir aisle.

147 William Wentworth, 2nd Earl of Strafford (1626–95), and his 1st wife, Lady Henrietta Mary Stanley (1630–85). By J. van Nost, the elder (d. 1729). All Saints Chapel (in the extreme SE. corner of the cathedral).

Grinling Gibbons, who received £100 for it (Plate 146). Lamplugh with moustache and small beard looks like another survivor from the days of Charles I; the archbishop's upright stance is shared only with a few laymen of the highest rank and family. While his predecessor Sterne is portrayed in the process of waking and getting up, Lamplugh is fully on his feet, as if anticipating the General Resurrection. One can but hope such confidence is not misplaced.[42]

Meanwhile, less typically, 1689 also saw commemorated the wife of the previous year's lord mayor of York. Even this may be more explicable by the fact that she had been the daughter of a prominent neighbouring landowner.[43] One of the greatest family names in seventeenth-century Yorkshire is commemorated from the 1690s by what Dr. Friedman calls 'a most spectacular monument for its date in England' (Plate 147). William Wentworth, second Earl of Strafford, did not play any political role comparable to that of his father—the man who might have been England's equivalent of Cardinal Richelieu if Charles I, as it was said, had known 'either how to make himself, or to be made great'. The burial in January 1686 of the second Earl's first wife, Henrietta Mary, née Stanley, a descendant of the de la Trémouilles and so of the great house of Orange, provoked what may have been either a xenophobic riot or an outburst of popular anti-clerical and anti-aristocratic feeling at the Minster. Was she perhaps suspected of popery, and thus regarded as ineligible for burial in a Protestant church? Be this as it may, her devoted husband directed in his will that no less than £700—a vast sum at that date—should be spent on their joint funeral monument. The commission almost certainly went to John van Nost the elder, a first generation immigrant like other leading artists of the period. This dramatic stone composition (outer wall of All Saints' Chapel in the extreme south-east corner of the church) includes two larger than life-size standing figures; the use and control of detail to enhance the effect of the whole seems indeed to deserve that over-worked term 'baroque'. The entrance to the Wentworth family vault can be seen in the flooring immediately outside the chapel railings. The Earl's second wife,

[42] *DNB*; Gunnis, *Dictionary*, p. 170; Addleshaw, *400 Years*, quoting Bodl., MS. Autograph, d. 11, p. 335; Morrell, *Yorks Mons.*, Pl. XXXVIII; Pevsner, *York and E.R.*, p. 107.

[43] Lady Maria Raynes or Raines (alabaster tablet on north choir wall): Morrell, *York Mons.*, p. 39 and Pl. XXIX (a); Addleshaw, Additional Notes, TS., noting similarity to Lady Elizabeth Stapleton's monument by Samuel Carpenter (1660–1713) in Snaith Church, West Riding; for her own family, the Conyers of Bowlby, see Surtees Soc. xxxvi, *Dugdale's Visn. of Yorks.*, p. 340; Clay (ed.), *Dugdale's Visn. of Yorks.* i. 275; Gunnis, *Dictionary*, p. 82, does not list it under Carpenter; for Snaith, see also N. Pevsner, *Yorkshire: The West Riding* (Buildings of England, Harmondsworth, 1959), p. 483, (rev. edn. Enid Radcliffe, 1967), p. 490. For her husband, see C. B. Knight, *A History of the City of York From . . .A.D. 71 to . . . A.D. 1901* (2nd edn. 1944), p. 493.

also Henrietta, this time of the French ducal house of de la Rochefoucauld, outlived him by many years and was buried in St. James's, Westminster.[44]

The other aristocratic monument of this epoch presents something of a historical curiosity (Plate 148). At some date after her death in 1708, a tripartite wall monument (north choir aisle, outer wall), was erected in honour of Lady Mary Fenwick, eldest daughter of Charles Howard, first Earl of Carlisle—and thus aunt of the third Earl who employed Vanbrugh to build Castle Howard. The left-hand panel commemorates her father, whose bust also surmounts the whole composition, above the central panel in her own memory. The inscription is notable, firstly for getting the Earl's dates wrong (*c.* 1621–76, instead of *c.* 1628–84), secondly for suppressing completely all mention of his pro-Parliamentarian, Cromwellian career before 1660. Young Charles Howard was sheriff of Cumberland in 1649–50, and a little later was captain of Cromwell's Lifeguard under the Protectorate and then deputy major-general for the three northernmost counties in 1655–6. His dates are given correctly on his tombstone near the foot of the monument. Carlisle is not the only ex-servant of the English Republic buried in York whose Interregnum career was suppressed in his monumental inscription.[45] The right-hand panel of the Fenwick memorial, is, if anything, even stranger. For it commemorates Lady Mary's husband, Sir John (*c.* 1645–97), without mentioning that he was beheaded after being attainted for treason against King William III, after the 'Assassination Plot' of 1696. The inscription merely records that he and his children are buried in London: *suppressio veri* could hardly go further. It seems a remarkable comment on the feeling against William in some aristocratic and clerical circles that such a monument could have been erected so soon after.[46]

The last Stuart archbishop, John Sharp (1645–1714; at York 1691–1714), seems to have been exemplary in performing his duties. Coming, it is said, from a divided family background in Bradford with a Puritan father and Royalist mother, he forfeited the confidence of James II in 1686 when he was dean of Norwich and a fashionable London preacher, but was

[44] *Complete Peerage*, 'Strafford'; *DNB*, 'van Nost, the Younger d. 1780'; Gunnis, *Dictionary*, pp. 279–82, 282; Morrell, *York Mons.*, p. 39, Pl. XXXI; T. F. Friedman, further information kindly communicated to the author.

[45] The other is Sir Thomas Herbert 'of Tintern': see M.I. in St. Crux parish hall off Pavement; *DNB*, supplemented and corrected by Norman H. Mackenzie, 'Sir Thomas Herbert of Tintern: A Parliamentary Royalist', *Bull. Inst. Hist. Res.* xxix (1956), 32–86; and Aylmer, *The State's Servants* (1973), pp. 274–6.

[46] *DNB*, 'Fenwick', 'Howard'; *Complete Peerage*, 'Carlisle'; Skaife, 'Burial Res.', no. 91; PRO, *Lists and Indexes*, ix, *Sheriffs of England*; Aylmer, *State's Servants*, pp. 97, 195; Williams, 'Brasses of Y.M.'; Morrell, *York Mons.*, p. 40 (again favouring Carpenter's authorship); National Monuments Register, Notes (ascribe it to James Hardy, *c.* 1632–*c.* 1721, for whom see Gunnis, *Dictionary*, pp. 187–8, not, however, listing this work for him or for Carpenter: ibid., p. 82).

appropriately rewarded in the next reign. His real heyday came under Queen Anne, to whom he was almoner and personal confidant. Despite these preoccupations, Sharp devoted much energy to attempting the reform of the Church in his diocese and to the repair of the cathedral; some fire damage was sustained by the Minster in 1711, though not as severe as in 1829 and 1840. While in politics he was a committed 'Court' and 'Tory' man, whose successive patrons were Heneage Finch, later first Earl of Nottingham, Henry Bennett Lord Arlington, and—until Sharp's Anglicanism overcame his royalism—James himself, Sharp none the less seems to have risen on his own merits and abilities without advantage of birth or connection. Moreover, though a strong controversialist and an enemy of Dissent, he was not a persecutor. He died at Bath, whether when taking the waters is not recorded. This time Francis Bird's authorship of the monument is undisputed; again the archbishop's figure is recumbent but rising (Plate 149). Substantial restoration had to be undertaken by Sharp's descendants to make good the fire damage after 1829. As a memorial, it is pleasant, indeed unexceptionable of its kind, if perhaps a trifle bland; like others at the extreme east end of the cathedral, it seems to have little in common with the beauty and spirituality of the great window above it.[47]

No other archbishop was commemorated in the Minster until the nineteenth century. Minor figures whose monuments or memorial tablets date from the early Hanoverian period are almost all people directly or indirectly connected with the cathedral itself: the subdean, a canon, two maiden ladies, a mother and her daughters.[48]

One of the grandest aristocratic monuments in the Minster, to Thomas Watson-Wentworth (1665–1723) and his wife Alice, was licensed by the dean and chapter in 1730 (Plate 150). Dr. Colvin has established that it was designed by the architect William Kent, but the actual work was carried out by Giovanni Battista Guelfi, who had been brought to England by Lord Burlington. That discerning patron was soon to discard him in favour of another, superior sculptor, and Dr. Whinney believes that Guelfi secured

---

[47] *DNB*; Morrell, *York Mons.*, pp. 40–1; Addleshaw, *400 Years*; Whinney, *Sculpture in Britain*, Ch. 10; Esdaile, *AntJ* xxii; Gunnis, *Dictionary*, p. 55; all authorities except Esdaile agree on Bird (1667–1731).

[48] e.g. William Pearson (*c.* 1660–1716), a tablet with coat of arms above, on outer wall of north choir aisle (Foster, *Al. Oxon.*, p. 1134; Venn, *Al. Cant.* I. iii. 332; M.I.); Samuel Terrick (*c.* 1668–1719), rectangular tablet with shield above, Lady Chapel (Le Neve, *Fasti*, pp. 210, 227; Venn, *Al. Cant.* I. iv. 215, for his sons only; Morrell, *York Mons.*, Pl. XLIX (a); M.I.); the Misses Penelope and Joanna Gibson, oval with heads of cherubs, in St. Stephen's Chapel (Venn, *Al. Cant.* I. ii. 211, for their father; Surtees Soc. xxxvi, *Dugdale's Visn. of Yorks.*, p. 73); Mrs. Mary Thornhill and her two daughters (*c.* 1657–1727), wall tablet, with urn on top and foliage decoration. I have not seen this; was it totally destroyed in the fire of 1829? (see Foster, *Al. Oxon.*, p. 1480; Clay (ed.), *Dugdale's Visn. of Yorks.* i. 82–3; Hargrove, *Hist. York* ii. 101, gives a fuller description).

this commision by virtue of his monument to ex-Secretary of State George Craggs in Westminster Abbey. Thomas Watson was the third son of Edward Lord Rockingham, and Anne, sister of the second and childless Earl of Strafford; he took the additional surname of Wentworth on succeeding to his uncle's Yorkshire estates in 1695. He is portrayed standing and his wife is sitting; the whole, carved out of pieces of white stone (inner side of north choir aisle), gives an effect of grandeur rather than beauty.[49] The combination of an architect to design and a carver or firm of craftsmen to execute, instead of a single sculptor, later became quite usual, often with less happy results.

The next major clerical monument was more controversial, and by no means aesthetically compelling. Henry Finch (*c.* 1665–1728), sixth or seventh son of Heneage, lord keeper of the great seal and then lord chancellor and Earl of Nottingham, moved from Cambridge on to a rapid escalator of clerical preferment: prebendary of Ely at 26 and of York at 30, Henry was dean by 37, holding this position for twenty-six years until his death. Meanwhile, his elder brother Edward (*c.* 1664–1738), likewise a fellow of Christ's, varied this pattern by studying at the Inner Temple and sitting as M.P. for Cambridge University (1690–5); following his parliamentary experience, he was ordained and obtained a York prebend in 1704; other livings and prebends followed. He was a chaplain to Queen Anne and a minor composer of church music. When Dean Henry died, he was buried—as he had every right to be—towards the eastern end of the cathedral. As 'senior president' (or canon residentiary), in the absence of a dean, Edward Finch chaired a chapter meeting on 27 October 1728; on inspection of the late dean's burial-place, it was then decreed that 'Mr [*sic*] Edward Finch' could erect a monument 'against the N.W. side of the pillar near this place', of eight feet width and ten feet height, or more as required, being the first pillar from the east end of the church on the south side of the middle aisle.[50] The monument was to be permitted to have three busts: of the late dean, of Mr. Edward Finch, and of his wife, with suitable

[49] Complete Peerage, 'Rockingham', 'Strafford'; *DNB*, 'James Craggs, Junior'; Gunnis, *Dictionary*, p. 183; H. M. Colvin, *A Biographical Dictionary of English Architects, 1660–1840* (1954), p. 346; Whinney, *Sculpture in Britain*, Ch. 11; Addleshaw, *400 Years*. The description in John Britton's *The History and Antiquities of the Metropolitical Church of York; illustrated* (folio, 1819; and as part of a series on cathedrals, large qto. 1819), p. 64, suggests that the monument began its career at the east end of the south choir aisle, unless he confused it with the Strafford (on the same wall but inside All Saints' Chapel), which seems unlikely. See also Morrell, *York Mons.*, p. 41, Pl. XXXV.

[50] Presumably at the east end of the inner side of the south nave aisle; Britton (op. cit.) again has it 'at the E end of the church'; after the second fire it was moved to its present site (on the outer wall of the south choir aisle, towards the east end: E. A. Gee, Notes, quoting Burdekin, *An Account of the alarming and destructive fire in York Minster on February 2, 1829* (York, 1829), p. 16, and Chapter Acts, 1844, p. 77).

148 Charles Howard, 1st Earl of Carlisle
(c. 1628–85), his daughter Lady Mary Fenwick
(d. 1708), and her husband, Sir John Fenwick
(c. 1645–97), who was beheaded after
attainder. By either James Hardy of
Northumberland (c. 1632–c. 1720), a one-time
assistant to Latham, or Samuel Carpenter
(1660–1713). N. choir aisle.

150 Thomas Watson-Wentworth
(1665–1723), and his wife Alice, née
Proby. By William Kent (1684–1748) and
G. B. Guelfi of Bologna (fl. in England
1714–34). N. choir aisle (inner wall)

149 John Sharp (1645–1714), Archbishop
from 1691, and Almoner to Queen Anne.
By Francis Bird (1667–1731); restored
after 1829. Lady Chapel (under S. corner
of E. Window).

inscriptions; it was also approved that Canon Edward and his wife could be buried next to his brother. This was agreed at another chapter meeting, with the new dean, Richard Osbaldeston, presiding on 11 November 1729. Licence was to be granted to Mr. Edward Finch, his heirs, and executors accordingly; shortly afterwards mention is made of a £100 legacy from Dean Henry to the Minster library, though there is of course no question of this having been a precondition. So far, so good: burial fees were not mentioned.[51]

Then in 1730 instructions were issued for a decanal visitation on Osbaldeston's part. On 9 December the dean and chapter's registrar, one Mr. Jubb, was ordered to call on Mr. Edward Finch, and to require him to come to the chapter meeting with the key of the chest which contained the dean and chapter's seal, or else to hand over the key to Jubb, in the name of the dean and chapter. After he had resolutely refused either to attend in person or to give Jubb the key, and after other canons had then been sent to call on him also without success, since he refused to come to his front door in a state of undress or to allow them to enter his house, it was ordered that the box should be broken into and Finch proceeded against for contempt. On 17 December he was duly condemned by 6 votes to 1 (presumably his own) for contempt in the matter of the key. But in making his formal protestation in self-defence, Finch produced a letter from William Wickham, Esquire, showing that no fees had been paid for the burial of Dean Tobias Wickham (1620–97), son of that Archdeacon Henry (d. 1641) whose wife was commemorated in the 1620s; he also declared that no fees had been paid for the burial of the next dean, Thomas Gale (d. 1702), who like Wickham has no monument; there is an inscription on his tombstone behind the high altar. Finch's point appears to have been accepted; for the new key to the strong box was then handed over to him. The normal burying fee payable to the clerk of the vestry was £3, though there may well have been other customary tips or gratuities.[52]

After all this fuss, the monument (Plate 151), erected after the death of Edward's widow, Mary Finch, was commissioned from the fashionable foreign-born sculptor Michael Rysbrack (1694–1770), who had already executed in 1723 or 4 a bust of the Finches' elder brother Daniel, second Earl of Nottingham, 'Dismal' as he was known in political circles from his temperamental pessimism. Rysbrack had also done a terracotta head of

---

[51] YML, H7, Chapter Acts, 1728–47, fos. 29–32^v; *DNB*, 'Heneage Finch'; *Complete Peerage*, 'Nottingham'; Venn, *Al. Cant.* I. ii. 138.

[52] YML, H7, fos. 54^v–57^v, 61–62^v, 64; Skaife, 'Burial Reg.', nos. 112, 126, 135. But a 'pall fee' of £7 was paid for the Earl of Strafford in 1695, and one of £8 for the Dowager Countess of Carlisle in 1708 (Skaife, nos. 122, 137).

Canon Edward (presumably from life) which is much superior to the stone bust of the monument. Mrs. Esdaile may be going too far in describing this as 'one of the dullest monuments in York Minster'; but what might have been among the most exciting artistically speaking, falls far short, achieving only technical competence.[53]

Other monuments of the 1730s are in a minor key,[54] but the later 1740s are more notable. Thomas Lamplugh, grandson of the archbishop, himself canon residentiary and rector of Bolton Percy to the south-west of the city, has an elegant pyramidal wall monument with a shield at the top and urns at the bottom corners, apparently by Charles Mitley of York (1705–58). Like his other designs it is derivative, being unusual for York and reminiscent of many triangular or pyramidal designs in southern English churches (Plate 152).[55]

One of the Minster's only two commemorations of naval officers provides the finest monument of the mid-eighteenth century. This was how it came about. Robert Medley senior (1650–1708) originally hailed from the Isle of Axholme in Lincolnshire, also incidentally the home of James Torre, the York antiquary, whose first wife was buried in the Minster in August 1693 and who was himself remarried there barely eight months later.[56] Medley came to York to practise as an advocate in the church courts, and married one Dorothy Grimston, member of a minor East Riding landed family. She was a child of the second marriage of her father William (1619–64), the main line, seated at Grimston Garth, descending from his first marriage. Robert and Dorothy's only surviving child, Henry Medley (c. 1687–1747) entered the Royal Navy in 1703; he attained flag rank in 1744, and became vice-admiral in command of the Mediterranean fleet shortly after. During the War of the Austrian Succession he soon began to make a great deal of prize money. He had earlier married Ann Gooch, whose mother was a Grimston of the main (Garth) line, so that his wife was his own step-second-cousin; but she died in 1734 and their only child too died young, leaving the

---

[53] Esdaile, *English Church Mons.*, p. 105; M. I. Webb, *Michael Rysbrack Sculptor* (1954), p. 215; M. Whinney, *English Sculpture 1720–1830* (V & A Museum, 1971), Pl. no. 4.

[54] e.g. Archdeacon John Richardson (1675–1735), mural tablet with columns, shield, etc. above; possibly by Charles Mitley, in St. Stephen's Chapel (Le Neve, *Fasti*, pp. 149, 157, 173, 227; Venn, *Al. Cant.* I. iii. 452; Morrell, *York Mons.*, Pl. LII (a); Addleshaw, Additional Notes; Dr. Samuel Breary (c. 1670–1735), succentor and prebendary, rectangular compartment with angel's head at top and pediment above that; a long genealogical inscription; possibly designed by Kent (Morrell, *York Mons.*, Pl. LIII (b); Venn, *Al. Cant.* I. i. 209; Addleshaw, Additional Notes), also in St. Stephen's Chapel.

[55] Foster, *Al. Oxon.*, p. 873; *Burke's Landed Gentry* (1937 Centenary edn.), pp. 256–7; Morrell, *York Mons.*, p. 60 and Pl. LVI (Ch. IV lists other pyramidal compartments dating from 1726 to 1758); E. A. Gee, Notes, quoting Newby Hall MSS., letter from Mitley's sister, Mrs. Carr, to Mrs. Worsley, 1755.

[56] For Torre, see Skaife, 'Burial Reg.', no. 116.

admiral to grow old and rich without direct heirs. Late in 1744 he wrote
instructing his cousin and friend Thomas Grimston (1702–51) to buy an
estate for him at Kilnwick (also in the East Riding), presumably in
anticipation of his retirement. The purchase went through rather slowly
but was eventually completed for £9,000 in May 1747. Shortly before his
death (on 5 August) Admiral Medley made a new will, leaving all his real
property, including the new Kilnwick estate, to his Grimston cousin, and a
£7,000 cash legacy to his other heir, a nephew in York; he directed that he
should be buried in St. Michael-le-Belfry church, but apparently said
nothing about a monument. His body was embalmed, and according to the
family historian then pickled in pure naval rum, and duly transported
home. Four months later a solemn cortège wound into York, and the funeral
took place on 10 December. Already the previous month it seems to have
been assumed that a monument would be erected in his memory, for the
York carver Richard Fisher, lately arrived from Ripon, solicited the
commission. But in the spring of 1748 Medley's London banker who also
acted as man-of-business for Grimston, advised the latter to discourage
Fisher. And it seems likely to have been he who suggested instead the well-
known London sculptor Henry later Sir Henry Cheere (1703–81).
Permission was obtained from the dean and chapter on 10 February 1749,
and Cheere duly received £262 10s. for the completed commission; the iron
railings (which were not replaced after the fire of 1829) cost another £6 14s.
Almost immediately Thomas Grimston commissioned Carr of York to begin
rebuilding operations at Kilnwick; he largely reconstructed the family
home at Grimston Garth too, but was only to survive his step-cousin by a
few years. There is a fine wall tablet to him in Kilnwick church, also by
Cheere; Richard Fisher's son John (1735–1804), however, executed the
memorial tablet there to Grimston's son John (1725–80); it was by no means
as handsome. Cheere's monument for Admiral Medley (on the outer wall of
the north choir aisle, towards the east end; Plate 153), is rated by Dr.
Friedman as 'the master-piece of post-medieval sculpture in the Minster'.
At its centre is a large portrait bust, among the finest pieces of eighteenth-
century figure-carving, and as a whole it surpasses Rysbrack's memorial to
the Finches, and Guelfi's to Watson Wentworth. Its superiority to van
Nost's Strafford, or John Fisher's Savile (discussed below), is more
debatable, but may be conceded to Dr. Friedman who has done so much to
reawaken interest in Cheere's work.[57]

[57] *DNB*; M. Edward Ingram, *Leaves from a Family Tree. Being the Correspondence of an East Riding Family* (Hull and London, 1951), esp. pp. 5, 8, 11, 14–15, 18–20, 113, 210–11, Pedigree facing p. 98, Pls. III and IX; Gunnis, *Dictionary*, p. 99; Whinney, *Sculpture in Britain*, Ch. 16; T. F. Friedman, *The Man at Hyde Park Corner* (Catalogue of Sir Henry Cheere Exhibition, 1974), pp. 7–8, Pl. no. 8. I am extremely grateful to Dr. Friedman for his help.

151 Henry Finch (1664–1728), Dean of York from 1702, and his brother Edward (1662–1737), Canon from 1704, with Edward's wife (d. 1741). By J. M. Rysbrack (1694–1770), erected in 1738. S. choir aisle (possibly moved from E. end of cathedral in 1844).

153 Henry Medley (d. 1747), Vice-Admiral. By Sir Henry Cheere (1703–81), 1749, costing £262-10-0. The inscription explains Medley's connection with the East Riding family of Grimston. N. choir aisle.

152 Thomas Lamplugh, junior (c. 1687–1747), grandson of the Archbishop, and Canon of York. Possibly by Charles Mitley (1705–58), this is a type of monument common elsewhere, though not in York Minster. S. choir aisle.

Mention has already been made of Richard Fisher and his son John. The 'Fishers of York' formed a three- or four-generation dynasty of craftsmen, stone-carvers, and wood-workers spanning more than a century. The founder of the family, Richard Fisher, is a shadowy figure, a man of mystery and legend. Since he did not, so far as is known, himself execute any funeral monument in the Minster, it may well be asked by what right he appears in this chapter. The answer is itself a part of the mystery.

In 1907 the widow of a General Fisher, apparently the last direct male descendant, presented to the dean, A. P. Purey-Cust, as a gift for the Minster, a work which had remained in Fisher's family's possession ever since it was shown at the Society of Artists' Exhibition in 1761. This is a white marble statuette (about half life-size) of Christ Carrying the Cross (Plate 154). For a provincial carver of that date it is a remarkable achievement. Firstly, the sheer standard of technical accomplishment puts its author on a level with the best figure sculptors of the days: Rysbrack, Roubiliac, Scheemakers, Cheere. Secondly, the iconoclastic element even in the moderate Protestantism of the Church of England had strongly discouraged artistic representation of Jesus Christ, as of the other Persons of the Trinity. However, in one sense it is not an original work at all, since it is a 'mirror-image' copy, much reduced in scale, of Michelangelo's 'Risen Christ with the Cross' in the church of Santa Maria Sopra Minerva in Rome (Plate 155); and it could only have been executed by someone who had either been in Rome himself, or had seen an engraving based on the Michelangelo statue, perhaps in London. It is not clear whether the Society of Artists realized this when they exhibited it in 1761, or indeed whether the then dean did so when he accepted it in 1907. But that should not be allowed to detract too much from Fisher's achievement. It may be excessive caution to write this and not call it Richard Fisher's, but the extant records say 'by Fisher', and it is oral family tradition, not committed to writing until the later nineteenth century, which ascribes the Christ, and the Jupiter with the Swan, given to the Yorkshire Philosophical Society at the same date, to Richard and not to his son John. We known that Richard Fisher was living in Minster Yard, to the south side of the cathedral, in the parish of St. Michael-le-Belfry, from 1746, when his arrival in York from Ripon was publicly advertised and custom solicited on his behalf as a carver, until 1755. From 1756 into the 1760s his house there appears to have been empty, and to have been one of several located together which eventually fell into decay. The 'Fishers' (plural) signed a monument in the Minster dated to 1773 (see below), but this could have been John and his brother Samuel (1738–80s); in 1780 the two brothers are found residing and with a workshop in the parish of St. Helen's Stonegate, while Richard Fisher's

155 'The Risen Christ'. By Michelangelo, in Santa Maria Sopra Minerva, Rome; commissioned 1514, completed 1520.

154 Christ with the Cross. ? by Richard Fisher (fl. in Yorks 1730–55); exhibited 1761; presented to York Minster 1907.

widow Alice was buried in St. Michael-le-Belfry in 1773. Where had Richard Fisher come from, and where did he disappear to?

The earliest documented reference is in the parish register of Ripon, where the cathedral was also the parish church. Richard Fisher of Scriven, Knaresborough, was married to Alice Broadley or Brodly of Ripon in 1730; their first recorded child, Hannah, was baptized there eleven months later. In 1733 Richard Fisher was employed by John Aislabie as a wood-carver for work on the interior of Studley Royal House near Ripon; in 1737–8 he was working for Horatio, brother of Sir Robert Walpole, later Lord Walpole of Wolterton, in Norfolk; by 1738, apparently after some disagreement with Walpole, Fisher was back at Ripon; in 1741 he did some work at Castle Howard; in 1746, as we have seen, he moved to York, but in the following year was again employed as a carver at Studley Royal, this time by John Aislabie's son William (c. 1700–81). He is also known to have done work at Newby Hall, and almost certainly worked elsewhere in the north of England during the 1730s–40s. So much for the known facts.

According to the family tradition, not written down until 1879 or later, he was the scion of a Jacobite noble house, who appeared in Ripon after the collapse of the 1715 Rebellion, as a disguise took the name of Fisher—which was common in the area—and trained himself to earn his living as a carver. He had received a classical education, spoke fluent French, and was also an accomplished painter and musician. He called his favourite horse after the Jacobite heroine Jenny Cameron, but preserved the mystery of his birth to the last, forbidding his wife ever to speak of it, and failed—even if he wished—to reveal it when finally struck speechless on his deathbed. Much the same tradition has come down through two separate lines of female descendants, with minor variations.

What are we to make of all this? First of all, Fisher was by no means a common name in that part of Yorkshire. There are none in Ripon parish registers for many years before 1719, while none at all appear in those of Knaresborough. Secondly, the family story confuses the 1715, led by James Edward, the 'Old Pretender', with the 1745, led by the 'Young Pretender', Charles Edward. Thirdly, while it would seem deliberate provocation rather than camouflage to call one's horse after a Jacobite heroine, the lady in question, although she may have come to greet the prince in 1745, was regarded in pro-Hanoverian, anti-Jacobite circles as no better than she might have been, and there was nothing to admire save boldness and unconventionality about her, after 1715, as opposed to 1745. The name could equally have been used in contemptuous bravado.

An alternative theory, canvassed by the late Katherine Esdaile, offers as Richard Fisher's putative father Lewis Watson, first Earl of Rockingham

(1655–1724), whose brother's monument has already been discussed. The Marquis of Rockingham is also said to have been Fisher's patron and to have persuaded him to settle in York. So far from living in St. Michael-le-Belfry parish, his residence is given as a house at the junction of St. Saviourgate and Spen Lane, almost opposite St. Anthony's Hall. As is all too often the case, no references are provided.

Another account would relate Richard to James Fisher, of Deptford and Camberwell, sculptor (1682–1722), who did some work for Lord FitzWilliam. The latter's son or grandson became heir to the great Watson-Wentworth inheritance when the second Marquis of Rockingham died without issue in 1782. Again, ingenuity and plausibility have outrun any known facts.

An alternative advanced by the early twentieth-century York antiquary, J. W. Knowles, at least has the merit of economy and fits the geographical and chronological evidence. John Aislabie's head gardener for the 'emparking', or landscaping, work at Studley Royal was one William Fisher. That he was an unusual sort of gardener is evident from his work, while the local historian Thomas Gent dedicated his *History of Ripon* to him in 1733. From 1719 to 1731 a steady stream of William Fisher's offspring were christened at Ripon; these include a daughter Hannah in 1729. William died in 1743, his widow Hannay surviving him until 1772; his will refers to an eldest unnamed son being already provided for; if this son was by the same marriage, he was probably another William (1719–53). It is, however, possible that William Fisher had already been married when he came to Ripon to work for Aislabie, and had a son Richard by a former wife—his second wife being a good deal his junior. In this way one can reconcile Richard's eldest child being born in the same year as his (hypothetical) father's youngest. The coincidence of the name Hannah, for daughters of both and wife of the elder, is striking to say the least.[58]

[58] Algernon Graves, *The Society of Artists of Great Britain 1760–1791; The Free Society of Artists 1761–1783. A Complete Dictionary* . . . (1907), p. 92; A. P. Purey-Cust, *Walks round York Minster* (Leeds, 1907), Postscript; *York Jour.* 15 July 1746; *YH* 13 Nov. 1790; *Y.Cour.* 15 Apr. 1811, 11 Dec. 1815; YML, Parish Records of St. Michael-le-Belfry, DEP/P/M, 21, Churchwardens' Accounts and Assessments, 1730–52; ibid. 22, Accounts (only), 1751–85; BIHR, Account Book of Surveyors of St. Helen's Stonegate, 1763–1810, Y/HEL/17; L. Goldscheider, *The Sculpture of Michelangelo* (New York, 1940), p. 15 and Pls. 85–8, or *Michelangelo: Paintings, Sculpture and Architecture* (4th edn. 1964), Pls. 155–6. I am extremely grateful to Professor H. W. Janson, of New York University, for advice on this point, and for other generous help. Yorks. Par. Reg. Soc., *Register of St. Michael-le-Belfry*, pt. 2, p. 282; T. Gent, *The Antient and Modern History of the Loyal Town of Ripon* (York, 1733); J. R. Walbran, *A Pictorial Pocket Guide to Ripon and Harrogate: with topographical observations on Studley Royal* . . . (Ripon, 1844); *Studley Royal Near Ripon: A Short Description and History* (4 pp., n.d.); *Country Life*, 25 July and 1 Aug. 1931, 25 July and 15 Aug. 1957, 10 Aug. 1961, 8 and 15 Dec. 1966; Geoffrey Beard, 'Studley Royal: A Yorkshire Landscape Garden', *Leeds Art Calendar*, no. 48 (1961),

[cont.]

Meanwhile, Richard Fisher's Jupiter has been allowed to fall into sad disrepair by the Philosophical Society, while his Christ having first been housed in the Zouche Chapel, off the south choir aisle, was then moved to St. John's Chapel (on the west side of the north transept).

There are eight definite Fisher monuments dating from the 1770s to 1790s, a ninth from 1810, and possibly one or two others unsigned or unidentified. In the earliest of them (Plate 156), Dr. John Dealtry (d. 1773), M.D., a physician of the city, receives a warm tribute to his medical skill and devotion; his epitaph is said to have been composed by William Mason, canon of York, author and connoisseur (for whom see below). The monument is unusual in being one of the only two where the main figure is not a bust or statue of the person commemorated but an allegorical figure, in this case of Hygeia the Greek goddess of health; neo-classicism could hardly be taken further than by having a pagan deity, albeit an admirably benevolent one, in a Christian cathedral.[59] Mrs. Pulleyn (d. 1786), widow, herself a Sterne by birth, has a slightly more ambitious mural tablet than some, being topped off with an urn.[60] In the same year another tablet records the death of a judge. Sir Thomas Davenport (1734–86), M.P. for Newton in Lancashire and sergeant-at-law, a firm adherent of Lord North, was more distinguished as a lawyer than as a parliamentarian. He died presumably of jail-fever contracted while presiding over the York assizes.[61]

10–16; G. Beard, *Georgian Craftsmen and their Work* (1966), pp. 53, 176. For the real and mythical Jenny Camerons see James Ray of Whitehaven, *A Compleat History of the Rebellion* . . . (York, 1749), pp. 23–39; Robert Chambers, *History of the Rebellion of 1745–6* (7th edn. 1869), p. 49 n. 1, pp. 251–2 n. 1; Robert Forbes, ed. H. Paton, *The Lyon in Mourning* (Scottish History Soc., xx, 1895), i. 293; Alan Graeme, 'The Mystery Woman of the '45. Too many Jean Camerons', *Scots Mag.* xv (1931), 17–28; R. C. Jarvis, 'Fielding, Dodsley, Marchant and Ray: Some Fugitive Histories of the '45', pt. ii, *Notes and Queries*, 189 (1945), p. 120 and n. 68. Ripon Cathedral parish registers, searched *c.* 1680–1760; Knaresborough registers, *c.* 1680–1740; BIHR, PCY, York Wills, 1743; Gunnis, *Dictionary*, p. 146; *Complete Peerage*, 'FitzWilliam', 'Walpole'; sources already given for Aislabie and Watson-Wentworth; Esdaile, *YAJ* xxxvi. 88–90; J. W. Knowles, 'York Artists' (2 vols., YCA, 1927), i. 165; the late R. Gunnis, Additional Notes deposited at the Victoria and Albert Museum (I am grateful to Mr. John Physick for letting me have copies of these); Miss Corita Myerscough, letters and copies of nineteenth-century family documents. I am grateful to Miss Myerscough herself, and to Mr. Richard Reid, carver of York, for help in this connection and generally over Fisher's work; likewise to Mr. John Cornforth of *Country Life* and Mr. Hans Fletcher of the Royal Academy of Arts, for responding to my queries about Richard Fisher, and the latter for confirming that there are no additional, unpublished materials for the 1761 Exhibition.

[59] St. Stephen's Chapel, north wall, near railings; Venn, *Al. Cant.* I. ii. 25; Morrell, *York Mons.*, Pl. LXII; Addleshaw, *400 Years.*

[60] St. Stephen's Chapel, north wall; C. Pullein, *The Pulleyns of York* (1915)—see Cliffe, *Yorks. Gentry*, p. 407; Morrell, *York Mons.*, Pl. LXVII; Venn, *Al. Cant.* I. iii. 406; Gunnis, *Dictionary*, p. 146; Addleshaw, *400 Years.*

[61] North choir aisle, at east end of north wall; Foster, *Al. Oxon. 1715–1886* (4 vols., 1887–8), p. 342; Morrell, *York Mons.*, Pl. LXVI; Addleshaw, *400 Years*; L. Namier and J. Brooke, *History of Parliament, The House of Commons 1754–1790* (3 vols., 1964), ii. 302–3.

156 John Dealtry (1708–73), M.D. By the Fishers, no date; with relief figure of Hygeia, the Greek goddess of health. St. Stephen's Chapel (extreme NE. corner of the cathedral).

158 Sir George Savile, M.P., 8th Bart. (1726–84), buried at Thornhill. By J. Fisher—the most ambitious of the Fisher monuments. N. choir aisle.

Much the most striking Fisher monument, however, and sculpturally the only one of major interest, is to the Yorkshire political notability Sir George Savile, Bt. (1726–84). Member of Parliament for the county from 1759 to the year before his death, he was a consistent radical or 'Country' Whig who never accepted public office. A larger than life-size standing figure in white stone (Plate 158) shows Savile holding a copy of the famous Yorkshire freeholders' petition of 1780, demanding more drastic reforms than those which Edmund Burke was currently propounding. The statue has one main weakness, in the eyes which convey an unhappy impression of sightlessness. Otherwise it compares favourably with Nollekens's bust of Savile, also apparently posthumous (now in the York City Art Gallery), and with any other eighteenth-century work in the Minster. It was erected in 1789, and it is interesting to speculate what the reputation of a radical Whig might have been even a few years later, whether Savile would have followed Charles James Fox or Burke in the great ideological rift over the French Revolution which convulsed the Whigs in the 1790s.[62]

Additional Fisher tablets record an officer killed in the amphibious attack on Toulon in 1793, when Napoleon Bonaparte distinguished himself in action,[63] and a neighbouring landowner who led a blameless and truly private life but was notable for his benefactions to the poor.[64]

The next group of monuments chronologically are the work of two sculptors whose working lives spanned the late eighteenth and early nineteenth centuries: Michael Taylor (1760–1846) is represented by several mostly quite plain tablets from the 1790s–1800s.[65] For example, Francis Croft, who died aged 31 in 1807, is commemorated together with his parents. His father John (d. 1820, aged 88) had been a successful port-wine merchant who retired to York after working at Oporto, and became an amateur antiquary and civic worthy, serving as sheriff in 1773. Their

[62] At present against outer wall of north choir aisle, at the west end; *DNB*; Ian R. Christie, 'Sir George Savile, Edmund Burke and the Yorkshire Reform Programme', *YAJ* xl (1960), 205–8; Morrell, *York Mons.*, p. 83, Pl. LXV; Whinney, *Sculpture in Britain*, Ch. 21; Whinney, *English Sculpture*, Pl. no. 35; Addleshaw, *400 Years*; T. F. Friedman, private information.

[63] Captain Pelsant Reeves, north choir aisle; Gunnis, *Dictionary*, p. 146. The inscription of course makes no mention of the future Emperor of the French; Reeves was a Berkshire man himself, and the tablet was erected by a brother officer.

[64] Richard Wharton of Carlton, Esq. (1730–94); *Lincoln's Inn Admission Reg.*, p. 433; Harl. Soc. xlix, W. Musgrave, *Obituary*, vi. 246; Morrell, *York Mons.*, Pl. LXXII; Gunnis, *Dictionary*, p. 146; Addleshaw, *400 Years*.

[65] e.g. John Farr Abbott (d. 1794, aged 38), small plain tablet in north choir aisle, by Taylor, ? 1795; Rev. Richard Thompson and his wife Anne (d. 1795 and 1791, aged *c.* 70 and 76), stone tablet with urns on top, at east end of north choir aisle, by Taylor (Morrell, *York Mons.*, p. 84, Pl. LXIX) or by the Fishers (Addleshaw, Additional Notes); Lady Mary Hoar, née Howard (d. 1798, aged 22), mural tablet with triangular top, relief urn and shield above, south choir aisle, next Archbishop Lamplugh,

[cont.]

monument, surmounted by an urn and a shield in relief, may well be by Taylor.[66] The last Fisher monument, of 1810, must presumably be by the third generation of the family: John (1786–1839) or possibly one of his brothers.[67] Meanwhile, the Italian, London-based craftsman Francesco Bernasconi (*fl.* 1800–35) had been employed by the dean and chapter and had carried out some good-quality restorations on the de Gray tomb and its canopy, and on the canopy of Archbishop Bowet's tomb in the Lady Chapel.[68] A letter from Bernasconi's agent to the dean and chapter makes it clear that the bills submitted covered all the work undertaken, and refers to several 'monuments', although only the two are named in the bills. There seem only to be two works by Richard Westmacott the elder, later a knight (1775–1856).[69] One of 1810 (Plate 159) is of more interest than any other monument of the period, later than Fisher's of Savile. It commemorates William Burgh of Bootham, York (1741–1808), who had been born in Ireland, the heir to large estates there, and had sat as an M.P. in the Irish Parliament from 1769 to 1776. Burgh lived in York for nearly forty years, and was a friend of William Wilberforce, the great abolitionist, as well as of Canon William Mason. Although entirely self-educated, he ventured into theology, attacking the Unitarians and defending the doctrine of the Trinity. For this the University of Oxford made him a D.C.L. in 1788. He was also a collector and connoisseur, and owned the so-called Rokeby Milton—Samuel Cooper's fine miniature which subsequently passed from him to the Morritts and so to the present owners of Rokeby. It is in fact a portrait, probably the best there is, of Cromwell's secretary of state, John Thurloe, and not of the great Puritan poet.[70] The Burgh monument includes

by Taylor (Gunnis, *Dictionary*, p. 381; *Complete Peerage*, 'Wicklow'); Edward Tipping, Esq. (d. 1798, aged 35), mural tablet with dove and urn above inscription, swag below, in All Saints' Chapel, signed by Taylor (Morrell, *Yorks Mons.*, Pl. LXVIII; J. O'Hart, *The Irish and Anglo-Irish Landed Gentry (1884; repr. Dublin and New York, 1969)*; *Irish Pedigrees* (2 vols., Dublin, 1892); F. A. Crisp, *Visitation of Ireland*, pt. 5 (1911), p. 17. Elizabeth and Albinia Chaloner (d. 1798 and 1836, aged 52 and 45), stone tablet (?) by Taylor in north choir aisle (Addleshaw, *Additional Notes*; Clay (ed.), *Dugdale's Visn. of Yorks.*, pt. vi, p. 234).

[66] In south choir aisle; *DNB*, 'John Croft'; Morrell, *York Mons.*, Pl. LXXVI (d); Addleshaw, *Additional Notes*.

[67] Ensign Henry Whittam, drowned in the River Ouse, aged 25 or 26 (1809), commemorated by his brother officers of the Craven militia; large white on black oval tablet with urn above, south choir aisle (signed).

[68] Addleshaw, *400 Years*; Gunnis, *Dictionary*, p. 51; further repairs to Bowet were ordered in 1819, became urgently necessary after 1829, and were carried out in or just after 1844 (E. A. Gee, *Notes*).

[69] YML, E4 (a), Fabric Accounts, 1661–1827, fos. 89–94ᵛ; E3, Rolls and Loose Bills, including William Price's letter of 22 Nov. 1803.

[70] See G. Williamson, *Portraits of John Milton* (for Christ's College, Cambridge, 1908), pp. 15–17; Margaret Toynbee, 'An attempt to identify the subject of the so-called Milton miniature at Rokeby', *Connoisseur* (July 1923), pp. 151–3; Bernard Barr and John Ingamells (comps.), *A Candidate for Praise: William Mason 1725–97 Precentor of York* (Exhibition Catalogue, York, 1973), pp. 45–6.

the other large allegorical female figure of the time—probably a personification of Faith—holding a cross and a copy of his book *On the Holy Trinity*. While his career was no doubt admirable by many standards, this cultured defender of orthodoxy was among the many Englishmen whose comfortable, leisured way of life depended on the ill-rewarded toil of the Irish peasantry; like his friend Wilberforce, he need not have looked outside the British Isles to champion victims of exploitation and injustice.[71] Taylor, though not Westmacott, was also called upon to carry out restoration work on earlier tombs, such as a statue and finial on the canopy gable of Archbishop Greenfield's in St. Nicholas's Chapel (on the east side of the north transept).[72] This renewed interest in the tombs of the thirteenth- and fourteenth-century archbishops was surely no accident, coming when it did, but an indicator of changing tastes and values.

We are indeed at the time of the Gothic Revival, on the eve of the Tractarian or Oxford movement—and of Victorianism. It is perhaps fitting to pause and take stock. An excessively adulatory view has scarcely been taken here of the seventeenth- and eighteenth-century sculpture in the Minster. But, as a reminder of how low a view the spokesmen of a succeeding epoch can have of their predecessors' work—and of how quickly and completely tastes can change—let us turn to John Britton, F.S.A., whose splendid illustrated folio volume on the Minster appeared in 1819. 'Very few of the monuments of this church', he writes, 'are interesting, either as works of art, or subjects of antiquity'; and, comparing the de Gray monument with later works, he refers to Archbishop Savage's chest-tomb (d. 1507; erected soon after) as 'one of the latest examples of the elegant English sculpture which, towards the end of the sixteenth century, was corrupted and debased by the intermixture of Grecian and Roman architecture'. And of the post-Restoration archiepiscopal tombs at the eastern end of the church he writes 'these, notwithstanding the labour and expense profusely lavished in erecting them, display examples of every fault which should be avoided in monumental sculpture and architecture'.[73]

Although the revolution in style achieved by the Gothic Revival was surprisingly swift and complete, there was—as with all such movements— an overlap between the old and the new. Nor were all Gothicists such fanatical enemies of the Renaissance as John Britton was. Some artists went on working very much as they always had done, other adapted, or

---

[71] *DNB*; Gunnis, *Dictionary*, pp. 423–8; Whinney, *Sculpture in Britain*, Ch. 25; Addleshaw, *400 Years*. I am grateful to Professor Janson for the identification with 'Faith'.

[72] Addleshaw, *400 Years*, citing Browne, *History*, p. 318.

[73] John Britton, *History and Antiquities of the Metropolitical Church of York*, pp. 59, 60, 62.

tried to accommodate themselves to the new canons of taste. This can to some extent be documented visually by examining the works of such men as Taylor and Westmacott, both of whose active careers as monumental sculptors spanned the medieval revivalism of Britton, the elder Pugin, Sir Walter Scott, and others. In this movement of ideas Britton's originality is perhaps underrated, even by the best authorities.[74] At York the overlap of old and new can be seen in Taylor's tablet (extreme east end of the north choir aisle) to the Hon. Dorothy Langley (d. 1824, aged 65; erected about 1828), which has a kind of Gothic shrine over the top of it.[75]

By the 1840s the victory of the new style was almost total. The monument to William Wickham (1761–1840) illustrates the final stages of this process. He was a descendant of that Jacobean archdeacon whose wife's monument is in the north choir aisle, and also had York connections on his mother's side from the Lamplugh family. After a conventional but thorough education in Geneva as well as at Oxford and Lincoln's Inn, he was called to the bar and then became a bankruptcy commissioner in 1790. Wickham had married into an influential Swiss family; his French was faultless; and on the outbreak of war with the revolutionary Republic he was put in charge of the Aliens Division of the Home Office, but his real chance came in the autumn of 1794 when the foreign secretary sent him to Berne, nominally as envoy and chargé d'affaires, in reality to co-ordinate the counter-revolutionary activities of French *émigrés*, or such as were thought by Wickham to deserve encouragement in the form of English gold. From this underworld of political intelligence and secret diplomacy, he was recalled to become under-secretary in the Home Department (1797–9); he was sent abroad again to direct counter-revolutionary activities against the French Republic (1799–1802), though this phase of his work is less well documented. He was again recalled and served for two years as chief secretary for Ireland in the Addington administration

---

[74] For a proper account see Kenneth Clark, *The Gothic Revival: An Essay in the History of Taste* (1928; rev. edn. 1949; repr. 1962, paperb. edn. NY 1974); also T. S. R. Boase, *English Art 1800–1870* (Oxford Hist. of Engl. Art, x, Oxford, 1959), esp. Chs. I, VII, IX, but for sculpture and statuary see also Chs. V and XII. For Britton, see also *DNB*.

[75] *Complete Peerage*, 'Middleton'; Morrell, *York Mons.*, Pl. LXXXI; Gunnis, *Dictionary*, p. 381; Addleshaw, *400 Years*; J. Hunter, *Familiae Minorum Gentium*, iii. 979–80 (Harl. Soc. xxxix). Note too the kind of lettering used (gold on black) for the tablet to George Hoar (d. 1813) and his wife Frances (d. 1761), at west end of north choir aisle, possibly by Taylor (Addleshaw, Additional Notes), or that on the tablet of Archdeacon John Eyre (c. 1758–1830), the same location, ? Taylor (Foster, *Al. Oxon. 1715–1886*, p. 441; Venn, *Al. Cant.* II. ii. 448; Addleshaw, Additional Notes). For Westmacott, the case depends on whether he or Charles King (*fl.* 1809–40) was the carver of Lady Downe's monument (d. 1812, aged 72, erected 1836), near west end of north choir aisle, with large, ornate incised lettering on stone (*Complete Peerage*, 'Downe'; pedigree also in M.I.; Gunnis, *Dictionary*, pp. 228, 427, 429, negative for both; Addleshaw, Additional Notes).

(1802–4); by this time an M.P. (for a small Wiltshire borough), and indeed briefly a lord of the treasury in 1806, Wickham never seems to have been a politician of much consequence, and when the Whig ministry of 'The Talents' broke up in 1807, he retired from public life. His monument (between Mrs. Hodson and Sir William Gee, on the south choir aisle wall) is by John Ely Hinchcliffe (1777–1867) who served as Flaxman's assistant from 1808 to 1826. The mural tablet is embellished with columns and a pediment, and has an armorial shield below. Here we can perhaps begin to see that mixture of stylistic eclecticism, revivalism, and technical virtuosity which characterizes so much Victorian art.[76]

An even less distinguished but depressingly symptomatic product of these influences can be seen in the earliest of a long series of monuments commemorating military men and army units in the nineteenth and twentieth centuries. Major Oldfield, C.B., of the Bengal Light Cavalry and a colonel in the Indian Army (1805–50), was a hero of the north-west frontier, at the relief of Jellalabad in 1842, and then in the conquest of the Punjab, at the Battle of Maharajapore (1843), dying on active service at Nakodah a few years later. His family originally came from the West Riding; his grandfather moved and became lord mayor of York, and his father served as a judge in the civilian administration of the East India Company, retiring to Lendal in York; one elder brother was also a judge in India and another a colonel in the Indian Army. Here indeed was the pattern of imperial rule taking shape in York. The major's memorial was entrusted to Matthew Skelton, 'one of the least distinguished of the York statuaries', who produced a large, ornate stone and marble wall monument, with heavily incised lettering, paid for by the hero's brother officers of the 5th Regiment (Plate 160). If the dates given on it are correct, Oldfield must have begun his service in India at the age of 15: such was the cost of Empire.[77]

William Markham (1719–1807), who reigned over the see of York for thirty years, is the first archbishop to be commemorated in the Minster since Sharp (d. 1714). Of his six predecessors, two were translated to Canterbury, one was buried in the Cambridge College of which he was master and benefactor, two others in London, and one privately at

---

[76] *DNB*; Morrell, *York Mons.*, p. 109, Pl. LXXXIII; Gunnis, *Dictionary* p. 202; his career has recently been explored in W. R. Fryer, *Republic or Restoration in France? 1794–7* (Manchester, 1965), and Harvey Mitchell, *The Underground War against Revolutionary France. The Missions of William Wickham 1794–1800* (Oxford, 1965).

[77] Quotation from Gunnis, *Dictionary*, p. 353. He and Addleshaw, *400 Years*, give conflicting dates for Skelton and for the erection of the monument; the latter is surely correct. For the Oldfield family see Burke's *Landed Gentry* (1937 centenary edn.); and for the campaigns in question, *The Cambridge History of India*, v, *British India 1497–1858*, ed. H. H. Dodwell (Cambridge, 1929), Chs. xxviii and xxix.

Bishopthorpe.[78] Markham's tomb was ordered to be replaced in 1844, that is, after the second fire, but it must have been the first in 1829 by which it was nearly destroyed. His imposing stone chest-tomb with black marble top is apparently the combined work of three men. It was designed by A. Salvin (1799–1881), one of the high priests of the Gothic Revival, and jointly executed by Charles Raymond Smith (1799–1888) of Grosvenor Place, London, and Thomas Willement (1786–1871) of Hornsea. It is hard to know whether it should be called an imitation, in the sense of being a replica of medieval chest- or box-tombs, but it is certainly unusual and in contrast to those of previous archbishops in not having an effigy.[79] Perhaps it did have one (but unrecorded) before the fire.

The next major monument in date was that of the redoubtable Edward Venables Vernon (1757–1847), archbishop for thirty-nine years, who took the name of Harcourt after inheriting that family's estates in Oxfordshire but declined a peerage from Lord Melbourne; his great-grandson became Viscount Harcourt in 1917. The *Dictionary of National Biography* portrays him as a sweet-tempered, gentle person, but says nothing about his archiepiscopate. Nineteenth-century memoirs and other sources suggest, on the contrary, that he was touchy if not quarrelsome, and he must in his latter years have been an awe-inspiring not to say terrifying figure. The stone effigy by Matthew Noble (1818–76), himself a Yorkshireman who went to London and made good, suggests to the modern visitor the very image of an 'eminent Victorian' (Plate 161). But we must remember that Vernon-Harcourt was already in his thirties when the French Revolution broke out, and that over twenty-eight years of his tenure at York preceded the queen's accession. His almost Gladstonian features must surely reflect a fashion in portraiture as much as the reality.[80]

The only other monument of this period on the same scale commemorates—very fittingly—one of the cathedral's and the city's most generous benefactors of modern times. Dr. Stephen Beckwith (c. 1770–1843), apparently the last descendant of a long prominent York family, an Edinburgh graduate, practised medicine for many years from his house in Coney Street, latterly retiring across the river to Bishophill.

---

[78] See *DNB*, 'Sir William Dawes', 'Lancelot Blackburne', 'Thomas Herring', 'Matthew Hutton' (the second archbishop of York of this name), 'John Gilbert', 'Robert Hay Drummond'.

[79] In the Lady Chapel; *DNB*, also for Salvin and Willement; Addleshaw, *400 Years*; E. A. Gee, Notes, citing Chapter Acts, 1844, p. 77; nothing in Gunnis, *Dictionary*, pp. 355–6, under Smith.

[80] In the nave; *DNB*, also 'Noble'; *Complete Peerage*, 'Harcourt'; of his sixteen children, at least four received preferment within the province if not the diocese (refs. in Le Neve, *Fasti*); Morrell, *York Mons.*, Pl. LXXXIV (b); Gunnis, *Dictionary*, pp. 274–5; Addleshaw, *400 Years*. See also ch. VII, 'The 19th Century'. I am grateful to Mr. George Wilmot, lately curator of the Yorkshire Museum, for further information about nineteenth-century ecclesiastical disputes in York.

159 William Burgh (1741–1808) D.C.L., of Bootham, York, though born in Ireland, with a personification of Faith. By Sir Richard Westmacott (1755–1856), 1810. S. choir aisle.

160 Major C. E. T. Oldfield, C.B. (1804–50), Lieutenant-Colonel in the Bengal cavalry. By Matthew Skelton (1798–1878), 1852, a relatively early example in York of 'Victorian Gothic'. S. choir aisle.

161 Edward Venables Vernon-Harcourt (1757–1847), Archbishop for nearly 39 years; he declined a peerage but took the name Harcourt in order to inherit estates in Oxfordshire; for his relations with the Dean and Chapter, see Ch. VII. By Matthew Noble (1818–76), 1855. Nave.

When the contents of his will became known early in January 1844, his benefactions were said to total £40,000; these included £2,000 for the renovation of the Minster's bells, £3,000 for the restoration of the chapter-house, £10,000 for the Philosophical Society's Museum, £5,000 for the Blind School (by then in the King's Manor), £5,000 towards a new penitentiary, and at least another £6,000 or £7,000 odd to various schools, hospitals, and parochial charities. Considering the value of money in the 1840s, this must surely make Beckwith one of the greatest philanthropists York has known before the rise of the Rowntrees. His life-size recumbent effigy was carved by Joseph Bently Leyland (1811–51) of Halifax, whose father Robert Leyland was better known as a naturalist than he as a sculptor. The present chest-tomb base was executed by the Minster stoneyard staff in 1954, and the whole monument has been moved from its original site in the chapter-house vestibule to the north choir aisle.[81]

The regimental memorials of the 1850s and 1860s are a new feature, reflecting the Victorian 'burdens of Empire'. There are hierarchical differences among them: some commemorate officers only, in others the officers are named and the 'Other Ranks' merely enumerated, whereas in some all are named—rank by rank. In trying to account for the appearance of such collective memorials, we must remember that these were volunteer armies; apart from the naval press-gangs there was no general conscription for military service outside Great Britain from 1713 until 1916. And from this epoch too dates the association of particular regiments with individual cathedrals and other churches, leading—usually in the early twentieth century—to the consecration and furnishing of chapels as regimental memorials.[82]

The earliest such monument in York Minster is that by Edward Richardson (1812–69) to the officers and men of the 51st, King's Own—later

---

[81] *List of Graduates in Medicine in the University of Edinburgh from MDCCV to MDCCCLXVI* (Edinburgh, 1867), p. 27; Edward Baines, *Historical Directory and Gazetteer of the County of York* . . . ii (Leeds, 1823), p. 75; *The Times*, 4 Jan. 1844; *Gentleman's Magazine*, N.S., xxi, for Jan.–Jun. 1844, p. 221; xxii, for Jun.–Dec. 1844, p. 657; *DNB*, 'Leyland'; G. A. Auden (ed.), *A Handbook to York and District* . . . (London and York, 1906); Robert H. Skaife, 'Biographical Sketches of Eminent Citizens' (YCL), p. 229; Morrell, *York Mons.*, Pl. LXXXIV (a); Gunnis, *Dictionary*, pp. 239–40 (misdates it to 1845); Addleshaw, *400 Years* (citing *York Gazette* for 12 May and 9 June 1849); *VCH York*, pp. 338, 422, 424, 432–3, 443, 447; A. Stacpoole *et al.* (eds.), *The Noble City of York* (York, 1972); R. Cant, 'The Minster', p. 40; Pevsner, *York and E.R.*, p. 108. The various branches of the Beckwith family can be traced in numerous sources for York and Yorkshire from the sixteenth to the eighteenth centuries.
[82] General Sir Charles Deedes, *A Short History of the Chapel of the K.O.Y.L.I. in York Minster* (n.d. [1947–8]); The Revd. Chancellor G. Austen, *The West Yorkshire Regt. Its History and Memorial Chapel* (n.d. [1928–9]). I am grateful to Mr. C. B. L. Barr and Canon R. Cant for these references and for further information about regimental chapels in the Minster. There is room for a study covering the whole country.

Yorkshire—Light Infantry Regiment, killed or died in Burma 1852–3, erected in St. John's Chapel in 1855 (Plate 162). It is a mural tablet with a large but reduced figure of an officer facing to the left, in white stone; the surrounding, slate-coloured background has columns of names; it was commissioned, and paid for, by the surviving officers. The whole effect is not unpleasing, and the principal figure, despite the criticisms to which Richardson was subjected for some of his work, is at least competent.[83] Then in 1858 John Birnie Philip (1824–75) executed a stone tablet with carved figures and the names in brass, to the memory of Lieutenant-Colonel Willoughby Moore and his comrades, mainly N.C.O.s, of the 6th Inniskilling Dragoons who perished on the troopship *Europa* when it caught fire and sank only some two hundred miles away from Plymouth, taking horses and supplies out to the Crimea (Plate 163). Moore refused to leave the ship before all his men had done so, and this cost him his life; the representation is a kind of romanticized naturalism, but somehow the full horror of fire at sea has escaped the artist; a brother officer who died at Balaclava is also commemorated.[84] The Crimean memorial of the 19th Regiment, also known as the 1st Yorkshire North Riding Regiment, and more familiar as the Green Howards, was designed by John Hardman Powell (1828–95), son-in-law of A. W. N. Pugin, and executed by John Hardman of Birmingham. It comprises a large pictorial brass wall tablet with representations of Christ and various angels and saints; it commemorates officers only.[85] Only the connoisseur of Victorian Gothic is likely to savour its full joys. By contrast, Richardson's memorial to the dead of the 33rd, Duke of Wellington's Regiment manages to name all ranks, using incised lettering on a stone tablet, and generally displays restraint.[86] But for the present writer's taste, much the best of this group is that by John Bedford (1821–64) of London commemorating the 13 officers and 360 men—all unnamed—of the 84th, York and Lancaster Regiment who died in India during the Mutiny and Rebellion in 1857–9 (Plate 164). Erected in 1863, this is a relatively simple stone mural tablet, with the figures of two

---

[83] St. John's Chapel is on the west side of the north transept. *DNB*, 'Richardson'; Gunnis, *Dictionary*, pp. 320–1; Addleshaw, *400 Years*.

[84] South choir aisle, immediately west of entrance to Zouche Chapel. *The Times*, 17, 19, 20, 21, 24, and 27 June 1854; Gunnis, *Dictionary*, pp. 300–1 (nothing under Philip, but this is after Gunnis's terminal date); Addleshaw, *400 Years*, correcting George Benson, *Handbook to the Cathedral Church of St. Peter, York* (York, 1893; 5th edn. 1914), pp. 114 and 119, who ascribes the design to Giles Gilbert Scott.

[85] South choir aisle, just west of vestry door. Addleshaw, *400 Years*; *DNB*, 'A.W.N. Pugin'; Pevsner, *York and E.R.*, p. 107.

[86] All Saints' Chapel, now dedicated to the Duke of Wellington's Regt., in extreme south-east corner of the church. *DNB*, 'Richardson'; Gunnis, *Dictionary*, pp. 320–1 (not listed); Addleshaw, *400 Years*.

162 King's Own Yorkshire Light Infantry (51st Regiment), Burma 1852–3; note the long lists of names, other ranks as well as officers. By Edward Richardson (1812–69). St. John's Chapel (W. side of N. transept).

163 Lieutenant-Colonel Willoughby Moore and other members of the 6th Inniskilling Dragoons, lost in the *Europa*, 1854. By J. B. Philip (1824–75), 1858. S. choir aisle.

164 84th (York and Lancaster) Regiment, India, 1857–9; 13 officers and 360 men, but no names are given. By J. Bedford of London (d. 1875), 1863. S. choir aisle.

soldiers—fine manly fellows—facing inwards; though commissioned by their surviving comrades, the monument conveys the ethos of contemporary attitudes towards the army at its best: Gunnis damns it with faint praise, as 'conventional but not too unfortunate'.[87] No doubt misfortune is a relative term, aesthetically as otherwise.

And, just to remind us what the Victorians could do, the same part of the cathedral boasts another monument of the same date. This commemorates the worthy William Mason (1724–97) and his nephew W. H. Dixon (1783–1854)—the clergyman and antiquary, not the amateur historian of the same name and initials (Plate 165). By F. A. Skidmore (1816–96) of Coventry, it consists of a brass tablet set into a kind of pre-Raphaelite shrine, with stone figures of Christ as the Good Shepherd, and of the two Marys. Goodness knows what Mason would have made of it all; at least in this life he had a sense of humour.[88]

Matthew Noble was also commissioned to carve the effigy of Vernon-Harcourt's successor, Archbishop Thomas Musgrave (1788–1860). The base is by John Raphael Brandon (1817–77). Again, technical competence and a certain forbidding severity are its most obvious characteristics.[89]

The 1870s have left us only three monuments, all connected with premature, not to say violent, death. Frederick Grantham Vyner, fourth son of a wealthy family with historic Yorkshire connections, was captured with his travelling companions by Greek brigands not ten miles from Athens after visiting the battlefield of Marathon. After a series of blunders in the negotiations, which were conducted with the leader of the kidnappers by the British minister and the Greek authorities against the stormy, even treacherous background of Greek party conflict, he and three other hostages were murdered on 21 April, 1870 ten days after their capture. Vyner, who was nicknamed the 'dormouse' because his travelling companions had so much difficulty getting him up in the morning, was evidently a young man of some charm, who even endeared himself to his captors. But the iron rules of brigandage, which should have been well known to those negotiating at the other end, required that no hostages be recovered alive if the ransom terms were not met. Vyner faced, and finally met, death courageously; but the inscription oversimplifies in

---

[87] South choir aisle, east of vestry door. Gunnis, *Dictionary*, pp. 44–5; Addleshaw, *400 Years*.

[88] South choir aisle. *DNB*; Venn, *Al. Cant.* II. ii. 307; Morrell, *York Mons.*, Pl. LXXXV; Addleshaw, *400 Years*; Barr and Ingamells, *A Candidate for Praise*.

[89] Nave. *DNB*, also 'Brandon' and 'Noble'; Morrell, *York Mons.*, Pl. LXXXVI (a); Gunnis, *Dictionary*, pp. 274–5, dating it to 1860; Addleshaw, *400 Years* (correctly, 1864); D. A. Jennings, *The revival of the Convocation of York 1837–1861* (Borthwick Papers, no. 47, York, 1975) has additional material on the archbishop's role; see Ch. VII above.

saying that he refused to purchase his freedom at the expense of others, for it is very doubtful whether the brigand leader would have allowed the substitution of Lord Muncaster's Swiss courier, who heroically offered himself as a substitute, even if Vyner had agreed to consider this. The large mural tablet by Thomas Earp (1827–93) of stone and coloured marble resembles a tombstone set into the wall.[90]

Another regimental memorial commemorates the officers and men of the Duke of Wellington's Regiment who lost their lives in India 1857–67 and in Abyssinia 1867–8. It enumerates the men after naming the officers, in white incised lettering on a large but not too elaborate mural tablet; executed by a London firm, Gaffin of Regent Street, commissioned by the present and ex-officers of the regiment, it is characteristic if unremarkable.[91]

Finally, Lieutenant Henry Lee of the Third Dragoon Guards was killed falling from his horse in Phoenix Park, Dublin, in 1876. The officers and men of his regiment and his ex-comrades of the 47th commissioned another London firm, this time Burke's from near Oxford Street, who produced a relatively simple stone mural tablet.[92]

The eminent mid-Victorian dean of York, the Honourable Augustus Duncombe (1814–80) is buried at Helmsley in the North Riding, but prominently commemorated in the Minster (Plate 166). The second son of a lord and grandson of an earl, he became a prebendary of York in 1841, and is said to have subsequently declined a Scottish bishopric. His recumbent effigy, life-size or larger in stone and white marble on a chest-tomb, has two angels supporting his pillow and three choir-boys holding what is presumably a scroll of church music at his feet. Picturesquely sentimental rather than beautiful, this is at least an appropriate monument to one who did so much to revive the musical quality and interest of the Minster services.[93]

[90] South choir aisle, towards west end. Foster, *Al. Oxon., 1715–1886*, p. 1476; Addleshaw, *400 Years*; Romilly Jenkins, *The Dilessi Murders* (1961), for Vyner see esp. pp. 22–3, 25, 48, 50, 60, 67, 74, 77, 171–2, plate facing p. 50. This excellent study puts the kidnapping and killings into their proper historical context; I owe my knowledge of its relevance to the reference in Dean Addleshaw's booklet.

[91] All Saints' Chapel, next the railings. Gunnis, *Dictionary*, p. 160 (for T. & E. Gaffin, but this work is beyond his terminal date); Addleshaw, *400 Years*.

[92] South choir aisle, towards west end. M.I.; Addleshaw, *400 Years*.

[93] South-east corner of south transept, immediately on the right on entering by the south transept door. *DNB*, 'G. E. Street (1824–81)', responsible for the main tomb; The Fine Art Society, *British Sculpture 1850–1914* (Exhibition Catalogue, 1968), p. 20, for E. (later Sir Edward) Boehm, who carved the effigy with its embellishments; Foster, *Al. Oxon., 1715–1886*, p. 394; *Complete Peerage*, 'Feversham'; Le Neve, *Fasti*, p. 175; Addleshaw, *400 Years*; Pevsner, *York and E.R.*, p. 108. See Chs. VII and IX above.

The 1880s produced a variety of monuments to ecclesiastical.worthies and others. Several of them, whether executed in brass or stone, have inscriptions in elaborate, often nearly illegible pseudo-Gothic lettering. Some of those commemorated certainly deserve better. William Hey (1811–82), son of a Derbyshire clergyman, had a highly successful academic career at Cambridge before becoming headmaster of the Proprietary or Collegiate School at Clifton, York, in 1838–9. It had catered for middle-class parents, prepared to pay fees and dissatisfied with what York could offer educationally, at St. Peter's and Archbishop Holgate's schools—both of which were then at a low ebb. In the mid-1840s a successful merger was arranged between Clifton and St. Peter's, the former provided the site, most of the pupils and—of decisive importance—the headmaster, the latter the name and a minority of masters and pupils. On this basis the modern school of St. Peter's, York, has really been built, and by any standards Hey's headship was crucial. Already in orders and beneficed, in 1864 he gave up the school on becoming a canon residentiary, ending his days as archdeacon of Cleveland and rural dean of Easingwold (1874–82), He was also vicar of St. Olave's in Marygate, York, the preparatory school of that name—now part of St. Peter's—having been launched in the house opposite St. Olave's Church. An amateur entomologist of some repute, as well as a sound classical scholar, Hey was clearly an inspiring head; his friends and admirers founded two memorial scholarships of £15 a year each, plus fees in the case of boarders, as well as erecting a memorial. This is a rectangular tablet in red, white, and black stone, with heavily incised lettering. So far the attribution is not known.[94]

Robert Baker, M.R.C.S. (1803–80), was buried in York cemetery, but his colleagues commissioned a memorial executed by G. F. Bodley (1827–1907), with whose works from this time until his death the Minster is—aesthetically speaking—all too well endowed. Son of a York pharmacist, Baker was trained as an apothecary and then as a surgeon in Hull and London, and was town surgeon of Leeds during the 1830s cholera epidemic. But his real career was to be in the field of public health, and what is now known as industrial medicine. From 1858 to 1878 he was one of two inspectors of factories, responsible for the enforcement of legislation concerning health and safety as well as hours of work in half the country, including the Midlands and north-west. And it was the 'Certifying Surgeons' under the Factory Acts who commemorated 'his life long work in

[94] North choir aisle. A. Raine, *History of St. Peter's School: York A.D. 627 to the Present Day* (n.d. [1925 or 6]), pp. 122–4, 157–8; Venn, *Al. Cant.* II. iii. 352. Unfortunately these two authories differ on some details of Hey's career, as to dates, etc.

165 William Mason (1724–97), Canon and
Precentor, and his nephew, W. H. Dixon
(1783–1854), Canon of York. By F. A. Skidmore
of Coventry (1816–96), 1862, showing the height
of the Gothic Revival among York monuments.
S. choir aisle.

166 The Hon. Augustus Duncombe (1814–80),
Dean from 1858, for whom see also ch. VII. By
G. E. Street (1824–81) and Sir J. E. Boehm, Bart.
(1834–90), 1882. S. transept.

promoting and extending Factory legislation in the interests of the artisan classes'. If this had been the permissible hyperbole of a monumental inscription, it would still be unusual, but the records show Baker as a pamphleteer in favour of the Factory Acts as early as 1851, and advocating the appointment of workshop subinspectors by local government authorities in 1871; in 1859 he joined in the great controversy over hours of work in relation to wages, denying that women's rates of pay had fallen since the Ten Hours Act had come into force. Although he was omitted from the *DNB*, Baker's career has recently been described in detail.[95]

A more orthodox career was that of William Dalla Husband, F.R.C.S. (1817–92), whose father was lord mayor of York in the late 1850s. He was a surgeon and then consultant at the County Hospital, and took a leading part in the affairs of the British Medical Association, becoming chairman or president of the council (1868 or 1869 to 1871) and then treasurer (1874–81), before his enforced retirement through ill-health. His work helped to ensure that the B.M.A. should represent the entire qualified medical profession, anticipating its later emergence as a major professional 'pressure group'. The rectangular brass tablet with stone border has the typical would-be Gothic lettering of the later nineteenth century.[96] Looking back to Drs. Beckwith and Baker and, still further, to Dr. Dealtry and some way forward to others, we may thus fairly add medical men to those categories of royalty, ecclesiastics, aristocrats, naval and military heroes, who are visibly commemorated in the Minster.

By contrast, the main claim to fame of the Rev. Stephen Creyke (1795 or 1796–1883) was the fact of his having been the longest-standing member of the cathedral chapter at the time of his death. His family had been established in the East Riding in the seventeenth century; his grandfather, a country clergyman, had supported the Jacobite cause in the eighteenth century, but his father had had a successful career as a naval officer, as did two of his elder brothers, one rising to flag rank. Creyke had a successful university career himself, but gave up his Oxford fellowship after only two years—presumably to marry rather than to burn—and became a prebendary of York in 1841; he was a canon residentiary from 1857 to 1873, but, more importantly, archdeacon of York and the West Riding 1845–66;

[95] North choir aisle. *DNB*, 'Bodley'; Addleshaw, *400 Years*; B. L. Hutchins and A. Harrison, *A History of Factory Legislation* (Westminster, 1903), p. 230, App. A, by G. H. Wood, p. 294, refs. in Bibliog.; W. R. Lee, 'Robert Baker: the first Doctor in the Factory Department', pt. I, '1803–1858', pt. II, '1858 onwards', *Brit. Jour. of Industrial Medicine*, 21 (1964), 85–93, 167–79. I am grateful to Canon Cant for lending me his correspondence with Mr. Mark Baker, Dr. Baker's great-grandson.
[96] North choir aisle. M.I.; V. G. Plarr, *Lives of the Fellows of the Royal College of Surgeons of England*, ed. D'Arcy Power, W. G. Spencer, and G. E. Gask (2 vols., Bristol, 1930), i. 585–6; E. M. Little, *History of the British Medical Association 1832–1932* (n.d. [1930s]), pp. 207–8, 337–8.

from 1865 to his death he enjoyed the pleasant living of Bolton Percy. His surviving sons commissioned the brass tablet with stone surrounds; whether it was a product of the same workshop as Hey's, Husband's, and other monuments of the 1880s and 1890s with similar lettering is not certain, but seems likely.[97]

G. F. Bodley was employed by the 65th (York and Lancaster) Regiment in 1886, to commemorate the 1st Battalion's casualties in New Zealand 1845–66, India 1871–84, and finally the Sudan 1884—a reminder of how thinly the 'thin red line' was indeed spread. In this case all the names have been crowded on.[98]

George Trevor (1809–88) must surely have rivalled Creyke's record, having been a canon of York for forty-one years. His career, however, was less typical and more interesting. The sixth son of a Somerset gentleman, apparently without influential connections, he began as a clerk at India House in 1825, and was a youthful friend of Benjamin Disraeli, whether with the same tastes and proclivity for getting into debt is not clear. Rather unusually at that time, Trevor only went to the university in his early twenties; he took orders after that, and in 1836 went out to Madras as a chaplain in the service of the East India Company. He returned, graduated M.A., and became rector of All Saints, Pavement, York, in 1847, also a prebendal canon. By then he had begun to make his mark as an author and ecclesiastical controversialist. He organized support in Yorkshire for the missionary work of the S.P.G., but more to the point was a strong high churchman and helped to revive the Northern Convocation. He was rewarded with honorary doctorates of divinity from Hartford, Connecticut, and from Durham before the end of his life; it was a long way from the young Disraeli. Whatever his views on ecclesiology, he is ill served by a very ornate brass tablet with lettering and surrounds.[99]

Another educationist and cleric, like Hey, is commemorated from the late 1880s. Frederick Watkins, son of a clergyman, educated at Cambridge, fellow of Emmanuel College, whose main interest for posterity might seem to be his friendship with the great Charles Darwin, likewise sacrificed his fellowship on the altar of matrimony. He pursued his career in another branch of the growing nineteenth-century bureaucracy, serving as one of Her Majesty's Inspectors of Schools from the 1840s to 1873; he retired on becoming rector of Marston, to the west of the city, and was made

[97] North choir aisle. M.I.; Foster, *Al. Oxon., 1715–1886*, p. 317; Clay (ed.), *Dugdale's Visn. of Yorks.* viii. 452.

[98] South choir aisle, towards west end. *DNB*, 'Bodley'; Addleshaw, *400 Years*.

[99] North choir aisle. *DNB*; Le Neve, *Fasti*, p. 168; Foster, *Al. Ox., 1715–1886*, p. 1438; Jennings, *Revival of Convocation*.

archdeacon of York (and the West Riding) the year after that during which time he was also a prebendary of York. His monument, similar in style to Hey's combines red, white, and black stone or marble, but has relief patterns as well as incised lettering.[100]

A reminder of York's military connections is afforded by the memorial to Lieutenant-General C. F. T. Daniell (1827–89), who was in command of the Northern Military District, later known as Northern Command, from 1886. This has been adapted to provide a kind of mock-archway over the rectangular doorway into the vestry.[101] Of much the same date is the 19th, then Princess of Wales's Regiment's memorial to its dead in Egypt and the Sudan, 1884–7, further west along the same wall; this one too manages to get on all the names, being erected by their comrades past and present.[102]

Edward Hailstone (1818–90) is appropriately commemorated as a major benefactor of the Minster library, though in fact his brass memorial tablet was erected by his nephew, Samuel. His father, Samuel Hailstone senior (1768–1851), was a successful Bradford solicitor, an amateur botanist of some note, and an ardent bibliophile. Edward continued his father's legal practice, also his collection of books and other antiquities. He produced *A Catalogue of a Collection . . . relating to the County of York* in 1858, and a rather scrappy biographical compendium, *Portraits of Yorkshire Worthies* (2 vols., 1869). His prior connections were with the West Riding more than with the city of York, and he retired to Walton Hall near Wakefield. But the younger Hailstone wished the family collection of books, pamphlets, and manuscripts to be kept together, and to be accessible for scholars and other serious readers. This explains one of the Minster library's largest modern benefactions, including its hundreds of Civil War and Interregnum tracts from the 1640s and 1650s.[103]

The 1890s produced monuments to two more archbishops, the last until the mid-twentieth century. William Thomson (born 1819; at York 1863–90) enjoyed the longest reign since Vernon-Harcourt's.[104] Thomson's effigy, by Sir John Hamo Thornycroft (1850–1925), with tomb-chest by the ubiquitous Bodley, has a dog at his feet; the whole thing is said to have cost no less than £2,000, a considerable sum for the 1890s; it is not clear who

---

[100] North choir aisle. M.I.; Venn, *Al. Cant.* II, vi. 365; information from Dr. D. M. Smith.

[101] South choir aisle, over vestry door. M.I.

[102] South choir aisle, west end. M.I.

[103] Now north choir aisle, previously south aisle of nave. *DNB; Yorks Genealogist with . . . Bibliographer*, ii (1890), 244–5; info. from C. B. L. Barr.

[104] Only archbishops subsequently translated to Canterbury have been appointed so young since then: Cosmo Gordon Lang (1864–1945) at 44 in 1908, and William Temple (1881–1944) at 47 in 1928 (*20th-Century DNB*).

paid.[105] By contrast, his successor William Connor Magee, who sounds misleadingly like an Ulster presbyterian, one of the great orators of the nineteenth century, died in the year of his appointment and election (1891). He was buried at his previous see of Peterborough; in 1896 Bodley executed a mural tablet of brass set in stone, the modesty of the memorial perhaps corresponding to the brevity of Magee's tenure at York.[106]

The affluence and respectability of such late nineteenth- and early twentieth-century 'academic' sculptors as Boehm, Bodley, Thornycroft, Milburn, Tapper, and Mackenall, are striking. This is in contrast with the social and economic standing of even so eminent a seventeenth-century sculptor as Nicholas Stone, and other carvers of his time and before; more surprisingly, this also applies to later seventeenth-century and most eighteenth-century ones. It is perhaps a legacy of Sir Joshua Reynolds and the early academicians that artists in modern Britain have tended either to be conformist, respectable, and—if professionally successful— materially well rewarded, or else rebellious, 'bohemian', and—all too often—impoverished. Clearly there are many exceptions, and these lines of division have often been crossed. Prosperous academicians can dress and behave like eccentric 'bohemians'; rebels against the establishment can become successful and wealthy, especially in times of rapid change in fashions of taste and in aesthetic standards. But in so far as York is representative of the work done in cathedrals, the swing has definitely been towards 'academicism', respectability, and worldly success.

As we move from the nineteenth into the twentieth century, much the same kinds of people continue to be commemorated. The York antiquary James Raine (1830–96), himself the son of a distinguished Durham cleric and scholar, who was canon and librarian at York, has a tablet by Bodley with the characteristic pseudo-Gothic lettering.[107] More war heroes, from the Matabeleland campaign of 1896,[108] the Tirah campaign of 1897–8 on the North-West Frontier of India,[109] and then the South African War of 1899–1902,[110] are represented by both individual and collective memorials

---

[105] Against north-east wall of south transept. *DNB*, also 'J. H. Thornycroft (1850–1925)'; Morrell, *York Mons.*, p. 109 and Pl. LXXXVII; Addleshaw, *400 Years*; E. A. Gee, Notes, citing G. Benson, *New Handbook to York* (3rd edn., York, 1904), pp. 46–7.

[106] *DNB*; Addleshaw, *400 Years*. Near west end of north choir aisle.

[107] North choir aisle. M.I.; *DNB*, 'James Raine (1791–1858)'; Addleshaw, *400 Years*.

[108] South choir aisle, just east of Zouche Chapel door. Captain Frederick Rershaw [should surely be Renshaw], and Capt. Francis Shadwell: M.I.

[109] South choir aisle, high up towards west end. For the 2nd Battn. Princess of Wales's Yorks. regt., erected by O.R.s as well as by officers. M.I.

[110] South choir aisle, between the two doorways: Capt. Wombwell and Lieut. Wilson, 1901 and 1900 respectively: M.I.; Addleshaw, Additional Notes. South choir aisle, near west end: Capt. W. M.

[cont.]

(Plate 167). In line perhaps with Baker and Husband is Anthony Buckle (d. 1900), for thirty years superintendent of the Wilberforce School for the Blind (in the King's Manor), who is described as having been poet, artist, and philanthropist, as well as—both literally and metaphorically—a guide to the blind. He too has a brass, erected as it says by those who have appreciated his good works.[111] More surprising is the memorial to the first Prince of the royal house since William of Hatfield in the fourteenth century.[112] Albert Victor Christian Edward, Duke of Clarence and Avondale (1864–92), elder brother of the future King George V, was second in succession to the throne when he died in the influenza epidemic of 1892. Whatever the charm and youthful popularity of 'Eddy', as the young prince was familiarly known, it is most unlikely that he would, if he had lived, have been as successful a constitutional monarch in the early twentieth century as his younger brother. His recent biographer effectively clears him from the preposterous charge (first given public currency only in 1970) that he was the notorious murderer of East End prostitutes in 1888–9, 'Jack the Ripper'; but at the same time does not disguise his other failings. As against this he 'had the gift of inspiring affection'. He was stationed at York with his regiment, the 10th Hussars, in 1887–8, and had been made a freeman of the city in July 1888. There was also a more personal link in the friendship between the house of Windsor and the lords Brownlow, of whose family the then dean was a cadet member. This, together with the almost hysterical popular emotions aroused by the royal family in the wake of Queen Victoria's Diamond Jubilee, no doubt explains why Dean Purey-Cust himself commissioned George Walker Milburn (1844–1941) to produce a suitable memorial, the result being a white marble, or imitation marble, shield with gilt lettering, erected in 1900.[113]

Marter, King's Dragoon Guards, & Brigade Major, 14th Brigade South African Field Force: gilded lettering and embossed corners on white rectangular tablet: M.I. All Saints' Chapel: Duke of Wellington's Regt., officers and men all named, on a large brass: M.I. St. John's Chapel: K.O.Y.L.I., all ranks, stone with bronze figures by Bodley: M.I., *DNB*, 'Bodley'; Addleshaw, *400 Years*. South choir aisle, just east of vestry door: York & Lancaster Regt., 1st & 3rd Battns., 1st & 2nd Volunteer Battns., names of officers and of men, in brass set into white marble, with battle honours and roses carved as surrounds: M.I.

[111] Towards west end of north choir aisle: M.I.; Addleshaw, Additional Notes.

[112] See Ch. IV above.

[113] South choir aisle; *DNB*, 'Albert Victor'; *Complete Peerage*, 'Clarence'; Addleshaw, *400 Years*; Michael Harrison, *Clarence: The Life of H.R.H. the Duke of Clarence and Avondale (1864–1892)* (1972). Mr. Harrison argues very strongly for the identification of the Ripper with the Prince's one-time Cambridge tutor, J. K. Stephen (1859–92), member of the famous intellectual family of that name; and—perhaps with less cogent evidence—for Eddy's own patronage of a notorious homosexual brothel, whose activities were exposed in 1889–90. If either of these suggestions is correct, the Prince was indeed on the edge of the criminal underworld, and in the former case of the psychotic half-world too.

G. F. Bodley's work culminates in a series of specially commissioned works of the 1900s. These are monumental sculptures, but with only indirect memorial connections, on each of the four inner or interior columns of the Lady Chapel, between the screen behind the high altar and the east wall of the church. Of those commemorated, William of Wykeham (1324–1404) was indeed a canon of York from 1362 amongst his numerous other preferments, but had no other connection with the Minster; John Thoresby, archbishop 1352–73, was a benefactor of the cathedral whose own tomb has disappeared (unless it is the anonymous, much restored perpendicular stone monument in the north aisle of the nave); Henry Lord Percy of Alnwick (1322–68), heir to the earldom of Northumberland, was also a benefactor of York; so too was Walter Skirlaw, bishop of Durham, 1388–1406, whose connection was certainly closer than Wykeham's since he was at one time archdeacon of the East Riding, as well as holding a York prebend, and paid for substantial quantities of building work. In each case there is a brass tablet at rather high eye-level on the same column. These seem to have provided more of an outlet for the sculptor's energies than genuine commemorations; fortunately it is possible to enjoy the other features of the presbytery and the Lady Chapel without Bodley's additions being too obtrusive.[114] His work ended in 1907 with a statue of St. Cuthbert, bishop of Lindisfarne (d. 687), in the south transept, this time at ground level.[115] The burden was then taken up by G. W. Milburn, with his 'St. Edwin', king of Northumbria (d. 632), whose statue was commissioned for the choir sanctuary,[116] and—more tenuous for any direct connection with York—with his Edward VII (d. 1910), executed in 1911 under the supervision of W.J. (later Sir Walter) Tapper (1861–1935), for the same location.[117] Tapper served as architect and adviser to the dean and chapter from 1908 until the year of his death, and is himself commemorated by a tablet—happily of modest style and dimensions—in St. Stephen's Chapel.[118]

Meanwhile, the more obscure and less famous were not forgotten. In 1907 a retired army officer who had been a member of the cathedral's congregation for fifty years was accorded a rectangular mural tablet with

---

[114] *DNB*, for all and 'Bodley'; *Complete Peerage*, 'Percy of Alnwick'; Addleshaw, *400 Years*. For the possible Thoresby mon. in nave see Morrell, *York Mons.*, pp. 3, 5, Pl. IV(a); Pevsner, *York and E.R.*, p. 108, quoting J. Hutchinson. The alternative identification, Dean Higden or Hygdon (d. 1536) is less likely.

[115] *DNB*; Addleshaw, *400 Years*. See Chs. I and III above for more about St. Cuthbert.

[116] *DNB*; Addleshaw, *400 Years*. I have found Milburn's career, and other references to his works, difficult to trace. For King Edwin, see Chs. I and III above.

[117] Addleshaw, *400 Years*.

[118] M.I.; *Who Was Who, 1929–40* (1941 or 2).

black lettering on white marble with black surrounds and an armorial shield above, top left.[119] With tragic irony, the King's Own Yorkshire Light Infantry commemorated their dead in the Peninsular War of a hundred years before only in 1913, on the eve of a far greater and more terrible holocaust. Tapper supervised the carving which was carried out by the firm of Farmer and Brindley. The officers and N.C.O.s are named and the Other Ranks (610 of them) enumerated. The memorial includes a bust of Lieutenant-General Sir John Moore (1761–1809), colonel of the regiment, and hero of Corunna—the 'Dunkirk' of the Napoleonic Wars, subject of the famous poem, learnt by generations of English schoolchildren: 'Not a drum was heard, not a funeral note . . .'.[120] Tapper was also responsible for commemorating a canon and hymnologist who died in 1913,[121] and a little later there is a rectangular brass to the chapter clerk and chamberlain of the cathedral, 1907–14.[122]

The earliest memorial directly arising from World War One is to Rear-Admiral Sir Christopher Cradock (1862–1914), who went down with his ship at the Battle of Coronel, a disastrous minor British defeat in the South Pacific. It comprises an aesthetically distressing bust with surrounding figures, by Frederick William Pomeroy (1857–1924) whose work—perhaps fortunately—is not otherwise represented.[123]

Meanwhile, one of the more interesting figures of modern York was commemorated by G. W. Milburn in 1917. Dr. Tempest Anderson (1846–1913), the son of a York doctor, was educated at St. Peter's, and then—surprisingly unless he was a non-Anglican—like W. D. Husband before him, at the flourishing new medical school attached to University College, London, where he proceeded M.D. and D.Sc. and of which he later became a fellow (a rare and coveted honour); he returned to York and practised as an oculist, living for the rest of his life in Stonegate (Plate 168). Whatever his medical skill or dedication, Anderson's real contribution lay elsewhere. He was a keen amateur photographer and explorer, naturalist, and geologist; and he was interested in what we should call environmental

[119] West end of south choir aisle: Capt. E. C. Starkey, late 13th Hussars, of Tang Hall (now a suburb of York), d. 1906: M.I.; Addleshaw, Additional Notes.

[120] St. John's Chapel; *DNB*, 'Moore'; Addleshaw, *400 Years*.

[121] Towards west end of north choir aisle: Canon John Julian (1839–1913). Nearly illegible relief lettering on white stone: M.I.; E. A. Gee, citing *York Diocesan Gazette* (1914), p. 42; *Who Was Who, 1897–1915* (1920).

[122] Just west of door on outer wall of north choir aisle: James Ramsay (d. 1915): M.I.

[123] East side of north transept, towards chapter-house entrance. *20th-Century DNB*; Addleshaw, *400 Years*; A. J. Marder, *From the Dreadnought to Scapa Flow*, ii, *The War Years: to the Eve of Jutland* (1965), Ch. VI, pt. i, Maps 3 and 4, Pl. V, i; for Pomeroy, see also M. H. Spielman, *British Sculpture & Sculptors of Today* (1901); The Fine Art Soc., *British Sculpture 1850–1914*.

problems, which were then described as questions of housing and open spaces. He also took an active part in local government, and became sheriff of York. Above all, he was for many years the leading figure in the Yorkshire Philosophical Society: a member from 1875, and Honorary Curator of Comparative Anatomy from 1877, he was president from 1906 until his death. He made constant, arduous journeys in pursuit of his interest in volcanoes and earthquakes, and on the last of these he died in the Red Sea—presumably of heat-stroke. For the restrained tone of the obituary in the Society's proceedings—from what it avoids saying—one senses that he was a controversial president; but he was certainly a vigorous one, and it is fitting that as a major benefactor of the Society he should be commemorated by the Tempest Anderson Hall, a large auditorium, which was added to the museum building. His own religious position is not clear; but as luminary and benefactor of modern York he certainly earns his place in the Minster.[124]

Returning to the Great War of 1914–18, winners of the Victoria Cross were accorded individual memorial tablets.[125] But the others remain in a collective if glorious anonymity, like the 8,814 officers, N.C.O.s, and men of the York and Lancaster Regiment killed or died on active service 1914–19, and the 9,447 of all ranks of the King's Own Yorkshire Light Infantry (Plate 169).[126] In certain war memorials of the 1890s to 1940s there is what one can only describe as an unattractive attempt to spiritualize war and christianize the martial virtues: a kind of religious-cum-aesthetic equivalent of the 'war to end wars' and of 'homes fit for heroes'. Whatever

---

[124] North choir aisle. Addleshaw, *400 Years*; Yorkshire Philosophical Soc., *Annual Reports* for 1913 and 1914; *Who Was Who, 1897–1915*; H. H. Bellot, *University College London 1826–1926* (1929), esp. Chs. V, VIII, IX, is useful for the background but does not mention Anderson (or anyone else except professors) by name. The chapter on 'Societies of York' in Stacpoole *et al., The Noble City*, pp. 883–8, adds nothing, although the author, Miss M. G. Willoughby, presumably had access to the Society's unpublished records. Anderson was unlucky to miss inclusion in the *20th-Century DNB*, especially considering some of the high-flown mediocrities who are in it.

[125] e.g. south choir aisle, towards west end: Major Herbert Augustine Carter (awarded V.C. for heroism in Somaliland before the First World War; d. 1916, in the campaign in German East Africa), of 101st Grenadiers, Indian Army—the hero with angel and cross behind, rect. tablet at foot, by Sir Edgar Bertram Mackenall of Melbourne and London (1863–1931) (for whom see *20th-Century DNB*): M.I.; Addleshaw, *400 Years*. I am grateful to Mr. Barr for help on this. Captain Arthur Forbes Gordon Kilby (d. in Flanders, 1915), tablet and bust by Tapper, carved Farmer & Brindley, in St. Nicholas Chapel (east side of north transept): Addleshaw, *400 Years*; Brigadier Sir John Smythe, *The Story of the Victoria Cross 1856–1963* (1963), pp. 189–90, 203.

[126] South choir aisle, east of vestry door. Bronze rectangular tablet on white marble surround, regimental arms at top: M.I. (apparently otherwise unrecorded). St. John's Chapel, designed by Charles Frank Annesley Voysey (1857–1941), executed by W. Bainbridge Reynolds (1855–1935), mural tablet, stone or metal on marble or imitation: Morrell, *York Mons.*, Pl. LXXXVIII; *DNB*, 'Voysey'; Addleshaw, *400 Years*; M.I.

168 Tempest Anderson, M.D., D.Sc. (1846–1913), oculist, naturalist, and seismologist; President and benefactor of the Yorkshire Philosophical Society. A mural tablet by G. W. Milburn (1844–1941) is in the N. choir aisle.

167 K.O.Y.L.I., South Africa, 1899–1902, all ranks. By G. F. Bodley (1827–1907), 1903; stone with figures in bronze. St. John's Chapel.

169 6th Battalion of the K.O.Y.L.I., 1914–19. By Eleanor Fortescue-Brickdale (1871–1945), stone and bronze, 1921. St. John's Chapel.

their other failings, this particular feature is happily absent from the mid-Victorian military monuments, and seems to have disappeared from some erected since the Second World War. It should surely be possible to honour the nation's dead, to commemorate the fallen from a particular regiment, locality, or institution, and yet avoid confusing Christian saints and angels with the gods of war, officers' swords with the Cross of Jesus.[127]

A wealthy Anglo-Irish peer who died while serving in 1918 but not as a war casualty is commemorated with an individual stone tablet, which fails to explain his connection—if any—with York.[128] More congruous is that to Sir Edward Green of Wakefield, first Baronet (1831–1923), and his wife, Dame Mary, née Lycett (d. 1902), whose memorial tablets were erected by their sons, Sir Edward Lycett-Green, second Baronet (1860–1940), and Lieut.-Col. Francis William Green, F.S.A. (1861–1954); but it is really the third generation of Lycett-Greens who should be honoured in York, for their collection of paintings forms the largest and best part of the City Art Gallery's present holdings.[129]

War memorials apart, almost all the monuments of the last half-century commemorate persons directly connected with the Minster itself. For example, Dean Purey-Cust (1828–1916) has a mural tablet, designed by Tapper and executed by J. Whitehead and Sons of Kennington Oval.[130] R. C. Green (d. 1936), clerk of the works for forty-two years, a rectangular tablet with incised lettering, is nearby to him.[131] There is an interwar military memorial, and then a joint one for the two world wars.[132] Although

---

[127] See e.g. the memorial to the 6th Battn. of the K.O.Y.L.I., erected 1921, in St. John's Chapel by Eleanor Fortescue-Brickdale (1871–1945), whose true talent was for water-colours and stained glass windows, a mural tablet with figure (angel of death) with sword transmogrified into Cross, in stone and bronze: Morrell, *York Mons.*, Pl. LXXXIX; *Who Was Who, 1941–50* (1952); Addleshaw, *400 Years*.

[128] North transept: Victor Henry George Francis, 5th Marquis Conyngham (1883–1918); he was a lieut. in the Wilts. Regt. and then served in the S. Irish Horse; stone tablet, erected 1919, by Walter Henry Brierley (1862–1926): *Complete Peerage*, 'Conyngham'; Burke's *Peerage, Baronetage and Knightage*; Addleshaw, *400 Years*.

[129] On east wall of south transept. Venn, *Al. Cant.* II. iii. 127; *Who Was Who, 1929–40*; Burke's *Peerage, Baronetage and Knightage*, 'Green of Wakefield'; M.I.; J. Ingamells, ch. on 'Painting and Sculpture in York, 1700–1970', in *The Noble City*, pp. 855–74 and refs. there to growth of the City Art Gallery's collections.

[130] West side of south transept, combined with a War Memorial to the Old Boys of the Cathedral Choir School: Foster, *Al. Oxon., 1715–1886*, p. 330; *Who Was Who, 1916–28* (1929); Addleshaw, *400 Years*; see Ch. XII below.

[131] On north wall of St. Stephen's Chapel: Robert Charles Green, clerk of the works 1895–1936, rectangular stone tablet with incised lettering: M.I.

[132] St. George's Chapel: stone mural tablet to the officers of the West Yorks. Regt., who died on active service 1927–40, designed by Tapper, executed by J. Whitehead & Sons: Addleshaw, *400 Years*. St. George's Chapel, also, the Prince of Wales's or W. Yorks Regt., 1914–19 and 1939–45, stone cenotaph

[cont.]

not a piece of sculpture in the normal sense, the most unusual and interesting of the World War Two memorials is the astronomical clock in the north transept. The clock itself was designed by Dr. Robert Atkinson and Mr. C. J. Westcott of Greenwich Observatory, the case and surrounds by Sir A. E. Richardson, the decoration being largely by H. J. Stammers, and the frieze by Maurice Lambert, the only sculptor involved. It commemorates British, Commonwealth, and Allied airmen who died while based on stations in Yorkshire, Durham, and Northumberland, 1939–45.[133] The medical connection is maintained by two well-designed, modest wooden tablets to Arthur Hedley Visick, surgeon (1897–1949), and John Anthony Magnus, eye specialist (1900–66), both on the inner side of the south choir aisle, just east of Archbishop Dolben. Down by the great east window is a plain stone floor slab, by D. G. B. Kindersley, to Cyril Garbett (1875–1955, at York 1942–55), both the only twentieth-century archbishop to be commemorated in the Minster, and perhaps the one who inspired most affection in the clergy of cathedral and diocese.[134]

Here and in some of the lesser recent tablets we can see a welcome return to the artistic virtues of proportion and restraint, from which the great artist is emancipated but which seem to have so largely deserted the more humdrum designers and craftsmen, and those who commissioned and supported their work, between about the 1840s and the 1940s. It may not too rashly be predicted that, unless there is a drastic change of policy by the dean and chapter, or by whoever else may assume responsibility in the future, some memorial tablets will continue to be placed in the Minster in years to come. But the days of monumental sculpture, on any ambitious scale, would seem to be past. Moreover, with a very few exceptions, the monuments and inscriptions are more noteworthy for their contribution to social history than for their strictly artistic quality.

I am grateful to Mr. C. B. L. Barr for his constant and generous help in the preparation of this chapter; my thanks are also due to the staffs of the Borthwick Institute, the York City Library, and the Minster Library, and of the other libraries where I have worked, in London, Oxford, Princeton, and York.

---

with case holding two books of names (the alabaster figure of St. George and the Dragon is seventeenth-century English work, moved from elsewhere) designed Sir Albert E. Richardson (1880–1964), executed by the Minster stoneyard staff: Addleshaw, *400 Years; Who Was Who, 1961–70* (1972). Field-Marshal Sir Cyril John Deverell (1874–1947), colonel of the same Regt., erected 1949, designed and executed Denis Tegetmeier & Lawrence Cribb, plain mural tablet with inscription: *20th-Century DNB*; E. A. Gee, Notes; M.I.

[133] Addleshaw, *400 Years.*

[134] Lady Chapel: *DNB, 1951–60*; Friends of York Minster, *Ann. Rept. 1957*; Addleshaw, *400 Years.* Note also Herbert Nowell Bate (1871–1941), dean of York 1932–41, on north wall of St. Stephen's Chapel, plain rect. tablet with incised lettering: *Who Was Who, 1941–50*; see Ch. XII below; M.I.

CHAPTER XI

The Minster Library

C. B. L. Barr

The history of books at York Minster, though long, is not continuous: much in the early stages constitutes not so much a history as a chain of disconnected episodes, forerunners rather than origins of the present Minster library. Over the centuries individual volumes and collections of books at the Minster have served different functions, the differences reflecting in part the general history of libraries, the church, and culture, in part the particular circumstances of the Minster.

The missionaries Paulinus and James the Deacon must surely have carried bibles, and either they or shortly afterwards Wilfrid and Eddius, who taught Gregorian chant,[1] probably brought Gregory's 'antiphonary and missal', first attested by Egbert c. 750.[2] Wilfrid's benefactions to the Minster included a two-volume copy of the gospels in richly decorated covers, perhaps, like his similar gift to Ripon, 'written in letters of gold on purple parchment and illuminated'.[3] A service book which survives, albeit in a later (tenth- or eleventh-century) copy, is Egbert's pontifical, the earliest known from England.[4]

With Egbert there is evidence of the first true library at the Minster, attached to the cathedral school. The statutory teaching conducted in espiscopal households had been carried out at York and extended to lay pupils as well as clergy already by Wilfrid and his successors.[5] From the 730s Egbert and his successor Albert, stimulated perhaps partly by this

---

[1] Bede, *HE* ii. 20 and iv. 2; Eddi (Eddius Stephanus), *Vita Wilfridi*, Chs. 14 and 47.
[2] A. W. Haddan and W. Stubbs, *Councils and ecclesiastical documents*, iii (1871), 412; W. Apel, *Gregorian chant* (1958), p. 48.
[3] *Fabric Rolls*, p. 223; Eddi, *Vita Wilfridi*, Ch. 17; Bede, *HE* v.19.
[4] Paris, Bibliothèque nationale, MS. lat. 10575; ed. W. Greenwell (Surtees Soc. xxvii, 1853). See *Dictionnaire d'archéologie chrétienne et de liturgie*, iv. 2 (1921), 2211–20; V. Leroquais, *Les pontificaux* (1937), ii. 160–4 and 255–6.
[5] Eddi, *Vita Wilfridi*, Ch. 21; Bede, *HE* v. 20; Dixon and Raine, *Fasti Ebor.*, pp. 85–7, 92–3.

tradition of York episcopal teaching, partly by advice from Bede,[6] partly by the elevation of their see to an archbishopric (735), systematically extended casual household instruction to form a regular school. The subjects taught there, as described in verse by Alcuin,[7] approximate to the standard elements of the *quadrivium* and the *trivium*, the seven liberal arts which constituted the regular medieval school syllabus, with the addition of two of the three higher faculties, law and Scriptural divinity, which at a later period were the marks of a university. The international reputation of the York school rested not only on its teaching but largely on the size and quality of the supporting library. Credit for building this up, a process which must have taken many years, is due partly to Egbert but principally to Albert. An error by William of Malmesbury ascribed the creation of the library to Egbert, and this was constantly repeated until Alcuin's works were printed and Albert given his due.[8] Albert travelled several times through Frankland and Italy in search of books to bring home or to copy for the York library.[9] In the 740s and afterwards Egbert and Albert in turn sent books to Boniface at Fulda and Lul at Mainz, and *c.* 773 Liudgar returned to Frisia from his studies at York 'bene instructus, habens secum copiam librorum'.[10] In 778, when Albert retired from the see, he designated Alcuin as his heir to the 'treasury of books . . . which were an aid to study and to wisdom'.[11]

Alcuin's catalogue of the contents of the library, though in verse and composed after his departure from York, may be taken as generally accurate.[12] He says it is incomplete, but it names forty authors; no titles are given, but collected works are no doubt intended in most cases. The names may be grouped according to the subjects of the school curriculum. The Church Fathers are represented by Jerome, Hilary, Ambrose, Augustine, Athanasius, Orosius, Gregory, Leo, Basil, Fulgentius, Cassiodorus,

---

[6] Bede, 'Epistola ad Ecgbertum', in *Opera historica*, ed. C. Plummer (1896), i. 405–6.

[7] Alcuin, 'Carmen de pontificibus et sanctis ecclesiae Eboracensis', ll. 1430–48, in *Hists. York* i.349–98, and E. Dümmler (ed.), *Poetae Latini aevi Carolini*, i (*Monumenta Germaniae Historica, Poetae Latini medii aevi*, 1, 1881), pp. 169–206.

[8] Malmesbury, *Gesta regum* (Rolls Ser. 90), i (1887), p. 68, and *Gesta pontificum* (Rolls Ser. 52, 1870), p. 246; Higden, *Polychronicon* (Rolls Ser. 41), vi (1876), pp. 238–41; J. Leland, *Commentarii de scriptoribus Britannicis* (1709), p. 121, repeated by Drake, *Ebor.*, p. 483; W. Camden, *Britannia* (1590), p. 571. Corrected (e.g.) by T. Gale (1699) in Drake, *Ebor.*, p. 528, and F. Froben (ed.), *Alcuini Opera* (1777), i. 66.

[9] Alcuin, 'Carmen' 1453–8; id., 'Epitaphium Aelberhti', in Dümmler, op. cit., p. 206.

[10] Boniface in E. Dümmler (ed.), *Epistolae Merowingici et Karolini aevi*, i (*M.G.H. Epist*, 3, 1892), pp. 346–7 (= *EHD* i. 757–8) and 376–7; Lul in Dümmler, *Epistolae*, pp. 412–4 (= *EHD* i. 768); Altfrid, 'Vita Liudgeri', in *M.G.H. Scriptores*, ii (1829), pp. 407–8.

[11] Alcuin, 'Carmen' 1525–34, and letter in Haddan and Stubbs, iii (1871), 501–4.

[12] Alcuin, 'Carmen' 1535–61.

Chrysostom, Aldhelm, Bede, Victorinus (which?), and Boethius; history, apparently including natural history, by Pompeius Trogus, Pliny, and Aristotle; rhetoric by Cicero; poetry by Sedulius, Juvencus, Alcimus Avitus, Clemens, Prosper, Paulinus, Arator, Fortunatus, Lactantius; classical poetry by Virgil, Statius, and Lucan; grammar by Valerius Probus, Phocas, Donatus, Priscian, Servius, Eutyches, Pompeius, and Charisius Comminianus. The books are said to represent the writers of Rome, Greece, the Hebrews, and Africa, all probably in Latin. The list corresponds well with texts otherwise known to be current in Britain at the time.[13] Something of the quality as well as the extent of the York library may be gauged from the way in which Alcuin, though at Aachen and later at Tours he had the support of all the resources of Charlemagne and his empire, never felt that he had succeeded in assembling another library equal to the one which he had left at York.[14] Fifty years after Alcuin's death, *c.* 852, the noted scholar Lupus Servatus, abbot of Ferrières, asked to borrow from York for copying a group of four texts, two of which he subsequently requested from Rome.[15] The importance of Lupus's enquiry is that he thought it worth writing to York first when he could have applied at once to Rome; and this attests the continued existence and reputation of the York library on the eve of the Danish invasion. This is the last that we hear of it as a living collection: in 866–7 the fate which Alcuin lamented when it befell the monastery of Lindisfarne in 793 struck his own former cathedral, where the school and library must have shared the fate of the city and Minster ravaged and burnt by the Danes.[16] In the next two centuries almost the only tangible evidence, not of a library but of a single book, is the surviving volume of the 'York Gospels' (Plate 1 above). Its contents show it to have been written and illuminated at Canterbury in the opening years of the eleventh century, and brought to York *c.* 1020 by Wulfstan. A series of oaths written on the flyleaves shows it to have been in use at the Minster as an oath-book at least from the thirteenth century to the sixteenth, and identify it in an early sixteenth-century inventory of about ten precious gospel-books then in the Minster treasury. Alone of these volumes, all probably dating from before the Norman Conquest or not long after, this survived the despoliation of the treasury *c.*1547, albeit bereft of its silver cover 'not well gilded', because of its administrative function; it was noted at the Minster

[13] J. D. A. Ogilvy, *Books known to the English, 597–1066* (1967), *passim*.

[14] Alcuin in *EHD* i. 786.

[15] Lupus, *Correspondance*, ed. L. Levillain (1935), ii. 74–81 (=Haddan and Stubbs, iii. 634–6, *EHD* i. 807–9) and 120–5.

[16] Simeon of Durham, *Historia Dunelmensis ecclesiae* (Rolls Ser. 75), i (1882), pp. 50–1 and 54–5; Alcuin, letters 16–21, esp. 16, in E. Dümmler (ed.), *Epistolae Karolini aevi*, ii (*M.G.H. Epist.* 4, 1895).

in 1625 and, after its removal under the Commonwealth, was restored to its home in 1668. From then until modern times it was kept neither with the library nor among the muniments, but, again because of its regular use as oath-book, in the chapter clerk's office, thus escaping scholarly attention until the nineteenth century and becoming part of the library only in the twentieth.[17] It is fortunate that this volume at least, unlike any remains of Egbert's library which may have escaped the sacking of the Danes, survived the similar destruction of 1069, when 'the Minster of St. Peter was destroyed by fire'. 'In the library of St. Peter's, which . . . Alcuin extolled with marvellous praise for its great wealth of books . . . now there is nothing . . . for these treasures . . . were destroyed by the savagery of the Danes and the violence of William the Bastard.'[18] The effect of these violent destructions should not, however, be exaggerated. They only effected at a stroke what would otherwise have been effected gradually by a lack of leadership in school and library evidenced by the nature of the exhortations and instructions which Alcuin after his departure from York found it necessary to send to Eanbald and others. The *raison d'être* of the York library was as an educational tool, and its demise is a natural consequence of the fact that 'the call of Alcuin from York to the Palace School marks the transference of the primacy of letters from Britain to France'.[19] That the physical destruction of the library was in turn completed by an invader from France is one of the ironies of history. If it is correctly argued that Charlemagne's *Admonitio generalis* and capitulary *De litteris colendis* were largely the work of Alcuin and laid the foundation of the Carolingian renaissance and through it of the schools and universities of medieval Europe with their scriptoria and libraries, then the ultimate effect of the school of York and the first Minster library through Alcuin's removal to the Continent was immeasurably greater than if it had somehow survived his departure and the destruction of the Danes and the Normans.[20]

[17] YML, MS. Add. 1. J. P. Gilson's pamphlet *Description* of 1925 now needs correction and supplementation, e.g. N. R. Ker, *Catalogue of manuscripts containing Anglo-Saxon* (1957), pp. 468–9; H. R. Lyon (ed.), *A Wulfstan manuscript* (Early English manuscripts in facsimile 17, 1971), pp. 31–2 and App.; T. A. M. Bishop, *English caroline miniscule* (1971), p. 22; J. J. G. Alexander and C. M. Kauffmann, *English illuminated manuscripts, 700–1500: catalogue* [of an exhibition] (Brussels, 1973), pp. 28–9. For 1625 see Bodl., MS. Dodsworth 125, fo. 172, and *YAJ* xxxii (1936), 21; for 1668 see Chapter Acts, 1634–1700, part ii, fo. 128ʳ, and *Fabric Rolls*, p. 357. First mentioned in D. Rock, *The church of our fathers* (1849), i. 297 and ii. 357–8, and *Fabric Rolls*, pp. 84, 223, 357.
[18] Florence of Worcester, *Chronicon*, ii (1849), p. 4; J. Leland, *Collectanea*, iii (1774), pp. 36–7.
[19] H. Rashdall, *The universities of Europe in the middle ages* (new edn. 1936), i. 272.
[20] A. Boretius (ed.), *Capitularia regum Francorum*, i (*M.G.H. Leges* 2.i, 1883), pp. 78–9; Rashdall, op. cit. i. 29; E. S. Duckett, *Alcuin, friend of Charlemagne* (1951), pp. 124–6; J. Boussard in *La scuola nell' occidente latino dell' alto medioevo* (Settimane di studio del Centro italiano di studi sull' alto medioevo, 19, 1972), pp. 418–21.

Thomas of Bayeux, the first Norman archbishop of York, provided his new Minster with 'clergy, books, and ornaments'. These books were service books for the new style of liturgy which he introduced, not the beginnings of a fresh library, as was supposed by the twelfth-century chronicler of the archbishops and others, who had to blame the great fire of 1137 to account for the absence of information about such a library.[21] With the Minster, despite Thomas's rebuilding of the pre-Conquest refectory and dormitory, developing into not a monastic but a secular cathedral, there was no regular need, and no provision in its thirteenth-century statutes, for a communal library. The *magister scholarum*, afterwards styled chancellor, had the duty of giving theological lectures in the Minster precinct, but nothing is known of his performance of this obligation at this period, let alone of any connected collection of books.[22] In the twelfth century, however, there developed at many cathedrals 'great activity in procuring manuscripts', and it is unfortunate that nothing has been found to confirm the attractive conjecture that the group of volumes of this period among the Minster manuscripts may represent the known scholarly nature of Archbishop Roger.[23] The absence of a communal library at the Minster is in accord with the wills of the Minster clergy, who from the thirteenth century to the fifteenth regularly bequeathed their books either to friends or to their universities or colleges. A statute made in 1294 and repeated in 1369 ordered inventories to be made of chapter movables, including books; doubtless this refers primarily to service books and perhaps to muniments, but no surviving inventory of either is earlier than the sixteenth century.[24] The earliest of the few remaining medieval service books from the Minster is a pair, apparently the second and third parts of a twelfth-century five-volume bible (Plate 170). From the fifteenth century comes a large volume containing two collections of saints' lives, Capgrave's alphabetical set complete, and four months of the scarce chronologically arranged legendary of Pietro Calo.[25] Visitations show constant deficiencies in the service books from the fourteenth to the sixteenth centuries.[26] Something of a one-volume ready-reference library was presented *c.* 1270 by Canon John Le Cras; this was a copy of Hugutio's 'Summa super derivationem compositionem

[21] Hugh, *York*, pp. 10–11; W. H. Frere, 'York service books', in *Y.M. Hist. Tr.*, and in *A collection of his* [Frere's] *papers* (Alcuin Club Collections 35, 1940), p. 160; the chronicle in *Hists. York* ii. 108; Drake, *Ebor.*, p. 483 (more correctly, p. 61).

[22] Hugh, *York*, pp. 10–11; *York Statutes*, p. 6.

[23] K. Edwards, *The English Secular Cathedrals* (2nd edn. 1967), p. 210; I owe the suggestion to Dr. Margaret Buxton.

[24] *York Statutes*, pp. 33 and 35; the inventories are mostly in M2 (2).

[25] YML, MSS. XVI.Q.3–4 and XVI.G.23.

[26] *Fabric Rolls*, pp. 243–5, 252, 267.

170 Two inscriptions showing that the books in which they were written were at the Minster in the middle ages, the latter specifically in the Library as part of the Newton bequest in 1414: A, in volume three of a multi-volume Bible, was written in the twelfth century, and reads *Hic est Liber s(an)c(t)i Pet(r)i de Eborac(o)* ('This book belongs to St Peter's, York'); B, evidently written in or shortly after 1414, reads *Liber eccl(es)ie metropolitice b(eat)i Petri Ebor, Ex dono mag(ist)ri Joh(ann)is de Neuton Thesaur(arii) eiusde(m)* ('This book belongs to the metropolitical church of St Peter, York, by the gift of Master John de Neuton, treasurer of the same') (Y.M.L., MS XVI.Q.3, and Trinity College, (Cambridge, MS R.5.40, partly erased).

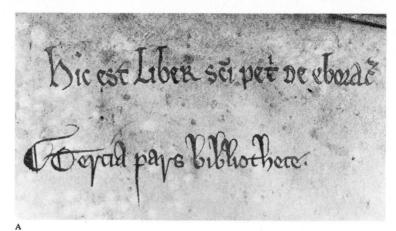

A

B

A

B

171 Two views of the building erected *c.* 1420 to hold the Minster Library on the upper floor and continuing in use as the Library until 1810: B, from the south-west, is a detail from an engraving by F. Vivares, 1750, after a drawing by Joseph Baker; A, from the south-east, is by David Whiteley, 1976.

significationem et interpretationem vocabulorum', specially written for the Minster and ordered to be chained in the choir.[27] A century later there was nothing at the Minster to cause it to be included with the eleven Yorkshire libraries used in Henry of Kirkstead's national 'Catalogus scriptorum ecclesiae'.[28] Archbishop Melton's books bequeathed to the Minster by his executor as late as 1378–9 were apparently to be sold for the benefit of the fabric fund. The bequests by Subdean John de Waltham in 1384 of 'librum qui dicitur Catholicon ad remanendum imperpetuo in ecclesia Ebor', and by Canon Thomas Walworth in 1409 of 'unam Bibliam in duobus voluminibus et Archidiaconum in Rosario, in librario ejusdem ecclesiæ pro perpetuo permansuros', are exceptional.[29] The latter is the first apparent mention of a library at the post-Norman Minster; nothing more than a book-chest can be meant. If one did not already exist to receive these bequests it was perhaps provided in consequence of a chapter decree of 1411 'ut ordinaretur unum commune librarium et securum pro libris ecclesie in eo fideliter conservandis', though in its context of a visitation record abounding with an exceptional number of complaints this chest or perhaps cupboard was more probably intended for the choir books or muniments.[30]

A Minster library proper, however, did come into existence shortly afterwards. In general at the universities and the secular cathedrals the opening of the fifteenth century was 'the age of library building',[31] and at York in particular the continuous building and rebuilding, which had occupied all the Minster's finances and the energy of its treasurers since 1070, was at last drawing to a close, and it was in fact a treasurer who took the first action towards founding a library. In 1414 John Newton, besides a handful of books for Peterhouse and various friends and parish churches, bequeathed to the Minster 'in subsidium et relevamen librariae faciendae' his collection of thirty-five manuscripts bound in at least forty volumes. The titles comprise biblical texts and commentaries, the fathers, three legal texts, a volume of historians, one of Petrarch, another containing Walter Hilton and Richard Rolle, and a book called *Speculum moralium*, with other treatises described as written by Alcuin, 'once a canon of the church of York', and other texts, 'for reading in chapter'. A codicil adds a further

---

[27] YML, MS. XVI.Q.13; T. Kelly, *Early public libraries* (1966), p. 25; A. B. Emden, *Biographical Register of the University of Oxford* (3 vols., 1957–9), ii. 1127.

[28] R. H. Rouse in *Speculum*, xli (1966), pp. 471–99; T. Tanner, *Bibliotheca Britannico-Hibernica* (1748), p. xxiv, nos. 139–46 and 159–61.

[29] *Testamenta Eboracensia*, i (Surtees Soc. iv, 1836), pp. 105 and 353; Emden, op. cit. iii. 1974 and 1977–8.

[30] YML, L 2 (3)a, Visitation Book, 1409–17, etc., fo. 37ᵛ; misdated and misinterpreted by Drake, *Ebor.*, App., p. lxxvi.

[31] E. A. Savage, *Old English Libraries* (1911), pp. 112 and 186.

thirty-five books of canon and civil law which in default of certain conditions being fulfilled by Newton's family were 'to be delivered to the chapter of York to remain in their library in perpetuity, for the salvation of my soul and of all the faithful departed'. If these last words are reminiscent of the foundation of a chantry, then Newton was certainly more successful in establishing a monument to his memory than a chantry would have been.[32] A few of his books can be identified. Still in the library are two legal texts, a Bartolus de Saxoferrato dated 1401 and a Cynus Pistoriensis; a handsome twelfth-century volume of homilies may be Newton's 'librum pulcrum de diversis sermonibus'.[33] His composite historical manuscript of Bede, Alfred of Beverley, and William of Malmesbury survives as three separate volumes at Oxford, and a solitary flyleaf from an Augustine with inscriptions recording Newton's and the Minster's ownership remains in the binding of another manuscript now at Cambridge.[34]

The supplementary books listed in Newton's codicil were 'to be deposited in a chest within the vestry of the cathedral . . . of which chest, for greater security, the subtreasurer is to have one key, the keeper of the vestry a second, and my brother Thomas a third'. But the principal significance of the bequest as a whole is less that, by thus avoiding mention of any library or librarian, it confirms the non-existence of an earlier library at the Minster, than the effect of this sudden accession of forty or more volumes where perhaps none had been before. The vestry and adjoining annexes on the south side of the choir, all built or rebuilt towards the end of the fourteenth century, could not conveniently accommodate the two or more large chests necessary to contain so many books, let alone facilities for reading them, and only four years after Newton's bequest we find a new building to house the library with the choristers' school below being erected on the west side of the south transept (Plate 171), where the school had previously been held, with the active support of Newton's friend and executor Thomas Haxey, himself this year appointed treasurer. He gave the lead which is recorded as being used to cover the roof in 1418–19, the walls being already in position, and the internal timberwork was fitted in the following year. The oblong room, measuring 44 ft. by 24 ft., is now internally subdivided, but, typically of libraries of its period, was built on the south side of the much taller Minster and on the upper floor, both to catch as much light as possible and to protect the books from flood and

[32] *Test. Ebor.* i. 364–71; A. B. Emden, *Biographical Register of the University of Cambridge* (1963), pp. 421–2.

[33] YML, MSS. XVI.P.5–7, XVI.P.8, XVI.P.12.

[34] Bodl., MSS. Rawlinson B.199, B.200, and C.162; Trinity College, Cambridge, MS. 728; N. R. Ker, *Medieval libraries of Great Britain* (2nd edn. 1964), p. 216; Emden, *Register of Cambridge*, pp. 421–2.

rising damp. The library was 'enlightened by nine windows, viz. one at the west end and four on each side', which until a date between 1690 and 1736 contained a series of heraldic shields including the arms of Haxey. The east end abutted the south transept, and access was by a spiral staircase in the north-east corner. In this room in 1421–2 forty volumes were chained, probably to a series of long lecterns projecting from both long walls between the windows and forming a central corridor, and their covers were fitted with title labels of vellum covered with a protective layer of horn.[35]

While a few Minster clergy continued to leave books either to their former universities or to be sold for the fabric fund, this now became the exception. The normal practice, begun already in 1418 by Archdeacon Stephen Scrope, whose arms duly appeared in the library windows, and continued throughout the fifteenth century, was to leave at least some of their books to the Minster library, sometimes after a friend who was to enjoy them during his lifetime. Two benefactors were careful to specify that the library should receive such of their books as it did not already possess, but a small number of books which were standard texts in theology and law were bequeathed to the library several times over. There is nothing to show whether the Minster library followed the regular practice of academic libraries in such cases of chaining the best copy for security and reference and keeping the others unchained, perhaps in a chest, and available for loan. By 1456 twenty-two additional books required to be chained. Once at least, in 1470, the library was used for transaction of Minster legal business.[36] In 1536 a Minster inventory records ten antiphonars and twelve graduals 'in libris in choro et librario', the latter unmistakably meaning a chest or cupboard, quite distinct from the 'Librarie' which the same document describes as containing 'bookes of law and dyvynite and stories [i.e. history] and other faculties ix^{xx} xiij', i.e. 193 books, a fivefold increase in the 122 years since Newton's foundation bequest.[37] It is fortunate that we have this confirmation of the library's size at this date, otherwise a statement made two years earlier would have been open to mis-apprehension. In 1534 John Leland came to York in pursuance of the king's commission 'to peruse the libraries of all cathedrals, abbies, priories, colleges, &c.' At the Minster he lamented the departed splendour of Alcuin's library and recorded only two books. Both are uncommon texts—neither has ever been printed—and with the evidence of the inventory we can be confident that Leland was only concerned with rarities that might be worth

[35] *Fabric Rolls*, pp. 36–40 and 45–6; Torre, 'Minster', p. 131.

[36] Scrope: *Test. Ebor.*, i. 385–9; duplicates: ibid. iii (Surtees Soc. xlv, 1865), pp. 89–90 and 91–2; 1456: *Fabric Rolls*, p. 67; 1470: Harrison, *Medieval College*, pp. 104–5.

[37] Purvis in *YAJ* xxxv (1943), 390–2.

adding to the royal library and consequently ignored the bulk of everyday books in the Minster collection. But the two volumes which he thought worth mentioning at the Minster were little compared with twenty-one at St. Mary's Abbey, seven at Durham, and twenty at St. Paul's.[38]

Leland's report and the inventory in 1534–6 mark the end of a long period of relatively stable development and the beginning of changes contemporaneous with the Reformation. Only a few books in the collection survived the next quarter-century. There is no indication that the Minster library suffered from the sudden wholesale dispersal which overtook monastic libraries, or from the destruction which was perpetrated in many academic libraries. Manuscript texts were in any case being replaced by printed books, and, with the Reformation coinciding with what would otherwise have been a gradual process of modernization, what actually took place was more complex than a simple process of replacement. Several factors influenced the events. Manuscripts, which were now becoming old, out-of-date, and hard to read, were replaced by printed books, which were clean, new, more accurate, up-to-date, and easier to read, and had now come to be regarded as respectable for institutional libraries. The limited evidence of wills suggests a falling-off of bequests in this period, and in any case these would have brought old books rather than new. There is no evidence of gifts or bequests of money, let alone grants from chapter funds, to buy new books for the library. Accessions were presumably limited and haphazard, and it is unlikely that enough new books came to York in the middle of the sixteenth century for there to have been any need to discard old books to make room for them, as happened at some Oxford colleges. After the Reformation bibles and the Church Fathers continued in demand; pre-Reformation 'roman' commentaries, theological treatises, and liturgies were replaced by their reformed equivalents, and the fundamental texts of law, ecclesiastical and common, but less so of civil law, would be retained for occasional reference but not automatically replaced for constant continued use. This probably worked smoothly enough over the period 1535–53, but was upset by the double reversal of the Marian Counter-Reformation and the return to Protestantism under Elizabeth: a library with slender resources for acquisition may withstand one such change, but three in a quarter of a century can hardly have left a coherent collection at the end.[39] There were also physical criteria for what was and what was not

[38] Leland, *Collectanea*, iii, pp. 36–7 (York Minster), 14 and 37 (St. Mary's), 41 (Durham), 47–8 (St. Paul's)
[39] See in general C. E. Wright, 'The dispersal of the libraries in the sixteenth century', in F. Wormald and Wright (eds.), *The English library before 1700* (1958), pp. 148–75, and N. R. Ker, 'Oxford college libraries in the sixteenth century', in the *Bodleian Library Record*, vi. 3 (1959), pp. 459–515, esp. 473–97.

kept. An obsolete book was more likely to be removed by an acquisitive individual if it was portable than if it was a large heavy tome; and, while parchment had a second-hand value for bookbinders and goldbeaters, an unwanted paper book was worthless rubbish. Thus it is more than pure accident that the few volumes from the medieval library which remained at the Minster over this period are predominantly large paper volumes of legal texts, the books which have been removed via private possessors to other libraries are smaller volumes of historical and patristic literature, and a common patristic text of Augustine which would soon be replaced survives as bookbinder's material.

The year 1547 illustrates both the negative and the positive sides of these changes. It is marked by the despoliation of the Minster treasury and of all but one of the sumptuous Saxon and Norman gospel-books, and the disappearance of the great mass of Minster charters, assiduously calendared by the chapter clerk, Thomas Water, in the 1520s and 1530s and reported to the royal visitors in 1536, and never heard of again. All this, however, relates to books which were 'treasures' and muniments, and for the library proper a more positive development occurred. As part of the general ecclesiastical visitation made in the first year of Edward VI's reign a set of twenty-two royal injunctions was issued to all the cathedrals and specifically to York. The eighth ran thus: 'Item they [the dean and chapter] shall maike a librarie in some convenient place within theire churche within the space of one yeare . . . and shall leye in the same Saynte Augustyne's, Basill, Gregorie, Nazanzene, Hierome, Ambrose, Chrisostome, Cipriane, Theophilact, Erasmus, and other good writers' workes.'[40] Most of these, as standard Church Fathers, will already have been in the York library. Whether a copy of Theophylact's *Enarrationes* on the Gospels and Epistles, Basle 1540–1, with the note 'Liber ecclesiae Eborum pertinens Cancellario eiusdem' was purchased in accordance with the injunction is uncertain in view of the mention of the chancellor. Erasmus's paraphrase on the New Testament, bought in 1551–2, was not for the library but for the Minster itself, in compliance with other injunctions of 1547.[41]

These royal injunctions of 1547 were followed by two archiepiscopal ones in thirty-five years. In 1552 Archbishop Holgate ordered that three keys to the library door be kept by three vicars choral, who were to accompany anyone other than a dignitary or canon while they were in the library and allow no harm to be done to the books; 'Musculus'

---

[40] *York Statutes*, pp. 58–62 at p. 59; W. H. Frere and W. M. Kennedy (eds.), *Visitations and injunctions*, ii (Alcuin Club Collections 15, 1910), p. 136.

[41] Theophylact: YML, XXI.E.12 (1–2); Erasmus: *Fabric Rolls*, p. 136 (rev. date, E 1/82); injunctions: Frere and Kennedy, op. cit. ii. 117–18 with note.

Commentaries upon Mathue, and John Brentius upon Luke, Calvyne and Bullinger upon the Epistles, Erasmus' Annotacions on the Newe Testament' were to be provided before next Whitsuntide. In 1572 Archbishop Grindal directed that no book or document 'be tayken out of the tresorye, revestrye, or librarie, except he that tayketh the same write his name in a booke to be provided for the same purpose, testifyeing the contentes of the same wrytinge, and byndinge himself to restore the same againe'.[42]

The first concern of both archbishops was for security; doubtless they were attempting to put an end to the laxity which had allowed the disappearance of the greater part of the medieval manuscript library. As with Newton's chest and most medieval valuables there were to be three keys and three key-holders, but it is not clear whether in this case the keys were to open three locks or one. The library is envisaged as being used both for reading, by canons and others, and for loan. As regards the contents, the 'ancient Doctors of the churche' specified by King Edward were probably in the library, but more Protestant commentaries on the New Testament were required. All are represented in the library today by sixteenth-century editions, mostly rather later and probably replacements for any volumes purchased in consequence of Holgate's injunctions.

In the years following Grindal's visitation several minor works undertaken in the library testify to its upkeep and regular use. The roof was repaired _c._ 1574, some books were bound in 1576, and six volumes chained _c._ 1579. At some date between the surviving fabric rolls of 1587 and 1607 the library began to be regularly cleaned at a fee of ten shillings a year. Apart from a copy of bishop Jewel's _Apologie_ or _Defence of the Apologie c._ 1569, all recorded expenditure on books at this period is for communion books, Geneva psalters, and bibles for the Minster services.[43]

Subdean Edmund Bunny, chaplain to Archbishop Grindal and a fluent Calvinist writer and evangelical preacher, is recorded on his monument, in his will, and in the 'liber donorum', as a benefactor to the library on his death in 1618. No list of his bequest survives, but three printed books and one manuscript can be identified as his.[44] In 1624 eight dozen chains were bought for the library, but it is not clear whether these were for Bunny's books, for miscellaneous acquisitions over a period, or to replace old chains which were broken.[45]

---

[42] _York Statutes_, pp. 75–6 and 86.

[43] _Fabric Rolls_, pp. 113–19; the entries for _c._ 1574 and _c._ 1579 (pp. 116–7) have been redated; that for 1576 is from E 2 (21), fo. 17[r].

[44] _DNB_; Drake, _Ebor._, p. 509; _The Friends of York Minster Annual Report_, 23 (1951), p. 12 and Pl. III; YML, _Catalogue_ (1896), pp. vi, 205, 227, 366; _Fabric Rolls_, pp. 314–16; YML, M 2 (2)e and L 2 (2)b.

[45] _Fabric Rolls_, p. 119, requiring correction from E 3/63/1.

Four years later chains old and new and the little library of one or two hundred volumes suddenly became a thing of the past. In 1628 the library received a benefaction that at a stroke changed a commonplace small medieval-style collection into an important large and up-to-date one which immediately became—as it again is today—the largest and most active cathedral library in England. 'Dux femina facti', exclaimed the writer of a tablet recording the Minster's gratitude, appropriating words of Virgil's. The benefactress of York was Frances Matthew, a very different woman from the Queen of Carthage, but a remarkable person none the less.

She was a woman of exemplary wisdom, gravity, piety, bounty, and indeed in other vertues not onely above her sex, but the times . . . One excellent act of hers, first derived upon this church, and through it flowing upon the country, deserveth to live as long as the church itself. The library of the deceased archbishop, consisting of above three thousand books, she gave entirely to the publick use of this church.[46]

Her husband, Tobie Matthew (Plate 172), archbishop 1606–28, had been a lifelong book collector, and his books, valued after his death at £600, constituted the largest private library in England at the time. Two of his books originate from his native Bristol; another he acquired in his first year at Oxford, 1559–60.[47] He remained there for twenty-four years, as undergraduate, fellow, head in turn of two houses, public orator, and vice-chancellor, 'respected for his great Learning, Eloquence, Authority, countenance given by the Queene, and the great Ones'.[48] He was a benefactor to the libraries of his colleges of Christ Church and St. John's, and afterwards to the new Bodleian Library.[49] His own library was as wide in its contents as his interests and his circle of friends. Biblical and liturgical texts, the Church Fathers, the ancient classics, history secular as well as ecclesiastical, religious controversies, philosophy and theology, dictionaries and grammars are all to be expected and all well represented. So are canon and civil law, geography and atlases, alchemy and medicine, mathematics and the natural sciences. In all subjects the breadth and quantity of his reading are attested by the marks which he made as he read. The only notable gap in his collection is English literature, but that would have been regarded as ladies' reading to be kept by Frances and not

---

[46] *Liber donorum*, fo. 1ʳ; Virgil, *Aeneid*, i. 364; Drake, *Ebor.*, p. 512.

[47] YML, Inc. X.G.17, Inc. I.E.19. XIII.M.1.

[48] Sir John Harrington, *Nugae antiquae* (new edn. 1792), i. 228.

[49] N. R. Ker in *Bodl. Library Rec.*, p. 499; W. H. Stevenson and H. E. Salter, *The early history of St. John's College* (Oxford Hist. Soc. N.S. 1, 1939), pp. 198–9; W. D. Macray, *Annals of the Bodleian Library* (2nd edn. 1890), p. 420; G. W. Wheeler (ed.), *Letters of Sir Thomas Bodley to Thomas James* (1926), pp. 23, 25.

admitted to a cathedral library. At Oxford he acquired not only the books which he bought for study and teaching, but gifts and dedications from friends and colleagues in university and church and at court, clergy and lay, men of law and of medicine, poet, lexicographer, and librarian, English, French, and Italian. In 1583 he left Oxford for the north, there to spend the rest of his career, at Durham as dean from that year and bishop from 1595, and finally at York as archbishop from 1606 and a member of the Council of the North from 1609. In the north, remote from the book trade and the bookish friends of Oxford, he received the six-monthly Frankfurt book fair catalogues; twenty-seven issues dated 1596–1623 remain.[50] In 1594 he asked William Camden to procure a book for him.[51] At Durham, apparently from individuals and from neglected corners of the cathedral, he acquired many volumes from the former monastic library. At York he appears to have acted as censor for the Council of the North, himself keeping copies of books which he banned as religiously or politically undesirable, and on at least one occasion apparently keeping a book confiscated from an executed recusant.[52]

There is no contemporary list of the 'above three thousand books' from Matthew's library given in 1628, but many of them can be identified. The catalogue of the library compiled a decade or so later contains some 3,069 entries, most of which must have been his. A few have his arms as archbishop stamped on the cover, one binding bears his initials T.D. as bishop of Durham.[53] Many contain his signature in the various forms 'Tobie Matthew', 'Tobias Dunelm̃', 'Tobias Eboraceñ', sometimes added long after he received a book; not a few have his motto, 'Vita Christus mors lucrum'. In others it is possible to recognize, with varying degrees of probability, his style of underlining, marginal marks, and particularly his handwriting in annotations, features already remarked on in his lifetime by his former chaplain, Canon John Favour, in a dedicatory preface of 1619. He addresses his patron as one 'who hath not onely read all the Ancient Fathers with a diligent eye, but hath also noted them with a judicious pen', and mentions 'those Multitudes of authors, sacred, profane, old, new, friends, and foes, with whose works your Graces great and good Library is plentifully furnished'.[54] Only a few volumes, all duplicates, are known to

---

[50] YML, XV.L.76–8; Agnes Cuming, 'Frankfurt book-fair catalogues', in *The book collector*, viii 1 (spring 1959), p. 71; H. G. Pollard and A. Ehrman, *The distribution of books by catalogue* (1965), pp. 70–84.
[51] W. Camden *et al., Epistolæ*, ed. T. Smith (1691), p. 53.
[52] YML, XVIII.D.10, XV.R.25(2).
[53] C. Davenport, *English heraldic book-stamps* (1909), p. 294; YML, XI.N.10.
[54] YML, XVIII.A.37 (*STC* 10716).

have been given away other than to the Minster library, some to friends and a group of thirteen or more to the new town library of his native Bristol.[55]

The arrival of over three thousand books in a library furnished to house at the most two hundred brought not only a sense of gratitude but also a physical and financial problem. King Charles had the intention of providing some money, but a fine of £1,000 which he granted to the Minster for several purposes, one of them the salary of a library keeper, was entirely spent without anything remaining for the library.[56] The cost of refitting the library was met mainly by Matthew's former colleagues on the Council of the North, four of them contributing a total of £40.[57] With this the old long lecterns were replaced by double-sided cases with three or four shelves in each, accompanied by an additional two shelves of smaller books 'in archivis'. This may mean books shelved below a projecting desk, or in low cases, perhaps the old lecterns adapted, standing between the new tall cases. The books were not now chained, but they stood in the manner of a chained library of books shelved upright, with fore-edge to the front. There were thirteen bays, i.e. three double-sided peninsula cases standing between the four windows on each long wall, and an odd single-sided case, probably against the unbroken east wall. A piece of furniture called a *musaeum* stood just inside the door, 'ad dextram ingredientis', for manuscripts and other particularly valuable books. There was a broad subject arrangement: bays 1–4 and 9–13 were theology, including sections for the Fathers and biblical texts and commentaries; 5 was history, 6 classics, 7 law, with a single shelf of science and medicine, and 8 was history and classics together. This reorganization was probably completed *c.* 1638, when 2s. 6d. was spent on 'ten sheetes of parchment for a frame for the library';[58] this may have been for the benefactors' board (Plate 173) and for indicator boards at the end of each bay. In the same year Sir Henry Slingsby, one of the contributors to the furnishing, recorded a visit to the library, where he met Canon Timothy Thurscross.[59] He described him as in the habit of being in the library from six to ten o'clock every morning, and it may be conjectured that what Thurscross was doing in the library for these long hours was arranging the books on the shelves, writing titles and

[55] J. Raine (ed.), *The correspondence of Dr. Matthew Hutton* (Surtees Soc. xvii, 1843), p. 188; *FAR* 35 (1963), pp. 19–20 (Adams B 1022); BL, C.64.dd.2 (Davenport, op. cit.); Ampleforth Abbey Library C.V.150 c (*STC* 17114); N. Mathews, *Early printed books and manuscripts in the City Reference Library, Bristol* (1899), pp. vii–ix, etc.; *A catalogue of books in the Bristol Reference Library . . . printed abroad . . . 1473 to 1700* (1956), *passim*.

[56] Drake, *Ebor.*, p. 522; *Fabric Rolls*, pp. 319–28.

[57] Liber donorum, fo. 2^r.

[58] Fabric roll, E 3/64.

[59] H. Slingsby, *Diary* (1836), pp. 7–9.

shelf-numbers on the foredges, and compiling the catalogue of the library which was certainly written at about this date (Plate 174). Nothing survives of Thurscross's handwriting except a few signatures which vary considerably over almost forty years, and the identification cannot be positively confirmed, but several points support it. Thurscross knew Matthew and two of the library benefactors, and was something of a scholar. He later gave the Minster library some important reference works, and left enough books to found three vicarage libraries.[60] He spent the long early mornings of a York winter in the unheated library in a year when he was seeking mortification because of a troubled conscience over having committed simony to obtain two livings which he then resigned. Did he arrange and catalogue the library as a penance? His catalogue, if it is his, is a competent performance. It is alphabetical, in the manner of the period, as far as the second letter of each heading; the choice of heading is not as systematic as might be desired, and there is no statement of imprint or format. There are, however, shelf-numbers, in the form of three arabic numerals, denoting respectively bay (*subsellis*), shelf (*classis*), and running number (*numerus*). *Subsellis* was used at St. John's College, Cambridge, for similar new cases erected in 1628, and *classis* regularly has the same meaning,[61] never elsewhere being used of a shelf, as here.

While the library was being refurnished and reorganized, individual donations continued to be made. Most notable was a gift of several hundred volumes from Ferdinando Lord Fairfax, who with his son Sir Thomas was in command of the parliamentarian forces which captured York in 1644, and as governor of the city thereafter issued orders to safeguard the archives both of the chapter and of the archbishopric, and instructed the corporation to pay the salary of the library keeper.[62] He had known Matthew, and probably his own books were already in the library when he thus saw to its care with the dean and chapter in no position to do so, and prevented any sacking of the library of York as happened in similar circumstances at some other cathedrals. Fairfax's books included a number formerly belonging to archbishops Richard Neile and (perhaps) John Williams, and a collection of medical books from Dr. William Mount, domestic chaplain to Lord Burghley and master of the Savoy. In 1641 and 1647, when the city and county of York petitioned Parliament for the founding of a university at York, 'the advantage of a library which is there

[60] Liber donorum, fo. 2ʳ; N. R. Ker, *Parochial libraries* (1959), p. 92.

[61] R. Willis and J. W. Clark, *The architectural history of the university of Cambridge*, iii (1886), pp. 438–9, 453; J. W. Clark, *The care of books* (1901), p. 243.

[62] Liber donorum, fo. 2ʳ; *YAJ* xlii. 2 (1968), 214; A. Raine (ed.), 'Proceedings of the Commonwealth Committee for York', in C. E. Whiting (ed.), *Miscellanea*, vi (YAS Rec. Ser. cxviii, 1953), pp. 3–6.

172 Archbishop Tobie Matthew, whose collection of 3,000 books given to the Minster Library after his death in 1628 first turned it into a large and widely used library: the portrait, dated 1624, hangs in the Library, and is inscribed with the motto 'Vita Christus, Mors Lucrum' ('Christ is life, riches are death'), adapted from Philippians i.21, which is written in many of his books as a mark of ownership, sometimes with his signature and sometimes without it (Y.M.L., I.L. 23).

173 The text of the wooden benefactors' board set up in the Library c. 1638, as copied by Thomas Comber to serve as the title-page for the *Liber donorum* begun by him in 1685–6.

NOMINA

Virorum Illustrium, aliorumq, bonarum

Artium Fautorum,

QUI

(Post immensam variamq, rei Litterariæ Supellectilem e Musæo Reverendissimi in Christo Patris ac Domini, Domini

TOBIÆ MATHEW,

Archiepiscopi Eboracensis,

æternæ memoriæ viri,

Huc translatam post obitum illius per munificentiam insignis fæmina,

FRANCISCÆ MATHEW,

dicti Dom: Archiepiscopi vidua)

BIBLIOTHECAM

Hujus Ecclesia Cathedralis & Metropolitica suis impensis & liberalitate ornarunt & auxerunt

Dux Fæmina facti.

already' was one of the factors urged in favour of the scheme; neither date was suitable for such a petition to have any hope of success.[63] The continuing accessibility of the library under the Commonwealth is attested by the will of the Hebrew scholar and anti-Puritan writer Christopher Cartwright, who in 1658 bequeathed Buxtorf's Hebrew bible 'to the Publique Librarie in Yorke Minster'.[64]

As under the Commonwealth, so at the Restoration use of the library continued. In 1661 the fine paid by the bookseller Francis Mawburne for a lease from the chapter was £50 'and Dr. Hammond's works'. In 1666 the Yorkshire clergyman Marmaduke Carver's book *A discourse of the terrestrial paradise* made acknowledgement of 'having the benefit of the library of the Cathedral-Church of St. Peters in York'.[65] Probably in 1671 there was drawn up a catalogue of the library's forty-three manuscripts, possibly made for Archbishop Sheldon of Canterbury; a copy of this was made *c.* 1675, and a third version, apparently written for Bishop Edward Stillingfleet, claims to be derived from notes made by Gerard Langbaine of Oxford, who died in 1658.[66] In 1672 the chapter paid for the return of some books borrowed by a clergyman who had died outside York.[67] In 1678 the volume of the York Gospels, 'long escaped from the archives of the church, when and how is not known', was mysteriously returned by the executors of Henry King, bishop of Chichester, who had died in 1669, and at once rebound.[68] In 1681 the 'sweeping and cleansing' or 'keeping' of the library, which since 1661 had been done by the organ-blower for 10s., afterwards £1 6s. 8d. a year, was transferred to the clerk of the vestry at the increased salary of £6 a year.[69] In 1685 Archbishop Dolben, finding at his visitation that neglect of Holgate's injunctions about security had rendered the library, 'though much encreased since that time . . . wholy useless in a place which much needs such an help to good learning', ordered the books to be properly catalogued, duplicates exchanged for other books, and three vicars appointed 'to waite by turnes two houres every morneing and two houres every afternoone, keeping the library open . . . and taking care that the bookes be not purloined or damnified by such as shall pretend there to study'. A year later Dolben died, and 376 titles were given to the library by

[63] G. W. Johnson (ed.), *The Fairfax correspondence: memoirs of the reign of Charles I* (1848), ii. 274–80.

[64] YML, *Catalogue* (1896), pp. xii, 42.

[65] YML, Register of Leases etc., 1640–1702, We, fos. 13ᵛ–14ᵛ, with BIHR, V.1662–3; Wing C 718–9 (YML, IX.M.12), fo. A8ᵛ.

[66] Bodl., MSS. Tanner 88, fos. 110ʳ–111ᵛ; Tanner 268, fos. 20ᵛ–25ᵛ; BL, MS. Harl. 695, pp. 628–30.

[67] *Fabric Rolls*, p. 139.

[68] Chapter Acts, 1634–1700, part ii, fo. 128ʳ; *Fabric Rolls*, p. 357 (partly incorrect).

[69] Chapter Acts, 1634–1700, part ii, fo. 32ᵛ; Fabric Accounts, E 4 a and E3/65/5–36; St. Peter's Accounts, E 2 (22).

his executors.[70] In obedience to his injunctions the library was reorganized by the precentor, Thomas Comber (Plate 175). Within six months he put the three major collections, Matthew, Fairfax, and Dolben, into a single subject sequence, wrote a model author catalogue of the printed books, fully alphabetical and complete with imprints and formats, a 'reall' or subject catalogue, no longer extant, and a register of benefactions from the time of the Matthew gift, with a copy of the donors' board serving as a title (Plate 173); he sold duplicates at convocation and spent £80 on new books and £30 on binding and additional shelves. Analysis of the shelf-marks in the catalogue shows the thirteen bays increased to sixteen, the special shelves 'in archivis' abolished, and between four and seven shelves in each bay; the subject arrangement, slightly improved from the previous system, again grouped the various branches of theology at the end of the room nearest the entrance. Truly could Comber write, 'I left the library in exact order.'[71]

It may have been Comber again, though direct evidence does not begin until 1707, who initiated an income for the library by appropriating to it the fee of £1 paid in lieu of a collation by a new canon at his installation, and £2 by a dignitary. These sums were doubled in 1730 and again in 1780, and, though irregular in frequency, were the only income for the library until the nineteenth century.[72] Accounts recording the expenditure of this money, mainly on new books from local booksellers, survive from 1716, and from the middle of the century are accompanied by some of the actual bills, which in many cases supply fuller details of the purchases.

One set well illustrates the way in which the library was for long built up from chance donations and at intervals reduced to order by the occasional active librarian of whom Comber is an outstanding example. The set is Cardinal Baronius's *Annales ecclesiastici*.[73] The first catalogue has the entry 'Baronij Annales 9 vol: 5:3:1–9', and the volumes, except the sixth, still have the shelf-numbers 1–9 on the foredge. Volumes 1 and 2 were certainly Matthew's, 6 was certainly Fairfax's, and the other six may have belonged to either. Matthew also had two epitomes, first a 1601–3 edition covering to A.D. 1000, and then a 1614 edition summarizing the complete twelve-volume set to A.D. 1198. The library's copy of volumes 10 and 11, bound together, was Fairfax's, and is entered first in Comber's catalogue of 1687 in the form 'X Vol: . . . II.C.1–10'. This suggests that Fairfax's contribution did not come till after the compilation of the earlier catalogue, and that his

[70] *York Statutes*, pp. 101–2; Liber donorum, fos. 3ʳ–15ʳ (rectos only); T. Comber, *Autobiographies*, ed. C. E. Whiting, i (Surtees Soc. 156, 1946), pp. 16, 52.
[71] Comber, op. cit., pp. xlv–xlvi, 16–17, 52.
[72] E 2(5), Common Account, 1677–1707; H 13/1, Jurisdiction Account, 1716–1813, fos. 2–4.
[73] YML, II.E.4–14 and 17, XI.K.33.

B

174 A page (A) from the Library's first catalogue, *c.* 1638, probably written by Timothy Thurscross(e), whose signature is appended (B) to show the similarity in script.

A

A

175 Thomas Comber, who reorganized the Library in 1685–7: the portrait (A) is from a mezzotint attributed to George Lumley of York, *c.* 1700 (reproduced by courtesy of York City Art Gallery); the note (B), in his hand, shows him presenting a book to the Library in 1688 (Y.M.L., MS XVI.L.8).

B

volume 6, distinguished from the rest of the set by the absence of a foredge number, was intruded into an existing Matthew set of the first nine volumes in which the sixth was either inferior or lost. Probably Matthew's volume 6 and Fairfax's volumes 1–5 and 7–9 were among the duplicates sold in 1686. Comber will have been keen to complete the library's set, and one can imagine the feeling of satisfaction with which he entered in the donors' book 'Mr. William Calvert M.A. gave the XIIth Tome of Cardinal Baronius Annals in Folio' and altered the author catalogue to read 'XI Vol: ad An: 1198, II.C.1–10^2.' His satisfaction, however, was short-lived, for on the next page of the Liber donorum Calvert has written that he had not given but lent volume 12 to Comber, and had it returned to him to keep his own set complete. The library had the last word, however, for in 1711 Calvert was made a canon, and instead of paying the installation fee he gave a book. No doubt this was his copy of Baronius volume 12, now come to the library a second time, for the cover bears his initials W.C. There remains another complication in the history of this volume: the stamp incorporating these initials is known to have belonged not to William Calvert but to William Crashawe, a canon of the Minster who died in 1626. He had a considerable library, and among many bequests of books to individuals and institutions his will, made in 1621, lists three volumes given 'to the publique librarie of St. Peters in Yorke' and 'a Coffer to keepe them in'. How Crashaw's Baronius, which is not mentioned in his will, passed to Calvert is not certain, but one of his residuary legatees of unspecified books was Trinity College, Dublin, where a Baronius would have been a duplicate and where Calvert entered as an undergraduate in 1672; more simply, both men spent most of their careers in Yorkshire and the bulky set may have found its way from one to the other with less travelling.[74] Whatever the truth of this, the Crashaw–Calvert copy of volume 12 thus came to the library in 1711, but did not join its fellows on the shelf until more than a century later. The continuation by H. Spondanus, published in two volumes in 1678 and shelved with volumes 1–11 since the 1687 catalogue, is probably one of Comber's purchases. It thus took two gifts, a purchase, and the complicated acquisition of volume 12 for the library, mainly through Comber, to build up its complete set of fourteen volumes.

Yet something else regularized by Comber was the lending of books from the library. Before him there is no record; partly in his hand is a series of loans of *c.* 1691–2 to several dignitaries and canons, and from 1716 there is a continuous series of loans registers. The dignitaries borrowing in 1691–2

---

[74] P. J. Wallis in *Transactions of the Cambridge Bibliographical Soc.* ii.3 (1956), pp. 213–28, and in *Transactions of the Hunter Archaeological Soc.* viii.2–5 (1960–3); G. D. Burtchaell and T. U. Sadleir, *Alumni Dublinenses* (new edn. 1935), p. 128; YML, VII.G.7 (Adams F 907) is part of Crashaw's bequest.

included 'Mr Precentor'. The earlier entries refer to Comber himself, the later ones, after his departure for the deanery of Durham, to his successor, James Fall. Fall had the experience, as executor of Archbishop Robert Leighton of Glasgow in 1684, of constituting his friend's books into the Leighton Library at Dunblane, and at his own death in 1711 Fall followed his example in becoming a library benefactor. Perhaps feeling that the main part of his collection would largely duplicate the contents of the Minster library, he bequeathed 'to the Dean and Chapter of York all my French and Italian books, to be . . . deposited in their publick library and remaine there for ever, as a testimony of the respect and honour I have for that Reverend and learned Society'. These books were mostly acquired in 1680–3 when he travelled in France and Italy as tutor to the two sons of Lord Queensberry, but a few volumes have dates which show that he must have acquired them after this journey.[75]

In 1715 the executors of Archbishop Sharp presented ten manuscript volumes compiled by James Torr, 'a learned student of ecclesiastical antiquities'. These comprised extracts made in the 1680s and 1690s from the archiepiscopal and capitular archives at York and from other sources, manuscript and printed, and the main group gives a detailed classified documentary history of the Minster in a volume by itself, and of every church in the diocese.[76] This is still today the fullest comprehensive account of the ecclesiastical history of the diocese until the end of the seventeenth century, and remains one of the most important and most constantly used of the gifts received by the library. One of the early users of the Torr manuscripts was Francis Drake, who acknowledged the 'extraordinary favour' of being allowed to borrow them and keep them at home as long as he needed for his work on his own history of York, published in 1736. This and Drake's other loans are entered in the borrowers' registers, which in their first continuous century from 1716 to 1820 record 1,242 loans to over 179 borrowers. Comparison of these York records with similar ones at seven other cathedrals shows that York was open to a far larger circle of borrowers than the others, apparently through the tradition which it still proudly maintains of affording access not just to the Minster and other clergy, as was commonly the practice, but to anyone who would make profitable use of the books in the library.[77]

[75] F. Leishman, 'Principal Fall of Glasgow', in *Transactions of the Glasgow Archaeological Soc.* N.S. vii. 3 (1924), 342–50; J. Fall, *Memoires of my Lord Drumlangrig's . . . travells abroad*, ed. H. H. Dalrymple (1931).

[76] Liber donorum, fo. 17ʳ; *DNB* Torre (his own spelling is Torr); YML, L 1(2)–(10).

[77] E. Brunskill, *18th century reading* (York Georgian Soc., 1950); Brunskill's analysis by author and borrower is YML, MS. Add. 217/1; P. Kaufman, 'Reading vogues at English cathedral libraries of the eighteenth century', 4 parts in the *Bull. of the New York Public Library*, lxvii–lxviii (1963–4).

Dean Henry Finch, who died in 1728, seems to have been the first person to bequeath money to the library, the large sum of £100. Two thirds of this was spent on a set of Rymer's *Foedera*, and the rest went towards a series of other standard major works of permanent value in the fields of theology, church history, and church law, which were being wisely purchased at this period. The foresight displayed by whoever made the selection is amply demonstrated by the regular use which many of the purchases of this period still receive today, as well as when they were newly bought. While gifts mostly brought in old books, purchases were usually of new publications. One of the first borrowers was often Laurence Sterne, who made thorough use of his loans from the Minster library.

In the 1730s there came the large and important collection of Marmaduke Fothergill (Plate 176). He was a non-juror, and had spent his long enforced retirement between 1689 and his death in 1731 collecting, reading, and annotating an excellently chosen library of theological and historical books. In addition he had some historical and musical manuscripts from the widow of the antiquary Matthew Hutton, and a collection of printed editions of Latin and Greek authors assembled by the classical scholar John Price. The topic which he studied most extensively was the history of the English liturgy, and in pursuance of this he collected and annotated all the principal editions of the Book of Common Prayer and many of the pre-Reformation liturgies, both printed and manuscript, from which much of it was derived, including a remarkable number of the rare texts of the medieval Use of York. To any book without a good printed index he added one of his own making, and on the title he generally gave a reference to Nicolson's *English historical library*, Wood's *Athenæ Oxonienses*, or some other bio-bibliographical reference work. He bequeathed this collection of over 1,500 volumes to his former parish at Skipwith, accompanied by his own classified and author catalogue, but the parishioners failed to provide a special building to accommodate the library and in default Fothergill's widow made it over to the dean and chapter.[78]

In 1751 the library's first book-plate was printed, bearing simply the words 'York Minster Library' and the date within a frame. In 1774 the library bought what was probably its first fireplace, perhaps at the instigation of two cataloguers less hardy than Thurscross in 1638. John Coulthred, minister of Hickleton near Doncaster, transcribed the neat new catalogues of the Fothergill collection in 1773 for one guinea and of the main library in 1774–5 for five guineas; the numbers of books in the two catalogues are given as 1,520 and 4,162; there were separate sections for

---

[78] Drake, *Ebor.*, pp. 379–80; Venn, *Alumni Cantabrigienses*, I.ii.165.

Fall's collection of French and Italian books, which had been augmented, and for the manuscripts. The making of these new catalogues was supervised and the books rearranged in subject order in preparation for them by William Richardson, vicar choral, who was paid ten guineas 'for his trouble' in 1775.[79]

Tables and chairs were bought in 1778, and in 1780 the installation fees paid to the library were doubled. Two men who both used the library regularly at this period and presented it with their own publications were Alexander Hunter, the medical and agricultural writer and editor of the works of John Evelyn, and the 'lay theologian' William Burgh, a friend of precentor William Mason. John Fountayne, who borrowed frequently during his long tenure of the deanery, 1747–1802, and whose third wife was one of the handful of ladies who used the library in the eighteenth century, gave Rapin's *History of England* and, by his will, the five great volumes of Gough's *Sepulchral monuments*. The last was one of the most important gifts of the period, together with Tanner's *Notitia monastica* in 1799 and Gough's *British topography* a year later, both from canons of the Minster and both still in regular use. Few books were bought in Fountayne's time, and with the increase in installation fees the library fund reached the remarkably large balance of £163 1s. in 1801. Then Chancellor George Markham, who a year later succeeded Fountayne as dean, began to show the active policy towards the library which he and his family pursued for the next quarter-century. George was always the leading figure in this, but his father, archbishop 1777–1807, two of his brothers and a sister, a brother-in-law and a brother's brother-in-law (both dignitaries of the Minster), a nephew, and his daughter and her husband were all occasional benefactors to the library.[80] But the use and appeal of the library were not confined to the chapter and its connections: a North Riding parson presented the library's first Shakespeare, a fourth folio, and there were gifts from the two prominent unitarian scholars John Kenrick and Charles Wellbeloved, and the eccentric but learned York surgeon James Atkinson; descendants of Archbishop Sharp gave books by and about him and other members of the family, including a wide-ranging collection of pieces by Granville Sharp; and in 1802 the Record Commissioners began to give their invaluable publications to York as they did to other cathedral libraries.

---

[79] This William Richardson, vicar choral and curate in charge of St. Michael-le-Belfrey 1772–1821, vicar of Huntington 1789–1802, curate in charge of St. Sampson's, York, 1802–21, subchanter 1803–21, buried at St. Michael-le-Belfrey 1821, is to be distinguished from two others of the same name afterwards associated with the library: below, nn. 84 and 85.

[80] Sir C. R. Markham, *Markham memorials* (1913), ii.51–2, 68–9, 91; Liber donorum, fos. 18^v–24^r and 32^r.

Under Dean Markham's guidance purchases for the first time in the library's history outstripped gifts. Already in 1802 he himself began a 'List of Books not in York Minster Library, which (if approved of) may be purchased'. Not only individual titles but also categories of books were selected and bought, Latin and Greek classics, church history, Bouquet's and Muratori's standard collections of French and Italian medieval chronicles, and the Church Fathers. Many of this last group were in the Benedictine or other best editions then readily available from the dispersal of French monastic libraries after the revolution; most of these were the editions afterwards reprinted by Migne in the Latin and Greek series of his *Patrologia*, which partly for this reason was not afterwards purchased for the library, a decision reasonable at the time but unfortunate from the point of view of the twentieth century. London booksellers were used to a considerable extent, but the local dealers, notably Todd and the shop successively run by Tesseyman, Wolstenholme, and Marsh, were not neglected and demonstrated their goodwill by occasional gifts. When a request for a 5 per cent discount from the London trade was granted but countered by charges for carriage which till then had been free the Minster wisely stopped asking for the discount. Subscriptions for new publications included *Archaeologia* and the *Philosophical Transactions*, Dibdin's edition of Ames's *Typographical antiquities*, Halfpenny's *Fragmenta vetusta*, and Whitaker's *Craven* and *Richmondshire*.

This expansion of the library necessitated increased physical care of the books. Already in 1794 they had been cleaned for a guinea, and in 1802 the library chimney was cleaned and the floor scoured. In 1801–2 and 1805–11 binders did regular repairs and lettering. But these were small jobs, and the big physical need of the library was for space, a need exacerbated by the accelerated expansion. The total stock now numbered close on 6,000 volumes, and it was clear that neither shelves nor room could hold more. On the floor below the diocesan archives were equally overcrowded, and there was nowhere else near enough to take an overflow. The only practical course was to seek completely fresh accommodation for the library. Markham's choice fell on a semi-ruinous building on the north side of the Minster, the thirteenth-century chapel of Archbishop Roger's palace, which had been abandoned in the sixteenth century and had become derelict and disreputable. The dean and chapter now took it over and demolished most of the buildings, the first step being the repair and conversion of the chapel as the new Minster library. The work was begun in 1803, and about 1810 the new five-light window inserted at the west end in imitation of the blocked east window was glazed with the arms of the chapter, each contributing three guineas as the cost of his own shield; the

Markham arms are appropriately conspicuous by their repetition. The books were moved into their new home in May 1810, under the supervision of Dean Markham and two vicars choral, William Bulmer and James Dallin.

The books occupied the north and east walls of the former chapel, again an upper room, where the windows had been blocked. Fourteen cases here and a fifteenth adjacent to them at the east end of the south wall each held from fourteen to eighteen shelves; under the west window a sixteenth case, lockable, held the manuscripts and specially important printed books selected partly by Dibdin in 1815 and partly by Archdeacon Henry John Todd, who was librarian at Lambeth Palace. A broad arrangement by subject placed miscellaneous books on medicine, science, music, and civil law in bay I, ecclesiastical history and biography in II, secular history and biography, chronology, geography, topography, antiquities, and voyages in III–V, Latin and Greek classics in VI and VII, the latter also containing dictionaries and grammars, Church Fathers in VIII and IX, church councils and canon law in X, bibles and liturgies in XI, divinity—expository, controversial, and practical—in XII–XV. Shelf H, immediately below the light gallery which afforded access to the upper shelves, contained periodicals and long sets. In the centre of the room a series of tables and low cupboards numbered XVII provided space for reference books and music as well as readers.

Once the books were installed in their new home a great deal of repairing and lettering was done. Thomas Peck, who had been doing this for six years already, for the next three years increased his work sixfold. In 1815, after the bibliomaniac Dibdin's dramatic visit to the library late at night, when he enthused over some Caxtons and rare continental incunables shown him by Archdeacon Eyre but was unsuccessful in persuading the chapter to sell him any of them, he put the library in touch with the leading London binder of the day, Charles Lewis, who the next year rebound sixty manuscripts and important printed books. Regular binding work was done locally, mainly by James and Oliver Sumner, until the 1840s.[81] The books on each shelf were arranged in order of size, so that pasteboard covers kept off dust, and paper labels supplied by the printers of the *York Courant* and the *York Chronicle* were pasted on the spines to indicate the shelf-numbers.

An incidental consequence of the removal of the library from the Minster was that the books were not, like the chapter and diocesan archives, endangered by the fires which consumed the choir in 1829 and the nave in 1840. On neither occasion was the wing, in which the library had been and

---

[81] T. F. Dibdin, *The bibliographical decameron*, iii (1817), pp. 254–9 and 416–19; C. Ramsden, *London bookbinders* (1956), pp. 9, 13–16, 96 (Lewis); id., *Bookbinders of the United Kingdom, outside London* (1954), p. 158 (Sumner).

the muniments still were kept, directly affected by the flames, but the hasty precautionary evacuation of the archives caused confusion, damage, and perhaps loss which the library books were providentially spared. One book loaned to a clergyman and presumably kept by him in the choir or vestry was lost in the first fire, but a more extensive and more serious loss on that occasion was that of a considerable proportion of the Minster music, which was naturally kept in the choir. The current choir books were quickly recopied from what survived, but some valuable older music was utterly lost; this included a quantity of Purcell, some of which happened to have been transcribed during the musical festival of September 1828 by Vincent Novello, who presented some of his transcripts and printed editions.[82]

A remarkable physical innovation introduced in 1827–31 was a door leading directly into the main library room from the adjoining new deanery erected by the autocratic Dean Cockburn. The door, in time surmounted with a case numbered XVIII containing six shelves of small books, remained until the demolition of the deanery in 1938. While Cockburn did not show the consuming interest in the library that Markham had done, he was sufficiently interested to place a number of orders with his regular bookseller, characteristically without consulting or informing chapter or the librarian, and in 1841, when he was in dispute with chapter, it ordered an extra lock to be fixed on this door. Of the six occupants of the deanery while this communicating door was in existence probably Purey-Cust (1880–1916) will have availed himself of it most frequently.

The first sizeable gift to come to the library in its new building was the happy consequence of an eighteenth-century friendship. William Burgh, who has already been mentioned as a regular user of the library between 1773 and 1783, had collaborated with Precentor Mason in literature, politics, and social welfare. He died in 1808, and in pursuance of his widow's will in 1819 the library received 328 volumes, mostly books that he had collected in preparation for a projected history of religious thought in the later eighteenth century; this went some way towards making up for the library's meagre purchases during that period.[83]

Although the cost of the new library building was charged not to the small library account but to the Minster fabric fund, the intensive purchasing and binding initiated by Dean Markham turned the sizeable credit balance of 1801 into a small deficit five years later. Immediate solvency was attained by Archbishop Vernon Harcourt's uniquely large

---

[82] YML, M 7 (S) and P 282/1–35, parts 7–10.
[83] On Burgh see above, p. 463; *DNB*; C. B. L. Barr and J. A. S. Ingamells, *A Candidate for Praise: William Mason* (1973), pp. 16–17, 64–5 and 76–7; his books are listed partially in the Liber donorum, fos. 25[r]–28[r], and apparently fully in the 1831 shelf-catalogue, vol. iv, II.a–k.

installation fee of £50 in 1808, and gifts totalling £70 for books from two of the dignitaries in 1809 and 1811. In the longer view, however, the irregular income from installation fees could never maintain an active library such as the Minster now enjoyed, and at once in 1808 chapter established a new and much enhanced library fund. The installation fees continued until Parliament in the 1840s stripped the canons of their prebendal income, but they were now supplemented and subsequently replaced by a sixth part of the profits of the lease of the rectory of Bubwith. This had been formerly assigned to St. Peter's account, which henceforward received a sixth instead of its former third part of these profits. Whereas the income from fees averaged less than £13 a year in the period 1780–1810, the Bubwith estate brought the library over £125 a year in the first five years and thereafter a regular £80. The purchase of between sixty and a hundred volumes a year, however, more than kept pace with this sixfold increase in the library's income, and the year 1817 again ended with a debit balance. Inevitably purchasing slowed down abruptly to about twenty items a year, including the subscriptions to *Archaeologia*, the *Philosophical Transactions*, the Bampton Lectures, *Monumenta Germaniae Historica*, Richardson's *Monastic ruins of Yorkshire*, Browne's *York Minster*, and a few others. Occasional large payments in the 1820s continued to bring debit balances in some years, but restraint in the 1830s gradually reduced the deficit and after 1838 a credit balance was maintained and steadily increased, the largest expenditure being the librarian's salary.

The library keeper, who since 1681 had normally been the vestry clerk, saw to the locking and unlocking of the door, the sweeping of the floor, and the recording of loans. His salary since 1702 of £4 as keeper, plus £1 6s. 8d. for the cleaning, was paid from St. Peter's account until 1840 and thereafter from the library account. With the library now outside the Minster and impossible for the vestry clerk to supervise regularly, and the increased activity of the library needing more attention than the occasional services of a dean or canon who happened to be interested, it became necessary to appoint a librarian. The salary was £25 a year, paid out of the library fund, reduced to £20 in 1841 at the same time that the keeper's inclusive salary of £5 6s. 8d. became a charge to the library fund. The first four holders of the office were all vicars choral. First was James Dallin, 1811–38, described as 'both obliging and competent in his office'. He presented several books himself, and in 1831 supervised the making of a shelf-catalogue.[84] He died

---

[84] Dibdin, op. cit. iii. 256; Liber donorum, fos. 24^r and 34^r–37^r. The catalogue was written for £50 by a second William Richardson (see also nn. 79 and 85), M.A. and sub-librarian at St. John's College, Cambridge, 1822, vicar choral and incumbent of St. Michael-le-Belfrey 1829–37, when he died (Venn, *Al. Cant.* II.v.296).

in 1838, not long after a remarkable announcement, almost an advertise-ment, had appeared in the *Yorkshire Gazette* of 9 December 1837:

THE CATHEDRAL LIBRARY.—The wishes of the Dean and Chapter, respecting the use of their library, not being generally known, we are authorized to state, that any gentleman resident in York, or the suburbs, may have the loan of books from the library, by leave from the Dean or the Residentiary; but ap-plication may be made to them through the Librarian, who fulfils the intentions of his superiors in affording every possible facility of access to their valuable collection of theological and other works. The number of volumes in the library amount to nearly 8000—a considerable part of them having been bequests and gifts, to be for ever attached to the Cathedral. The collection consists chiefly of works which were published before, or at the beginning of, the last century; and contains authors in the various departments of literature—only about half the volumes being theological. There is a good collection of the classics, and the fathers of the Christian church, most of them in the best editions; with some valuable works on Rabbinical learning, ecclesiastical and general history, and antiquities; the principal of the ancient authors de re medica, and some good specimens of manuscripts, and early printed books. A very considerable portion of the works are in the learned or modern foreign languages. The Librarian's ordinary days of attendance at the library are Mondays, Wednesdays, and Fridays, at 12 o'clock.

Dallin's successor, William Richardson,[85] held office as librarian for only a few months in 1839. In 1841 Archbishop Harcourt, in the course of a visitation occasioned by his and the chapter's dispute with Dean Cockburn, issued injunctions which contained three items regarding the library. An order that library funds were not to be spent without authority of chapter was clearly directed at Cockburn, who had ordered books without consultation. 'In observance of ancient usage'—of thirty years' standing!—'one of the vicars-choral shall be appointed to fill the office of librarian'; and 'Rules and regulations for the due management and augmentation of the chapter library, and for such an extensive use of the books as may be consistent with their safe custody and careful preservation, shall be drawn up at a chapter meeting'.[86]

Edward John Raines, who had first been proposed as librarian early in 1840, was appointed late in 1841 and held office until 1857. It is not clear

[85] Also of St. John's College, Cambridge, B.A. 1835, curate of Kirkby Malham and Arncliffe, probably 1839–43, perpetual curate of Stainforth near Giggleswick 1843–65, died 1865 (Venn, op. cit.).
[86] *York Statutes*, pp. 108–9.

whether the stream of petty library business which is recorded in the chapter acts and minutes in these years is the result of a fussy nature, of a close interest and control by chapter, or of prudent caution after the difficulties and irregularities of the immediately preceding years. Owing to the reduction in salary he attended for one hour on two instead of three days a week, and in 1842 a deputy was appointed to attend for three hours on three other days; the latter, who was the chapter clerk's son and assistant, resigned after a few months owing to the pressure of his other duties; two successors did not hold office long, and after 1848 the post seems to have remained unfilled. This extension of the library's services was in response to a request by 'several gentlemen', whose spokesman was the solicitor Joseph Munby. Only five keys were to be issued, to the dean, the canon in residence, the librarian, the library keeper, and the chapter clerk for the use of the chapter. Consideration was given to protecting the manuscripts from damp. The existing author catalogue still related to the arrangement of the books in the old building, and Raines was asked to prepare a new catalogue to be 'printed and circulated . . . to facilitate the use of the library'; in 1848–51 he was granted a total of £50 for assistance in preparing the catalogue for press. In 1842 strict regulations for borrowing were issued, two stoves with chimney-pipes leading out of the windows were installed in place of the open fire, and extra shelves were built between and beneath the windows on the south wall of the main room, which could then contain all the books.

A set of rules probably drafted in this year and in part approved by chapter on 24 November ordered the sublibrarian to attend on four days a week. The clergy of the diocese and any other applicants should have access on six days a week during the hours laid down. Borrowers were to have not more than four books at once, were not to keep them longer than a month, and were to pay the cost of carriage and a small weekly sum for each book. Only duplicates were to be borrowed; a catalogue of them was to be drawn up in consultation with Canon Edward Churton and printed, but seems never to have been completed. In a period when much library borrowing was conducted by post this limitation will not have encouraged the printing of a complete catalogue for circulation.

Some applications for loans were approved and some were not. A volume each of *Archaeologia* and the *Philosophical Transactions* were lost from the library in 1843, and after unsuccessful inquiries replacements were bought. In 1844 the privilege of using the library was granted to members of the British Association then meeting in York. The restrained rate of purchasing forced on the chapter by the deficits of the 1830s had become the rule, with no canon showing an initiative to purchase and the librarian not of sufficiently senior standing to do so himself even if he had the inclination, and perhaps above all because of an awareness of financial difficulties to come, purchases remained regrettably few. By 1869, after forty-five years of little buying, the balance of the library fund had risen to over £345.

The Cathedrals Commission of 1852–4 reported that the library had a stock of 8,000 books, perhaps something of an underestimate, as the same figure had been given in 1837 and, with no significant accessions in the interval, 9,000 was given in 1870. The size of the library was equal to that of St. Paul's and exceeded only by Durham; all others were much smaller. The library's only financial support was from the Bubwith lease, which was nearly expired and could not be renewed. Durham, with £200, was the only library with an income as large as York's, but the Durham fund seemed assured for the future while the York one was doomed. York and Durham again stood out for generosity to readers, York opening to the public on five days a week, and Durham accessible to all responsible persons.[87]

In 1857 Raines resigned as librarian, and two years later he died. A few months before his death he presented his two-volume catalogue of the library, written on paper watermarked 1854. His successor was Thomas Falkner, who held office from 1858 to 1872.

In 1869 the Bubwith lease fell in, the estate had to be surrendered to the Ecclesiastical Commissioners, and the library ceased to have any income. The outlook for the library was bleak indeed, and it was largely owing to the unflagging energy and scholarly interest of one man that the library did not stagnate but on the contrary flourished for the next quarter-century as never before. This was James Raine (Plate 177), son of the librarian of Durham Cathedral, and from 1855 until his death in 1896 a prolific historical author and editor. He had held livings in York since 1856 and been made a canon in 1865; in 1888 he became a residentiary, and in 1891 chancellor.[88] Chapter at once invested £300 of the sum standing in the library account, and appointed a committee of four, including Dean Duncombe and Raine, 'to draw up a scheme for the future management of the Library'. A circular letter drawn up by the committee was printed and issued in April 1870. A statement of the library's financial straits since the cessation of the Bubwith lease showed that, despite exemption from rates since 1843, taxes amounted to £25 a year, more than the income from the £300 investment. The chapter wished to keep up its library, add to it, and

[87] *First report of H.M.'s Commissioners, appointed . . . 1852, to inquire into . . . the cathedrals* (1854), pp. 3, xlix–l, and App., pp. 25–6.
[88] W. Stubbs in YML, *Catalogue* (1896), pp. xxvii–viii; Yorkshire Philosophical Soc., *A.R. for 1896* (1897), pp. xvi–xvii; F. Boase, *Modern English biography*, iii (1901), cols. 15–16; A. H. Thompson, *The Surtees Society, 1834–1934* (Surtees Soc. cl, 1939), pp. 1, 42, 49, 265, etc.

A

176 Marmaduke Fothergill, whose important collection came to the Library after his death in 1731: the upper part of two pages from his own classified catalogue (A), showing the quarto and folio sections of class G, 'Classici', and his signature (B) from one of his books (Y.M.L., II.M.20).

B

177 James Raine, who was active to improve and exploit the Library, 1870–96; the portrait was posthumously painted in 1906 by his son H. Keyworth Raine, apparently from a photograph (reproduced by courtesy of York City Art Gallery).

open it to the public, but the public would have to assist. Gifts were solicited, both of books for the library and money for investment. An annual subscription of a guinea would allow consultation for three hours on three days a week, and the borrowing of all except reference and rare books. A fire, writing materials, and other facilities would be provided. Donations already listed totalled £140, and were increased to £194 15s. by the end of the year; subscriptions already promised numbered fifteen, and forty-two were received during the year. Some £105 was spent on books, as against £10 the year before, £33 was spent on furniture, and a further £100 was invested. The total investment of £400 yielded £17 a year, just over a fifth of the former income. Raine was asked to see to the printing of a complete catalogue. The fabric fund paid for fitting up the upstairs ante-room and installing a fire-place, and the books were insured for £5,000. To commemorate this revitalization of the library a second window was filled with the shields of present and former members of chapter.[89]

This activity attracted gifts: in 1871 seventy-three volumes of Thomas Hearne's historical works from the former subdean, the Hon. Stephen Willoughby Lawley; in 1873 the historical manuscript collections of John Richard Walbran of Ripon, from Edward Akroyd of Halifax at a cost to him of £175; in 1874 several thousand volumes illustrating religious thought in the seventeenth and eighteenth centuries from the late Archdeacon Churton, one of the committee of 1869 and long a benefactor to the library; in 1875 260 volumes from the late Robert Davies, an outstanding antiquarian and authority on the history of printing in York. In 1883 Raine printed a catalogue of over 2,000 modern books added to the library since 1870, i.e. excluding the four gifts just mentioned, and in 1884 there followed a catalogue of 500 volumes that year bequeathed by the liturgical scholar Canon T. F. Simmons. In an introduction to the former catalogue Raine gave an eloquent justification of the expansion of the library and a declaration of intent to build it up still further and throw it open even more. 'Nearly eleven centuries have passed away since Alcuin laid upon his Brethren at York the burden of loving and extending learning. In his day they had won for themselves a name; it must not be tarnished or forgotten in ours! What Chapter in Europe has such a heritage of honour and glory?'

Already in 1878 Herbert Edward Reynolds, librarian of Exeter Cathedral, in a lively and incisive survey of 'Our cathedral libraries', observed that the York library had grown from 8,000 volumes in 1852–4 to 11,000, while its only peers in size Durham had increased from 11,000 to 21,000 and St. Paul's had remained at 8,000. The York opening times, however, had

---

[89] YML, D 2/1875/11; P. Gibson in A. Stacpoole *et al.* (eds.), *The Noble City of York* (1972), pp. 220–1.

decreased from five days a week to three, being now exceeded by six cathedrals. Besides York only Canterbury could boast both radiators and a fire. Reynolds put his finger on the fundamental cause of many of the difficulties and inadequacies of all cathedral libraries when he ventured to say, truly, that the clergy do not read what they ought or as much as they ought, and that for other potential readers it is generally too daunting to have to apply formally to a dean and chapter, however ready to grant permission they may be. The cathedrals which together owned some 90,000 books should take active steps towards 'increasing the public utility of our cathedral libraries . . . these invaluable treasures'.[90] York under Raine must have gladdened Reynolds's remarkably forward-looking spirit, in every respect except the smallness of the library's financial resources.

By the time that Reynolds was writing this was again a critical problem. By 1881 the forty-two subscribers of 1870 had been reduced to seven. Despite regular subventions from the fabric fund, rising from £25 in 1874 to £75 in 1881, an over-all deficit on the library fund was increasing alarmingly. Raine, convinced of the library's worth to the Minster and the community and backed by his chapter, courageously continued to buy the books that the library needed, particularly in the field of history. Ker is surely right in saying that only because Raine demanded it did the dean and chapter spend more than £3,000 on the library in the quarter-century that he was librarian.[91] But this faith in the future, glorious though it was, needed to be backed by hard cash. Hope came from the Cathedral Establishment Commissioners. In 1879 a questionnaire issued by them asked chapter for particulars of 'The cathedral library, its present condition and use, and the funds by which it is supported,' and in 1881 chapter was informed of its right under a new statute to apply for pecuniary aid. The amounts asked for included £100 for a librarian, Raine having received no salary for his performance of the office, and £200 for the library. After a series of hopeful negotiations no grant for the library or librarian seems to have been made. In 1882 the accumulated deficit of over £350 in the library account was paid from the fabric account, and in 1882–5 £100 a year from the same source was voted for the library. In 1885 there was apparently still hope of receiving an annual grant for the library, and Raine was given a salary of £80. A year later, however, the library's £400 of railway stocks was sold for nearly £500 to pay off its deficit, and in 1890 the fabric fund had to extinguish a further library deficit of nearly £800.[92]

[90] H. E. Reynolds in the Library Association's *Transactions and proceedings of the second annual meeting* (1878), pp. 32–43; also issued separately, 14 pp.

[91] N. R. Ker, 'Cathedral libraries', in *Library history*, i. 2 (autumn 1967), at p. 43.

[92] YML, M 1(4) VIII and XII; D 10/PR II; E 5 a, fo. 211.

A week previously, on 2 April, two notable donations demonstrating the regard in which the library was held outside the chapter perhaps helped to smooth the way. The dean reported that Pope Leo XIII had presented the facsimile edition of the New Testament portion of the Codex Vaticanus, and Raine announced 'the largest and most valuable gift ever received' by the library. This was the culmination of Raine's efforts to create a local history collection, now accomplished at one stroke by the bequest of Edward Hailstone.[93] The 'Hailstone Yorkshire Collection' brought some 10,000 printed books, including unrivalled collections of Civil War tracts, local printing, history and literature, newspapers, and playbills, together with a vast quantity of archives, maps, prints, and drawings. So thoroughly had Hailstone collected throughout his long life that his library remains the most comprehensive collection of the earlier printed material relating to the county as a whole. To house the collection a monstrous case was built in the centre of the main library room, thirty-six feet long and thirteen feet high, costing £400.

In 1896 there finally appeared Raine's printed catalogue of the library, originally proposed in 1848 and entrusted to him in 1870. It contained some 14,000 books, of which 6,000 had come in his time, half by purchase and half by gift, but did not include the 10,000 additional items in the Hailstone collection. Ker describes it as 'the last and biggest and best of ten catalogues [of cathedral libraries] printed between 1859 and 1896'.[94] It is prefaced by a historical survey of the library, which Ker likewise describes as still probably the best account of any cathedral library, and to which the present writer cannot but be enormously indebted. This was Raine's last work, partly corrected on his death-bed, and Bishop Stubbs added an eloquent tribute to him.

Raine dated his preface in March 1896; he died on 20 May. Rarely can it have been so true that the death of a man dramatically marked the end of an era for the institution with which he was connected, as was the case with Raine and the Minster library. For a quarter of a century he had striven with learning and energy to make it a better library—better housed, better equipped, better used, but above all better stocked. 'His thorough single heartedness and sincerity', wrote Stubbs, himself once Lambeth librarian, 'attracted the confidence of all who came into association with him . . . it was very largely to his personality, to the interest which his zeal inspired, to the trust that was reposed in his faithfulness and in his judgment, that the great benefactions, which late years have seen made to the Library, are due.

[93] *DNB*, art. Samuel Hailstone, his father; Boase, op. cit. i (1892), col. 1275; Y.P.S. *A.R. for 1890* (1891), p. 15; G. W. T[omlinson] and J. R[aine] in *YAJ* xi (1891), 204–7.
[94] Ker, 'Cathedral libraries', p. 43.

Men who loved their books had a pleasure in leaving or giving them, where under his care they might hope for them to be treasured and preserved.'[95] But for a librarian by his scholarly enthusiasm to gain the confidence of others with similar enthusiasm and scholarship is one thing; to keep the support of one's dean and chapter over a period of continuous and even increasing financial difficulty is, as others since have found, another and more difficult task. Raine succeeded; and it is very largely due to him and to the dean and chapter who supported him that the Minster library first grew from good to outstanding, and that after more than half a century of indifferent history after him it remained of sufficient quality for its potential once again to be realized, released, and developed. 'Raine', as Ker concluded, 'is one of the great cathedral librarians.'

A memorial fund to him was established. With its aid a commemorative brass was put up in the north choir aisle of the Minster, and nearly five hundred books acquired from his collection, besides the many which he had given in his lifetime. Further, a brick extension to the north of the library which had been erected by Dean Duncombe as a laundry for the deanery was fitted up to house Raine's and other recently acquired books in two rooms, known as the Raine Room and the Cust Room.

Raine's two successors, canons Henry Temple (1896–1900) and John Watson (1900–25), though perfectly able, lacked the vital spark which made him and his library stand out. They lacked his ubiquitous literary and historical connections, and the infectious enthusiasm and energetic busyness necessary in a time of financial weakness. Nevertheless, a manuscript calendar of the dean and chapter muniments contained in a foolscap ledger was completed in 1905 by Alfred Gibbons, editor of the *Northern genealogist* and of several volumes of Lincoln wills. This calendar has served well until the present day, a proposed reorganization and re-listing begun by Reginald M. Glencross in 1919–20 not being completed because its elaboration made it too expensive. The financial weakness itself had more than one cause—the end of the income from the Bubwith estate and the failure of the Ecclesiastical Commissioners to replace it with any specific and adequate endowment for the library; the failure of the fund instituted in 1870 to raise a sum sufficient to provide an adequate alternative endowment—no failure of Raine's, but a simple lack of sufficient people in the small York area for whom it was worth paying a regular subscription for their non-fiction book requirements—and the rise in prices brought about by the First World War. Above all, the creation and growth of other libraries academic and public in York and Yorkshire, where

[95] YML, *Catalogue* (1896), p. xxvii.

a century before the Minster library had been virtually the only library in any sense open to the public, greatly lessened the need for its largely antiquarian contents. Recent history and literature were more plentifully and conveniently obtained at the public library, which since 1892 had in effect been providing a similar service free of charge to a wider public, and the provision of current theology for the clergy was still regarded as their private duty and not that of a diocesan or cathedral library. The York Subscription Library, founded in 1794, had similar problems and ceased to function in 1917.[96] The Minster library at least continued its existence.

In the years 1918–21 a series of statements, reports, and replies to questionnaires on the Minster finances included similar information about the library. It had no income of its own, but was allotted £200 a year from the fabric fund, on the grounds that the library was formerly in the Minster itself and that this sum covered maintenance which would not be reckonable as a separate charge if the library were still in the Minster. The salaries of the librarian and assistant came to £100 a year; rates, taxes, water, heating, lighting, and insurance, together with a few books and subscriptions, came to between £50 and £76 a year. In 1923 a committee of chapter discussed the present organization and future possibilities of the library, taking particulars about other cathedral libraries into consideration. The committee suggested to chapter that one of the two open mornings each week should be changed to an afternoon, a fee should be charged for borrowing, a standing library committee should meet quarterly, and C. E. Sayle of the University Library at Cambridge be asked to act as consultant director, as he did for Worcester Cathedral library. Chapter formally adopted the report, but no action was taken on it.[97]

Three contacts with the British Museum occurred at this period. In 1918 the Museum wrote asking that in the event of any sale from the Minster library they should be given the first opportunity of buying five unique volumes; this letter was probably no more than gentle speculation following the publication of Seymour de Ricci's *Census of Caxtons* in 1909 and E. G. Duff's *Fifteenth-century English books* in 1917. At the same time W. Barclay Squire, superintendent of the music room at the British Museum, suggested the sale of some of the old music in the library to pay for the binding of the rest. 'Strong objection was raised against any sale.' In 1924 the chapter clerk took the York Gospels to London to be examined by J. P. Gilson, principal keeper of manuscripts, at the latter's request, and a year later a pamphlet description of the manuscript was printed. In 1925, no

[96] O. S. Tomlinson in Stacpoole, op. cit., pp. 975–7, 981–4.

[97] YML, M 1(4) XV; D 10/MA/3/10–11; D 10/MA/2; Chapter Minutes, 23 Nov. 1923, also 8 Oct. and 31 Dec.

doubt in the course of preparatory work for the *Short-title catalogue of books printed in England . . . 1475–1640*, which was published in the following year, the Museum inquired about two or three unique books in the library, and on 2 October the administrative chapter resolved to recommend to the larger chapter that these books should be sold if large sums could be obtained, 'the money to be devoted to endowment purposes', presumably for the library. Four days later the larger chapter held a 'protracted and serious discussion' about the library, but the only point recorded was that Watson's serious ill-health made it necessary to ask him to resign from the post of librarian, the important duties of which he was unable to perform.[98]

In November 1925 chapter appointed as librarian Frederick Harrison, a vicar choral. There is nothing to indicate whether this change of policy after three successive canon librarians was intended to put a minor department in its place, to give it a head who could be ordered and not requested to act in a certain way, to fill a position which no canon wished to occupy, to revert to the practice enshrined in Vernon Harcourt's injunctions and effective until Raine's appointment, or simply to recognize the potential of an energetic young historian and up-and-coming ecclesiastical administrator among the Minster clergy, who had already acted as choir librarian, published a booklet on the Minster glass, and begun to transcribe the medieval archives of the vicars choral, as well as editing the *York Journal of Convocation* and the *York Diocesan Calendar*. While Harrison's abilities were recognized, none the less he was very junior in standing at the Minster, and for his first seven years as librarian he had no way to make his voice heard in chapter. It was unfortunate that he had no authority in chapter precisely when the authoritative voice of an established and respected librarian turned out to be most needed.

Harrison began enthusiastically and energetically, and had the support of chapter. He was at once allowed £20 to replace and bind books. Some valuable books and manuscripts which could not be kept safe from fire in the library were removed to a safe in the Zouche Chapel until a new safe could be bought. A set of ten library rules was drawn up, published in the *Diocesan Calendar* for 1927 and printed as a separate sheet. Borrowers were to be approved by the librarian and confirmed by the dean or a residentiary; they might have up to three books at a time, all to be returned at Christmas. An experiment in opening on one morning, one afternoon, and one evening each week failed, and opening reverted to two mornings. Exhibition cases were to be provided, and in addition to a vicar choral as senior assistant a junior assistant was appointed. A cleaner began work,

[98] Chapter Minutes, 1 Oct. 1918, 7 Mar. 1924, 2 and 6 Oct. 1925.

electric lighting was installed for the first time, and the fire insurance was divided between two companies. All this was done in little more than a year. The success of Harrison's energetic beginnings as librarian is evident from the annual loan figures. These had dropped to under a hundred in the previous fifteen years, but quickly rose to three figures for the rest of the 1920s and in the following decade were regularly over 200 and three times over 300.

The activities of the Cathedrals Commission of 1925–6 overlapped the librarianships of Watson and Harrison. The chapter's reply to the initial questionnaire, after mentioning that the deputy often had to take the place of the very aged librarian and that there were practically no funds for additions, emphasized that the library was used by students from far beyond the diocese, a particular attraction being the music manuscripts, then being studied for the series of *Tudor church music*; there was very little borrowing. The archives were described as catalogued, much improved in condition in the previous thirty years, and readily at the service of students. A special subcommission met at York in February 1926, and Harrison was among those who gave evidence. The report, after a summary account of the contents of the library, expressed confidence in the new librarian. Books other than valuable ones were available for borrowing by clergy and trustworthy laymen, but not many were lent. Binding repairs needed £50 a year, and there should be money for additions. 'It may be worth consideration whether some of the unique volumes should not be offered to the British Museum, and the proceeds used for the library.' It was unfortunate that this last sentence was the commission's only proposal for meeting the needs outlined immediately before.[99]

Later in 1926 chapter welcomed the suggestion from one of its number that the Minster library, which was being used almost exclusively for historical and musical study, should be made more useful in the field of theology.[100] The decrease in the number of academically experienced parish clergy brought about by reforms at the universities, combined with the fall in the real incomes of the clergy, was at this time creating a new demand for standard theology to be made available for borrowing, and the chapter acted wisely in encouraging the Minster library to provide this service and not by default stimulating the creation of a separate diocesan library. No money was made available for this purpose, but it was largely met by gifts from Canon J. H. Rawdon in 1915–16, Canon E. S. Hore in 1926, Canon S. A. Scott Ram in 1928, and Dean Lionel Ford in 1932.

[99] YML, M 1(4) XVI, Sect. XII; M 1(4) XXI.
[100] Chapter Minutes, 11 Nov. 1926.

It is now necessary to say something of the saddest episode in the library's history: the sale of a number of rare books in 1930. Public knowledge of the circumstances of what unfortunately seems to be the most widely known event in the library's history is distorted in the extreme, owing ultimately to the chapter's unfortunate secrecy at the time and its discretion immediately afterwards, when those who had given advice in private declined to defend it in public, and more directly to the grossly fictionalized account given in the biography of one of the leading *dramatis personae*, which received considerable public attention on its publication in 1960. Dean Ford presented an impassioned defence in the spring and summer reports of the Friends of the Minster in 1931, and a more balanced, wholly accurate, but very summary account, based on the documents by a recent treasurer of the Minster, Canon (now Dean) G. W. O. Addleshaw, lies hidden in the Church Assembly's *Report of proceedings* for 1961.[101] There is not space here to give the detailed narrative and explanation which would be desirable.

The background of repeated approaches from the British Museum has been mentioned, and the repetition had its effect: the definite refusal of 1918 turned into the serious consideration of 1925, which was repeated as a recommendation by the Cathedrals Commission in 1926. The purpose of this was simply to provide an endowment for the fundless library, but it was apparently felt that to gain enough capital to make the sum invested really adequate the sacrifice of books would be too great, if it was desirable at all, and it was better for the library to continue doing as much as possible on the small amounts that chapter could make available. It is unfortunate that admirable national scholarly projects in bibliography and musicology sowed the seeds, and that publication of the Cathedral Commission's report scattered them wide. The latter was followed in 1927 by a letter from the notorious American entrepreneur of the book trade, Dr. A. S. W. Rosenbach, directed incorrectly to Archbishop Lang, asking to discuss the question of selling books from the Minster library. At the same time another approach was made by the British Museum direct to Harrison, asking to have first choice of five books not in the Museum. Neither approach met with any encouragement.

That would probably have been the end of the matter, had it not been for events entirely unconnected with the library. In 1929 Sir Walter Tapper, the Minster's consulting architect, pressed the urgency of major structural repairs which ten years earlier he had advised were necessary for the safety

---

[101] E. Wolf and J. F. Fleming, *Rosenbach* (1960), pp. 329–37, and particularly pp. 7–8; Church Assembly, *Report of proceedings*, xli. 1 (spring 1961), pp. 181–3.

of the Minster. The sum of £50,000 was needed to carry out the work. The chapter was at a loss to raise such a sum: benefactors on such a scale could not be found, and in Ford's words 'appeals seemed to have ceased to appeal'. Acting now through an intermediary, Rosenbach offered anonymously to save the Minster by buying the York Gospels for £30,000. The dean refused to sell the Gospels, but was prepared to consider parting with the two unique Caxtons, which had no particular connection with the Minster. Chapter sought advice from Sir Stanford Downing and Professor A. Hamilton Thompson, respectively the most eminent ecclesiastical lawyer and ecclesiastical historian of the day, and in the circumstances of Tapper's urgent recommendation they agreed that the dean and chapter had the power to sell. Chapter decided not to sell any manuscripts, and to part only with printed books having no special connection with the Minster. An approach to the British Museum produced only a low offer, and Rosenbach was offered the two Caxtons for £20,000. He offered £16,500, making up the balance of the £20,000 wanted in exchange for thirty-three other books. The deal was concluded in 1930. One can understand the feeling of satisfaction with which the dean saw an awkward task accomplished and, as he thought, the Minster saved, and the gratitude which he and chapter felt towards Harrison, who had so successfully carried out a duty which he more than any other of those most closely involved seems to have genuinely regretted from the first. None of the books sold had any York connections, indeed two were of specifically American interest, but several had formed part of the Matthew and Fothergill gifts. A few were 'ecclesiastical' in content, a couple of Sarum liturgies and in particular the two volumes of Erasmus's New Testament of 1519, printed on vellum and with the editor's autograph inscription to Bishop Cuthbert Tunstall of Durham; this is probably the only item for which the Minster was underpaid. Though a number of the books sold would figure well in exhibitions, it is but rarely that any of them is missed in the library for its contents. Inquiries after the books come mainly from the Continent of Europe and from America, from students to whom the books are as accessible in their present locations as they would be in York. The two unique items among the Caxtons were immediately sold to the John Pierpont Morgan library. Many of the other books were offered in an unpriced catalogue issued by Rosenbach in January 1931. Some were bought mainly by American libraries and collectors, one unique Scottish book went to the National Library of Scotland, but a fair number were never sold and remain in the possession of the Rosenbach Foundation in Philadelphia.

Those are the facts. The question remains, were the dean and chapter right to sell the books? Their consulting architect insisted that the work was essential and urgent, and his opinion was not challenged. Had his advice been ignored and the parapets left to collapse, the roofs to let in water, and the windows to fall in, accusations of neglect would rightly have been brought against the chapter. As it happened, the money realized even by the sale of the books was inadequate for the architect's main recommendations, relatively few of them were carried out, and the Minster did not collapse; this does not prove that his advice was wrong in the light of technical knowledge at the time and the safety margin necessary for a building such as the Minster. Such financial advice as was available at the time could suggest no way of raising the money except by public appeals, which had failed seven times in the previous twelve years, or by selling treasures; fund-raising was not then the sophisticated business that it is today. Legal and historical opinion advised that the books could be sold, subject to certain safeguards in selection; in general these were observed, except for the inclusion in the sale of a few books from the Matthew and Fothergill gifts. The British Museum complained that it was not in the event allowed to buy the Caxtons, but the price it was prepared to pay was about half of what Rosenbach paid. If the object of the exercise was to raise money, then it was not only right but incumbent on the Minster to raise as much money as possible: if domestic *pietas* was rightly overruled by an overriding need to sell for money, then national *pietas* was equally rightly overruled by the need to sell for the highest price. The decision to maintain secrecy, a decision not entirely of the chapter's making—Rosenbach himself was secretive at first, and the Morgan Library insisted on secrecy at one delicate stage—had unfortunate consequences, and the dean afterwards recognized that a public statement voluntarily issued promptly after the sale, if it was not possible earlier, would have been wiser than the reluctant admission forced out of the Minster by public bewilderment and indignation a year later. By starting from a defensive position the chapter inevitably got a bad press, which did it no good in respect of public goodwill and did the library in particular considerable harm as regards public esteem and confidence for a number of years. But on the main point of the sale itself, Dean Ford and his chapter were and remained satisfied that they had done the right thing, that they had had no alternative but to act as they did, and that they had done it well. Looked at from forty-five years later, however, while of the several sales from cathedral libraries which have taken place in the last half-century this one probably had the most justification, it was against the trust implicit in the gifts of the Matthew and Fothergill collections, it deprived the library of some fine books which gave it no inconsiderable part of its reputation and which for various reasons people were prepared to come a long way to see, and it damaged public respect and potential benefactors' confidence in the library as a secure and permanent repository. Several features of the whole affair were regrettable if not culpable, and it is strenuously to be hoped that the temptation will never for any reason recur, whether over books or any other of the ancient treasures and heritage of the Minster.

There is one compensation. With the £20,000 raised by the sale of books too little to complete Tapper's programme of restoration, what was done was mainly in the way of routine repair work, paid for out of regular income, so that much of the money remained unspent in the Special Fabric Restoration Fund. There Dean Milner-White found it, and in 1945 chapter under his guidance, recognizing its source, converted it into a Minster Library Fund. At last the library had an endowment and a fund of its own, one which today admittedly goes only a small way towards meeting the expenses of running the library as it should be run, but is a great improvement on any previous fund available to the library; its existence did much to make the modern revival of the library a financial possibility.

This episode over, the library continued much as before. The most considerable gift until the end of the Second World War came on the death of Mrs. Eliza Gutch in 1931, several hundred scholarly volumes on popular antiquities and folklore (including extensive runs of the Folklore Society's *Journal* and monograph series), subjects to which she had herself made many contributions.

As regards the structure of the library, in 1933–4 the glass, lead, and stonework of the west window were repaired, and at the same date Dean Bate abandoned the hundred-year-old deanery and sealed the communicating door with the library. In 1937–8 the deanery was demolished, and the wall and buttress of the library made good where the two had been joined.

In 1933, on the recommendation of M. R. James, who in 1925 began a still uncompleted catalogue of the library's manuscripts and in 1929 made a report on the Minster glass, H. R. Creswick, a young 'expert librarian' who had been on the staff of the University Library at Cambridge for seven years, was invited to 'report on the condition and needs of the Library'. His report ran to twenty-nine pages, and only a summary was presented to chapter by Dean Bate in 1934.[102] His recommendations made provision for much-needed accommodation for books, but left no space for readers. The details of the shelving and arrangement of books were closely copied from the practice at his own library, where they were perfectly suitable, but they

[102] Full report in Milner-White papers, YML, Acc. 1975/8, XI/1, with related papers; summary in Chapter Minutes, 2 Jan. 1934; James's report in Chapter Minutes, 17 Sept. 1929.

were totally unfitted to the scale and needs of the York collection. Some discarding of the more modern books was suggested, and the establishment of a policy for new acquisitions. A committee of chapter, including Harrison and Hamilton Thompson, was established to consider the report and make recommendations, but seems never to have met. Parts of the report were implicitly critical of Harrison, who took strong exception to them, and his resignation was only averted by the dean's discretion in presenting only an abbreviated form of the report to chapter and not pressing for action upon it. In this way a beginning which if wisely handled might have resulted in valuable and necessary improvements to the library petered out ineffectually. The only point on which action was taken was the proposed discarding, which was to be left to Harrison's judgment and was in fact performed by him. The other main proposals would in any case have required a considerable amount of money, which was not available.

A decline in the running of the library followed. It is hard to say how far this was due to lack of money and how far to Harrison's disillusionment and frustration after the abortive report coming hard on the heels of the sale. When the vicar choral who had been assistant librarian and the lady assistant resigned in 1934 and 1936 after six and ten years' service respectively, neither was at once replaced. Harrison was regularly in attendance on the two mornings each week that the library was open, welcoming and helping serious visitors and a circle of regular readers. New Minster statutes, first drafted by 1931 and finally authorized in 1936, included a provision that if the chancellor were not the librarian, then he was to exercise some supervision over him, and it was doubtless in consonance with this that Chancellor George Austen rather than Harrison was sometimes regarded as librarian, an appreciative American visitor going so far as to present a bronze portrait bust of Austen to the library in 1927, six years before his death. A draft statute empowering chapter to spend money on buying books and on maintaining the library 'as a place of research' was deleted, perhaps because it was undesirable to commit them to an expense without a fund to pay for it. Harrison was made a non-residentiary canon in 1932 and promoted chancellor three years later.[103]

In 1936 Dean Bate placed before chapter a statement which was indirectly to have far-reaching consequences for the library. The diocesan registry now occupied most of both floors of the original library building and a hundred-year-old annexe. This was quite unsuitable both for the storage and use of the vast series of archives and for current administration, and it was proposed to erect a new archive building on the north side of the

[103] YML, M 1(4) XX–XXII; Chapter Minutes, 4 Feb. and 4 Oct. 1927.

library and linked to it, so that library and archives could be conveniently used together. The initiative for this important and visionary scheme officially came from Archbishop William Temple, who may have been prompted by advisers such as Hamilton Thompson. Chapter gave general approval, provided that no cost fell on it. To make room for the new wing it would be necessary to remove the existing extension to the library, containing the Raine and Cust rooms, and rehouse the books from them. In 1938 the Pilgrim Trust granted £5,000 for the building and fittings, and it was hoped that the chapter archives would be found room to join their diocesan counterparts in close association with the library. In 1939 the old laundry building was emptied of its books, which were put on the floor of the library, and it was demolished. The outbreak of war prevented any further progress.[104]

During the war the archives, manuscripts, and most valuable printed books were put into a variety of safe storage places, which made them inconvenient to use. Visiting parties and readers decreased considerably. Requests for loans to exhibitions, which had been gladly acceded to in peacetime, were now refused for reasons of security. Special insurance against war damage was taken out. From 1942 Harrison read periodic papers to chapter about the library and the muniments and their contents. These papers were a symptom of the increased interest in the library displayed by Eric Milner-White, dean from 1941. Never before had a dean thought and worked for the Minster library with such zest, vision, and practicality. When he first saw the library it was probably in the worst state it had ever been in, and with at best a doubtful prospect for the future; he did much himself and encouraged others to do more for its improvement and revitalization, until it became almost inevitable that it should have what he liked to call the library's little 'renaissance'. When he died in 1963 it was thanks almost entirely to him and to others inspired by him that the library once again had a place in the Minster, the city, and the world of scholarship, and was on the way to becoming the largest, fastest-expanding, and most active cathedral library in England.[105]

In 1943 there came the first imaginative and expensive purchase; it was an item absolutely right for the Minster library, an illuminated fifteenth-century Book of Hours of the Use of York.[106] The cost, £425, was defrayed

[104] Chapter Minutes, 10 Nov. 1936; 16 Mar. 1937; 21 Jan., 10 and 17 Mar., 25 Apr., 14 July, 10 Nov. 1938; 21 Mar., 6 Oct., 24 Nov., 16 Dec. 1939; 13 Jan., 2 July, 26 Oct. 1940; 18 Jan. 1941; correspondence in Milner-White papers, Acc. 1975/8, X/1.

[105] P. N. Pare and D. B. Harris, *Eric Milner-White: a memoir* (1965), pp. 82–3, is right in spirit but needs correction in several points of fact.

[106] YML, MS. Add. 2; *FAR* 16 (1944), pp. 14–18 with Pl. 3, and 17 (1945), pp. 27–8; Chapter Minutes, 8 Dec. 1943.

out of the Special Fabric Restoration Fund, i.e. the proceeds of the sale of 1930. The next year saw the existing shelves and tables in the lower hall moved and new shelves built. On these a newly appointed assistant librarian, Miss Elizabeth Brunskill, began to shelve, arrange, and catalogue the thousands of modern books which had been allowed to remain on the floor since 1939; this work was completed in 1950. At the same time a songman began to clean the older books in the upper hall. All this and more that was in Milner-White's mind needed money, and to help provide money for purchases, repairs, and staff he founded a society of Friends of the Minster Library as a branch of the Friends of the Minster, and invited subscriptions and donations. His dream was that in twenty years' time the library would have a permanent assistant librarian, staff for upkeep and cleaning, a capital fund of £10,000, an income of £100 from subscriptions, and a new extension with space and facilities to house books, manuscripts, and readers in proper warmth and light, with room for exhibitions. Most of this vision became a reality within his notional time limit, if not in the way which he envisaged. The new Friends of the Library unfortunately never became as numerous as Milner-White had hoped, eight life members and seven subscribers, and they came to exist chiefly as a channel for his own frequent gifts of money and books, mostly disguised with characteristic modesty and impish humour under the name of 'Philologus'.[107] In 1945 the Special Fabric Restoration Fund and some related sums comprising the residue of the money fetched by the sale of books in 1930 were constituted into a proper Minster Library Fund.[108] In 1946 six handsome bookcases were bought to supplement the simpler shelving being erected by the Minster joiners. In 1946–8 the registry scheme was revived, new plans drawn up, and a further £10,000 granted by the Pilgrim Trust, but the builders' estimate came to over £50,000 and as no other funds could be made available the whole plan was abandoned.[109] While the gifts of 'Philologus' were mostly fine and expensive books of art history, many of them illustrative of the stained glass and sculptures of the Minster, sizeable gifts of mainly theological books came from the Rev. J. W. E. Walker in 1942 and 1946–7, the Marquis of Normanby in 1949, and the Rev. E. A. S. Littlewood in 1953–4. Useful collections of music had been given in 1932 and 1942, and another followed in 1946.

The hard work of reorganization was rewarded by an increase in readers, many of them serious students, and Harrison's correspondence grew in

[107] *FAR* 16 (1944), pp. 19–22; 17 (1945), pp. 22–6 and 34; etc.
[108] Chapter Minutes, 28 Aug. 1945; *FAR* 18 (1946), p. 39, and 19 (1947), p. 18.
[109] Chapter Minutes, 28 May, 13 Aug. 1946; 7 June 1949; Milner-White papers, Acc. 1975/8, X/1.

proportion. In 1949 he began to exhibit and lecture on the muniments both of the chapter and of the vicars choral to the series of summer schools on archives and historical research, organized initially by the York Civic Trust as a first step towards having a university in the city. In 1951 and subsequently the library lent books, manuscripts, and playbills to exhibitions forming part of the York Festivals of the Arts. In 1959 an extensive exhibition illustrating the history of science was arranged by the library for a meeting of the British Association.

By the 1950s, however, Harrison's health was failing, and he found the work of the library an increasing strain. While personal acquaintances and known scholars continued to be welcomed to the library, it was the strenuous efforts of Miss Elizabeth Brunskill, assistant librarian for more than a quarter of a century, that kept it accessible to the public at large. Harrison retired from all his posts in 1956 and died a year later.

The new chancellor and librarian, Canon Reginald Cant, helped to turn the dean's ideas and inspiration into reality with shrewd common sense and discreet efficiency, giving the library not only activity but stability. The library was thus enabled to attain a position where, even when it was bound to be affected by the financial problems of the Minster as a whole, it was never allowed to fall into the background or re-enter the doldrums from which it had been rescued.

In June 1957 Canon Cant's first account of the library was published in the report of the Friends, accompanied by his ideas for development in the future. In July an external report on the library was drawn up by Dr. A. N. L. Munby, librarian of King's College, Cambridge.[110] He saw the library as having a threefold function: to preserve and make available the inherited collections, to maintain and extend the modern collections in subjects likely to be the object of academic research in York, and to provide theological reading for the clergy. The archives should be brought from the Zouche Chapel to the library, and the Hailstone collection should be brought down from its place in the middle of the upper hall. Catalogues should be completed and improved, and the bibliographical aids necessary for this would have to be acquired. The old bindings needed to be treated with leather-dressing, and more extensive repairs were desirable. Liaison with other local libraries might suggest subjects to concentrate on and subjects better left to them. Lapsed periodical subscriptions should in some cases be restarted, and sources of revenue should be energetically sought. 'The Library has been starved of funds for half a century . . . The promotion

---

[110] *FAR* 29 (1957), pp. 5–6 and 24–8, and 30 (1958), pp. 12, 15–16, 27–8, 43; Munby's report in Milner-White papers, Acc. 1975/8, XI/1.

and diversion of benefactions for library uses is long overdue.' Voluntary assistance might be obtained both from local individuals and perhaps from the neighbouring universities, who frequently sent researchers, and perhaps the proposed university of York might become a reality and take the Minster library under its wing. Munby's report was deliberately framed at a modest level so that it would remain within the library's capacity. Its realism, moderation, and professionalism led to immediate action on most of its recommendations. Ceilings were cleaned, leather polish was applied, the music was catalogued by a specialist, bibliographical reference books were bought or given, and miscellaneous gifts testified to the public interest in the library. Most dramatically, a donation from the dean made possible the building in 1959–60 of an extension to contain the muniments brought from the Zouche Chapel and the Hailstone collection brought down from the centre of the upper hall. Lighting and heating were renewed and improved. Shabby furniture was replaced by better pieces. The library, so long starved of money, was costing far more than its own income to run, and the treasurer, Canon Addleshaw, found ways for the chapter to divert more money to it, at least for the time being. In 1960 the foundation of the university was officially approved and interest was immediately shown in library facilities. This stimulated the appointment in 1961 of a full-time professional assistant, whose experience and interests coincided happily with many of the varied contents of the library. For the first time it could now open daily to readers and visitors. This sudden extension of facilities was appreciated slowly by the regular users who had long been accustomed to two mornings a week, but quickly by tourists, students from St. John's College, and readers from outside the city. Although the new assistant had been appointed primarily to re-catalogue the library, the effect of full-time opening was that the greater part of his time had to be devoted to assisting readers and visitors, answering correspondence and telephone inquiries, selecting books old and new for purchase, liaising with other local libraries and learned institutions and societies, and attending to the perpetual physical and administrative needs of a living organization in a largely medieval building.

The University of York appointed its own librarian in 1962 and admitted its first students in 1963. Many of these were studying History and English, and the contribution which the Minster library made towards their studies at both undergraduate and research level was recognized in 1964 when the university offered to take over the full-time staffing of the library, the staff to be responsible both to the university librarian and to the canon librarian. With rules wisely kept to a minimum and control by both librarians exercised benevolently the assistant librarian, afterwards promoted sub-librarian, who was in day-to-day charge of the library, was able to give the lie to the ancient proverb, 'Nemo potest dominis servire duobus'. The co-operation thus effected between Minster and university has been beneficial not only to both institutions but above all to the library itself: the Minster has its library under regular professional care which it could not itself have afforded to continue for long, and the university has full access to one of the major national collections of early printed books, local history, and other materials which would not otherwise have been available in York. The library has a constant stream of users for all parts of its collections, and its books, old and not so old, are not dead 'museum objects' for preservation and display but what they were intended to be and should remain, living objects to be read. The university provided not only staff and readers but photographic and interlibrary loan facilities and other benefits of library co-operation; the Minster, as a centre both of worship and religion, of music and art, and of architecture and archaeology, provided topics, advisers, and inquiries in these and allied fields. There are frequent visiting parties from conferences, universities, colleges, and schools. Individual readers and inquiries in person, by telephone, and by post come from all over the world. Library schools send not only visiting groups of students but individuals to gain experience in books and methods not readily available elsewhere. There is constant collaboration with research projects, local, national, and international, in the fields of history, architecture, bibliography, literature, music, maps, newspapers, drama, and much else. The staff make the resources of the library better known by exhibitions and catalogues, and by publication themselves as well as by encouraging and assisting publication by others in their own specialities.

As the use of the library has grown and the subjects actively studied in it have widened, so the policy of accessions has had to try to keep up with what readers expect and ought to find there now and in the future. Miscellaneous acquisitions after 1890, almost all gifts, brought a total of 30,000 volumes in 1961, and by 1976 this has been more than doubled again to over 60,000. While regular purchasing brings in not much less than a thousand volumes a year and small donations add a hundred or two, gifts of large collections make up the balance of this growth. In 1955 Garbett, the only archbishop since Maclagan to end his ministry in York, bequeathed his collection of theology, literature, history, and political thought for a library in a Bishopthorpe Palace transformed into an ecclesiastical conference and retreat centre; his successors thought better of such a transformation of the traditional archiepiscopal residence, and, after an attempt to administer the collection as a diocesan clergy library a stone's throw from the Minster library proved unsuccessful, in 1965 it was placed on permanent deposit there, with an annual grant from Garbett's trustees, to help keep the current theology up to date as a clerical lending collection. Almost the whole of Milner-White's library was given to the Minster library at his death in 1963. The Milner-White and the Garbett collection received not long afterwards were broadly similar in period and in breadth of coverage as well as in scale, each numbering between 4,000 and 5,000 volumes, and despite a certain amount of duplication of standard works were usefully complementary one to the other. Dean Richardson's library, bequeathed as an addition to the Garbett collection in 1975, was similar in size but very different in content, comprising almost entirely academic theology of the previous thirty years and a virtually complete series from the same period of the publications of the Student Christian Movement, of which he had for a time been literary director. Purchases of individual books other than new publications have concentrated on filling gaps in the collection, gaps significantly less in the periods and topics covered by Raine and Hailstone than in most others. Purchases of early printed books are of necessity very few: examples are some Civil War tracts complementary to the existing collection, additional works by archbishops Sharp and Herring, Dean Gale, Precentor Comber, Chancellor Waterland, Bishop Cosin, and, perhaps most important as well as most costly, additions to the library's holdings of manuscripts and printed texts of the medieval liturgies of the Use of York, a category of book which as much as any other should be preserved and studied at the Minster library. Thanks more to Fothergill than to continuous preservation the library already had a good collection of these, and, besides the Book of Hours purchased in 1943, was able in the 1960s to buy, aided by donations from individuals and trusts, three further manuscript volumes, a *horae* and two breviaries, and a unique printed *horae* of 1520. Other purchases, gifts, and deposits include a fourteenth-century Bede previously unknown to scholars; the unique parliamentarian battle-plan of Marston Moor to join the library's parallel royalist plan; a charter recording a donation to the Minster fabric in the 1240s, and another recording confraternity between the priories of Mount Grace and Coldstream in 1531; and a list in Frances Matthew's hand of the births and baptisms of all her children accompanied by the names of the godparents who were her husband's friends at successive stages of his career in that age of patronage.[111]

[111] *FAR* 37 (1965), pp. 3, 28–9 with Pls. 2–3 (*horae*, YML, MS. Add. 67); 38 (1966), pp. 23–4 with Pl. 4 (breviary, MS. Add. 68); 39 (1967), p. 28 (breviary, MS. Add. 115); 42 (1970), p. 16 (Marston Moor, MS. Add. 258; G. R. Smith, *Without touch of dishonour: the life and death of Sir Henry Slingsby* (1968), pp. 179–81 and plate facing p. 77); 43 (1971), p. 11 (Mount Grace, MS. Add. 284); MS. Add. 285 (thirteenth-century gift); 47 (1976), p. 33 (Matthew, MS. Add.322).

To house its doubled and still growing contents, its constant stream of readers and its increased staff, the library has required considerable extra space. In addition to the new north wing of 1960, which holds the Hailstone collection with the muniments in a separate strong-room, there was added in 1963 a second extension, again financed partly by Dean Milner-White and partly by chapter, serving as a reading-room, containing reference books on shelves provided by the Friends and the important collections of incunables, Civil War tracts, and York printing in a triple-fronted cupboard given by Dean Richardson. The accommodation in the main lower hall was doubled in 1965 by new shelves provided by Archbishop Garbett's trustees to hold his and other books. A third extension was added in 1970–1, with the help of grants from two trusts, in the form of a two-storey stack-room with sliding shelves on the upper floor to hold the maximum number of books, mainly new acquisitions; this wing also contains a microfilm reader and ultra-violet lamp.[112] Whether another extension to house the constantly increasing contents and users of the library will ever be a financial possibility is an open question.

Largely through the link with the university library the staff of the Minster library has grown considerably from the solitary full-time assistant appointed in 1961. He now has two full-time assistants, one of them professional, a part-time archivist, a part-time typist, and a part-time cleaner who performs his essential service to books as well as building. This group of paid staff is reinforced by a number of part-time volunteers, and without their willing help it would be impossible to maintain the existing level of services. It is entirely appropriate that the ancient Minster library, whose first period of greatness was shared with the proto-university school of York, should enjoy its present period of usefulness and vitality in collaboration with the modern University of York. What the Minster by itself maintained and provided for many centuries, and what, largely through the vision and activity of Eric Milner-White, has been passed on to the present generation as a treasure-house of knowledge, is having its value to the community continued and enhanced by this partnership between Church and Gown. In words recently written to the present author by a scholarly churchman who has known and used the library for forty years, 'The development of the Library is one of the greatest achievements in the life of the Minster in the twentieth century.'

Any historical account of York Minster library must owe much to James Raine's preface to the printed Catalogue *of 1896 and repeat much of what is there said. Specific references to it are given above only in cases where it is the sole printed source.*

[112] *FAR* 32 (1960), pp. 10–11 and 25–6 with Pl. 3; 33 (1961), pp. 6–7; 35 (1963), p. 19; 36 (1964), pp. 18 and 22; 38 (1966), pp. 25–6; 42 (1970), p. 16; 43 (1971), pp. 10–11 with plate.

A

178 Two views of the Minster Library at the present day: the exterior from Dean's Park (A) by David Whiteley, and the interior of the main hall (B) by the R.C.H.M.

B

CHAPTER XII

From 1916 until 1975

Reginald Cant

The new dean, William Foxley Norris, installed in March 1917 at the age of 58, had had a long experience of parochial life in Yorkshire and in post-war years was to be much involved in the work of the newly formed Church Assembly. His main objects during his nine years at York were to bring the Minster into closer relationship with the diocese, to improve its finances in order to carry out necessary repairs to the fabric and glass, to provide better furnishings for the interior of the building, and to maintain and enrich its daily worship.[1] They were to be among the chief concerns of deans and chapters throughout this period.

For these purposes the resources which Norris inherited were hardly adequate. The constitution, as it then operated, is described in his answers to a questionnaire in 1921 from the committee on the property and finances of the church set up by the Assembly after the war.[2] The only 'chapter' recognized by immemorial custom consisted of the dean and thirty canons who met quarterly, exercised patronage, and acted in every way as the statutory governing body. Chapter minutes reveal that at the thirty-six meetings of Norris's time the average attendance was eleven.[3] There were four residentiaries, but the only accommodation provided for them, the new residence built in 1824 (to the north-west of Dean's Park) and occupied in turn by the canons for periods of three months, had been abandoned in 1919 on grounds of expense. Their duty of residence was understood to be constituted by attendance at the daily morning and evening services. Their stipends from the capitular fund were augmented (from 1917) by the Ecclesiastical Commissioners to £500 and they each received one-quarter of the rent from the letting of the residence as a housing allowance. It was 'manifestly wholly inadequate in these modern days and unless the sum can

---

[1] *YP* 29 Sept. 1937, obituary notice.
[2] YML, D10/M.
[3] YML, H12/2, 3/ Minutes of Meetings of Chapter and of Committees of Chapter, 1909–19, 1919–29.

be increased it will be impossible to get men of standing to take canonries'. It was desirable to return to the original intention of the constitution, that the precentor should be qualified in music, the chancellor have charge of education, and the treasurer be experienced in business and finance. 'These would be invaluable nowadays for diocesan work in these three departments.' On his arrival Norris continued the monthly meetings which the residentiaries had begun during the interregnum between deans. His colleagues in 1917 were George Austen, rector of Whitby, aged 76, who was to resign the chancellorship a few months before his death at the age of 95; John Watson, rector of All Saints, Pavement, York, aged 68, who had charge of the library and by 1925 was totally incapacitated;[4] Francis Gurdon, suffragan bishop of Hull, aged 55; and Charles Bell, canon missioner of the diocese and from 1920 vicar of St. Martin's and St. Helen's, York, aged 49. Norris followed recent precedent in holding the precentorship until he relinquished it to Bell in 1925.

In 1924 the Church Assembly set up a commission to inquire into the constitution and requirements of cathedrals, and to advise on these very matters, viz. the provision to be made for deans, canons, minor canons, and other officers and servants; the maintenance of the services and the fabric; the provision of residence houses, and choir schools. Each cathedral was investigated by a subcommission, the report of the commission was presented in 1927, and, after lengthy debate and some revision, the Cathedrals Measure 1931, became law. Supplemented by an amendment measure in 1934, it provided for a body of cathedral commissioners to assist the cathedral authorities to revise their statutes and to prepare schemes for enabling cathedrals 'to adapt themselves to the needs and opportunities of the age', and empowered the Ecclesiastical Commissioners to contribute an annual sum, decided—and increased—each year by the Assembly, to be divided among all the cathedrals. In the first year the sum was £18,000; by 1962 it had risen to £250,000. The Cathedrals Measure was to be described later as 'the last of four great statutory reforms carried out in the early days of the Assembly', the others dealing with the deployment of the clergy, church property, and clergy pensions (Church Assembly, *Report of Proceedings*, xxxviii, 11 November 1958).

Thus many of Norris's wishes were eventually implemented. Houses were acquired for the residentiaries in 1937, although not all were assigned until 1945. The revised constitution and statutes of 1936 provided for the revival of the office of treasurer, which was subsequently held by a succession of able men, Arthur England, archdeacon of York, George

[4] YML, H12/3/ Minutes etc., 6 Oct. 1925.

Addleshaw (1946–63), later dean of Chester, Basil Smith, who died in office in 1969, and David Galliford (1970–5), later bishop of Hulme. They provided also for the appointment by chapter of an administrative committee consisting of dean, residentiaries, and one non-residentiary elected for a term by chapter. Stipends were raised to £800 and departmental duties were defined. The arrangement lasted until the further revision of 1968, when the number of non-residentiaries on the committee was increased to two, the precentor's responsibilities enlarged by providing that he should normally hold the office of chamberlain and thus be in effective charge, with the dean, of all events inside the minster, and a retirement age of 70 fixed for residentiaries, compulsory unless the archbishop determined otherwise. In one respect Norris's wishes were not fulfilled. Experience caused the next Cathedrals Commission (1958) to question the wisdom of uniting residential canonries with diocesan posts, and to recommend that there should be in every cathedral a dean and two residentiaries holding no other benefice or 'demanding' diocesan office but engaged solely in cathedral work (defined, however, as including assistance of a pastoral or theological nature to the bishop in his cure of souls in the whole diocese) and that the Church Commissioners should provide their stipends.[5] These recommendations were carried out in the Cathedrals Measure 1963 and embodied in the revised statutes of 1968. It marked the decisive acceptance by cathedrals of the reforms in church finance begun in the nineteenth century whereby ecclesiastical revenues were systematically allocated for the performance of ecclesiastical work rather than awarded, haphazard, for the maintenance of ecclesiastical persons.

A second list of questions, this time from the newly set up Cathedrals Commission of the Church Assembly, in 1926, just after Norris had left for the deanery of Westminster, asked what powers in respect of the cathedral and its services belonged to the dean as dean and as distinct from dean and chapter. The guarded reply of the residentiaries was that it was very difficult to answer this with any statutory authority but by custom the dean's powers were very large.[6] In spite of the democratic constitution (all members of chapter having equal voice and vote, and the dean having no casting vote) strong decanal initiative was a characteristic of the whole period. Bate was to maintain that 'the dean is really the chapter, and as such responsible for the major portion of the administrative work' and Milner-

---

[5] *Cathedrals in modern life*, Report of the Cathedrals Commission of the Church Assembly, 1961. The Church Commission was formed by the fusion of the Ecclesiastical Commissioners and Queen Anne's Bounty in 1948.
[6] YML, Milner-White papers (Acc. 1968/9), V/1.

White was told by 'a very responsible person' that a cathedral could be adequately administered by a dean and two curates.[7]

The 1921 answers describe the other officers and servants of the Minster. The chapter clerk, a layman, was paid 'about £380' to keep the accounts and chapter records, collect rent and other income, pay accounts, let property, and act generally as secretary and receiver for the chapter. He was assisted, part-time, by one of the lay clerks, of whom there were ten or twelve, paid £120 a year. The three minor canons formed the corporation of vicars choral, paid from their own endowments, which yielded an income of about £1,400. They were allowed to hold benefices within six miles of the Minster and two of them did so. Their duties were to provide two of their number to be responsible for daily matins and evensong, to assist at holy communion, and to sing services as required. Complaints from and about the vicars recur in chapter minutes before the corporation was abolished in 1936. The vicars remained as paid employees of the dean and chapter with their senior retaining the title and responsibility of *succentor vicariorum*. In 1934 the duties of sacrist were assigned to one of the vicars. In the statutes of 1936 the office of chamberlain as well as that of sacrist was tenable by a vicar, and from then until the 1960s the day-to-day management of events in the Minster was to be in the hands of the dean and a vicar choral who was also chamberlain. Milner-White enjoyed an especially close relationship with the able young vicars of his day, and favoured this pattern of administration. Previously, since 1919, the chamberlain, then a lay officer, had exercised a general supervision over vergers and police and seen to 'the inside management of affairs and the minster services'.[8] The organist in 1921 was master of the music under the precentor (at that time the dean) who chose the music and supervised the behaviour of the choir. The organist was paid a salary of £400. The songmen were appointed by the dean and most of them had other jobs. There were four vergers (£150 plus 'commission'), three policemen (£170), two sextons (£170), one winter-time stoker (£140). The dean and chapter were no longer financially responsible for St. Peter's School, but there was a day school for their twenty choristers which cost them £380 annually, including the lay headmaster's salary. The clerk of works received £225 and a house, and his staff consisted of a clerk, seven masons, one carver, three joiners, one bricklayer, and six labourers. The wage bill was three times what it was in 1914 and fewer men were employed.[9] There was no pension scheme for any lay employees:

---

[7] *YH* 21 May 1932. YML, Milner-White papers (Acc. 1968/9), n.d. (1939?).
[8] YML, H12/2/ Minutes etc., 3 and 31 July 1919.
[9] *York diocesan gazette* (1921), p. 123.

discussion of the subject began in 1938,[10] but it does not seem to have been continued, and it was not until 1965 that a scheme was introduced. Paid holidays of one week were introduced in 1931.

The dean reported in 1921 that the fabric 'on the whole' was in good repair, but heavy expense on the roof was imminent and repairing was 'always going on'. On 6 February 1919 the chapter clerk had replied to a correspondent that there was no truth in the widely entertained belief that, if repairs ceased, the dean and chapter would forfeit the building; however, if repairs did cease it would soon fall into decay. 'There is always more to do than we can pay for.'[11] The words describe the Minster's financial plight during this whole period. Norris soon discovered that, contrary to the report he had received, such money as there was was well managed,[12] but that there was never enough. There were four main funds: capitular estates (from which the stipends of the dean and canons were paid); fabric; the Duncombe trust (for purposes of the fabric fund); and St. Peter's (for Minster services).[13] In 1919, the first post-war year, the income from the two largest funds was (fabric) £6,231 and (St. Peter's) £2,639; the expenditure respectively was £5,981 and £3,470. The total deficit, from all funds, which Norris inherited rose in that year to £2,991. In 1925, his last year, there was a surplus of £84.[14] A fee of sixpence was charged for entrance to the Lady Chapel, crypt, and tower, and brought in £1,000 a year. 'The deans of England' resolved to double their charges,[15] but 'astonishing' news reached the chapter clerk in 1920 that at Chester all fees had been abolished and that voluntary offerings exceeded the previous charges. 'It will lead to much discussion by my dean and canons.'[16] York, however, did not follow suit until 1927. These sources of income provided only for ordinary maintenance, and there was nothing available for extraordinary need. Nor was money likely to come from the public. An ambitious proposal to raise a large sum for the fabric by appeal was dropped in the face of rising costs and economic stringency,[17] and when in 1926 Norris asked 2,165 Yorkshiremen to give £5 each the total received was £545.[18]

The one major fund-raising effort undertaken after the First World War

[10] YML, H 12/5 Minutes etc., 24 May 1938.
[11] YML, D 4/10/ Dean and Chapter Letter Book, 1917–20, 516.
[12] YML, H 12/2/ Minutes etc., 2 July 1918.
[13] *Y. dioc. gaz.* (1918), p. 206.
[14] YML, H30, v, vi, Auditors' Reports, 1910–18, 1919–30.
[15] YML, H 12/3/ Minutes etc., 30 Sept. 1920.
[16] YML, D 4/11/ Letter Book, 1920–3, 123.
[17] YML, H 12/2, 3/ Minutes etc., 7 Oct. 1919, 20 Apr. and 6 July 1920.
[18] YML, H 12/4/ Minutes etc., 1929–38: Regular Chapter 28 Jan. 1930.

was for the restoration of the glass. The decision to remove some of the windows was taken immediately after the old dean's death by the residentiaries on the advice of the Minster architect and with active support from the archbishop.[19] They needed cleaning and re-leading before reinstatement, and an appeal for £50,000 for this purpose was launched in November 1920. It had been well prepared: the Duke of York spoke for it at a meeting in the chapter-house, the Lord Lieutenant, Lord Scarbrough, and civic, county, and military leaders gave their support. Towns, organizations, and private individuals sponsored particular windows. A new vicar choral, Frederick Harrison, who was to write an authoritative book on the glass,[20] was appointed paid secretary and travelled far and wide giving popular lectures on behalf of the appeal. A committee of the best available experts in the country advised on the work and answered criticisms of the methods used in it.[21] The clerk of works, R. C. Green, supervised its execution. Fifty-five of the 109 ancient windows were thought to need immediate attention. The pre-war cost would have been £200–£230 a window; now it was over £600, not including stonework. Masons' pay had increased from ninepence an hour to 2s. $2\frac{1}{2}$d.; labourers' from sixpence to 1s. $11\frac{1}{2}$d. The cost of lead had increased from £12 to £54 a ton. At first the money came in well. Pierpoint Morgan, a friend of Lang's, gave 2,000 dollars and in the first year £15,000 was raised. Thereafter the pace slackened, and the public seemed to be apathetic. After two years the dean and Harrison painted a gloomy picture of crumbling masonry and sagging windows: a great heritage in danger of total loss. The president of the Royal Academy and the director of the Victoria and Albert Museum agreed in proclaiming the urgency of the task and the advisory committee expressed full confidence in the way the work was being done. When Norris left, £32,000 had been received and Harrison declared 'we shall carry on'. Indeed the work never quite ceased until the target figure was achieved on the eve of the Second World War, when practically all the ancient windows were once more removed and the work began all over again.[22]

The brightest episode in the story of the restoration of the glass concerned the Five Sisters window. A separate appeal was launched in 1923, after an imaginative suggestion had been made that it should commemorate the women of the empire who had given their lives in war.

[19] YML, H 12/2 Minutes etc., 26 and 28 Dec. 1916. J. G. Lockhart, *Cosmo Gordon Lang* (1949), pp. 253–4.

[20] *The painted glass of York* (1927).

[21] YML, D 4/10, 11/ Letter Books, 1917–20, 851; 1920–3, 500; D10/F, 5 June 1924; D/FAB, envelope 1928.

[22] YML, D10/F, Y.M. Windows Preservation Fund 1920–6.

One thousand four hundred names were inscribed on oak screens nearby, the young Earl of Feversham, through his guardians, gave lead which had been stripped from the roof of Rievaulx Abbey at the Reformation and been recently rediscovered in the grounds, and on Midsummer Day 1925 the Duchess of York, in the presence of 800 relatives of the dead women and 2,000 of the 32,000 subscribers, unveiled the restored window.[23]

There is little doubt that the object which engaged Norris's deepest feelings was the improvement of the interior of the building. He was himself an amateur painter of merit, and designed the great crucifix (a memorial to the old boys of the Song school fallen in war) which in 1975 still hung on the west wall of the south transept. Since 1908 the Minster's consultant architect had been Walter Tapper, described by Dean Bate at his death in 1935 as 'a simple christian man who believed intensely in the sacramental character of beauty'.[24] Norris and Tapper co-operated closely in planning what both regarded as the restoration of the medieval beauty of the Minster, and bequeathed to it some of its most striking features. In January 1918 Norris complained to a specially invited gathering of church people that no cathedral in Europe was so meanly furnished as York's. Chapels lacked altars, nearly all movable furniture and hangings needed restoration. The building should be a house of prayer as well as the delight of architects and archaeologists. Four years later he wondered if anyone cared: 'the only accommodation by the high altar, which ought to be full of splendour, is an old dining room chair or two and a deal bench. . . . It ought to be a blaze of splendour and magnificence . . . and is furnished in a way you would not furnish your back passages'.[25]

The post-war years provided an opportunity which Norris seized. It lay in the strong feelings in many people's minds of gratitude for a great deliverance and sorrow at its great cost of human life. The intensity of patriotic sentiment is illustrated by, for example, Bell's Christmas Day sermon in 1916 in which he could credibly claim that the allied armies were fighting for 'the sacredness of womanhood and childhood' against barbarism[26] and by the fact that on 'military Sunday' nine years later 10,000 people attended services in the Minster and 30,000 visited it.[27] In this atmosphere money denied to appeals for the fabric came readily from Yorkshire regiments wishing to commemorate their dead. The chapels thus provided, by Norris's persuasion, helped to give the 'glow and glory of

[23] YML, D2, 15 Feb., 20 June 1923; H12/3/ Minutes etc., 8 Oct. 1923. *YH* 6 June 1924, 25 June 1925.
[24] Laurence A. Turner was responsible for the work. YML, H12/4/ Minutes etc., 8 Oct. 1935.
[25] *YH* 19 June 1922.
[26] *YH* 26 Dec. 1916.
[27] *YH* 4 May 1925.

colour and gilding' which he and Tapper thought the building needed. The chapels were All Saints' at the east end of the south choir aisle, reopened on 12 May 1923 for the Duke of Wellington's Regiment; St. John's, in the west aisle of the north transept, on 9 May 1925, for the King's Own Yorkshire Light Infantry, and St. George's, in the corresponding position on the south side, 20 March 1926, for the West Yorkshire Regiment. For each of them Tapper, with the help of an inspired north country craftsman, Bainbridge Reynolds, provided painted wrought iron screens, and furnished them with High-Renaissance altars, two of them in coloured marble. These features were novelties in Anglican cathedrals at the time and met with some criticism, but had the enthusiastic approval of Archbishop Lang.[28] In 1923 the Lady Chapel was refurnished and embellished: a large new altar table of solid English marble was provided by a private donor and the carved stone reredos was painted and gilded. Norris characteristically admonished the congregation at its dedication how easily the Minster could be spoiled by vulgar decorations and shabby fittings, and asked them to remember after whom the chapel was named.[29] In 1926 the Zouche Chapel was reopened for worship and altars were placed in the crypt and nave.[30]

The pattern of Sunday and weekly worship had necessarily been modified during the war. Late Sunday evening nave services had been abandoned and, save exceptionally, were not resumed: it was now felt that their effect would be to diminish the surrounding parish church congregations; on the rare occasions when they were held they attracted between three and four thousand people.[31] Towards the end of the war Military Sunday, instituted by Purey-Cust, was resumed and for many years was one of the most popular of the special services. Norris gave much thought to the presentation of the sung eucharist. As early as July 1917 he reported that he had consulted Walter Frere, the leading English liturgical scholar of the day, on its improvement, 'having regard to any York use known to him'.[32] *The English Hymnal* was introduced in 1919 (and was in turn replaced by *Ancient and Modern Revised* in 1967). In 1924 an anonymous donor (it was Lord Halifax) offered to give eucharistic vestments and the chapter approved their use.[33] Thereafter a large collection was built up, largely by gift. On 15 November 1924 the dean and residentiaries made regulations concerning vesture at the eucharist. At late

[28] YML, D10/F 3 Dec. 1925.
[29] *YP* 7 May 1923.
[30] 'The book of records' in Y.M. sacristy.
[31] *YP* 1 Jan. 1921.
[32] YML, H12/2/ Minutes etc., 26 July 1917.
[33] Ibid., 23 Apr. 1924. J. G. Lockhart, *Charles Lindley, Viscount Halifax* (1936), ii.174.

plain celebrations the surplice was to be used; at early services and at sung eucharists on Sundays and red-letter days, white vestments, gold on high festivals. All prayers, except the consecration, were to be monotoned. The use of the natural voice was inappropriate.[34] Some years later the *Yorkshire Post* was to remark, with a touch of exaggeration, that Norris desired to elevate the services of the Minster to the front rank of Anglo-Catholic practice (21 May 1932). In the main the pre-war order persisted: on Sunday, holy communion at 8 a.m. and 11.45 a.m. (sung); matins (sung) at 10.30 a.m. and evensong at 4 p.m.; the litany was recited at 3 p.m.; on ordinary weekdays communion at 8 a.m., matins and evensong sung daily (except on choir holidays) at 10 a.m. and 4 p.m.; on red-letter days matins said at 7.45 a.m. and a sung eucharist replacing 10 o'clock matins. Daily evensong in the 1920s attracted a congregation of about thirty, and plain services about six people.[35] On Easter Day (27 March) 1921 there were 285 communicants, 110 of them at 11.45 a.m. At Easter 1925 (12 April) there were 293, 152 of them at 11.45 a.m. At the two services on Sunday, 31 July 1921 there were 98 communicants, on 2 August 1925, 79.[36] Numbers remained at this level through most of the period, but increased noticeably towards the end. Changing habits encouraged communion at the later service, and on Easter Day 1974 (14 April) there was a total of 417, over half of them at 11.30 a.m.

The four deans who followed Norris were alike in important respects. They were much the same age on taking office: Lionel Ford (1926–32) and Herbert Bate (1932–41) were both 61, Eric Milner-White (1941–63) 57, Alan Richardson (1964–75) 58, and all four died in office. All were scholarly men, and had achieved distinction in their ecclesiastical careers. Ford came from the headmastership of Harrow and had 'a vast clan' of ecclesiastical relatives, including Edward Talbot, bishop of Winchester, as father-in-law; Bate had had an academic career at Oxford for eleven years after taking his degree and had subsequently been a residentiary canon of Carlisle; Milner-White came from a Cambridge fellowship and had had the care of King's Chapel since the end of the First World War; Richardson came from a professorship of theology at Nottingham and had previously been a residentiary of Durham. They all belonged, with whatever nuances, to the High Anglican tradition of churchmanship, Ford and Milner-White being more explicitly 'Anglo-Catholic' in their allegiance; and all, at least to an observer, were of the currently prevalent liberal catholic school of theology, Richardson with a more markedly biblical and ecumenical

---

[34] YML, H12/3 Minutes etc., 15 Nov. 1924; D2 Miscellaneous Documents, 1911–19.
[35] YML, Milner-White's papers (acc 1968/9), V/1.
[36] YML, S4/2g/ Register of Services. *VCH York*, L. W. Cowie, 'Worship in the Minster', pp. 355–7.

emphasis. All inhabited an intellectual world different from that of Purey-Cust, who had once proclaimed from the Minster pulpit that the revised version of the Scriptures (1881–5) had kindled a flame which threatened the very destruction of the Word of God.[37] At York they all faced the same continuing tasks, if with different emphasis, yet with a similar dedication and resourcefulness.[38] Because the tasks were the same it is convenient to take them as the themes for the remainder of the period and to see how each dean, with his chapter, dealt with them. They were, as for Norris, to cultivate relations with the diocese and, increasingly, with the wider Church and with the community of the north; to care for the fabric and its artistic treasure, and therefore to busy themselves with raising money; to continue Norris's embellishment of the interior of the building; and to maintain the worship and extend its appeal. All four deans and their chapters would have agreed that the last was the prime activity of a cathedral, and that the members of the cathedral foundation, clergy and choir especially, were committed to it by law, by history, and by personal conviction. A fascinating but largely indescribable feature of the period is the tension between the claims of the outside world and the liturgical life of the cathedral community: for example, between the expectation of the ever-increasing numbers of tourists in the 1970s to have unimpeded access to the building and the desire of clergy, choir, and congregation for peace and quiet in which to offer choral worship.

Throughout this period relations between archbishop and Minster were cordial. Lang supported Norris's policies, presided over the Cathedrals Commission of 1926, and piloted the subsequent measures, with difficulty, through the Church Assembly, thus helping to give cathedrals a new and more secure foundation for their work.[39] For Ford he had warm personal friendship; of Bate Temple said he would rather spend an evening with him than with any other of his friends.[40] Garbett recorded 'a growing affection and admiration' for Milner-White, and Ramsey, who had known him since his own boyhood, wrote appreciatively of him after his death.[41] Archbishop Coggan, the first archbishop of the century to come from the

---

[37] *YH.* 26 Dec. 1916, obituary.

[38] C. A. Alington, *Lionel Ford* (1934); H. N. Bate, *Faith and Order* (1927); P. Wilkinson, *Eric Milner-White, 1884–1963* (privately printed for King's College, Cambridge, 1963); P. Pare and D. Harris, *Eric Milner-White 1884–1963* (1965). A. M. Ramsey, *From Gore to Temple* (1960), places Milner-White, and J. J. Navone, S. J., *History and faith in the thought of Alan Richardson* (1966), places Richardson in the succession of *Lux Mundi*.

[39] Lockhart, *Lang*, pp. 297–8, 378, 455.

[40] F. A. Iremonger, *William Temple* (1948), p. 372.

[41] C. H. Smyth, *Cyril Foster Garbett* (1959), p. 339. Harris and Pare, *Milner-White*, pp. 93–106, 'Epilogue' by A. M. Ramsey.

evangelical tradition, gave ready and effective support to the great fund-raising operations from 1967 onwards as well as displaying personal friendliness towards the clergy and lay staff. Increasingly, however, archbishops were immersed in the administration of the Church of England, travelled in the worldwide Anglican communion of which they were outstanding leaders, and took their indispensable parts in ecumenical activities. Only Temple of all recent visitors of the Minster exercised his right of visitation, in 1931, and no significant result followed save the authorization of monthly residence.[42] The Minster continued to be used for archbishop's services, such as ordinations and consecrations of new bishops for the northern province, and for diocesan occasions, such as the choirs' festival, revived in July 1928: but the diocese had, officially, no financial or constitutional responsibility for the upkeep of its cathedral church, and no voice in its affairs save through the archbishop as visitor and individual members of chapter, all of whom, normally, were appointed by the archbishop and beneficed within the diocese. Deans and residentiaries contributed to the diocese and the wider Church through such activities as serving on diocesan committees, convocation, and synod, preaching, post-ordination training, lecturing, conducting retreats, writing; but the administration of the Minster, and an increasing pastoral ministry (encouraged by the requirements of the Cathedrals Measure 1963 that the dean and two canons should be 'solely engaged' in cathedral work and the admission that they had a cure of souls), absorbed their time and energy. The constitution of the Minster and its current *modus operandi* remained untouched by the changes in diocesan administration which took place in the 1970s in the wake of the Adair Report[43] which, at the request of the archbishop, surveyed the organization of the diocese.

An event which brought the Minster prominently to the notice of diocese and public in Ford's day was the celebration of the 1,300th anniversary of its founding in 1927. The holy year began and ended with crowded midnight services. For the main celebrations, in the octave of St. Peter (28 June–6 July), a special altar was set up in the nave and a platform for the choir. Ford preached at the first evensong on the text from Revelation 21:3 'the tabernacle of God is with men' and spoke of the 'open minster', a mother church spreading out maternal arms, calling men to holiness. The eucharist was sung daily, choirs and organists of almost all the northern cathedrals shared in the worship, and each day save one there was a sermon from a distinguished visiting preacher. Lang considered that the great

[42] YML, H12/4 Minutes etc., 1929–38: Regular Chapter, 12 Oct. 1931.
[43] John Adair, *A report on the diocese of York* (July 1970), pp. 52–5, on relations of Minster and diocese.

anniversary services had reached a climax of beauty and were a pattern of worship to the Church of England.[44] The year saw a contribution to the historiography of the Minster in the publication of a series of essays, edited by A. Hamilton Thompson, *York Minster Historical Tracts*; the introduction of central heating and loudspeakers; and the first broadcast evensong, which began the making of a new and powerful link between the Minster and a wider, often non-church-going, public. Parish pilgrimages began well, with 95 in 1927, but dwindled to 4 in 1930. A result of the year which was to be of lasting benefit was the founding of the Friends of York Minster in May 1928. In four years the membership rose from 770 to 1,412. It helped to convert the new-found enthusiasm for the Minster into tangible form, and the annual reports from June 1929 provided a year-by-year chronicle of the domestic history of the Minster, bringing the dean and chapter into touch with a wider circle of well-wishers than they had previously known. The formation of this independent body helped to enlist wide support for the preservation and adornment of the building and for the promotion of activities associated with it.

Bate's years were overshadowed by the worsening economic condition of the country. On 8 July 1934 the Minster received the pilgrimage of the unemployed, sharing the attempt by all the cathedrals to identify themselves with the national suffering and to stimulate the demand for remedial action. As the shadows of war fell precautions for the safety of the building had to be taken, staff was depleted, visitors dwindled, and much of the euphoria of 1927 evaporated. Nevertheless, he was able quietly to implement the revision of statutes following the 1931 Cathedrals Measure, to arrange for proper celebrations of the centenary of the Oxford movement in 1933 and of the 200th anniversary of the conversion of John Wesley in 1938; to guide St. Peter's School through a difficult year in 1937 and ensure its continuity;[45] and to replace the impracticable deanery of 1827–31 by a smaller modern building (begun in 1938 and financed by a £7,000 loan secured by a sinking fund policy with the Yorkshire Insurance Company).[46] Milner-White touched the life of Minster, church, and community creatively: as chairman of the York Academic Trust he helped to bring the university to York; he cared for the amenities of the city and was a founder of the Civic Trust in 1946; he was provost of the northern division of the Woodard schools, and served on the literary panel of the *New English Bible*. As chairman of the diocesan advisory committee he exercised his

---

[44] Lockhart, *Lang*, pp. 296–7. *Church Assembly, Report of Proceedings* (16 Nov. 1927), pp. 432–46.
[45] F. J. Wiseman, *The recent history of St. Peter's school, York* (York, 1967), p. 82.
[46] YML, H12/4, 5/ Minutes etc., 3 July 1934, 10 Apr. 1945. Minutes of Administrative Committee, 30 July 1966.

discriminating taste decisively in the parish churches of the diocese. In his time the Minster was brought before the world by the televising on 8 June 1961 of the wedding of the Duke of Kent and Miss Katharine Worsley in the presence of the Queen, sixty-two members of the royal family, and 2,500 guests. Perhaps the most enduring influence of the Minster on the surrounding community at this time was provided by the increasing number of special services, devised by the dean with rare skill and making a designed missionary impact.[47] This ministry was extended in his successor's time and clearly met a felt need.

During the thirties a small group of scholars began a quiet, but in the long run extremely important, work on the records housed on the Minster premises in what was then the probate registry and by the seventies had become a shop and choir practice room, where they lay under thick dust, uncatalogued, unindexed, unusable by scholars, and in danger of total loss. The task of clearing out and reordering this vast and valuable collection devolved principally upon an incumbent of the diocese, later to become a member of chapter, J. S. Purvis. It was an enormous achievement, placing later generations of church historians in his debt.

It was in the decade 1964–74 that the Minster was brought more fully into touch with the public than it had been for centuries, and the occasion for this was largely provided by the peril to the fabric disclosed in 1967. No deans or chapters of this period were unmindful of their responsibility for the building or unaware of the need for more money in order to discharge it. Correspondence in 1927 between Ford and the director of the Building Research Station reveals the concern that was felt at the weathering of the external stone, and a petition dated 23 March 1927 protesting against the noise and vibration caused by the stoneyard saw claimed that the foundations were endangered.[48] A thanksgiving fund was opened in 1927 and one-third of the unearmarked contributions went to overseas cathedrals. Four years later the total stood at £12,427.[49] In January 1930 the dean announced to the chapter that £52,236 was needed to repair the central tower, choir and nave roofs, parapet, and the remaining unrestored windows: but it was felt that in the worsening economic climate a public appeal was pointless.[50] The need and the impotence to meet it explain two decisions that were made at this time which, with hindsight, might appear misguided but which in the circumstances were defensible. After the sale of

[47] *York Quarterly* (Feb. 1959), Milner-White, 'Special services: a liturgical need'.
[48] YML, D3/2–3 Letters, 1927–8.
[49] YML, D2 Misc. Docs., 1920–30.
[50] YML, H12/4. Minutes of Regular Chapter, 28 Jan. 1930.

library books[51] Ford could report in 1932 that the central tower was now enclosed in a 'great sheath of scaffolding' and that its repair, with Clipsham stone (said to be impervious to coal smoke) instead of the previously used Tadcaster stone, was under way and that the choir roofs were being re-leaded.[52] A more fateful step, so far as the future financial position was concerned, was taken on 29 October 1931 when the dean reported the receipt of a letter from the Ecclesiastical Commissioners regarding a proposed exchange of capitular estates for a fixed annual payment, and the letter was favourably received by chapter and negotiations were begun.[53] In 1935 an agreement was signed, to become effective in 1938, whereby nearly three hundred acres of arable and grass land in the Yorkshire parishes of Melbourne, Borrowby, Dalton, Nether Silton, Topcliffe, and Wharram-le-street and the Nottinghamshire parish of Misterton, valued at £11,876, and some twenty-six properties in the centre of York (half of them in the Shambles) valued at £19,053 were handed over for an annual payment of £1,048.[54] An indication of what was lost to the chapter is that in 1973 the rents yielded by about double the number of such city properties then in the possession of the dean and chapter produced a total income of twenty times this sum. Yet at the time it seemed a prudent transaction. In those years the rents were small, and many of the lettings were charitable in intention. Repairs were minimal and the property deteriorated. In 1933 Canon Lindsay Dewar vehemently reminded the chapter that it was becoming a body of slum landlords.[55] Not until 1966 was the decision taken to put the management of property into the hands of agents with instructions, as leases fell in, to put property into good order and charge economic rents. By that time help from the local authorities was available for improvements and for the careful renovation of listed buildings.

In 1934 the state of the north transept roof was serious enough to delay the scheme for housing the residentiaries. The restoration, which entailed re-roofing in copper and rebuilding the wooden ceiling, was begun, interrupted by the war, and completed in 1951. By this time an appeal for £250,000 had been made on 1 June 1950 'to York, to Yorkshire, to Great Britain and to the world' for the repair of the west front. The total was eventually achieved, but the work went slowly through shortage of labour, and scaffolding still obscured the west front seventeen years later when the

[51] See Ch. XI.
[52] *Friends of York Minster Annual Report*, 1932 (henceforth *FAR*).
[53] YML, H12/4 Minutes of Regular Chapter, 29 Oct. 1931.
[54] Order in Council, 6 May 1938, schedule (A scheme for ... York). YML, Acc 1967/8, Correspondence and Statements; Acc 1969/5, Correspondence.
[55] YML, H12/4/ Minutes of Regular Chapter, 1 Feb. 1933.

fund was wound up and a new appeal, the most dramatic and most successful of the century, was launched.[56] A warning of the peril that evoked it was given in 1958, when Albert Richardson (Minster architect since 1947) reported that two buttresses on the south side of the nave, restored in 1905–6, had moved out of perpendicular and showed cracks of a very dangerous type. Richardson maintained that the damage was caused by traffic vibrations from Deangate. The city authorities, not entirely convinced, but willing to help, agreed to take the steps necessary to control the traffic, and eventually a ban on vehicles of more than three tons' weight unloaded was secured. In the course of the debate the city engineer made the ominous suggestion that the main source of the trouble might lie in inadequate foundations. But 1958 was not a propitious year for embarking on further expense. In spite of his gratifying success in increasing the Minster's income from investments by 50 per cent since the war, and doubling their capital value, the dean had to inform the chapter at the end of 1958 that there was not enough money to pay for the heating of the Minster that winter. 'If inflation does not cease, if wages rise any more, the prospect for a great church is very dark.'[57]

In 1965–6 the newly appointed architect (henceforth known as the surveyor of the fabric), Bernard Feilden, carried out a careful inspection of the entire fabric. Supported by a second professional opinion, and by the findings of an initial exploratory excavation at the base of one of the central tower piers, which showed severe cracking and deformation of masonry below floor level, he warned the dean and chapter that unless remedial work was undertaken forthwith the central tower would collapse: very soon, within fifteen years, the structure would be too delicate to undergo the drastic repairs necessary. Preparations began for the largest appeal ever made for any ecclesiastical building in Britain. The eleventh Earl of Scarbrough accepted the archbishop's invitation on behalf of the dean and chapter to become high steward (a new post provided for, presciently, in the statutes then under revision) and to lead the campaign. To assist him he set up a network of area chairmen in Yorkshire (which, as he remarked, for the purpose included the city of London), and professional fund-raisers were employed. The appeal was launched in May 1967. The size of the sum required, two million pounds, the urgency of the need, the technical

---

[56] *FAR* (1950) 4–6; (1951), pp. 3–5. YML, H12/5 Minutes etc., 1941–54, 6 Dec. 1949 onwards. Appeal Brochure, 1950. *YEP* 27 Jan. 1958, reported a shortage of labour on the west front.

[57] There was extensive reporting of the debate in the local Press from November 1958 onwards. *Yorkshire Evening Press*, 18 Feb. 1959, summarizes the report of the city engineer to the joint committee of the streets and buildings and the watch and fire services committee of the city council, 10 Feb. 1959 (CRA/BVW). YML, Milner-White papers (Acc. 1968/9), I, I/1.

179 The eastern wall of the Minster, 1968, supported by raking shores while new foundations were inserted.

interest of the engineering and architectural work, and the archaeological investigation of the site which from the beginning went on alongside the restoration, aroused wide public interest, and the amount was achieved in 1972. Approximately one-quarter of the sum had been provided by Yorkshire local authorities, whose attention had been personally directed by the responsible Minister, then Anthony Greenwood, to the clause in the Historic Buildings Act 1962 which tacitly permitted them to contribute to ecclesiastical buildings still in use. In five years the strength of the foundations of the four piers supporting the central tower had been doubled, the tower itself re-roofed and the upper part strengthened by the insertion of a steel girdle in the stonework under the windows. New foundations were inserted at the west and east ends, much grouting and repair carried out to interior stonework. The nave and choir were washed and their ceilings painted. The year 1972, amid a blaze of publicity, saw the celebration of the 500th anniversary of the consecration of the completed building on 3 July 1472, and of the successful completion of the major repairs. The royal maundy was distributed in the Minster for the first time since Charles I distributed it in 1639, there were great services in the octave of St. Peter matching those of 1927 in popularity, a flower festival in July which attracted tens of thousands of visitors, and *son et lumière* nightly in the late summer and early autumn. In these years which coincided with a national boom in tourism, more people than ever entered the building. The city tourist office estimated that in 1973 two million visitors came to York: most of them must have included the Minster in their visit.[58]

The vast increase in tourist traffic in the 1960s and 1970s made a twofold impact on the dean and chapter. They improved their facilities for receiving and helping their visitors: much voluntary help, gladly given, was recruited to provide stewards to keep open the chapter-house through the summer, and a company of instructed voluntary guides to show people round, in addition to the existing Minster chaplains who began in 1947, was formed (1965); with the co-operation of St. John's College of Education better educational provision was made for the increasingly numerous school parties (1972); the staff was augmented by two sisters of the Order of the Holy Paraclete (1972); St. William's College, of which the dean and

---

[58] The literature concerning the restoration is abundant, but much of it ephemeral. The documentary sources are closed to public inspection until approximately the end of the century. The most informative publications available are D. J. Dowrick and P. Beckmann, 'York minster structural restoration', *Proceedings of the Institution of Civil Engineers* (1971), Supplement (vi), Paper 7415S; Bernard M. Feilden, 'The Restoration of York Minster' in *The Noble City of York*, ed. A. Stacpoole *et. al.* (York, 1972) pp. 409–46, and *The Wonder of York Minster*, (York), 1976, which also contains the paper by Dowick and Beckmann; and an account of the five years 1967–72 by the dean, Alan Richardson, in *FAR* (1972), 3–14.

180 The interior of the nave, 1972, while cleaning and re-decoration were in progress. ▷

chapter had become the legal trustees, was used for the refreshment and reception of visitors (1974); a shop was opened (1969); an underground area beneath the central crossing, created during the repair of the foundations, was used as a display gallery, amid the modern foundations, to become known as the 'Undercroft', for archaeological remains and treasure, and attracted in the two years after its opening (1972) over half a million paying visitors. The second result of the increased numbers of visitors was a steep rise in income. Partly this came from increased giving in collections and boxes; but most of the money came from admissions to the tower, the chapter-house, and undercroft and from purchases in the shop. In a period of rapid inflation, and with no financial help for the ordinary maintenance of the building and its work beyond their own resources, the dean and chapter needed this money to pay the ever-increasing running costs. In 1974 there were over a hundred names on the Minster payroll, excluding clergy and choristers, and the budget for necessary and ordinary expenditure was for the sum of £250,000. For some special works grants were available from the Department of the Environment—the washing of the exterior in 1973 and the restoration of the surroundings, especially Dean's Park in 1974, to both of which the city of York also contributed. Even so, the needs of the building were not completely met, and in May 1974 a fresh appeal, this time for covenanted subscriptions to bring in an annual income of £75,000 to pay stoneyard wages for the repair of external stonework according to a thirty-year programme, was launched. The money was necessary if the budget was to be balanced. Links with the public were strengthened by the regular issue of a Minster newsletter from 1967, and by its more ambitious successor, the *York Minster News*, from 1973–5. The teaching ministry of the Minster was extended by the revival of a lecture society in 1965, which each winter provided a forum for theological instruction and debate.

Two activities aroused special interest: archaeology and the care of the glass. The site on which the Minster stood was known to be, potentially, one of the most important in Europe, and the excavations made necessary by the restoration yielded impressive archaeological results. The only previous investigation in this period had been conducted by Charles Peers (who succeeded Tapper as architect in 1935) in the crypt. He presented his report in 1930 in the belief that he had uncovered the Saxon foundations of the Alma Sophia church described by Alcuin. Later scholars came to the conclusion that he was mistaken, but his work had saved them much trouble. Between 1967 and 1972 extensive remains of the Roman legionary fortress headquarters building and of the Norman cathedral of Thomas were uncovered; the tombs of two thirteenth-century archbishops, de Gray

181 The choir ceiling, 1970, in process of decoration.

182 The north-west pier of the central tower; strengthening of
its foundations was one of the first tasks of the restoration in 1967.

and de Ludham, were opened and their contents, apart from the human remains, removed for exhibition in the undercroft; and the tomb of St. William, the twelfth-century archbishop canonized in 1227, was removed from the nave and re-erected in the western crypt and a small austerely furnished chapel for ecumenical use formed round it. The contents of the coffin were examined by experts in 1974.[59] For centuries the Minster had attracted the interest of scholarly antiquarians: in the last years of this period, thanks to the Royal Commission on Historical Monuments (England), the University of York, and the Minster's own archaeological team, it received more sustained professional attention than ever before.

The windows removed during the Second World War underwent the most extensive restoration of their history at the hands of Milner-White, who secured the indispensable financial support of the Pilgrim Trust at the rate, from 1950–62, of £1,500 yearly. The Minster glaziers, under his personal direction, undertook the 'jigsaw puzzle' work of sorting out intrusions in the glass and of restoring it to its original state or, when this, through lack of knowledge or of suitable glass, proved impossible, making a coherent and aesthetically pleasing pattern, using the most appropriate glass, in age or appearance, that was available. A 'bank' was carefully built up for this purpose. Milner-White had his critics among art historians but at the time secured considerable approval for his work. The Pilgrim Trust supported him unreservedly; on 19 November 1960 W. I. Croome, chairman of the Cathedrals Advisory Committee, wrote to him, referring flatteringly to the work of the glass shop, but recommending the appointment of an academic consultant and reference to the Glass Research Institute, Sheffield, for technical advice; and on 21 July 1962 Peter Newton of the Barber Institute (later to become academic consultant to the York Glaziers Trust) wrote to him praising his wonderful work on the windows. When, soon after his death, the Pilgrim Trust, with the dean and chapter, set up the York Glaziers Trust, in enlarged and re-equipped premises, to undertake the restoration of any good glass, and in particular the Minster glass, the nucleus of professional expertise was provided by the craftsmen whom he had inspired. Work on the glass continued into the 1970s, with further aid from the Pilgrim Trust and with an increasingly precise and wide knowledge of the physical composition of the glass itself, thanks to the

[59] C. R. Peers, 'Recent discoveries in the crypt of York minster', a paper read to the Society of Antiquaries, 11 Dec. 1930; summarized, *FAR* (1931), 23–30. B. Hope-Taylor, *Under York minster: archaeological discoveries 1966–71* (York, 1971). H. G. Ramm *et al.*, 'The tombs of archbishops Walter de Gray and Godfrey de Ludham in York Minster, and their contents,' *Archaeologia*, ciii (1971), 101–47. *FAR* (1969), 7–12. The report on the archaeological investigations of 1967–74 is not yet published.

researches of Roy Newton of the Sheffield Institute and to co-operation with the Physics Department of the University of York.[60]

Despite lack of capitular resources all the deans of the period were able to pay considerable attention to the interior furnishing and adornment of the Minster. Money for the purpose came from individuals and organizations, and the Friends especially made generous grants. In this area various factors counted: the personal taste of deans, and of those to whose advice they listened, notably the consultant architects, and to some extent their type of churchmanship also. Since there was a limit to what even a building as large as the Minster could contain, difficult decisions about the replacement of furniture and ornaments had sometimes to be made and did not always command general approval. The new sacristies completed in 1936 were of Ford's inspiration: always he cared passionately for the worship of the Minster and they were necessary for its reverent conduct. In the late 1930s, under the direction of two successive architects, Tapper and Peers, the choir sanctuary was refurnished and provided with a new high altar of noble proportions in memory of the second Viscount Halifax (died 1934).[61] In February 1934 Bate reported the gift from Lord Halifax of the ring given to his father by Cardinal Mercier and set in the stem of a Breton chalice. It was a precious gift, rich in ecumenical significance: but few could then have foreseen the day, nearly half a century later, when in the same sanctuary a successor of Mercier, Cardinal Suenens, accompanied by the archbishop of York, would unveil a plaque commemorating the Malines conversations in which Halifax had taken a leading part, but which to all appearance had collapsed in irremediable failure in 1926, nor could they have foreseen the new friendship which would begin then between Suenens and Archbishop Coggan.[62]

Each dean attracted numerous gifts, but Milner-White more than any set out to collect them. In his first letter to the Friends he said he came to York as a lover, and his enthusiasm proved to be infectious. The annual reports chronicle the gifts which poured in, each of them to occupy its providentially ordained place: in 1942 new red hangings for the high altar, and a rare collection of vestments which received a glowing account in 1943; new nave choir stalls by Richardson in 1944, oak stalls by Thompson of Kilburn to a design by Peers for the Lady Chapel in 1945, a font cover by

[60] YML, Milner-White papers (Acc. 1968/9), Box II/7, correspondence with Pilgrim Trust; Box II/6 for correspondence with Croome and Newton. York Glaziers Trust, Research programme newsletters, 1972.

[61] YML, H12/4/ Minutes etc., 31 Jan. 1936.

[62] *The visit of cardinal Suenens to York minster, 27 April 1969* (published by the Friends of York Minster, York, 1969. Until 1975 the chalice was thought to be Flemish.

J. N. Comper in 1946 ('York minster should possess the most wonderful baptistery in our christian land'); statues in wood, altar crosses, and candlesticks in precious metals in 1947—and so the stream went on until the year of his death which saw the gift of 150 specially bound prayer books for congregational use in the choir, the furnishing of the Paternoster Chapel in the nave, and a new dustcover for the altar in St. John's Chapel. The most remarkable of the furnishings of his time was an astronomical clock, whose making entailed the co-operation of scientist, technologist, and artist and which was a memorial to the 23,000 allied airmen from camps north of the Humber who fell in attack or defence during the Second World War. It was completed and erected in the north transept in 1955.[63] From 1964 onwards, at a time when there was an increasing interest in church embroidery, a widening range of materials, and a new boldness in design and choice of colour, there were notable additions to the furnishings, outstanding among them a Laudian-type throw-over for the nave altar, presented by the Women's Institutes of Yorkshire in 1971, and a dossal in heraldic red for the All Saints' Chapel. Popular exhibitions of modern ecclesiastical vestments and altar furnishings were held in the chapter-house during the York Festivals of the Arts from 1966 onwards. The choir stalls were stripped and cleaned, and the policy inaugurated half a century before by Norris and Tapper of introducing colour into the building found its boldest expression in the high-lighting of the pulpitum in red and gold. All these additions were gifts: the stream of generosity flowed as freely as ever.

The heart of the Minster's worship remained, as always, the recitation of the divine office. All the deans and chapters of the period were unanimous in their approval of cathedral-style worship, and the musical tradition was maintained so far as circumstances allowed. Matins was rarely sung on weekdays after 1967, but daily choral evensong, except on choir holidays (and then, frequently, a visiting choir would undertake the duty), remained, and was omitted only once during the five years' turmoil of restoration, 1967–72. The point at which changing practice in the Church at large impinged most visibly on the cathedral pattern of worship was in the presentation of the eucharist. Norris and Ford took much care: in 1926 there was 'prolonged discussion' by the dean and residentiaries of the ceremonial to be used and it was decided that on high festivals three vested ministers, celebrant, deacon, and subdeacon should officiate. In 1929 this became customary at every sung eucharist when practicable and continued so throughout the period. Ford doubted whether there was anything in Europe to surpass the Minster's Sunday eucharist.[64] Only minor

[63] *The astronomical clock in York minster* (Y.M. picture books) (York, n.d.).
[64] Alington, *Ford*, Ch. ix.

modifications were subsequently made, and an explanatory booklet for use by worshippers, composed by the precentor, Charles Bell, at this time, was still in use in 1975. With the coming of liturgical revision in the 1960s there were cautious innovations: a plain second series eucharist at 8.45 a.m. on Sundays and on one weekday and very occasionally, with a suitable adaptation of the traditional ceremonial, sung on a red-letter day during the week; the third series rite was used in the first year of its life, 1973, and again in 1975, on Fridays in Lent; the Lady Chapel was reordered to provide for the westward position at a free-standing altar. In 1930 the dean and residentiaries approved in principle the reservation of the blessed sacrament for sick communion:[65] at first All Saints' Chapel was used, later the Zouche Chapel. A Christmas crib was introduced in the same year, and its blessing on Christmas Eve became a popular event. Small changes in rite and ceremony were made (a greater use of the natural voice in prayers, 'deep reverences' instead of genuflexions) in 1934.[66] Milner-White shared Ford's enthusiasm, introduced in 1942 the additional Sunday celebration at 8.45 a.m., and designed his special services so as to supplement the provision of the Book of Common Prayer while remaining as near as possible to it in structure, content, and language. Particularly appealing were paraliturgical compilations like his version of the nine lessons and carols for Christmas Eve and the Epiphany procession, beginning in the darkened nave and concluding in brilliant light with the symbolic furnishing of the bare altar. In the last decade of this period fresh efforts were made (by revising the lectionary and extending the scope of the intercessions) to increase the popular appeal of daily evensong and to provide more flexible special services. The most significant addition to seasonal observances was the Easter Eve ceremony of lighting the paschal candle and blessing the font. The 'Thursday candle', with prayers for unity, was introduced in 1964. Popular lunch-hour services in Lent and for other short periods were held, eucharists provided at later hours, and the nave made available to the vicar of St. Michael-le-Belfrey, David Watson, for evening services, which were exceptionally well attended, and for other religious gatherings. Watson's evangelical preaching ministry in York and beyond was one of the most striking features of the religious scene during the last years of our period, and the dean and chapter gladly welcomed his congregations into the mother church of the north.

At the conclusion of a book such as this the temptation to peer into an unpredictable future is hardly to be resisted. For the next few years the practical question uppermost in the minds of deans and chapters will be how

[65] YML, H12/4/ Minutes etc., 1929–38, 15 Dec. 1930.   [66] Ibid. 31 Oct. 1934.

to raise the money to discharge their responsibilities as guardians of the building, its glass, and monuments. If the appeal of 1974 were to fall far short of its aim the alternative to imposing an entrance charge would be to watch the slow decay of their heritage. The question which the remoter future may be expected to answer is not whether but when state aid will become available in sufficient quantity to lift the responsibility from them. Barring catastrophe, it is unlikely that either the public or the government in the future will be less concerned with the conservation of historic buildings than they were in the 1970s. At some time in the future that second career of the Minster of which Dr. Harvey spoke at the end of Chapter IV, as the greatest ancient monument in England, will be crowned when it passes finally into the care of the public authorities. The procedures by which public aid could be given are already informally taking shape through consultations held between Minster, local authority, and government department, and the arrangements for supervision worked out, in connection with specific grants already received.

State aid need not preclude or hinder the use of the Minster for religious purposes, either for worship according to the Anglican cathedral tradition, so long as musical resources are available, or for joint ecumenical use. It would certainly entail some modification of the autonomy of the dean and chapter, but hardly of any powers that a modern dean and chapter would want to retain: the 'island of privilege' of which Dr. Cross wrote in her chapter has ceased to exist. Constitutionally and legally, however, deans and chapters remain enclaves within the Church organization. A serious alteration in the relations between Church and State, or a union of the Church of England with other Churches would raise again the question of the cathedral in the life of the modern Church. So long as the Church of the future has a territorial or a diocesan system it will need the use of large central buildings for church occasions: but it may not accept the need for these buildings to remain in the care of deans and chapters, and certainly not if the church of the future is the hidden church of the dispersion which some prophesy. It may well be that the great building whose story we have told will prove more durable than the present constitutional status of its guardians.

INDEX

All entries refer to page numbers; entries in **bold** refer to illustrations
Page numbers followed by 'n' refer to footnotes
Key to numbering of York Minster windows is on p. 314